Standard Catalog of®
MILITARY
FIREARMS

1870 TO THE PRESENT

THE COLLECTOR'S PRICE & REFERENCE GUIDE
1st Edition

NED SCHWING

Front Cover:
Cover photo by Paul Goodwin. He can be reached at 229
East 4th Street, Newport, KY 41071, 606-431-7606
Colt Model 1873 and accessories courtesy Tommy Hass, Jr.

Back cover:

Vickers MK1 machine gun, Courtesy Robert Segel
Model 1927 Thompson, Private NFA collection, Photo Paul Goodwin
H&K MP5 A3 KAC submachine gun, Courtesy H&K

© 2001 by
Krause Publications, Inc.

Published by

**krause
publications**

700 E. State Street • Iola, WI 54990-0001
Telephone: 715/445-2214

Please call or write for our free catalog of publications.
Our toll-free number to place an order or obtain a free catalog is 800-258-0929
or please use our regular business telephone 715-445-2214.

Library of Congress Catalog Number: 2001088596
ISBN: 0-87341-997-9

Printed in the United States of America

"Tools or weapons, if only the right ones can be discovered, form 99 percent of victory."

Major General J.F.C. Fuller, 1936

"After God, we should place our hopes of safety in our weapons, not in our fortifications alone."

Emperor Mauricius Flavius Tiberius, 600 AD

CONTENTS

—— DIRECTORY ——

ACKNOWLEDGMENTS

Orvel Reichert is a collector World War II-era semi-automatic pistols, especially the P38, and has been an invaluable help in sorting out a sometimes confusing array of pistol variations. He can be reached at P.O. Box 67, Vader, WA 98593, 360-245-3492, email address: mr.p38@localaccess.com

Joe Gaddini, of SWR, has provided invaluable technical assistance on Class III firearms and suppressors. He can be reached at 119 Davis Road, Suite G-1, in Martinez, GA 30907, 706-481-9403.

Thanks to Eric M. Larson for his knowledgeable information on Federal gun laws.

A special thanks to Simeon Stoddard, curator of the Cody firearms Museum, for his research and contribution on the M1 Garand rifle.

Nick Tilotta is an expert on Thompson submachine guns. He helped to explain all of the subtle differences between models and variation. He can be reached at P.O. Box 451, Grapevine, Texas, 817-481-6616.

Don Westmoreland is a serious student of Japanese and German World War II automatic weapons. His knowledge was extremely valuable.

Stan Andrewski, a crackerjack gunsmith, can be reached at 603-746-4387 for those who desire nothing but the best in the way of repair and refinishing work on their Class III firearms.

Dan Shea, editor and publisher of the *Small Arms Review*, lent his mastery of Class III firearms.

Ted Dawidowicz of Dalvar, USA made photos available of currently imported Polish military firearms. He may be reached at 740 E. Warm Springs Rd. Ste. #122, Henderson, NV 89015, 702-558-6707.

I want to thank Jim Allee of I.D.S.A. Books for his expert advice concerning the scope of this book based on his encyclopedic knowledge of military books. He was also generous with the use of his extensive personal library. Jim can be reached at P.O. Box 1457-G, Piqua, OH 45356, 937-773-4203.

Blake Stevens, Collector Grade Publications, shared his vast knowledge of military firearms as well as photos from his first-class publications. Blake can be reached at 905-342-3434.

A special thanks to all the manufacturers and importers who supplied us with information and photographs on their products.

Ted Willems and Bruce Wolberg of *Gun List* have been most helpful with information and locating hard-to-find firearms.

Ricky Kumor, Sr. spent much of his valuable time making constructive suggestions and sharing his bottomless expertise of military firearms.

James Rankin gave freely of his vast experience as an author and small arms expert to steer this book in the right direction. His assistance is gratefully acknowledged.

Mark Keefe, editor of the *American Rifleman*, is a keen student of military firearms. He was particulay helpful on Lee-Enfield rifles with small but important details that are so useful to the collector.

A special note of appreciation to Chuck Karwan, one of the contributing editors of this book, who gave unselfishly of his enormous store of knowledge of military firearms.

Richard R. Wray, one of the deans of the Class III community with 50 years of experience, and Ken Keilholtz with over 30 years of experience, both extremely knowledgable Class III collectors, gave generously of their time and expertise to make this a more useful and more accurate publication. Photos of their comprehensive collections are seen throughout this book.

J. R. Moody, a contributing editor, willingly gave of his time and expertise based on his years of practical hands-on experience with Class III weapons and sniper rifles.

Many thanks to Pedro Bello for sharing his extensive experience and knowledge of machine pistols.

I want to thank the contributing editors to this publications who have gone out of their way to give of their time and knowledge to make this a better book. Any errors or omissions in this book are entirely the editor's responsibility.

PHOTO CREDITS

Many of the large format photos in this book were taken by Paul Goodwin, a photographer of exceptional ability.

A special acknowledgment to Kris Leinicke, curator of the Rock Island Arsenal Museum, for allowing us full access to the museum's outstanding firearms collection.

Karl Karash supplied photos from his personal Colt 1911 collection.

Jim Rankin has an extensive library of photos he was kind enough to share with the readers.

Robert Fisch, curator of the museum at the United States Military Academy at West Point was most helpful and cooperative in sharing that institutions wonderful treasure trove of historically important firearms.

Robert Segel lent photos of his superb collection of vintage machine guns, beautifully photographed and displayed.

Many thanks to Charles Kenyon for the use of photos for his forthcoming book on Luger pistols.

Chuck Karwan shared many photos from his extensive photo archives of military firearms.

Ricky Kumor, Sr. photographed many of the rare and high quality military weapons that flow through his shop.

INTRODUCTION

When the decision was made to publish a price and reference guide to military firearms a host of parameters had to be addressed and established. For example, what exactly is a military firearm? If we include those firearms used in combat then we might as well include all firearms. Most militaries used whatever was available at the time. On the other hand, if we only include those firearms designed and used exclusively for and by militaries, then this book would be very small. The military firearms that are included in this book are generally thought of as combat weapons, as opposed to the miriad of guns that were purchased by militaries as training guns or general purpose non-combat weapons, although some of those are included as well. In the end this book is an attempt to combine those firearms that are thought of as military and so marked, even if they were available on a commercial basis. The parameters set for the scope of this book are arbitary and the sole responsibility of the editor.

Because this publication is not an encyclopedic work of military small arms, it covers only those military firearms that the collector in North America can expect to locate and purchase. Therefore, a number of military firearms are not listed in this book. These omissions are particularly noticeable for current military firearms, both domestic and foreign, that have not been released for civilian sale. We have not included any experimental weapons or prototypes because of their lack of availability to the general collector.

This publication goes to great lengths to show the reader what he or she may expect to find in the way of markings on various military small arms. Large format photos have been used to illustrate important features and markings that the collector may encounter. The military collector knows better than most firearms collectors that markings help to determine rarity, eras of use, issuing services, and a host of other important information. Good quality photos go a long way in helping the begining collector and reminding the verteran where and what these markings should be.

We do, however, try to give the collector a comprehensive look at collectable military firearms from 1870 to the present day.

Good luck with your collecting and be safe in your shooting.

Ned Schwing
Editor

GRADING SYSTEM

In the opinion of the editor all grading systems are subjective. It is our task to offer the collector and dealer a measurement that most closely reflects a general consensus on condition. The system we present seems to come closest to describing a firearm in universal terms. We strongly recommend that the reader acquaint himself with this grading system before attempting to determine the correct price for a particular firearm's condition. Remember, in most cases condition determines price.

NIB-New in Box
This category can sometimes be misleading. It means that the firearm is in its original factory carton with all of the appropriate papers. It also means the firearm is new; that it has not been fired and has no wear. This classification brings a substantial premium for both the collector and shooter.

Excellent
Collector quality firearms in this condition are highly desirable. The firearm must be in at least 98 percent condition with respect to blue wear, stock or grip finish, and bore. The firearm must also be in 100 percent original factory condition without refinishing, repair, alterations or additions of any kind. Sights must be factory original as well. This grading classification includes both modern and antique (manufactured prior to 1898) firearms.

Very Good
Firearms in this category are also sought after both by the collector and shooter. Firearms must be in working order and retain approximately 92 percent metal and wood finish. It must be 100 percent factory original, but may have some small repairs, alterations, or non-factory additions. No refinishing is permitted in this category. Both modern and antique firearms are included in this classification.

Good
Modern firearms in this category may not be considered to be as collectable as the previous grades, but antique firearms are considered desirable. Modern firearms must retain at least 80 percent metal and wood finish, but may display evidence of old refinishing. Small repairs, alterations, or non-factory additions are sometimes encountered in this class. Factory replacement parts are permitted. The overall working condition of the firearm must be good as well as safe. The bore may exhibit wear or some corrosion, especially in antique arms. Antique firearms may be included in this category if their metal and wood finish is at least 50 percent original factory finish.

Fair
Firearms in this category should be in satisfactory working order and safe to shoot. The overall metal and wood finish on the modern firearm must be at least 30 percent and antique firearms must have at least some original finish or old refinish remaining. Repairs, alterations, nonfactory additions, and recent refinishing would all place a firearm in this classification. However, the modern firearm must be in working condition, while the antique firearm may not function. In either case the firearm must be considered safe to fire if in a working state.

Poor
Neither collectors nor shooters are likely to exhibit much interest in firearms in this condition. Modern firearms are likely to retain little metal or wood finish. Pitting and rust will be seen in firearms in this category. Modern firearms may not be in working order and may not be safe to shoot. Repairs and refinishing would be necessary to restore the firearm to safe working order. Antique firearms will have no finish and will not function. In the case of modern firearms their principal value lies in spare parts. On the other hand, antique firearms in this condition may be used as "wall hangers" or as an example of an extremely rare variation or have some kind of historical significance.

Pricing Sample Format

NIB	Exc.	V.G.	Good	Fair	Poor
550	450	400	350	300	200

PRICING

The prices given in this book are <u>RETAIL</u> prices.

Unfortunately for shooters and collectors, there is no central clearinghouse for firearms prices. The prices given in this book are designed as a guide, not as a quote. This is an important distinction because prices for firearms vary with the time of the year and geographical location. For example, interest in firearms is at its lowest point in the summer. People are not as interested in shooting and collecting at this time of the year as they are in playing golf or taking a vacation.

It is not practical to list prices in this book with regard to time of year or location. What is given is a reasonable price based on sales at gun shows, auction houses, *Gun List* prices, and information obtained from knowledgeable collectors and dealers. The firearms prices listed in this book are **RETAIL PRICES** and may bring more or less depending on the variables discussed above. If you choose to sell your gun to a dealer you will not receive the retail price but a wholesale price based on the markup that particular dealer needs to operate. Also, in certain cases there will be no price indicated under a particular condition but rather the notation "N/A" or the symbol "—". This indicates that there is no known price available for that gun in that condition or the sales for that particular model are so few that a reliable price cannot be given. This will usually be encounter only with very rare guns, with newly introduced firearms, or more likely with antique firearms in those conditions most likely to be encountered. Most antique firearms will be seen in the good, fair and poor categories.

One final note. The prices listed here come from a variety of sources: retail stores, gun shows, individual collectors, and auction houses. Due to the nature of business one will usually pay higher prices at a retail store than at a gun show. In some cases auctions will produce excellent buys or extravagant prices, depending on any given situation. Collectors will sometimes pay higher prices for a firearm that they need to fill out their collection when in other circumstances they will not be willing to pay market price if they don't have to have the gun. The point here is that prices paid for firearms is an ever-changing affair based on a large number of variables. The prices in this book are a **GENERAL GUIDE** as to what a willing buyer and willing seller might agree on. You may find

the item for less, and then again you may have to pay more depending on the variables of your particular situation.

Sometimes we lose sight of our collecting or shooting goals and focus only on price. Two thoughts come to mind. First, one long time collector told me once that, "you can never pay too much for a good gun." Second, Benjamin Franklin once said, "the bitterness of poor quality lingers long after the sweetness of a low price."

In the final analysis, the prices listed here are given to assist the shooter and collector in pursuing their hobby with a better understanding of what is going on in the marketplace. If this book can expand one's knowledge, then it will have fulfilled its purpose.

There is one pricing comment that should be made about military firearms in particular. The prices given in this book for foreign firearms are for guns that do not have an importer's stamp affixed to them. This stamping became a federal requirement in 1968. The importer's stamp was required to be placed on the receiver or frame of the firearm in a conspicuous location. To many collectors this makes little difference in their collecting. To others it makes a significant difference and this group will pay more for firearms without an importer's stamp.

Note also that the prices listed below for Class III weapons reflect the gun only with one magazine and no accessories. The prices for medium and heavy machine guns do not include bipods or tripods. These necessary items are extra. Buyer and seller should note that machine gun mounts come in various configurations. Mounts may range in price from several hundred dollars to several thousand dollars depending on type.

A futher caution regarding the buying and selling of Class III firearms. These weapons are highly restricted by federal law. Some states do not allow its citizens to own these firearms. Because the value of these Class III firearms lies not only in the historical and techinical significance of the weapon, it also lies in the grandfathered paper that accompanied each gun. These values sited in this publication can change overnight if federal or state law changes. Be aware. Be cautious.

ADDITIONAL CONSIDERATIONS

Perhaps the best advice is for the collector to take his time. Do not be in a hurry and do not allow yourself to be rushed into making a decision. Learn as much as possible about the firearms you are interested in collecting or shooting. Try to keep current with prices through *Gun List* and this publication. Go to gun shows, not just to buy or sell but to observe and learn. It is also helpful to join a firearms club or association. These groups have older, experienced collectors who are glad to help the beginner or veteran. One of the best starting points in firearms collecting is to read as much as possible. There are many first-rate publications available to the beginner and veteran collector alike that will not only broaden his knowledge of a particular collecting field but also entertain and enlighten as well.

In the preparation of this book I have encountered a vast number of models, variations, and subvariations. It is not possible to cover these in the kind of detail necessary to account for every possible deviation in every model produced. The collector needs to read in- depth studies of models and manufacturers to accomplish this task. Knowledge and experience together fashion the foundation for successful collecting.

Firearms collecting is a rewarding hobby. Firearms are part of our nation's history and represent an opportunity to learn more about their role in that American experience. If done skillfully, firearms collecting can be a profitable hobby as well.

AUCTION HOUSE CREDITS

The following auction houses were kind enough to allow the Catalog to report unusual firearms from their sales. The directors of these auction concerns are acknowledged for their assistance and support.

Amoskeag Auction Company, Inc.
  250 Commercial Street, Unit #3011
  Manchester, NH 03101
  Attention: Jason or Melissa Devine
  603-627-7383
  603-627-7384 FAX

Butterfield & Butterfield
  220 San Bruno Avenue
  San Francisco, CA 94103
  Attention: James Ferrell
  415-861-7500 ext. 327
  415-861-8951 FAX

Old Town Station Ltd.
  P.O. Box 15351
  Lenexa, KS 66285
  Attention: Jim Supica
  913-492-3000
  913-492-3022 FAX

Rock Island Auction Company
  1050 36th Avenue
  Moline, IL 61265
  Attention: Patrick Hogan
  800-238-8022
  309-797-1655 FAX

THE EDITOR

Ned Schwing is the author of:

The Winchester Model 42, Winchester's Finest: The Model 21, Winchester Slide Action Rifles, Volume I: The Model 1890 and Model 1906, Winchester Slide Action Rifles, Volume II: The Model 61 and Model 62, The Browning Superposed: John M. Browning's Last Legacy, For the past 10 years he has been the editor of the *Standard Catalog of Firearms.* He is also the firearms contributor to the *Standard Catalog of Winchester.* His articles have appeared in the *American Rifleman, Guns Illustrated, Shooting Sportsman, Waffen Digest, Double Gun Journal,* and other firearm publications.

CONTRIBUTING EDITORS

Bob Ball
  Springfield Armory & Mauser rifles
  P.O. Box 562
  Unionville, CT 06085

Scott Bennett
  Modern Military weapons
  2557 E. Loop 820 N.
  Fort Worth, TX 76118
  817-595-2485

David Bichrest
  Winchester lever action rifles
  P.O. Box 177
  Wiergate, TX 75977-0177
  409-787-4671

John Callahan
  Savage Historian
  53 Old Quarry Road
  Westfield, MA 01085

Bruce Canfield
  U.S. Military firearms
  P.O. Box 6171
  Shrevport, LA 71136

Jim Cate
  J.P. Sauer pistols
  406 Pine Bluff Dr.
  Chattanooga, TN 37412
  423-892-6320

Steve Hill
  Spotted Dog Firearms
  Class III Firearms
  Scottsdale, AZ
  602-538-2769

Doug MacBeth
  Acme Firearms
  Class III firearms
  Scottsdale, AZ
  602-762-0429

Karl Karash
  Colt Model 1911 & 1911A1
  288 Randall Road
  Berlin, MA 01503
  978-838-9401
  FAX 987-589-2060

Chuck Karwan
  Colt New Service, Browning High-Power,
  Lee-Enfield, Webley revolvers
  958 Cougar Creek Road
  Oakland, OR 97462
  541-459-4134

Richard M. Kumor Sr.
c/o Ricky's Gun Room
WWII era military firearms
P.O. Box 286
Chicopee, MA 01021
413-592-5000
413-594-5700 FAX
e-mail Rickyslnc@aol.com
Website rickysinc.com

Gale Morgan
Luger and Mauser pistols
Pre-World War I pistols
P.O. Box 72
Lincoln, CA 95648
916-645-1720

J.R. Moody
Contemporary Military small arms
c/o Ned Schwing
Krause Publications
700. E State St.
Iola, WI 54990

Charles Pate
U.S. Military handguns
c/o Ned Schwing
Krause Publications
700. E State St.
Iola, WI 54990

Jim Rankin
Walther pistols & pre-war auto pistols
3615 Anderson Road
Coral Gables, FL 33134
305-446-1792

Orvel Reichert
World War II-era semiautomatic
pistols
P.O. Box 67
Vader, WA 98593
360-245-3492
email:mr.p38@localaccess.com

Howard Resnick
19th century military handguns
141 S. Smoke Raod
Valpariso, IN 46385
219-477-1045

Joe Schroeder
Steyer/Mannlicher pistols
P.O. Box 406
Glenview, IL 60025
847-724-8816
827-657-6500
847-724-8831 FAX

John Stimson, Jr.
High Standard pistols
540 W 92nd Street
Indianapolis, IN 46260
317-831-2990

Jim Supica
Smith & Wesson
P.O. Box 15351
Lenexa, KS 66285
913-492-3000

Nick Tilotta
Great Western Firearms Co.
Thompson sub-machine guns
P.O. Box 451
Grapevine, TX 76099
817-481-6616
FAX-817-251-5136

Don Westmoreland
Class III Curio & Relic guns
c/o Ned Schwing
Krause Publications
700. E State St.
Iola, WI 54990

Bibliographical Notes:

There are a number of excellent comprehensive books on military history for the period that this volume covers. Perhaps the best, at least in my opinion, are two outstanding studies by Edward Ezell. They are: *Small Arms of the World*, 12th edition, Stackpole Books, 1983, and *Handguns of the World*, Stackpole Books, 1981. For early military revolvers the two volume work by Rolf H. Muller, *Geschichte und Technik der Europaischen Militarrevolver*, Journal-Verlag Schwend, 1982 is excellent. For modern military weapons *Jane's Infantry Weapons* gives a broad overview, with technical data, of just about any modern military weapon in use in recent times. Donald Webster's book on *Military Bolt Action Rifles, 1841-1918*, Museum Restoration Service, 1993 filled some important gaps in information on early bolt action rifles. There are additional titles that are of interest and offer beneficial information: *Pistols of the World*, 3rd ed., Hogg and Weeks, DBI Books, 1992. *Rifles of the World*, John Walter, DBI books, 1993. *Military Small Arms of the 20th Century*, 7th ed., Hogg and Weeks, Krause Publications, 1999. *Small Arms Today*, 2nd ed., Edward Ezell, Stackpole Books, 1988. *The Greenhill Military Small Arms Data Book*. Ian Hogg, Greenhill Books, 1999. *Modern Machine Guns*, John Walter, Greenhill Books, 2000. *The Encyclopedia of Modern Military Weapons*, Chris Bishop, ed., Barnes & Noble , 1999. *The World's Submachine Guns*, Vol. I, Thomas B. Nelson, 1964. *The World's Assault Rifles*, Vol. II, Musgrave and Nelson, 1967. *The World's Fighting Shotguns*, Vol. IV, Thomas F. Swearengen, Ironside, 1978. *Flayderman's Guide to Antique American Firearms...and Their Value*, 7th edition, Krause Publications, 1998. I have endeavored to give the reader a listing of helpful books of specific weapons at the beginning of each section, where applicable, so that he may easily pursue additional information that is outside the scope of this book.

COLLECTING MILITARY FIREARMS

by Chuck Karwan

I have been collecting military firearms for about 42 years. That's not bad for a guy 54 years old. My first rifle was a British .303 Mark III* Lee-Enfield of WWI vintage that cost $14.95 at Newman & Sterns sporting goods store in downtown Cleveland, Ohio. In case you were wondering, my mother was with me at the time and I carried the rifle home on the city bus with nary a glance from fellow passengers. The next one was bought mail order. It was a Swiss Vetterli .41 rimfire M78 Sharpshooter's rifle that cost me $14.95 in paper route money plus shipping from Golden State Arms.

Since those grand old innocent days, I have had several hundred military rifles, pistols, shotguns, and legally registered machine guns pass through my hands. I have actively collected them along a variety of different themes resulting in the acquisition of a considerable amount of experience and information covering a wide field.

It has been an immensely interesting, educational, and enjoyable hobby. It has also been quite cost effective. By that I mean that when I have sold or traded off a specimen from my collection I have virtually always made a profit that at least offset the rate of inflation and more often than not resulted in enough extra profit to allow me to buy something else for my collection.

If you were to total up all the firearms ever made in the world, I believe that you would find that well over 90% were originally made for military use. Only in the United States would you find that civilian arms production is even remotely comparable to military production. That is because we are the only country in the world with a big population with a large legal market for non-military sporting and defensive firearms.

For the same reason, the U. S. has been the dumping ground for much of the world's unwanted military surplus small arms since just after the American Civil War. Very few other countries offered a significant market for such guns. Prior to the Civil War improvements in military arms came about rather slowly so military firearms generally wore out before they became obsolete and surplus. In the period of the Civil War and for the next fifty years saw the world's militaries go from muzzle loaders to single shot breechloaders to black powder repeaters to early smokeless powder repeaters. Each stage made the previous models obsolete and surplus. The field of military handguns paralleled this with percussion revolvers being replaced with cartridge revolvers then by faster loading and ejecting revolvers then by semiautomatics. Then along comes the World Wars and huge production of arms that were surplus after the wars ended.

Various countries exported practically all of their obsolete former arms to the U. S. In some cases collectors from countries like Switzerland have had to come to the U. S. to fill out their collections because more specimens were here than in their native land.

Today the only other countries left with a significant number of military arms collectors are Germany, Switzerland, Norway, and Finland often with substantial restrictions. While England, Sweden, Canada, Australia, Belgium, and New Zealand used to have many military arms collectors, the left wing socialist governments in those countries have made it extremely difficult to impossible for collectors to continue.

I have had a number of "authorities" tell me that the days of large quantities of military surplus guns being available are all but over. Barring the passing of some new legislation to ban importation of military surplus arms, nothing could be further from the truth. There are huge numbers of obsolete military guns in circulation both in the United States and on the international market. Periodically the latter are sold and eventually make there way to the U. S. for sale to collectors and shooters.

While many traditional sources for such guns, like England, have begun to dry up there are many as yet untapped or barely tapped sources still available. For example there are mammoth quantities of obsolete military surplus guns in Russia. One reliable source reports that there are 20 million Mosin-Nagant rifles alone, not to mention many others. These include large amounts of captured German and other origin equipment from WWII as well as huge amounts of other obsolete Soviet equipment from the same period. Reportedly, a substantial number of American made Winchester M95 7.62x54Rmm muskets made for the Czar's army in WWI have recently been located and will be available in the near future.

Similarly there are also large quantities of surplus military guns still in China. Taiwan also has large quantities but has yet to release any of it. Currently a good variety of such guns are coming out of former Soviet republics and former Iron Curtain countries that are now independent.

There are also still large quantities of such guns in Latin America and Asia. Just recently, the Gibbs Rifle Company imported original German 11mm G71/84 Mauser rifles and G88 8x57mm rifles as well as Austrian M1886 11mm and M1888/90 8x50Rmm Mannlicher rifles from Ecuador. Since these were all made well before 1898 they are legally antiques. It's hard to believe that there would be quantities of guns over 110 years old still in storage some where but there's your proof. I would bet good money that these aren't the only antique military guns still out there let alone guns of more recent vintage.

The legal significance of "antique" status is that they can be brought into the country without paying duty and with virtually no restriction. Similarly they can be sold without federal paperwork (Form 4473) and may be shipped interstate directly to an individual without going through a dealer just like all guns could be prior to 1968.

Military surplus gun collecting was doing fine in the U. S. until 1968. Thanks largely to over reaction to some prominent assassinations and the complicity of American gun manufacturers that did not want to compete against cheap military surplus guns, the Gun Control Act of 1968 banned the importation of military surplus guns. Fortunately, several large importers of such guns, such as Interarms, Century Arms, and Springfield Sporters had warehouses full enough to keep a limited selection of surplus guns on the U. S. retail market in quantity for many years there after. For those of us interested in military arms, that period was pure torture. A lot of extremely neat and desirable military surplus guns were imported into Canada at that time but were unavailable in the U. S.

Fortunately in 1986 the federal law was changed to allow the importation of most guns classified as "Curios and Relics" by the ATF. All manually operated and semiautomatic military firearms made before 1946 had been previously declared to be "Curios and Relics". Thus, this law allowed the importation of most of the obsolete military surplus guns on the world market. Since many military arms made after 1946 were also on the Curio and Relic list or were later added to it, the pool of military surplus arms available for importation increased even further. Examples of the latter include the Soviet SKS carbines and the Indian 2A1 .308 Lee-Enfields to name just a couple.

That's the good news, the bad news is that President Clinton used executive orders and special trade agreements to prevent the importation of many such guns from China, Russia, and other sources.

It remains to be seen if President Bush will let these stand or not.

Most military long arms originating after WWII are not importable because they are capable of full automatic fire or are not classified as a Curio & Relic though there are exceptions.

One aspect of military arms collecting that must be understood is the fact that what is rare today can often become common over night if large quantities are imported from overseas. Naturally this will have a very negative effect on the market value of such guns. Examples from the recent past include the unique roller locked Czech Vz52 pistol and the East German version of the Makarov pistol. Both pistols had a market value of $700 to $800 among collectors because of their rarity. Then large quantities of these pistols were imported and sold for just a little over $100. It did not please those few that already had such guns but it sure did please the rest of us that didn't.

This brings up another important point. Prior to 1968 imported military surplus guns were not marked with importer's markings. After 1986 when importation recommenced, such marking was required by import regulations. Initially collectors holding guns without importer's markings tried to make a big deal out of the fact that their guns didn't have them. However, few people were willing to pay a several hundred percent premium just to avoid the importer's stamp. Most importers are currently using an extremely small stamp and are putting it in an unobtrusive place so collectors are even less critical.

While it is desirable to have a specimen not "blemished" by an importer's stamp, the difference in market value for two otherwise identical specimens, one with and one without importer markings, has steadily dropped. In most cases the difference is as little as 10% or even less. Most collectors would much rather have a minty specimen with an importer's stamp than a significantly inferior condition specimen without one.

Unlike most commercial arms it is common for military arms to have many of their parts serial numbered. Generally the receiver will have a serial number and then other parts will be marked with the last several digits of that number. It is highly desireable that all of these numbers match. It is common enough to find the numbers mixed after a gun has been rebuilt or modified at an arsenal. However, in the case of rifles in particular it is important that the bolt's number match that of the receiver otherwise the rifle may suffer with problems like excessive headspace.

The key factors in judging a military arm are originality of all parts including matching numbers, percent of original finish or arsenal refinish, soundness and condition of the wood or grips, and bore condition.

Among military arms collected, by far the largest area is the manually operated rifles. The big five of manually operated military rifles with regard to production numbers are the German designed M98 type Mausers (somewhere between 50 and 100 million made), the Russian Mosin-Nagant rifles (30+ million made), the British Lee-Enfields (11+ million made), the Japanese Type 38 and 99 Arisakas (7+ million made), and the Austro-Hungarian Mannlicher M95 straight pull (6+ million made). Other large categories include the French Lebel and Berthier rifles, the Italian Carcanos, the various Krags, the American made Enfields (P14 and M1917), the Mannlicher turnbolts, the Swiss Schmidt-Rubin, and the M1903 Springfield family just to name some of the other major players.

The Mauser rifle field also includes not only the M98 types, by far the most common, but also the many pre-M98 varieties including the G71, G71/84, the M1889, '90, and '91 series, as well as the M1893, 94, 95, and 96 series some of which stayed in production well into WWII. As you can see, just in the field of breech loading military rifles the number of guns and potential sub-fields of interest are enormous.

The nature of military organizations is that there are probably 100 or more rifles produced for every handgun made. Consequently handguns are as a rule much less common and typically more expensive than rifles of the same origin and vintage. Their personal nature and small size make military handguns popular for collecting.

Unfortunately, the change of law in 1986 that allowed the importation of Curio & Relic military surplus guns has additional requirements for handguns before they can qualify for importation. Basically military surplus handguns must meet the same arbitrary safety and size requirement "sporting criteria" as commercial imported handguns. This keeps out many of the small military handguns as

well as such guns as the Russian Tokarev because it has no manual safety.

Everything said earlier about the enjoyment of shooting military rifles also applies to shooting military handguns except for the availability of matches.

There are endless persistent myths that surround various military guns. Many stem from a prejudice against weapons used by our enemies, ignorance of the facts, or just an arrogant belief that nobody else can make a gun as good as we can. The simple fact is that practically all military arms, no matter the country of origin, are quite safe in design and construction even if they may be relatively crude in finish.

One common myth is that the roughly finished simplified Type 99 7.7mm Arisaka rifles produced by the Japanese late in WWII are made from suspect materials and are liable to blow up if fired. In actuality the results of several blow up tests of such rifles indicate that the crudest "Last Ditch" Arisaka ever made is probably stronger than the best U. S. M1903 Springfield ever made.

A similar myth talks about the crude Jap rifles made with cast receivers that are totally unsafe to shoot. It is true that such "guns" do exist and they are unsafe to fire with ball ammunition. The point totally missed is that such guns were Japanese training rifles originally intended to only fire blanks!

Yet another Arisaka myth says that the safety of the Type 38 and 99 Arisakas is awkward to use. In actuality it is probably the simplest, strongest, fastest, and easiest to use manual safety found on any military rifle.

The Russian Mosin-Nagant rifle action is often characterized as weak when actually, like the Japanese Arisakas, it is one of the strongest of the military rifles.

The British Lee Enfield series is often criticized as being "inaccurate" because of its rear locking bolt and two piece stock. In my considerable experience, with good ammunition the Lee-Enfields will more than hold their own in the accuracy department with the service rifles of any country. Indeed I have won more than a couple bets shooting Lee-Enfields for accuracy against Mausers, M1903 Springfields, and other rifles.

One military rifle that has received more than its share of myths is the U. S. M1917. It is commonly put forth that it was only used as a training rifle in WWI when in actuality it was the primary rifle of the American Expeditionary Force with more than three quarters of the American rifleman using the M1917. It is often portrayed as only being used as a training rifle in WWII when it actually saw a tremendous amount of action by the Philippine Army, the Free French, the Nationalist Chinese, and other allies as a primary rifle and by the Canadians, the British, and the U. S. as a secondary rifle.

It is also commonly said that the M1917 is not very accurate because its bore is oversized because it was based on an English .303 P14 design. The truth is that the M1917 rifle's bore has tighter specifications than that of the M1903 Springfield. Given match grade ammunition the M1917 is the single most accurate military service rifle, on the average, of all the ones I have tested. Testing examples made by all three of the original manufacturers, every one would consistently shoot less than one inch groups at one hundred yards with match grade ammunition.

Another myth that is often repeated is that the M1903 Springfield was the most accurate service rifle of its day. My tests indicate that the M1903 is not even in the top five! Consistently out shooting service grade M1903s are Finnish M28/30 and M39 Mosin-Nagant rifles, Swedish Mausers, the Canadian Ross Mark III, the British P14, the Swiss K31 Schmidt-Rubin, and the U. S. M1917. I bring all this up to illustrate the excellence of many foreign and domestic military rifles in their design, accuracy, strength, and other features. I could write a whole book on the myths that surround just military rifles alone.

Most people that collect military arms enjoy shooting them. One of the major reasons Mausers and Lee-Enfields are so popular is that high quality American made ammunition is readily available for most caliber variations. Then there is the military surplus ammunition.

As this is being written 8x56Rmm ammunition for many of the Mannlicher M95 rifles is available in quantity in original Mannlicher clips at great prices for the first time in many years. In spite of the fact that the ammunition was all made in the 1930s and early 1940s it has proven to be sure fire and of quite high quality.

Recently an enormous amount of 8x57mm ammunition was sold off by Turkey. It varies from several decades old to relatively recent manufacture and is being sold for as little as 7¢ per round shipping included. This is a fantastic buy. There are many other examples available and it is quite uncommon to find a military rifle or pistol for which ammunition is not available from some source.

There is one big catch about using surplus ammunition. Most of it has corrosive priming that leaves highly corrosive chemical salts in the bore of the gun after it is shot. If these corrosive salts are not cleaned out within a few hours after shooting, the bore will begin to rust and can soon become irreparably pitted.

Another problem is that most of the modern bore cleaners or solvents will not dissolve these corrosive salts. The only commonly available commercial bore cleaner rated for cleaning corrosive priming residue is Hoppe's No. 9. In its absence one can use warm water since the salts are also easily dissolved in water. Be sure to dry the bore thoroughly and then protect it with a coat of a preservative oil or grease.

In a pinch, the destructive action of the corrosive priming can be delayed for a short while by giving the bore a good coat of a water displacing oil like WD40. However, the bore can still rust under the oil if cleaning is delayed too long.

An other important aspect to remember is that if you shoot corrosive primed ammunition in a gas operated semiautomatic or machine gun, the corrosive residues end up in the gas system as well.

Consequently, the gas system has to be thoroughly cleaned of corrosive residues or it will quickly begin to rust as well. This extra effort is such a pain in the butt that I refuse to shoot any of my gas operated guns like my Swedish Ag42, Egyptian Hakim, or French M49/56 with corrosive primed ammunition.

There is a recent trend for many gun clubs to have shooting matches restricted to as issued military rifles or with a military rifle category. They are immense fun. The Civilian Marksmanship Program, formerly known as the DCM, also sponsors matches only open to as issued U. S. service rifles and carbines of WWI and WWII. These are called John C. Garand matches in honor of the designer of the M1 Garand.

I take great delight in showing up at local rifle matches with some oddball military rifle and doing reasonably well with it. At one particularly memorable match I shot a mildly tuned Canadian Longbranch No. 4 Lee-Enfield. In the prone phase I shot a clean 100 with 7Xs beating out all the other competitors, some of which were shooting commercial target and military match rifles. How sweet it was! Even if it only amounts to some informal target shooting or plinking, do not overlook this aspect of military arms collecting.

Similarly I find it to be fun to take some of my military guns out hunting. I have shot prairie dogs with an M1903A3, several deer with Lee-Enfields, squirrels and other small game with several different military .22 training rifles, a deer with a French FR-F1 sniper rifle, and many others. I find that I learn a lot about how the gun handles and shoots under field conditions when hunting and I find such experiences highly enlightening and enjoyable.

I have previously mentioned the term Curio & Relic several times as it applies to most military surplus arms. What many collectors do not know is that here is a Federal Curio & Relic Collector's license. This license costs only $30 for three years, has minimal record keeping requirements, and is easy to obtain.

It is not a license to be a dealer in such guns. However, it does allow a collector to buy guns classified as Curio & Relics directly through the mail or in states other than your residence. Also a Collector's License holder does not have to undergo a background check when purchasing Curio & Relic firearms. Since many full automatic weapons have Curio & Relic status, a Collector License holder can purchase such guns directly, where it is legal under local law. All transfer taxes must still be paid and other requirements for a sale of a machine gun to a private citizen met, but it cuts out the inconvenience and expense of having to go through a Class 3 dealer.

When a Collector's License holder purchases any firearm not classified as a Curio & Relic, then all legal restrictions and requirements demanded of a non-license holder must be complied with. A serious collector of military firearms of the Curio & Relic kind should definitely consider obtaining a Federal Collector's License.

There are countless approaches to collecting military arms. Some do it by country or by type such as Mausers, Lee-Enfields, carbines, or semiautomatics. Others do it by historical association such as wars. One fellow I know collects military rifles made in the U. S. for foreign countries. Another collects sniper rifles. One friend collects military bolt actions chambered for rimmed cartridges.

Whatever makes your clock tick can work. I have collected Tokarev pistol variations, Browning High Powers, Springfield M1903s, Lee-Enfields, Ross rifles, oddball conversions, military match rifles, and just plain whatever took my fancy.

I find that I get more enjoyment out of collecting variety than sameness. That is, having several different Lee-Enfield models is more fun than having a bunch of Tokarev pistols that are all virtually identical except for the markings.

A big part of the enjoyment in military arms collecting is in the hunt just as in any other collecting endeavor. However, unlike many other gun collecting fields it is entirely possible to find many interesting pieces for under $100 and $200 will buy the majority of military surplus rifles and a surprising number of handguns.

As this is written there is a large variety of Mausers, Lee-Enfields, Mosin-Nagants, and M95 Mannlichers on the market at very low prices. Some like the German made Turkish Mausers can be bought for not much over $50 in decent shape.

It is a common mistake to think that models on the market may be available for a long time.

Sometimes they are but sometimes they are only available for a very short time. Once the availability of a gun model from the distributors dries up, invariably the market value goes up steeply. Do not procrastinate!

The other day I was cleaning a Turkish M1903 Mauser just a few feet from one of my favorite Lee-Enfields, an Australian made Mark III. It suddenly dawned on me that these rifles could have faced each other at Gallipoli or at some other battle. As I have done many times before with such guns I thought, " If they could only talk."

CLASS III FIREARMS

by J. R. Moody

The 1920s and early 1930s in this country were years that encompassed much change. The free spirited and roaring 1920s were very different from the previous staid Victorian years. Speakeasy's, drinking parties, and high living were the order of the day, even though there was a legal prohibition against alcohol. But legality aside, people drank anyway. This indifference to the law gave way to black markets, spawning racketeers and gangsters like Al Capone.

Gangsters, being gangsters, utilized the ends justify the means philosophy. They used any weapon that seemed appropriate, most notably the Thompson sub-machine gun, to exterminate rival gangs, police, or whomever stood in their way. The Thompson fired .45 caliber bullets at a rate of between 600 and 1,000 rounds per minute. This was quite extraordinary for its day.

The police, not wanting to be outdone in the arms race, also bought Thompson sub-machine guns as did the FBI. The amazing fact at the time was that any person could purchase a machine gun or any other firearm without any registration or background check whatsoever. This enabled the underworld to utilize these deadly weapons even to the extent of mail order purchase.

In 1934 Congress put a stop to this unregulated situation by enacting the 1934 National Firearms Act. This act did not ban the acquisition of any automatic weapons, it just halted convicted felons and gangsters from purchasing them. After this act became law any individual desiring to purchase a machine gun, silencer, short barrel rifle or shotgun, had to comply with an FBI background check, get local law enforcement approval, and pay a $200 one time tax for each NFA firearm. This law apparently stopped most of the criminal use of these types of weapons.

The law has not stopped the unregistered, stolen, or illegally smuggled machine guns from being used by criminals in their illegal activities, however. But, accordingly to one top ATF official, registered NFA weapons are used in virtually no crimes in this country. In fact, in the 60 years that this law as been in effect only one NFA registered weapon was used in the commission of a crime, and that was a crime of passion.

Today the ATF, or Alcohol, Tobacco, and Firearms Agency, oversees the registration of automatic firearms from its NFA branch. The agency makes certain that no criminal can qualify for the legal possession of any NFA weapon. But, criminals are unlikely to pay a $200 transfer tax and wait approximately three months to take possession of a NFA firearm after it is legally transferred.

It cannot be stressed enough that the possession of an unregistered machine gun, silencer or short barreled rifle or shotgun can result in a $10,000 fine and/or 10 years in jail. Always obey the law.

As a historian I view the machine gun as a significant force that changed the course of military history over the last 100 years. Despite its historical impact some are uncertain as to precisely what the term machine gun means. A machine gun can fire continuously with one pull of the trigger, and when the trigger is released the gun stops firing. This vast increase in firepower has changed military tactics from their first widespread use in World War One to the present day.

Under the broad heading of machine guns are three distinct types. The first type is the sub-machine gun which is a short, handy, lightweight weapon typically firing a pistol caliber such as the .45 ACP, 9mm, or 7.62 Tokarev. Sub-machine guns are the most controllable in full automatic fire due to the low power cartridges used. One can be taught to shoot a target in full automatic fire without the gun veering or pulling up away from the line of fire. The downside of sub-machine guns is their limited penetration and range, usually no more than 150 meters.

Historically, the sub-machine gun played a major role in many conflicts all over the world. During World War II U.S. troops used the M1 Thompson or M3 sub-machine in many battles. The German soldier used the MP40 in every part of the war. The Russian soldier attacked with vigor using the PPSH41 or Burp gun as it was sometimes called. In the 1956, 1967, and 1973 Arab-Israeli conflicts, the Israeli soldier fielded the Uzi sub-machine gun against his attackers. The Uzi was designed to work very reliably, even in desert sand. This Israeli gun reached new levels of convenience with its compact size and amazing accuracy.

Sub-machine guns enjoyed their heyday in most armies during World War Two, Korea, and the early years of Vietnam because of their small size and portability. After the 1960s most armies adopted the assault rifle in some form. Assault rifles, the second type of machine gun, closely match the handy size and weight of the sub-machine gun, but with increased range to over 800 meters, and better accuracy and penetration. The success of the assault rifle doomed many sub-machine guns to a limited military role.

The assault rifle usually refers to a lightweight select fire rifle capable of both semi-automatic and full automatic fire. The German army first adopted them in

World War II, calling them *Sturmgewer*, meaning assault rifle in German. They used an intermediate caliber cartridge, the 8mm Kurtz. It was not as large or powerful as a full size rifle cartridge but it was more controllable in automatic fire than a full power rifle cartridge. The 8mm Kurtz exhibited more range and penetration than comparable sub-machine ammunition. This assault rifle was very successful, so successful that the Russians copied this concept and designed their own assault rifle, the famous AK47. The United States version of its assault rifle was the Stoner designed M16. Both the Russian and U. S. assault rifles used intermediate caliber ammunition.

Today, the AK47 and M16 are the most prolific infantry rifles in the world. However, the term assault rifle has been badly misused in the American press by referring to any semi-automatic rifle or even pistol as an assault rifle. They might as well refer to a baseball bat as an assault rifle.

The third and last variation of the machine gun is also its largest in size and weight. This group is referred to as simply machine guns, both light and heavy. Most are tripod mounted and belt fed using full power rifle ammunition. This group of machine guns made its debut in World War I. The Germans used the Maxim machine gun while the United States and British forces used the US1917 Browning and British Vickers respectively. All these guns were water cooled and quite large. They were capable of sustained fire for long periods of time because of their water cooled barrel jackets and the continuous belts of ammunition. Being tripod mounted, they were very accurate out to 1,000 yards and beyond.

During World War II, the Germans innovated and designed a quick change barrel system in their MG34 and MG42 machine guns. This lightened the soldier's load and enabled these weapons to be used more efficiently. The barrel change is significant because it still allows a high rate of fire by changing a hot barrel for a cool one before becoming overheated. Today, most contemporary armies utilize these same systems in the U.S. M60 machine gun, the Belgium FN MAG, and the heavy machine guns like the Browning .50 caliber.

All the above automatic firearms and many more are available to qualified individuals who would like to own a piece of history. One can feel how these pieces of history really worked and how advances in technology effected history. Historical military firearms collectors know the desirability of a rare mint condition Winchester M1 Garand or a like-new 75-year-old Colt single action Army revolver, but rare and desirable NFA weapons are much more difficult to obtain. There are many reasons for this. Many of these machine guns came back to this country as war trophies from World War II, Korea, or Vietnam where they were used in actual combat. The condition of most of these war weapons is less than excellent. Only Interarms and a few other importers brought collectible machine guns into the United States during the 1960s. One important fact to remember is the basic law of supply and demand. The NFA weapon's market has a small supply and a large demand. This always drives prices upward. It is estimated that there are only about 155,000 registered NFA firearms in the hands of individuals in the U. S.

The market price for NFA weapons as been steadily increasing, although in the past year or so the increase has been quite dramatic. Twenty years ago a new M16 rifle cost approximately $350; today it's about $4,500. During the same period a German light machine gun, the MG42, cost about $900. Today, if one can be found, its cost is approximately $10,000 or more. The most important aspects of the pricing formula are rarity, desirability, and historical significance. Keep in mind that these guns are not bought on the world market at prices much lower than private sales to individuals. These guns bring a premium because the buyer is in essence purchasing the grandfathered registration paperwork of the weapon plus the weapon itself.

In order to better understand the pricing structure of NFA weapons it is necessary to understand the different chronological sequences that NFA weapons went through. There were periods of time which gradually decreased the incoming supply of NFA weapons entering the NFA registry. The Gun Control Act of 1968 was one of the most crucial. Pursuant to NFA weapons the 1968 Act stipulated that no more imported machine guns could be brought into the system. As a result pre-1968 imported guns command a premium because of their original manufacture. During 1968 the NFA branch of the ATF allowed a one-year amnesty period so that returning servicemen from Vietnam could register their war trophies. It was during this period that many AK47s, PPSH41s, and MP40 machine guns were put into the system. Many more U.S. and foreign manufactured guns were also registered at this time as well. All of these guns command a premium because of their originality and registration.

Domestic production of NFA weapons continued until 1986 when the 1986 Gun Control Act prohibited the registration of domestic machine guns. Thus the door was closed to any further production of machine guns available to individuals. NFA weapons already registered could remain in the system and be transferred to qualified individuals. This situation drove prices higher and continues to do so. This group of weapons consist of many desirable semi-automatic that were legally converted into fully automatic weapons. These include the HK94s converted to the MP5, the HK91s converted to the G3, and the HK93 converted to the HK33. There were many Browning .30 and .50 caliber machine guns manufactured during this time frame as well. But remember pedigree determines price. An original pre-1968 Israeli-manufactured Uzi will fetch over $9,000 where as a U.S. manufactured Uzi built during the same time period will only bring $3,000.

Those individuals who wish to be Class 3 dealers in machine guns have many more NFA weapons to choose from especially the newer, more contemporary designs. Pre-1986 dealer samples, imported before 1986, can be transferred between dealers only and retained personally by them after they surrender their Class 3 licenses.

Only people who wish to engage in active business of buying and selling machine guns should do this as it entails much more paperwork and responsibility. These dealers samples can only be transferred to other dealers. Some of these contemporary guns are very rare and desirable. For example, a pre-1986 dealer sample FN MAG machine gun in excellent condition will bring upwards of $60,000 because only about six of these guns were imported into the country before 1986. Supply and demand rule here.

Post-1986 dealer samples are even more restrictive. Only dealers who can produce a law enforcement letter wishing to demonstrate these weapons can obtain them. Unlike the pre-1986 samples these post-1986 samples cannot be retained after their license is surrendered. It is for this reason that post-1986 dealer sample prices are not given.

People from all walks of life own and shoot these rare firearms. Sub-machine matches are held around the country for those interested in the competitive aspects of shooting these NFA weapons. Collecting and shooting NFA firearms is as interesting, perhaps more so, as the more traditional firearms. It is always important to keep in mind that these NFA firearms are heavily regulated and strict federal rules must be adhered to. Always follow NFA rules. When in doubt call or write the ATF for clarification.

J. R. Moody, a degreed historian, has been collecting and shooting Class III firearms for twenty years because he enjoys the historical and technological aspects of these firearms. He competes successfully at sub-machine matches across the country. On several occasions he has defeated the National Champion. In addition he works as a consultant to Knight's Armament Company, one of the country's leading small arms contractors to U.S. military forces and law enforcement agencies.

ADVISORY: For those readers who are interested in advancing their knowledge and understanding of Class III firearms it is recommended that they subscribe to *Small Arms Review*, a first rate publication that has many informative and useful features. There are sections on the law, new products, and illuminating articles on all aspects of NFA weapons and their history. *Small Arms Review* may be contacted at Moose Lake Publishing, 223 Sugar Hill Rd., Harmony, ME 04942. Telephone 207-683-2959 or FAX 203-683-2172. E-mail SARreview@aol/com. Website-http://www.smallarmsreview.com.

NOTE: *The prices listed for Class III firearms reflect the most current information as of publication date. Class III firearms are very volatile with rapid and sudden price changes. It is highly recommended that the latest market prices be verified in a particular market prior to a sale.*

Of interest to military collectors is the following exchange between the Subcommittee on Appropriations in the House of Representives for the 106th Congress, Jim Kolbe, Arizona, Chairman and the Director of the ATF Mr. Buckles. For those interested in submitting feedback they should contact the Honorable Ernest J, Istook, Jr., Chiarman, Subcommittee on the Treasury, Postal Service, and General Government, House of Repre-sentqative, B-307 Rayburn House Office Building, Washington, D.C. 20515. Telephone 202-225-5834. Thanks to Eric Larson for making the information available to the *Standard Catalog of Military Firearms* and its readers.

SUBCOMMITTEE ON THE TREASURY, POSTAL SERVICE, AND GENERAL GOVERNMENT APPROPRIATIONS

JIM KOLBE, Arizona, Chairman FRANK B. WOLF, Virginia STENY H. HOYER, Maryland ANNE M. NORTHUP, Kentucky CARRIE P. MEEK, Florida JO ANN EMERSON, Missouri DAVID E. PRICE, North Carolina JOHN E. SUNUNU, New Hampshire LUCILLE ROYBAL-ALLARD, California JOHN E. PETERSON, Pennsylvania VIRGIL L GOODE, JR., Virginia NOTE: Under Committee Rules, Mr. Young, as Chairman of the Full Committee, and Mr. Obey, as Ranking

CURIOS AND RELICS

Question: The Administration wants to eliminate the rider related to the definition of curio or relic firearms: Provided Further, That no funds appropriated here shall be used to pay administrative expenses or the compensation of any officer or employee of the United States to implement an amendment or amendments to 27 CFR 178.11 or remove any item from ATF Publication 5300.22 as it existed on January 1, 1994.

Curios or relics are firearms as such by virtue of their age (more than 50 years old), or by certification by museum curators or by the Secretary of the Treasury (through ATF) that they are primarily of interest to collectors.

This rider was first enacted in the mid-1990s to prevent the BATF from administratively redefining curio or relic firearms to allow a broad ban on importations of curios or relics. In addition, it provides a general protection from the process under which curios or relics are defined.

Director Buckles, what policy is AU pursuing which would require changes in the curio or relic list or in the definition of curios or relics, or in the importation standards for curios or relics?

Answer: Prior to 1984, the only significance to classification of a firearm as a curio or relic was that licensed collectors could obtain such firearms in interstate commerce.

A 1984 amendment to the GCA allows the importation of surplus military firearms if they are curios or relics. When most classifications of military firearms as curios or relics were made, they addressed a fixed and limited number of firearms already in the United States. The classifications were based upon a determination that these firearms were sufficiently rare in the United States, no additional quantities would be available by virtue of the import prohibition, and all such firearms were of distinct interest to collectors.

The 1984 amendments coupled with the lifting of restrictions on communist-bloc countries in the 1990s resulted in the availability of large quantities of firearms in the world market at relatively low prices. For example, prior to 1984 the Russian SKS rifle was very rare in the U.S. and commanded prices in excess of $2000. When large quantities of the weapons became available for sale in the U.S., the selling price dropped to below $200. In this context, ATF has been concerned that classifications of these firearms as curios and relics is inconsistent with the regulatory definition and the limited purpose behind the 1984 amendment to the GCA.

Under the existing regulatory definition any firearm that is more than 50 years old qualifies as a curio or relic. Right now any weapon made prior to March, 1950 is a curio or relic and every day more firearms become 50 years old. Many of these weapons are primarily of interest to collectors and are properly classified as curios or relics. However, there are many weapons more than 50 years old that have no particular collector interest.

ATF has received applications to import large numbers of these weapons into the United States. It is apparent that most of these are not being imported as collectors' items. The quantities imported, sale prices, and marketing strategies of the importers are geared to large quantity commercial distribution. These factors are inconsistent with a determination that the weapons are of special interest to collectors by reason of some quality other than is associated with firearms intended for sporting use or as offensive or defensive weapons.

If the appropriation restriction is lifted, ATF will consider publication of a notice of proposed rulemaking seeking public comment on a proposal to require that importers seeking to import surplus military curio or relic firearms provide evidence that a particular firearm is primarily of interest to collectors.

ARGENTINA

Argentine Military conflicts, 1870-Present

During the latter part of the 19th century Argentina suffered from political instability and military coups. This instability continued into the 20th century. Argentina adopted a pre-Axis neutrality during World War II and finally entered the war on the Allied side in 1945. With military coup in 1944 Colonel Juan Peron rose to power and implemented a popular dictatorship. The subsequent 30 years saw Peron and his wives come and go in power with the eventual coup in 1976 that led to a repressive military junta led by General Galteri. In 1982 Argentina occupied the Falkland Islands and was defeated by the British in the war that followed. The balance of its 20th century history is marked by economic difficulties and austerity measures.

NOTE: Argentina manufactures most of its small arms in government factories located in different locations around the country. This factory is known as the *"Fabrica Militar de Armas Portatiles "Domingo Matheu""* (FMAP "DM"). It is located in Rosario.

HANDGUNS

Argentina also used a small number of Star Select fire pistols for its special forces. See *Spain, Handguns, Star Model M.*

FN Model 1935 GP

Designated by the Argentine military as the "Browning Pistol PD." Licensed from FN and manufactured by FMAP "DM." Since 1969 Argentina has built about 185,000 of these pistols some of which have been sold commercially. This 9x19 caliber pistol is marked on the left side of the slide, "FABRICA MILITAR DE ARMAS PORTATILES "D.M." ROSARIO, D.G.F.M., LICENCIA F N BROWNING, INDUSTRAI ARGENTINA."

Exc.	V.G.	Good	Fair	Poor
425	325	275	225	150

BALLESTER—MOLINA

Argentine D.G.F.M.

(Direccion General de Fabricaciones Militares) made at the F.M.A.P. (Fabrica Militar de Arms Portatiles (Military Factory of Small Arms)) Licensed copies SN 24,000 to 112,494 (Parts are Generally interchangeable with Colt. Most pistols were marked D.G.F.M. - (F.M.A.P.). Late pistols were marked FM within a cartouche on the right side of the slide. These pistols are found both with and without import markings, often in excellent condition, currently more often in refinished condition, and with a seemingly endless variety of slide markings. None of these variations have yet achieved any particular collector status or distinction, unless "New In Box." A "New In The Box" DGFM recently sold at auction for $1200. In fact many of these fine pistols have and continue to be used as the platforms for the highly customized competition and target pistols that are currently popular.

Exc.	V.G.	Good	Fair	Poor
550	425	350	275	225

Argentine Made Ballester Molina

Un-Licensed, Argentine re-designed versions (parts are NOT interchangeable with Colt except for the barrel and magazine). These pistols are found both with and without import markings. Pistols without import markings usually have a B prefix number stamped on the left rear part of the mainspring housing and are often in excellent to New original condition. The vast majority of currently available pistols are found in excellent but refinished condition. Only the pistols with no import markings that are in excellent to New original condition have achieved any particular collector status. Most of these pistols that are being sold today are being carried and shot, rather than being collected. 99%-100% = Exc + 40%; Refinished = Fair/Poor.

Courtesy Karl Karash collection

Courtesy Karl Karash collection

Exc.	V.G.	Good	Fair	Poor
425	300	250	185	135

SUBMACHINE GUNS

Shortly after World War II Argentina purchased a number of Beretta Model 38A₂ directly from Beretta. The Argentine military also used the Sterling Mark 4 and the Sterling Mark 5 (silenced version) purchased directly from Sterling against British forces during the Falkland War. The Argentine Coast Guard purchased HK MP5A2 and MP5A3 guns from Germany.

The Argentines have also produced a number of submachine guns of its own design and manufacture. The PAM 1, PAM 2, the FMK series, and the Mems series were or are all Argentine submachine guns. It is doubtful if any of these guns were imported into the U.S. prior to 1968 and are therefore not transferable.

RIFLES

In 1879 the Argentine army adopted the Remington Rolling rifle in .43 caliber as its standard issue rifle. This was followed by the Mauser Model 1891 rifle.

The Model 1909 was replaced by the FN FAL series of rifles. This was the standard rifle of the Argentine armed forces. About 150,000 of these rifles have been issued in various configurations and the majority of these were manufactured in Argentina at FMAP "DM" Rosario.

Argentina has also used the U.S. M1 carbine, the Beretta BM59 rifle, and the Steyr SSG sniper rifle.

MAUSER

M1891 Rifle

This rifle was made in Germany with a 19.1" barrel and 5-round magazine. Full stock with straight grip stock with half-length upper handguard. Rear sight V-notch. Chambered for the 7.65x53mm cartridge. Weight is about 8.8 lbs. Marked with Argentine crest on receiver ring.

Exc.	V.G.	Good	Fair	Poor
400	350	300	150	90

M1891 Carbine

Full stock with straight grip. Front sight protectors and sling loops attached to bottom of stock behind the triggerguard. Turned down bolt. Barrel length is 17.6". Caliber is 7.65x53mm. Weight is about 7.2 lbs.

Exc.	V.G.	Good	Fair	Poor
395	350	300	200	150

M1909 Rifle

Based on the Gew design and fitted with a 29" barrel and tangent rear sight graduated to 2000 meters. Almost full stock with pistol grip. The 5-round magazine fits in a flush box magazine with hinged floor plate. Chambered for the 7.65x53mm cartridge. Some of these rifles were made in Germany and about 85,000 were built in Argentina. Argentine crest on receiver ring. Weight is about 9 lbs.

Courtesy Rock Island Auction Company

Exc.	V.G.	Good	Fair	Poor
500	425	375	250	175

M1909 Sniper Rifle w/o scope

Same as above but for bent bolt and scope. Some telescopes were German-made for the Argentine army.

Exc.	V.G.	Good	Fair	Poor
1200	900	750	600	400

M1909 Cavalry Carbine

Built by the German company DWM and Argentine companies as well. This 7.65x53mm rifle has a full-length stock with straight grip and 21.5" barrel. Upper handguard is 2/3 length. Bayonet fittings. Weight is about 8.5 lbs. About 19,000 of these carbines were produced in Argentina between 1947 and 1959.

Exc.	V.G.	Good	Fair	Poor
400	350	300	225	150

M1909 Mountain Carbine

Sometimes referred to as the Engineers model. This is a cut down Model 1909 rifle with 21.25" barrel with bayonet lug. Rear sight graduated to 1400 meters. Weight is about 8.5 lbs.

Exc.	V.G.	Good	Fair	Poor
400	350	300	225	150

FN FAL (Argentine Manufacture)

A number of these have been imported into the U.S. in semi-automatic configuration. Marked, "FABRICA MILITAR DE ARMAS PORTATILES-ROSARIO, INDUSTRAI ARGENTINA."

Exc.	V.G.	Good	Fair	Poor
2500	2000	1250	900	450

SHOTGUNS

Mossberg Model 500

In 1976 the Argentine navy acquired the Mossberg Model 500 in 12 gauge.

Exc.	V.G.	Good	Fair	Poor
600	500	400	200	100

MACHINE GUNS

The Argentine military has used a wide variety of machine guns from various sources. Obsolete guns include the Browning Model 1917 water-cooled gun. More current machine guns are the Browning .50 caliber M2 HB, the FN MAG, the French AAT-52, and the MG3.

Argentine Maxim Model 1895

This gun was sold to Argentina from both British and German sources. Standard pattern early Maxim gun with smooth brass water jacket and brass feed plates. Most likely chambered for the 7.65x53mm Mauser cartridge. Rate of fire was about 400 rounds per minute. Weight of the gun was approximately 60 lbs. Marked in Spanish on the receiver as well as the country of manufacture.

Pre-1968 (Rare)

Exc.	V.G.	Fair
15000	13000	12000

Pre-1986 conversions

Exc.	V.G.	Fair
8500	7500	7000

Pre-1986 dealer samples

Exc.	V.G.	Fair
N/A	N/A	N/A

British Maxim Nordenfelt M1895 in 7.65mm • Courtesy Private NFA Collection • Paul Goodwin Photo

AUSTRIA AUSTRIA-HUNGARY HUNGARY

Austrian/Hungarian Military conflicts, 1870-Present

In 1867 the Austro-Hungarian monarchy ruled this important and critical part of Europe. Germany and Austria-Hungary entered into an alliance called the Dual Alliance and later, in 1882 when Italy joined, the Triple Alliance. In the same year Serbia and Romania joined this group as well. Eventually this partnership between Germany and Austria-Hungary pitted them against England and France for control of Europe. With the advent of World War I and the defeat of the Dual Alliance the Austrian-Hungarian rule came to an end. In 1918 German Austria became a republic. The small nation was beset by social, economic, and political unrest throughout the 1920s and in 1934 a totalitarian regime was established. Austria became part of the German Third Reich in 1938. After the end of World War II, Austria was restored to a republic and occupied by the allies until 1955 when it became a sovereign nation. Austria joined the European Union in 1995.

Hungary followed a similar history after 1918, as did Austria. In 1941 Hungary joined the Axis Alliance and in 1944 was invaded by the USSR. In 1946 a republic was established but was overthrown by a Communist coup in 1948. In 1956 an anti-Communist revolution was suppressed by Soviet military forces. In 1990 democratic reform swept the country. In 1994 the Socialists won control of the government with the result that economic and social reforms are almost nonexistent.

HANDGUNS

Model 1870

This revolver is built on a Lefaucheux-Francotte double action solid frame with fixed cylinder with mechanical rod ejection. It is chambered for the 11.3mm cartridge and fitted with a 7.3" round barrel. The non-fluted cylinder holds 6 rounds. The frame and barrel were iron not steel. Checkered wooden grips with lanyard loop. Built by the Austrian firm of Leopold Gasser, and marked "L.GASSER, WIEN, PATENT, OTTAKRING." Weight is about 53 oz., or 3.3 lbs. making it one of the heaviest military service revolvers on its time. When the Model 1878 was introduced and adopted by the Austro-Hungarian army the Model 1870 was sold to the Balkan States and was sometimes referred to as the "Montenegrin" revolver.

Military Unit Marked

Exc.	V.G.	Good	Fair	Poor
900	600	400	250	150

Non-Unit Marked

Exc.	V.G.	Good	Fair	Poor
750	500	350	225	150

Model 1870/74 Gasser Trooper's model

Similar to the above model but built with cast steel instead of iron. It was issued from 1874 to 1919. Built by the Austrian firm of Leopold Gasser. Weight is still about 53 oz.

Military Unit Marked

Exc.	V.G.	Good	Fair	Poor
900	600	400	250	150

Non-Unit Marked

Exc.	V.G.	Good	Fair	Poor
750	500	350	225	150

Model 1878 Officer's model

Because the Model 1870 revolver was so heavy and large Johann Gasser, Leopold younger brother, designed a smaller version chambered for the 9mm (9x26) cartridge. The barrel length was 4.8" and the overall length was reduced as well. The weight of this revolver was about 27 oz.

Exc.	V.G.	Good	Fair	Poor
750	500	350	200	150

Model 1898 Rast & Gasser

This model was built on the Schmidt-Galand double action solid frame with 8-round cylinder with loading gate and mechanical ejection rod. Chambered for the 8mm cartridge and fitted with a 4.5" round barrel. The caliber was too light to be effective as a military sidearm. The firing pin was a spring loaded frame mounted plunger instead of the more common hammer mounted type. Checkered wooden grips with lanyard loop. In service from 1898 to 1938. Weight is about 33 oz.

Model 1898 • Paul Goodwin Photo

Short Grip

Exc.	V.G.	Good	Fair	Poor
400	200	150	120	90

Short Barrel

Exc.	V.G.	Good	Fair	Poor
3500	2000	1200	400	200

STEYR
Osterreichische Waffenfabrik Gesellschaft GmbH, Steyr (1869-1919)
Stery-Werke AG (1919-1934)
Stery-Daimler-Puch, Steyr (1934-199)
Stery-Mannlicher GmbH, Steyr (1990-)

Steyr Model 1893 Gas Seal Test Revolver

Chambered for the 8mm cartridge this 7 shot 5.5" barrel revolver was built by Steyr as a prototype for the Austrian army. Less than 100 were built. Several different variations. It is recommended that an expert be consulted prior to a sale.

Exc.	V.G.	Good	Fair	Poor
15000	9000	5000	2000	—

Roth Steyr Model 1907

Based on the patents granted to Karel Krnka and Georg Roth, the 8mm Model 1907 had a rotating barrel locking system and was the first self-loading pistol adopted by the Austro-Hungarian army. Add 20% for early Steyr examples without a large pin visible on right side of frame, or for those made in Budapest instead of Steyr.

Courtesy Joseph Schroeder

Exc.	V.G.	Good	Fair	Poor
950	600	500	350	250

Steyr Hahn Model 1911

The Steyr Hahn was originally introduced as a commercial pistol but was quickly adopted by the Austro-Hungarian, Chilean, and Romanian militaries. Magazine capacity is 8 rounds. Weight is about 30 oz. Commercial examples were marked "Osterreichische Waffenfabrik Steyr M1911 9m/m" on the slide, have a laterally adjustable rear sight, and are rare. Austrian militaries are marked simply "STEYR" and the date of manufacture, while those made for Chile and Romania bear their respective crests. During WWII the Germans rebarreled a number of Steyr Hahns to 9mm Parabellum for police use, adding "P.08" to the slide along with appropriate Waffenamt markings.

Courtesy Orvel Reichert

Commercially marked

Exc.	V.G.	Good	Fair	Poor
1350	1000	750	500	350

P.08 Marked Slides

Exc.	V.G.	Good	Fair	Poor
800	500	350	200	125

Austrian Military

Exc.	V.G.	Good	Fair	Poor
400	300	200	150	100

FEG (Frommer) Stop Model 19

Introduced in 1912 and took a whole new approach compared to any of the pistols this company had produced to that point. It is still unconventional as it uses two recoil springs in a tube above the barrel and resembles an air pistol in this way. It is chambered for 7.65mm or 9mm short and has a 3.75" barrel. The detachable magazine holds 7 rounds, and the sights are fixed. This locked-breech action, semiautomatic pistol was a commercial success. It was used widely by the Austro-Hungarian military during WWI. It was manufactured between 1912 and 1920.

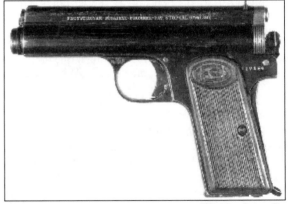

Courtesy James Rankin

Exc.	V.G.	Good	Fair	Poor
300	225	200	150	100

Model 1929

A blowback-operated semiautomatic chambered for the 9mm short cartridge. It has an external hammer; and the barrel was retained, as the Browning was, by four lugs. This was a simple and reliable pistol, and it was adopted by the military as a replacement for the Stop. This model was manufactured between 1929 and 1937. It was also produced in .22 Long Rifle.

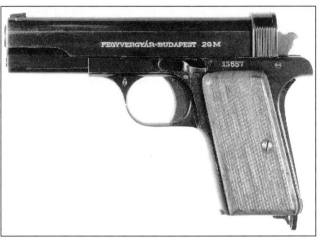

Courtesy James Rankin

Exc.	V.G.	Good	Fair	Poor
400	300	200	175	125

Model 1937

An improved version of the Model 1929 and was the last of Frommer's designs. It appeared a year after his death. This model is similar to the Model 1929, with a grooved slide to make cocking easier. It was adopted as the M1937 by the Hungarian Military, and in 1941 the German government ordered 85,000 pistols chambered for 7.65mm to be used by the Luftwaffe. These pistols were designated the "P Mod 37 Kal 7.65." They were also marked "jhv," which was the German code for the Hungarian company. These German pistols also have a manual safety, which is not found on the Hungarian military version and bears the Waffenamt acceptance marks. This model was manufactured from 1937 until the end of WWII.

Nazi Proofed 7.65mm Version

Exc.	V.G.	Good	Fair	Poor
275	250	200	150	100

9mm Short Hungarian Military Version

Exc.	V.G.	Good	Fair	Poor
250	225	175	125	75

Model 48 (7.62mm)

This is a Hungarian copy of the Soviet 7.62mm TT33 pistol. The pistol has a molded plastic grips with the Hungarian coat of arms.

Hungarian M48 • Courtesy Chuck Karwan

Exc.	V.G.	Good	Fair	Poor
225	175	150	100	75

Tokagypt

A licensed copy of the TT33 pistol produced by Fegyvergar (FEG) of Hungary. Chambered for the 9mm cartridge, and intended for but never issued to Egyptian army in the 1950s. Barrel length is 4.5" and magazine capacity is 7 rounds. Manual thumb safety. Weight is approximately 32 oz.

Hungarain Tokagypt • Courtesy Chuck Karwan

Exc.	V.G.	Good	Fair	Poor
750	650	500	350	150

NOTE: For pistols without markings deduct 25%. For pistols with importer stamps deduct 50%.

PA-63

An aluminum frame copy of the Walther PP in a slightly larger size. Chambered for the 9mm Makarov cartridge. This was the standard Hungarian service until recently.

Exc.	V.G.	Good	Fair	Poor
165	135	120	90	75

R-61

This model is a smaller version of the PA-63. Chambered for the 9mm Makarov. This model is slightly longer than a Walther PPK and was intended for issue to high ranking officers, CID, and police units.

Exc.	V.G.	Good	Fair	Poor
185	150	130	100	80

Glock 17

Adopted by the Austrian military in 1983. This model is chambered for the 9mm Parabellum cartridge. It is a double action only semiautomatic that has a 4.49" barrel and a 17-shot detachable magazine. The empty weight of this pistol is 21.91 oz. This pistol is offered with either fixed or adjustable sights at the same retail price. The finish is black with black plastic grips. It is furnished in a plastic case with an extra magazine. This pistol was introduced in the U.S. 1985 and is still currently produced.

NIB	Exc.	V.G.	Good	Fair	Poor
600	450	325	300	275	175

Note: Add $70.00 if equipped with Meprolight night sights. Add $90 if equipped with Trijicon night sights. Add $30 if equipped with adjustable sights.

SUBMACHINE GUNS

Steyr-Solothurn MP 30

Introduced in 1930 and built at the Steyr plant under license from the Swiss firm Solothurn. It was adopted by the Austrian police. Chambered for the 9x23 Steyr cartridge and fitted with a 7.8" jacketed barrel. It is fed by a 32-round magazine and has a rate of fire of about 500 rounds per minute. Wood buttstock with unusual upswept appearance. It is select fire. Weight is about 9.5 lbs. Produced from 1930 to 1935 with approximately 6,000 manufactured.

Pre-1968

Exc.	V.G.	Fair
4500	4200	3800

Pre-1986 conversions

Exc.	V.G.	Fair
N/A	N/A	N/A

Pre-1986 dealer samples

Exc.	V.G.	Fair
2000	1850	1700

Steyr-Solothurn S1-100 (MP 34(o))

This gun machine was designed in Germany, perfected in Switzerland, and built in Austria. Steyr-Solothurn was a shell company established to enable the German company Rhein-metall to evade the restrictions of the Versailles Treaty that prevented them from producing military small arms. The gun was used by the Austrian army as well as the Germany army. It is chambered for the 9x23 Steyr cartridge as well as others. The German army used them in 9mm Parabellum while Austrian troops used the gun chambered for the 9mm Mauser cartridge. The gun was also sold to Portugal where it was designated the Model 42. Barrel length is almost 7.8". Magazine capacity is 32 rounds. Rate of fire is about 500 rounds per minute. Fixed wooden butt and forearm. Weight is approximately 9.5 lbs. Produced from 1934 to 1939. On this gun a magazine loading device is built into the magazine housing.

Pre-1968

Exc.	V.G.	Fair
4800	4500	4000

Pre-1986 conversions

Exc.	V.G.	Fair
N/A	N/A	N/A

Pre-1986 dealer samples

Exc.	V.G.	Fair
2500	2250	2000

Steyr Mpi69

Built in Austria this submachine gun is chambered for the 9mm cartridge. It was adopted by the Austrian army in 1969. The gun features a 10" barrel and 25- or 32-round magazine. It has a rate of fire of 550 rounds per minute. It is marked "STEYR-DAIMLER-PUCH AG MADE IN AUSTRAI" on top of the receiver. The folding stock is metal. The gun weighs about 7 lbs. Production stopped in 1990.

Photo Courtesy Private NFA Collection

Pre-1968 (Rare)

Exc.	V.G.	Fair
8000	7500	7000

MP 34 • Paul Goodwin Photo

Pre-1986 conversions

Exc.	V.G.	Fair
N/A	N/A	N/A

Pre-1986 dealer samples

Exc.	V.G.	Fair
2500	2250	2000

Model 39

Produced by Danuvia in Budapest this submachine gun is chambered for the 9x25mm Mauser Export cartridge. It is fitted with a 19.5" barrel and a full stocked rifle-style wooden stock. Magazine capacity is 40 rounds. The magazine folds into a recess in the forward part of the stock. Fitted with a bayonet lug. Gun features a two-part bolt design. Introduced in the late 1930s but not issued until 1941. Weight is about 8 lbs. Rate of fire is approximately 750 rounds per minute. About 8,000 were produced.

NOTE: It is not known how many, if any, of these guns are in the U.S. and are transferable. Prices listed below are estimates only.

Pre-1968

Exc.	V.G.	Fair
6500	6000	5500

Pre-1986 conversions

Exc.	V.G.	Fair
4500	4000	3500

Pre-1986 dealer samples

Exc.	V.G.	Fair
N/A	N/A	N/A

Model 43

This model, introduced in 1942, is an improved version of the Model 39. It has a shorter barrel at 16.5", a folding stock, pistol grip, and an improved magazine. Weight is about 8 lbs. Rate of fire and caliber remains the same. Produced until 1945.

NOTE: It is not known how many, if any, of these guns are in the U.S. and are transferable. Prices listed below are estimates only.

Pre-1968

Exc.	V.G.	Fair
6500	6000	5500

Pre-1986 conversions

Exc.	V.G.	Fair
4500	4000	3500

Pre-1986 dealer samples

Exc.	V.G.	Fair
N/A	N/A	N/A

Model 48

This is a Hungarian copy of the Soviet PPSh-41 submachine gun. See also *Russia Submachine Guns.*

Pre-1968

Exc.	V.G.	Fair
7000	6500	6000

Pre-1986 conversions

Exc.	V.G.	Fair
4500	4000	3500

Pre-1986 dealer samples

Exc.	V.G.	Fair
3250	2750	2250

RIFLES

MANNLICHER
Built by Steyr & Fegyvergyar

Model 1885

This was the first magazine rifle used by Austria-Hungary and the first straight-pull rifle used as a general issue shoulder arm. This model required that a clip be used to load the box magazine, loose cartridges could not be loaded. Like the U.S. M1 Garand empty clips were ejected up from the receiver when empty. Chambered for the 11.15mmx58R black powder cartridge. Barrel length is 31" with two barrel bands. Box magazine held 5 clip loaded rounds. Weight was about 10 lbs. Only about 1500 of these rifles were built.

Model 1886-Courtesy West Point Museum • Paul Goodwin Photo

Model 1888/1890-Courtesy West Point Museum • Paul Goodwin Photo

Exc.	V.G.	Good	Fair	Poor
1200	900	700	500	300

Model 1886

This rifle was produced in large numbers and adopted for general service use. This model is similar to the Model 1885 but unlike the M85 the clip of this rifle ejected out of the bottom of the magazine. Still chambered for the 11.156x58R black powder cartridge. Barrel length was 30". After 1888 most of these rifles were converted to 8x50R smokeless powder. Two barrel bands with pistol grip stock. This rifle was made at Steyr. Weight was slightly under 10 lbs.

Exc.	V.G.	Good	Fair	Poor
400	300	200	100	75

Model 1888

This model is the same as the Model 1886 except chambered for the 8x50R black powder cartridge.

Exc.	V.G.	Good	Fair	Poor
550	400	250	150	100

Model 1888/1890

This variation is the result of the change-over from black powder to smokeless. This model was chambered for the 8x50R smokeless powder cartridge with a stronger bolt locking wedge. Barrel length was 30". New sights were added to accommodate the new cartridge. These sights were graduated. This model was also made at Steyr. A number of these were sold to Bulgaria, Greece, and Chile. A number of these rifles were used during WWI and some were found in irregular units during WWII.

Exc.	V.G.	Good	Fair	Poor
400	275	200	150	75

Model 1890 Carbine

This model represented a departure from previous models not only in design but incorporated a stronger action to better handle the 8x50R smokeless cartridge. On this model the bolt head contained the extractor. The result of this new design was that the trigger was behind the end of the bolt handle. Barrel length was 19.5" with a single barrel band and no handguard. There is no bayonet lug on this rifle. The box magazine capacity was 5 rounds of clip loaded ammunition. Weight is about 7 lbs.

Exc.	V.G.	Good	Fair	Poor
650	450	300	200	100

Model 1895 Infantry Rifle

Chambered for the 8x50R cartridge this straight pull bolt action rifle was fitted with a 30" barrel with an integral clip loaded magazine and wooden handguard. This model has essentially the same action as the Model 1890 Carbine. Fitted with leaf sights. Weight is about 8 lbs. Produced from 1895 to about 1918 both at Steyr and Budapest. The rifle was marked with either of these two locations on top of the receiver ring along with "M95."

This was the primarily shoulder arm of the Austro-Hungarian army during WWI and was made in huge quantities. The rifle was also used by Bulgaria and Greece. Many of these models were used in Italy during WWII as well as the Balkans during that same period of time.

NOTE: In the 1930s both Austria and Hungary converted large numbers of these rifles to 8x56Rmm. Many of these rifles were converted to carbines at the same time. Converted rifles will have an "S" or "H" stamped over the chamber.

Between the two world wars many Model 95s were converted to 8x57mm short rifles and fitted with 24" barrels. These rifles used the standard Mauser stripper clip instead of the Mannlicher system. Receivers were marked M95M and M95/24. Yugoslavia was the main user of these rifles.

Courtesy Richard M. Kumor, Sr.

Exc.	V.G.	Good	Fair	Poor
250	200	125	75	50

Model 1895 Sharpshooter's Rifle

Same configuration as the Infantry rifle except for the addition of double set triggers. Rare.

Exc.	V.G.	Good	Fair	Poor
750	600	500	400	200

Model 1895 Sniper Rifle

Same as the Sharpshooter's rifle but fitted with a telescope sight. Extremely rare.

Exc.	V.G.	Good	Fair	Poor
3000	2500	2000	—	—

Model 1895 Cavalry Carbine

Essentially the same as the Infantry rifle with a shorter barrel. Barrel length is 19.5". The sling swivels are located on the side on the stock and there is no bayonet lug or stacking hook. Weight is about 7 lbs. Produced until 1918.

Exc.	V.G.	Good	Fair	Poor
400	350	275	—	—

Model 1895 Short Rifle (Stuzen M95)

This model was designed for non-Cavalry use as it was fitted with a bayonet lug and sling swivels on the underside of the rifle. It was also fitted with a stacking hook attached to the barrel band. When the bayonet is attached a blade sight is integral with the bayonet barrel ring for sighting purposes. Weight is about 7.5 lbs.

Exc.	V.G.	Good	Fair	Poor
400	275	200	125	75

FEGYVERGYAR
Fegyver es Gepgyar Resvenytarsasag, Budapest, (1880-1945)
Femaru es Szersazamgepgyar NV (1945-1985)
FEG Arms & Gas Appliances Factory (1985-)

Model 35 Rifle

This turn-bolt rifle is based on the Romanian Model 1893 Mannlicher turn bolt but chambered for the 8x56mm cartridge. It is clip loaded with a full-length stock (two-piece

around receiver) and full upper handguard. Barrel length is 23.5". Magazine capacity is 5 rounds. Weight is about 9 lbs.

Exc.	V.G.	Good	Fair	Poor
400	275	200	125	75

Model 43 Rifle

This is a Model 35 redesigned on the German Model 98 and chambered for the 7.92mm cartridge. Barrel length is 23.75". Magazine capacity is 5 rounds fixed box. Rear sight is tangent with notch. Weight is approximately 8.5 lbs. Almost full stock with German bayonet fittings. Issued to the Hungarian army in 1943. Rare.

Exc.	V.G.	Good	Fair	Poor
550	350	250	125	75

Model 48 (Mosin-Nagant)

This is a Hungarian copy of the M91/30 Mosin Nagant Soviet rifle chambered for the 7.62mm cartridge. Barrel length is 28.5". Five-round magazine. Weight about 8.5 lbs. Exported world-wide.

Exc.	V.G.	Good	Fair	Poor
85	60	40	—	—

NOTE: Model 48 Sniper rifle was also made in Hungary and it is the same as the Soviet M91/30 Sniper rifle. See *Russia, Rifles.*

STEYR
Osterreichische Waffenfabrik Gesellschaft GmbH, Steyr (1869-1919)
Stery-Werke AG (1919-1934)
Stery-Daimler-Puch, Steyr (1934-199)
Stery-Mannlicher GmbH, Steyr (1990-)

Model 1895 Steyr Rifle • Courtesy West Point Museum • Paul Goodwin Photo

Model 95 Rifle (Model 31)

A number of Model 95 rifles and short rifles were modified to accept the 8x56mm cartridge after World War I. The letter "H" is stamped on the barrel or the receiver. This is a straight pull rifle with 19.6" barrel and a 5-round fixed magazine. Weight is approximately 7.5 lbs.

Exc.	V.G.	Good	Fair	Poor
125	80	65	40	25

NOTE: The Steyr-built Model 1895 was adopted by the Netherlands and that country's arsenal produced these rifles. Values are about the same as the Austrian-built rifles.

Model 1903

Built for Greece in 6.5x54mm.

Exc.	V.G.	Good	Fair	Poor
400	275	200	125	75

NOTE: For Carbine version add a 50% premium.

Model 1904

Similar to the Dutch Model 1895 but chambered for 8x57mm rimless cartridge. Many of these rifles were sold to China and about 11,000 were sold to the Irish Ulster Volunteer Force.

Exc.	V.G.	Good	Fair	Poor
300	175	125	75	50

NOTE: For Irish Ulster marked versions add a 30% premium.

Model SSG-PI

This model features a black synthetic stock originally designed as a military sniper rifle. Fitted with a cocking indicator, single or double set trigger, 5-round rotary magazine, or 10-round magazine. Receiver is milled to NATO specifications for Steyr ring mounts. Barrel length is 26". Rifle weighs about 9 lbs. Offered in .308 Win.

NOTE: This model was originally called the SSG 69.

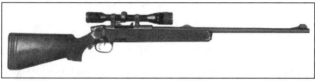

NIB	Exc.	V.G.	Good	Fair	Poor
1700	1300	1000	—	—	—

Steyr AUG (Armee Universal Gewehr)

Produced by Steyr-Mannlicher beginning in 1978 this rifle is chambered for the 5.56x45mm cartridge. It is a bullpup design with a number of different configurations. Barrel lengths are 13.6" in submachine gun configuration, 16.3" in carbine, 19.8" in rifle, and 24.2" in a heavy barrel sniper configuration. Magazine is 30 or 42 rounds. Carry handle is an optic sight of 1.5 power. Adopted by Austrian army and still in production. Weight is 7.7 lbs. in rifle configuration. Rate of fire is about 650 rounds per minute.

Photo Courtesy Private NFA Collection

Pre-1968

Exc.	V.G.	Fair
N/A	N/A	N/A

Pre-1986 conversions

Exc.	V.G.	Fair
8000	7500	7000

Pre-1986 dealer samples

Exc.	V.G.	Fair
7500	7300	7000

Steyr AUG (Semiautomatic Version)

As above but in semiautomatic only. Two versions. The first with green furniture and fitted with a 20" barrel. The second with black furniture and fitted with a 16" barrel.

First Model

NIB	Exc.	V.G.	Good	Fair	Poor
3900	3250	2250	—	—	—

Second Model

NIB	Exc.	V.G.	Good	Fair	Poor
4200	3700	2750	—	—	—

HUNGARIAN AK CLONES

AKM-63

A close copy of the AKM but with plastic furniture. Fitted with a vertical grip under the forend. Weigh about 1/2 lb. less than the Russian ARM.

Pre-1968

Exc.	V.G.	Fair
18000	15000	13000

Pre-1986 conversions

Exc.	V.G.	Fair
8000	7000	6000

Pre-1986 dealer samples

Exc.	V.G.	Fair
9000	8000	7000

AKM-63 (Semiautomatic version)

This semiautomatic version of the AKM-63 is in a pre-ban (1994) configuration.

Exc.	V.G.	Good	Fair	Poor
1400	1100	800	—	—

NOTE: Add 20% for folding stock (AMD-65-style).

AMD-65

This model is an AKM-63 with a 12.5" barrel, two port muzzle brake, and a side folding metal butt. Rate of fire is about 600 rounds per minute. Weight is approximately 7 lbs.

Pre-1968

Exc.	V.G.	Fair
18000	15000	13000

Pre-1986 conversions

Exc.	V.G.	Fair
8000	7000	6000

Pre-1986 dealer samples

Exc.	V.G.	Fair
9000	8000	7000

NGM

This assault rifle is the Hungarian version of the AK-74 chambered for the 5.56x45mm cartridge. Fitted with a 16.25" barrel. Magazine capacity is 30-round box type. Rate of fire is about 600 rounds per minute. Weight is approximately 7 lbs.

Pre-1968

Exc.	V.G.	Fair
N/A	N/A	N/A

Pre-1986 conversions

Exc.	V.G.	Fair
10000	9500	9000

Pre-1986 dealer samples

Exc.	V.G.	Fair
N/A	N/A	N/A

MACHINE GUNS

Hungary was supplied with a wide variety of Soviet machine guns after World War II from the RPD to the DShK38. Many of these machine guns were later copied by the Hungarians while retaining the Soviet model designations.

Model 07/12 Schwarzlose

The gun was designed by Louis Strange and built by Waffenfabrik Solothurn A.G., a Swiss factory. Chambered for the 8mm cartridge as well as the 7.92x57mm Mauser and the 6.5x54R Dutch. It was adopted by Austria-Hungary in 1905. It was also sold to the Dutch and Germans as well. It saw use in WWI. Barrel length was 24.4" and rate of fire was about 400 rounds a minute. Fed by a 250-round belt. The gun was produced from 1912 to 1918. Marked "MG SCHWARZLOSE M7/12" on the rear of the receiver. Weight is about 44 lbs.

NOTE: The predecessor to this gun was the Model 1907. Its rate of fire was about 400 rounds per minute, and it was fitted with a smaller oil reservoir. An aircraft version of the Model 07/12 was the Model 07/16 which had a rate of fire of about 600 rounds per minute. Early versions were water-cooled, later versions were air-cooled with slotted barrel jacket. Last version had no jacket.

Pre-1968

Exc.	V.G.	Fair
18000	16000	15000

Pre-1986 conversions

Exc.	V.G.	Fair
N/A	N/A	N/A

Pre-1986 dealer samples

Exc.	V.G.	Fair
N/A	N/A	N/A

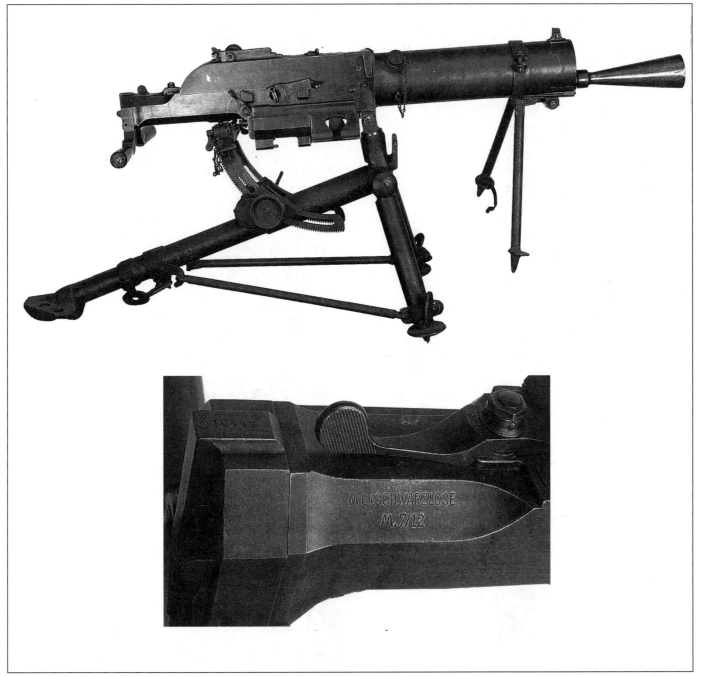

Model 07/12 Schwarzlose • Private NFA Collection • Paul Goodwin Photo

AUSTRALIA

Australian Military Conflicts, 1870-Present

The period of the last quarter of the 19th century was marked by colonization and westward expansion similar to that in the U.S. In 1901 the various colonies were federated as states into a Commonwealth of Australia. Australia fought on the side of Great Britain in both world wars. Australia sent troops to Vietnam in the 1960s and 1970s.

HANDGUNS

The Australian military currently uses the Browning Model 1935 designated the L9A1. These guns were manufactured by Inglis during World War II and since by FN. Chambered for 9mm cartridge. The first FN built pistols were purchased in 1963.

Australian Model L9A1 Pistol

This model is the standard British issue 9mm Model 1935 pistol built by FN under contract. Marked, "PISTOL, SELF-LOADING" instead of "PISTOL, AUTOMATIC." First ordered in June of 1963.

Exc.	V.G.	Good	Fair	Poor
650	550	400	200	150

SUBMACHINE GUNS

Australian military forces currently use its own designed and produced F1 submachine gun as well as the HK MP5 and MP5SD. The Sterling L34A1 silenced version is also used by special operations units.

Owen

This Australian submachine is chambered for the 9mm cartridge. It features a top mounted 33-round magazine and quick release barrel attachment. The barrel is 9.75" long and the rate of fire is 700 rounds per minute. Weight is about 9.25 lbs. It was produced from 1941 to 1944. Marked "OWEN 9MM MKI LYSAGHT PK AUSTRALIA PATENTED 22/7/41" on the right side of the frame.

Pre-1968

Exc.	V.G.	Fair
4500	3500	3000

Pre-1986 conversions

Exc.	V.G.	Fair
N/A	N/A	N/A

Pre-1986 dealer samples

Exc.	V.G.	Fair
2000	1500	1000

Austen Mark I

Introduced in 1943 this gun is a take off on the British Sten with a folding butt similar to the MP 40. Chambered for the 9mm cartridge and fitted with an 8" barrel with forward grip. Uses a 28-round box magazine. Rate of fire is approximately 500 rounds per minute. Weight is about 9 lbs. About 20,000 were produced between 1943 and 1945 by Diecasters and Carmichael in Australia.

Pre-1968

Exc.	V.G.	Fair
4500	3500	3000

Pre-1986 conversions

Exc.	V.G.	Fair
N/A	N/A	N/A

Pre-1986 dealer samples

Exc.	V.G.	Fair
2000	1500	1000

F-1

First introduced in 1962 this submachine gun was built by the Australian arsenal at Lithgow. Chambered for the 9mm cartridge and fitted with an 8" barrel, this gun has a round receiver with a wooden buttstock with pistol grip and perforated barrel jacket. The 34-round magazine is top mounted.

Owen • Paul Goodwin Photo

Weight is about 7 lbs. Rate of fire is approximately 600 rounds per minute.

NOTE: It is not known how many, if any, of these guns are in the U.S. and are transferable. Prices listed below are estimates only.

Pre-1968

Exc.	V.G.	Fair
10000	9500	9000

Pre-1986 conversions

Exc.	V.G.	Fair
N/A	N/A	N/A

Pre-1986 dealer samples

Exc.	V.G.	Fair
N/A	N/A	N/A

RIFLES

In 1985 the Australian Defense Ministry adopted the Steyr AUG 5.56mm F8 rifle as its service rifle. Australia also uses the British Parker Hale M82 Sniper Rifle, as well as the U.S. M16A1 rifle.

L1A1 Rifle

This is the British version of the FN-FAL in the "inch" or Imperial pattern. Most of these rifles were semiautomatic only.

This rifle was the standard service rifle for the British army from about 1954 to 1988. The rifle was made in Great Britain under licence from FN. The configurations for the L1A1 rifle is the same as the standard FN-FAL Belgium rifle. Only a few of these rifles were imported into the U.S. They are very rare. This "inch" pattern British gun will also be found in other Commonwealth countries such as Australia, New Zealand, Canada, and India.

NOTE: Only about 180 Australian L1A1s were imported into the U.S. prior to 1989. These are rare and in great demand.

Exc.	V.G.	Good	Fair	Poor
6000	4500	—	—	—

MACHINE GUNS

Between 1925 and 1930 the Australian firm of Lithgow built the Vickers machine gun. Later, between 1938 and 1940, the same company built the Bren gun in .303 caliber. Approximately 12,000 Vickers and 17,000 Bren guns were built in Australia during this period. After World War II the Australian military adopted the U.S. M60 machine, the Browning 1919A4, and the .50 caliber Browning M2HB. More recently that country's military uses the Belgian FN MAG, and the German MG3.

Austrialian L1A1 Rifle • Courtesy Blake Stevens, The FAL Rifle

BELGIUM

Belgian Military Conflicts, 1870 to the Present

Throughout the last quarter of the 19th century Belgium experienced rapid economic growth that led to colonization, mainly in the Belgium Congo. Germany occupied Belgium in both World War I and World War II. Belgium became a member of NATO in 1949 where that organization's headquarters are located in Brussels.

Bibliographical Notes:

The best overview of Belgian military firearms are two books by Claude Gaier; *FN 100 Years, The Story of the Great Liege Company, 1889-1989*, 1989 and *Four Centuries of Liege Gunmaking*, 1985.

HANDGUNS

E. & L. NAGANT

Model 1878 Officer's (Fluted Cylinder)

This 6-shot double action centerfire revolver is chambered for the 9mm cartridge. Solid frame with fixed cylinder sliding rod ejection. Octagon barrel is 5.5". Issued to Belgian officers it is marked with the Nagant address and logo. Wooden checkered grips with lanyard loop. Weight is about 33 oz. Produced from 1878 to 1886.

Exc.	V.G.	Good	Fair	Poor
1750	900	500	300	200

Model 1883 (Non-Fluted Cylinder)

This model was also chambered for the 9mm centerfire cartridge. Fitted with a 5.5" octagon barrel. Wooden checkered grips with lanyard loop. A simplified version of the Model 1878 Officers revolver. This model was used by NCOs, artillery, and troops in the Belgian army from 1883 to 1940.

Exc.	V.G.	Good	Fair	Poor
1250	750	400	275	150

Model 1878/86 Officers (Fluted Cylinder)

This 6-shot revolver was issued to officers in the Belgian army. Chambered for the 9mm cartridge and fitted with a 5.5" octagon barrel. Checkered wooden grips with lanyard loop. Produced from 1886 to 1940.

Exc.	V.G.	Good	Fair	Poor
1500	850	450	300	175

Model 1883/86

Similar to the Model 1878/86 Officers but issued to NCOs as a regular sidearm. Cylinder is non-fluted. The hammer rebounds slightly after the revolver has been fired.

Exc.	V.G.	Good	Fair	Poor
1250	750	400	275	150

GAVAGE, ARMAND

A 7.65mm caliber semiautomatic pistol with a fixed barrel and a concealed hammer. Similar in appearance to the Clement. Markings with "AG" molded into the grips. Some (1,500 est.) have been found bearing German Waffenamts. Manufactured from 1930s to 1940s.

Exc.	V.G.	Good	Fair	Poor
400	300	225	150	100

FABRIQUE NATIONALE

NOTE: For historical and technical information see Blake Stevens, *The Browning High Power Automatic Pistol*, Collector Grade Publications, 1990.

Model 1903

A considerable improvement over the Model 1900. It is also a blowback-operated semiautomatic; but the recoil spring is located under the barrel, and the firing pin travels through the slide after being struck by a hidden hammer. The barrel is held in place by five locking lugs that fit into five grooves in the frame. This pistol is chambered for the 9mm Browning long cartridge and has a 5" barrel. The finish is blued with molded plastic grips, and the detachable magazine holds 7 rounds. There is a detachable shoulder stock/holster along with a 10-round magazine that was available for this model. These accessories are extremely rare and if present would make the package worth approximately five times that of the pistol alone. There were approximately 58,000 manufactured between 1903 and 1939. This model was one of the Browning patents that the Eibar Spanish gunmakers did so love to copy because of the simplicity of the design.

It should be noted that during World War I the Spanish supplied almost one million Model 1903 copies for the French army.

Courtesy Richard M. Kumor, Sr.

Exc.	V.G.	Good	Fair	Poor
500	425	375	275	175

Model 1910 "New Model"

Chambered for 7.65mm and 9mm short. It has a 3.5" barrel, is blued, and has molded plastic grips. The principal difference between this model and its predecessors is that the recoil spring on the Model 1910 is wrapped around the barrel. This gives the slide a more graceful tubular appearance instead of the old slab-sided look. This model has the triple safety features of the 1906 Model 2nd variation and is blued with molded plastic grips. This model was adopted by police forces around the world. It was manufactured between 1912 and 1954.

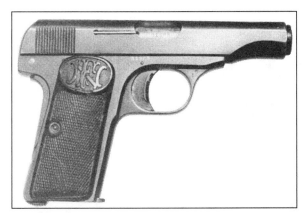

Courtesy Orvel Reichert

Exc.	V.G.	Good	Fair	Poor
375	250	200	150	125

Model 1922

Similar to the Model 1910, with a longer 4.5" barrel and correspondingly longer slide. This model was a military success, and approximately 200,000 were produced during the WWII German occupation of Belgium in 1940-1944. These pistols that bear the Waffenamt acceptance marks are known as the "Pistole Modell 626(b)," and are chambered for 7.65mm only. These pistols would bring a 10% premium. There were approximately 360,000 of these pistols produced during the German occupation. There are a number of subvariations that may effect value. There were also contracts from France, Yugoslavia, and Holland, as well as Belgian military versions. They were manufactured between 1912 and 1959.

Exc.	V.G.	Good	Fair	Poor
275	225	175	125	100

Model 1935

The last design from John Browning and was developed between 1925 and 1935. This pistol is known as the Model 1935, the P-35, High-Power or HP, and also as the GP (which stood for "Grand Puissance") and was referred to by all those names at one time or another. The HP is essentially an improved version of the Colt 1911 design. The swinging link was replaced with a fixed cam, which was less prone to wear. It is chambered for the 9mm Parabellum and has a 13-round detachable magazine. The only drawback to the design is that the trigger pull is not as fine as that of the 1911, as there is a transfer bar instead of a stirrup arrangement. This is necessary due to the increased magazine capacity resulting in a thicker grip. The barrel is 4.75" in length. It has an external hammer with a manual and a magazine safety and was available with various finishes and sight options and was furnished with a shoulder stock. The Model 1935 was used by many countries as their service pistol as such there are many variations. We list these versions and their approximate values. There are books available specializing in this model, and it would be beneficial to gain as much knowledge as possible if one contemplates acquisition of this fine and highly collectible pistol.

Prewar Commercial Model

Found with either a fixed sight or a sliding tangent rear sight and is slotted for a detachable shoulder stock. It was manufactured from 1935 until 1940.

Wood Holster Stock-Add 50%.

Fixed Sight Version

Exc.	V.G.	Good	Fair	Poor
600	525	475	375	275

Tangent Sight Version

Exc.	V.G.	Good	Fair	Poor
1000	850	675	550	400

Prewar Military Contract

The Model 1935 was adopted by many countries as a service pistol, and some of them are as follows:

Belgium

Exc.	V.G.	Good	Fair	Poor
1200	1050	900	600	375

Canada and China (*See John Inglis & Company*)

Denmark

Exc.	V.G.	Good	Fair	Poor
1250	1100	950	650	400

Great Britain

Exc.	V.G.	Good	Fair	Poor
1150	1000	850	550	325

Estonia

Exc.	V.G.	Good	Fair	Poor
1200	1050	900	600	375

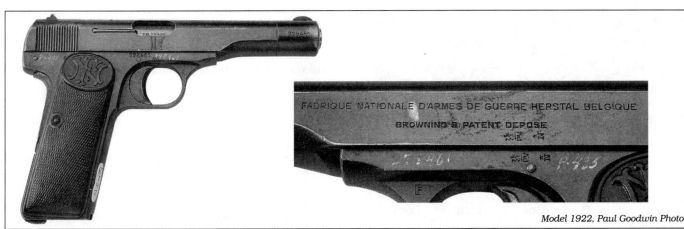

Model 1922, Paul Goodwin Photo

Holland

Exc.	V.G.	Good	Fair	Poor
1250	1100	950	650	400

Latvia

Exc.	V.G.	Good	Fair	Poor
1500	1350	1050	775	500

Lithuania

Exc.	V.G.	Good	Fair	Poor
1250	1100	950	650	400

Romania

Exc.	V.G.	Good	Fair	Poor
1500	1350	1050	775	500

German Military Pistole Modell 640(b)

In 1940 Germany occupied Belgium and took over the FN plant. The production of the Model 1935 continued, with Germany taking the output. The FN plant was assigned the production code "ch," and many thousands were produced. The finish on these Nazi guns runs from as fine as the Prewar Commercial series to downright crude, and it is possible to see how the war was progressing for Germany by the finish on their weapons. One must be cautious with some of these guns as there have been fakes noted with their backstraps cut for shoulder stocks, producing what would appear to be a more expensive variation. Individual appraisal should be secured if any doubt exists.

Fixed Sight Model

Paul Goodwin Photo

Exc.	V.G.	Good	Fair	Poor
500	450	400	300	250

Tangent Sight Model - 50,000 Manufactured

Courtesy Orvel Reichert

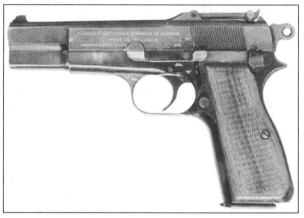

Courtesy Orvel Reichert

Exc.	V.G.	Good	Fair	Poor
850	750	700	550	400

Captured Prewar Commercial Model

These pistols were taken over when the plant was occupied. They are slotted for stocks and have tangent sights. There were few produced between serial number 48,000 and 52,000. All noted have the WaA613 Nazi proof mark. Beware of fakes!

Exc.	V.G.	Good	Fair	Poor
1500	1400	1150	750	500

Postwar Military Contract

Manufactured from 1946, and they embody some design changes—such as improved heat treating and barrel locking. Pistols produced after 1950 do not have barrels that can interchange with the earlier model pistols. The earliest models have an "A" prefix on the serial number and do not have the magazine safety. These pistols were produced for many countries, and there were many thousands manufactured.

Fixed Sight

Exc.	V.G.	Good	Fair	Poor
475	425	375	300	250

Tangent Sight

Exc.	V.G.	Good	Fair	Poor
750	675	575	400	300

Slotted and Tangent Sight

Exc.	V.G.	Good	Fair	Poor
1500	1050	750	500	400

Mauser/FN Model 1889 • Paul Goodwin Photo

Sultan of Oman

This is the only post war Hi-Power that is designated a Curio and Relic pistol. It has a tangent sight. The grip is slotted to accept a shoulder stock which is a legal accessory to this model. Less than 50 of these pistols were brought into the U.S. Canceled contract military sidearm for Oman. Very rare.

NIB	Exc.	V.G.	Good	Fair	Poor
6000	5750	4500	—	—	—

NOTE: For pistols with no shoulder stock deduct $1,000.

SUBMACHINE GUNS

Prior to 1940 Belgium used the MP28 (Model 34) as its standard military submachine gun.

FN also manufactured, under license from Israeli Military Industries (IMI), a copy of the UZI submachine gun.

Vigneron M2

This sub gun was issued to the Belgian army in 1953. It was also used by those same forces in the Belgian Congo. Many of these guns were taken by Congo forces after independence. A number of Vigneron guns may be found over much of Central Africa. The gun is chambered for the 9mm cartridge and has a wire folding stock. Barrel length is 11.75" with the rear portion of the barrel finned. A muzzle compensator is also standard. Magazine capacity is 32 rounds. Rate of fire is about 600 rounds per minute. Capable of select fire. Markings are found on the right side of the magazine housing and read, "ABL52 VIG M1." Also on the right side of the receiver is stamped "LICENCE VIGNERON." Weight is about 7.25 lbs. The gun was in production from 1952 to 1962.

Pre-1968

Exc.	V.G.	Fair
9000	8000	7000

Pre-1986 conversions

Exc.	V.G.	Fair
N/A	N/A	N/A

Pre-1986 dealer samples

Exc.	V.G.	Fair
4000	3500	3000

RIFLES

NOTE: For historical information, technical data, and photos on the FN-FAL rifle see Blake Stevens', *The FAL Rifle, Classic Edition*, Collector Grade Publications, 1993.

MAUSER (FN)

Model 1889 Rifle

The Mauser rifle that Fabrique Nationale was incorporated to manufacture. It is chambered for 7.65mm and has a 30.5" barrel. The magazine holds 5 rounds. The unique feature that sets the Belgian rifle apart from the Mausers made by other countries is the thin steel tube that encases the barrel. This was the first Mauser to use a charger loaded detachable box magazine. The sights are of the military type. The finish is blued, with a walnut stock.

Exc.	V.G.	Good	Fair	Poor
350	300	225	150	100

M1889 Carbine with Bayonet

Barrel length is 21". Fitted for a bayonet. Weight is about 7.5 lbs.

Exc.	V.G.	Good	Fair	Poor
375	350	235	160	100

M1889 Carbine with Yataghan

Barrel length is 21". Fitted for a unique bayonet. Weight is about 7.5 lbs.

Exc.	V.G.	Good	Fair	Poor
375	350	250	200	150

M1889 Carbine Lightened

Fitted with a 15.75" barrel and turned down bolt. A slotted sling bracket mounted on left side of buttstock.

Model 1889 Carbine • Paul Goodwin Photo

Model 1935 Short Rifle • Courtesy West Point Museum • Paul Goodwin Photo

Exc.	V.G.	Good	Fair	Poor
375	320	250	175	100

M1889 Carbine Lightened with Yataghan

Same as above but with longer stock. A unique bayonet was also issued with this carbine.

Exc.	V.G.	Good	Fair	Poor
375	320	250	175	100

M1890 Turkish Rifle

Captured Turkish Model 1890 rifles with Belgian rear sight similar to the Model 1889 rifle. No handguard. Original Turkish markings remain. Belgian proofs.

Exc.	V.G.	Good	Fair	Poor
350	275	250	200	100

M1916 Carbine

Similar to the Model 1889 with Yataghan bayonet but with different bracket on buttstock.

Exc.	V.G.	Good	Fair	Poor
350	275	225	175	125

M1935 Short Rifle

This model is very similar to the German 7.92 Kar 98k and uses the M98 bolt system. It is fitted with a 5-round flush magazine. Barrel length is 23.5". Weight is about 9 lbs.

Exc.	V.G.	Good	Fair	Poor
400	350	300	225	125

M50 Short Rifle

Post war surplus rifle converted to .30-06 caliber. Barrel length is 23.2". Tangent leaf rear sight graduated to 2000 meters. Marked "B/ABL/ DATE." Weight is approximately 9 lbs.

Exc.	V.G.	Good	Fair	Poor
350	300	250	200	100

M1889/36 Short Rifle

This model is a converted Model 1889 with a 23.5" barrel with wooden handguard. The upper barrel band and front sight are of the Model 1935 type. The bolt system appears similar to the Model 98. Chambered for the 7.65mm Mauser cartridge. Weight is about 9 lbs.

Exc.	V.G.	Good	Fair	Poor
250	200	150	90	60

M35/46 Short Rifle

Similar to the M50 short rifle.

Exc.	V.G.	Good	Fair	Poor
350	200	150	100	60

M24/30 .22 Caliber Training Rifle-Army

This is a military training rifle in .22 caliber built for the Belgian army after World War II.

Exc.	V.G.	Good	Fair	Poor
400	300	250	175	125

M24/30 .22 Caliber Training Rifle-Navy

Same as above but for the Belgian navy.

Exc.	V.G.	Good	Fair	Poor
400	300	250	175	125

FN M30 Postwar Short Rifle (M24/30)

Built after WWII for the Belgian army. It uses the standard M98 action.

Exc.	V.G.	Good	Fair	Poor
350	300	250	200	135

FABRIQUE NATIONALE

Model 1949 or SAFN 49

A gas-operated semiautomatic rifle chambered for 7x57, 7.92mm, and .30-06. It has a 23" barrel and military-type

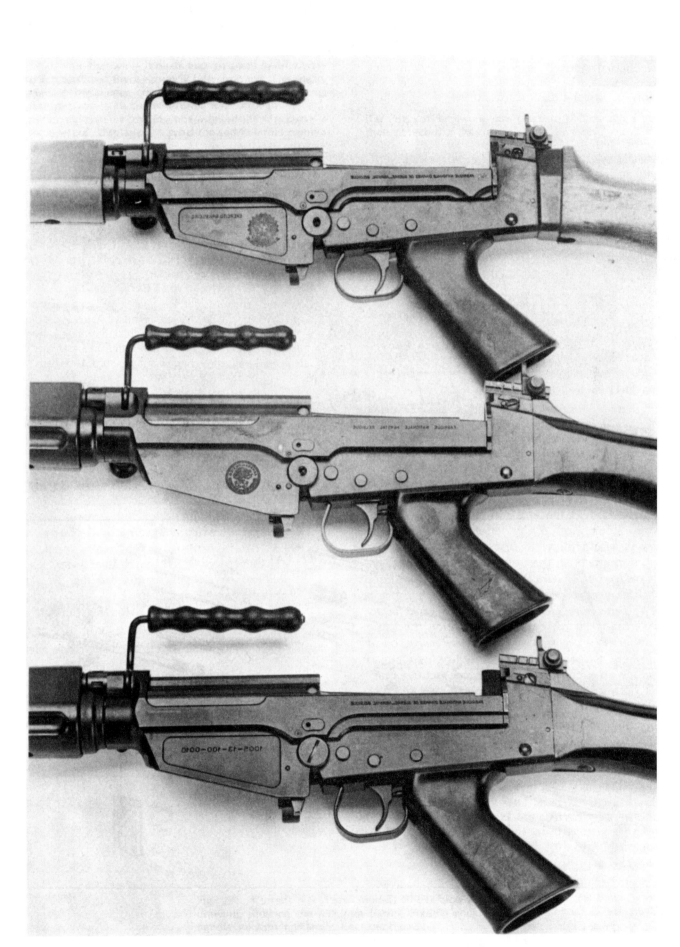

FAL Receivers: Top - Type 2; Middle - Type 3; Bottom - Type 1 • Courtesy Blake Stevens

sights. The integral magazine holds 10 rounds. The finish is blued, and the stock is walnut. This is a well-made gun that was actually designed before WWII. When the Germans were in the process of taking over Belgium, a group of FN engineers fled to England and took the plans for this rifle with them, preventing the German military from acquiring a very fine weapon. This model was introduced in 1949, after hostilities had ceased. This model was sold on contract to Egypt, chambered for 7.92mm; to Venezuela, chambered for 7x57; and to Columbia, Indonesia, Belgium, and Luxembourg chambered for the .30-06.

NOTE: The Egyptian model has recently been imported in large numbers and is worth approximately 25% less. For .30-06 caliber-Add 20%.

Courtesy Richard M. Kumor Sr.

Exc.	V.G.	Good	Fair	Poor
500	400	300	225	150

Model 30-11 Sniper Rifle

Chambered for the 7.62 NATO cartridge. It has a 20" heavy barrel and Anschutz sights. There is a flash suppressor mounted on the muzzle. It is built on a highly precision-made Mauser bolt action fed by a 9-round, detachable box magazine. The walnut stock is rather unique in that the butt is made up of two parts, with the rear half being replaceable to suit the needs of different-sized shooters. It is issued with a shooting sling, bipod, and a foam-lined carrying case. This is a rare firearm on the commercial market as it was designed and sold to the military and police markets.

Courtesy Jim Supica, Old Town Station

Exc.	V.G.	Good	Fair	Poor
5000	4500	3500	2750	2000

FN-FAL

A gas-operated, semiautomatic version of the famous FN battle rifle. This weapon has been adopted by more free world countries than any other rifle. It is chambered for the 7.62 NATO or .308 and has a 21" barrel with an integral flash suppressor. The sights are adjustable with an aperture rear, and the detachable box magazine holds 20 rounds. The stock and forearm are made of wood or a black synthetic. This model has been discontinued by the company and is no longer manufactured.

The models listed below are for the metric pattern Type 2 and Type 3 receivers, those marked "FN MATCH." The models below are for semiautomatic rifles only. FN-FAL rifles in the "inch" pattern are found in the British Commonwealth countries of Australia, India, Canada, and of course Great Britain. These rifles are covered separately under their own country headings.

50.00-21" Rifle Model

NIB	Exc.	V.G.	Good	Fair	Poor
3100	2700	2300	1900	1200	1000

50.63-18" Paratrooper Model

NIB	Exc.	V.G.	Good	Fair	Poor
3200	2800	2400	2000	1300	1100

50.64-21" Paratrooper Model

NIB	Exc.	V.G.	Good	Fair	Poor
2800	2400	2000	1800	1200	1000

50.41-Synthetic Butt H-Bar

NIB	Exc.	V.G.	Good	Fair	Poor
2800	2400	2000	1800	1200	1000

50.42-Wood Butt H-Bar

NIB	Exc.	V.G.	Good	Fair	Poor
2800	2400	2000	1800	1200	1000

FN FAL "G" Series (Type I Receiver)

Converted semiautomatic FAL. These rifles are subject to interpretation by the BATF as to their legal status. A list of BATF legal serial numbers is available. This information should be utilized prior to a sale in order to avoid the possibility of the sale of an illegal rifle. There was a total of 1,160 legal "G" Series FN FAL rifles imported into this country.

Standard

NIB	Exc.	V.G.	Good	Fair	Poor
5000	4500	4000	3000	2000	1000

Lightweight

NIB	Exc.	V.G.	Good	Fair	Poor
5000	4500	4000	3000	2000	1000

NOTE: There are a number of U.S. companies that built FN-FAL receivers and use military surplus parts. These rifles have no collector value as of yet.

FN FAL-Select Fire Assault Rifle

First produced in 1953, this 7.62x51mm select fire rifle has been used world-wide. It is fitted with a 20.8" barrel and a magazine that holds 20 rounds. It is available in several different configurations. Weight is about 9.8 lbs. Marked "FABRIQUE NATIONALE HERSTAL." Markings will also indicate many other countries would made this rifle under license from FN.

Photo courtesy FN

Pre-1968 (Rare)

Exc.	V.G.	Fair
9000	8500	8000

18" Para Model • Courtesy Blake Stevens, The FAL Rifle

21" Para Model • Courtesy Blake Stevens, The FAL Rifle

FN Heavy Barrel Model • Courtesy Blake Stevens, The FAL Rifle

Pre-1986 conversions

Exc.	V.G.	Fair
5500	5000	4500

Pre-1986 dealer samples

Exc.	V.G.	Fair
4000	3500	3000

FN CAL

Chambered for the 5.56x45mm cartridge and designed with a rotary bolt. It is fitted with an 18.2" barrel and has a magazine capacity of 20 or 30 rounds. Weight is about 6 lbs. With folding stock. Produced from 1966 to 1975 and is marked "FABRIQUE NATIONALE HERSTAL MOD CAL 5.56MM" on the left side of the receiver. This rifle was not widely adopted. A rare rifle. Only about 20 of these rifles were imported into the U.S.

NIB	Exc.	V.G.	Good	Fair	Poor
7500	6500	5000	3000	—	—

FN CAL-Select Fire Assault Rifle

Chambered for the 5.56x45mm cartridge and designed with a rotary bolt. It is fitted with an 18.2" barrel and has a magazine capacity of 20 or 30 rounds. It rate of fire is 650 rounds per minute. Weight is about 6 lbs. With it folding stock. Produced from 1966 to 1975 and is marked "FABRIQUE NATION-ALE HERSTAL MOD CAL 5.56MM" on the left side of the receiver. This rifle was not widely adopted.

Photo Courtesy Private NFA Collection

Pre-1968 (Rare)

Exc.	V.G.	Fair
9500	9000	8500

Pre-1986 conversions

Exc.	V.G.	Fair
7500	7000	6800

Pre-1986 dealer samples

Exc.	V.G.	Fair
5500	5000	4500

FNC

A lighter-weight assault-type rifle chambered for the 5.56mm cartridge. It is a gas-operated semiautomatic with an 18" or 21" barrel. It has a 30-round box magazine and is black, with either a fixed or folding stock. This model was also discontinued by FN. The same problem with fluctuating values applies to this weapon as to the L.A.R., and we strongly advise that one research the market in a particular geographic location as prices can fluctuate radically.

Standard-Fixed stock, 16" or 18" barrel

NIB	Exc.	V.G.	Good	Fair	Poor
3000	2800	2500	2000	1500	1000

Paratrooper Model-Folding stock, 16" or 18" barrel

NIB	Exc.	V.G.	Good	Fair	Poor
3000	2800	2500	2000	1500	1000

NOTE: The above prices are for Belgian-made guns only.

FN FNC-Select Fire Assault Rifle

This model, introduced in 1979, took the place of the CAL. Chambered for the 5.56x45mm cartridge and fitted with a 17.5" barrel, it weighs about 8.4 lbs. It has a 30-round magazine capacity. Rate of fire is 700 rounds per minute. Fitted with a metal folding stock. This model will accept M16 magazines. Marked "FNC 5.56" on left side of receiver. This rifle was adopted by the Belgian, Indonesian, and Swedish military.

Pre-1968

Exc.	V.G.	Fair
N/A	N/A	N/A

Pre-1986 conversions

Exc.	V.G.	Fair
5500	4500	4000

Pre-1986 dealer samples

Exc.	V.G.	Fair
4000	3800	3500

FN BAR Model D (Demontable)

Photo courtesy Jim Thompson

This was the FN version of the Browning automatic rifle. It is fitted with a quick change barrel, pistol grip, and can be modified to either a belt-fed or box magazine configuration. It was offered in a variety of calibers from 6.5 Swedish Mauser to the 7.92x57mm Mauser. It is fitted with a 19.5" barrel and has a rate of fire of either 450 or 650 rounds per minute. Weight is about 20 lbs. Marked "FABRIQUE NATIONALE D'ARMES DE GUERRE HERSTAL-BELGIQUE" on left side of receiver.

FN sold about 700 Model Ds to Finland in 1940 which the Finns used during their "Winter War" with the Russians. These Finnish BARs were chambered for the 7.63x54R cartridge. Also a small number of FN guns were sold to China (2,000) and Ethiopia in the 1930s. These BARs were chambered for the 7.92x57mm Mauser cartridge. After World War II FN sold its Model 30 BAR to a number of countries around the world.

Pre-1968 (Very Rare)

Exc.	V.G.	Fair
12000	10000	9000

Pre-1986 conversions

Exc.	V.G.	Fair
N/A	N/A	N/A

Pre-1986 dealer samples

Exc.	V.G.	Fair
3500	3250	3000

MACHINE GUNS

Fabrique Nationale has a long history of manufacturing John M. Browning's firearms. These firearms include the Browning Model 1917, M1919, and .50 caliber heavy gun. The light machine were chambered in a variety of calibers and sold around the world by FN. During World War II the FN factory was occupied by German troops but after the war in 1945 when production finally returned to normal levels. The Belgians produced the air-cooled Browning guns in 7.62x63mm (.30-06) for the Belgian army. When NATO adopted the 7.62x51mm cartridge FN designed and built the FN MAG machine gun.

FN MAG (Mitrailleuse d'Appui Generale)

First produced in Belgium in 1955 this machine gun is chambered for the 7.62x51mm cartridge. It is fitted with a 21.3" quick change barrel and has an adjustable rate of fire of 700 to 1000 rounds per minute. It is belt-fed with metal links. The basic configuration uses a wooden buttstock, smooth barrel with bipod attached to gas cylinder, pistol grip, and slotted flash hider. The gun can also be attached to a tripod as well as used with an anti-aircraft mount. Weight is about 22 lbs. Marked "FABRIQUE NATIONALE D'ARMES DE GUERRE HERSTAL BELGIUM" on the right side of the receiver. This gun is still in production and is in use by over 80 countries world-wide.

There is an aircraft version of this gun designated the Model 60-30 (single mount) or 60-40 (twin mount). The gun can also be mounted in a coaxial configuration such as a tank or armored vehicle.

Pre-1968 (Extremely Rare, only 1 known)

Exc.	V.G.	Fair
85000	—	—

Pre-1986 conversions

Exc.	V.G.	Fair
N/A	N/A	N/A

Pre-1986 dealer samples

Exc.	V.G.	Fair
60000	58000	55000

NOTE: This is an extremely rare machine gun with prices based on scarcity and high demand.

FN Minimi

Designed as a squad automatic weapon (SAW) and chambered for the 5.56x45mm cartridge this machine gun has a rate of fire of 700 rounds per minute and is equipped with a 30-round magazine or 100 to 200-round boxed belts. The quick change barrel length is 18" and weight is about 15 lbs. Marked "FN MINIMI 5.56" on the left side of the receiver. First produced in 1982 this gun is called the M249 machine gun in the U.S. army. It is also in service in a number of other countries.

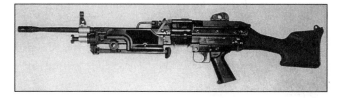

Photo Courtesy Private NFA Collection

Pre-1968

Exc.	V.G.	Fair
N/A	N/A	N/A

Pre-1986 conversions

Exc.	V.G.	Fair
N/A	N/A	N/A

Pre-1986 dealer samples (Extremely Rare, only 6 known)

Exc.	V.G.	Fair
50000	45000	43000

CANADA

Canadian Military Conflicts, 1870-Present

In 1867, under the British North America Act, the Dominion of Canada was created. In 1982 the British Parliament in London gave Canada's constitution full self control. Because Canada has such close ties to Great Britain much of Canada's military history closely follows Great Britain, especially during both World Wars and Vietnam.

HANDGUNS

INGLIS, JOHN & COMPANY

Introduction by Clive M. Law

This firm manufactured Browning Pattern .35 semiautomatic pistols for the Canadian, Chinese and British governments. Pistols are parkerized dark gray and include black plastic grips and a lanyard ring. Premium paid for pistols which still display the Canadian "Lend-Lease" decal on the front grip strap. Fewer than 160,000 pistols were manufactured between 1943 and 1945. Add $350 for original Canadian-produced wood stocks. Prices shown here are for original finish unaltered pistols, prices lower for recent Chinese and British imports.

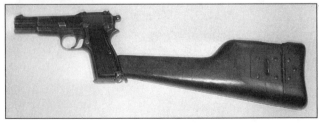

Courtesy Richard M. Kumor, Sr.

Mk. 1 No. 1 (Chinese marked)

The first 4,000 pistols destined for the Chinese government included a six character Chinese marking on the slide, as well as a serial number which incorporated the letters "CH." Includes a tangent rear sight and a stock slot.

Exc.	V.G.	Good	Fair	Poor
2000	1650	1400	950	800

Mk. 1 No. 1

Identical to the Chinese-marked model but without the Chinese characters.

Exc.	V.G.	Good	Fair	Poor
1100	1000	925	825	750

Mk. I No. 1*

Externally identical to the No. 1 Mk. 1 but the slide includes the marking Mk. 1*. This mark may be factory applied, or applied in the field after conversion.

Paul Goodwin Photo

Exc.	V.G.	Good	Fair	Poor
695	600	475	425	375

No. 2 Mk. 1

The first 10,000 pistols made for Canada/Britain display the standard slide legend, fixed rear sight in the distinctive Inglis "hump" and no stock slot. All No. 2 type pistols will incorporate the letter "T" within the serial number.

Exc.	V.G.	Good	Fair	Poor
1000	925	850	775	675

No. 2 Mk. 1*
Identical to the No. 2 Mk. 1 externally but the slide includes the marking Mk. 1*. This mark may be factory applied, or applied in the field after conversion. Some examples imported from England or New Zealand may include the "No. 2" stamped or engraved on the slide.

Paul Goodwin Photo

Exc.	V.G.	Good	Fair	Poor
600	550	475	425	375

No. 2 Mk. 1* slotted
A small quantity of pistols, mostly in the 3Txxx range, were made up from Chinese frames and include the stock slot. Beware of fakes.

Exc.	V.G.	Good	Fair	Poor
1300	1150	925	625	500

DP Pistols
Approximately 150 No. 1 type pistols, some with the Chinese inscription, were made up as display and presentation pistols. Serial numbers will range from DP1 to DP150 approximately.

Exc.	V.G.	Good	Fair	Poor
2400	2000	1750	1450	1200

Inglis Diamond
In the last week of production, Inglis marked a small quantity of pistols with their trademark, the word Inglis within a diamond. Both the No. 1 and No. 2-style pistols were affected. Some pistols remained in the white while others were parkerized. It is believed that fewer than 50 pistols were marked.

Exc.	V.G.	Good	Fair	Poor
2500	2250	1900	1650	1200

New Zealand Issue
Only 500 pistols were acquired by New Zealand in the 1960s. A serial number list will soon be published which will identify 400 of these pistols. A small quantity was modified, and marked, by the NZ Special Air Service.

Exc.	V.G.	Good	Fair	Poor
1000	800	650	575	525

British Issue
A large quantity of pistols have been imported from the British Ministry of Defense over the past several years. These pistols often display a black "paint" finish and may be marked "FTR" (Factory Thorough Repair) or "AF" (meaning unknown).

Exc.	V.G.	Good	Fair	Poor
575	525	500	475	425

Dutch Issue
The Netherlands used over 10,000 Inglis pistols. Early versions display a small crown over W mark on the rear sight while later models will have Dutch serial numbers, Belgian proofs and Belgian barrels.

Exc.	V.G.	Good	Fair	Poor
2500	2300	2100	1800	1600

Belgian Issue
Belgium received 1,578 pistols as aid from Canada in the 1950s. These remained in use with the Gendarmerie until recently. Some pistols will display a grey "paint" finish and have numbered magazines. These have been wrongly identified as Danish navy in the past.

Exc.	V.G.	Good	Fair	Poor
3000	2500	2300	2100	1700

SUBMACHINE GUNS

Sterling-Canadian C1
Chambered for the 9mm cartridge this submachine gun features a 7.75" barrel collapsible metal stock. The rate of fire is 550 rounds per minute. Weight is about 6 lbs. Produced from 1953 to 1988. Still made in India under license. Marked "SMG 9MM C1" on the magazine housing.

The Canadian version of the Sterling is much like the British except for a 30-round magazine without rollers as followers, a different type bayonet (FAL), and internal modifications. A 10-round magazine is also available. Designated the "C1" by the Canadian military. It was first produced in Canada in the late 1950s.

Photo Courtesy Private NFA Collection

Pre-1968 (Very Rare)

Exc.	V.G.	Fair
9000	8000	7000

Pre-1986 conversions

Exc.	V.G.	Fair
5000	4500	4500

Pre-1986 dealer samples

Exc.	V.G.	Fair
5000	4500	3250

RIFLES

ROSS RIFLE CO.

Designed in 1896 by Sir Charles Ross, this straight pull rifle was manufactured in a variety of styles. Due to problems with the bolt design, it never proved popular and was discontinued in 1915.

Mark I

This rifle was adopted by the Canadian military in 1903. Barrel length is 28". Chambered for .303 caliber with a "Harris Controlled Platform Magazine" that can be depressed by an external lever to facilitate loading. Magazine capacity is 5 rounds. Marked "ROSS RIFLE COM. QUEBEC CANADA" on left side of receiver. About 5,000 of these rifle were built.

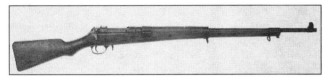

Courtesy Buffalo Bill Historical Center, Cody, Wyoming

Exc.	V.G.	Good	Fair	Poor
500	350	250	150	100

Mark I Carbine

As above, with a 26" barrel without bayonet lug.

Exc.	V.G.	Good	Fair	Poor
450	300	250	200	150

Mark II

Introduced in 1905 with a modified rear sight, longer handguard, no receiver bridge. Marked "ROSS RIFLE CO. QUEBEC CANADA 1905."

Exc.	V.G.	Good	Fair	Poor
500	350	250	150	100

Mark III

Built between 1910 and 1916 with improved lockwork and stripper clip guides. Extended single column 5-round box magazine. Barrel length is 30". Marked "ROSS RIFLE CO." over "CANADA" over "M10" on receiver ring. About 400,000 of these rifles were produced with about 67,000 sent to England's Home Guard.

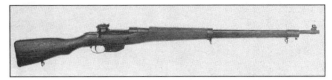

Courtesy Buffalo Bill Historical Center, Cody, Wyoming

Exc.	V.G.	Good	Fair	Poor
500	350	275	175	125

Mark III*

As above, with a magazine cutoff.

Exc.	V.G.	Good	Fair	Poor
450	300	250	200	150

Ross Military Match Rifle

A .280 Ross or .303 caliber straight pull military-style rifle with a 30" barrel having peep sights. Blued with a walnut stock. Similar in appearance to the Mark III except for flush magazine with .280 version.

Exc.	V.G.	Good	Fair	Poor
825	600	400	250	125

C1/C1A1 (FN FAL)

Canada was one of the first countries to adopt the FN-FAL rifle. This is a semiautomatic version with 21" barrel. Twenty-round box magazine. The rear sight on the C1 is a revolving disk with five different sized openings. Ranges calibrated from 200 to 600 yards; numbered 2 to 6 on the sight. The sight may be folded when not in use. Weight is about 9.5 lbs. About 1959 the C1 was modified to use a 2-piece firing pin and a plastic carry handle replaced the wooden type. Both types of rifles utilize the long prong flash hider on the muzzle.

C1A1 • Courtesy West Point Museum • Paul Goodwin Photo

Exc.	V.G.	Good	Fair	Poor
2500	2000	1500	1000	500

NOTE: For C1/C1A1 registered as NFA firearms see prices listed below:

Pre-1968 (Rare)

Exc.	V.G.	Fair
9000	8500	8000

Pre-1986 conversions

Exc.	V.G.	Fair
5500	5000	4500

Pre-1986 dealer samples

Exc.	V.G.	Fair
4000	3500	3000

C2/C2A1

This is Canada's version of the FN heavy barrel Squad Light Automatic Rifle. Select fire with a rate of fire of about 700 rounds per minute. Barrel length is 21". Magazine capacity is 30 rounds. Weight is approximately 15 lbs. Built by Long Branch Arsenal, Ontario.

Pre-1968 (Rare)

Exc.	V.G.	Fair
10000	9000	8000

Pre-1986 conversions

Exc.	V.G.	Fair
6000	5500	5000

Pre-1986 dealer samples

Exc.	V.G.	Fair
5000	4500	4000

C7/C8 (M16A2)

In 1985 the Canadian firm of Diemaco began producing a Canadian version of the Colt M16A2 rifle. There are differences between the Colt-built M16 and the Diemaco version. However, due to import restrictions on Class 3 weapons no Diemaco M16s were imported into the U.S. for transferable civilian sale. Therefore, no Diemaco lowers are available to the civilian collector. There are Diemaco uppers in the U.S. that will fit on Colt lowers. The 20" rifle version is designated the C7 while the 16" carbine version is called the C8. There are a number of other Diemaco Canadian uppers that may be seen in the U.S. such as the LMG and 24" barreled version. Prices should be comparable with Colt uppers.

MACHINE GUNS

NOTE: Canada used the Lewis and Vickers machine guns during World War II. The Toronto firm of John Inglis produced Mark I and Mark II Bren guns in .303 caliber in large quantities for British and Canadian troops. Begining in 1943 Canada produced almost 60 percent of the total Bren gun production for World War II. Canada also uses the Browning Model 1919A4, called the C1 machine gun in 7.62mm (.308) as its primarily light machine gun.

See Great Britian Machine Guns, Bren.

CHINA & PEOPLE'S REPUBLIC OF

Chinese Military Conflicts, 1870 to 2000

By 1870 China was affected by foreign influence from Great Britain, France, Germany, and Russia. The central government in China was furthered weakened by its defeat in the Sino-Japanese War of 1894-1895. The decade of the 1890s ended with China's fierce attempt to overthrow foreign influence with the Boxer Rebellion, 1898 to 1900. The period of the early 20th century was marked by internal strife which eventually led to Chinese warlords gaining control of the government in 1916. These warlords were eventually ousted in 1927 by the Nationalist leader Chiang Kai-shek in alliance with the Communists. The year 1927 marked the beginning of a long Chinese civil war between the Nationalist and the Communists ending with the Communists Long March of 1934-35 and their exile. In 1931 Japan occupied Manchuria and in 1937 the Japanese mounted a full scale invasion of China. Both the Nationalist and the Communists fought in an uneasy alliance against the Japanese. By the end of World War II the civil war again ignited and the Communists became victorious in 1949 when the People's Republic of China was proclaimed. China entered the Korean War on the side of the North Koreans in 1950. In the last 50 years China has been occupied with intellectual turmoil (Cultural Revolution) and other domestic turmoil.

HANDGUNS

MAUSER

Between the two world wars the Chinese military purchased a number of Mauser 1896 pistols directly from Mauser and other commercial sources. These purchases consisted mainly of Bolos and Model 1930s. In addition to these purchases China made its own copies of the Mauser broomhandle as well as the Astra. See Germany, Handguns, Mauser for more detailed descriptions and prices.

CHINA STATE ARSENALS

Type 51/54 Pistol (TT33)

A 7.62mm semiautomatic pistol with a 4.5" barrel and 8-shot magazine. This model was produced in a number of communist countries. It is essentially a Soviet Tokarev TT-33.

NOTE: for cut-aways add 200%.

TT33 • Courtesy Richard M. Kumor Sr.

Exc.	V.G.	Good	Fair	Poor
500	450	375	225	100

From top to bottom; M20 export model, K54, K51
Courtesy Chuck Karwan

Type 59 Makarov

This semiautomatic pistol is similar in appearance to the Walther PP pistol and is chambered for the 9mm Makarov (9x18mm) cartridge. It has a double action trigger and is fitted with fixed sights. Barrel length is 3.6" and overall length is 6.4". Weight is approximately 25 oz. Magazine capacity is 8 rounds.

Exc.	V.G.	Good	Fair	Poor
150	100	80	60	50

Type 80

A Chinese version of the Mauser 96 pistol chambered for the 7.63x25mm cartridge. Fitted with a 7" barrel and detachable 10- or 20-round magazine, this pistol is capable of select fire. Weight is approximately 40 oz. see Mauser Schnellfeuer.

SUBMACHINE GUNS

Type 43/53

This is a Chinese copy of a Soviet PPS 43 built during the Korean War.

Pre-1968

Exc.	V.G.	Fair
5500	5000	4500

Pre-1986 conversions

Exc.	V.G.	Fair
N/A	N/A	N/A

Pre-1986 dealer samples

Exc.	V.G.	Fair
N/A	N/A	N/A

Type 50/ Vietcong K-50M

This model is a Chinese copy of the Soviet PPSh-41 submachine gun. It is chambered for the 7.62 Soviet pistol cartridge. Barrel is 10.5" and magazine capacity is 25, 32, or 40 rounds. Rate of fire is 600 rounds per minute. Weight is approximately 7.5 lbs. Unlike the Soviet model this gun features a telescoping metal stock and no muzzle compensator. Markings are located on top of the receiver.

Pre-1968

Exc.	V.G.	Fair
7000	6500	6000

Pre-1986 conversions

Exc.	V.G.	Fair
N/A	N/A	N/A

Pre-1986 dealer samples

Exc.	V.G.	Fair
N/A	N/A	N/A

RIFLES

MAUSER

Mauser Rifles

The Chinese used a wide variety of Mauser rifles from the Gew 71 to the Chinese Model 1924. Some of these are marked with Chinese characters and others are not. Generally speaking these Chinese Mausers are worth approximately the same as their German counterparts.

For in-depth information on Chinese Mausers see Robert W.D. Ball's, *Mauser Military Rifles of the World*, 2nd Edition, Krause Publications, 2000.

NOTE: For prices *see Germany, Rifles, Mauser.*

Type 53

This is a Chinese copy of the Soviet Model 1944 Mosin-Nagant carbine.

Exc.	V.G.	Good	Fair	Poor
200	150	125	75	50

Type 56 Carbine (SKS)

A 7.62x39mm semiautomatic rifle with a 20.5" barrel and 10-shot fixed magazine. Blued with oil finished stock. This rifle was a standard service arm for most Eastern Bloc countries prior to the adoption of the AK47.

Pre-Ban Rifles

Exc.	V.G.	Good	Fair	Poor
400	300	—	—	—

NOTE: The importation of post-ban SKS rifles has resulted in an oversupply of these rifles with the result that prices are less than $100 for guns in excellent condition. However, this situation may change and if that occurs the price will adjust accordingly. Study local conditions before purchase or sale of this firearm.

North Korean Type 56 Carbine (SKS)

Same overall design as the Chinese version but with high quality fir and finish. Reddish-brown laminated stock. Rare.

Pre-Ban Rifles

Exc.	V.G.	Good	Fair	Poor
1400	1000	800	600	300

Chinese Type 56 Rifle

A close copy of the AK-47 and first produced in 1958, this select fire rifle is chambered for the 7.62x39mm cartridge. It is fitted with a 16" barrel and has a magazine capacity of 30 rounds. This model has a folding bayonet hinged below the muzzle. Weight is about 8.4 lbs. Rate of fire is 600 rounds per minute. Markings on left side of receiver. Still in production. This rifle was adopted by Chinese forces and was seen in Cambodia as well.

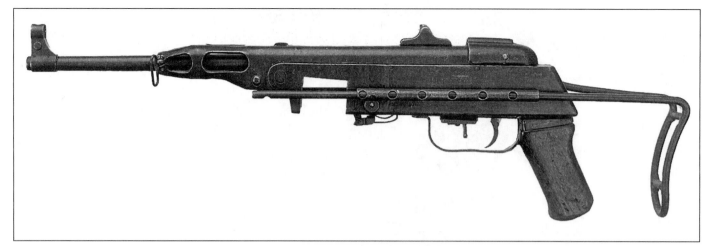

Chinese Type 50 • Paul Goodwin Photo

Type 53 Rifle • Courtesy West Point Museum • Paul Goodwin Photo

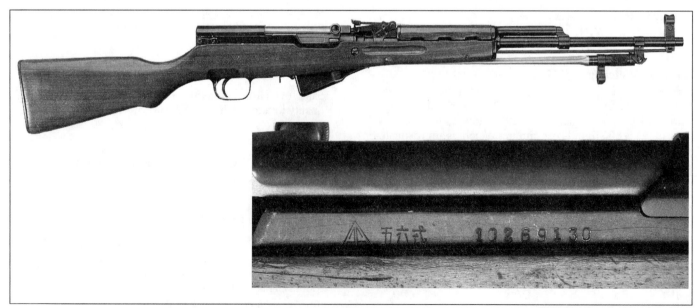

SKS Carbine • Paul Goodwin Photo

Chinese Type 56-1 • Paul Goodwin Photo

Another variation of the Type 56 was the Type 56-1 which featured prominent rivets on the metal butt. No bayonet. There is also the Type 56-2 which as a metal folding buttstock. No bayonet. There is also the Type 56-C with plastic furniture, side folding butt with cheekpiece and improved sights.

Pre-1968

Exc.	V.G.	Fair
15000	11000	9500

Pre-1986 conversions

Exc.	V.G.	Fair
6000	5500	5000

Pre-1986 dealer samples

Exc.	V.G.	Fair
7000	6000	5000

Type 56 (AK Clone semiautomatic versions)

Imported from China in semiautomatic versions and built by Poly Tech and Norinco in different styles and configurations, some of which are listed below.

Milled Receiver-Poly Tech

Exc.	V.G.	Good	Fair	Poor
1500	1200	800	500	250

Stamped Receiver-Poly Tech

Exc.	V.G.	Good	Fair	Poor
1100	800	500	300	150

Stamped Receiver-Norinco

Exc.	V.G.	Good	Fair	Poor
950	700	450	250	150

NOTE: For folding stock version add 20%.

Type 79

A Chinese copy of the Soviet Dragunov SVD sniper rifle.

Exc.	V.G.	Good	Fair	Poor
3000	2500	1500	1000	750

MACHINE GUNS

NOTE: See also *Great Britain, Machine Guns, Bren MK2.*

Type 24

The Chinese designation for the Russian Model 1910 Maxim purchased from the Russians.

Pre-1968

Exc.	V.G.	Fair
15000	12000	10000

Pre-1986 conversions

Exc.	V.G.	Fair
10000	9000	8000

Pre-1986 dealer samples

Exc.	V.G.	Fair
N/A	N/A	N/A

Type 26

This is the Czech wz 26 purchased in the 1930s.

Pre-1968

Exc.	V.G.	Fair
15000	14000	13000

Pre-1986 conversions

Exc.	V.G.	Fair
13000	12500	12000

Pre-1986 dealer samples (Rare)

Exc.	V.G.	Fair
N/A	N/A	N/A

Type 53

This is a Chinese copy of the Soviet DPM machine gun.

Pre-1968

Exc.	V.G.	Fair
13000	11000	11000

Pre-1986 conversions

Exc.	V.G.	Fair
8000	7000	6000

Pre-1986 dealer samples

Exc.	V.G.	Fair
N/A	N/A	N/A

Type 54

The Chinese made a variation of the Soviet DShK 38/46 gun.

Pre-1968

Exc.	V.G.	Fair
—	35000	30000

Pre-1986 conversions

Exc.	V.G.	Fair
—	27000	—

Pre-1986 dealer samples (Rare)

Exc.	V.G.	Fair
—	20000	20000

Type 56

This is a Chinese copy of the Soviet Model RPD light machine gun.

Pre-1968 (Very Rare)

Exc.	V.G.	Fair
38000	35000	35000

Pre-1986 conversions

Exc.	V.G.	Fair
N/A	N/a	N/A

Pre-1986 dealer samples (Rare)

Exc.	V.G.	Fair
20000	20000	20000

Type 57

This is a Chinese copy of the Soviet SG-43.

Pre-1968

Exc.	V.G.	Fair
25000	20000	18000

Pre-1986 conversions

Exc.	V.G.	Fair
20000	18000	15000

Pre-1986 dealer samples (Rare)

Exc.	V.G.	Fair
N/A	N/A	N/A

Type 58

This is a licensed Chinese made copy of the Soviet RP-46.

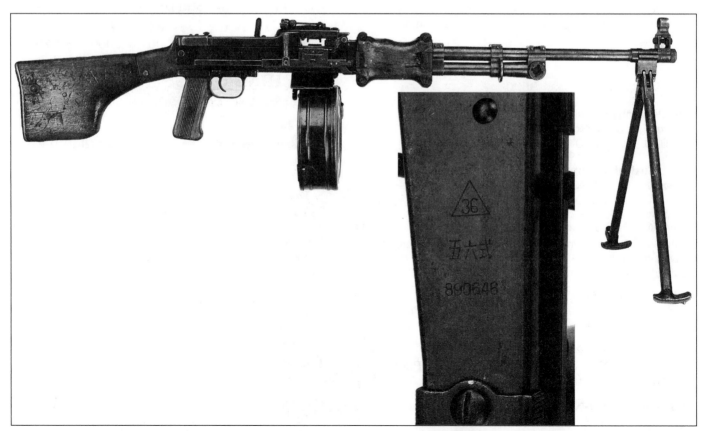

Type 56 • Courtesy West Point Museum, Paul Goodwin Photo

Type 57 with mount • Courtesy West Point Museum, Paul Goodwin Photo

Pre-1968				**Pre-1986 dealer samples (Rare)**		
Exc.	**V.G.**	**Fair**		**Exc.**	**V.G.**	**Fair**
19000	18000	16000		N/A	N/A	N/A

Pre-1986 conversions		
Exc.	**V.G.**	**Fair**
10000	9000	8000

Type 58 • Courtesy West Point Museum, Paul Goodwin Photo

CZECHOSLOVAKIA

Czechoslovakian Military Conflicts, 1918-1993

Czechoslovakia, as an independent nation, was born at the end of World War I from the ruins of the Austro-Hungarian Empire. In 1939 the country was invaded and occupied by Germany. After the war ended in 1945 Czechoslovakia was re-established under Communists rule. Czechoslovakia became the independent state of the Czech Republic in 1993.

Bibliographical Notes:

Perhaps the best general work on Czech firearms is *Czech Firearms and Ammunition*, by Dolinek, Karlicky, and Vacha, Prague, 1995. Jan Still, *Axis Pistols*, 1986.

NOTE: The term "vz" stands for model (*Vzor*) in Czech. This abbreviation is used in place of the English word Model. The author has sometimes used both terms but never together.

HANDGUNS

Most Czech handguns are of domestic design and manufacture. See below.

CZ 1922

Semiautomatic pistol chambered for the .380 ACP (9x17mm short) cartridge. Barrel length is 3.5". Magazine capacity is 8 rounds. Weight is approximately 22 oz. Adopted by the Czech army in 1922 and called the M22. This was the first Czech designed and manufactured service semiautomatic pistol. It was based on a German locked breech design and made under license from Mauser. Blued with checkered plastic grips. Manufactured between 1921 and 1923. Because of production difficulties only about 22,000 were built.

Exc.	V.G.	Good	Fair	Poor
650	500	350	200	150

CZ 1924

The first large production military pistol produced by CZ. It is a locked-breech pistol with a 3.5" rotating barrel chambered for the 9mm short cartridge, external hammer and a magazine safety. It features a rounded slide and is blued with a wrap-around walnut grip. Magazine capacity is 8 rounds. The slide is marked, "Ceska Zbrojovka A.S. v Praze." Weight is approximately 24 oz. About 170,000 of these pistols were produced between 1922 and 1938.

NOTE: For Nazi-Proofed add 50%.

Exc.	V.G.	Good	Fair	Poor
475	375	300	200	100

NOTE: A limited number of pistols have been noted marked, "CZ 1925" and "CZ 1926." There are various minor design changes on each model, and it is conjectured that they were prototypes that were manufactured on the road to the production of the less complicated, blowback-operated CZ 1927 pistol.

CZ 1927

A semiautomatic pistol chambered for the 7.65mm cartridge (.32 ACP), marked the same as the CZ 1924, but the cocking grooves on the slide are cut vertically instead of sloped as on the earlier model. This model was blued with checkered, wrap-around, plastic grips. These early guns were beautifully made and marked, "Ceska Zbrojovka AS v Praze."

This version remained in production during the German occupation of Czechoslovakia between 1939 and 1945. Occupation pistols are marked, "BOHMISCHE WAFFENFABRIK IM PRAG." The Germans used the code "fnh" on these wartime pistols and designated the model the "PISTOLE MOD 27(T)." The finish declined as the war progressed, with the very late guns rough but functional. There are several subvariations of this pistol that may affect value (see Still). A total of about 450,000 were produced during the German occupation. After the war, these pistols continued in production until 1951. There were almost 700,000 manufactured.

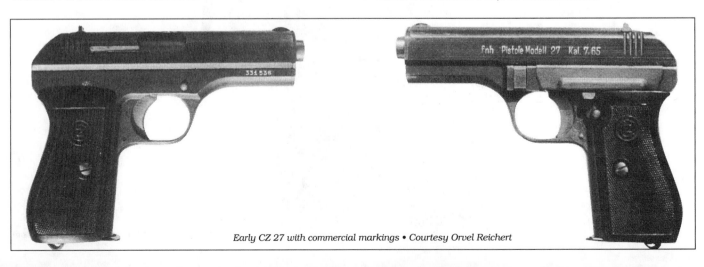

Early CZ 27 with commercial markings • Courtesy Orvel Reichert

NOTE: For Nazi-Proofed add 50%.

Exc.	V.G.	Good	Fair	Poor
450	375	300	200	165

NOTE: Some of these pistols were made with an extended barrel for the use of a silencer. This variation brings a large premium. Less than 10 CZ27s were made in .22 caliber. An expert opinion is suggested if a sale is contemplated.

CZ 1938

This odd pistol has been rated as one of the worst military service pistols ever manufactured. It is chambered for the 9mm short cartridge (.380 Auto) and has a 4.65" barrel. Except for a few examples with a conventional sear and slide safety it is double action-only with exposed hammer, and difficult to fire accurately. It utilizes an 8-round, detachable box magazine; and the slide is hinged at the muzzle to pivot upward for ease of cleaning and disassembly. It is well made and well finished but is as large in size as most 9mm Parabellum pistols. Production began in 1938, and the Germans adopted it as the "Pistole Mod 39" on paper; but it is doubtful that any were actually used by the German army. It now appears that the P39(t), which is the Nazi designation, were all sent to Finland and a large number with "SA" (Finnish) markings have recently been surplused along with their holsters. A few SA marked guns have been modified by the Finnish army to function single or double action. Almost 1,000,000 of these pistols were manufactured.

Exc.	V.G.	Good	Fair	Poor
450	400	350	250	175

CZ 1938-Nazi Proofed (P39(t))

Fewer than 1,000 of these pistols were Nazi proofed late in the war. E/WaA76 acceptance stamp on left frame and barrel.

Exc.	V.G.	Good	Fair	Poor
—	1500	1250	600	300

CZ 1950

This is a blowback-operated, semiautomatic, double action pistol chambered for the 7.65mm cartridge with a 3.75" barrel. Magazine capacity is 8 rounds. Weight is about 23 oz. It is patterned after the Walther Model PP with a few differences. The safety catch is located on the frame instead of the slide; and the triggerguard is not hinged, as on the Walther. It is dismantled by means of a catch on the side of the frame. Although intended to be a military pistol designed by the Kratochvil brothers, it proved to be under powered and was adopted by the police. There were few released on the commercial market.

CZ 1950 • Courtesy Chuck Karwan

Exc.	V.G.	Good	Fair	Poor
275	200	150	100	75

Model 1970

This model was an attempt to correct dependability problems with the Model 50. There is little difference to see externally between the two except for markings and the grip pattern. Markings are, "VZOR 70 CAL 7.65." Production began during the 1960s and ended in 1983.

Courtesy Rock Island Auction Company

Exc.	V.G.	Good	Fair	Poor
250	200	150	100	75

CZ 1952

Since the Czechoslovakian army was not happy with the under powered CZ 1950 pistol, they began using Soviet weapons until 1952, when this model was designed. It was designed for a new cartridge known as the 7.62mm M48. It was similar to the Soviet cartridge but loaded to a higher velocity. This is a single action, semiautomatic pistol with a 4.5" barrel. It has a locked breech that utilizes two roller cams. Magazine capacity is 8 rounds. This was an excellent pistol that has been replaced by the Soviet Makarov, a pistol that is decidedly inferior to it.

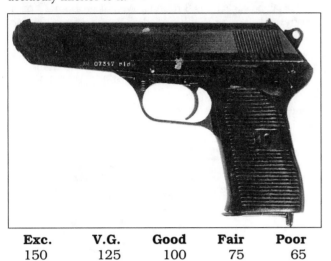

Exc.	V.G.	Good	Fair	Poor
150	125	100	75	65

CZ 75 B

Introduced in 1994 this CZ model is an updated version of the original CZ 75. It features a pinned front sight, a commander hammer, non-glare ribbed barrel, and a squared triggerguard. Also offered in 40 S&W chamber. Offered in both commercial and military version the CZ75B is used by more than 60 countries around the world in 9mm. Approximately 1,250,000 military pistols are in service. The Czechs use the pistol in their Special Forces units.

NIB	Exc.	V.G.	Good	Fair	Poor
450	350	300	250	175	125

NOTE: For .40 S&W add $30. For glossy blue add $20, for dual tone finish $25, and for nickel add $25. For tritium night sights add $80.

CZ 82/83

This is a fixed barrel .380 caliber pistol. It features an ambidextrous safety and magazine catch behind the triggerguard. The pistol is stripped by means of a hinged triggerguard. Barrel length is 3.8", overall length is 6.8", and weight is about 23 oz.

The Model 82 designation is the military model, while the Model 83 is the commercial version. The Model 83 is offered in 3 calibers; the 9x18, .380, and 9mm. The military Model 82 is offered in only 1 caliber, the 9mm Makarov. The Model 82 is the side arm of the Czech army. The Model 82 is no longer in production, but the Model 83 is currently manufactured.

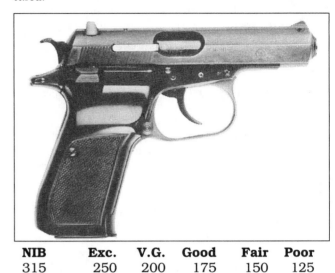

NIB	Exc.	V.G.	Good	Fair	Poor
315	250	200	175	150	125

SUBMACHINE GUNS

The Czechs built the CZ 247 and the CZ 47 after World War II but did not adopt these guns for its own military use. Instead they were exported to South America and other countries. These submachine guns are chambered for the 9mm Parabellum cartridge and are similar in appearance to the CZ 1938 gun but with a 40-round magazine.

CZ 23/25

The Model 23 has a wooden stock while the Model 25 has a folding metal stock, otherwise all other dimensions are the same. Introduced in 1948 this submachine gun is chambered for the 9mm cartridge. Magazine capacity is 25- or 40-round box type. Rate of fire is about 600 rounds per minute. Weight is approximately 8 to 8.5 lbs. depending on model. This gun introduced the hollow bolt that allows for the short length of the gun (17.5" with butt folded, 27" with butt extended) and was copied in the UZI. The magazine well is located in the pistol grip, another feature copied by the UZI. The trigger mechanism is designed so that light pressure gives semiautomatic fire while full trigger pressure gives full automatic fire. Weight of the gun is about 7 lbs. A variation of this model is called the Model 24/26 and is the same except for the caliber; 7.62mm.

NOTE: Prices listed are estimates only.

Pre-1968

Exc.	V.G.	Fair
9000	8000	7000

Pre-1986 conversions

Exc.	V.G.	Fair
N/A	N/A	N/A

Pre-1986 dealer samples

Exc.	V.G.	Fair
5000	4500	4000

ZK 383

This submachine gun was first introduced in 1933. It is chambered for the 9mm Parabellum cartridge and fitted with a 12.8" quick change barrel with jacket. Adjustable rate of fire from 500 to 700 rounds per minute by means of a removable insert in the bolt. This model fitted with a bipod. Rear sight is a V-notch tangent graduated to 800 meters. Weight is about 9.5 lbs. This gun was sold to Bulgaria, some South American countries and was used by the German army from 1938 to 1945.

A variation of this model called the ZK 383P was used by police units and does not have a bipod or quick change barrel. The ZK 383H was a limited production version with a folding magazine housing fitted to the bottom of the gun rather than the side.

Pre-1968

Exc.	V.G.	Fair
8000	7000	6500

Pre-1986 conversions

Exc.	V.G.	Fair
N/A	N/A	N/A

Pre-1986 dealer samples

Exc.	V.G.	Fair
N/A	N/A	N/A

Skorpion Samopal vz61

Introduced in 1960 this weapon is sometimes referred to as a machine pistol because of its size. Chambered for the 7.65x17SR Browning (.32 ACP) cartridge. Export models of this gun are chambered for the 9x17mm (.380 ACP(vz63)), 9x18mm Makarov (vz64) and the 9x19mm Parabellum (vz68). The gun has a 4.5" barrel and is fitted with a wooden pistol grip. Overall length with butt folded in 10.5", with butt extended the length is 20.5". Weight is approximately 3 lbs. Rate of fire is about 700 rounds per minute. A licensed copy is made in Yugoslavia called the Model 84.

Pre-1968

Exc.	V.G.	Fair
N/A	N/A	N/A

Pre-1986 conversions

Exc.	V.G.	Fair
N/A	N/A	N/A

Pre-1986 dealer samples (Rare)

Exc.	V.G.	Fair
9500	9000	8500

RIFLES

Immediately after World War I the Czechs continued to use the Mannlicher Model 1895 rifle until 1924 when they began production of their own Mauser action rifles.

Skorpion • Courtesy West Point Museum • Paul Goodwin Photo

MAUSER
Ceskoslovensha Zbrojovaka (ZB), Brno

NOTE: In 1924 the Czechs began to manufacture a number of Mauser designed rifles for export, and for its own military use. Czech Mausers were based on the Model 98 action. Many of these rifles were sold to other countries and will be found under *Germany, Mauser, Rifles.*

M1898/22 Rifle

Manufactured by CZ in Brno this rifle is based on the Mexican Model 1912 with a Model 98 action. It is half cocked with a full-length upper handguard with pistol grip. Chambered for the 7.92x57mm Mauser cartridge. Barrel length is 29" with a 5-round integral magazine. Weight is about 9.5 lbs. This rifle was used by Turkey as well as other countries.

Courtesy Rock Island Auction Company

Exc.	V.G.	Good	Fair	Poor
100	90	70	40	25

VZ23 Short Rifle

Used by the Czech army this 7.92x57mm rifle was fitted with a 21.5" barrel and 5-round magazine. Tangent leaf rear sight graduated to 2000 meters. Most were marked, "CZECHOSLO-VAKIAN FACTORY FOR ARMS MANUFACTURE, BRNO" on the receiver ring. Weight is about 9 lbs.

Exc.	V.G.	Good	Fair	Poor
120	100	80	60	40

VZ 24 Short Rifle

Chambered for the 7.92x54mm cartridge and fitted with a 23.25" barrel. Weight is about 9 lbs. This was the standard Czech rifle prior to World War II and was used by a number of countries such as Romania, Yugoslavia, and China. This rifle was also used by the German army at the beginning of WWII.

Exc.	V.G.	Good	Fair	Poor
100	80	60	40	25

VZ12/33 Carbine

This rifle was produced primarily for export. It has a pistol grip stock with 3/4 length upper handguard and two barrel bands fairly close together. Bolt handle is bent down. Barrel length is 21.5" with 5-round magazine. Rear leaf sight is graduated to 1400 meters. Weight is about 8 lbs. Country crest on stamped on receiver.

Exc.	V.G.	Good	Fair	Poor
125	110	90	75	50

VZ16/33 Carbine

Designed for paramilitary units this rifle has a 19.25" barrel. Chambered for the 7.92x57mm cartridge as well as other calibers depending on country. Magazine capacity is 5 rounds. Tangent rear leaf sight graduated to 1000 meters. Czech crest stamped on receiver ring. This rifle formed the basis on the German Model 33/40 paratroop carbine used during WWII.

Exc.	V.G.	Good	Fair	Poor
300	260	220	160	120

CZECH STATE

Model 24 (VZ24)

This rifle marks the first Czech produced military rifle for the Czech army. It was based on the Mauser 98 action. The rifle was in wide use by other countries such as Germany prior to WWII. Chambered for the 7.92mm cartridge and fitted with a 23" barrel, this model had a 5-round non-detachable box magazine. The rear sight was graduated from 300 to 2000 meters in 100 meter increments. Weight is about 9 lbs.

Exc.	V.G.	Good	Fair	Poor
275	175	100	75	50

NOTE: Prices are for rifles with matching numbers and original markings.

Model ZH29

Introduced in 1929 this semiautomatic rifle was designed by Emmanuel Holek of CZ at Brno. It is chambered for the 7.92x57mm cartridge and is fitted with a 21.5" barrel with aluminum cooling jacket over the barrel. Fitted with a bayonet lug. The detachable box magazine has a 10- or 25-round capacity. Weight is about 10 lbs. Exported to Thailand and Ethiopia. Very rare.

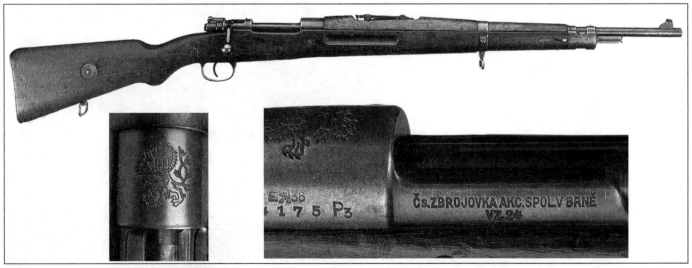

Czech VZ 24 with receiver markings and crest • Paul Goodwin Photo

Exc.	V.G.	Good	Fair	Poor
9500	8500	7500	—	—

Model ZK420S

Chambered for the 7.92x57mm cartridge this rifle was first introduced in 1942 but did not appear in its final form until 1946. It was also offered in 7mm, .30-06, 7.5mm Swiss. This was a gas operated semiautomatic rifle with 21" barrel with upper handguard. The detachable magazine has a 10-round capacity. Front sight is hooded. Rear sight is notched tangent with ramp. Weight is about 10 lbs. Not adopted by Czech military but tested by many countries. Built by CZ, Brno in limited numbers. Very rare.

Exc.	V.G.	Good	Fair	Poor
10500	9000	8000	—	—

Model 52

Chambered for 7.62x45 caliber this gas operated semiautomatic rifle is fitted with a 20.5" barrel. This model has a full stock with pistol grip. Folding non-detachable bayonet. Hooded front sight and notched tangent rear sight with ramp. Detachable box magazine with 10-round capacity. Weight is about 9.7 lbs. First produced in 1952.

Exc.	V.G.	Good	Fair	Poor
400	300	250	—	—

Model 52/57

Similar to the Model 52 except chambered for the 7.62x39 cartridge.

Courtesy Richard M. Kumor Sr.

Exc.	V.G.	Good	Fair	Poor
650	500	400	300	150

Exc.	V.G.	Good	Fair	Poor
750	600	500	400	200

Vz 58

First produced in 1959 this select fire assault rifle is chambered for the 7.62x39mm Soviet cartridge. Its appearance is similar to an AK-47 but it is an entirely different design. It is gas operated but the bolt is locked to the receiver by a vertically moving block similar to the Walther P-38 pistol. Early rifles were fitted with a plastic fixed stock while later rifles used a folding metal stock. Barrel length is 16". Rate of fire is about 800 rounds per minute. Weight is approximately 7 lbs. Production ceased in 1980. Made at CZ Brno and Povaske Strojarne. The two versions of this gun are designated the vz58P with fixed stock and the vz58V for metal folding stock.

Pre-1968

Exc.	V.G.	Fair
9500	8500	8000

Pre-1986 conversions

Exc.	V.G.	Fair
N/A	N/A	N/A

Pre-1986 dealer samples

Exc.	V.G.	Fair
7000	6500	6000

MACHINE GUNS

The Czechs used the Steyr-built Schwarzlose Model 7/24 adopted to 7.92mm immediately after World War I. Czechoslovakia has also used the Soviet SG43 and the Soviet DT. Today the Czech army uses the ZB 59 as its primary machine gun. The ZB 59 is called a universal machine gun when mounted on a bipod. It is also used by the Czech military with a light barrel.

ZB vz26

Manufactured by CZ Brno this weapon is a light air-cooled gas operated select fire machine gun chambered for the 7.92x57mm Mauser cartridge. Fitted with a 23.7" finned bar-

Vz 58 • Courtesy West Point Museum, Paul Goodwin Photo

Model 1954 Sniper Rifle

This rifle, introduced in 1954, is built on a Mosin Nagant 1891/30 action and fitted with a 28.7" barrel chambered for the 7.62x54mmR cartridge. Magazine capacity is 5 rounds. Half stock with pistol grip and handguard. Rifle is supplied with a telescope. Weight is approximately 11.5 lbs. Built by CZ in Brno.

ZB 26 with both left and right side receiver markings • Paul Goodwin Photo

rel, it has a rate of fire of 500 rounds per minute. It is fed by a 20- or 30-round box magazine. Bipod and carry handle standard. Wooden butt with pistol grip. Quick change barrel. It was adopted by over two dozen countries around the world. It was the fore-runner of the famous British Bren gun (model designation ZGB33). Produced from 1925 to 1945. On left side of receiver marked, "BRNO", and on right side marked," LEHKY KULOMET ZB vz26." Weight is about 21 lbs. This gun was and still is used in large numbers throughout the world.

Zb made small improvements to the vz26 along with the date of the improvements. These guns are essentially the same as the ZB 26 but are known as the ZB vz27 and vz28.

Pre-1968

Exc.	V.G.	Fair
15000	14000	13000

Pre-1986 conversions

Exc.	V.G.	Fair
13000	12500	12000

Pre-1986 dealer samples

Exc.	V.G.	Fair
N/A	N/A	N/A

ZB vz30

This weapon has an outward appearance almost identical to that of the vz26 but with the exception of a new bolt move-

ment design differently from the vz26. It has a 26.5" finned barrel, and uses a 30-round top mounted straight box magazine. The rate of fire is about 600 rounds per minute. Weight of the gun is approximately 21 lbs. This model was adopted by China, Spain, and Iran. Between 1939 and 1945 it was also used by the German army.

Pre-1968

Exc.	V.G.	Fair
18000	17000	16000

Pre-1986 conversions

Exc.	V.G.	Fair
14000	13500	13000

Pre-1986 dealer samples

Exc.	V.G.	Fair
N/A	N/A	N/A

ZGB vz30 (vz32/33/34)

Same as the vz30 but modified to fire the British .303 cartridge. Uses a curved 20-round magazine to accommodate the .303 cartridge. Improved versions of this gun are known as the vz 32, the vz33, and the vz34. These later versions use a 30-round magazine and a slightly shorter barrel. Reduced rate of fire to 500 rounds per minute.

Pre-1968

Exc.	V.G.	Fair
18000	17000	16000

Pre-1986 conversions

Exc.	V.G.	Fair
14000	13500	13000

Pre-1986 dealer samples

Exc.	V.G.	Fair
N/A	N/A	N/A

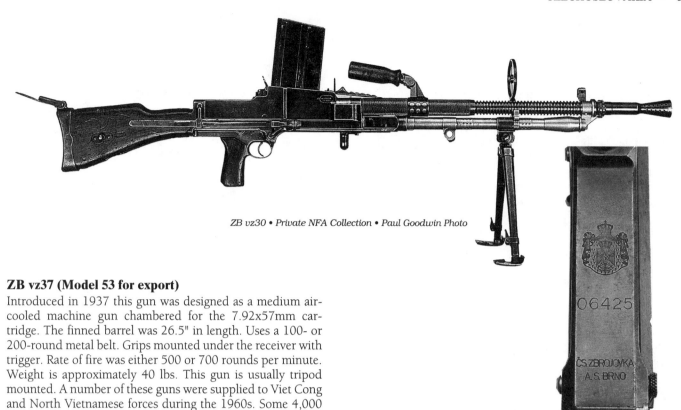

ZB vz30 • Private NFA Collection • Paul Goodwin Photo

ZB vz37 (Model 53 for export)

Introduced in 1937 this gun was designed as a medium air-cooled machine gun chambered for the 7.92x57mm cartridge. The finned barrel was 26.5" in length. Uses a 100- or 200-round metal belt. Grips mounted under the receiver with trigger. Rate of fire was either 500 or 700 rounds per minute. Weight is approximately 40 lbs. This gun is usually tripod mounted. A number of these guns were supplied to Viet Cong and North Vietnamese forces during the 1960s. Some 4,000 were sold to Israel in 1949. Many more were exported to the Middle East and Africa.

Pre-1968 (Very Rare)

Exc.	V.G.	Fair
30000	25000	20000

Pre-1986 conversions

Exc.	V.G.	Fair
N/A	N/A	N/A

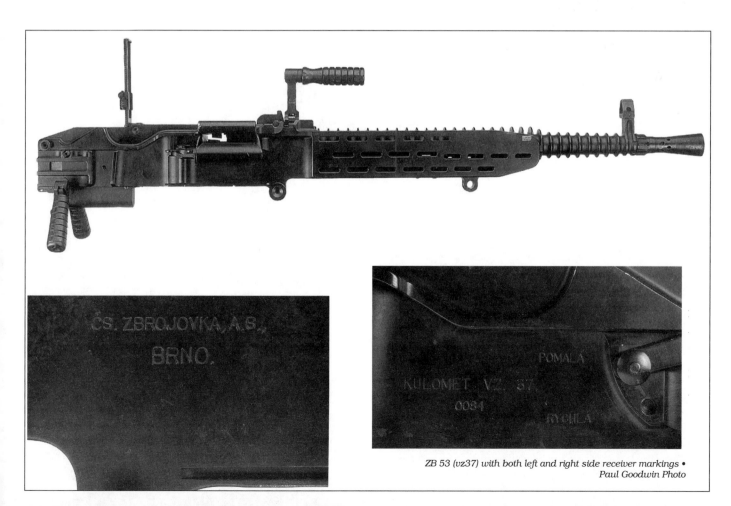

ZB 53 (vz37) with both left and right side receiver markings •
Paul Goodwin Photo

Pre-1986 dealer samples

Exc.	V.G.	Fair
N/A	N/A	N/A

vz52/57

This gun is based on the ZB vz30. It is chambered for the 7.62x39 rimless cartridge (Warsaw Pact). The gun was originally chambered for the 7.62x45 rimless cartridge (vz52). Barrel length is 27" and is quick change. It is fed by a 100-round belt or 25-round detachable box magazine. Rate of fire is 900 rounds per minute with box magazine and about 1,100 rounds per minute with belt. Weight is about 17.5 lbs. with bipod. This is a select fire weapon with the finger pressure on the trigger determining full auto or single round fire. The gun was introduced in the 1952. This gun is often seen in Central America.

Pre-1968 (Very Rare)

Exc.	V.G.	Fair
25000	22500	20000

Pre-1986 conversions

Exc.	V.G.	Fair
N/A	N/A	N/A

Pre-1986 dealer samples

Exc.	V.G.	Fair
N/A	N/A	N/A

DENMARK

Danish Military Conflicts, 1870-Present

After losing part of its territory to Prussia and Austria in 1862 Denmark concentrated its energies on improving its domestic economic and social conditions. Denmark maintained a peaceful coexistence with its European neighbors until it was occupied in 1940 by the German army. Following the end of the war, Denmark joined Nato in 1949, and in 1973 joined the European Union.

HANDGUNS

In addition to the handguns listed below the Danes used the Browning Hi-Power 9mm pistol designated the Model 46. They also used the Swedish Model 40 Lahti, called the Model 40S by the Danes. In the late 1940s the Danes adopted the SIG 9mm Model 47/8 pistol (P-210-2).

Model 1871

This 6 shot revolver was built on a Lefaucheux-Francotte solid frame fixed cylinder with non-mechanical ejection. This is an 11mm pin-fire revolver. Octagon barrel length is 5". Weight is about 34 oz. Smooth wooden grips with lanyard loop. Built by the Belgian firm of Auguste Francotte. Issued to the Danish navy from 1871 to 1882.

Exc.	V.G.	Good	Fair	Poor
750	500	375	200	125

Model 1871/81

This model is a converted center-fire 11mm Model 1871. The conversion was done at the Danish navy yard in Copenhagen in 1881. All other specifications are the same as the Model 1871.

Exc.	V.G.	Good	Fair	Poor
600	375	200	125	75

Model 1865/97

This revolver is built on the Chamelot-Delvigne solid frame fixed cylinder action with non-mechanical ejection. It was originally issued to the Danish navy in 1865 as a 11mm pin-fire sidearm and was later converted in Kronberg to 11.45mm center-fire revolver. The revolver is fitted with a lever-type safety that blocks the hammer from the cylinder when engaged. Barrel length is 5". Checkered wood grips with lanyard loop located behind the hammer. Weight is about 30 oz. Issued to Danish navy from 1897 to 1919.

Exc.	V.G.	Good	Fair	Poor
1750	1000	600	350	200

Model 1882

This revolver was built on the Lefaucheux-Francotte solid frame fixed cylinder with non-mechanical ejection. Capacity was 6 rounds and the gun was chambered for the 9mm cartridge. The half-round half-octagon barrel was 5.5". This revolver was issued to Danish NCOs from 1888 to 1919.

Exc.	V.G.	Good	Fair	Poor
1200	650	400	200	125

Model 1886

This revolver was chambered for the 9.5mm cartridge and fitted with a 3" barrel. Built by Auguste Francotte in Liege, Belgium and issued to military police units in the Danish army beginning in 1886.

Exc.	V.G.	Good	Fair	Poor
500	350	200	125	75

Model 1891

This revolver employed top break hinged frame with latch. This model was chambered for the 9mm cartridge and fitted with a 6.3" half-round half-octagon barrel. Checkered wooden grips with lanyard loop. Built by J.B. Ronge in Liege, Belgium. Weight is about 33 oz. Issued to Danish navy units from 1891 to 1941.

NOTE: A training version of this revolver was also used by the Danish navy and was chambered for the 5.1mm cartridge. All other specifications are the same.

Standard Model

Exc.	V.G.	Good	Fair	Poor
1000	500	350	250	150

Model 1891/96 Training Version

Exc.	V.G.	Good	Fair	Poor
3500	1750	800	500	300

Bergmann-Bayard Model 1908

Built by the Belgium firm of Pieper SA from 1908 to about 1914. Caliber is 9mm with 4" barrel. Many foreign contracts were built in this model.

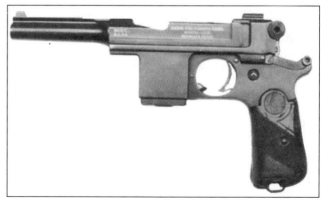

Courtesy Rock Island Auction Company

Exc.	V.G.	Good	Fair	Poor
1250	950	700	400	200

Bergmann-Bayard Model 1910-21

After WWI Pieper could no longer supply Bergmann-Bayard pistols to the Danish army, so Denmark made their own at their two national arsenals, Haerens Rustkammer and Haerens Tojus as the Model 1910-21. Most pre-war Pieper-made pistols were modified to 1910-21 configuration during the post-war years.

Courtesy Rock Island Auction Company

Exc.	V.G.	Good	Fair	Poor
1500	1100	850	700	300

P210 (Model 49)

See *Switzerland, Handguns, SIG*

SUBMACHINE GUNS

The Danish military has also used the Finnish Suomi MP 41, the Swedish Model 37/39, and the HK MP5A2 and MP5A3 submachine gun.

Danish Hovea M49

Introduced in 1949 this submachine gun is chambered for the 9mm Parabellum cartridge and fitted with an 8.5" barrel. Folding metal butt. Magazine capacity is 35 rounds. Rate of fire is about 600 rounds per minute. Weight is approximately 7.5 lbs. This gun was originally developed by Husqvarna for the Swedish army. Denmark purchased the rights and built the gun for its own forces.

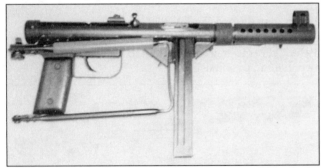

Courtesy private NFA collection

Pre-1968

Exc.	V.G.	Fair
9000	8000	7000

Pre-1986 conversions

Exc.	V.G.	Fair
N/a	N/A	N/A

Pre-1986 dealer samples

Exc.	V.G.	Fair
N/A	N/A	N/A

Madsen M50

This submachine gun was produced from 1945 to 1953 by the Danes. It is chambered for the 9mm cartridge and is fitted

with a 7.8" barrel. Its rate of fire is about 500 rounds per minute. Marked "MADSEN" on the right side of receiver. Weight is approximately 7 lbs.

This gun has some unusual features, such as a flat receiver with barrel attached with locking nut that when unscrewed allows the left side of the receiver to fold back to expose the right side, which contain all the moving parts. Fitted with a quick change barrel. Very simple design allows for fast and economical construction.

Photo Courtesy Private NFA Collection

Pre-1968

Exc.	V.G.	Fair
4000	3500	3000

Pre-1986 conversions

Exc.	V.G.	Fair
2900	2500	2000

Pre-1986 dealer samples

Exc.	V.G.	Fair
2500	2000	1500

RIFLES

More recently Danish military forces have used the U.S. M16A1 rifle, the HK G3, the M1 Garand converted to 7.62 NATO and the Enfield Model 1917 rifle.

KRAG JORGENSEN

The Krag rifle was developed in Norway and first adopted by Denmark for standard issue through World War II. For a list of U.S. models and prices see *United States, Rifles, Krag Jorgensen*. For those collectors who are interested in the Danish Krags the only major difference, other than caliber, lies in the operation of the loading gate. Prices listed below are for unaltered Danish Krags. The forerunner of the U.S. Krags was the Model 1889 rifle.

NOTE: All Danish Krag's are chambered for the 8x57Rmm cartridge.

Danish Model 1889

This rifle was developed by Ole Krag and Eric Jorgensen. It used a single forward bolt locking lug plus a bolt guide rib. Chambered for the 8x58Rmm cartridge the rifle was fitted with a 33" barrel with full stock and no pistol grip. The barrel is fitted with a full-length metal handguard on the barrel. A flush loose-loaded box magazine was used. The bolt handle was straight. There were a number of different carbine versions but all of these were full stocked and fitted with 23.5" barrel with bayonet lugs on all but one variation: the artillery carbine (see below). These guns are marked prior to 1910 "GEVAERFABRIKEN KJOBENHAVN" [date] over "M89" on the left

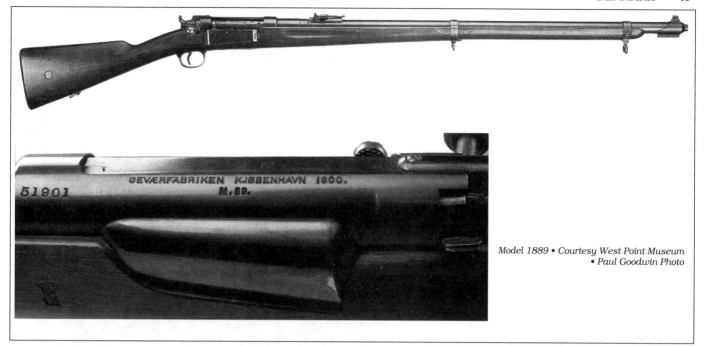

Model 1889 • Courtesy West Point Museum
• Paul Goodwin Photo

side of the receiver. Approximately 140,000 of these rifles and carbines were manufactured prior to 1930. During the German occupation in WWII the Germans reintroduced the rifle for its own use.

Exc.	V.G.	Good	Fair	Poor
350	300	250	150	100

Model 1889 Infantry Carbine
Introduced in 1924 this model is a converted Model 1889 rifle with metal barrel jacket and bayonet stud. Barrel length is 24". Tangent rear sight. Magazine capacity is 5 rounds. Weight is about 8.5 lbs. Marked "F" before the serial number.

Exc.	V.G.	Good	Fair	Poor
450	400	300	200	100

Model 1889 Artillery Carbine
Similar to the Infantry carbine and also introduced in 1924 this model features a turn down bolt handle, a triangle shaped upper sling swivel and a hanger stud on the left side of the stock.

Exc.	V.G.	Good	Fair	Poor
450	400	300	200	100

Model 1889 Engineer Carbine
This model was introduced in 1917. It is fitted with a wooden handguard and a slightly shorter barrel, about 1/2". Marked with "I" before the serial number.

Exc.	V.G.	Good	Fair	Poor
450	400	300	200	100

Model 1889 Cavalry Rifle
Introduced in 1914 this model is fitted for a bayonet. Has a straight bolt handle. Marked with "R" before the serial number.

Exc.	V.G.	Good	Fair	Poor
350	300	250	150	100

Model 1928 Sniper Rifle
This model is based on the Model 1889 with half stock but fitted with a 26" heavy barrel, micrometer rear sight and hooded front sight. Wooden handguard. Turned down bolt. Similar in appearance to the U.S. 30 caliber-style "T" rifle. Weight is approximately 11.5 lbs.

Exc.	V.G.	Good	Fair	Poor
950	800	600	400	200

MADSEN

Model 47
Sometimes referred to as the Madsen light military rifle this post-WWII bolt-action rifle was sold to Colombia in limited quantities of 5,000 guns. Fitted with a rubber buttplate. Chambered in a number of calibers including the .30-06. Barrel length was 23" with a magazine capacity of 5 rounds. Weight was about 8 lbs.

Courtesy Richard M. Kumor Sr.

Exc.	V.G.	Good	Fair	Poor
500	425	300	—	—

NOTE: Add $75 for rifles with numbered matching bayonet.

MACHINE GUNS
After World War II Denmark used the British Bren gun chambered for the .303 caliber, the Swedish Model 37 6.5mm gun, the U.S. Model 1919 A4 and A5 version, the .50 M2 Browning. More recently the Danes use the Germany MG 42/59.

Madsen
This was the first practical light machine gun. It was produced from 1897 to 1955. It is chambered for several calibers from 6mm to 8mm. It is fitted with a 22.7" barrel and a top feeding 25-, 30-, or 40-round magazine. Rate of fire is 450 rounds per minute. Its weight is approximately 20 lbs. Marked "MADSEN MODEL" on the right side of the receiver. Found all over the world during a fifty year period.

Chilean Madsen Model 1950 with receiver markings and crest • Paul Goodwin Photo

Pre-1968

Exc.	V.G.	Fair
10000	9000	8000

Pre-1986 conversions

Exc.	V.G.	Fair
N/A	N/A	N/A

Pre-1986 dealer samples

Exc.	V.G.	Fair
3500	3250	3000

Madsen-Satter

First produced in 1952 this belt-fed machine gun is chambered for the 7.62x51mm Nato cartridge. Designed to be used on a tripod for sustained fire it had a rate of fire of 650 to 1000 rounds per minute (adjustable). Fitted with a 22" barrel. Weight is approximately 23.4 lbs. Marked "MADSEN-SETTER" on left front side of receiver. Many South American countries used this gun as do many other countries around the world. Produced stopped on this gun in 1960 in Denmark but continued under license to Indonesia until the 1970s.

Photo Courtesy Private NFA Collection

Pre-1968 (Very Rare)

Exc.	V.G.	Fair
25000	23000	22000

Pre-1986 conversions

Exc.	V.G.	Fair
N/A	N/A	N/A

Pre-1986 dealer samples (Rare)

Exc.	V.G.	Fair
20000	18000	17000

FINLAND

Finnish Military Conflicts, 1870-Present

Finland was annexed by Russia in 1809 but allowed the Finns considerable independence throughout the 19th century. Finnish nationalism began to grow during the latter part of the 19th century and by the early 20th century Finland established its own parliament in 1906. Finnish independence was declared in 1917. Beginning in 1918, a civil war erupted in which the White Guard aided by German troops defeated the leftist Red Guard supported by the Soviet Union. As a result of this conflict a republic was established in 1919. In 1939 Soviet troops invaded Finland and by 1940 Finnish forces were defeated, despite a heavy cost to the Soviet troops. Finland joined the German attack on the Soviet Union in 1941. Finland was again defeated by Soviet forces by 1944. Finland was then forced to expel the Germans which resulted in a massive loss of life and property to the Finnish people. A 1947 treaty between - Finland and The Soviet Union ceded some Finnish territory to the Soviets and in 1948, the Finns signed a mutual defense pact with the Soviets. During the post-war period Finland attempted to stay neutral and preserve its independence. By 1990 with the collapse of the Soviet Union, the 1948 treaty was now moot and in 1995, the Finns joined the European Union.

NOTE: The Finns established their own arms factory soon after independence. It was called *Souojeluskuntain Ase-ja Konepaja Oy* (SAKO). In 1926 the Finns constructed a state rifle factory called the *Valtion Kivaaritehdas* (VKT, later Valmet). Also in the 1920s another state arms plant was built called *Tikkakoski* (TIKKA).

HANDGUNS

NOTE: During the 1920s and 1930s the Finnish army relied primarily on the Model 1895 Russian Nagant revolver and the Spanish 7.65mm self-loading pistols, the Ruby (Model 19). During World War I the Finns were supplied with the Mauser M1896 Broomhandle in a late wartime commercial configuration. In the early 1920s the Finns adopted a commercial model of the DWM Luger, called by the Finns the Model 23. By the late 1920s the Finnish military decided to adopt and domesticly produced a 9mm self-loading pistol of their own. It was called the Lahti.

The Finns, more recently, have used the FN M1935 in 9mm and the French MAB PA-15 pistol in 9mm.

M35 Lahti

This 9x19mm semiautomatic pistol was adopted in 1935 and built at VKT. This pistol is a locked-breech semiautomatic that features a bolt accelerator that does much to make this a reliable firearm. This pistol is the same as the Swedish Model 40 Lahti, 4.7" barrel and 8-round magazine, except that it has a loaded chamber indicator on top of the pistol, a different assembled recoil spring, and the Finnish pistol's grips are marked "VKT." Finnish army markings on top of slide. This pistol was designed to function in extreme cold and has a reputation for reliability. About 5,700 wartime Lahti pistols were produced.

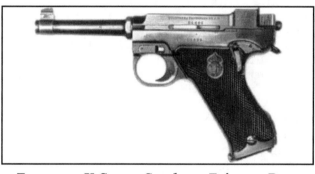

Exc.	V.G.	Good	Fair	Poor
1250	1000	800	550	300

Model 1931 • Paul Goodwin Photo

SUBMACHINE GUNS

The first Finnish submachine gun was developed by Aimo Lahti in 1922. This gun later became the Model 1926 with only about 200 built in 7.65mm caliber. A perfected design was later built called the Model 1931 Suomi. Since the end of World War II the Finns have used the Sten Mark II and Mark III gun.

Suomi Model 1931

First produced in Finland in 1931 this submachine gun is chambered for the 9mm cartridge. It was widely used by Scandinavian armies as well as several countries in South America. It features a 12.25" barrel with wooden stock and 71-round drum magazine. Box magazine capacity is 20 or 50 rounds. Rate of fire is 900 rounds per minute. Weight is about 10 lbs. Marked on the end cap and left side of the receiver. Production stopped in 1944. A total of about 80,000 were produced by TIKKA.

This gun was also made in Sweden where it was designated the Model 37-39. In Switzerland it was called the Model 43/44, in Denmark it was made by Madsen.

Pre-1968

Exc.	V.G.	Fair
7500	6500	6000

Pre-1986 conversions

Exc.	V.G.	Fair
N/A	N/A	N/A

Pre-1986 dealer samples

Exc.	V.G.	Fair
4500	4000	3500

Suomi Model 1944

This Finnish gun is based on the Russian Model PPS-43, but the Model 1944 fires the 9mm cartridge. It is fitted with a 9.66" barrel and accepts a 36 box magazine or 71-round drum magazine. Rate of fire is 650 rounds per minute. Weight is about 6.35 lbs. Production stopped in 1945. Marked on left side of receiver. TIKKA built about 10,000 of these guns.

Pre-1968

Exc.	V.G.	Fair
7500	6500	6000

Pre-1986 conversions

Exc.	V.G.	Fair
N/A	N/A	N/A

Pre-1986 dealer samples

Exc.	V.G.	Fair
4500	4000	3500

RIFLES

NOTE: All Finnish military rifles are built on Russian Model 1891 Mosin Nagant actions. These are as follows:

Model 1891 (Finnish Army Variation)

Basically a Russian Model 1891 but with a Finnish two-piece stock, sights calibrated to meters, trigger modified to two stage pull, and frequently with the addition of sling swivels. Large numbers of captured Russian Model 1891s were reconfigured this way as late as 1944. Many, but not all, have Finnish-made barrels with a length of 31.6".

Exc.	V.G.	Good	Fair	Poor
150	125	100	75	60

Model 1891 Dragoon (Finnish Army Variation)

Basically a Russian Model 1891 Dragoon rifle modified as above with a side mounted Mauser Kar 98 type sling. Barrel length is 28.8". Rare.

Exc.	V.G.	Good	Fair	Poor
250	200	150	100	75

Model 1924 Civil Guard Infantry Rifle

This model was made by Valmet and consisted of new heavy Swiss or German barrels fitted to reworked Model 1891 Russian actions. Chambered for 7.62x54R cartridge and fitted with 32" barrels. Box magazine capacity was 5 rounds. Weight is about 9.4 lbs.

Exc.	V.G.	Good	Fair	Poor
150	125	100	75	50

Model 1924 Civil Guard Carbine

As above but with 24" barrel. Very Rare.

Exc.	V.G.	Good	Fair	Poor
650	500	400	300	150

Model 1927 Army Short Rifle

This rifle, also made by Valmet, is a shorter version of the Model 1924 and fitted with a 27" barrel. It has a full stock with bayonet lug with peep rear sight and front sight guards. Weight is about 9 lbs.

Exc.	V.G.	Good	Fair	Poor
150	125	100	75	50

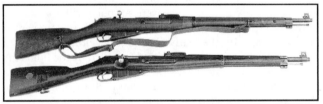

M27 Rifle on top and M27 Carbine at bottom • Courtesy Chuck Karwan

Model 1927 Carbine

Similar to the Model 1927 rifle but fitted with a 24" barrel and turned down bolt. Side mounted sling. About 2,500 were produced. Very rare as most were converted to rifles.

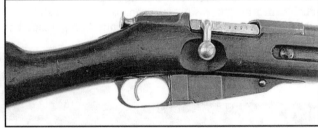

M27 Carbine action at bottom • Courtesy Chuck Karwan

Exc.	V.G.	Good	Fair	Poor
250	200	150	100	75

Model 1928 Civil Guard Short Rifle

Similar to the Model 1927 but with two piece stock. Built by SAKO.

Exc.	V.G.	Good	Fair	Poor
300	250	200	150	100

Model 1928/30 Civil Guard Short Rifle

This is the same as the Model 1928 Short Rifle but with an improved magazine and different rear sight. Built by SAKO.

Exc.	V.G.	Good	Fair	Poor
350	300	250	200	150

Model 1939 Short Rifle (Army and Civil Guard)

Similar to the Model 1927 but with larger diameter bore to accommodate a heavier bullet. Two piece stock with pistol grip and new rear sight fitted to this model. Barrel length is 27". Weight is about 10 lbs. Produced by SAKO, TIKKA, and VT.

Exc.	V.G.	Good	Fair	Poor
175	150	140	90	50

NOTE: Add a 20% premium for SAKO-built rifles.

TRG-21

The receiver is similar to the TRG-S but the polyurethane stock features a unique design. The trigger is adjustable for length and two-stage pull and also for horizontal or vertical pitch. This model also has several options that would affect the price; muzzle brake, one-piece scope mount, bipod, quick detachable sling swivels, and military nylon sling. The rifle is offered in .308 Win. only. It is fitted with a 25.75" barrel and weighs 10.5 lbs.

NIB	Exc.	V.G.	Good	Fair	Poor
3500	2750	1850	—	—	—

TRG-22

This model is similar to the TRG-21 but meets the exact specifications to comply with the Finish military requirements. Introduced in 2000.

NIB	Exc.	V.G.	Good	Fair	Poor
2700	2000	—	—	—	—

TRG-41

Exactly the same as the TRG-21 except chambered for the .338 Lapua Magnum cartridge.

NIB	Exc.	V.G.	Good	Fair	Poor
4350	3500	2500	1500	—	—

TRG-42

This model is similar to the TRG-41 but meets the exact specifications to comply with the Finish military requirements. Introduced in 2000.

NIB	Exc.	V.G.	Good	Fair	Poor
3100	2300	—	—	—	—

Valmet M62

Based on the AK-47 but with internal differences built by Valmet. SAKO also built many of these rifles. Perforated plastic forend and handguard. Tube butt. Barrel length is 16.5". Magazine is 30 rounds. Rate of fire is about 650 rounds per minute. Weight is about 9 lbs.

NOTE: There are number of different versions of this rifle: the M62-76-a Finnish AKM; the M62-76M-plastic stock; M62-76P-wood stock; M62-76T-tubular steel folding stock.

Pre-1968

Exc.	V.G.	Fair
N/A	N/A	N/A

Pre-1986 conversions

Exc.	V.G.	Fair
5000	4750	4500

Pre-1986 dealer samples

Exc.	V.G.	Fair
4000	4000	3850

Valmet M62S

A semiautomatic version of the M62 imported for sale in the U.S. by Interarms.

NIB	Exc.	V.G.	Good	Fair	Poor
2500	1750	1200	850	500	250

Valmet M71

A different version of the M62 with solid plastic butt and rear sight in front of chamber. Sheet metal receiver. Chambered for the 7.62x39mm and the 5.56x45mm cartridges. Weight reduced to 8 lbs.

Pre-1968

Exc.	V.G.	Fair
N/A	N/A	N/A

Pre-1986 conversions

Exc.	V.G.	Fair
5000	4750	4500

Valmet Model 78 • Courtesy Chuck Karwan

Pre-1986 dealer samples

Exc.	V.G.	Fair
4000	4000	3850

Valmet M71S

A semiautomatic version of the M71 imported for sale in the U.S. by Interarms.

NIB	Exc.	V.G.	Good	Fair	Poor
2000	1500	1200	850	500	250

Valmet M76

This model has a number of fixed or folding stock options. It is fitted with a 16.3" barrel and has a magazine capacity of 15, 20, or 30 rounds. Its rate of fire is 700 rounds per minute. It is chambered for the 7.62x39mm Soviet cartridge or the 5.56x45mm cartridge. Weight is approximately 8 lbs. Marked "VALMET JYVAKYLA m78" on the right side of the receiver. Produced from 1978 to 1986.

There are a total of 10 variants of this model.

Pre-1968

Exc.	V.G.	Fair
N/A	N/A	N/A

Pre-1986 conversions

Exc.	V.G.	Fair
8000	7000	6500

Pre-1986 dealer samples

Exc.	V.G.	Fair
4000	4000	3850

NOTE: For rifles in 7.62x39mm caliber add a 20% premium. For rifles chambered for .308 caliber deduct $2,500.

Model 78 (Semiautomatic)

As above, in 7.62x51mm, 7.62x39mm, or .223 with a 24.5" heavy barrel, wood stock, and integral bipod. Semiautomatic-only version.

NIB	Exc.	V.G.	Good	Fair	Poor
1750	1350	1000	850	600	300

MACHINE GUNS

During the early years the Finns used the Maxim Model 09, Maxim Model 21, and the Maxim Model 32, all chambered for the 7.62mm cartridge.

Lahti Saloranta Model 26

Designed and built as a light machine gun this model was chambered for the 7.62mm rimmed cartridge. Fitted with a 20-round box magazine or a 75-round drum magazine. The rate of fire was about 500 rounds per minute. Weight is approximately 23 lbs. This gun was also chambered for the 7.92mm cartridge for sale to the Chinese prior to World War II.

Pre-1968

Exc.	V.G.	Fair
10000	9000	8500

Pre-1986 conversions

Exc.	V.G.	Fair
N/A	N/a	N/A

Pre-1986 dealer samples

Exc.	V.G.	Fair
N/A	N/A	N/A

Valmet M62

First introduced in 1966 this machine gun is chambered for the 7.62x39mm cartridge. Designed as a light air-cooled machine gun it is based on the Czech ZB26. Fitted with a wood butt with pistol grip and 18.5" heavy barrel with bipod. Fed by a 100-round metal link belt with a rate of fire of about 1000 rounds per minute. Gun weighs approximately 18 lbs. Produced between 1966 and 1976.

Pre-1968

Exc.	V.G.	Fair
N/A	N/A	N/A

Pre-1986 conversions

Exc.	V.G.	Fair
6500	6000	5500

Pre-1986 dealer samples

Exc.	V.G.	Fair
4500	4000	3500

Valmet M78

This model is a heavy barrel version of the Valmet M76. Barrel length is 18.75". It is offered in 7.62x39mm and 5.56x45mm calibers. Marked "VALMET Jyvaskyla M78" on the right side of the receiver. Rate of fire is about 650 rounds per minute and magazine capacity is 15 or 30 rounds. Weight is about 10.3 lbs. Produced from 1978 to 1986.

Photo Courtesy Private NFA Collection

Pre-1968

Exc.	V.G.	Fair
N/A	N/A	N/A

Pre-1986 conversions

Exc.	V.G.	Fair
7500	7000	6000

Pre-1986 dealer samples

Exc.	V.G.	Fair
5000	4500	4000

NOTE: For guns chambered for 7.62x39 add 20%.

FRANCE

French Military Conflicts, 1870-Present

With the French defeat in the Franco-Prussian War, 1870-1871, Napoleon III was ousted and the Third Republic established. France was involved in overseas colonial expansion in North Africa and Indochina. The French army bore the brunt of heavy fighting during World War I. France surrendered to Germany in 1940 and was occupied by German troops. In unoccupied France the Vichy government was headed by Marshall Petain. General Charles de Gaulle led the Free French government in exile. In the summer of 1944 the allied armies drove the German troops out of France and when the end of the war came in 1945 a Fourth Republic was formed in 1946. The French army received a stunning defeat in Indochina at Dien Bien Phu (1954) and other elements of the French military were busy in Algeria in that country's war for independence against France. In 1958 Charles de Gaulle returned to power to lead the Fifth Republic and attempted to restore French world prestige. France was involved with the U.S. in Desert Storm in Kuwait as well as a NATO member in various "peacekeeping" ventures.

HANDGUNS

NOTE: At the outbreak of the Franco-Prussian War the French military purchased a large number of revolvers from Colt's, Remington, and Starr. These revolvers were percussion arms.

Bibliographical Note: For additional historical information, technical data, and photos see Eugene Medlin and Jean Huon, *Military Handguns of France, 1858-1958*, Excalibur Publications, 1993.

Model 1870 Navy (Navy Contract)

This 6-shot solid frame fixed cylinder revolver uses a mechanical ejection system. Chambered for the 11mm cartridge and fitted with a 4.7" round barrel. Smooth wooden grips with lanyard loop. Adopted by the French navy in 1870 and remained in service until 1900. Built by the French firm "LEFAUCHEUX" in Paris. Marked "E LEFAUCHEUX" on the top of the frame, and on the right side "BVT. S.G.D.G. PARIS" with a naval anchor on the butt cap of the grip. This revolver was the first centerfire handgun to be adopted by any nation's military. About 6,000 revolvers were built under contract.

A modified version of this pistol was built by the French arsenal at St. Etienne (MAS) designated the Model 1870N. About 4,000 of these revolvers were produced and are marked, "MODEL 1870" on the top strap and "MODIFIE N" on the right side of the sighting groove. The military arsenal proof of MAS is on the cylinder and the underside of the barrel.

Revolvers fitted with military extractors have the extractor located along the barrel while civilian revolvers have the extractor located offset from the barrel.

Military Extractor

Exc.	V.G.	Good	Fair	Poor
5000	3500	2000	1000	500

Civilian Extractor

Exc.	V.G.	Good	Fair	Poor
3000	2000	1500	600	300

Model 1873 Navy

Built on a Chamelot-Delvigne type locking system with a solid frame, fixed cylinder, and mechanical rod ejection. Chambered for the 11mm cartridge and fitted with a 4.7" half-round half-octagon barrel. Non-fluted cylinder. It is both a single and double action revolver. Finish was left in the white. Marked, "MRE D'ARMES ST. ETIENNE" on the right side of the frame. On top of the barrel marked, "MLE 1873 M" or "NAVY." There are many other small markings on the revolver as well. Weight is approximately 36 oz. Used by the French navy for its NCOs from 1874 to 1945. Built by French military armory at St. Etienne. Between 1873 and 1886 approximately 350,000 of these revolvers were produced.

Model 1873 with barrel and frame markings • Paul Goodwin Photo

NAVY

Exc.	V.G.	Good	Fair	Poor
950	600	500	300	175

"MLE 1873"

Exc.	V.G.	Good	Fair	Poor
400	300	200	100	75

ARMY

Exc.	V.G.	Good	Fair	Poor
400	350	200	150	100

Model 1874

The Model 1874 was essentially the same as the Model 1873 but with a fluted cylinder. Used by French naval officers from 1878 to 1945. Between 1874 and 1886 approximately 36,000 of these revolvers were produced.

ARMY

Exc.	V.G.	Good	Fair	Poor
750	550	400	300	175

NAVY

Exc.	V.G.	Good	Fair	Poor
2500	1500	750	350	200

Model 1892

Chambered for an 8mm centerfire cartridge and has a 4.6" barrel with a 6-shot cylinder. Weight is about 30 oz. It is erroneously referred to as a "Lebel," but there is no certainty that Nicolas Lebel had anything to do with its design or production, but was the chairman of the selection board that chose the design. This revolver is a simple double action, with a swing-out cylinder that swings to the right side for loading. The design of this weapon is similar to the Italian Model 1889. There is one redeeming feature on this revolver, and that is a hinged side plate on the left side of the frame that could be swung away after unlocking so that repairs or cleaning of the lockwork could be performed with relative simplicity. The cartridge for which this weapon was chambered was woefully inadequate. This revolver remained in use from its introduction in 1893 until the end of WWII in 1945, mainly because the French never got around to designing a replacement.

NOTE: There are a number of commercial variations of this revolver, some of which are Spanish-made copies and others are St. Etienne commercial examples.

NAVY (Anchor of butt)

Exc.	V.G.	Good	Fair	Poor
600	400	200	150	100

ARMY

Exc.	V.G.	Good	Fair	Poor
400	250	175	125	75

Model 1892 "A Pompe"

As above, except that the cylinder latch is a sleeve around the ejector rod that can be moved forward to release the cylinder.

Exc.	V.G.	Good	Fair	Poor
750	500	250	125	75

Le Francais Model 28 Type Armee

A unique pistol chambered for the 9mm Browning cartridge. It is a large pistol, with a 5" barrel that was hinged with a tip-up breech. This is a blowback-operated semiautomatic pistol that has no extractor. The empty cases are blown out of the breech by gas pressure. The one feature about this pistol that is desirable is that it is possible to tip the barrel breech forward like a shotgun and load cartridges singly, while holding the contents of the magazine in reserve. This weapon has fixed sights and a blued finish, with checkered walnut grips. It was manufactured in 1928 and built by Manufrance.

Model 1892 with frame markings • Paul Goodwin Photo

Exc.	V.G.	Good	Fair	Poor
1250	950	750	500	200

Le Francais Police Model (Type Policeman)

A blowback-operated, double action semiautomatic that is chambered for the .32 ACP cartridge. It has a 3.5" barrel and a 7-round magazine. It has the same hinged-barrel feature of the Model 28 and is blued, with fixed sights and Ebonite grips. This model was manufactured 1913 to 1914.

Courtesy James Rankin

Exc.	V.G.	Good	Fair	Poor
800	650	450	300	150

Le Francais Officers Model (Pocket Model)

May also be referred to a "Staff Model." Also a blowback-operated semiautomatic chambered for the .25 ACP cartridge. It has a 2.5" barrel and a concealed hammer. It has fixed sights and the finish is blued. The grips are Ebonite. This model was manufactured between 1914 and 1938 in two variations: early and second type.

Early Variation Pocket • Courtesy James Rankin

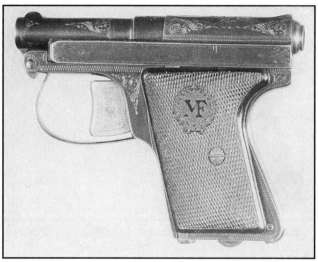

Second Variation Pocket • Courtesy James Rankin

Exc.	V.G.	Good	Fair	Poor
300	250	200	150	100

Model 1935A

A 7.65mm French Long caliber semiautomatic pistol with a 4.3" barrel. Magazine capacity is 8 rounds. Fixed sights. Weight is about 26 oz. Eventually became known as the Model 1935A. This pistol was designed and built for the French military and about 10,000 were produced up to June 20, 1940 when the factory, SACM (*Societe Alsacienne des Constructions Mecaniques*, Cholet, France), was occupied by German troops. About 24,000 were built and used by the German army during World War II.

Courtesy Richard M. Kumor Sr.

German Waffenamt Model (7.65mm Pistole 625f)

Exc.	V.G.	Good	Fair	Poor
475	425	250	125	100

Standard Model

Exc.	V.G.	Good	Fair	Poor
375	250	125	100	75

Model 1935S

As above, with locking ribs on slide and a 4.3" barrel. Built by MAC Chatellerault, MAS, SAGEM, and MF (Manufrance). About 85,000 pistols were produced between 1939 and 1953.

Exc.	V.G.	Good	Fair	Poor
250	150	125	100	75

MAB Model D

This semiautomatic pistol is built along the lines of the FN Model 1910. Built in Bayonne, France (MAB). Chambered for the 7.65mm cartridge. Early examples had a steel frame and later ones had an alloy frame. German army test and acceptance marks stamped on pistol. About 50,000 were produced during World War II.

Exc.	V.G.	Good	Fair	Poor
500	400	300	350	150

MAS Model 1950

A 9mm Parabellum caliber semiautomatic pistol with a 9-shot magazine. Blued, with ribbed plastic grips.

Exc.	V.G.	Good	Fair	Poor
525	425	350	275	200

MAS G1

This is a Beretta 92G which is a double action only 9mm pistol with decocking lever. Barrel length is 4.9". Magazine capacity is 15 rounds. Weight is about 34 oz. Military marked.

Exc.	V.G.	Good	Fair	Poor
N/A	—	—	—	—

MAB PA-15

This pistol is a French military version of the commercial Unique Model R Para. Chambered for the 9mm Parabellum cartridge and fitted with a 4.5" barrel. Magazine capacity is 15 rounds. Weight is about 38 oz. Sources indicate that this pistol was never officially adopted by the French military. However, a target version of this pistol, the F1 Target, was adopted by the French air force and army.

Exc.	V.G.	Good	Fair	Poor
550	450	300	200	100

UNIQUE

When the French Vichy government signed an armistice with Germany in 1940 the Germans occupied Handaye in France, the site of *Manufacture D'Armes Des Pyrenees*. This factory then produced for the German army the Model 16 and Model 17.

Model 16

Chambered for the 7.65mm cartridge this pistol was fitted with a 7-round magazine. German army proof test and acceptance stamp. Hard rubber grips. About 2,000 were built under German supervision.

Exc.	V.G.	Good	Fair	Poor
250	175	150	100	75

Model 17

Similar to the above but with a 9-shot magazine. About 30,000 of these pistols were built under German control.

Exc.	V.G.	Good	Fair	Poor
300	250	200	150	100

Unique Kriegsmodell

This is an improved Model 17 with exposed hammer. Approximately 18,000 were manufactured under Germany occupation.

Exc.	V.G.	Good	Fair	Poor
500	400	300	200	100

SAVAGE

Model 1907 (French Model)

A .32 or .380 semiautomatic pistol with a 3.75" or 4.25" barrel depending upon caliber and a 9- or 10-shot magazine. Blued with hard rubber grips. The .380 caliber model is worth approximately 20% more than the values listed below. This pistol was sold to the French government during World War I and used by the French military. These guns were not stamped with French acceptance marks. The first shipment was made in 1914. Most of these pistols were fitted with a lanyard ring. French contract Model 1907 pistols were chambered for the 7.65mm cartridge and are fitted with a chamber indicator. Approximately 27,000 of these pistols were sold to France.

Courtesy Orvel Reichert

Exc.	V.G.	Good	Fair	Poor
300	250	200	125	75

SUBMACHINE GUNS

The French used the German 9mm Erma submachine prior to World War II. The first French designed and built submachine gun was the MAS 35, designated the SE-MAS Type L, chambered for the 7.65 long pistol cartridge and built at Manufacture d'Armes de St. Etienne, St. Etienne, France. This gun was quickly superseded by the more common MAS 38.

MAS 38

Built in France and chambered for the 7.65mm French Long cartridge. Fitted with an 8.75" barrel and a magazine capacity of 32 rounds. Fitted with a fixed wooden butt. Rate of fire is about 650 rounds per minute. Uses a folding trigger for safety. Weight is approximately 6.5 lbs. On the left side of the receiver marked "CAL 7.65 L MAS 1938." Produced from 1938 to 1946.

NOTE: This gun may be seen chambered for the 7.65mm Soviet cartridge after capture by the Viet Minh during the French Indo-China war.

Private NFA Collection • Photo by Gary Gelson

Courtesy West Point Museum • Paul Goodwin Photo

Pre-1968

Exc.	V.G.	Fair
3000	2500	2000

Pre-1986 conversions

Exc.	V.G.	Fair
N/A	N/A	N/A

Pre-1986 dealer samples

Exc.	V.G.	Fair
N/A	N/A	N/A

MAT 49

This French submachine gun was first produced in 1949 and is still in production. Built at the French arsenal at Tulle using a stamped steel frame and receiver. It is chambered for the 9mm cartridge and fitted with a 9" barrel. The magazine housing acts as a forward grip and folds forward under the barrel. Fitted with an ejection port cover. It was used by French forces and is still found in former French colonies. The magazine capacity is 32 rounds and the weight is about 8 lbs. Rate of fire is 600 rounds per minute. Markings are "M.A.T. MLE 49 9M/M" on the left side of the receiver.

Pre-1968

Exc.	V.G.	Fair
6500	5500	5000

Pre-1986 conversions

Exc.	V.G.	Fair
N/A	N/A	N/A

Pre-1986 dealer samples

Exc.	V.G.	Fair
N/A	N/A	N/A

RIFLES

GRAS

Model 1874 & M1874/M14 & M80

An 11x59Rmm caliber bolt action single shot rifle with a 32" barrel with a walnut stock, two iron barrel bands and a metal tip. The bayonet is a spike blade with a wood handle and a brass butt cap. Many of these rifles were converted early in WWI to 8x50.5Rmm Lebel caliber by sleaving the barrel and rechambering. This converted rifle was designated the 1874/M14. Many of the conversions were fitted with wooden handguards. The rifle was built at Chatellerault, Mutzig, Tulle and so marked.

There was a Musketoon version, model designation M1874, with 27" barrel and 3 brass barrel bands. The Musketoon did not have a bayonet lug. It was made at St. Chatellerault and so marked.

A Carbine version was also built at St. Etienne and so marked. It was designated the M80 and was fitted with a 20" barrel with two brass barrel bands.

Rifle

Exc.	V.G.	Good	Fair	Poor
1250	850	650	450	150

Musketoon

Exc.	V.G.	Good	Fair	Poor
1500	1150	800	550	200

Carbine

Exc.	V.G.	Good	Fair	Poor
1500	1150	800	550	200

Model 1878 & 1878/M84 Navy

This rifle was produced at Steyr on contract with the French navy and marines. It was fitted with a 29" barrel and cham-

MAT 49 with receiver markings • Paul Goodwin Photo

bered for the 11x59R Gras cartridge. It has a 6-round magazine tube in the forend. The rifle was loaded through the action with the bolt open. These rifles will probably be marked "STEYR MLE. 1878 MARINE" on the left side of the receiver.

The 1878/M84 variation had the magazine extending slightly beyond the forend cap. The 1878/84 was produced at Chatellerault and St. Etienne. It was not made by Steyr.

Exc.	V.G.	Good	Fair	Poor
600	450	200	100	50

LEBEL

The Lebel system was invented by Nicolas Lebel in 1886. The French replaced the single shot Gras Model 1874 rifle with this weapon. This was the first successful smallbore rifle and sent the rest of the European continent into a dash to emulate it. The Lebel was chambered for the 8mm Lebel cartridge with smokeless powder. The Lebel system was used until it was made obsolete by the Berthier rifle in the 1890s.

Model 1886 "Lebel"

Chambered for the 8mm Lebel cartridge. While the cartridge was the first to use smokeless powder the rifle was based on the old Gras Model 1874. It has a 31" barrel and holds 8 shots in a tubular magazine that runs beneath the barrel. This design is long and heavy and was not in use for long before being replaced by the more efficient box magazine weapons, such as those from Mauser. This rifle has a two-piece stock with no upper handguard. It is held on by two barrel bands, and a cruciform bayonet could be fixed under the muzzle. Weight of the rifles was about 9.5 lbs. Although this rifle was made obsolete rather quickly, it did have the distinction of being the first successful smokeless powder smallbore rifle; there were shortened examples in use until the end of WWII. This rifle was made at Chatellerault, St. Etienne, and Tulle arsenals and so marked.

Courtesy Richard M. Kumor, Sr.

Exc.	V.G.	Good	Fair	Poor
600	450	200	100	50

Model 1886/M93/R35

A shorter version of the above. Fitted with a 17.7" barrel and a 3-round tubular magazine. Weight was about 7.8 lbs. Issued in 1935.

NOTE: Add 50% for Nazi marked models.

Courtesy Richard M. Kumor, Sr.

Exc.	V.G.	Good	Fair	Poor
500	300	200	150	75

BERTHIER-MANNLICHER

Adolph Berthier was a French army officer. He developed his new design to accommodate the new, more modern 8mm cartridge. His bolt action rifles employed Mannlicher-style

clips which were used to form part of the box magazine design. These clips fell out of the bottom of the action when the last round was chambered. Most of the Berthier rifles used 3 round clips.

Model 1890 Cavalry Carbine

This bolt action model a sling swivels mounted on the left side of the stock. The carbines did not have a bayonet lug. One piece stock had a straight grip without a handguard. The stock just forward of the triggerguard was swelled giving a potbelly appearance. This swell contained the magazine. Stock had two cross bolts. Bolt handle was extra long. Barrel length was 17.7". Weight was approximately 6.8 lbs. These carbines were built at Chatellerault and St. Etienne arsenals and so marked in script on the left side of the receiver.

Exc.	V.G.	Good	Fair	Poor
400	325	250	150	75

Model 1892 Artillery

This model was similar in appearance to the Model 1890 carbine with the exception that it was fitted with a bayonet lug and bottom sling swivels. No handguard.

Exc.	V.G.	Good	Fair	Poor
400	325	250	150	75

Model 1892/M16

This is a conversion of the Model 1892 with the addition of a 5-round extended magazine and upper handguard. Conversion was done during WWI, hence the 1916 designation.

French Model 1892/16 • Courtesy Richard M. Kumor, Sr.

Exc.	V.G.	Good	Fair	Poor
225	175	125	90	70

NOTE: For rifles originally chambered for .22 rimfire add 100%.

Model 1902

This model was based on the Model 1890 and 1892 carbines. It was designed for use by colonial troops in Indo-China. It was fitted with a 25" barrel with no upper handguard. One piece stock with straight grip with swell for magazine in front of triggerguard. Long bolt handle. Two cross bolts. These rifles were built at Chatellerault, St. Etienne, and Tulle arsenals, and so marked on the left side of the receiver. Weight was about 8 lbs.

Model 1902 • Courtesy West Point Museum • Paul Goodwin Photo

Exc.	V.G.	Good	Fair	Poor
225	150	100	75	50

Model 1907

Similar to the Model 1902 but with a 31.5" barrel. No upper handguard. Other specifications the same as the Model 1902 except weight was about 8.5 lbs.

Model 1907/15 • Courtesy West Point Museum •
Paul Goodwin Photo

Exc.	V.G.	Good	Fair	Poor
250	200	150	100	75

Model 1907/15

Similar to the Model 1907 except for a straight bolt design. Barrel length was 31.5" with upper handguard. Besides being built at the three French arsenals, this rifle was also made by Remington-UMC on contract in 1914 and 1915. These examples are so marked on the left side of the receiver. Weight is about 8.25 lbs.

Exc.	V.G.	Good	Fair	Poor
250	200	150	100	75

Model 1916 Rifle

Similar to the Model 1907/15 except fitted with a 5-round extended magazine.

Exc.	V.G.	Good	Fair	Poor
250	200	150	100	75

Model 1916 Carbine

This is a Model 1916 rifle with a 17.7" barrel and 5-round magazine. Weight is about 7 lbs.

Courtesy Rock Island Auction Company

Exc.	V.G.	Good	Fair	Poor
300	250	200	150	100

Model 1907/15-M34

This model was fitted with a 23" barrel and a new Mauser-type 5-round staggered column magazine. Clips were no longer needed in this design. It was chambered for the 7.5x54 rimless cartridge. Weight is about 8 lbs. Some of these rifles were used during WWII.

French Model 1907/15-M34 • Courtesy Richard M. Kumor, Sr.

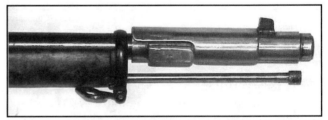

French Model 1907/M34 • Courtesy Richard M. Kumor, Sr.

Exc.	V.G.	Good	Fair	Poor
600	500	350	250	100

Model 1886/74/1917 Signal Rifle

A scarce variation of the military issue rifle.

Courtesy Richard M. Kumor, Sr.

Exc.	V.G.	Good	Fair	Poor
850	600	300	175	75

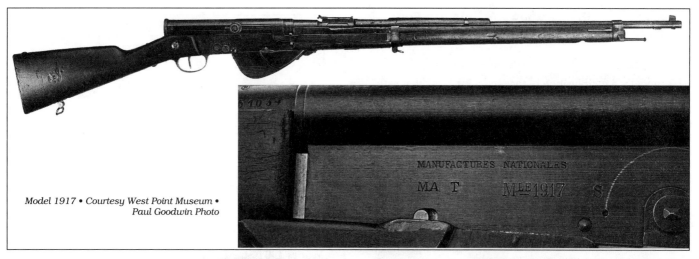

Model 1917 • Courtesy West Point Museum • Paul Goodwin Photo

FRENCH STATE ARSENALS
MAS, MAT

Model 1917

An 8x50mm Lebel caliber semiautomatic gas operated rifle with a 31.4" barrel, 5-shot half-oval charger loaded magazine, and full-length walnut stock with cleaning rod. Weight is about 11.5 lbs. Produced by MAT.

Exc.	V.G.	Good	Fair	Poor
1500	1200	800	—	—

Model 1918

As above in an improved version, with a 23.1" barrel. Uses a standard cartridge charger. Weight is about 10.5 lbs.

Exc.	V.G.	Good	Fair	Poor
1700	1400	800	—	—

MAS 36

A 7.5x54mm caliber bolt action rifle with a 22.6" barrel and 5-shot magazine. Bolt handle slants forward. Blued with a two piece walnut stock. Weight is about 8.25 lbs. The standard French service rifle from 1936 to 1949. The post-war version of this rifle has a grenade launcher built into the end of the barrel.

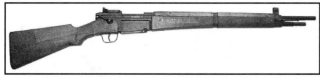

Courtesy Rock Island Auction Company

Exc.	V.G.	Good	Fair	Poor
225	175	150	100	75

MAS 36 CR39

As above, with an aluminum folding stock and 17.7" barrel. Weight is about 8 lbs. Designed for parachute and mountain troops. This is a rare variation.

Courtesy Richard M. Kumor, Sr.

MAS 36 Para rifle in arsenal refinish with wooden stock Courtesy Richard M. Kumor, Sr.

Exc.	V.G.	Good	Fair	Poor
900	800	300	125	90

MAS 44

This model was the first semiautomatic adopted by the French military. It was built in 1944. It later developed into the Model 49.

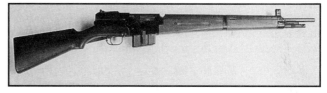

Courtesy Richard M. Kumor, Sr.

Exc.	V.G.	Good	Fair	Poor
375	300	225	150	100

MAS 49

Introduced in 1949 this model is a 7.5x54mm gas operated semiautomatic rifle with a 22.6" barrel and full-length walnut stock. It has a grenade launcher built into the front sight. Fitted with a 10-round magazine. No bayonet fittings. Weight is about 9 lbs.

Courtesy Richard M. Kumor, Sr.

MAS 49 Sniper Rifle • Courtesy Richard M. Kumor, Sr.

Exc.	V.G.	Good	Fair	Poor
375	300	225	150	100

MAS 49/56

This model is a modification of the Model 49. It is fitted with a 20.7" barrel. Principal modification is with NATO standard grenade launcher. A special grenade sight is also fitted. This model has provisions to fit a bayonet. Weight is about 8.5 lbs.

Courtesy Richard M. Kumor, Sr.

Exc.	V.G.	Good	Fair	Poor
400	300	250	175	100

Model FR-F 1 Sniper Rifle

Introduced in 1964 this 7.5x54mm rifle is based on the MAS 36 and uses the same style two-piece stock with pistol grip. Barrel length is 22" with bipod attached to forend. Barrel is fitted with a muzzle brake. Fitted with open sights but 3.8 power telescope often used. Magazine capacity is 10 rounds. Many of these rifles were converted to 7.62mm caliber.

Exc.	V.G.	Good	Fair	Poor
5500	4500	4000	—	—

Model FR-F 2 Sniper Rifle

A 1984 improved version of the F 1 rifle. The forearm has a plastic covering. The bipod is now attached to a yoke around the barrel, and the barrel is covered with a thermal sleeve to reduce heat. The features and dimensions the same as the F 1.

Exc.	V.G.	Good	Fair	Poor
6500	5500	5000	—	—

FAMAS F 1 Assault Rifle

Introduced in 1980 this bullpup designed rifle is chambered for the 5.56x45mm cartridge and fitted with a 19.2" barrel with fluted chamber. Select fire with 3 shot burst. Muzzle is designed for grenade launcher and fitted with flash hider. This model is also fitted for a bayonet and a bipod. Magazine capacity is 25 rounds. Rate of fire is about 950 rounds per minute. Weight is approximately 8 lbs.

Pre-1968

Exc.	V.G.	Fair
N/A	N/A	N/A

Pre-1986 conversions

Exc.	V.G.	Fair
N/A	N/A	N/A

Pre-1986 dealer samples

Exc.	V.G.	Fair
8000	7500	7000

FAMAS F 1 Rifle

Same as above but in semiautomatic version only. Scarce.

FAMAS Rifle • Courtesy Chuck Karwan

Exc.	V.G.	Good	Fair	Poor
8000	6000	—	—	—

MACHINE GUNS

Model 1907 St. Etienne

Built by the French arsenal MAS this is a reversed gas action gun chambered for the 8x50R Lebel cartridge. It was an unsuccessful attempt to improve on the Hotchkiss gun. The rate of fire is between 400 and 500 rounds per minute and is regulated by changing the gas cylinder volume. Barrel jacket is half-length over a 28" barrel. Fitted with spade grips with trigger. Fed by 24 or 30 metal strips. Weight is approximately 57 lbs. with tripod. This gun was not able to withstand the rigors of trench warfare and was withdrawn from combat in Europe.

Model 1907 St. Etienne • Robert G. Segel Collection

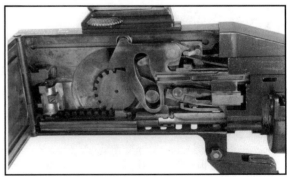

Model 1907 St. Etienne blow forward mechanism
Robert G. Segel Collection

Pre-1968

Exc.	V.G.	Fair
10000	9000	8000

Pre-1986 conversions

Exc.	V.G.	Fair
N/A	N/A	N/A

Pre-1986 dealer samples

Exc.	V.G.	Fair
N/A	N/A	N/A

Model 52 (AAT Mle.52)

Introduced in 1952 as a general purpose machine gun with light 19" quick change barrel with flash hider and bipod. This gun employs a blowback operation with two-piece bolt and fluted chamber. Chambered for the 7.62mm cartridge. The buttstock is a single piece metal folding type. Rate of fire is about 700 rounds per minute and is belt-fed from the left side. Weight is about 21 lbs.

A heavy barrel of this gun is built around a 23.5" heavy barrel. Weight is about 24 lbs. Gun is usually placed on a U.S. M2 tripod. All other specifications same as light barrel version.

Pre-1968

Exc.	V.G.	Fair
18000	16000	14000

Pre-1986 conversions

Exc.	V.G.	Fair
N/A	N/A	N/A

Pre-1986 dealer samples

Exc.	V.G.	Fair
N/A	N/A	N/A

Hotchkiss Model 1914

This model is an improvement over the original Model 1897 gun but with steel cooling fins instead of brass. Otherwise it remains an air-cooled gun chambered for the 8x50R Lebel cartridge. It is fed by a 24- or 30-round metal strip or by a 250-round belt. Its rate of fire is about 500 rounds per minute. Barrel length is 31" and weight is about 55 lbs. The tripod for the Hotchkiss weighed another 55 lbs. by itself. In production from 1914 to 1930. Marked "MILTRAILLEUSE AUTOMATIQUE HOTCHKISS M1914 SDGD CALIBERE ———" on left side of receiver. The gun was used by the French army in both WWI and WWII. During WWI it was used by a number of Allied forces as well. After World War II the gun appeared with French forces in Indo-China where the Viet Minh and later the Viet Cong used the gun.

Model 1914 Hotchkiss • Robert G. Segel Collection

NOTE: An earlier version of this gun, the Model 1909, was fitted with brass cooling fins instead of steel. The original design of the Hotchkiss was the Model 1897. This gun was fed by 30 round metal strips and had a rate of fire of about 600 rounds per minute. Similar in appearance to the Model 1909.

Pre-1968

Exc.	V.G.	Fair
8000	7000	6000

Pre-1986 conversions

Exc.	V.G.	Fair
N/A	N/A	N/A

Pre-1986 dealer samples

Exc.	V.G.	Fair
N/A	N/A	N/A

Chauchat Model 1915 (C.S.R.G.)

This model is a light air-cooled machine gun using a long recoil operation with a rotating bolt. It is chambered for the 8x50R Lebel and features an 18.5" barrel with barrel jacket. The 20-round magazine is a semi-circular type located under the receiver. Wooden buttstock and bipod. Rate of fire is about 250 rounds per minute. Used during WWI. The gun was inexpensively built and was not considered combat reliable.

A U.S. version firing the .30-06 cartridge was designed and built by the French and called the Model 1918. Used by U.S.

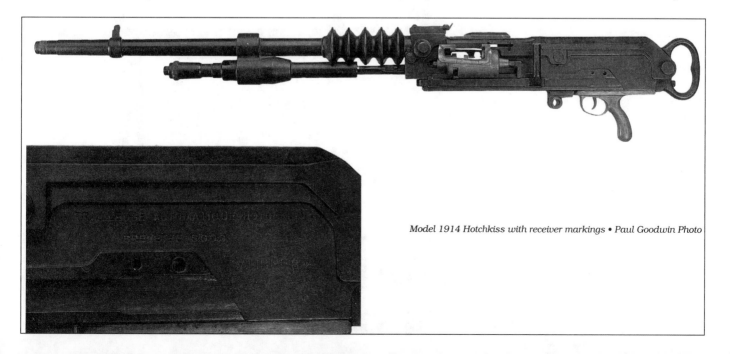

Model 1914 Hotchkiss with receiver markings • Paul Goodwin Photo

forces during WWI the M1918 has a 16-round magazine and a rate of fire of about 300 rounds per minute. U.S. military purchased about 19,000 of these gun chambered for the .30-06 cartridge.

After World War I Belgium used the M1918 chambered for the 7.65mm cartridge and by Greece (Gladiator) chambered for the 8mm Label, and in England where it was designated the Chauchard.

Chau-chat Model 1915 with "C.S.R.G." stamped on the receiver with serial number • Paul Goodwin Photo

Pre-1968

Exc.	V.G.	Fair
3500	3000	2000

Pre-1986 conversions

Exc.	V.G.	Fair
N/A	N/A	N/A

Pre-1986 dealer samples

Exc.	V.G.	Fair
N/A	N/A	N/A

Chatellerault M1924/M29

This is an air-cooled light gas piston machine gun that the French referred to as an automatic rifle. It is chambered for the 7.5x54mm French cartridge. Fitted with a 19.7" barrel with flash hider and bipod. Wooden butt and forearm. Select fire with two triggers. Fed by a 25-round detachable top mounted box magazine. Rate of fire is about 500 rounds per minute. Weight is approximately 24 lbs. with bipod. Introduced in 1929 the gun was used extensively in combat by French troops.

Another version of this model is known as the M1931A introduced in 1931. It is essentially an M1924/29 for use on a tank as a fixed place machine gun with tripod. Fitted with a 23" heavy barrel. The gun can use a 36-round box magazine or 150-round drum, both of which attach to the right side of the gun. Its rate of fire is 750 round per minute.

Pre-1968

Exc.	V.G.	Fair
6500	6000	5500

Pre-1986 conversions

Exc.	V.G.	Fair
N/A	N/A	N/A

Pre-1986 dealer samples

Exc.	V.G.	Fair
N/A	N/A	N/A

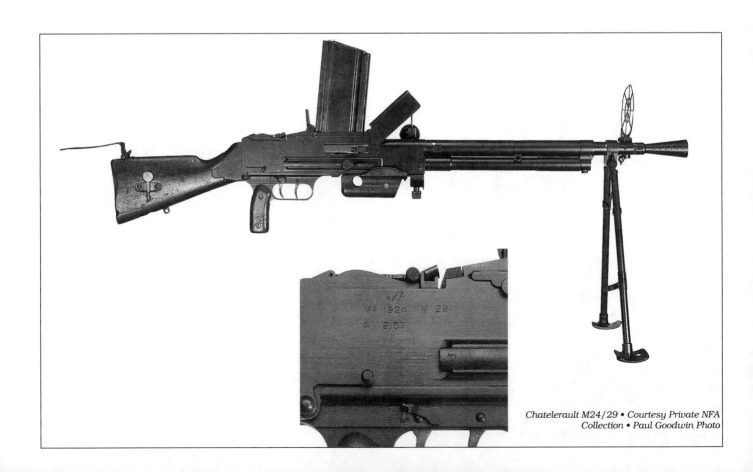

Chatelerault M24/29 • Courtesy Private NFA Collection • Paul Goodwin Photo

GERMANY

German Military Conflicts, 1870-Present

Prussia, under Otto von Bismark, achieved unification of the German states with victories in the Austro-Prussian War of 1866 and the Franco-Prussian War of 1870-1871. In 1871 William I of Prussia was named emperor of Germany and the nation's economic and military power began to grow and spread throughout the world. The outbreak of World War I was in part due to German expansion, threatening British and French interests. With the end of World War I, and Germany's defeat, came a period of political and economic instability that led to the rise of the Nazi party. In 1933 Adolf Hitler was named chancellor of Germany. With the invasion of Poland on September 1, 1939 World War II began. After the war ended parts of eastern Germany were absorbed by Poland and Russia. In 1949 West and East Germany were formed. The military weapons in this section cover Germany up to the formation of both East and West Germany with the post-war period only concerned with firearms produced in West Germany. East German military firearms are covered under the Russian, U.S.S.R. section. Both East and West Germany were reunited in 1990.

HANDGUNS

Bibliographical Note: For information on a wide variety of German military handguns see Jan Still, *Axis Pistols*, 1986.

REICHS REVOLVER
Germany

There are two basic versions of the German Standard Service Revolver designed by the Small Arms Commission of the Prussian army in the 1870s. Revolvers of this type were produced by the Erfurt Royal Arsenal, F. Dreyse of Sommerda, Sauer & Sohn, Spangenberg & Sauer, and C. H. Haenel of Suhl. Normally, the maker's initials are to be found on an oval above the triggerguard.

Model 1879

A 10.55mm caliber revolver with a 7.2" stepped octagon barrel, 6-shot cylinder and fixed sights. Standard finish is browned with smooth walnut grips having a lanyard ring at the base. These revolvers are fitted with a safety catch. In use from 1882 until 1919.

Exc.	V.G.	Good	Fair	Poor
1000	700	500	300	200

NOTE: Add 20% for Mauser-built revolvers.

Model 1883

As above with a 5" stepped octagon barrel and round bottom grips with lanyard loop. The finish on early production guns was browned, and on the balance of production, the finish was blued. In use from 1885 until 1919. Mauser-built M1883s are rare.

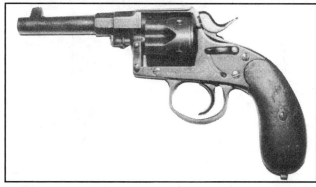

Exc.	V.G.	Good	Fair	Poor
750	500	375	250	175

NOTE: For Mauser-built revolvers add 250%.

STEYR

Steyr Hahn Model 1911

The Steyr Hahn was originally introduced as a commercial pistol but was quickly adopted by the Austro-Hungarian, Chilean, and Romanian militaries. Commercial examples were marked "Osterreichische Waffenfabrik Steyr M1911 9m/m" on the slide, have a laterally adjustable rear sight, and are rare. Austrian militaries are marked simply "STEYR" and the date of manufacture, while those made for Chile and Romania bear their respective crests. During WWII the Germans rebarreled a number of Steyr Hahns to 9mm Parabellum for police use, adding "P.08" to the slide along with appropriate Waffenamt markings.

Courtesy Orvel Reichert

Commercially marked

Exc.	V.G.	Good	Fair	Poor
1350	1000	750	500	350

German WWII Issue (P.08 marked)

Exc.	V.G.	Good	Fair	Poor
800	500	350	200	125

DREYSE

Dreyse 7.65mm

As above, but chambered for the 7.65mm cartridge, with a 3.6" barrel and a 7-shot magazine. The slide marked "Dreyse Rheinmetall Abt. Sommerda." Blued with plastic grips.

Courtesy Orvel Reichert

Exc.	V.G.	Good	Fair	Poor
350	250	175	100	75

Dreyse 9mm

As above, but chambered for the 9mm cartridge with a 5" barrel and an 8-shot magazine. The slide marked "Rheinische Mettellwaaren Und Maschinenfabrik, Sommerda." Blued with plastic grips.

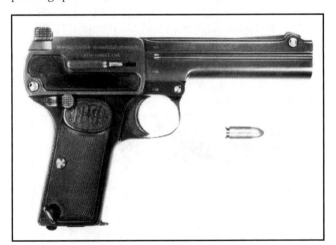

Courtesy James Rankin

Exc.	V.G.	Good	Fair	Poor
3000	2000	800	450	300

MAUSER

MODEL 1896 "BROOMHANDLE MAUSER PISTOL"

Manufactured from 1896 to 1939, the Model 1896 Pistol was produced in a wide variety of styles as listed below. It is recommended that those considering the purchase of any of the following models should consult Breathed & Schroeder's, *System Mauser*, Chicago, 1967 as it provides detailed descriptions and photographs of the various models. See also Wayne Erickson and Charles Pate, *The Broomhandle Pistol, 1896-1936,* 1985.

NOTE: A correct, matching stock/holster will add approximately 40 percent to value of each category.

"BUYER BEWARE" ALERT by Gale Morgan: Over the past several years large quanities of "Broomhandle" Mausers and Astra "copies" have been imported into the United States. Generally these are in poor or fair condition and have been offered for sale in the $125 to $300 price range, primarily as shooters or parts guns. Over the past year or so, a cottage industry has sprung up where these very common pistols have been "converted" to "rare, exotic, near mint, original" specimens selling well into the four figure price range. I have personallly seen English Crest, the U.S. Great Seal, unheard-of European dealers, aristocratic Coats-of-Arms, and Middle East Medallions beautifully photo-etched into the magazine wells and rear panels of some really common wartime commercials with price tags that have been elevated to $2,500 plus. They are quite eye-catching and if they are sold as customized/modified Mausers, the seller can price the piece at whatever the market will bear. However, if sold as a factory original-BUYER BEWARE.

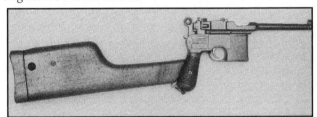

Courtesy Wallis & Wallis, Lewes, Sussex, England

Turkish Contract Cone Hammer

Chambered for 7.63mm Mauser cartridge and fitted with a 5.5" barrel. Rear sight is marked in Farsi characters. Grips are grooved walnut with 21 grooves. Proof mark is a 6 pointed star on both sides of the chamber. Marked in Turkish script and bearing the crest of Sultan Abdul-Hamid II on the frame. Approximately 1,000 were sold to Turkey.

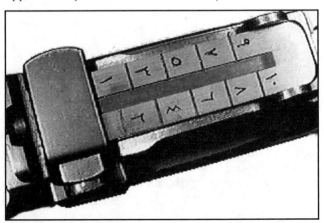

Courtesy Gale Morgan

Exc.	V.G.	Good	Fair	Poor
11000	8000	6500	3000	2000

Contract Transitional Large Ring Hammer

This variation has the same characteristics of the "Standard Cone Hammer" except the hammer has a larger, open ring. It is fitted with a 5.5" barrel and an adjustable sight marked from 50 to 500 meters. Grips are walnut with 23 grooves. Some of these pistols were issued to the German army for field testing.

Courtesy Gale Morgan

Exc.	V.G.	Good	Fair	Poor
3500	2800	2500	1150	800

Model 1899 Flat Side-Italian Contract

Similar to the above, with a 5.5" barrel, adjustable rear sight and the frame sides milled flat. Left flat of chamber marked with "DV" proof. A "crown over AV" is stamped on the bottom of the barrel. All parts are serial numbered. Approximately 5,000 were manufactured in 1899.

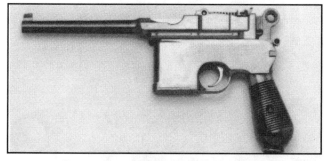

Courtesy Butterfield & Butterfield, San Francisco, California

Exc.	V.G.	Good	Fair	Poor
4000	3000	1500	1200	900

Contract Flat Side

Fitted with a 5.5" barrel with adjustable rear sight marked 50 to 500 meters. Grips are walnut with 23 grooves. The proof mark is the German military acceptance proofs. This model was used for field test by the German army in 1899 or 1900. Number of pistols is unknown but most likely very small.

Exc.	V.G.	Good	Fair	Poor
2700	2200	1500	1000	750

Persian Contract

Persian rising sun on left rear barrel extension. Persian Lion crest in center of rear frame panel. Barrel length is 5.5" and grips are walnut with 34 grooves. Adjustable rear sight marked from 50 to 1000 meters. Prospective purchasers should secure a qualified appraisal prior to acquisition. Serial numbers in the 154000 range.

Exc.	V.G.	Good	Fair	Poor
4200	3500	2250	1400	1000

Standard Wartime Commercial

Identical to the prewar Commercial Model 96, except that it has 30 groove walnut grips and the rear of the hammer is stamped "NS" for new safety. A number of these have the Austrian military acceptance marks in addition to the German commercial proofs. These pistols were also used by the German army as well.

Courtesy Gale Morgan

Exc.	V.G.	Good	Fair	Poor
1800	1300	1000	500	350

9mm Parabellum Military Contract

As above, in 9mm Parabellum caliber with 24 groove grips, stamped with a large "9" filled with red paint. Rear sights are adjustable with 50 to 500 meter markings. This model has German military acceptance marks on the right side of the chamber. Fit and finish on these pistol are poor. Some example have the Imperial German Eagle on the front of the magazine well. About 150,000 of these pistols were built for the German government.

Exc.	V.G.	Good	Fair	Poor
2200	1700	1200	700	450

A Mauser 9mm military contract was sold at auction for $2,185. Red "9" on grips. Correct holster and shoulder stock. Condition wasexcellent.
Amoskeag Auction Co., Inc., March, 2000

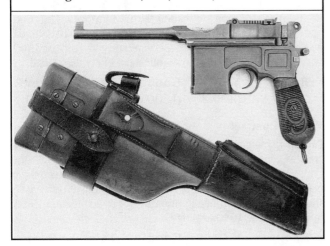

1920 Rework

A Model 96 modified to a barrel length of 3.9" and in 7.63mm Mauser or 9mm Parabellum caliber. Rear sight on this model is fixed. German military acceptance marks are located on right side of the chamber. Often encountered with police markings.

Courtesy Gale Morgan

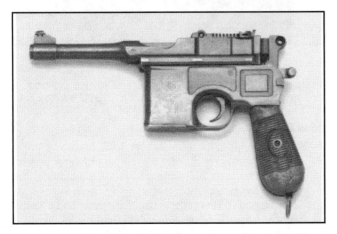

Courtesy Butterfield & Butterfield, San Francisco, California

Exc.	V.G.	Good	Fair	Poor
1300	1000	500	400	350

Late Postwar Bolo Model

Chambered for the 7.63mm Mauser cartridge and fitted with a 3.9" barrel. Rear sight marked for 50 to 500 meters or 50 to 1000 meters. Grips are walnut with 22 grooves. Some of these pistols will bear Chinese characters. The Mauser banner trademark is stamped on the left rear panel.

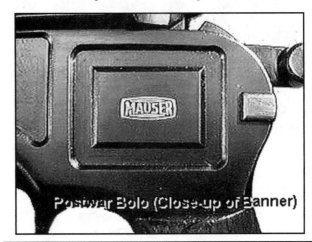

Courtesy Gale Morgan

Exc.	V.G.	Good	Fair	Poor
3000	2500	1500	750	500

Early Model 1930

A 7.63mm caliber Model 96 with a 5.2" stepped barrel, 12-groove walnut grips and late style safety. The rear adjustable sight is marked in 50 to 1000 meters. Some of these pistols have Chinese characters on the left side of the magazine well.

Courtesy Gale Morgan

Exc.	V.G.	Good	Fair	Poor
2700	2200	1200	800	500

Late Model 1930

Identical to the above, except for solid receiver rails.

Exc.	V.G.	Good	Fair	Poor
2500	2000	1000	700	400

Model 1930 Removable Magazine

Similar to the above, but with a detachable magazine. Prospective purchasers should secure a qualified appraisal prior to acquisition. Too rare to price.

Mauser Schnellfeuer (Model 712 or Model 32)

This is not a submachine gun but rather a machine pistol. Chambered for 7.63mm Mauser cartridge. Barrel length is 5.5" and rear sight is adjustable from 50 meters to 1000 meters. Walnut grips with 12 grooves. This pistol is often encountered with Chinese markings as it was very popular in the Orient. Approximately 100,000 were produced. Rate of fire is between 900 and 1,100 rounds per minute. It should be noted that the Model 712 was used to some limited extent by the Waffen SS during World War II as well as the German Luftwaffe. Stamped with army test proof.

NOTE: The prices listed below are for guns with commercial markings and correct Mauser Schnellfeuer stock. Schnellfeuer stocks are cut larger inside to accommodate selector switch. For German army acceptance stamped pistols add 5% to 10% depending on condition. For pistols without stock or incorrect stock deduct $750 to $1,000.

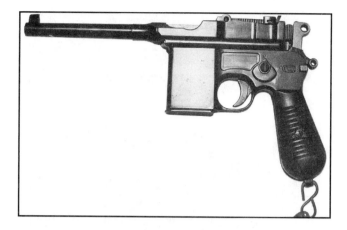

Photo Courtesy Joseph Schroeder

Pre-1968

Exc.	V.G.	Fair
7500	7000	6500

Pre-1986 conversions

Exc.	V.G.	Fair
N/A	N/A	N/A

Pre-1986 dealer samples

Exc.	V.G.	Fair
3000	3000	2500

CHINESE MAUSERS

The Chinese government purchased a large quantity of Mauser pistols directly from Mauser and continued to do so until they began purchasing Browning Hi-Power pistol from FN in the mid 1930s. The Chinese bought many Bolos and Model 1930 pistols. Some of these pistols are marked with Chinese characters, many are not. The Chinese also made their own copies of Mauser Broomhandles as well as Astras. Some of the more encountered varieties are listed here.

CHINESE MARKED, HANDMADE COPIES

Crude copies of the Model 96 and unsafe to fire.

Exc.	V.G.	Good	Fair	Poor
500	400	350	250	175

Taku-Naval Dockyard Model

Approximately 6,000 copies of the Model 96 were made at the Taku-Naval Dockyard. Values listed below include a correct shoulder stock/holder.

Exc.	V.G.	Good	Fair	Poor
2500	1500	1000	500	400

Shansei Arsenal Model

Approximately 8,000 Model 96 pistols were manufactured in .45 ACP caliber at the Shansei Province Arsenal in 1929. Magazine capacity is 10 rounds.

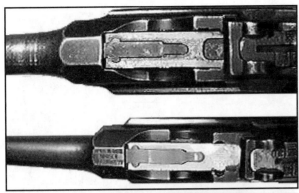

Shansei Panel Marking

Courtesy Gale Morgan

Exc.	V.G.	Good	Fair	Poor
5000	3500	2250	1500	1300

NOTE: Within the past several years, a large quantity of Model 96 pistols exported to or made in China have been imported into the United States. It has been reported that some *newly* made copies of the Shansei .45 were recently exported from China. **Proceed with caution.**

NOTE: Copies of the Model 96 were made by Unceta (Astra), Eulogio Arostegui (Azul) and Zulaica y Cia (Royal) and marketed by the firm of Beistegui Hermanos. These copies are covered in their own sections of this text.

LUGER

Bibliographical Note: See Charles Kenyon's, *Lugers at Random*, Handgun Press, 1969 for historical information, technical data, and photos. See also Jan Still, *Axis Pistols*, 1986.

Just before the turn of the twentieth century, Georg Luger (1849-1923) redesigned the Borchardt semiautomatic pistol so that its mainspring was housed in the rear of the grip. The resulting pistol, the German army's Pistole '08, was to prove extremely successful and his name has become synonymous with the pistol despite the fact his name never appeared on it.

The following companies manufactured Luger pattern pistols at various times:

1. DWM - Deutsch Waffen und Munitions - Karlsruhe, Germany

2. The Royal Arsenal of Erfurt Germany

3. Simson & Company - Suhl, Germany

4. Mauser - Oberndorf, Germany

5. Vickers Ltd. - England

6. Waffenfabrik Bern - Bern, Switzerland, *see Switzerland, Handguns, Luger.*

7. Heinrich Krieghoff - Suhl, Germany

NOTE: The model listings below contain the commonly accepted Lugers that are considered military issue. It should be pointed out that in wartime commercial pistols were often diverted to military use if necessary.

DEUTSCH WAFFEN UND MUNITIONS

1900 Swiss Contract

4.75" barrel, 7.65mm caliber. The Swiss Cross in Sunburst is stamped over the chamber. The military serial number range is 2001-5000; the commercial range, 01-21250. There were approximately 2,000 commercial and 3,000 military models manufactured.

Wide Trigger-Add 20%.

Paul Goodwin Photo

Exc.	V.G.	Good	Fair	Poor
5500	4000	2000	1500	1000

1900 American Eagle

4.75" barrel, 7.65mm caliber. The American Eagle crest is stamped over the chamber. The serial range is between 2000-200000, and there were approximately 11,000-12,000 commercial models marked "Germany" and 1,000 military test models without the commercial import stamp. The serial numbers of this military lot have been estimated at between 6100-7100.

Paul Goodwin Photo

Exc.	V.G.	Good	Fair	Poor
4500	3200	1500	850	600

1900 Bulgarian Contract

An old model, 1900 Type, with no stock lug. It has a 4.75" barrel and is chambered for the 7.65mm cartridge. The Bulgarian crest is stamped over the chamber, and the safety is marked in Bulgarian letters. The serial range is 20000-21000, with 1,000 manufactured. This is a military test model and is quite rare as most were rebarreled to 9mm during the time they were used. Even with the 9mm versions, approximately 10 are known to exist. It was the only variation to feature a marked safety before 1904.

Paul Goodwin Photo

Exc.	V.G.	Good	Fair	Poor
12000	8000	4000	2500	1800

1902 American Eagle Cartridge Counter

As above, with a "Powell Indicating Device" added to the left grip. A slotted magazine with a numbered window that allows visual access to the number of cartridges remaining. There were 50 Lugers altered in this way at the request of the U.S. Board of Ordnance, for U.S. army evaluation. The serial numbers are 22401-22450. Be especially wary of fakes!

Paul Goodwin Photo

Exc.	V.G.	Good	Fair	Poor
28000	20000	14000	5000	3500

1904 Navy

6" thick barrel, 9mm caliber. The chamber area is blank, and the extractor is marked "Geladen." The safety is marked "Ge-

sichert." There were approximately 1,500 manufactured in the one- to four-digit serial range, for military sales to the German navy. The toggle has a "lock" comparable to 1900 types.

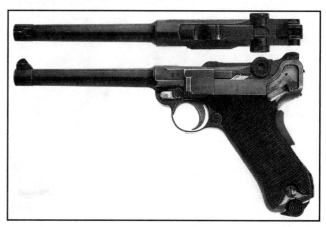

Paul Goodwin Photo

Exc.	V.G.	Good	Fair	Poor
40000	30000	16000	6000	4500

1906 U.S. Army Test Luger .45 Caliber

5" barrel, .45 ACP caliber. Sent to the United States for testing in 1907. The chamber is blank; the extractor is marked "Loaded", and the frame is polished under the safety lever. The trigger on this model has an odd hook at the bottom. Only five of these pistols were manufactured.

Exc.	V.G.	Good	Fair	Poor

Too Rare to Price

1906 Swiss Military

As the Swiss Commercial, with the Geneva Cross in shield appearing on the chamber.

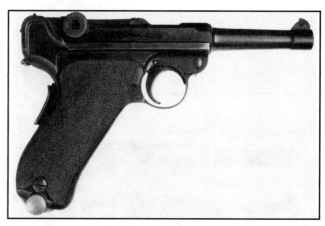

Courtesy Rock Island Auction Company

Exc.	V.G.	Good	Fair	Poor
4500	3100	2000	900	700

1906 Swiss Police Cross in Shield

As above, with a shield replacing the sunburst on the chamber marking. There were 10,215 of both models combined. They are in the 5000-15215 serial number range.

Paul Goodwin Photo

Exc.	V.G.	Good	Fair	Poor
4700	3200	1800	1000	700

1906 Dutch Contract

4" barrel, 9mm caliber. It has no stock lug, and the chamber is blank. The extractor is marked "Geleden" on both sides, and the safety is marked "RUST" with a curved upward pointing arrow. This pistol was manufactured for military sales to the Netherlands, and a date will be found on the barrel of most examples encountered. The Dutch refinished their pistols on a regular basis and marked the date on the barrels. There were approximately 4,000 manufactured, serial numbered between 1 and 4000.

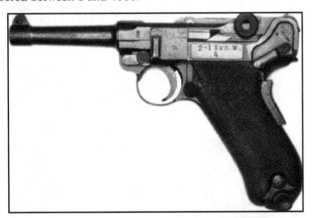

Courtesy Gale Morgan

Paul Goodwin Photo

Exc.	V.G.	Good	Fair	Poor
4200	3000	1500	800	600

1906 Royal Portuguese Navy

4" barrel, 9mm caliber, and has no stock lug. The Royal Portuguese Naval crest, an anchor under a crown, is stamped above the chamber. The extractor is marked "CARREGADA" on the left side. The frame under the safety is polished. There were approximately 1,000 manufactured with one- to four-digit serial numbers.

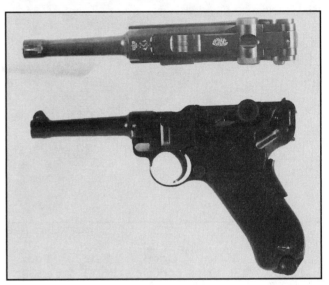

Exc.	V.G.	Good	Fair	Poor
12000	9000	6500	4000	2500

1906 Royal Portuguese Army (M2)

4.75" barrel, 7.65mm caliber. It has no stock lug. The chamber area has the Royal Portuguese crest of Manuel II stamped upon it. The extractor is marked "CARREGADA." There were approximately 5,000 manufactured, with one- to four-digit serial numbers.

Exc.	V.G.	Good	Fair	Poor
3000	2500	1200	600	500

1906 Republic of Portugal Navy

4" barrel, 9mm caliber. It has no stock lug, and the extractor was marked "CARREGADA." This model was made after 1910, when Portugal had become a republic. The anchor on the chamber is under the letters "R.P." There were approximately 1,000 manufactured, with one- to four-digit serial numbers.

Exc.	V.G.	Good	Fair	Poor
11000	9000	5500	3500	2500

1906 Brazilian Contract

4.75" barrel, 7.65mm caliber. It has no stock lug, and chamber area is blank. The extractor is marked "CARREGADA", and the frame under the safety is polished. There were approximately 5,000 manufactured for military sales to Brazil.

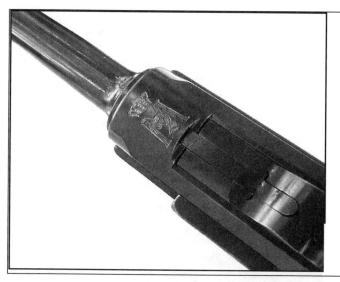

1906 Royal Portuguese Army (M2), Paul Goodwin Photo

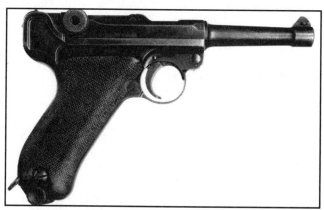

Paul Goodwin Photo

Exc.	V.G.	Good	Fair	Poor
3000	2400	1100	750	450

1906 Bulgarian Contract

4.75" barrel, 7.65mm caliber. It has no stock lug, and the extractor and safety are marked in cyrillic letters. The Bulgarian crest is stamped above the chamber. Nearly all of the examples located have the barrels replaced with 4" 9mm units. This was done after the later 1908 model was adopted. Some were refurbished during the Nazi era, and these pistols bear Waffenamts and usually mismatched parts. There were approximately 1,500 manufactured, with serial numbers of one- to four-digits.

Courtesy Rock Island Auction Company

Exc.	V.G.	Good	Fair	Poor
9500	7000	5000	3500	1500

1906 Russian Contract

4" barrel, 9mm caliber. It has no stock lug, and the extractor and safety are marked with cyrillic letters. Crossed Nagant rifles are stamped over the chamber. There were approximately 1,000 manufactured, with one- to four-digit serial numbers; but few survive. This is an extremely rare variation, and caution should be exercised if purchase is contemplated.

Exc.	V.G.	Good	Fair	Poor
14000	12000	6500	4000	2500

1906 Navy 1st Issue

6" barrel, 9mm caliber. The safety and extractor are both marked in German, and the chamber area is blank. There is a stock lug, and the unique two-position sliding Navy sight is mounted on the rear toggle link. There were approximately 12,000 manufactured for the German navy, with serial numbers of one- to five-digits. The wooden magazine bottom features concentric rings.

NOTE: Many of these pistols had their safety changed so that they were "safe" in the lower position. Known as "1st issue altered." Value at approximately 20% less.

Courtesy Gale Morgan

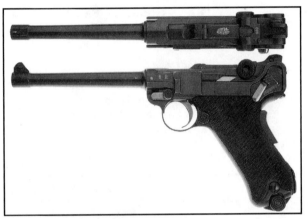

Paul Goodwin Photo

Exc.	V.G.	Good	Fair	Poor
4200	3500	2000	1300	950

1906 Navy 2nd Issue

As above, but manufactured to be safe in the lower position. Approximately 11,000 2nd Issue Navies manufactured, with one- to five-digit serial numbers—some with an "a" or "b" suffix. They were produced for sale to the German navy.

Paul Goodwin Photo

Exc.	V.G.	Good	Fair	Poor
3600	2700	1500	950	700

1908 Navy

As above, with the "Crown M" military proof. They may or may not have the concentric rings on the magazine bottom. There were approximately 40,000 manufactured, with one- to five-digit serial numbers with an "a" or "b" suffix. These Lugers are quite scarce as many were destroyed during and after WWI, although a total of 40,000 were produced.

Exc.	V.G.	Good	Fair	Poor
3600	2700	1500	1100	800

1914 Navy

Similar to the above, but stamped with the dates from 1914-1918 above the chamber. Most noted are dated 1916-1918. There were approximately 30,000 manufactured, with one- to five-digit serial numbers with an "a" or "b" suffix. They are scarce as many were destroyed or altered as a result of WWI, even though about 40,000 were built.

> A DWM 1914 Navy was sold at auction for $6,600. Pistol has all matching serial numbers with matching stock, three matching magazines, all marked with Naval acceptance proofs. All accessories. Condition was very good to excellent.
> Faintich Auction Service, June 2000

Paul Goodwin Photo

Exc.	V.G.	Good	Fair	Poor
3500	2500	1500	950	700

1908 Military 1st Issue

4" barrel, 9mm caliber. This was the first Luger adopted by the German army. It has no stock lug, and the extractor and safety are both marked in German. The chamber is blank. There were approximately 20,000 manufactured, with one- to five-digit serial numbers—some with an "a" suffix.

Exc.	V.G.	Good	Fair	Poor
1500	850	600	500	350

1908 Military Dated Chamber (1910-1913)

As above, with the date of manufacture stamped on the chamber.

Exc.	V.G.	Good	Fair	Poor
1200	900	600	500	350

1914 Military

As above, with a stock lug.

Exc.	V.G.	Good	Fair	Poor
1000	800	650	500	350

1914 Artillery

Fitted with an 8" barrel and chambered for the 9mm Parabellum cartridge, it features a nine-position adjustable sight that has a base that is an integral part of the barrel. This model has a stock lug and was furnished with a military-style flat board stock and holster rig (see Accessories). The chamber is dated from 1914-1918, and the safety and extractor are both marked. This model was developed for artillery and machine gun crews; and many thousands were manufactured, with one- to five-digit serial numbers—some have letter suffixes. This model is quite desirable from a collector's standpoint and is rarer than its production figures would indicate. After the war many were destroyed as the allies deemed them more insidious than other models, for some reason.

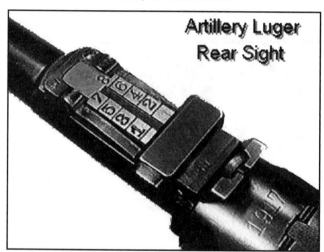

Courtesy Gale Morgan

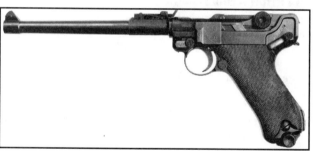

Courtesy Rock Island Auction Company

Exc.	V.G.	Good	Fair	Poor
2400	1800	1300	900	600

NOTE: For models stamped with 1914 date add 50%.

DWM Double Dated

Has a 4" barrel, 9mm cartridge. The date 1920 or 1921 is stamped over the original chamber date of 1910-1918, creating the double-date nomenclature. These are arsenal-reworked WWI military pistols and were then issued to the German military and/or police units within the provisions of the Treaty of Versailles. Many thousands of these Lugers were produced.

Courtesy Rock Island Auction Company

Exc.	V.G.	Good	Fair	Poor
900	700	550	400	300

1920 Police/Military Rework

As above, except that the original manufacture date was removed before the rework date was stamped. There were many thousands of these produced.

Exc.	V.G.	Good	Fair	Poor
800	650	500	350	300

1920 Navy Carbine

Assembled from surplus Navy parts with the distinctive two position, sliding navy sight on the rear toggle link. Most are marked with the export stamp (GERMANY) and have the naval military proofmarks still in evidence. The safety and extractor

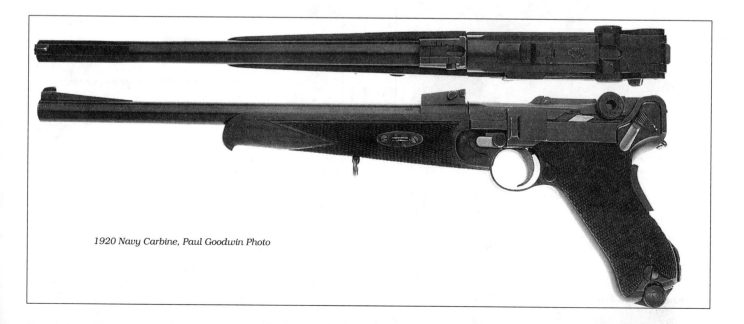

1920 Navy Carbine, Paul Goodwin Photo

are marked, and rarely one is found chambered for the 9mm cartridge. Few were manufactured.

Exc.	V.G.	Good	Fair	Poor
6250	5000	3000	1800	900

1923 Dutch Commercial & Military

Fitted with a 4" barrel, 9mm caliber. It has a stock lug, and the chamber area is blank. The extractor is marked in German, and the safety is marked "RUST" with a downward pointing arrow. This model was sold commercially and to the military in the Netherlands. There were approximately 1,000 manufactured in the one- to three-digit serial range, with no letter suffix.

Exc.	V.G.	Good	Fair	Poor
3200	2400	1000	850	550

Royal Dutch Air Force

Fitted with a 4" barrel, 9mm caliber. Marked with the Mauser Oberndorf proofmark and serial numbered in the 10000 to 14000 range. The safety marked "RUST."

Exc.	V.G.	Good	Fair	Poor
3500	2500	1000	800	550

VICKERS LTD.

1906 Vickers Dutch

Has a 4" barrel, 9mm caliber. There is no stock lug, and it uses a grip safety. The chamber is blank, and the extractor is marked "Geleden." "Vickers Ltd." is stamped on the front toggle link. The safety is marked "RUST" with an upward pointing arrow. Examples have been found with an additional date as late as 1933 stamped on the barrel. These dates indicate arsenal refinishing and in no way detract from the value of this variation. Arsenal reworks are matte finished, and the originals are a higher polished rust blue. There were approximately 10,000 manufactured in the 1-10100 serial number range.

Paul Goodwin Photo

Exc.	V.G.	Good	Fair	Poor
3500	2800	1800	1200	750

ERFURT ROYAL ARSENAL

1908 Erfurt

Has a 4" barrel, 9mm caliber. It has no stock lug, and the year of manufacture, from 1910-1913, is stamped above the chamber. The extractor and safety are both marked in German, and "ERFURT" under a crown is stamped on the front toggle link. There were many thousands produced as Germany was involved in WWI. They are found in the one- to five-digit serial range, sometimes with a letter suffix.

Exc.	V.G.	Good	Fair	Poor
1000	850	600	400	350

1914 Erfurt Military

Has a 4" barrel, 9mm caliber. It has a stock lug and the date of manufacture over the chamber, 1914-1918. The extractor and safety are both marked in German, and the front link is marked "ERFURT" under a crown. The finish on this model is rough; and as the war progressed in 1917 and 1918, the finish got worse. There were many thousands produced with one- to five-digit serial numbers, some with letter suffixes.

Courtesy Rock Island Auction Company

Exc.	V.G.	Good	Fair	Poor
1000	800	600	400	350

1914 Erfurt Artillery

Fitted with an 8" barrel, 9mm caliber. It has a stock lug and was issued with a flat board-type stock and other accessories, which will be covered in the section of this book dealing with same. The sight is a nine-position adjustable model. The chamber is dated 1914-1918, and the extractor and safety are both marked in German. "ERFURT" under a crown is stamped on the front toggle link. There were a great many manufactured with one- to five-digit serial numbers, some with a letter suffix. This model is similar to the DWM Artillery except that the finish is not as fine.

Paul Goodwin Photo

Exc.	V.G.	Good	Fair	Poor
2500	1600	1100	800	600

Double Date Erfurt

Has a 4" barrel, 9mm caliber. The area above the chamber has two dates: the original 1910-1918, and the date of rework, 1920 or 1921. The extractor and safety are both marked in

German, and this model can be found with or without a stock lug. "ERFURT" under a crown is stamped on the front toggle link. Police or military unit markings are found on the front of the grip straps more often than not. There were thousands of these produced by DWM as well as Erfurt.

Exc.	V.G.	Good	Fair	Poor
750	600	500	400	350

WAFFENFABRIK BERN

See *Swiss, Handguns, Bern*

SIMSON & CO.
SUHL, GERMANY

Simson & Co. Rework

Fitted with a 4" barrels, and chambered for either the 7.65 or 9mm caliber. The chamber is blank, but some examples are dated 1917 or 1918. The forward toggle link is stamped "SIMSON & CO. Suhl." The extractor and safety are marked in German. Most examples have stock lugs; some have been noted without them. The only difference between military models and commercial models is the proofmarks.

Exc.	V.G.	Good	Fair	Poor
1500	1200	900	600	500

Simson Dated Military

Has 4" barrel, 9mm caliber. There is a stock lug, and the year of manufacture from 1925-1928 is stamped above the chamber. The extractor and the safety are both marked in German. The checkered walnut grips of Simson-made Lugers are noticeably thicker than others. This is an extremely rare variation. Approximately 2,000 were manufactured with one- to three-digit serial numbers, and few seem to have survived.

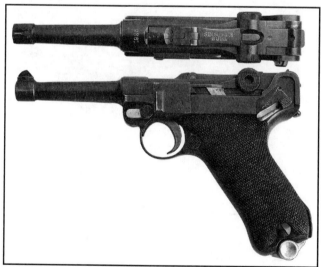

Paul Goodwin Photo

Exc.	V.G.	Good	Fair	Poor
3200	2200	1800	900	650

Simson S Code

Has a 4" barrel, 9mm caliber. The forward toggle link is stamped with a Gothic S. It has a stock lug, and the area above the chamber is blank. The extractor and the safety are both marked. The grips are also thicker. There were approximately 12,000 manufactured with one- to five-digit serial numbers—some with the letter "a" suffix. This pistol is quite rare on today's market.

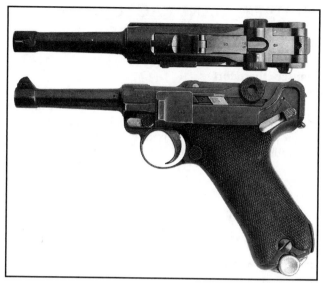

Paul Goodwin Photo

Exc.	V.G.	Good	Fair	Poor
4000	3000	1500	1000	750

EARLY NAZI ERA REWORKS MAUSER

Produced between 1930 and 1933, and normally marked with Waffenamt markings.

Deaths Head Rework

Has a 4" barrel, 9mm caliber. It has a stock lug; and a skull and crossbones are stamped, in addition to the date of manufacture, on the chamber area. This date was from 1914-1918. The extractor and safety are both marked. The Waffenamt proof is present. It is thought that this variation was produced for the 1930-1933 era "SS" division of the Nazi Party. Mixed serial numbers are encountered on this model and do not lower the value. This is a rare Luger on today's market, and caution should be exercised if purchase is contemplated.

Exc.	V.G.	Good	Fair	Poor
2500	1500	950	600	450

Kadetten Institute Rework

4" barrel, 9mm caliber. It has a stock lug, and the chamber area is stamped "K.I." above the date 1933. This stood for Cadets Institute, an early "SA" and "SS" officers' training school. The extractor and safety are both marked, and the Waffenamt is present. There were only a few hundred reworked, and the variation is quite scarce. Be wary of fakes.

Exc.	V.G.	Good	Fair	Poor
3200	2500	1100	800	600

Mauser Unmarked Rework

4" barrel, 9mm caliber. The entire weapon is void of identifying markings. There is extensive refurbishing, removal of all markings, rebarreling, etc. The stock lug is present, and the extractor and safety are marked. The Waffenamt proofmark is on the right side of the receiver. The number manufactured is not known.

Exc.	V.G.	Good	Fair	Poor
1450	1000	850	600	450

MAUSER MANUFACTURED LUGERS 1930-1942 DWM

Mauser Oberndorf

4" barrel, 9mm caliber. It has a stock lug, blank chamber area and a marked extractor and safety. This is an early example of Mauser Luger, and the front toggle link is still marked DWM as leftover parts were intermixed with new Mauser parts in the production of this pistol. This is one of the first Lugers to be finished with the "Salt" blue process. There were approximately 500 manufactured with one- to four-digit serial numbers with the letter "v" suffix. This is a rare variation.

Exc.	V.G.	Good	Fair	Poor
3800	3000	2000	1500	900

Courtesy Richard M. Kumor, Sr.

Exc.	V.G.	Good	Fair	Poor
4500	3500	2200	1200	1000

1935/06 Portuguese "GNR"

4.75" barrel, 7.65mm caliber. It has no stock lug but has a grip safety. The chamber is marked "GNR," representing the Republic National Guard. The extractor is marked "Carregada"; and the safety, "Seguranca." The Mauser banner is stamped on the front toggle link. There were exactly 564 manufactured according to the original contract records that the Portuguese government made public. They all have four-digit serial numbers with a "v" suffix.

S/42 G Date

As above, with the chamber stamped "G", the code for the year 1935. The Gothic lettering was eliminated, and there were many thousands of this model produced.

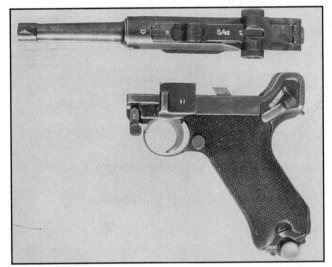

Courtesy Orvel Reichert

Paul Goodwin Photo

Exc.	V.G.	Good	Fair	Poor
3200	2700	1600	900	750

Exc.	V.G.	Good	Fair	Poor
1700	1250	900	650	450

S/42 K Date

4" barrel, 9mm caliber. It has a stock lug, and the extractor and safety are marked. This was the first Luger that utilized codes to represent maker and date of manufacture. The front toggle link is marked S/42 in either Gothic or script; this was the code for Mauser. The chamber area is stamped with the letter "K," the code for 1934, the year of manufacture. Approximately 10,500 were manufactured with one- to five-digit serial numbers—some with letter suffixes.

Dated Chamber S/42

4" barrel, 9mm caliber. The chamber area is dated 1936-1940, and there is a stock lug. The extractor and safety are marked. In 1937 the rust blue process was eliminated entirely, and all subsequent pistols were salt blued. There were many thousands manufactured with one- to five-digit serial numbers—some with the letter suffix.

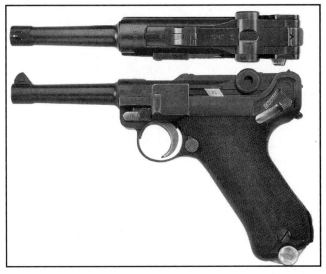

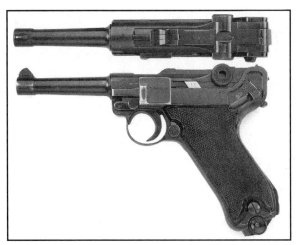

Paul Goodwin Photo

Exc.	V.G.	Good	Fair	Poor
1200	950	750	450	350

Persian Contract 4"

4" barrel, 9mm caliber. It has a stock lug, and the Persian crest is stamped over the chamber. All identifying markings on this variation—including extractor, safety and toggle—are marked in Farsi, the Persian alphabet. There were 1,000 manufactured. The serial numbers are also in Farsi.

Exc.	V.G.	Good	Fair	Poor
6500	5000	3500	2500	2000

Persian Contract Artillery

As above, with an 8" barrel and nine-position adjustable sight on the barrel. This model is supplied with a flat board stock. There were 1,000 manufactured and sold to Persia.

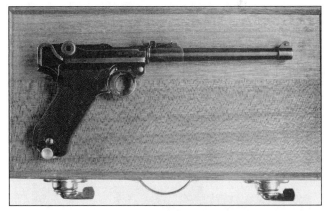

Courtesy Rock Island Auction Company

Exc.	V.G.	Good	Fair	Poor
3500	2850	1800	1300	1000

1934 Mauser Dutch Contract

4" barrel, 9mm caliber. The year of manufacture, 1936-1939, is stamped above the chamber. The extractor is marked "Geladen," and the safety is marked "RUST" with a downward pointing arrow. The Mauser banner is stamped on the front toggle link. Checkered walnut grips. This was a military contract sale, and approximately 1,000 were manufactured with four-digit serial numbers with a letter "v" suffix.

Paul Goodwin Photo

Exc.	V.G.	Good	Fair	Poor
1300	1100	750	500	400

NOTE: Rarest variation is early 1937 with rust blued and strawed parts, add 20%.

Code 42 Dated Chamber

4" barrel, 9mm caliber. The new German code for Mauser, the number 42, is stamped on the front toggle link. There is a stock lug. The chamber area is dated 1939 or 1940. There were at least 50,000 manufactured with one- to five-digit serial numbers—some have letter suffixes.

Exc.	V.G.	Good	Fair	Poor
1100	850	650	400	350

41/42 Code

As above, except that the date of manufacture is represented by the final two digits (e.g. 41 for 1941). There were approximately 20,000 manufactured with the one- to five-digit serial number range.

Exc.	V.G.	Good	Fair	Poor
1600	1350	900	700	500

byf Code

As above, with the "byf" code stamp on the toggle link. The year of manufacture, either 41 or 42, is stamped on the chamber. This model was also made with black plastic, as well as walnut grips. There were many thousands produced with the one- to five-digit serial numbers—some with a letter suffix.

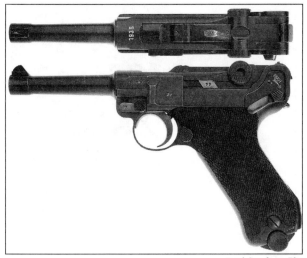

Paul Goodwin Photo

Exc.	V.G.	Good	Fair	Poor
3500	3000	2000	1100	850

1934 Mauser Swedish Contract

4.75" barrel, 9mm or 7.65mm caliber. The chamber is dated 1938 or 1939. The extractor and safety are both marked in German, and there is a stock lug. The front toggle link is stamped with the Mauser banner. There were only 275 dated 1938 and 25 dated 1939 in 9mm. There were only 30 chambered for 7.65mm dated 1939. The serial number range is four digits with the letter "v" suffix.

Exc.	V.G.	Good	Fair	Poor
3700	3000	2000	1500	700

1934 Mauser German Contract

4" barrel, 9mm caliber. The chamber is dated 1939-1942, and the front toggle link is stamped with the Mauser banner. There is a stock lug, and the extractor and safety are both marked. The grips are either walnut or black plastic. There were several thousand manufactured with one- to five-digit serial numbers—some with letter suffixes. They were purchased for issue to police or paramilitary units.

Exc.	V.G.	Good	Fair	Poor
2800	2300	1500	800	550

Austrian Bundes Heer (Federal Army)

4" barrel, 9mm caliber. The chamber is blank, and there is a stock lug. The extractor and safety are marked in German, and the Austrian federal army proof is stamped on the left side of the frame above the triggerguard. There were approximately 200 manufactured with four digit serial numbers and no letter suffix.

Exc.	V.G.	Good	Fair	Poor
2500	1850	1200	700	500

Mauser 2 Digit Date

4" barrel, 9mm caliber. The last two digits of the year of manufacture—41 or 42—are stamped over the chamber. There is a stock lug, and the Mauser banner is on the front toggle link. The extractor and safety are both marked, and the proofmarks were commercial. Grips are either walnut or black plastic. There were approximately 2,000 manufactured for sale to Nazi political groups. They have one- to five-digit serial numbers—some have the letter suffix.

Exc.	V.G.	Good	Fair	Poor
3000	1800	1200	900	550

KRIEGHOFF MANUFACTURED LUGERS

S Code Krieghoff

4" barrel, 9mm caliber. The Krieghoff trademark is stamped on the front toggle link, and the letter "S" is stamped over the chamber. There is a stock lug, and the extractor and safety are both marked. The grips are brown checkered plastic. There were approximately 4,500 manufactured for the Luftwaffe with one- to four-digit serial numbers.

Courtesy Rock Island Auction Company

Exc.	V.G.	Good	Fair	Poor
3750	3000	1800	950	750

Persian Contract 4", Paul Goodwin Photo

Grip Safety Krieghoff

4" barrel, 9mm caliber. The chamber area is blank, and the front toggle link is stamped with the Krieghoff trademark. There is a stock lug and a grip safety. The extractor is marked "Geleden," and the safety is marked "FEUER" (fire) in the lower position. The grips are checkered brown plastic. This is a rare Luger, and the number produced is not known.

Exc.	V.G.	Good	Fair	Poor
6000	4000	2800	1400	900

36 Date Krieghoff

4" barrel, 9mm caliber. It has a stock lug and the Krieghoff trademark on the front toggle link. The safety and extractor are marked, and the grips are brown plastic. The two-digit year of manufacture, 36, is stamped over the chamber. There were approximately 700 produced in the 3800-4500 serial number range.

Paul Goodwin Photo

Exc.	V.G.	Good	Fair	Poor
4500	3850	2200	1200	950

4 Digit Dated Krieghoff

As above, with the date of production, 1936-1945, stamped above the chamber. There were approximately 9,000 manufactured within the 4500-14000 serial number range.

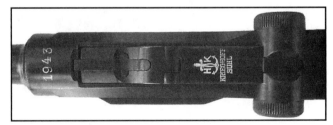

Courtesy Gale Morgan

Exc.	V.G.	Good	Fair	Poor
3750	3000	1850	950	750

LUGER ACCESSORIES

Detachable Carbine Stocks

Approximately 13" in length, with a sling swivel and horn buttplate.

Exc.	V.G.	Good	Fair	Poor
3600	2700	1500	700	500

Artillery Stock with Holster

The artillery stock is of a flat board-style approximately 13.75" in length. There is a holster and magazine pouches with straps attached. This is a desirable addition to the Artillery Luger.

Exc.	V.G.	Good	Fair	Poor
1200	850	500	400	300

Navy Stock without holster

As above, but 12.75" in length with a metal disc inlaid on the left side.

Exc.	V.G.	Good	Fair	Poor
1800	1400	850	500	400

NOTE: With holster add 100%.

Ideal Stock/Holster with Grips

A telescoping metal tube stock with an attached leather holster. It is used in conjunction with a metal-backed set of plain grips that correspond to the metal hooks on the stock and allow attachment. This Ideal Stock is U.S. patented and is so marked.

Exc.	V.G.	Good	Fair	Poor
2000	1400	1000	700	450

Drum Magazine 1st Issue

A 32-round, snail-like affair that is used with the Artillery Luger. It is also used with an adapter in the German 9mm submachine gun. The 1st Issue has a telescoping tube that is used to wind the spring. There is a dust cover that protects the interior from dirt.

Exc.	V.G.	Good	Fair	Poor
1000	800	600	350	300

Drum Magazine 2nd Issue

As above, with a folding spring winding lever.

Exc.	V.G.	Good	Fair	Poor
800	700	500	350	300

Drum Magazine Loading Tool

This tool is slipped over the magazine and allows the spring to be compressed so that cartridges could be inserted.

Exc.	V.G.	Good	Fair	Poor
600	550	500	300	200

Drum Magazine Unloading Tool

The origin of this tool is unknown and caution should be exercised prior to purchase.

Drum Carrying Case

The same caveat as above applies.

Exc.	V.G.	Good	Fair	Poor
250	200	125	100	50

Holsters

Produced in a wide variety of styles.

Exc.	V.G.	Good	Fair	Poor
350	275	150	60	50

LANGENHAN, FRIEDRICH

Langenhan Army Model

A blowback-operated semiautomatic pistol chambered for the 7.65mm Auto Pistol cartridge. It has a 4" barrel and a detachable magazine that holds 8 rounds. The pistol was made with a separate breechblock that is held into the slide by a screw. This feature doomed this pistol to eventual failure as when this screw became worn, it could loosen when firing and allow the breechblock to pivot upwards—and the slide would then be propelled rearward and into the face of the shooter. This is not a comforting thought. This pistol was produced and used in WWI only and was never offered commercially. It is marked "F.L. Selbstlade DRGM." The finish is blued, and the grips are molded rubber, with "F.L." at the top.

CAUTION: This is an unsafe weapon to fire.

Exc.	V.G.	Good	Fair	Poor
300	225	200	150	100

P-38

THE GERMAN WWII SERVICE PISTOL

Walther developed its German military service pistol, the P.38 or Model HP (Heerespistole), in 1937. It was adopted by the German military as its primary handgun in 1938. The background behind this adoption by the German military is an interesting one. In the 1930s, the German Army High Command wanted German arms manufacturers to develop a large caliber semiautomatic pistol to replace the Luger, which was difficult and costly to manufacture. The army wanted a pistol that was easy to manufacture as well as simple to assemble and disassemble. It also required a pistol that could be produced by several manufacturers if necessary and one whose parts would be interchangeable among manufacturers. Walther had just completed its Model HP for worldwide distribution and had the advantage over the other German companies. The German High Command approved Walther's design with only a few mechanical changes. This designation, the P.38, was not used by Walther on its commercial guns. Production began in late 1939 for both civilian and military use. Both military and commercial versions were produced throughout the war years. The civilian pistol was referred to as the MOD HP until late in the war, when a few were marked MOD P.38 to take advantage of the identity of the military pistol. In late 1942, Mauser and Spreewerke began production of the P.38. Mauser was assigned the code "BYF" and in 1945 the code was changed to "SVW." Spreewerke code was "CYQ." Late in the war the die stamp broke and the code appears as "CVQ."

The P.38 is a double action semiautomatic pistol that is short recoil operated and fires from a locked breech by means of an external hammer. It is chambered for the 9mm Parabellum and has a 5" barrel. The detachable magazine holds 8 cartridges and the front sight is adjustable for windage. Initially the finish was a high quality blue, but when the war effort increased less time was spent on the finish. The P.38 was equipped with two styles of plastic grips. Early pistols have a checkered grip and later grips are the military ribbed variety; the later style is much more common. The P.38 was produced by three companies and each had its own distinct markings and variations as outlined below. Despite the large number of variations that the P.38 collector will encounter, it is important for him to be aware that there are no known documented examples of P.38s that are factory engraved, nickel-plated, have barrels that are longer or shorter than standard, or built as military presentation pistols.

Collectors should be made aware of a final note. The P.38 pistol was first adopted over 50 years ago. During that period of time the pistol has seen use all over the world. After the end of WWI several governments came into possession of fairly large quantities of P.38s and used them in their own military and police agencies. Many countries have reworked these older P.38s with both original and new component parts. The former U.S.S.R. is the primary source of reworked P.38s. Many of these pistols have been completely refinished and reproofed by a number of countries. The collector should be aware of the existence of reworked P.38s and examine closely any P.38 carefully to determine if the pistol is original German military issue. These reworked pistols bring substantially lower prices than original P.38s.

NOTE: As of 1997 the Ukraine is now the primary source of pistols. Almost all are importer marked and have been cold dipped blued. Some are reworked and others are original except for the finish.

WALTHER COMMERCIAL

The Commercial version of the P.38 is identified by commercial proofmarks of a crown over N or an eagle over N. Production started at around serial number 1000 and went through serial number 26659. This was the first of the commercial pistols and was a high-quality, well made gun with a complete inscription on the left slide. A few of these early pistols were equipped with checkered wooden grips. The quality decreased as the war progressed. There are many variations of these commercial models and values can vary from $1,000 to $16,000. It is suggested that these pistols be appraised and evaluated by an expert. For postwar Walther P.38 pistols see the Walther section.

A few of the Walther Commercial Model variations are listed below:

MOD HP-Early w/High Gloss Blue

Courtesy Orvel Reichert

Exc.	V.G.	Good	Fair	Poor
2500	1750	1000	700	400

MOD HP-Early w/High Gloss Blue & Alloy Frame

Exc.	V.G.	Good	Fair	Poor
7500	5000	3500	2000	1000

MOD HP-Late w/Military Blue Finish

Exc.	V.G.	Good	Fair	Poor
1700	1400	1000	650	350

NOTE: Add $200 for "Eagle/359" on right side.

MOD P38-Late with Military Blue (1800 produced)

Exc.	V.G.	Good	Fair	Poor
2250	1700	1000	700	400

WALTHER MILITARY

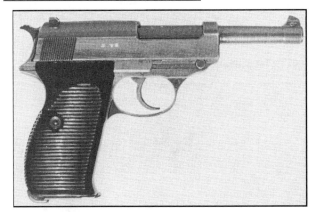

Courtesy Orvel Reichert

Courtesy Orvel Reichert

ZERO SERIES

This was the first of the military P.38s and they are well made with a high polish finish. These pistols have the Walther banner and the designation P.38. The serial number began with 01 and went through about 013714. The First Zero Series has a concealed extractor and rectangular firing pin. About 1,000 First Zero Series were built. The Second Zero Series has a rectangular firing pin and standard extractor, with a production of about 2,300. The Third Zero Series has a standard firing pin and standard extractor and has the highest production with 10,000 built.

Courtesy Orvel Reichert

First Issue Zero Series

Exc.	V.G.	Good	Fair	Poor
7500	5000	3500	2500	1500

Second Issue Zero Series

Exc.	V.G.	Good	Fair	Poor
6500	4000	3250	2000	1000

Third Issue Zero Series

Exc.	V.G.	Good	Fair	Poor
2500	1750	1250	800	500

480 CODE

This code was utilized by Walther in late 1940 and represents the first true military contract pistols. There were approximately 7,250 guns produced under this code. There are two subvariations: one with a round lanyard loop and the other with a rectangular lanyard loop.

Courtesy Orvel Reichert

Exc.	V.G.	Good	Fair	Poor
5000	3500	2500	1750	1000

"AC" CODES

This variation follows the 480 code.

"ac" (no date)

This variation has on the slide "P.38ac" then the serial number only. This is the first use of the "ac" code by Walther. There were approximately 2,700 pistols produced with this code and is the rarest of all military P.38s.

Courtesy Orvel Reichert

Courtesy Orvel Reichert

Exc.	V.G.	Good	Fair	Poor
7500	4800	3750	2800	2000

"ac40"

There are two types of "ac40s." The first variation is the ac with the 40 added, that is the 40 was hand stamped below the ac. There are about 6,000 of these produced. The second variation is the ac40 rolled on together. There are also about 14,000 of these produced as well. The "ac" 40 added is more valuable than the standard "ac40."

"ac40" (added)

Courtesy Orvel Reichert

Exc.	V.G.	Good	Fair	Poor
3500	2500	1750	1000	600

"ac40" (standard)

Courtesy Orvel Reichert

Exc.	V.G.	Good	Fair	Poor
2000	1200	950	700	500

"ac41"

There are three variations of the "ac41." The first variation has "ac" on left triggerguard and features a high gloss blue. About 25,000 of this variation were made. The second variation, about 70,000 were produced, also has a high gloss blue but does not have "ac" on the triggerguard. The third variation features a military blue rather than a high gloss blue and had a production run of about 15,000 pistols.

"ac41" (1st variation)

Courtesy Orvel Reichert

Exc.	V.G.	Good	Fair	Poor
1600	900	700	500	350

"ac41" (2nd variation)

Exc.	V.G.	Good	Fair	Poor
1250	750	600	450	300

Courtesy Orvel Reichert

"ac41" (3rd variation)

Exc.	V.G.	Good	Fair	Poor
1000	550	475	400	300

"ac42"

There are two variations of the "ac42" code. The first has an eagle over 359 stamped on all small parts as do all preceding variations and a production of 21,000 pistols. The second variation does not have the eagle over 359 stamped on small parts. This second variation has a large production run of 100,000 pistols.

Courtesy Orvel Reichert

Courtesy Orvel Reichert

"ac42" (1st variation)

Exc.	V.G.	Good	Fair	Poor
900	450	400	350	275

"ac42" (2nd variation)

Exc.	V.G.	Good	Fair	Poor
800	500	400	300	250

"ac43"

This code has three variations. The first is a standard date with "ac" over 43. It has an early frame and extractor cut. The second variation has the late frame and extractor cut. Both variations are frequently encountered because approximately 130,000 were built.

"ac43" (1st variation)

Courtesy Orvel Reichert

Exc.	V.G.	Good	Fair	Poor
650	400	300	250	200

"ac43" (2nd variation)

Exc.	V.G.	Good	Fair	Poor
550	350	300	250	200

"ac43" single line slide

This variation represents the beginning of the placement of the date on the same line with the production code. There were approximately 20,000 built in this variation.

Courtesy Orvel Reichert

Exc.	V.G.	Good	Fair	Poor
750	550	450	350	250

"ac44"

This variation also has the date stamped beside "ac" and is fairly common. About 120,000 were produced.

Courtesy Orvel Reichert

Exc.	V.G.	Good	Fair	Poor
600	400	300	250	200

Note: Add $50 for FN frame (Eagle/140).

"ac45"

This code has three variations. The first has all matching numbers on a plum colored frame. About 32,000 of this first variation were produced. The second variation has a capital "A" in place of the lowercase "a." The third variation has all major parts with factory mismatched numbers, with a single eagle over 359 on the slide. The first variation is the most common of this code.

"ac45" (1st variation)

Exc.	V.G.	Good	Fair	Poor
600	400	325	300	250

"ac45" (2nd variation)

Courtesy Orvel Reichert

Exc.	V.G.	Good	Fair	Poor
700	400	325	300	250

"ac45" (3rd variation)

Exc.	V.G.	Good	Fair	Poor
500	350	325	300	250

Note: Add $50 for pistols with Czech barrels; barrel code "fnh."

"ac45" Zero Series

This is a continuation of the commercial pistols with a military marked slide. This series has "ac45" plus the 0 prefix serial number on the left side as well as the usual P-38 roll stamp. It may or may not have commercial proofmarks. A total of 1,800 of these "ac45" Zero Series guns were produced in 1945. They are often seen with a plum colored slide.

Exc.	V.G.	Good	Fair	Poor
1500	900	700	450	325

MAUSER MILITARY

The following P.38s were produced by Mauser and are identified by various Mauser codes.

Courtesy Orvel Reichert

Courtesy Orvel Reichert

"byf42"

Approximately 19,000 P.38s were manufactured in this variation. Some of these pistols will have a flat blue finish.

Courtesy Orvel Reichert

Exc.	V.G.	Good	Fair	Poor
1400	950	700	500	300

"byf43"

A common variation of the P.38 with approximately 140,000 produced.

Courtesy Orvel Reichert

Exc.	V.G.	Good	Fair	Poor
650	400	300	250	200

"byf44"

Another common variation with a total production of about 150,000 guns.

Courtesy Orvel Reichert

Exc.	V.G.	Good	Fair	Poor
650	400	300	250	200

Note: Add $100 for dual tone finish that is a combination of blue and gray components.

AC43/44-FN slide
Exc.	V.G.	Good	Fair	Poor
1400	950	725	600	450

"svw45"

The Mauser code is changed from "byf" to "svw." This variation was produced until the end of the war when France took over production and continued through 1946. French-produced guns will have a 5-point star on the right side of the slide. A large number of these French pistols have been imported thereby depressing values.

"svw45"-German Proofed

Courtesy Orvel Reichert

Exc.	V.G.	Good	Fair	Poor
1500	900	650	450	300

"svw45"-French Proofed

Courtesy Orvel Reichert

Exc.	V.G.	Good	Fair	Poor
400	300	275	250	200

"svw46"-French Proofed

Courtesy Orvel Reichert

Exc.	V.G.	Good	Fair	Poor
500	450	400	350	300

MAUSER "POLICE" P.38

Mauser produced the only Nazi era Police P38 during the 1943 to 1945 period. It is generally believed that only 8,000 guns were serially produced although a few "oddballs" show up beyond that range.

Police guns are easily recognized by the appearance of a commercial proof (eagle over N) instead of the Military proof (eagle over swastika). They also have a civilian (Police) acceptance stamp (either an Eagle L or Eagle F).

The guns will have a stacked code with date below the code. Earliest guns were coded "byf" over 43 and later, "byf" over 44. In the late 1944 production, a group of slides manufactured for Walther at the FN plant in Belgium were received and used. These slides all have the "ac" over 43 or "ac" over 44 code. Finally, in 1945, a few "svw" over 45 coded guns were made. These Walther coded slides are hard to find....the 1945 guns are *quite* rare.

Because of the increased value of these guns, it is wise to have them examined by an expert before purchasing.

"byf/43"

Exc.	V.G.	Good	Fair	Poor
2200	1500	1200	800	500

"byf/44"

Exc.	V.G.	Good	Fair	Poor
2200	1500	1200	800	500

"ac/43"

Exc.	V.G.	Good	Fair	Poor
4000	3000	2000	1250	800

"ac/44"

Exc.	V.G.	Good	Fair	Poor
4000	3000	2000	1250	800

"svw/45"

Exc.	V.G.	Good	Fair	Poor
5200	4000	2250	1600	1000

SPREEWERKE MILITARY

Production of the P.38 began at Spreewerke (Berlin) in late 1942 and Spreewerke used the code "cyq" that had been assigned to it at the beginning of the war.

"cyq" (1st variation)

The first 500 of these guns have the eagle over 359 on some small parts and command a premium. Value depends on markings and an expert should be consulted for values.

Courtesy Orvel Reichert

Exc.	V.G.	Good	Fair	Poor
1250	950	750	600	500

"cyq" (standard variation)

There were approximately 300,000 of these pistols produced in this variation which makes them the most common of all P.38 variations.

Courtesy Orvel Reichert

Exc.	V.G.	Good	Fair	Poor
500	300	275	250	200

Note: If "A" or "B" prefix add $250.

A "cyq" series with an "A" prefix serial number.

Courtesy Orvel Reichert

"cyq" Zero Series

This variation features a Zero ahead of the serial number and only about 5,000 of these guns were produced.

Courtesy Orvel Reichert

Exc.	V.G.	Good	Fair	Poor
1000	500	400	350	275

NOTE: Add $250 for AC43 or AC44 marked "FN" slide.

MAUSER POCKET PISTOLS

Bibliographical Note: For historical information, technical data, and photos see Roy Pender, III, *Mauser Pocket Pistols, 1910-1946*, Houston, 1971.

Model 1914

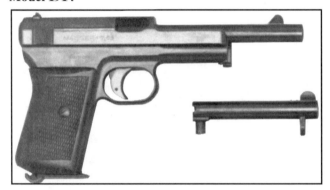

Courtesy Butterfield & Butterfield, San Francisco, California

A 7.65mm caliber semiautomatic pistol with a 3.5" barrel, fixed sights, and wrap-around walnut grips. The slide marked "Waffenfabrik Mauser A.G. Oberndorf A.N. Mauser's Patent" on the slide. The frame has the Mauser banner stamped on its left side. Manufactured between 1914 and 1934. Almost all model 1914 pistols built between serial numbers 40,000 and 180,000 will be seen with German military acceptance stamps. A few will have the Prussian Eagle stamped on the front of the triggerguard.

Courtesy Wallis & Wallis, Lewes, Sussex, England

Exc.	V.G.	Good	Fair	Poor
450	300	225	150	100

Model 1934

Similar to the Model 1910 and Model 1914, with the slide marked "Mauser-Werke A.G. Oberndorf A. N." It has the Mauser banner stamped on the frame. The reverse side is marked with the caliber and "D.R.P. u A.P." Manufactured between 1934 and 1939. Those with Nazi Waffenamt markings are worth approximately 20 percent more than the values listed below. Those marked with an eagle over the letter "M" (Navy marked) are worth approximately 100% more than the values listed below.

Courtesy Orvel Reichert

Courtesy Orvel Reichert

Courtesy Gale Morgan

Exc.	V.G.	Good	Fair	Poor
525	400	300	150	100

Model HSC

A 7.65mm or 9mm short caliber double action semiautomatic pistol with a 3.4" barrel, 7- or 8-shot magazine and fixed sights. Introduced in 1938 and produced in the variations listed below.

Courtesy Orvel Reichert

Low Grip Screw Model

As above, with screws that attach the grip located near the bottom of the grip. Highly-polished blue, checkered walnut grips and the early address without the lines and has the Eagle N proof. Some have been observed with Nazi Kreigsmarine markings. Approximately 2,000 were manufactured.

Exc.	V.G.	Good	Fair	Poor
3500	2500	1400	750	650

Early Commercial Model

A highly-polished blued finish, checkered walnut grips, the standard Mauser address on the slide, and the Eagle N proofmark. The floorplate of the magazine stamped with the Mauser banner.

Exc.	V.G.	Good	Fair	Poor
650	500	350	175	125

Transition Model

As above, but not as highly finished.

Exc.	V.G.	Good	Fair	Poor
525	400	300	150	100

Early Nazi Army Model

Highly polished with Waffenamt No. 135 or 655 markings. Checkered walnut grips. Acceptance marks are located on the left side of the triggerguard.

Courtesy Orvel Reichert

Exc.	V.G.	Good	Fair	Poor
650	550	400	200	125

Late Nazi Army Model

Blued or parkerized, with walnut or plastic grips, and the 135 acceptance mark only. It also has the Eagle N proof.

Exc.	V.G.	Good	Fair	Poor
450	375	250	150	100

Early Nazi Navy Model

Highly polished with checkered walnut grips and the eagle over "M" marking on the front grip strap.

Exc.	V.G.	Good	Fair	Poor
1000	800	550	400	300

Wartime Nazi Navy Model

Similar to the above, with the navy acceptance mark on the side of the triggerguard. Blued, with either checkered walnut or plastic grips. It has the standard Mauser address and banner and also the Eagle N proof.

Exc.	V.G.	Good	Fair	Poor
700	600	500	400	200

Early Nazi Police Model

Identical to the Early Commercial Model with an eagle over "L" mark on the left side of the triggerguard.

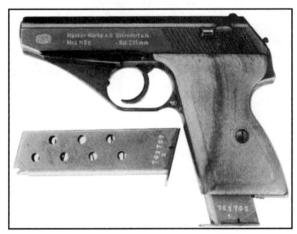

Courtesy Orvel Reichert

Exc.	V.G.	Good	Fair	Poor
600	500	425	250	175

Wartime Nazi Police Model

As above, with a three line Mauser address.

Exc.	V.G.	Good	Fair	Poor
500	400	350	250	175

Wartime Commercial Model

As above, without acceptance markings on the triggerguard.

Exc.	V.G.	Good	Fair	Poor
425	350	300	200	125

French Manufactured Model

Blued or parkerized with walnut or plastic grips and the triggerguard marked on the left side with the monogram "MR."

Exc.	V.G.	Good	Fair	Poor
325	275	225	150	100

SAUER, J. P. & SON

Bibliographical Note: For historical information, technical data and photos see Jim Cate's.

Text and prices by Jim Cate

SAUER MODEL 1913

FIRST SERIES, which incorporates an extra safety button on the left side of the frame near the trigger and the rear sight is simply a milled recess in the cocking knob itself. The serial number range runs from 1 to approximately 4750 and this first series is found only in 7.65mm caliber. All were for commercial sales as far as can be determined. Some were tested by various militaries, no doubt.

A. European variation—all slide legends are in the German language.

B. English Export variation—slide legends are marked, J.P. Sauer & Son, Suhl - Prussia, "Sauer's Patent" Pat'd May 20 1912.

Both were sold in thick paper cartons or boxes with the color being a reddish purple with gold colored letters, etc. Examples of the very early European variation are found with the English language brochure or manual as well as an extra magazine, cleaning brush and grease container. These were shipped to England or the U.S. prior to Sauer producing the English Export variation.

A. European variation:

Exc.	V.G.	Good	Fair	Poor
1100	900	650	400	250

B. English Export variation:

Exc.	V.G.	Good	Fair	Poor
1450	1150	800	500	300

Original box with accessories and manual: Add $500 if complete and in very good to excellent condition.

SECOND SERIES, extra safety button eliminated, rear sight acts as cocking knob retainer.

A. Commercial variation

Normal European/German slide markings are normally found; however it has been called to my attention that there are English Export pistols in this **SECOND SERIES** which have the English markings on the slide which are similar to those found on the **FIRST SERIES** of the Model 1913. This is applicable to both the 7.65mm and 6.35mm model pistols. These are exceptional scarce pistols and should command at least a 50% premium, perhaps more due to their rarity. This commercial variation had factory manuals printed in English, Spanish and German which came with the cardboard boxed pistols. With the original Sauer box accessories and manual: Add $300 if in very good to excellent condition.

Caliber 7.65mm variation

Exc.	V.G.	Good	Fair	Poor
450	375	300	250	100

Caliber 7.65 variation with all words in English (i.e Son, Prussia, etc.)

Exc.	V.G.	Good	Fair	Poor
700	575	450	300	200

Caliber 6.35mm variation

This particular pistol must be divided into three (3) subvariations.

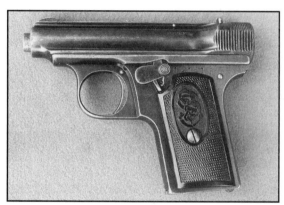

This variation appears to be in a serial number range of its own. The first subvariation appears to run from 1 to 40,000. It is highly doubtful if this quantity was manufactured. The second subvariation incorporates a Zusatzsicherung or Additional Safety which can be seen between the normal safety lever and the top of the left grip. It locked the trigger bar when in use. This second range appears to run from approximately serial number 40,000 to 51,000 which probably was continuous in the number produced. Lastly, the third subvariation examples were manufactured during or after 1926. The triggerguard has a different shape; the slide has a greater area of vertical milled finger grooves; the added Additional safety (Zusatzsicherung) now acts as the hold open device as well. These are found up to approximately 57,000. Then a few examples of the first subvariation are found from 57,000 up to about 62,500. This was, no doubt, usage of remaining parts.

Caliber 6.35mm first subvariation:

Exc.	V.G.	Good	Fair	Poor
350	300	250	150	75

Caliber 6.35mm second subvariation:

Exc.	V.G.	Good	Fair	Poor
350	300	250	150	75

Caliber 6.35mm third subvariation:

Exc.	V.G.	Good	Fair	Poor
450	375	300	200	100

Caliber 6.35mm English export variation (all words in English; i.e. Son, Prussia, etc.) Very Rare, only one example known.

Exc.	V.G.	Good	Fair	Poor
850	700	500	300	200

Please note that any commercial pistol could be special ordered with a factory nickel finish, special grip material (pearl, wood, etc.) as well as different types of engraving. It would be in your best interest to have these pistols examined by an expert.

B. Police variations

These will be of the standard German Commercial configuration but nearly always having the Zusatzsicherung (additional safety) added to the pistol. This safety is found between the regular safety lever and the top of the left grip. Police used both calibers, 7.65mm and 6.35mm but the 7.65 was predominant. After the early part of the 1930s the 6.35 was not available to police departments. Thus the 6.35mm police marked Sauer is rather scarce in relation to the 7.65mm caliber. A few in 7.65mm are dated 1920 on the left side of the frame and were used by auxiliary policemen in Bavaria. Normal police property markings are on the front or rear gripstraps. Most were originally issued with at least two magazines and a police accepted holster. The mags were usually numbered and the holsters are found with and without pistol numbers.

Caliber 6.35mm police marked but without Zusatzsicherung

Exc.	V.G.	Good	Fair	Poor
400	350	275	200	75

Caliber 6.35mm police marked with Zusatzsicherung

Exc.	V.G.	Good	Fair	Poor
450	375	275	200	75

Caliber 7.65mm police marked without Zusatzsicherung

Exc.	V.G.	Good	Fair	Poor
375	325	275	175	125

Caliber 7.65mm police marked with Zusatzsicherung

Exc.	V.G.	Good	Fair	Poor
400	350	275	175	125

NOTE: Add 10% for one correctly numbered magazine, or 20% if found with both correctly numbered magazines. Add 30% if found with correct holster and magazines.

C.R.F.V. (Reich Finanz Verwaltung)

This Sauer variation is rarely found in any condition. The R.F.V. markings and property number could be 1 to 4 digits. This variation is found in both calibers and were used by the Reich's Customs and Finance department personnel.

Caliber 6.35mm R.F.V. marked pistols

Exc.	V.G.	Good	Fair	Poor
800	650	500	350	250

Caliber 7.65mm R.F.V. marked pistols

Exc.	V.G.	Good	Fair	Poor
750	600	400	300	200

D. Imperial Military variations

These were normal German commercial variations of the time period having either the Imperial Eagle acceptance marking applied on the front of the triggerguard and having the small Imperial Army inspector's acceptance marking (crown over a scriptic letter) on the right side of the frame close to the Nitro proof; or having just the Imperial Army inspector's marking alone. Usually these pistols are found in the 40,000 to 85,000 range. However, the quantity actually Imperial Military accepted is quite low even though thousands were privately purchased by the officer corps. There are examples in 6.35mm which are Imperial Military accepted but these are very scarce.

Caliber 7.65mm Imperial Military accepted pistols

Exc.	V.G.	Good	Fair	Poor
550	450	350	275	150

Caliber 6.35mm Imperial Military accepted pistols

Exc.	V.G.	Good	Fair	Poor
700	500	375	300	150

E. Paramilitary marked Sauer pistols, of the 1925-35 period

A very few of the Model 1913 pistols will have been marked by paramilitary groups or organizations of this period. Usually this marking is no more than a series of numbers above another series of numbers, such as 23 over 12. These are found usually on the left side of the frame next to the left grip. Most of these numbers are indicative of property numbers assigned to a particular pistols belonging to a particular SA Group, Stahlhelm, or a right-wing organization such as the Red Front (early communist). Any pistol of this type should be examined by an expert to determine if it is an original example.

Exc,	V.G.	Good	Fair	Poor
350	300	275	200	100

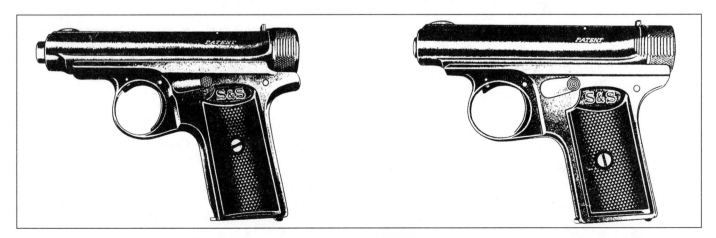

F. Norwegian police usage, post World War II

After the war was over many surplus German weapons were put back into use by the government of Norway. The Germans had occupied this country and large numbers of weapons remained when the fighting ended. This included a large number of surplus Sauer pistols being utilized by the police (POLITI) forces. Most of the Sauers that were used by the Politi which have been imported into the U.S. have been the Model 1913; however there were a number of the Model 1930 pistols which reached our country as well. All examples, regardless of the model, have the word POLITI stamped on the slide as well as a rampant lion on a shield under a crown marking. Following this is the property number and this number is also stamped into the left side of the frame. Most saw much usage during the postwar period. All are in 7.65mm caliber.

Exc.	V.G.	Good	Fair	Poor
350	300	200	150	100

MODEL 38 AND 38-H (H MODEL) VARIATIONS

A. MODEL 38

This pistol started at 260,000. It is Crown N Nitro proofed, has a cocking/decocking lever, and a loaded indicator pin, and is double action. It has a high polish blue; is in 7.65mm (the standard production pistol); is found without the thumbsafety on the slide; with a pinned mag release. VERY RARE.

1. One Line Slide Legend variation (about 250 produced)

Exc.	V.G.	Good	Fair	Poor
2500	1600	1200	600	300

2. Two Line Slide Legend variation C/N proofs, blued, with pinned magazine release, (about 850 produced) VERY RARE

Exc.	V.G.	Good	Fair	Poor
1850	1400	1000	500	275

3. Two Line Slide Legend variation C/N proofs, blued, magazine release button retained by a screw. RARE

Exc.	V.G.	Good	Fair	Poor
1000	850	600	400	275

NOTE: Add $250 for factory nickel; $350 for factory chrome; $1000 for engraving; $500 for NIROSTA marked barrel.

4. SA der NSDAP Gruppe Thuringen marked variation blued, C/N proofs, with mag release button held by a screw, VERY RARE

Exc.	V.G.	Good	Fair	Poor
3000	2000	1000	500	275

B. MODEL 38-H or H MODEL

This model has a thumbsafety on the slide, Crown N Nitro proof, high polish blued finish, a cocking/decocking lever, double action, and is found in 7.65mm caliber as the standard production pistol. This model is found only with the two line slide legend or logo. Type 1, variation 2.

1. Standard Commercial variation as described above:

Exc.	V.G.	Good	Fair	Poor
850	700	475	300	175

NOTE: Add $100 for factory nickel (factory chromed has not been identified); $1000 for factory engraving; $250 for exotic grip material; $500 for NIROSTA marked stainless barrel.

2. SA der NSDAP Gruppe Thuringia variation

Same as 1 above except having SA markings on slide, with blued finish, VERY RARE.

Exc.	V.G.	Good	Fair	Poor
2500	1800	600	350	200

NOTE: Add $700 for SA marked ankle holster in excellent condition.

3. L.M. MODEL

(Leicht Model–lightweight model); frame and slide made of DURAL (Duraluminum), in the 264800 range, with thumb safety, and regular black bakelite grips. EXTREMELY RARE.

Exc.	V.G.	Good	Fair	Poor
3850	3250	2500	1500	850

4. Police accepted variation; found with Police Eagle C acceptance on left triggerguard and having Crown N proofs. RARE.

Exc.	V.G.	Good	Fair	Poor
850	700	500	300	175

TYPE TWO MODEL 38-H (H MODEL)

There are no Model 38 pistols in the Type Two description, only the H Model with thumbsafety. These begin at serial number 269100 and have the Eagle N Nitro proofs, with a blued high polish finish and black bakelite grips. The normal caliber is 7.65mm.

A. H Model

1. Standard Commercial

Exc.	V.G.	Good	Fair	Poor
750	550	475	300	200

NOTE: Add $1500 for boxed examples complete with factory manual, clean ring rod, all accessories, extra magazine, etc. $250 for factory nickel, $350 for factory chrome, $1000 for factory engraving.

2. .22 Caliber variation, found in 269900 range

Slide and magazines are marked CAL. .22 LANG. (Some with steel frame and slides; some with Dural frames and slides). VERY RARE.

Exc.	V.G.	Good	Fair	Poor
2500	1800	1000	400	250

3. Jager Model

A special order pistol in .22 caliber which is similar in appearance to Walther's 1936 Jagerschafts pistol. VERY RARE, and watch for fakes.

Exc.	V.G.	Good	Fair	Poor
2500	1850	1200	600	250

4. Police Eagle C and Eagle F acceptance variations

These are the first Eagle N (post January 1940) police accepted pistols are found in the 270000 to 276000 ranges. (Add 25% for E/F).

Exc.	V.G.	Good	Fair	Poor
650	500	400	325	200

5. German Military variation

This is the first official military accepted range of 2000 pistols. It is in a TEST range found between 271000 to 273000. Two Eagle 37 military acceptance marks are found on the triggerguard.

Exc.	V.G.	Good	Fair	Poor
1200	900	675	475	300

6. Second Military variation

These pistols are found with the high polish finish but have only one Eagle 37 acceptance marks. The letter H is found on all small parts.

Exc.	V.G.	Good	Fair	Poor
600	425	350	275	175

7. Police Eagle C acceptance.

This variation includes the remainder of the high polish blued police accepted pistols.

Exc.	V.G.	Good	Fair	Poor
575	425	350	275	175

NOTE: Add $50 for matching magazine, $200 for both matching mags and correct police holster; $300 for both

matching mags and correct matching numbered, police accepted & dated holster.

TYPE THREE 38-H MODEL (H MODEL)

This terminology is used because of the change of the exterior finish of the Sauer pistols. Due to the urgency of the war, the order was received to not polish the exterior surfaces of the pistols as had been done previously. There was also a change in the formulation of the grip's material. Later in this range there will be found stamped parts, zinc triggers and magazine bottoms, etc. used to increase the pistol's production. Type Three has a full slide legend.

A. H Model

1. Military accepted with one Eagle 37 Waffenamt mark

Exc.	V.G.	Good	Fair	Poor
500	450	350	275	150

2. Commercial, having only Eagle N Nitro proof marks

Exc.	V.G.	Good	Fair	Poor
450	400	350	250	150

NOTE: See Type Two Commercial info above, prices apply here also.

3. Police accepted with the Police Eagle C acceptance

Exc.	V.G.	Good	Fair	Poor
500	425	350	250	150

NOTE: See Type Two Police info above, prices apply here also.

TYPE FOUR 38-H MODEL (H MODEL)

This is a continuation of the pistol as described in Type Three except the J.P. Sauer & Sohn, Suhl legend is dropped from the slide and only CAL. 7.65 is found on the left side. The word PATENT may or may not appear on the right side. Many are found with a zinc trigger.

A. H Model

1. Military accepted with one Eagle 37 Waffenamt mark

Exc.	V.G.	Good	Fair	Poor
500	450	350	275	150

2. Commercial, having only the Eagle N Nitro proofs

Exc.	V.G.	Good	Fair	Poor
450	400	350	250	150

NOTE: See Type Two Commercial info above, prices apply here also.

3. Police accepted with the Police Eagle C acceptance

Exc.	V.G.	Good	Fair	Poor
500	450	350	275	150

NOTE: See Type Two price info above, prices apply here also.

4. Eigentum NSDAP SA Gruppe Alpenland slide marked pistols

These unique pistols are found in the 456000 and 457000 serial number ranges. They have thumbsafety levers on the slides.

Exc.	V.G.	Good	Fair	Poor
2800	1800	1000	450	250

5. NSDAP SA Gruppe Alpenland slide marked pistols

These unique pistols are found in the 465000 serial number range. They have thumb safety levers on the slide.

Exc.	V.G.	Good	Fair	Poor
2800	1800	1000	450	250

6. H. HIMMLER PRESENTATION PISTOLS

These desirable pistols have a high polish finish with DEM SCHARFSCHUTZEN - H. HIMMLER on the left side of the slide (with no other markings), and J.P. SAUER & SOHN over CAL.7.65 on the right side (opposite of normal). These pistols came in imitation leather cover metal cases with cloth interiors having a cleaning brush, extra magazine and cartridges.

Exc.	V.G.	Good	Fair	Poor
15000	12000	8500	3500	1000

B. MODEL 38

To speed up production even more, the thumbsafety (Hand-sicherung-Hammer safety) was eliminated. The side continues to be marked only with CAL. 7.65. The frame's serial number changes from the right side to the left side at 472000 with overlaps up to 489000.

1. Military accepted with one Eagle 37 Waffenamt mark

Exc.	V.G.	Good	Fair	Poor
450	400	350	250	175

2. Commercial, having only the Eagle N Nitro proofs

Exc.	V.G.	Good	Fair	Poor
450	400	350	250	175

NOTE: See Type Two Commercial info above, prices apply here also.

3. Police accepted with the Police Eagle C acceptance

Exc.	V.G.	Good	Fair	Poor
575	450	400	300	200

4. Police accepted with the Police Eagle F acceptance

Exc.	V.G.	Good	Fair	Poor
475	400	350	250	175

NOTE: (3&4) See Type Two Police info above, prices apply here also.

TYPE FIVE MODEL 38 & H MODEL PISTOLS

There are two different basic variations of the Type Five Sauer pistols. Either may or may not have a thumb safety lever on the slide. The main criteria is whether the frame is factory numbered as per normal and follows the chronological sequence of those pistols in the preceding model. After the frames were used, which were already numbered and finished upon the arrival of the U.S. army, the last variation came about. Neither variation has any Nitro proof marks.

A. First variation

Factory numbered sequential frames starting on or near serial number 506800. Slides and breech blocks may or may not match.

Exc.	V.G.	Good	Fair	Poor
475	350	275	225	100

B. Second variation

Started with serial number 1; made from mostly rejected parts, generally have notched triggerguards, may or may not be blued, no Nitro proofs, slides may or may not have factory legends, etc. Approximately 300 assembled.

Exc.	V.G.	Good	Fair	Poor
750	500	300	200	100

NOTE: There are some pistols which have postwar Russian Crown N Nitro proofs. The Russians may have assembled a very few pistols after the U.S. army left this section after the war. Several have been found with newly made barrels in 7.65mm with a C/N proof.

WALTHER

Bibliographical Note: For technical details, historical information, and photos see James Rankin, *Walther*, Volumes I, II, and III, 1974-1981.

Model 6

A 9mm semiautomatic pistol. The largest of the Walther numbered pistols. Approximately 1,500 manufactured. Blued with checkered hard rubber grips with the Walther logo on each grip. Sometimes seen with plain checkered wood grips. Introduced 1915.

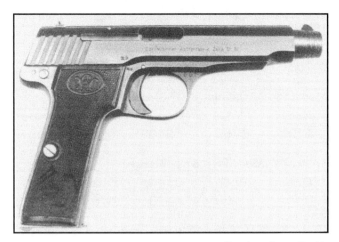

Courtesy James Rankin

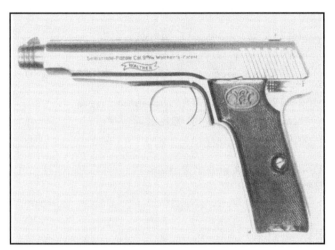

Courtesy James Rankin

Exc.	V.G.	Good	Fair	Poor
6000	4000	2500	1500	700

Model PP

Courtesy James Rankin

A semiautomatic pistol in .22, .25, .32 and .380 caliber. Introduced in 1928. It was the first successful commercial double action pistol. It was manufactured in finishes of blue, silver, and gold, and with three different types of engraving. Grips were generally two-piece black or white plastic with the Walther banner on each grip. Grips in wood or ivory are seen, but usually on engraved guns. There are many variations of the Model PP and numerous NSDAP markings seen on the

pre-1946 models that were produced during the Nazi regime. All reflect various prices.

Model PP .22 Caliber

Exc.	V.G.	Good	Fair	Poor
750	500	350	250	150

Model PP .25 Caliber

Exc.	V.G.	Good	Fair	Poor
5500	3500	2500	1500	600

Model PP .32 Caliber High Polished Finish

Exc.	V.G.	Good	Fair	Poor
450	325	275	225	175

Model PP .32 Caliber Milled Finish

Exc.	V.G.	Good	Fair	Poor
375	275	250	200	125

Model PP .380 Caliber

Exc.	V.G.	Good	Fair	Poor
950	750	550	475	350

Model PP .32 Caliber with Duraluminum Frame

Exc.	V.G.	Good	Fair	Poor
800	675	550	400	200

Model PP .32 Caliber with Bottom Magazine Release

Exc.	V.G.	Good	Fair	Poor
950	750	600	400	200

Model PP .32 Caliber with Verchromt Finish

Exc.	V.G.	Good	Fair	Poor
2000	1450	1000	700	400

Courtesy James Rankin

Courtesy Orvel Reichert

Model PP .32 Caliber in Blue, Silver or Gold Finish and Full Coverage Engraving

Blue

Exc.	V.G.	Good	Fair	Poor
3000	2500	2000	1200	700

Silver

Exc.	V.G.	Good	Fair	Poor
3500	3000	2500	1200	700

Gold

Exc.	V.G.	Good	Fair	Poor
4000	3500	3000	1200	700

NOTE: Add $250 for ivory grips with any of the three above.
Add $700 for leather presentation cases.
Add $500 for .22 caliber.
Add $1000 for .380 caliber.

Model PP .32 Caliber, Allemagne Marked

Exc.	V.G.	Good	Fair	Poor
850	700	550	325	250

Model PP .32 Caliber, A. F. Stoeger Contract

Exc.	V.G.	Good	Fair	Poor
2000	1450	1050	700	400

Model PP .32 Caliber with Waffenamt Proofs. High Polished Finish

Exc.	V.G.	Good	Fair	Poor
850	600	375	275	150

Model PP .32 Caliber with Waffenamt Proofs. Milled Finish

Exc.	V.G.	Good	Fair	Poor
450	375	325	250	150

Model PP .32 Caliber. Police Eagle/C Proofed. High Polished Finish

Exc.	V.G.	Good	Fair	Poor
800	475	375	250	150

Model PP .32 Caliber. Police Eagle/C and Police Eagle/F Proofed. Milled Finish

Exc.	V.G.	Good	Fair	Poor
600	400	375	275	150

Model PP .32 Caliber. NSKK Marked On The Slide

Exc.	V.G.	Good	Fair	Poor
2200	1500	850	550	300

NOTE: Add $700 with proper NSKK DRGM AKAH holster.

Model PP .32 Caliber. NSDAP Gruppe Markings

Exc.	V.G.	Good	Fair	Poor
2000	1500	1000	500	300

NOTE: Add $600 with proper SA DRGM AKAH holster.

Model PP .32 Caliber. PDM Marked with Bottom Magazine Release

Exc.	V.G.	Good	Fair	Poor
850	700	550	475	300

Model PP .32 Caliber. RJ Marked

Exc.	V.G.	Good	Fair	Poor
750	600	475	400	150

Model PP .32 Caliber. RFV Marked. High Polished or Milled Finish

Exc.	V.G.	Good	Fair	Poor
700	600	475	400	150

Model PP .32 Caliber. RBD Munster Marked

Exc.	V.G.	Good	Fair	Poor
2200	1750	1200	650	400

Model PP .32 Caliber. RpLt Marked

Exc.	V.G.	Good	Fair	Poor
950	750	475	375	200

Model PP .32 Caliber. Statens Vattenfallsverk Marked

Exc.	V.G.	Good	Fair	Poor
850	700	550	375	200

Model PP .32 Caliber. AC Marked

Exc.	V.G.	Good	Fair	Poor
450	375	300	250	150

Model PP .32 Caliber. Duraluminum Frame

Exc.	V.G.	Good	Fair	Poor
700	600	500	400	150

Model PP .380 Caliber. Bottom Magazine Release and Waffenamt Proofs

Exc.	V.G.	Good	Fair	Poor
1450	1000	700	500	300

Model PPK

A semiautomatic pistol in .22, .25, .32 and .380 caliber. Introduced six months after the Model PP in 1929. A more compact version of the Model PP with one less round in the magazine and one-piece wrap-around checkered plastic grips in brown, black, and white with the Walther banner on each side of the grips. The Model PPK will be found with the same types of finishes as the Model PP as well as the same styles of engraving. Grips in wood or ivory are seen with some of the engraved models. As with the Model PP there are many variations of the Model PPK and numerous NSDAP markings seen on the pre-1946 models that were produced during the Nazi regime. All reflect various prices.

Courtesy Orvel Reichert

Courtesy James Rankin

Model PPK .22 Caliber

Exc.	V.G.	Good	Fair	Poor
1100	700	475	325	175

Model PPK .25 Caliber

Exc.	V.G.	Good	Fair	Poor
5800	3800	1850	1000	500

Model PPK .32 Caliber. High Polished Finish

Exc.	V.G.	Good	Fair	Poor
550	450	325	250	150

Model PPK .32 Caliber. Milled Finish

Exc.	V.G.	Good	Fair	Poor
500	400	325	250	150

Model PPK .380 Caliber

Courtesy Orvel Reichert

Exc.	V.G.	Good	Fair	Poor
2200	1750	1300	750	375

Model PPK .32 Caliber with Duraluminum Frame

Exc.	V.G.	Good	Fair	Poor
950	800	600	400	200

Model PPK .32 Caliber with Verchromt Finish

Exc.	V.G.	Good	Fair	Poor
2500	1800	1200	700	350

Model PPK .32 Caliber in Blue, Silver or Gold Finish and Full Coverage Engraving

Blue

Exc.	V.G.	Good	Fair	Poor
3500	3000	2500	1200	700

Silver

Exc.	V.G.	Good	Fair	Poor
3750	3250	2750	1200	700

Gold

Exc.	V.G.	Good	Fair	Poor
4500	3750	3000	1200	700

Add $750 for ivory grips with any of the three above.
Add $700 for leather presentation cases.
Add $500 for .22 caliber.
Add $1000 for .380 caliber.

Model PPK .32 Caliber Marked Mod. PP on Slide

Exc.	V.G.	Good	Fair	Poor
5000	4000	2500	1500	1000

Model PPK .32 Caliber with Panagraphed Slide

Exc.	V.G.	Good	Fair	Poor
650	550	450	300	200

Model PPK .32 Caliber. Czechoslovakian Contract

Exc.	V.G.	Good	Fair	Poor
1850	1500	1000	550	300

Model PPK .32 Caliber. Allemagne Marked

Exc.	V.G.	Good	Fair	Poor
800	700	600	400	250

Model PPK .32 Caliber with Waffenamt Proofs and a High Polished Finish

Exc.	V.G.	Good	Fair	Poor
1200	800	550	400	250

Model PPK .32 Caliber with Waffenamt Proofs and a Milled Finish

Exc.	V.G.	Good	Fair	Poor
800	600	375	300	175

Model PPK .32 Caliber. Police Eagle/C Proofed. High Polished Finish

Exc.	V.G.	Good	Fair	Poor
675	575	450	300	175

Model PPK .32 Caliber. Police Eagle/C Proofed. Milled Finish

Exc.	V.G.	Good	Fair	Poor
650	500	375	275	175

Model PPK .32 Caliber. Police Eagle/F Proofed. Duraluminum Frame. Milled Finish

Exc.	V.G.	Good	Fair	Poor
900	700	550	350	225

Model PPK .22 Caliber. Late War, Black Grips

Exc.	V.G.	Good	Fair	Poor
1200	750	600	450	300

Model PPK .32 Caliber. Party Leader Grips. Brown

Exc.	V.G.	Good	Fair	Poor
2750	2550	2350	2250	2000

Model PPK .32 Caliber. Party Leader Grips. Black

Exc.	V.G.	Good	Fair	Poor
3250	3000	2750	2550	2500

NOTE: If grips are badly cracked or damaged on the two Party Leaders above, reduce $2000 each valuation.
Add $500 with proper Party Leader DRGM AKAH holster.

Model PPK .32 Caliber. RZM Marked

Exc.	V.G.	Good	Fair	Poor
900	700	500	400	300

Model PPK .32 Caliber. PDM Marked with Duraluminum Frame and Bottom Magazine Release

Exc.	V.G.	Good	Fair	Poor
2500	1800	1150	750	450

Model PPK .32 Caliber. RFV Marked

Exc.	V.G.	Good	Fair	Poor
2000	1750	1150	650	400

Model PPK .32 Caliber. DRP Marked

Exc.	V.G.	Good	Fair	Poor
800	650	550	450	275

Model PPK .32 Caliber. Statens Vattenfallsverk

Exc.	V.G.	Good	Fair	Poor
1400	1200	700	450	300

Model P 99 Military

Similar to the P99 but with military finish.

NIB	Exc.	V.G.	Good	Fair	Poor
625	475	375	—	—	—

HECKLER & KOCH

VP 70Z

This is a blowback-operated semiautomatic chambered for the 9mm Parabellum cartridge. It is striker-fired and double action only. The barrel is 4.5" long, and the double column magazine holds 18 rounds. The finish is blued, and the receiver and grip are molded from plastic. This model was discontinued in 1986.

NIB	Exc.	V.G.	Good	Fair	Poor
550	450	350	300	250	200

VP 70M

This is similar to the VP70Z except for a very important feature; when a shoulder stock is added the internal mechanism is altered to fire full automatic 3-round burst. When the shoulder stock is removed the pistol reverts back to semiautomatic. The rate of fire is a very high 2,200 rounds per minute. This version has no safety devices. First produced in 1972 and discontinued in 1986.

Pre-1968

Exc.	V.G.	Fair
N/A	N/A	N/A

Pre-1986 conversions

Exc.	V.G.	Fair
15000	—	—

Pre-1986 dealer samples

Exc.	V.G.	Fair
N/A	N/A	N/A

P9

This is a single action, delayed-blowback semiautomatic pistol chambered for 9mm or 7.65mm Parabellum. The action is based on the G-3 rifle mechanism and is single action only. The barrel is 4" in length, and the pistol has an internal hammer and a thumb-operated hammer drop and decocking lever. There is also a manual safety and a loaded-chamber indicator. The finish is parkerized, and the grips are molded plastic and well contoured. It has fixed sights. This model was manufactured between 1977 and 1984. This model is rarer than the P9S model. This was H&Ks first military pistol.

NIB	Exc.	V.G.	Good	Fair	Poor
1000	775	600	500	400	300

SUBMACHINE GUNS

MP18/1 (WWI)

This was the first German submachine and it was designed by Schmeisser in 1916. It was used by German military forces in WWI. The gun was chambered for the 9mm Parabellum cartridge. The barrel length is 7.5" and the snail magazine holds 32 rounds. The rate of fire is about 450 rounds per minute. Markings are "MP 18 L" above chamber and "C.G HANEL WAFFENFABRIK SUHL" on the left side of receiver. No longer produced after 1945. Weight is about 9 lbs.

Pre-1968

Exc.	V.G.	Fair
4000	3500	2500

Pre-1986 conversions

Exc.	V.G.	Fair
N/A	N/A	N/A

Pre-1986 dealer samples

Exc.	V.G.	Fair
1500	1400	1000

MP18/1 (Post-war)

Introduced into combat by German troops in 1918. Designed by Hugo Schmeisser and built by Bergmann. Chambered for 9mm cartridge. In place of the 32-round snail drum, a box magazine holds 20 or 32 rounds. The magazine is essentially the only difference between the WWI guns and the post-war examples. Barrel length is 8". Rate of fire is about 400 rounds per minute. Was in use from 1918 to 1930s. Weight is about 9 lbs.

Private NFA Collection • Photo by Gary Gelson

Pre-1968

Exc.	V.G.	Fair
4000	3500	3000

Pre-1986 conversions

Exc.	V.G.	Fair
N/A	N/A	N/A

Pre-1986 dealer samples

Exc.	V.G.	Fair
N/A	N/A	N/A

Bergman MP28

This model is an improved version of the MP18. It is fitted with a tangent sight and straight magazine. It also has a selector switch to allow for semi-auto fire. Rate of fire is approximately 500 rounds per minute. Chambered for a variety of caliber including 9mm Parabellum, 9mm Bergmann, 7.65mm Parabellum, 7.63mm, and .45 ACP. Magazine capacity is 20,

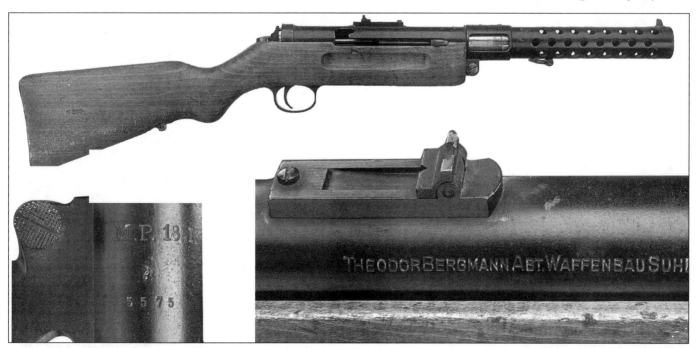

MP 18.I with markings • Paul Goodwin photo

32, or 50 rounds with special 25-round magazine for .45 ACP models. Built in Belgium by Pieper. Many of these guns were sold to South American countries. They were also used by German Police units including SS units. It was never adopted by the German army. Markings over the chamber are "MP 28 II SYSTEM SCHMEISSER PATENT." Weight is 8.8 lbs.

Courtesy Richard M. Kumor, Sr.

Pre-1968

Exc.	V.G.	Fair
4500	3500	2500

Pre-1986 conversions

Exc.	V.G.	Fair
N/A	N/A	N/A

Pre-1986 dealer samples

Exc.	V.G.	Fair
2000	1500	1200

Erma EMP

First developed in Germany in 1934 this submachine gun was chambered for the 9mm cartridge. It was fitted with a wooden vertical fore-grip. The gun was fitted with a 9.75" barrel with a 20- or 32-round magazine. The rate of fire was 500 rounds a minute. The weight was about 8.25 lbs. Marked "EMP" on rear receiver cap. Production ceased in 1945. This gun was used extensively in the Spanish Civil War.

Erma EMP • Paul Goodwin Photo

Pre-1968

Exc.	V.G.	Fair
4000	3000	3000

Pre-1986 conversions

Exc.	V.G.	Fair
N/A	N/A	N/A

Pre-1986 dealer samples

Exc.	V.G.	Fair
2000	1900	1700

H&K MP5

First produced in 1965 this submachine is quite popular world-wide, being in service in a number of countries. It is produced in 9mm, .40 S&W, and 10mm. It is offered in a number of variations. The basic model is fitted with an 8.75" barrel with retractable stock. Magazine capacity is 15 or 30

rounds. Rate of fire is 800 rounds per minute. Weight is approximately 5.5 lbs. Marked "MP5 KAL 9MMX19" on top rib of receiver.

Courtesy Richard M. Kumor, Sr.

Pre-1968 (Rare)

Exc.	V.G.	Fair
9500	9000	9000

Pre-1986 conversions

Exc.	V.G.	Fair
8000	7500	7000

NOTE: Add 15% for registered receiver using OEM parts.

Pre-1986 dealer samples

Exc.	V.G.	Fair
4700	4200	4000

HK MP5 K

This model is essentially the same as the MP5 with the exception of a 4.5" barrel. Weight is about 4.4 lbs.

Photo courtesy H&K

Pre-1968 (Rare)

Exc.	V.G.	Fair
N/A	N/A	N/A

Pre-1986 conversions

Exc.	V.G.	Fair
7000	6500	6000

NOTE: Add 15% for registered receiver using OEM parts.

Pre-1986 dealer samples

Exc.	V.G.	Fair
3900	3500	3000

HK MP5 SD

This variation of the MP5 uses a suppressor making it one of the quietest submachine guns ever. The barrel is ported so that supersonic 9mm ammunition can be used at subsonic levels. Rate of fire is 800 rounds per minute. Magazine capacity is 15- or 30-round magazines. Barrel length is 7.7" and weight is approximately 7 lbs. This model comes in six different configurations which may affect price.

Courtesy Heckler & Koch

Pre-1968

Exc.	V.G.	Fair
N/A	N/A	N/A

Pre-1986 conversions

Exc.	V.G.	Fair
8500	8000	7000

NOTE: Add 15% for registered receiver using OEM parts.

Pre-1986 dealer samples

Exc.	V.G.	Fair
5000	4800	4500

HK53

This submachine gun fires the 5.56x45mm cartridge. It is fitted with an 8.25" barrel and retractable stock. Magazine capacity is 25 rounds. Rate of fire is about 700 rounds per minute. Weight is approximately 6.7 lbs. Marked "MP53 KAL 5.56X45" on top rib of receiver. The gun is in service in several military and police units around the world.

Courtesy H&K

Pre-1968

Exc.	V.G.	Fair
N/A	N/A	N/A

Pre-1986 conversions

Exc.	V.G.	Fair
8000	7500	6500

Pre-1986 dealer samples

Exc.	V.G.	Fair
5000	4500	4000

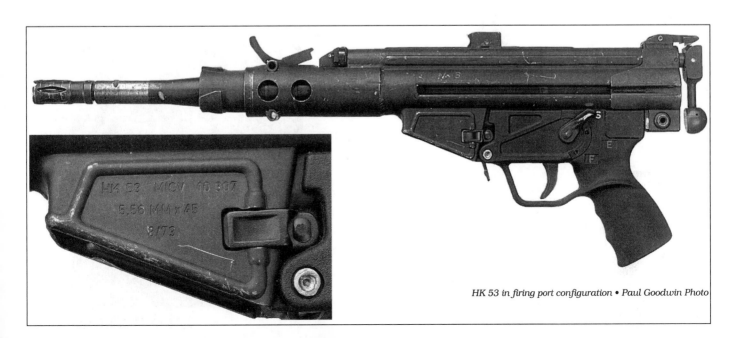

HK 53 in firing port configuration • Paul Goodwin Photo

Steyr-Solothurn (Solothurn SI-100 or MP34(o))

See *Austria, Submachine Guns, Steyr*

MP34/I & MP35/I

Similar in appearance to the MP28, and produced in Germany by Walther in Zella Mehlis. Chambered for the 9mm cartridge and fitted with a 7.8" or 12.6" barrel. Other calibers were offered such as the 9mm Bergmann, 9mm Mauser, .45 ACP, and 7.63 Mauser. Rear sight had a V-notch tangent graduated to 1000 meters. The gun had a cocking handle much like a rifle located at the rear of the receiver. Fitted with two triggers the outer one fired semiautomatic and the inner one fired full automatic. The 24- or 32-round magazine fed from the right side. Rate of fire was about 650 rounds per minute and weight is approximately 9 lbs. The MP35/I was a modified MP34/I and was used by the German SS. Built by Junker & Ruh. Many more MP35/I guns were built than MP34/I.

Private NFA Collection • Photo by Gary Gelson

signed by Vollmer and built by the Erma company. It is chambered for the 9mm cartridge and is fitted with a 9.75" barrel. It has a folding stock and a magazine capacity of 32 rounds. Its rate of fire is 500 rounds per minute. Full automatic fire only. Weight is approximately 9 lbs. Marked "MP38" on the rear receiver cap. Production ceased in 1940. Produced by Erma. This was the standard submachine gun of the German army during World War II. Over 1,000,000 were produced.

NOTE: In 1940 and 1941 some Model 38s were modified to prevent accidental discharges. By replacing the one-piece retracting handle with a two-piece one that incorporated a cutout which could be locked to prevent firing. This modified Model 38 is designated the Model 38/40.

Pre-1968 (Rare)

Exc.	V.G.	Fair
4500	4000	3500

Pre-1986 conversions (or U.S. manufactured parts)

Exc.	V.G.	Fair
N/A	N/A	N/A

Pre-1986 dealer samples

Exc.	V.G.	Fair
N/A	N/A	N/A

MP40

This model was the successor to the MP38 with faster manufacturing components. The steel receivers pressed with a corrugated magazine housing. The grip frame is pressed steel as well. Weight and barrel length are the same as the MP38 as is magazine capacity and rate of fire. This model was produced

Pre-1968

Exc.	V.G.	Fair
6000	5000	4000

Pre-1986 conversions

Exc.	V.G.	Fair
4000	3000	2500

Pre-1986 dealer samples

Exc.	V.G.	Fair
3000	2500	2000

MP38

This German submachine gun was first produced in 1938. It is often called the Schmeisser but that is incorrect. It was de-

MP 38 • Paul Goodwin Photo

from 1940 to 1945 by Erma. Marked "MP40" on the rear receiver cap. Approximately 1,000,000 of these guns were produced.

NOTE: There is a rare modification of this submachine gun designated the MP40/II, which is fitted with a magazine housing that holds two magazines. These magazines fit in a oversized sliding housing that moves laterally, allowing a full magazine to be moved into place when the first magazine becomes empty. Not developed until late 1943. Not considered a successful attempt to increase ammunition capacity.

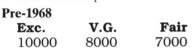

Pre-1968

Exc.	V.G.	Fair
10000	8000	7000

MP 40-Paul Goodwin Photo

Pre-1986 conversions (or U.S. manufactured receivers)

Exc.	V.G.	Fair
5500	4500	4000

Pre-1986 dealer samples

Exc.	V.G.	Fair
5000	4000	3500

MP41

This model was built by Schmeisser to compete with the official adopted military MP40. The gun was not adopted by the German army. The result is that very few of these guns exist. The MP40-style receiver and barrel were fitted to a wooden buttstock and a select fire mechanism was added. Weight is about 8 lbs. Marked "MP41 PATENT SCHMEISSER C.G.HAENEL SUHL" on the top of the receiver.

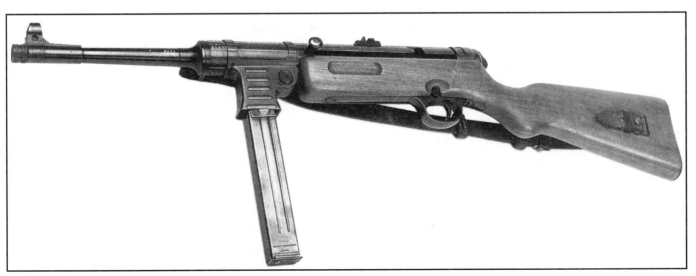

MP 41 • Private NFA Collection • Photo by Gary Gelson

Pre-1968 (Rare)

Exc.	V.G.	Fair
12000	9500	8000

Pre-1986 conversions

Exc.	V.G.	Fair
5500	5000	4500

Pre-1986 dealer samples

Exc.	V.G.	Fair
6000	5000	4000

Walter MPK and MPL

This German submachine gun was first produced in 1963. The MPK is a short barrel (6.7") version and the MPL is the long barrel (10.14") version. Magazine capacity is 32 rounds of 9mm. Rate of fire is 55 rounds per minute. Weight empty is 6.1 lbs. Markings are on the left side of the receiver. Production of this model ceased in 1985.

Photo Courtesy Private NFA Collection

Pre-1968 (Rare)

Exc.	V.G.	Fair
12000	10000	9000

Pre-1986 conversions

Exc.	V.G.	Fair
N/A	N/A	N/A

Pre-1986 dealer samples

Exc.	V.G.	Fair
2500	2000	1900

MAUSER MILITARY BOLT ACTION RIFLES FOR COUNTRIES NOT LISTED UNDER SEPERATE HEADING:

Argentina

See Argentina, Rifles, Mauser

Austria

M1914 Rifle

Exc.	V.G.	Good	Fair	Poor
675	500	425	225	100

Belgium

See Belgium, Rifles, Mauser

Bolivia

M1895 Rifle

Exc.	V.G.	Good	Fair	Poor
200	165	120	100	70

M1907 Rifle

Exc.	V.G.	Good	Fair	Poor
325	275	225	150	100

M1907 Short Rifle

Exc.	V.G.	Good	Fair	Poor
325	275	225	150	100

VZ24 Short Rifle

Exc.	V.G.	Good	Fair	Poor
400	350	275	225	125

M1933 Standard Model Export Model Short Rifle

Exc.	V.G.	Good	Fair	Poor
325	275	225	150	100

M1950 Series B-50 Rifle

Exc.	V.G.	Good	Fair	Poor
400	350	275	225	125

Brazil

M1894 Rifle

Exc.	V.G.	Good	Fair	Poor
275	225	125	100	75

M1894 Carbine

Exc.	V.G.	Good	Fair	Poor
250	200	125	100	75

M1904 Mauser-Verueiro Rifle

Exc.	V.G.	Good	Fair	Poor
325	250	200	150	100

M1907 Rifle

Exc.	V.G.	Good	Fair	Poor
325	250	200	150	100

M1907 Carbine

Exc.	V.G.	Good	Fair	Poor
300	250	200	150	100

M1908 Rifle

Exc.	V.G.	Good	Fair	Poor
275	225	125	100	75

M1908 Short Rifle

Exc.	V.G.	Good	Fair	Poor
250	200	150	100	70

M1922 Carbine

Exc.	V.G.	Good	Fair	Poor
225	175	130	90	60

VZ 24 Short Rifle

Exc.	V.G.	Good	Fair	Poor
250	195	125	90	75

M1935 Mauser Banner Rifle

Exc.	V.G.	Good	Fair	Poor
350	300	240	195	120

Courtesy Rock Island Auction Company

M1935 Mauser Banner Short Rifle

Exc.	V.G.	Good	Fair	Poor
350	300	240	195	120

M1935 Mauser Carbine

Exc.	V.G.	Good	Fair	Poor
350	300	240	195	120

M1908/34 Short Rifle

Exc.	V.G.	Good	Fair	Poor
295	250	195	150	90

M954 Caliber .30-06 Short Rifle

Exc.	V.G.	Good	Fair	Poor
295	240	180	125	90

Chile

M1893 Rifle

Exc.	V.G.	Good	Fair	Poor
250	200	150	100	60

M1895 Rifle

Exc.	V.G.	Good	Fair	Poor
250	200	150	100	60

M1895/61 7.62 NATO Conversion

Exc.	V.G.	Good	Fair	Poor
350	300	240	195	120

M1895 Short Rifle

Exc.	V.G.	Good	Fair	Poor
225	190	150	90	60

M1896 Carbine

Exc.	V.G.	Good	Fair	Poor
225	190	150	90	60

M1912 Steyr Rifle

Exc.	V.G.	Good	Fair	Poor
250	190	140	100	70

M1912 Steyr Short Rifle

Exc.	V.G.	Good	Fair	Poor
250	190	140	100	70

M1912/61 7.62 NATO Conversion

Exc.	V.G.	Good	Fair	Poor
350	300	250	200	125

M1935 Carabineros Carbine

Exc.	V.G.	Good	Fair	Poor
350	320	275	225	180

China

G71 Rifle

Exc.	V.G.	Good	Fair	Poor
400	325	250	190	120

J71 Rifle

Exc.	V.G.	Good	Fair	Poor
400	350	225	200	150

M1895 Rifle

Exc.	V.G.	Good	Fair	Poor
225	200	175	130	90

Hunyaug Rifle

Exc.	V.G.	Good	Fair	Poor
225	200	175	130	90

M1907 Rifle

Exc.	V.G.	Good	Fair	Poor
225	195	175	125	90

M1907 Carbine

Exc.	V.G.	Good	Fair	Poor
225	195	150	90	60

M1912 Steyr Rifle

Exc.	V.G.	Good	Fair	Poor
275	225	175	120	90

M98/22 Rifle

Exc.	V.G.	Good	Fair	Poor
250	200	160	110	90

FN M24 and 30 Short Rifles

Exc.	V.G.	Good	Fair	Poor
150	120	90	60	40

M21 Short Rifle

Exc.	V.G.	Good	Fair	Poor
175	150	120	90	50

Chiang Kai-shek Short Rifle

Exc.	V.G.	Good	Fair	Poor
165	130	100	80	50

VZ24 Short Rifle

Exc.	V.G.	Good	Fair	Poor
90	80	60	50	30

M1933 Standard Model Short Rifle

Exc.	V.G.	Good	Fair	Poor
190	170	140	110	90

M1933 Standard Model Carbine

Exc.	V.G.	Good	Fair	Poor
190	170	140	110	90

VZ24 with Japanese Folding Bayonet (copy)

Exc.	V.G.	Good	Fair	Poor
200	175	150	120	100

Colombia

M1891 Rifle (Argentine Pattern)

Exc.	V.G.	Good	Fair	Poor
120	90	75	55	35

M1904 Rifle

Exc.	V.G.	Good	Fair	Poor
190	160	130	100	75

M1912 Steyr Rifle

Exc.	V.G.	Good	Fair	Poor
170	130	110	90	55

Vz 23 Short Rifle

Exc.	V.G.	Good	Fair	Poor
170	130	110	90	55

Steyr-Solothurn A-G M1929 Short Rifle

Exc.	V.G.	Good	Fair	Poor
190	160	130	100	75

FN M24 and 30 Short Rifles

Exc.	V.G.	Good	Fair	Poor
150	120	100	75	45

VZ 12/33 Carbine

Exc.	V.G.	Good	Fair	Poor
170	130	110	90	55

FN M1950 Short Rifle

Exc.	V.G.	Good	Fair	Poor
170	130	110	90	55

Costa Rica

M1895 Rifle

Exc.	V.G.	Good	Fair	Poor
120	100	80	60	35

M1910 Rifle

Exc.	V.G.	Good	Fair	Poor
140	110	90	70	40

FN M24 Short Rifle

Exc.	V.G.	Good	Fair	Poor
130	110	90	70	40

Czechoslovakia

NOTE: See *Czechoslovakia, Rifles, Mauser*

Denmark

G98 Action Military Target Rifle (Model 52)

Exc.	V.G.	Good	Fair	Poor
300	250	200	150	100

K98k Action Military Target Rifle (Model 58)

Exc.	V.G.	Good	Fair	Poor
300	250	200	150	100

Dominican Republic

M1953 Rifle

Exc.	V.G.	Good	Fair	Poor
325	290	275	175	90

M1953 Short Rifle

Exc.	V.G.	Good	Fair	Poor
325	290	250	160	90

Ecuador

M71/84 Rifle

Exc.	V.G.	Good	Fair	Poor
175	150	100	80	50

M1891 Rifle (Argentine Pattern)

Exc.	V.G.	Good	Fair	Poor
125	90	70	50	30

M1907 Rifle

Exc.	V.G.	Good	Fair	Poor
150	120	90	70	45

M1910 Rifle

Exc.	V.G.	Good	Fair	Poor
150	110	80	60	50

VZ 24 Short Rifle

Exc.	V.G.	Good	Fair	Poor
80	60	50	30	20

VZ12/33 Carbine

Exc.	V.G.	Good	Fair	Poor
125	110	90	70	40

FN M30 Short Rifle

Exc.	V.G.	Good	Fair	Poor
110	90	70	60	40

El Salvador

M1895 Rifle

Exc.	V.G.	Good	Fair	Poor
125	90	80	60	40

VZ 12/33 Carbine

Exc.	V.G.	Good	Fair	Poor
125	110	90	70	40

Estonia

Czech Model L Short Rifle

Exc.	V.G.	Good	Fair	Poor
400	350	300	250	200

Ethiopia

FN M24 Carbine

Exc.	V.G.	Good	Fair	Poor
400	375	325	275	225

M1933 Standard Model Short Rifle

Exc.	V.G.	Good	Fair	Poor
450	375	350	300	250

M1933 Standard Model Carbine

Exc.	V.G.	Good	Fair	Poor
450	375	350	300	250

France

Post-WWII Modified K98k Carbine

Exc.	V.G.	Good	Fair	Poor
500	450	350	175	100

Greece

M1930 Short Rifle

Exc.	V.G.	Good	Fair	Poor
350	300	220	120	60

M1930 Carbine

Exc.	V.G.	Good	Fair	Poor
N/A	—	—	—	—

Guatemala

M1910 Rifle

Exc.	V.G.	Good	Fair	Poor
150	120	80	60	40

VZ25 Short Rifle (Model 24)

Exc.	V.G.	Good	Fair	Poor
175	130	90	70	40

VZ33 Carbine

Exc.	V.G.	Good	Fair	Poor
190	160	120	90	60

Haiti

FN M24/30 Short Rifle

Exc.	V.G.	Good	Fair	Poor
175	140	90	60	30

Honduras

G 71 Rifle

Exc.	V.G.	Good	Fair	Poor
300	250	200	130	90

M1895 Rifle (Chilean Pattern)

Exc.	V.G.	Good	Fair	Poor
150	110	90	60	25

M1933 Standard Model Short Rifle

Exc.	V.G.	Good	Fair	Poor
350	280	230	175	120

Iraq

Post-WWII 98k-style Carbine

Exc.	V.G.	Good	Fair	Poor
200	160	120	80	40

Ireland

G 71 Rifle

Exc.	V.G.	Good	Fair	Poor
400	325	250	200	150

Israel

Czech Post-WWII 98k Short Rifle

Exc.	V.G.	Good	Fair	Poor
275	225	190	125	80

FN 98k-style Short Rifle (8mm or 7.62 conversion)

Exc.	V.G.	Good	Fair	Poor
290	250	190	120	90

Japan

G 71 Rifle

Exc.	V.G.	Good	Fair	Poor
400	325	250	200	150

Latvia

VZ 24 Short Rifle

Exc.	V.G.	Good	Fair	Poor
190	150	110	80	60

Liberia

FN M24 Short Rifle

Exc.	V.G.	Good	Fair	Poor
200	160	75	80	40

Lithuania

FN M30 Short Rifle

Exc.	V.G.	Good	Fair	Poor
225	190	160	110	80

FN M246 Short Rifle

Exc.	V.G.	Good	Fair	Poor
275	250	200	130	100

Luxembourg

M1900 Rifle

Exc.	V.G.	Good	Fair	Poor
500	400	300	190	110

FN M24/30 Short Rifle

Exc.	V.G.	Good	Fair	Poor
175	140	90	60	30

Manchuria

Mukden Arsenal Rifle

Exc.	V.G.	Good	Fair	Poor
700	600	450	250	100

Mexico

See Mexico, Rifles, Mauser

Morocco

Post-WWII FN Carbine

Exc.	V.G.	Good	Fair	Poor
225	190	150	110	80

Netherlands

M1948 Carbine

Exc.	V.G.	Good	Fair	Poor
300	240	200	125	90

Nicaragua

VZ 23 Short Rifle

Exc.	V.G.	Good	Fair	Poor
300	250	200	125	90

VZ 12/33 Carbine

Exc.	V.G.	Good	Fair	Poor
350	300	225	140	100

Norway

K98k Reissued Short Rifle (.30-06)

Exc.	V.G.	Good	Fair	Poor
300	240	190	100	70

K98k Action Military Target Rifle (Model 59)

Exc.	V.G.	Good	Fair	Poor
325	280	210	140	90

Orange Free State

M1895 Rifle

Exc.	V.G.	Good	Fair	Poor
325	275	225	150	100

M1895 Chilean-marked Rifle

Exc.	V.G.	Good	Fair	Poor
325	275	225	150	100

M1896 Loewe & Co. Rifle

Exc.	V.G.	Good	Fair	Poor
350	275	225	175	100

M1897 DWM Rifle

Exc.	V.G.	Good	Fair	Poor
400	350	275	225	125

Paraguay

M1895 Rifle (Chilean Pattern)

Exc.	V.G.	Good	Fair	Poor
150	110	80	40	20

M1907 Rifle

Exc.	V.G.	Good	Fair	Poor
225	200	160	100	80

M1907 Carbine

Exc.	V.G.	Good	Fair	Poor
225	190	160	110	80

M1909 Haenel Export Model Rifle

Exc.	V.G.	Good	Fair	Poor
300	240	190	120	90

M1927 Rifle

Exc.	V.G.	Good	Fair	Poor
180	130	90	60	30

M1927 Short Rifle

Exc.	V.G.	Good	Fair	Poor
180	130	90	50	30

FN M24/30 Short Rifle

Exc.	V.G.	Good	Fair	Poor
225	190	150	100	80

M1933 Standard Model Short Rifle

Exc.	V.G.	Good	Fair	Poor
300	250	200	150	90

M1933 Standard Model Carbine

Exc.	V.G.	Good	Fair	Poor
300	250	200	150	90

Persia/Iran

M1895 Rifle

Exc.	V.G.	Good	Fair	Poor
200	150	120	90	70

FN M24/30 Short Rifle

Exc.	V.G.	Good	Fair	Poor
275	225	175	100	70

M98/29 Long Rifle

Exc.	V.G.	Good	Fair	Poor
425	350	300	250	150

VZ 24 Short Rifle

Exc.	V.G.	Good	Fair	Poor
350	300	250	200	100

M30 Carbine

Exc.	V.G.	Good	Fair	Poor
500	400	300	175	100

M49 Carbine

Exc.	V.G.	Good	Fair	Poor
550	450	300	175	100

Peru

M1891 Rifle M1891 Carbine

Exc.	V.G.	Good	Fair	Poor
175	140	100	75	35

M1895 Rifle

Exc.	V.G.	Good	Fair	Poor
190	150	100	75	35

M1909 Rifle

Exc.	V.G.	Good	Fair	Poor
425	350	275	225	100

VZ 24 Short Rifle

Exc.	V.G.	Good	Fair	Poor
325	275	225	150	100

VZ 32 Carbine

Exc.	V.G.	Good	Fair	Poor
275	225	150	100	65

M1935 Short Rifle (converted to .30-06)

Exc.	V.G.	Good	Fair	Poor
225	225	175	125	90

M1935 Short Rifle

Exc.	V.G.	Good	Fair	Poor
425	350	275	225	100

Poland

See Poland, Rifles, Mauser

Portugal

M1904 Mauser-Verueiro Rifle

Exc.	V.G.	Good	Fair	Poor
250	170	110	80	50

M904/M39 Rifle

Exc.	V.G.	Good	Fair	Poor
250	200	125	80	50

M1933 Standard Model Short Rifle

Exc.	V.G.	Good	Fair	Poor
300	250	200	150	90

M1933 Standard Model Carbine

Exc.	V.G.	Good	Fair	Poor
300	250	200	150	90

M937-A Short Rifle

Exc.	V.G.	Good	Fair	Poor
325	280	220	160	90

M1941 Short Rifle

Exc.	V.G.	Good	Fair	Poor
395	300	200	140	80

Romania

See Romania, Rifles

Saudi Arabia

FN M30 Short Rifle

Exc.	V.G.	Good	Fair	Poor
250	190	120	80	40

Serbia/Yugoslavia

See Yugoslavia, Rifles, Mauser

Slovak Republic

VZ 24 Short Rifle

Exc.	V.G.	Good	Fair	Poor
375	300	225	150	90

South Africa

M1896 ZAR Rifle

Exc.	V.G.	Good	Fair	Poor
395	300	250	180	100

ZAE M1896 B Series Rifle

Exc.	V.G.	Good	Fair	Poor
395	300	230	160	100

M1896 ZAR Loewe Long Rifle

Exc.	V.G.	Good	Fair	Poor
375	290	200	150	90

M1895/1896 C Series

Exc.	V.G.	Good	Fair	Poor
375	300	225	160	90

Spain

See *Spain, Rifles, Mauser*

Sweden

See *Sweden, Rifles, Mauser*

Syria

M1948 Short Rifle

Exc.	V.G.	Good	Fair	Poor
150	125	100	80	40

Courtesy Rock Island Auction Company

Thailand/Siam

G 71 Rifle

Exc.	V.G.	Good	Fair	Poor
350	300	200	150	110

M1903 (Type 45) Rifle

Exc.	V.G.	Good	Fair	Poor
225	175	140	110	90

M1904 Rifle

Exc.	V.G.	Good	Fair	Poor
325	290	260	190	150

M1923 (Type 66) Short Rifle

Exc.	V.G.	Good	Fair	Poor
225	175	150	120	90

Transvaal

G 71 Rifle

Exc.	V.G.	Good	Fair	Poor
450	400	300	200	150

Turkey

M1887 Rifle

Exc.	V.G.	Good	Fair	Poor
400	350	300	200	150

M1890 Rifle

Exc.	V.G.	Good	Fair	Poor
325	280	225	180	110

M1893 Rifle

Exc.	V.G.	Good	Fair	Poor
325	280	220	150	90

M1903 Rifle

Exc.	V.G.	Good	Fair	Poor
250	190	140	100	40

M1903/38 (converted to 8mm)

Exc.	V.G.	Good	Fair	Poor
225	190	160	110	80

M1905 Carbine

Exc.	V.G.	Good	Fair	Poor
395	300	200	110	60

M98/22 Rifle

Exc.	V.G.	Good	Fair	Poor
125	100	70	50	30

Courtesy Rock Island Auction Company

M38 Short Rifle

Exc.	V.G.	Good	Fair	Poor
125	100	70	50	30

M38 Short Rifle with Folding Bayonet

Exc.	V.G.	Good	Fair	Poor
150	120	80	60	30

Uruguay

G 71 Rifle

Exc.	V.G.	Good	Fair	Poor
350	300	200	150	110

M1895 Rifle

Exc.	V.G.	Good	Fair	Poor
175	140	90	60	30

M1908 Rifle

Exc.	V.G.	Good	Fair	Poor
190	160	130	100	70

M1908 Short Rifle

Exc.	V.G.	Good	Fair	Poor
190	130	130	100	70

FN M24 Short Rifle

Exc.	V.G.	Good	Fair	Poor
225	190	170	110	70

VZ 37 (937) Short Rifle

Exc.	V.G.	Good	Fair	Poor
400	300	200	120	80

VZ 37 (937) Carbine

Exc.	V.G.	Good	Fair	Poor
400	300	200	120	80

Venezuela

G 71/84 Rifle

Exc.	V.G.	Good	Fair	Poor
290	200	150	100	70

M1910 Rifle

Exc.	V.G.	Good	Fair	Poor
200	160	140	100	80

VZ 24 Short Rifle

Exc.	V.G.	Good	Fair	Poor
250	200	150	100	70

FN M24/30 Short Rifle

Exc.	V.G.	Good	Fair	Poor
400	300	200	120	80

FN M24/30 Carbine

Exc.	V.G.	Good	Fair	Poor
400	300	200	100	70

FN M24/30 Military Target Rifle

Exc.	V.G.	Good	Fair	Poor
350	300	200	125	90

Yeman

FN M30 Short Rifle

Exc.	V.G.	Good	Fair	Poor
300	220	175	110	80

RIFLES

For historical information, technical data and photos see Hans Dieter Gotz, *German Military Rifles and Machine Pistols, 1871-1945*, 1990 Schiffer Publishing.

MAUSER

Established in 1869 by Peter and Wilhelm Mauser, this company came under the effective control of Ludwig Loewe and Company of Berlin in 1887. In 1896 the latter company was reorganized under the name *Deutsches Waffen und Munition* or as it is better known, DWM.

For history and technical details see Robert W.D. Ball's, *Mauser Military Rifles of the World*, 2nd edition, Krause Publications, 2000.

NOTE: There are a number of variations to the Mauser rifle listed below that are found in various countries, approximately 54, throughout the world. These can be identified by the country crest stamped most likely on the receiver ring of the rifle. The rifles listed below form the basis of whatever variations that may be encounter elsewhere.

Model 1871

This was the first German metallic cartridge rifle. It was a 11x60Rmm caliber single shot bolt action rifle with a 33.5" barrel with bayonet lug, full-length stock secured by two barrel bands and a cleaning rod. There is no upper handguard on this model. This model did not have an ejector so that empty shells had to be removed manually. The rear sight was a leaf type with graduations out to 1600 meters. Weight was about 10 lbs. The barrel marked "Mod. 71" together with the year of production and the manufacturer's name of which there were several. First produced in 1875. Blued with a walnut stock.

Courtesy Milwaukee Public Museum, Milwaukee, Wisconsin

Exc.	V.G.	Good	Fair	Poor
750	500	400	300	150

Model 1871 Jaeger Rifle

As above, with a 29.4" barrel and finger grip extension behind the triggerguard. Weight about 10 lbs.

Courtesy Bob Ball

Exc.	V.G.	Good	Fair	Poor
800	650	550	450	300

Model 1871 Carbine

As above, with a 20" barrel and no bayonet lug. It was full stocked to the muzzle. Weight is about 7.5 lbs.

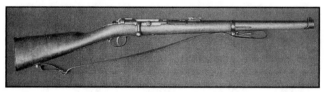

Courtesy Bob Ball

Exc.	V.G.	Good	Fair	Poor
750	500	425	350	225

Model 1871 Short Rifle

As above, but with upper and lower barrel bands and bayonet lug.

Exc.	V.G.	Good	Fair	Poor
700	500	425	350	225

Model 79 G.A.G. Rifle (Grenz-Aufsichts-Gewehr)

Fitted with a 25" barrel and built by Haenel in Suhl and so marked. It is also marked "G.A.G." Used by German border guards. It is full stock almost to the muzzle. It is chambered for the 11x37.5mm cartridge. Weight is about 7 lbs. Single shot.

Exc.	V.G.	Good	Fair	Poor
600	500	400	250	100

Model 71/84 Rifle

The Model 71 modified by the addition of a tubular 8-round magazine. This model was fitted with an ejector. Barrel length 31.5". Weight is approximately 10 lbs. Issued in 1886. About 900,000 were produced. Marked "I.G.MOD.71/84" on the left side of the receiver.

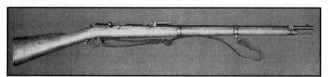

Courtesy Bob Ball

Exc.	V.G.	Good	Fair	Poor
750	600	500	350	275

Model 88 Commission Rifle

A 7.92x57mm caliber bolt action rifle with a 29" barrel, 5-shot magazine, full-length stock, bayonet lug and cleaning rod. Marked "GEW. 88" together with the year of manufacture and the maker's name. This was the first military to take a rimless cartridge. Weight is about 9 lbs. About 1,000,000 of these rifles were produced. Many of these rifles were later modified to charger loading therefore original Model 88 rifles are uncommon. These rifles were used in World War I by German, Austro-Hungarian, Bulgarian, and Turkish armies.

Exc.	V.G.	Good	Fair	Poor
300	250	200	150	90

Model 98 Rifle (Gewehr 98)

The best known of all Mauser rifles. A 7.92mm bolt action rifle with a 29" barrel, 5-shot flush fitting magazine, full-length stock, half-length handguard, cleaning rod and bayonet lug. Pre-1915 versions had a steel grommet through the buttstock and finger grooves on the forend. Marked "GEW. 98" together with the date of manufacture and maker's name. Weight is about 9 lbs. About 3,500,000 of these rifles were built from its introduction in 1898 to 1918.

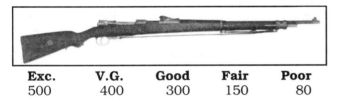

Exc.	V.G.	Good	Fair	Poor
500	400	300	150	80

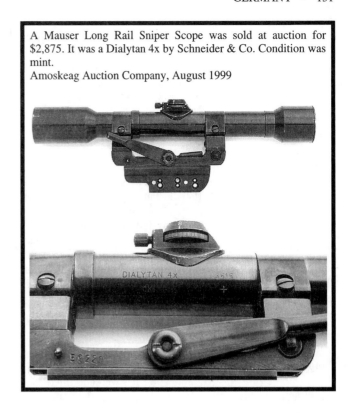

A Mauser Long Rail Sniper Scope was sold at auction for $2,875. It was a Dialytan 4x by Schneider & Co. Condition was mint.
Amoskeag Auction Company, August 1999

Model 98 Carbine • Paul Goodwin Photo

Model 98/98A Carbine

As above, with 17" barrel and full stock to the muzzle without handguard. Not fitted for a bayonet. Produced at the Erfurt arsenal in 1900 to 1902. About 3,000 were produced. In 1902 the Model 98A, with bayonet bar and cleaning rod, was also produced at Erfurt until 1905. Weight was about 7.5 lbs.

Exc.	V.G.	Good	Fair	Poor
800	650	400	250	150

Model 98 AZ Carbine/Model 98a

This model has the same stock as the Model Gew 98 but with the a slot through the buttstock. Barrel length was 24". Bolt handle was turn down type and the full stock went to the muzzle with full upper handguard. Fitted with a bayonet stud and curved stacking bar on the forearm cap. Magazine capacity is 5 rounds. Weight is about 8 lbs. Introduced in 1908 with about 1,500,000 total production. Stamped "KAR 98" on the left side of the receiver. After WWI these rifles were renamed the Model 98a. Fitted with a small ring receiver.

Exc.	V.G.	Good	Fair	Poor
400	300	225	150	100

Model 98 Transitional Rifle

As a result of the armistice Model 98 rifles were modified with a simple tangent rear sight, the markings ground off and arsenal refinished.

Exc.	V.G.	Good	Fair	Poor
400	300	225	150	100

Model 98 KAR 98b Rifle

Also a product of the armistice the Model 98 rifle was altered with the addition of a flat tangent rear sight, removed stacking hook, and a slot was cut for a sling in the buttstock. Otherwise this is a Model 98 rifle.

Exc.	V.G.	Good	Fair	Poor
350	300	275	200	150

Model 98k Carbine (Short Rifle)

This was the standard shoulder arm of the German military during World War II. Introduced in 1935 about 11,000,000 were produced. Barrel length is 23.6". Magazine capacity is 5 rounds of 7.92mm. Rear sight was a tangent leaf graduated to 2000 meters. Weight is about 8.5 lbs. Produced by a numbers of German arsenals using a variety of different identifying codes. Date of production is found on the receiver ring.

Courtesy Buffalo Bill Historical Center, Cody, Wyoming

Exc.	V.G.	Good	Fair	Poor
450	375	295	160	90

Model K98k Sniper Rifle (ZF 41)

A sniper version of the 98K with a ZF 41 scope mounted.

K98F Sniper Rifle • Courtesy Richard M. Kumor, Sr.

Exc.	V.G.	Good	Fair	Poor
2500	2000	1250	750	400

Model 98AZ • Courtesy West Point Museum • Paul Goodwin Photo

Model 33/40 • Courtesy West Point Museum • Paul Goodwin Photo

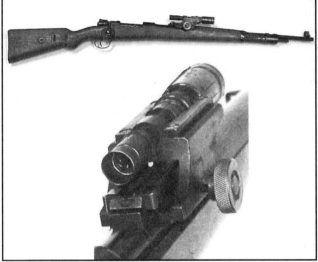

K98F Dual Rail Sniper Rifle • Courtesy Richard M. Kumor, Sr.

Model K98k Sniper Rifle (Dual Rail)

This sniper version is fitted with a dual rail scope mount. It is estimated that only about 25 of these rifles were built using this sight system.

Exc.	V.G.	Good	Fair	Poor
Too Rare to Price				

Model 1933 Standard Model Short Rifle

Introduced in 1933 and fitted with a 23.6" barrel full stock with pistol grip and finger grooves in forend. Short upper handguard. Weight is about 8.75 lbs. Used extensively by the German Condor Legion in the Spanish Civil War, 1936 to 1939. Stamped with Mauser banner on receiver ring with date of manufacture.

Exc.	V.G.	Good	Fair	Poor
350	275	225	150	100

Model 1933 Standard Model Carbine

Similar to the Model 98k but forearm has finger grooves. Mauser banner stamped on top of receiver ring with date of manufacture. Weight is about 8.5 lbs.

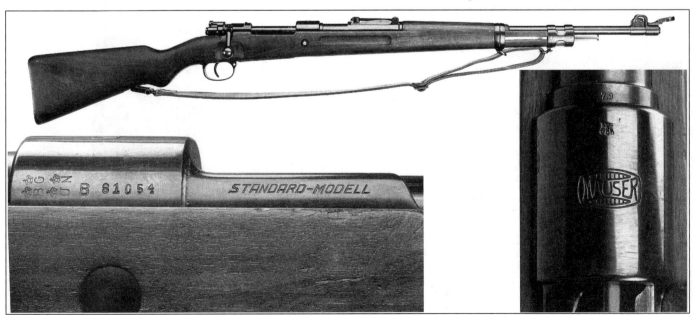

Model 1933 Standard Model • Courtesy West Point Museum • Paul Goodwin Photo

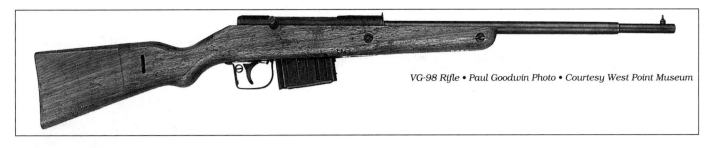

VG-98 Rifle • Paul Goodwin Photo • Courtesy West Point Museum

Exc.	V.G.	Good	Fair	Poor
600	500	375	200	125

Model 33/40 Carbine

This carbine was made in Brno in Czechoslovakia during World War II after it was occupied by the German army. This model featured a laminated stock with full upper handguard. Fitted with a 19.2" barrel and marked "G. 33/40" together with the year of production and the maker's code. Marked "dot" over the date or "945" over the date. Weight is about 8 lbs.

Exc.	V.G.	Good	Fair	Poor
750	600	400	300	200

Model 29/40 Rifle (G29o)

This rifle was built by Steyr for the German Luftwaffe. It has a bent bolt and an "L" marked stock. There is some confusion over the origins of this model and its correct designations and configurations. Consult an expert prior to a sale to avoid vexation.

Exc.	V.G.	Good	Fair	Poor
800	675	425	225	150

Model 24 (t) Rifle

This is the German version of the Czech vz 24 rifle built during the German occupation of that country during WWII.

Exc.	V.G.	Good	Fair	Poor
500	375	275	150	100

Model VG-98

These are crude half stocked 7.92mm weapons produced near the end of the war to arm the German population. Barrel length is about 21" and some use a 10-round magazine while other examples are single shot. Weight is about 7 lbs. It is made from parts of older often unserviceable Mausers. Will command premium prices.

Exc.	V.G.	Good	Fair	Poor
3000	2500	2000	1200	600

Model VG-1 (Volksturm Gewehr)

This rifle was made in the last days of WWII and is crudely made. It used the magazine of a semiautomatic Model 43 rifle. Beware of firing this weapon. It is poorly made but because of historical interest and high demand prices command a premium.

Courtesy Richard M. Kumor, Sr.

Exc.	V.G.	Good	Fair	Poor
4500	4000	3000	—	—

Model VG-2

Chambered for the 7.9mm cartridge and fitted with a 10-round G43 magazine. This semiautomatic rifle has a 21" MG 13 barrel with no bayonet lug. Cheaply built. Receiver is a "U" shaped stamping. Rare.

Exc.	V.G.	Good	Fair	Poor
5500	5000	4000	—	—

Model VG-5

Another last ditch, locally produced rifle made at the very end of World War II. Chambered for the 7.92mm cartridge. Stamped receiver. Magazine is MP44 type. Simply and poorly made.

Exc.	V.G.	Good	Fair	Poor
5500	5000	4000	—	—

Model 1918 Anti-Tank Rifle

Chambered for the 13x92SR cartridge this was the first Mauser anti-tank rifle. Barrel length is 39" and weight is about 37 lbs. The Mauser banner is stamped on the upper receiver over the date "1918." Used successfully by the Germans against Allied tanks during WWI.

Courtesy Amoskeag Auction Co., Inc.

An experimental Luger self loading rifle was sold at auction for $167,500.
Chambered for 7.92mm cartridge and fitted with a 27.5" barrel. Luger toggle action with "SYSTEM LUGER". Tang mounted safety. Oil-finished walnut stock. George Luger received patent No. 4126 in February of 1906 for this rifle. Weight of rifle was almost 10 lbs. Condition was excellent. Butterfield & Butterfield, November, 1999.

(Model 1918 Anti-Tank Rifle, contd.)

Exc.	V.G.	Good	Fair	Poor
4000	3000	2700	2200	1800

GERMAN WWII MILITARY RIFLES

Model G 41 Rifle(M)

First produced in 1941. Built by Mauser. Not a successful design and very few of these rifles were produced. These are extremely rare rifles today. Chambered for the 7.92mm Mauser cartridge. Semiautomatic gas operated with rotating bolt. It was full stocked with a 10-round box magazine. Barrel length is 21.5" and weight is about 11 lbs. A total estimated produced of this model is estimated at 20,000 rifles.

Courtesy Richard M. Kumor, Sr.

Exc.	V.G.	Good	Fair	Poor
—	6000	—	—	—

Model G 41(W)

Similar to the above model but designed by Walther and produced by "duv" (Berlin-Lubeck Machine Factory) in 1941. This rifles was contracted for 70,000 units in 1942 and 1943. Correct examples will command a premium price.

Courtesy Richard M. Kumor, Sr.

Exc.	V.G.	Good	Fair	Poor
3000	2500	1500	—	—

Model G 43 (W) (K43)

An improved version of the G 41(W), introduced in 1943, with a modified gas system that was the more typical gas a piston design. Full stocked with full-length handguard. Wood or plastic stock. Receiver has a dovetail for telescope sight (#43@4 power). Barrel length is 22" and magazine capacity is 10 rounds. Weight is approximately 9.5 lbs. It is estimated that some 500,000 of these rifles were produced. Used by the Czech army after WWII.

Exc.	V.G.	Good	Fair	Poor
2800	2500	1500	—	—

NOTE: Add 150% for original scope.

Courtesy Richard M. Kumor, Sr.

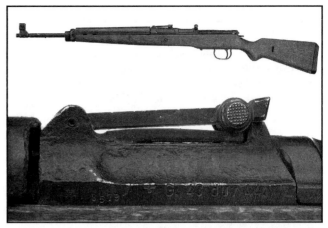

G43 left side with receiver markings, note rough finish
Paul Goodwin Photo

Exc.	V.G.	Good	Fair	Poor
1250	1000	750	250	100

A Walther G43 rifle sold at auction for $1,650 without the scope. The rifle had all matching numbers and was in very good condition. The scope for the G43 with mount sold separately for $1,760. It was in excellent condition with steel and rubber sunshade and original leather/cork lens cap.
Amoskeag Auction Company Inc., May 1999

Model FG42 (Fallschirmjager Gewehr)

This select fire 7.92x57mm rifle was adopted by the Luftwaffe for its airborne troops. It was designed to replace the rifle, light machine gun, and submachine gun. It incorporates a number of features including: straight line stock and muzzle brake, reduced recoil mechanism, and closed bolt semiautomatic fire and open bolt full auto fire. Rate of fire is about 750 rounds per minute. It had a mid-barrel bipod on early (1st Models, Type "E") models and front mounted barrel bipod on later (2nd Models, Type "G") models. Barrel attachment for pike-style bayonet. First Models were fitted with steel buttstocks, sharply raked pistol grips, and 2nd Models with wooden stocks and more vertical pistol grips. The 20-round magazine is left side mounted. Fitted with a 21.5" barrel the rifle weighs about 9.5 lbs. This breech mechanism was to be used years later by the U.S. in its M60 machine gun.

FG 42 with original German FG 42 ZF 4 scope and without scope and wooden buttstock • Courtesy Private NFA Collection • Paul Goodwin Photo

FG 42 with original German ZFG 42 scope and without scope and steel buttstock • Courtesy Private NFA Collection • Paul Goodwin Photo

Pre-1968

Exc.	V.G.	Fair
45000	35000	25000

Pre-1986 conversions

Exc.	V.G.	Fair
N/A	N/A	N/A

Pre-1986 dealer samples

Exc.	V.G.	Fair
N/A	N/A	N/A

NOTE: For rifles fitted with original German FG 42 scopes add between $5,000 and $10,000 depending on model. Consult an expert prior to a sale.

STURMGEWEHR GROUP

Because the German military thought the 7.92x57mm cartridge too powerful for their needs, a new cartridge was developed to provide less recoil, lighter weight, and less expensive production. This new cartridge, developed in the mid 1930s by Gustav Genschow, Polte, and others was called the 7.92x33mm Kurtz (Short) cartridge. The entire cartridge was 1.89" in length and had a bullet weight of 125 grains. This new cartridge was introduced in 1943 and spawned a new series of firearms designed for that cartridge.

MKb42(W)

This select fire open bolt machine carbine built by Walther was used on the Russian front. It was fitted with a 30-round box magazine and 16" barrel. Rate of fire was about 600 rounds per minute. It was fitted with a wooden stock and metal forearm. The rest of the weapon, with the exception of the barrel and bolt, was made from sheet metal to save cost and weight. Weight was about 9.75 lbs. A total of about 8,000 of these weapons were built by Walther.

Pre-1968(Very Rare)

Exc.	V.G.	Fair
18000	16500	15000

Pre-1986 conversions

Exc.	V.G.	Fair
N/A	N/A	N/A

Pre-1986 dealer samples

Exc.	V.G.	Fair
N/A	N/A	N/A

MKb42(H)

This was a similar design (open bolt) to the Walther version except for a 14.5" barrel and other internal differences. It was built by Haenel, and also saw extensive use on the Eastern Front. This version proved to be better than the Walther design. Its rate of fire was a somewhat slower 500 rounds per minute. Weight was approximately 11 lbs. Some 8,000 of these weapons were also produced.

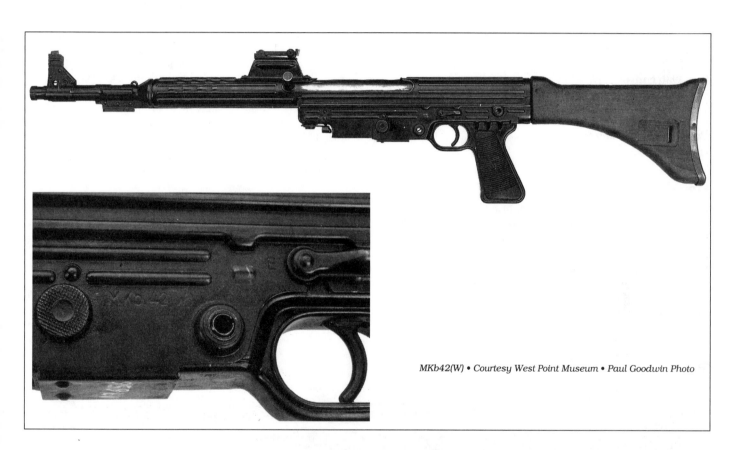

MKb42(W) • Courtesy West Point Museum • Paul Goodwin Photo

MP 43 • Paul Goodwin Photo

Pre-1968

Exc.	V.G.	Fair
14000	10000	8000

Pre-1986 conversions

Exc.	V.G.	Fair
N/A	N/A	N/A

Pre-1986 dealer samples

Exc.	V.G.	Fair
N/A	N/A	N/A

MP43, MP43/1

With some redesign this model was a newer MKb42(H). This weapon was adopted by the Waffenamt as standard issue in 1944. Original built by Haenel it was later produced by Mauser and Erma. This model was the forerunner of the MP44 and StG44.

Pre-1968

Exc.	V.G.	Fair
8500	7500	7000

Pre-1986 conversions

Exc.	V.G.	Fair
N/A	N/A	N/A

Pre-1986 dealer samples

Exc.	V.G.	Fair
N/A	N/A	N/A

MP 44

This German automatic rifle was first produced in 1943 and chambered for the 7.92x33 Kurz cartridge. Fitted with a solid stock and 16.3" barrel it has a magazine capacity of 30 rounds. The rate of fire is 500 rounds per minute. Weight is about 11.5 lbs. Marked "MP44" on top of the receiver. Production ceased in 1945. This rifle was used extensively on the Eastern Front during World War II.

Pre-1968

Exc.	V.G.	Fair
8500	7500	7000

StG44

This version of the MP43-Mp44 series is nothing more than a name change from the MP 44.

Pre-1968

Exc.	V.G.	Fair
8500	7500	7000

Pre-1986 conversions

Exc.	V.G.	Fair
N/A	N/A	N/A

Pre-1986 dealer samples

Exc.	V.G.	Fair
N/A	N/A	N/A

Model 86 SR

Introduced in 1993 this bolt action .308 is sometimes referred to as the Specialty Rifle. Fitted with a laminated wood and special match thumbhole stock or fiberglass stock with adjustable cheekpiece. Stock has rail in forearm and an adjustable recoil pad. Magazine capacity is 9 rounds. Finish is a non-glare blue. The barrel length with muzzle brake is 28.8". Many special features are found on this rifle, from adjustable trigger weight to silent safety. Mauser offers many options on this rifle as well that will affect the price. Weight is approximately 11 lbs.

NIB	Exc.	V.G.	Good	Fair	Poor
3300	2950	2500	1750	1250	750

Model 93 SR

Introduced in 1996 this is a tactical semiautomatic rifle chambered for the .300 Win. Mag. or the .338 Lapua cartridge. Barrel length is 25.5" with an overall length of 48.4". Barrel is fitted with a muzzle brake. Magazine capacity is 6 rounds for .300 and 5 rounds for .338 caliber. Weight is approximately 13 lbs.

NIB	Exc.	V.G.	Good	Fair	Poor
N/A	—	—	—	—	—

MKb42(H) • Courtesy West Point Museum
Paul Goodwin Photo

Pre-1986 conversions

Exc.	V.G.	Fair
N/A	N/A	N/A

Pre-1986 dealer samples

Exc.	V.G.	Fair
N/A	N/A	N/A

HECKLER & KOCH

Model 91

This rifle is recoil-operated, with a delayed-roller lock bolt. It is chambered for the .308 Winchester cartridge and has a 17.7" barrel with military-style aperture sights. It is furnished with a 20-round detachable magazine and is finished in matte black with a black plastic stock. This model is a semiautomatic version of the select fire G3 rifle. Some areas of the country have made its ownership illegal.

NIB	Exc.	V.G.	Good	Fair	Poor
3100	2750	2300	1550	1200	800

Model 91 A3

This model is simply the Model 91 with a retractable metal stock.

NIB	Exc.	V.G.	Good	Fair	Poor
3250	3000	2500	1600	1300	900

Model 93

This model is similar to the Model 91 except that it is chambered for the .223 cartridge and has a 16.4" barrel. The magazine holds 25 rounds, and the specification are the same as for the Model 91. This is a semiautomatic version of the select fire HK33 rifle.

NIB	Exc.	V.G.	Good	Fair	Poor
3100	2750	2300	1500	1200	800

Model 93 A3

This is the Model 93 with the retractable metal stock.

NIB	Exc.	V.G.	Good	Fair	Poor
3250	3000	2500	1650	1300	900

Model 94

This is a carbine version chambered for the 9mm Parabellum cartridge, with a 16.5" barrel. It is a smaller-scaled weapon that has a 15-shot magazine.

NIB	Exc.	V.G.	Good	Fair	Poor
4200	3850	3300	2750	2200	1500

Model 94 A3

This model is a variation of the Model 94 with the addition of a retractable metal stock.

NIB	Exc.	V.G.	Good	Fair	Poor
4500	3900	3400	2900	2300	1500

HK G3

First adopted by the German army in 1959. Chambered for the 7.62x51mm cartridge and fitted with a 17.5" barrel. Solid wooden stock on early models and plastic stock on later models (A3). Folding stock (A2) also offered. Magazine capacity is 20 rounds with a rate of fire of 550 rounds per minute. Weight is about 9.7 lbs. Marked "G3 HK" on left side of magazine housing. This select fire rifle has seen service with as many as 60 military forces around the world. There are several variations of this model.

Photo courtesy H&K

Pre-1968

Exc.	V.G.	Fair
9000	8750	8500

Pre-1986 conversions

Exc.	V.G.	Fair
7000	6500	6000

Pre-1986 dealer samples

Exc.	V.G.	Fair
4000	3800	3500

HK33

This model is a reduced caliber version of the standard HKG3. First produced in 1968 this model is chambered for the 5.56x45mm NATO cartridge (.223 caliber). This rifles is available in several variants, namely a sniper version with set trigger, telescope sight and bipod; a retractable stock version (A3); and a carbine version (12.68"). The HK33 features a 15.35" barrel without flash hider, and a magazine capacity of 25 or 40 rounds. The rate of fire is 750 rounds per minute. The rifle is marked "HK 33 5.56MM" with serial number on the left side of the magazine housing. The rifle is still in production and is in service in Chile, Brazil, various countries in southeast Asia, and Africa. Weight is approximately 8 lbs. for standard model.

HK33K • Photo courtesy H&K

Pre-1968 (Very Rare)

Exc.	V.G.	Fair
10000	9500	9000

Pre-1986 conversions

Exc.	V.G.	Fair
7500	7000	6800

Pre-1986 dealer samples

Exc.	V.G.	Fair
3500	3200	3000

NOTE: The HK33 K is the same as the HK33 with the exception of a 13" barrel. Prices may differ slightly for the 33 K version.

HK41

First produced in 1983 this 5.56x45mm chambered select fire rifle is fitted with a 17.5" barrel and has a magazine capacity of 30 rounds. Rate of fire is about 850 rounds per minute. Marked "HK G41 5.56MM" on the left side of magazine housing. This model will accept M16 magazines. This model is also available with fixed or retractable stock. Weight is 9.7 lbs.

Pre-1968

HK G41 • Courtesy H&K

Exc.	V.G.	Fair
N/A	N/A	N/A

Pre-1986 conversions

Exc.	V.G.	Fair
N/A	N/A	N/A

Pre-1986 dealer samples (Very Rare)

Exc.	V.G.	Fair
9000	8000	7500

PSG-1

This rifle is a high precision sniping rifle that features the delayed-roller semiautomatic action. It is chambered for the .308 Winchester cartridge and has a 5-shot magazine. Barrel length is 25.6". It is furnished with a complete array of accessories including a 6x42-power illuminated Hensoldt scope. Rifle weighs 17.8 lbs.

NIB	Exc.	V.G.	Good	Fair	Poor
14500	12500	9000	7500	6000	4000

Model SL8-1

This is a new generation .223 rifle modeled after the military Model G36 (not available to civilians) and introduced in 2000. It is built of carbon fiber polymer and is gas operated. Thumbhole stock with cheekpiece. Barrel length is 20.8". Magazine capacity is 10 rounds. Adjustable sights. Weight is approximately 8.6 lbs.

NIB	Exc.	V.G.	Good	Fair	Poor
1600	1200	—	—	—	—

Model USC

Introduced in 2000 this semiautomatic blowback carbine is derived from HK's UMP submachine gun (not available to civilians). Chambered for the .45 ACP cartridge and fitted with a 16" barrel. Skeletonized stock. Accessory rail on top of receiver. Adjustable sights. Magazine capacity is 10 rounds. Weight is approximately 6 lbs.

NIB	Exc.	V.G.	Good	Fair	Poor
1200	900	—	—	—	—

SHOTGUNS

SAUER, J. P. & SON

Luftwaffe Survival Drilling

A double barrel 12 gauge by 9.3x74R combination shotgun/rifle with 28" barrels. Blued with a checkered walnut stock and marked with Nazi inspection. Stampings on the stock and barrel breech. Normally, furnished with an aluminum case.

NOTE: Add 50% to prices below for case.

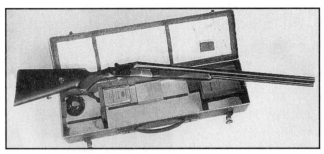

Courtesy Richard. M. Kumor, Sr.

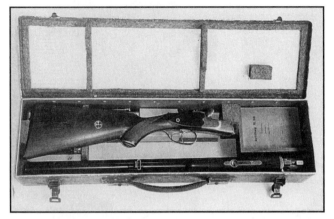

Courtesy Richard M. Kumor, Sr.

Exc.	V.G.	Good	Fair	Poor
6000	5500	3800	2500	—

MACHINE GUNS

Germany adopted the Maxim gun designated it the MG01 which was built on the Belgian Maxim pattern Model 1900. It was not until 1908 that Germany produced its own version of the Maxim called the MG 08.

Maxim '08 (MG 08)

Germany adopted this gun at the turn of the 20th century. In 1908 they began to produce the gun themselves. This was the standard German heavy machine gun during WWI. Chambered for the 7.92x57mm cartridge this gun had a rate of fire of 400 to 500 rounds per minute from its 28" barrel. It was fed with a 100 or 250-round fabric belt. The gun weighed about 41 lbs. with a sled mount weighing about 83 pounds. The gun was marked "DEUTCHE WAFFEN UND MUNITIONSFABRIKEN BERLIN" with the year of production on the left side of the receiver. The serial number was located on the top of the receiver. The gun was produced from 1908 to about 1918.

Pre-1968

Exc.	V.G.	Fair
15000	13000	12000

Pre-1986 conversions

Exc.	V.G.	Fair
9000	8000	7000

Pre-1986 dealer samples

Exc.	V.G.	Fair
N/A	N/A	N/A

Maxim '08/15

A more movable version of the Maxim Model '08. Chambered for the 7.92x57mm Mauser cartridge and fitted with a 28" water-cooled barrel with bipod, it weighs about 31 lbs. It is fed by a 50-round cloth belt with a rate of fire of 500 rounds per minute. Marked "LMG 09/15 SPANDAU" on top of the receiver.

Another version of this gun with an air-cooled slotted barrel jacket was used in aircraft. Called the IMG 08/15.

Pre-1968

Exc.	V.G.	Fair
8500	7500	7000

Pre-1986 conversions

Exc.	V.G.	Fair
N/A	N/A	N/A

Pre-1986 dealer samples

Exc.	V.G.	Fair
N/A	N/A	N/A

MG 08/15 • Courtesy West Point Museum • Paul Goodwin Photo

Dreyse Model 1915 • Courtesy Private NFA Collection • Paul Goodwin Photo

MG 34 with receiver markings • Paul Goodwin Photo

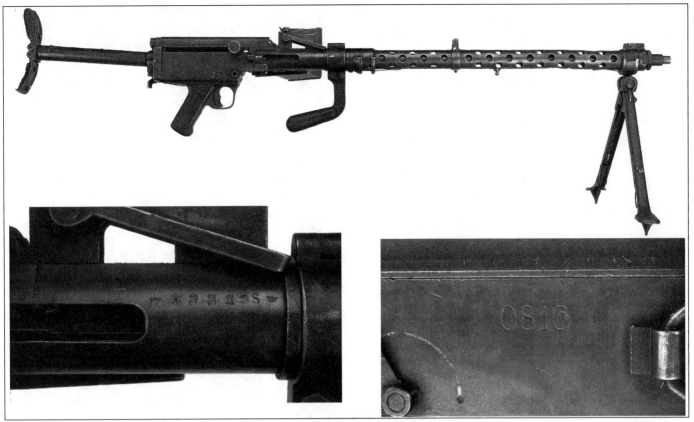

Dreyse Model 1910/15

Chambered for the 7.92x57mm Mauser cartridge this gun was based on the Louis Schmeisser patents of 1907. Built by Rheinmetall in Sommerda, Germany. Named in honor of Johann Niklaus von Dreyse who died in 1875. This is a water-cooled gun designed for sustained fire. Rate of fire is about 550 to 600 rounds a minute. Weight is approximately 37 lbs. Most of these guns were converted by Germany to MG13s during the 1930s so few original Dreyse still survive. Very rare in unaltered condition.

Pre-1968

Exc.	V.G.	Fair
20000	18000	17000

Pre-1986 conversions

Exc.	V.G.	Fair
N/A	N/A	N/A

Pre-1986 dealer samples

Exc.	V.G.	Fair
N/A	N/A	N/A

MG 13

In 1932 the German army adopted the MG 13 as its standard machine gun. Chambered for the 7.92x57mm cartridge and fitted with a 28" air-cooled barrel this gun is recoil operated. The butt is a single arm metal type with pistol grip. The bipod is attached close to the muzzle. A 25-round box magazine or a 75-round saddle drum magazine can be used. Weight is about 25 lbs. with bipod. The gun was built by Simson of Suhl, Germany and were built from a Dreyse.

NOTE: The 75-round drum for use with the MG 13 is rare because it uses a MG 15 drum with a special magazine extension to fit into the side of the MG 13 magazine well.

Pre-1968

Exc.	V.G.	Fair
15000	13000	11000

Pre-1986 conversions

Exc.	V.G.	Fair
N/A	N/A	N/A

Pre-1986 dealer samples

Exc.	V.G.	Fair
N/A	N/A	N/A

MG15 Aircraft Gun

Used by German Air Force in its bombers this air-cooled gun is chambered for the 7.92x57JS cartridge. Rate of fire is about 850 rounds per minute. Barrel length is 28". Saddle drum magazine with 75-round capacity was used. Weight is about 28 lbs. Built by Krieghoff. Made by Rheinmetall beginning in 1932.

Pre-1968

Exc.	V.G.	Fair
13000	12000	11500

Pre-1986 conversions

Exc.	V.G.	Fair
N/A	N/A	N/A

Pre-1986 dealer samples

Exc.	V.G.	Fair
N/A	N/A	N/A

MG15 Water-Cooled Ground Gun

A converted aircraft machine gun, this water-cooled model was used by ground forces from 1944 to 1945. Barrel length was 30" and weight is about 33 lbs. Chambered for the 7.92x57JS cartridge. Rate of fire is about 750 rounds per minute. Ammunition capacity is a 75-round saddle drum magazine. Built by Krieghoff.

Private NFA collection • Photo by Gary Gelson

Pre-1968

Exc.	V.G.	Fair
12000	11000	10500

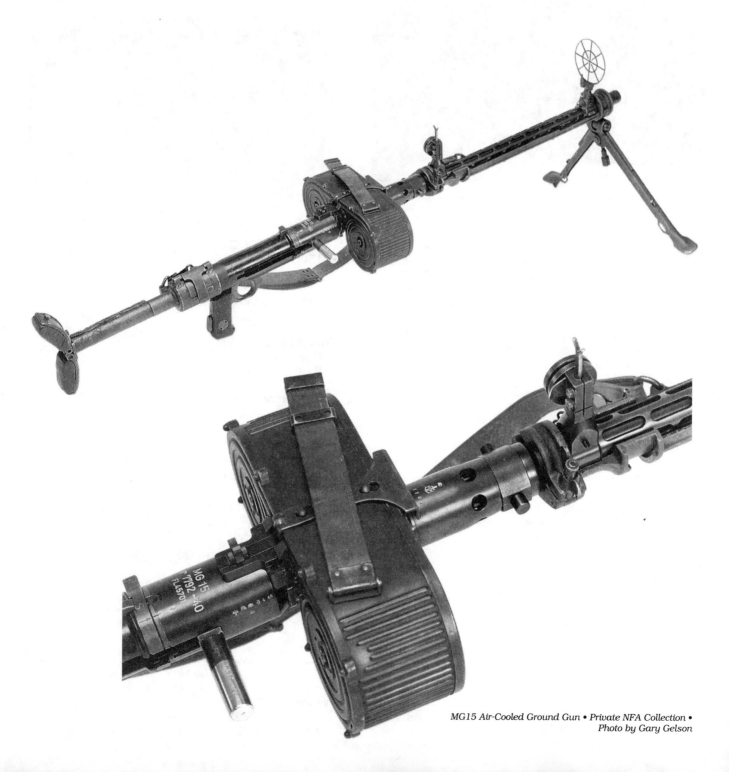

MG15 Air-Cooled Ground Gun • Private NFA Collection • Photo by Gary Gelson

Pre-1986 conversions

Exc.	V.G.	Fair
N/A	N/A	N/A

Pre-1986 dealer samples

Exc.	V.G.	Fair
N/A	N/A	N/A

MG15 Air-Cooled Ground Gun

Same as the aircraft gun but converted to ground use in 1944 and 1945 by attaching a bipod and single strut buttstock.

Pre-1968

Exc.	V.G.	Fair
13000	12000	11500

Pre-1986 conversions

Exc.	V.G.	Fair
N/A	N/A	N/A

Pre-1986 dealer samples

Exc.	V.G.	Fair
N/A	N/A	N/A

MG34

Designed and built by Mauser, this was the first general purpose machine gun to be produced in large numbers. It was introduced into the German army in about 1936, and stayed in production until the end of the war in 1945. Chambered for the 7.92x57mm Mauser cartridge this gun had a 25" barrel with a 50-round belt or 75-round saddle drum. Rate of fire was about 800 to 900 rounds per minute. Marked "MG34" with its serial number on top of the receiver. Weight was approximately 26.5 lbs. There were a number of different bipods and tripod mounts for this gun, as well as different gun configurations such as antiaircraft use, use in armored vehicles and one configuration where only automatic fire was possible. After WWII the gun was used by the Czechs, French, and Israelis as well as the Viet Cong. Superseded by the MG42.

Pre-1968

Exc.	V.G.	Fair
15000	13000	11000

Pre-1986 conversions

Exc.	V.G.	Fair
N/A	N/A	N/A

Pre-1986 dealer samples

Exc.	V.G.	Fair
N/A	N/A	N/A

MG42-MG42/59-MG1-MG3

This gun replaced the MG 34 and was chambered for the 7.92x57mm Mauser cartridge. It has a 20.8" quick change barrel and is fed by a 50-round belt. Its rate of fire is about 1,000 to 1,200 rounds per minute. The butt is synthetic with pistol grip. The gun weighs about 25 lbs. Marked "MG42" on the left side of the receiver. This gun was produced from 1938 until the end of the war in 1945. Its design was the result of wartime engineering which used roller locks, at the time a revolutionary design concept.

Post-war models, the MG42/59 followed by the MG1 then the MG3, are still in use by the German army. These post-war guns are chambered for the 7.62x51mm cartridge. These models utilize many important improvements in manufacturing and design, and are in use by many countries throughout the world. There are a numbered of licensed versions of the MG42/59 made in Austria, Italy, Spain, Portugal, Turkey, Yugoslavia, and Switzerland.

MG3 • Photo Courtesy Private NFA Collection

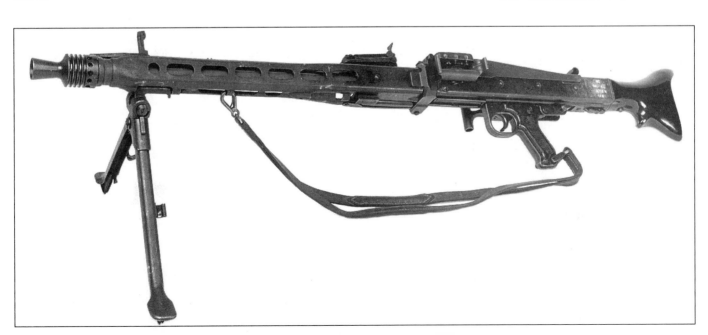

MG 42 • Private NFA Collection • Photo by Gary Gelson

Pre-1968

Exc.	V.G.	Fair
17000	15000	14000

Pre-1986 conversions

Exc.	V.G.	Fair
N/A	N/A	N/A

Pre-1986 dealer samples

Exc.	V.G.	Fair
12000	10000	9000

NOTE: For post-war guns add 50% premium.

HK11 (HK11A1-HK11E)

Designed as a light air-cooled machine gun chambered for the 7.62x51mm cartridge this gun uses a roller-delayed bolt. The quick change barrel is 17.7" long. Fixed synthetic stock with pistol grip and bipod. Uses a 20-round box magazine or 80 dual drum. Rate of fire is about 850 rounds per minute. Weight is approximately 15 lbs.

NOTE: There is no drum magazine on the HK 11A1.

Pre-1968

Exc.	V.G.	Fair
N/A	N/A	N/A

Pre-1986 conversions

Exc.	V.G.	Fair
13000	11000	9000

Pre-1986 dealer samples

Exc.	V.G.	Fair
13000	11000	9000

HK13 (HK13E)

This gun is similar to the HK11 but is chambered for the 5.56x45mm cartridge. Quick change 17.7" barrel. Fed by a 20-, 30-, 40-round box magazine, or 100-round dual drum. Rate of fire is about 800 rounds per minute. Weight is approximately 12 lbs.

NOTE: There are a number of variants to this model. The HK13C has a baked-on forest camouflage finish. The HK13E is a modernized version with selective improvements, such as a 3-round burst capability. The rifling has been changed to stabilize 62 grain bullets. The HK13E1 is the same as the HK13E with rifling twist to accommodate 54 grain bullets. The HK13S has a baked-on desert camouflage scheme.

Pre-1968

Exc.	V.G.	Fair
N/A	N/A	N/A

Pre-1986 conversions

Exc.	V.G.	Fair
12000	11000	9000

Pre-1986 dealer samples

Exc.	V.G.	Fair
12000	11000	9000

NOTE: There is a semiautomatic version of this gun. Value would be around $6,000 for one in excellent condition.

HK 21 (HK21E-HK23E)

These guns form a series of general purpose machine guns. The 21 series is chambered for the 7.62x51mm cartridge while the 23E is chambered for the 5.56x45mm cartridge. The HK 21 is fitted with a 17.5" barrel and has a rate of fire of 900 rounds per minute. Its weight is about 17 lbs. Marked on the top of receiver. The HK 21 was first produced in 1970 but is no longer in production , while the HK21E and 23E are still produced.

This series of guns has variations similar to the HK13 series of guns.

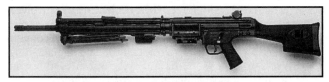

HK 23 • Courtesy H&K

HK 23E • Courtesy H&K

Pre-1968-Model 21 only

Exc.	V.G.	Fair
12000	11000	9000

Pre-1986 conversions

Exc.	V.G.	Fair
10000	9500	9000

Pre-1986 dealer samples

Exc.	V.G.	Fair
6000	6000	6000

NOTE: The HK21E and HK23E will bring a premium of 75% over the older HK21/2

GREAT BRITAIN

British Military Conflicts, 1870-Present

The period from 1870 to 1901 marked the height of Britain's economic, political, commercial, and military influence. During this period the far flung British empire required the country to police its possessions frequently with force. The British army was involved in Africa, Asia, the Middle East, and even Ireland during this period. The Boer War in the last years of the 19th century, for example, required extensive military presence in South Africa. In 1914 Britain entered World War I. By the end of the war in 1918 the country had exhausted its wealth and manpower. During the period between the two world wars Britain tried to consolidate its remaining power which led to the appeasement of Nazi Germany and eventually World War II in 1939. With the end of the war in 1945 Britain gave independence to many of its colonies and concentrated on domestic, economic and social affairs. In 1982 the country was involved in a successful military engagement with Argentina over the Falkland Islands. As a member of NATO Britain continued to carry out its military responsibilities.

HANDGUNS

NOTE: During World War I the British government contracted with two Spanish firms to build what was called the Old Pattern No.1 Mark I revolver by Garate y Compania and the Old Pattern No. 2 Mark I revolver by Trocaola, Aranzabal y Compania. Both companies were located in Eibar, Spain. These revolvers were chambered for the .455 caliber cartridge and were fitted with 5" barrels.

Britain also acquired Colt New Service and Smith & Wesson First Model and Second Model Ejector .455 revolvers from the U.S. Approximately 75,000 of these S&W and Colt revolvers were sent to England between 1914 and 1916.

Adams Model 1872 Mark 2, 3, and 4

A .450 caliber double action revolver with a 6" octagonal barrel and 6-shot cylinder. Blued with walnut grips. Built by Adams Patent Small Arms Company. Weight was about 40 oz. This was the first breechloading revolver issued to the British mounted units. In service from 1872 to 1919.

Exc.	V.G.	Good	Fair	Poor
—	1000	500	300	200

WEBLEY & SCOTT, LTD.

Bibliographical **Note:** For historical information, technical data and photos see William Dowell's, *The Webley Story*, Skyrac Press, 1987.

Mark I

A .455 caliber double action top break revolver with a 4" barrel and 6-shot cylinder. Blued with hard rubber grips. Manufactured from 1887 to 1894. Models issued to the Royal Navy have the letter "N" stamped on top of the frame behind the hammer.

Courtesy Faintich Auction Services, Inc. • Photo Paul Goodwin

Exc.	V.G.	Good	Fair	Poor
300	200	175	125	100

NOTE: Military version chambered for .455 cartridge only while commercial versions were chambered for the .442 and .476 cartridges.

Mark II

As above, with a larger hammer spur and improved barrel catch. Manufactured from 1894 to 1897.

Exc.	V.G.	Good	Fair	Poor
300	200	175	125	100

Mark III

As above, with internal improvements. Introduced in 1897.

Courtesy Rock Island Auction Company

Exc.	V.G.	Good	Fair	Poor
325	225	200	150	125

Mark IV

As above, with a .455 caliber and 4" or 6" barrel. Sometimes referred to as the "Boer War" model because it was supplied to British troops in South Africa between 1899 and 1902.

NOTE: This model was also commercially available in .22 caliber with 6" barrel, .32 caliber with 3" barrel, and .38 caliber with 3", 4", or 5" barrel.

Courtesy Faintich Auction Services, Inc. • Photo Paul Goodwin

Exc.	V.G.	Good	Fair	Poor
350	300	225	175	125

Mark V

As above, with a 4" (standard) or 6" barrel. Manufactured from 1913 to 1915.

Courtesy Faintich Auction Services, Inc. • Photo Paul Goodwin

Exc.	V.G.	Good	Fair	Poor
375	325	250	200	150

Mark IV .380 (.38S&W)

Webley produced a military version of its .38 revolver for military use during World War II. This model was intended to supplement the .38 Enfield revolvers.

Exc.	V.G.	Good	Fair	Poor
375	325	250	200	150

Mark VI

As above, with 6" barrel and square buttgrip. Introduced in 1915 and replaced in 1928.

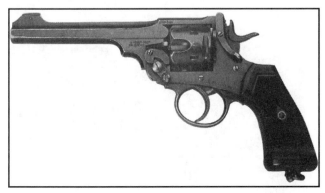

Courtesy Faintich Auction Services, Inc. • Photo Paul Goodwin

Exc.	V.G.	Good	Fair	Poor
350	300	250	175	125

Model 1913-Semiautomatic Pistol

The Model 1913 was the result of years of development in conjunction with the British government and was finally adopted in 1913 as the Model 1913 MK1N for Royal Navy issue. It has the same breech-locking system as the Model 1910, but has an external hammer and is chambered for the .455 Webley Self-Loading cartridge. About 1,000 Model 1913s were sold commercially and serial numbered along with the smaller caliber pistols. In 1915 a variation of the Model 1913 with butt slotted for a shoulder stock, an adjustable rear sight, and a hammer safety adopted for use by the Royal Horse Artillery. Shoulder stocks are very rare, and will double values shown for the RHA model. All militaries were numbered in their own series; about 10,000 made in both variations.

Model 1913

Exc.	V.G.	Good	Fair	Poor
1500	1200	800	500	300

Model 1913 (RHA model)

Courtesy Joseph Schroeder

Exc.	V.G.	Good	Fair	Poor
2500	2000	1500	850	600

ENFIELD ROYAL SMALL ARMS FACTORY

In 1879 the British army needed revolvers, and the Royal Small Arms Factory was commissioned to produce them. The result was that on August 11, 1880, the Enfield Mark I was accepted for duty.

Enfield Mark I Revolver

A 6-shot, hinged-frame, break-open revolver. It has an odd ejection system—when the barrel is pulled down, the cylinder moves forward; and the extractor plate remains in place, retaining the spent cartridges. This revolver is chambered for the .476 cartridge and has a 6-shot cylinder. The barrel is 6" long, and the finish is blued with checkered walnut grips. Weight is about 40 oz.

Exc.	V.G.	Good	Fair	Poor
350	225	175	140	100

Enfield Mark 2

The Mark 2 is similar externally, with some design improvements—such as a rounded front sight, taper-bored cylinders, an integral top strap, and plain grips. The Mark 2 was introduced in 1881 and was replaced by the Webley Mark I in 1887.

Exc.	V.G.	Good	Fair	Poor
350	225	175	140	100

Enfield-Produced Webley Mark 6

This model is identical to the Webley-produced versions. It is of .455 caliber and is stamped "Enfield" on the frame.

Exc.	V.G.	Good	Fair	Poor
350	250	175	140	100

Enfield No. 2 Mark I/Mark 1*

Originally chambered for the .380 (.38 S&W). It is a 6-shot, break-open double action, with a 5" barrel. The finish is blued, with black plastic checkered grips. This model was actually a modified Webley design and was adopted in 1932. In 1938 the bullet was changed from a 200-grain lead "soft-nosed" to a 178-grain jacketed, in response to pressure from the Geneva Conference.

Exc.	V.G.	Good	Fair	Poor
225	200	150	125	100

Enfield No. 2 Mark I*

The same as the Mark I with the hammer spur and single action lockwork omitted in response to the Royal Tank Regiment's fear that the spur would catch on the tank as the crews were entering and exiting their confines.

Exc.	V.G.	Good	Fair	Poor
225	200	175	150	125

NOTE: During WWII these pistols were also manufactured by Albion Motors Ltd. of Glasgow, Scotland. These pistols were produced between 1941 and 1943, and approximately 24,000 were made. They are marked "Albion" on the right side of the frame. These examples would not be valued differently than Enfield-made pistols. Enfield pistols with the marking "SM" or "SSM" will also be noted, and this refers to various parts produced by Singer Sewing Machine Company of England. These pistols were assembled at Enfield. Used until 1957, when the FN-Browning GP35 semiautomatic pistol replaced them.

Enfield No. 2 MK1-Paul Goodwin Photo

Enfield No. 2 Mark 1* • Courtesy West Point Museum • Paul Goodwin Photo

SUBMACHINE GUNS

NOTE: For historical information and technical details see Laider and Howroyd, *The Guns of Dagenham; Lanchester, Patchett, Sterling,* Collector Grade Publications, 1999. Laider, *The Sten Machine Carbine,* Collector Grade Publications, 2000.

Lanchester Mk1/Mk1*

The British submachine gun was produced from 1940 to about 1942. It is chambered for the 9mm cartridge and is fitted with a 7.75" barrel. The magazine capacity is 50 rounds. Rate of fire is 600 rounds per minute. Weight is about 9.5 lbs. This British gun is almost an exact copy of the Bergmann

Lanchester Mark I* • Courtesy West Point Museum • Paul Goodwin Photo

MP28. The magazine housing is made of brass. The bayonet lug will accept a Model 1907 pattern bayonet. Most of these weapons were issued to the Royal Navy and stayed in service there until the 1960s. Markings are "LANCHESTER MARK I" on the magazine housing.

The Mk1* has had the fire selector switch in front of the triggerguard removed thus making the weapon capable of full automatic fire only.

Pre-1968

Exc.	V.G.	Fair
4500	3500	3000

Pre-1986 conversions

Exc.	V.G.	Fair
N/A	N/A	N/A

Pre-1986 dealer samples

Exc.	V.G.	Fair
2000	1500	1500

NOTE: Add a premium of 15% for the Mark 1 version.

Sten Mark II

The Mark II is the most common version of the Sten models. It is chambered for the 9mm cartridge and features a removable stock and barrel. The magazine capacity is 32 rounds. Barrel length is 7.66". The rate of fire is 550 rounds per minute. Markings are located on top of the magazine housing and are stamped "STEN MK II." Weight is approximately 6.6 lbs. Produced from 1942 to 1944 with about two million built in Britain, Canada, and New Zealand.

Courtesy Richard M. Kumor, Sr.

Pre-1968

Exc.	V.G.	Fair
4000	3500	3000

Pre-1986 conversions (or U.S.-manufactured receivers)

Exc.	V.G.	Fair
3000	2500	2500

Pre-1986 dealer samples

Exc.	V.G.	Fair
2500	2000	1000

NOTE: The Mark II S is the silenced version of the Mark II. Fitted with a canvas foregrip. Weight is about 7.75 lbs. and rate of fire is about 450 rounds per minute.

Sten Mark III

This model was an improved version of the Marks 1 and 2, and featured a one-piece receiver and barrel jacket of welding tubing with a non-removable barrel. No flash hider. Built at Lines and Long Branch arsenals. All other specifications are the same as the Marks 1 and 2.

Pre-1968

Exc.	V.G.	Fair
4000	3500	3000

Pre-1986 conversions (or U.S.-manufactured receivers)

Exc.	V.G.	Fair
3000	2500	2500

Pre-1986 dealer samples

Exc.	V.G.	Fair
2500	2000	1000

Sten Mark V

This version of the Sten was first produced in 1944. It featured a wooden stock and pistol grip. The barrel could accept a bayonet. Finish was better than standard service of the period. Barrel length was 7.75" and magazine capacity was 32 rounds. Rate of fire was 600 rounds per minute. Weight was increased to 8.6 lbs. over the Mark II. Marked "STEN M.C. MK V" on top of the magazine housing. Production ceased on this version in 1946.

Pre-1968

Exc.	V.G.	Fair
4500	4250	3750

Pre-1986 conversions

Exc.	V.G.	Fair
3500	3000	2500

Pre-1986 dealer samples

Exc.	V.G.	Fair
2500	2000	1500

NOTE: The Mark VI is the silenced version of the Mark V. Fitted with a long barrel and silencer assembly. Weight is about 9.8 lbs. and rate of fire is about 450 rounds per minute.

Sterling Mk 4 (L2A3)

Chambered for the 9mm cartridge this submachine gun features a 7.75" barrel, 34-round side mounted magazine, collapsible metal stock. The last version of the Sterling, the Mk 4, is a result of a long line of improvements to the gun beginning with the Pachett. The Pachett was originally developed during WWII and produced by the Sterling Co. in Dagenham, England and the Royal Ordnance Factory in Fazakerley England. Next came the Mk 2 and the Mk 3 beginning in 1953 and the Mk 4 during the late 1950s.

It has seen wide use throughout the world having been adopted by the British army, New Zealand and approximately 40 other countries. The rate of fire is 550 rounds per minute. Weight is about 6 lbs. Produced from 1953 to 1988. Still made in India under license. Marked "STERLING SMG 9MM" on the magazine housing.

Photo Courtesy Private NFA Collection

Pre-1968 (Rare)

Exc.	V.G.	Fair
8000	7000	6000

Sten MK 5 with magazine housing markings • Paul
Goodwin Photo

Pre-1986 conversions

Exc.	V.G.	Fair
5000	4500	4500

Pre-1986 dealer samples

Exc.	V.G.	Fair
5000	4500	3250

Sterling L34A1

This is a silenced version of the L2A3 Mark 4 gun. The silencer is fitted with a short wooden forearm. Barrel length is the same as the unsilenced version. Weight is about 8 lbs.

Pre-1968 (Rare)

Exc.	V.G.	Fair
8000	7000	6500

Pre-1986 conversions

Exc.	V.G.	Fair
4500	4000	3500

Pre-1986 dealer samples

Exc.	V.G.	Fair
4000	3500	3000

RIFLES

NOTE: For historical information and technical data see: Reynolds, E.G.B., *The Lee-Enfield Rifle*, Herbert Jenkins, Ltd., 1960. *The Lee-Enfield Story*, Ian Skennerton, 1993. Stevens, Blake, *UK and Commonwealth FALs*, Vol. 2, The FAL Series, Collector Grade Publications, 1980. Skennerton has also writen a number of monographs on other British rifles that are well worth study by the collector.

MARTINI-HENRY

This single shot rolling block rifle was built on the Martini block action and a rifled barrel by Alexander Henry. Early rifles built prior to 1885 used a fragile rolled cartridge case while later post 1885 versions used a solid case. The British army built these rifles with three different buttstock lengths and marked the 1/2" shorter than standard rifles with an "S" on the stock while longer stocks were marked with an "L." Standard length buttstocks were not marked. Martini-Henry rifles and carbines were used by British military forces all over the world during the latter quarter of the 19th century. Produced by Enfield, BSA, and LSA.

Mark 1 Rifle

Chambered for the .577-450 Martini-Henry cartridge and fitted with a 33.2" barrel, this lever operated single shot rifle was fitted with a steel bayonet and was full stocked with no upper handguard. Weight is about 8.75 lbs. Introduced in 1874.

Exc.	V.G.	Good	Fair	Poor
1250	900	700	400	250

Mark 2 Rifle

Similar to the Mark 1 but with an improved trigger in 1877.

Exc.	V.G.	Good	Fair	Poor
1250	900	700	500	250

Mark 3 Rifle

An improved version introduced in 1879 of the Mark 2 with double lump barrel and wider breech block. Weight is slightly heavier than the Marks 1 and 2 at about 9 lbs.

Exc.	V.G.	Good	Fair	Poor
1250	900	700	500	250

Mark 4 Rifle

Introduced in 1887 this Mark was fitted with a longer lever, a thinner breech block with modified extractor, narrow buttstock with bayonet fitting to accommodate a P1887 sword bayonet. Weight is about 9.25 lbs.

Exc.	V.G.	Good	Fair	Poor
1250	900	700	500	250

Cavalry Carbine Mark 1

This configuration was introduced in 1877 and is a short version of the rifle with full stock, no handguard, front sight with protectors, and a reduced charge carbine cartridge; the .577-450 Martini-Henry Carbine cartridge. Barrel length is about 21.25". Weight is approximately 7.5 lbs.

Exc.	V.G.	Good	Fair	Poor
1500	1250	950	700	350

Artillery Carbine Mark 2

This model is similar to the Cavalry Carbine but with bayonet fittings. Introduced in 1879. Weight is about 7.7 lbs.

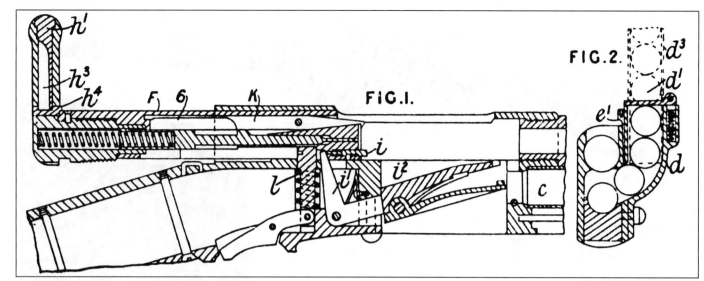

Burton Patent # 4046, Oct. 5, 1880 showing receiver and magazine hopper system in Fig. 2 • British Small Arms Patents

Exc.	V.G.	Good	Fair	Poor
1500	1250	950	700	350

LEE-METFORD

NOTE: The Lee-Metford rifles were produced at the Royal Small Arms Factory, Enfield; the Birmingham Small Arms Co.; Sparkbrook, Vickers, Birmingham, and the London Small Arms Co., and so marked on the right side under the bolt handle for rifles and on the left side for carbines.

The British used the MARK and * system to denote improvements. The "MARK" indicated a major design change or improvement. The "*" indicated a minor change.

TRIALS RIFLES

The first trials for magazine rifles for the British army began in 1880. There were a number of initial contenders which will not be covered here. By 1883 the number of serious competitors was reduced to those listed below.

Owen Jones

This model was an adaptation of the Martini action and fitted with a 33" barrel chambered for the .402 caliber Enfield-Martini cartridge. Five-round magazine. Folding rear sight graduated to 2,000 yards. Weight is about 10.5 lbs. An unknown number of these rifles were built with different type magazine feeds and styles.

Exc.	V.G.	Good	Fair	Poor
5000	4500	4000	2500	—

Lee-Burton

This rifle used the Lee action, the first British rifle to do so. Chambered for the .402 caliber Enfield-Martini cartridge and fitted with a 30.2" barrel. Built by Enfield. Magazine capacity is 5 rounds. Marked "ENFIELD 1886" of left side of the receiver. Weight is about 10 lbs. About 300 were produced.

Exc.	V.G.	Good	Fair	Poor
5000	4500	4000	2500	—

Improved Lee

These rifles were purchased directly from Remington in 1887. Chambered for the .43 caliber Spanish cartridge and fitted with a 32" barrel. Folding leaf rear sight was graduated to 1,200 yards. Magazine capacity was 5 rounds. Weighs approximately 10 lbs. Marked with the Remington address on the receiver. About 300 were used in the trials. The only indication that this is a trials rifle is the marking "WD" on the right side of the butt.

Exc.	V.G.	Good	Fair	Poor
3500	3000	2500	1500	—

.303 Magazine Rifle-1888 Trials Model

Developed from the Improved Lee but chambered for the .303 cartridge and fitted with a 30.2" barrel. No upper handguard. Magazine capacity is 7 rounds. Marked, "ENFIELD 1888." Weight is about 9 lbs. Some 387 of these rifles were produced.

Exc.	V.G.	Good	Fair	Poor
4000	3500	3000	1750	—

Mark I

A bolt action service rifle chambered for the .303 black powder British cartridge. It was designed by James Paris Lee and incorporated rifling developed by William Metford. This rifling was specifically designed to alleviate the problem of black powder fouling. 30.2" barrel and an 8-round, detachable box magazine located in front of the triggerguard. Furnished with magazine cutoff, it features military-type sights and a cleaning rod mounted underneath the barrel and a trap in the steel buttplate to house cleaning tools. Finger grooves in forend. The finish is blued, with a full-length walnut stock held on by two barrel bands. Weight is about 10 lbs. It was introduced in 1888. Approximately 358,000 were produced.

Exc.	V.G.	Good	Fair	Poor
550	400	300	200	100

Mark I*

Similar to the Mark 1 except that the safety catch was removed from the cocking piece and a brass disc was inletted into the buttstock for regimental markings. There were a number of internal improvements, as well as the fitting of a different, blade-type front sight and V-notch rear sight graduated to 1,800 yards. This model was fitted with an 8-round magazine. It was introduced in 1892.

Exc.	V.G.	Good	Fair	Poor
550	400	300	200	100

Lee-Metford Mark 1* • Paul Goodwin Photo

Mark II

Has a modified magazine that holds 10 rounds in a double column. A 1/2 length cleaning rod was located under the 30.2" barrel. No finger grooves in forend. Fitted with brass buttplate with long heel tang. Rear leaf sight graduated to 1,800 yards. No butt marking disk. It was introduced in 1892. Weight reduced to 9.25 lbs. About 250,000 were produced.

Exc.	V.G.	Good	Fair	Poor
550	400	300	200	100

Mark II*

Has a lengthened bolt, with the addition of a safety catch. Barrel length is 30.2". No finger grooves in forend. All parts are interchangeable with the Mark II rifle. It was introduced in 1895. About 13,000 were produced.

Exc.	V.G.	Good	Fair	Poor
500	400	300	200	100

Mark I Carbine

Has a 20.75" barrel. Rear sight is graduated to 2,000 yards. Buttstock is fitted with a marking disk. No bayonet fittings. Weight was about 7.5 lbs. It was introduced in 1894. Approximately 18,000 were produced.

Exc.	V.G.	Good	Fair	Poor
750	600	450	300	150

NOTE: Many Lee-Metford rifles were modified after 1902 to accept a stripper clip guide which required the removal of the dust cover. Such a modification results in a deduction of 10% from original Lee-Metford rifles.

military-styled. Rear leaf sight graduated to 1,800 yards. The stock is full-length walnut, and there is a cleaning rod beneath it. There is a magazine cutoff located on the right side of the receiver. There are two barrel bands and a bayonet lug. The upper handguard extended from the receiver ring to the rear sight. The buttplate is brass with extended upper tang with trap for cleaning equipment. Weight is about 9.25 lbs. This model was manufactured between 1895 and 1899. Approximately 315,000 were manufactured.

Paul Goodwin Photo

Exc.	V.G.	Good	Fair	Poor
850	750	600	400	200

Mark II • Courtesy West Point Museum • Paul Goodwin Photo

ENFIELD ROYAL SMALL ARMS FACTORY

NOTE: This series of rifles is marked by the presence of deeper Enfield rifling rather than the shallow Metford rifling. The same manufactureres that built the Lee-Metford built the Lee-Enfield along with Ishapore, India and Lithgow, Austrilia.

Lee-Enfield Mark I Rifle

Chambered for the .303 cartridge and has a 30" barrel. The attached box magazine holds 10 rounds, and the sights are

Lee-Enfield Mark I* Rifle

No attached cleaning rod, otherwise the same as the Mark I rifle. It was introduced in 1899. Almost 600,000 of these rifles were produced.

Exc.	V.G.	Good	Fair	Poor
850	750	600	400	200

NOTE: Many long Lee-Enfield rifles were modified for charger loading (stripper clip). Prices are 10% less than unmodified rifles.

Lee-Enfield Mark I Carbine

This model is the same as the Lee-Medford except for the Enfield rifling and so marked. Slight different rear sight marked "EC" on bottom right hand corner of leaf. Introduced in 1896. Rear sight leather protector is standard on this carbine. Weight is about 7.5 lbs. Approximately 14,000 were produced.

Exc.	V.G.	Good	Fair	Poor
750	650	500	300	150

Lee-Enfield Mark I* Carbine

Same as the Mark I carbine but with no cleaning rod and no left side sling bar. Rear sight leather protector. Introduced in 1899. A little more than 26,000 were produced.

Exc.	V.G.	Good	Fair	Poor
750	650	500	300	150

Lee-Enfield Mark I RIC Carbine

This model was converted from Lee-Enfield carbines and was fitted with a bayonet lug for a Pattern 1888 bayonet. This required a collar be added at the muzzle to increase the barrel diameter to accept the bayonet ring. It was first converted in 1905 for the Royal Irish Constabulary. About 11,000 were converted.

Exc.	V.G.	Good	Fair	Poor
450	350	200	100	75

No. 1 SMLE SERIES

The SMLEs were not designated No. 1s until the British changed their rifle nomenclature system 1926. Guns made prior to that date were marked "SMLE", not No. 1

SMLE Trials Rifle

About 1,000 of these rifles were built for trials in 1902. Fitted with a full-length handguard and a charger loading system. Barrel length is 25.2" with a .303 chamber. Sheet metal buttplate. Weight is about 8 lbs. A number of different features appeared on this rifle that were later incorporated into the regular production SMLE. Most of these rifles were converted to Aiming Tube Short Rifles in 1906 and are extremely rare.

Exc.	V.G.	Good	Fair	Poor
1200	950	700	400	200

No. 1 SMLE Mark I

Introduced in 1902 this was the first of the "Short, Magazine Lee-Enfield" or No. 1 series of rifles. It was fitted with a full stock with pistol grip and a 25.2" barrel. It also had a full upper handguard. Rear sight is leaf-type graduated to 2,000 yards. The bayonet mountings are integral with the nosecap. Magazine capacity was 10 rounds. Magazine cutoff on right side of receiver. Weight was about 8 lbs. A little more than 360,000 of these rifles were produced.

Exc.	V.G.	Good	Fair	Poor
650	550	400	300	150

No. 1 SMLE Mark I*

A minor modification of the SMLE Mark I. Introduced in 1906. Fitted with a buttplate trap and a new style butt sling swivel. About 60,000 of these rifles were produced.

Exc.	V.G.	Good	Fair	Poor
600	500	350	250	100

No. 1 SMLE Mark II

The Mark I and II Long Lee converted by fitting a shorter and lighter barrel (25.2"), modifying the action to accept a stripper clip, and fitting new sights. It was introduced in 1903. Approximately 40,000 Mark IIs were manufactured.

Exc.	V.G.	Good	Fair	Poor
225	200	175	150	100

No. 1 SMLE Mark II*

A modification of the Mark II SMLE to add features from the SMLE Mark III so that it would correspond with that model. Introduced in 1908. About 22,000 were converted.

Exc.	V.G.	Good	Fair	Poor
225	200	175	150	100

No. 1 SMLE Mark III

Chambered for .303 British and has a 25.2" barrel with a 10-round magazine. The magazine has a cutoff, and the sights are military-styled. The action is modified to accept a stripper clip and automatically eject it when the bolt is closed. Weight is approximately 8.5 lbs. This model was introduced in 1907. The Mark III was one of the more successful and famous British military rifles. It was used extensively in World War I and World War II. In many areas of the old British Commonwealth it is still used today. Almost 7,000,000 of these were produced.

NOTE: Add 30% for non-imported models.

Courtesy Richard M. Kumor Sr.

Exc.	V.G.	Good	Fair	Poor
185	125	100	60	30

No. 1 Mark III and Mark III* Drill Rifles

These rifles were modified for drill use and stamped "DP." They feature a firing pin with no tip and on occasion a bolt head with the firing pin hole welded closed.

Exc.	V.G.	Good	Fair	Poor
65	50	40	30	15

No. 1 Mark III Single Shot Rifles

Converted to single shot at Ishapore, India and have magazine well filled. Intended for use with "unreliable" Indian troops.

Exc.	V.G.	Good	Fair	Poor
125	100	85	60	30

No. 1 Mark III and Mark III* Grenade Launching Rifles

Built on the standard Mk III and Mk III* rifles with the addition of a wire wrapping on the front of the barrel. These rifles are usually marked "E.Y." to indicate only ball ammunition used be used in an emergency. A cup-type grenade launcher was fitted.

Exc.	V.G.	Good	Fair	Poor
165	115	100	70	40

Paul Goodwin Photo

NOTE: For rifles without launcher deduct $50.

Lee-Enfield .410 Musket
Built around the No. 1 Mark III rifle and converted in Ishapore, India to a single shot .410 shotgun. Intended for guard duty.

Exc.	V.G.	Good	Fair	Poor
80	60	50	40	20

No. 1 SMLE Mark IV
This model was Lee-Metford and Lee-Enfield rifles converted to Mark III configuration. The receiver was modified for a charger bridge and safety catch. The dust cover lugs were also removed from the bolt. Adopted in 1907. Almost 100,000 of these rifles were converted.

Exc.	V.G.	Good	Fair	Poor
150	120	95	75	50

Rifle Charger Loading Long Lee-Enfield Mark I/I*
These are converted Lee-Enfield rifles adapted to charger loading. Many of these rifles were used in the early days of World War I by the British Royal Navy. Over 180,000 of these rifles were produced.

Exc.	V.G.	Good	Fair	Poor
750	650	500	300	150

No. 1 SMLE Mark III*
This variation does not have a magazine cutoff, the rear sight windage adjustment, left side auxiliary long rang sights, a center swivel lug, or a brass buttstock marking disc. Over 2 million of this model were made during World War I. It was last built in England in 1944 by B.S.A. This model was also manufactured in India at Ishapore until the end of World War II, and in Australia at Lithgow through the 1950s, and are so marked. Weight is about 9 lbs.

No. 1 SMLE Mark III* H
Built only at Lithgow arsenal in Australia and features a heavier barrel marked with an "H" near the receiver.

Exc.	V.G.	Good	Fair	Poor
350	250	200	150	100

No. 1 SMLE Mark V
Similar to the Mark III except for the use of a receiver mounted wide aperture rear sight. The folding sight is graduated from 200 yards to 1,400 yards with even number on the right side and odd on the left. Serial numbers range from 1 to 9999, then an "A" prefix was used. The standard pattern 1907 sword bayonet was issued with the rifle. Between 1922 and 1924 only 20,000 were produced. A scarce model.

Courtesy Richard M. Kumor, Sr.

No. 1 Mark III • Courtesy West Point Museum • PaulGoodwin Ph*

Exc.	V.G.	Good	Fair	Poor
150	125	95	75	50

NOTE: For rifles built in Australia add 20%; for rifles built in India deduct 20%.

Close-up of Mark V rear sight • Courtesy Richard M. Kumor, Sr.

Exc.	V.G.	Good	Fair	Poor
600	500	300	—	—

No. 1 SMLE Mark VI

This model had the rear sight located on the receiver bridge. It also used a heavier barrel, lighter nose cap, and smaller bolt head than previous models. It did have the magazine cutoff. Checkered forend. There were three variants of this rifle: Pattern A introduced in 1926, Pattern B, introduced in 1929 to 1931 and Pattern C introduced in 1935. About 1,000 trials rifle were built in Pattern B.

Exc.	V.G.	Good	Fair	Poor
3500	2500	1500	—	—

NO. 4 SERIES

Rifle No. 4 Mark 1 Trials Model

Introduced in 1931 with about 2,500 being produced. This is a No. 1 Mark VI with the exception of the shape of the action, and designation markings. Some had no markings at all. Many were later converted to No. 4 Mark I (T) sniper rifles. Markings are commonly found on the right side of the butt socket.

Exc.	V.G.	Good	Fair	Poor
2000	1500	900	—	—

Rifle No. 4 Mark I

An improved version of the No. 1 Mark VI that featured a stronger action with an aperture sight. It was issued in 1931. It was redesigned in 1939 for mass production with shortcuts taken for wartime production. Barrel length is 25.2" with 10-round magazine. The barrel diameter is larger than the S.M.L.E. series and extended almost 3" out of the forend. Weight is about 8.75 lbs. This model was used extensively during WWII. It is still in use today. About 2 million of these rifles were produced but none were built at Enfield. Other factories such as Longbranch in Canada and Savage-Stevens.

NOTE: Add 30% for non-imports.

Courtesy Richard M. Kumor Sr.

Exc.	V.G.	Good	Fair	Poor
150	125	100	60	30

Rifle No. 4 Mark I*

This model was almost identical to the No. 4 Mark I but was produced in North America during WWII. The principal U.S. producer was Savage-Stevens (marked US PROPERTY); in Canada marked "LONG BRANCH." The Savage-Stevens guns have a "C" in the serial number for Chicoppe Falls and guns with "L" serial numbers were produced at Longbranch. This model differed from the Mark 1 in that the bolt-head catch was eliminated and a cut-out on the bolt head track was used for its removal. Over 2 million were produced during the war.

Exc.	V.G.	Good	Fair	Poor
150	125	95	75	50

Rifle No. 4 Mark 2

This model was fitted with a trigger that was pinned to the receiver rather than the triggerguard. Introduced in 1949. This rifle had a higher quality finish than its wartime predecessors.

Exc.	V.G.	Good	Fair	Poor
200	150	120	80	50

Rifle No. 4 Mark 1/2 (converted No. 4 Mark I) & No. 4 Mark 1/3 (converted No. 4 Mark I*)

These models have new trigger mechanism installed to more closely emulate the Mark 2 and upgraded components. The conversion required altering the old markings. This was done with an electric pencil instead of a stamp. The result is quite obvious.

Exc.	V.G.	Good	Fair	Poor
175	150	100	75	50

JUNGLE CARBINES

No. 1 Shortened & Lightened Rifle

Fitted with a 20" barrel and a shortened forend. The rear aperture sight is mounted on the charger bridge and graduated for 200 and 500 yards. Fitted for a blade bayonet. Weight is about 8.75 lbs. About 32 of these rifle were built at Lithgow. The serial number has a "XP" prefix.

NOTE: Extremely rare. Beware of fakes. Seek expert advice prior to a sale.

Exc.	V.G.	Good	Fair	Poor
N/A	—	—	—	—

Rifle No. 6 Mark I & Mark I/I (AUST)

This model was essentially a trials rifle built in Australia at Lithgow. Similar to the No. 5 but with a No. 1 receiver. Metal components have been milled for lightening. Barrel length is 20.5" with flash hider. The Mark I differs from the Mark I/I in rear sight. Rear sight is open and graduated to 2,000 yards on the Mark I and the Mark I/I uses an aperture sight graduated from 200 to 800 yards. Both models have serial numbers with a "XP" prefix. Each model has two variations of buttplates: one standard brass and the other composition padded with hinges at bottom for trap access.

NOTE: Beware of fakes. Seek expert advice prior to a sale.

Exc.	V.G.	Good	Fair	Poor
2500	2000	1000	—	—

Rifle No. 5 Mark 1

Also known as the "Jungle Carbine." It is chambered for the .303 British cartridge and has a 20.5" barrel with an attached flash suppressor and a shorter forend and handguard. It is furnished with a rubber buttpad and modified rear sight graduated to 800 yards. This was not a popular weapon with the soldiers who carried it, as the recoil was excessive due to the lighter weight. Weight is approximately 7 lbs. About 250,000 were built. This model has its own distinctive knife bayonet.

Courtesy Richard M. Kumor, Sr.

Exc.	V.G.	Good	Fair	Poor
450	400	300	175	125

SNIPER RIFLES

SMLE Sniper (Optical Sights)

These rifles are Mark III and Mark III* mounted with optical sights. These sights are comprised of a special front and rear sight that when used together form a telescope with a magnification of 2 to 3 power. About 13,000 of these rifles were fitted with these optical sights. Three different optical makers were used with Lattey being the largest. Conversions were performed by unit armorers beginning in 1915.

NOTE: Beware of fakes. Seek expert advice prior to a sale.

Exc.	V.G.	Good	Fair	Poor
3000	2500	2000	—	—

SMLE Sniper (Telescope Sights)

As above but fitted with conventional telescope sights made by Periscope, Aldis, Winchester, and others. A total of about 9,700 of these rifles were fitted with telescope sights using Mark III and Mark III* rifles during World War I.

NOTE: Beware of fakes. Seek expert advice prior to a sale.

Exc.	V.G.	Good	Fair	Poor
3000	2500	2000	—	—

No. 1 Mk III* H.T. (Australian) Sniper

Introduced toward the end of World War II this rifle used mostly rebuilt Mark III actions dating to between 1915 and 1918. Fitted with both high and low mounts. The standard bracket telescope tube is marked, "SIGHT TELESCOPE PATT 1918 (AUS)." These rifles are fitted with a heavy barrel. Only about 1,500 of these rifles were converted.

Exc.	V.G.	Good	Fair	Poor
2500	2000	1500	—	—

SCOPE NOTE: The No. 32 (Marks 1-3) scope was the most commonly used on British-made guns. The No. 32 and the Alaskan are not the same scope. About 100 Lyman Alaskan scopes were fitted to Longbranch No. 4 Mark 1*(T) rifles in 1944-1945. In addition to the British-made scopes, R.E.I. Ltd. in Canada made its own version of the No. 32 and these are usually found on Longbranch guns. The No. 67 scope, used on about 100 Longbranch (T)s was made by R.E.I. and differs from the design of the No. 32.

Rifle No. 4 Mark I (T) & Mark I* (T)

These are sniper versions of the No. 4 Mark I and the Mark1*. Fitted with scope mounts on the left side of the receiver and a wooden cheekpiece screwed to the buttstock. A No. 32 or a No. 67 (Canadian) telescope was issued with these rifles. Many of these rifles were converted by Holland & Holland. About 25,000 rifles using various telescopes were converted.

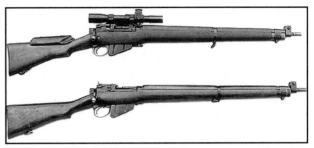

No. 4 Mk1(T) on top and Standard No. 4 Mk1 at bottom
Courtesy Chuck Karwan

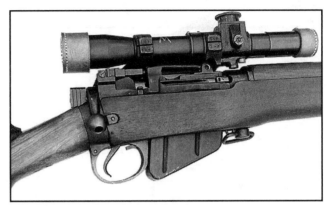

No.2 Mk1 (T) close-up of action and scope • Courtesy Chuck Karwan

Exc.	V.G.	Good	Fair	Poor
1200	800	650	425	350

NOTE: Prices above are for rifles in original wood case and scope numbered to the rifle. For rifles without case deduct 10%. A subvariation of this model has no scope fitted to the rifle and is not stamped with a "T" on the butt.

L42A1

Introduced in 1970 this rifle is a converted No. 4 (T) chambered for the 7.62mm cartridge. Half stocked with upper handguard with 27.6" heavy barrel. A converted No. 32 Mark 3 scope is used marked, "TEL. STRT. STG. L1A1." Weight is about 12.5 lbs. Some 10,000 were converted at Enfield.

NOTE: Prices listed below are for rifles with original wood case.

Exc.	V.G.	Good	Fair	Poor
1200	800	650	425	350

LEE-ENFIELD .22 CALIBER RIFLES

Short Rifle Mark I

This single shot .22 caliber model is converted from the Lee-Metford Mark I* rifle but with a 25" barrel. Introduced in 1907.

Exc.	V.G.	Good	Fair	Poor
550	450	300	200	100

Long Rifle Mark II

This single shot .22 caliber rifle was converted from long Lee-Enfield rifles. Adopted in 1912.

Exc.	V.G.	Good	Fair	Poor
550	450	300	200	100

Short Rifle Mark I*

This .22 caliber single shot conversion is modified from the Lee-Metford Mark I* rifle.

Exc.	V.G.	Good	Fair	Poor
1200	950	700	500	200

Short Rifle Mark III

This .22 caliber conversion is from the SMLE Mark II and Mark II*. Adopted in 1912.

Courtesy Rock Island Auction Company

Exc.	V.G.	Good	Fair	Poor
350	275	200	125	100

Rifle No. 2 Mark IV

This model uses converted SMLEs. Some of these conversions are fitted with new .22 caliber barrels and others use .303 barrels with .22 caliber bore liners. These rifles have special bolt heads. Weight is about 9 lbs.

Courtesy Rock Island Auction Company

Exc.	V.G.	Good	Fair	Poor
400	350	250	150	100

Rifle No. 2 Mark IV*

A subvariation of Rifle No. 2 Mark IV.

Exc.	V.G.	Good	Fair	Poor
400	350	250	150	100

Rifle C No. 7

This model was developed at the Long Branch Canadian arsenal. It is a single shot .22 caliber version of the No. 4. Canadian nomenclature is "Rifle "C" No. 7 .22 in Mark I. This model was also made by B.S.A. with a 5-round magazine. About 20,000 were produced.

Exc.	V.G.	Good	Fair	Poor
450	400	300	175	125

Rifle No. 7 Mark 1

This is a conversion of the No. 4, not a new rifle. Introduced in 1948. Different bolt from the Canadian version Rifle C No. 7 Mark 1. This rifle was intended for use at 25 yards. About 2,500 were built at BSA.

Exc.	V.G.	Good	Fair	Poor
450	400	300	175	125

NOTE: Be aware that A.G. Parker built a commercial version of this rifle. For those models deduct $100.

No. 5 Trials Rifle

This rifle was the forerunner of the No. 8. It was designed as a competition small bore rifle with special sights and half stock. It is fitted with a No.4 butt that has a checkered grip. The upper handguard is a No. 5 in length. It uses a No. 1 magazine converted to .22 caliber. It could be used as a single shot or magazine feed. Rear sight is micrometer graduated to 100 yards. Target tunnel front sight. Barrel length is 19". Weight is about 8.5 lbs. About 100 of these rifles were built.

Exc.	V.G.	Good	Fair	Poor
1000	800	600	—	—

Rifle No. 8 Mark 1

This rifle was adopted in 1950. This is a single shot rifle with 24" barrel fitted with a rear peep sight. Half stocked with three sling swivels the middle one attached in front of the triggerguard. Weight is 9 lbs. Approximately 17,000 of these rifles were produced.

Exc.	V.G.	Good	Fair	Poor
450	400	300	200	100

Rifle No. 9 Mark 1

This .22 caliber single shot conversion was done by Parker Hale using No. 4 rifles. Main differences are the bolt, barrel, magazine, and rear sight. The magazine is an empty case without spring or follower. Weight is about 9.25 lbs. The conversion was done between 1956 and 1960. About 3,000 of these rifles were converted for the Royal Navy.

Exc.	V.G.	Good	Fair	Poor
450	400	300	200	100

7.62x51mm CONVERSIONS & MANUFACTURE

NOTE: The NATO cartridge 7.62x51mm was agreed upon by NATO in December of 1953. Conversions began soon after that date.

L8 Series

This series consists of converted No. 4 rifles from .303 to 7.62mm. Conversions involved a new barrel, and a new magazine stamped, "CR12A." The old receiver marks were eliminated and new ones using an electric pencil were substituted. Some rear sights graduated to 1,300 *meters*, and other graduated to 1,000 *meters*. Series conversions are as follows:

L8A1 converted from No. 4 Mk2
L8A2 converted from No. 4 MK 1/2
L8A3 converted from No. 4 Mk 1/3
L8A4 converted from No. 4 MK I
L8A5 converted from No. 4 MK I*

Exc.	V.G.	Good	Fair	Poor
450	400	300	200	100

L39A1

This conversion uses a No. 4 Mark 2 action and is similar to a L42A1 sniper rifle without the scope. Fitted with target-type front and rear sights. Half stocked. Weight is about 10 lbs.

Exc.	V.G.	Good	Fair	Poor
1000	800	600	400	200

NOTE: For 7.62 NATO magazine add $75. For English match sights by Parker Hale add $125.

L42A1

See *Sniper Rifles.*

Rifle 7.62mm 2A and 2A1 (India)

This rifle is based on a No. 1 Mark III* rifle utilizing newly made receivers of stronger steel to handle the higher .308 pressures. The Indians referred to it as "EN" steel. New rear sight graduated to 800 meters. New detachable box magazine with 10-round capacity. The buttplate is cast alloy. Manufactured in India at Ishapore. Weight is about 9.5 lbs. Most imported rifles are in the 2A1 configuration.

Exc.	V.G.	Good	Fair	Poor
100	75	50	30	15

ENFIELD FENCING MUSKETS

These are not firearms but rather fabricated or converted rifles made to look and feel like the real thing. They were used for bayonet practice and drilling practice. There are a large number of variations, at least 17, and to cover each is beyond the scope of this book. The prices listed below only represent a possible range of prices. Some rifles were late converted to fencing muskets.

Exc.	V.G.	Good	Fair	Poor
125	100	75	50	20

OTHER BRITISH RIFLES

Boys Anti-Tank Rifle

Developed in the 1930s this rifle was chambered for the .55 caliber armor piercing cartridge. It was fitted with a 36" barrel with muzzle brake. It had a detachable 5-round box magazine. Weight was approximately 36 lbs. Available in two versions: a long barrel (36") and a short barrel airborne model. Not used much after 1940 due to inability to penetrate modern armor. Some of these rifles were used by the U.S. Marine Corp. in the Pacific during World War II.

NOTE: The Boys Rifle is listed as a destructive device by the ATF and is therefore subject to all NFA rules.

Exc.	V.G.	Good	Fair	Poor
3750	3000	2500	2000	1000

No. 3 Mark I (Pattern 14)

Built on a modified Mauser-type action and was chambered for the .303 British cartridge. It is fitted with a 26" barrel and 5-round magazine. It was a secondary-issue arm during WWI and was simpler to mass-produce than the SMLE. These rifles were produced in the U.S.A. by Remington and Winchester. There are a number of marks for this model divided between Remington, Eddystone, and Winchester.

The Mark IE was built at Remington Arms at Eddystone, Pennsylvania. The Mark IR were built at Remington Arms in Ilion, New York.

The Mark IW was built at Winchester Repeating Arms in New Haven, Connecticut.

Exc.	V.G.	Good	Fair	Poor
170	120	90	65	35

No. 3 Mark I* Pattern 14W(F) (T)

This is a No. 3 Mark I that has been converted to a sniper configuration. These rifles were built by Winchester during World War I. The (F) model has a long range aperture and dial sight along with the scope. On the (T) model the long range sights were removed. It is estimated that about 1,500 of these rifles were built. A rare rifle. Caution should be used prior to a sale.

Courtesy Richard M. Kumor, Sr.

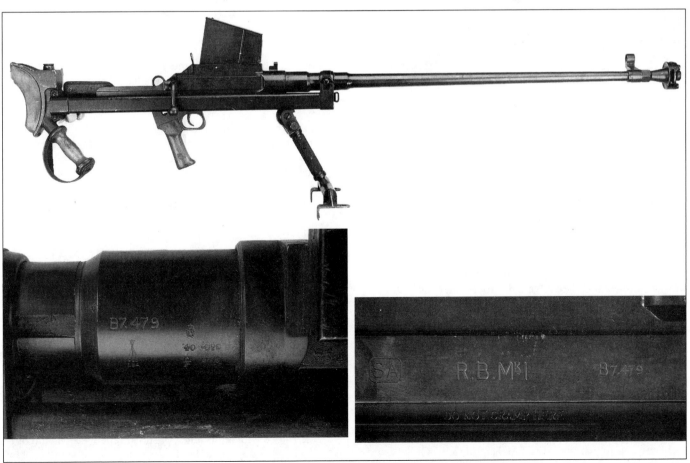

Boys Anti-Tank Rifle • Courtesy West Point Museum • Paul Goodwin Photo

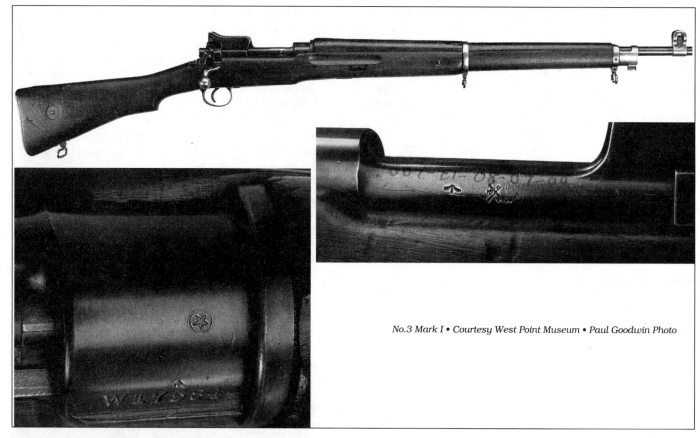

No.3 Mark I • Courtesy West Point Museum • Paul Goodwin Photo

Close-up of sniper scope and mount • Courtesy Richard M. Kumor, Sr.

Exc.	V.G.	Good	Fair	Poor
5000	4500	3500	—	—

STERLING

De Lisle Carbine

This rifle is built on a Lee-Enfield action with a .45 ACP caliber barrel fitted inside a large suppressor tube. Barrel length is 8.25". Magazine capacity is 8 rounds using a Colt Model 1911 magazine. Weight is about 7.5 lbs. About 100 to 150 of these rifles were built by Sterling during World War II for use in special operations. Most were destroyed after the war. All NFA rules apply to the purchase of these weapons.

Exc.	V.G.	Good	Fair	Poor
—	6000	5000	—	—

L1A1 Rifle

This is the British version of the FN-FAL in the "INCH" or Imperial pattern. Most of these rifles were semiautomatic only. This rifle was the standard service rifle for the British army from about 1954 to 1988. The rifle was made in Great Britain under licence from FN. The configurations for the L1A1 rifle is the same as the standard FN-FAL Belgium rifle. Only a few of these rifles were imported into the U.S. They are very rare.

This "inch" pattern British gun will also be found in other Commonwealth countries such as Australia, New Zealand, Canada, and India.

Exc.	V.G.	Good	Fair	Poor
—	6000	5000	—	—

NOTE: The only known pre-1986 L1A1 rifles imported into the U.S. are Australian and Canadian. See that country for prices. See *also Canada* for its C1 and C2 versions of the FN FAL.

There are a number of U.S. companies that build or import L1A1 rifles, imported rifles are in a sporter configuration) but these have no collector value. Rifles built with military surplus parts and U.S.-made receivers also have no collector value as of yet.

Exc.	V.G.	Good	Fair	Poor
N/A	—	—	—	—

ACCURACY INTERNATIONAL

This English company provides its rifles to military forces in over 40 countries, and these models have been used in Northern Ireland, Sri Lanka, Somalia, Bosnia, Rwanda, and in Desert Storm. Most of these rifles are currently NATO codified.

Model AW

Chambered for the 5.56 NATO cartridge and the 7.62x51 NATO cartridge this bolt action rifle is fitted with a 26" heavy match grade barrel with muzzle brake. Magazine capacity is 8 rounds for the 5.56 and 10 rounds for the 7.62x51. Olive green stock with adjustable buttstock. Bipod, scope, and other accessories are included in the complete kit. Prices below are for rifle only. Weight is about 14.25 lbs.

FN-FAL L1A1 Rifle • Paul Goodwin Photo

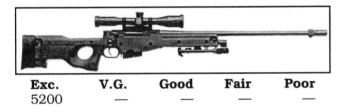

Exc.	V.G.	Good	Fair	Poor
5200	—	—	—	—

Model AWP

Similar to the Model AW but with black stock and metal and 24" barrel. Offered in .243 and .308 calibers. Weight is about 14 lbs.

Exc.	V.G.	Good	Fair	Poor
4300	—	—	—	—

Model AWS

A suppressed version of the AW model. Weight is about 13 lbs.

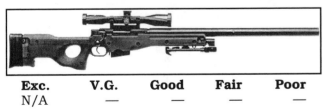

Exc.	V.G.	Good	Fair	Poor
N/A	—	—	—	—

Model AWM

Similar to the Model AW but chambered for the .300 Winchester Magnum or .338 Lapua Magnum cartridge. Fitted with a 26" barrel with muzzle brake. Magazine capacity is 5 rounds. Weight is about 15.5 lbs.

Exc.	V.G.	Good	Fair	Poor
5625	—	—	—	—

Model AW 50

Chambered for the .50 caliber Browning cartridge. Barrel length is 27" with muzzle brake. Magazine capacity is 5 rounds. Weight is about 33 lbs. Supplied with metal case, spare magazine, carry handle, cling, and tool kit.

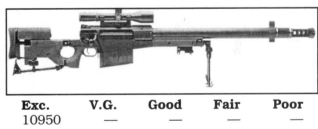

Exc.	V.G.	Good	Fair	Poor
10950	—	—	—	—

PARKER-HALE

M82

This bolt action rifle uses a Mauser 98 action fitted to a heavy 26" barrel chambered for the 7.62x51mm cartridge. Magazine capacity is 4 rounds. Used as a sniper rifle by the Australian, New Zealand, and Canadian military. Marked "PARKER-HALE LTD BIRMINGHAM ENGLAND 7.62 NATO" on top of the barrel. Produced from 1982 to about 1984.

Exc.	V.G.	Good	Fair	Poor
2500	2000	1500	850	—

M85

This is an improved version of the M82 with a Mauser 98 type bolt action designed to compete for a British military contract against the Accuracy International rifle. It did not win the trials. It is fitted removable 10-round magazine, 27.5" heavy barrel with iron sights, and telescope mounts on the receiver. Rifle is half stocked with adjustable buttplate. Bipod is attached to forend rail. Weight is about 12.5 lbs. with scope. Chambered for the 7.62x51mm NATO round.

Exc.	V.G.	Good	Fair	Poor
3500	3000	2500	1500	—

MACHINE GUNS

NOTE: For historical information and technical details see: Dugelby, *The Bren Gun Saga*, Collector Grade Publications, 1999. Goldsmith, *The Grand Old Lady of No Man's Land, The Vickers Machinegun*, Collector Grade Publications, 1994.

Bren MK1

Introduced in 1938 and designed in Czechoslovakia as the ZB vz26 this British version is chambered for the .303 British cartridge during the early part of its service. After WWII it was adapted to the 7.62x51mm cartridge. It was fitted with a top mounted magazine of 30 rounds. Rate of fire is 500 rounds per minute. The gun was set up to fire selectively as well. The gun has a 24.8" barrel and an empty weight of 22 lbs. The rear sight is a offset drum type. The buttstock has a hand grip and top strap. The bipod has fixed legs, and the cocking handle folds away. Marked "BREN MK" on the rights side of the receiver.

The Bren MK2 (1941) has a leaf type rear sight and a simplified buttstock. The Bren MK3 (1944) is lighter (19 lbs) and fitted with a shorter barrel (22.2"). The Bren MK4 (1944) has minor differences in the buttstock. The L4A1 (1958) is a converted MK 3 to 7.62mm caliber. The L4A2 (1958) is a converted MK3 with lighter bipod. The L4A3 is a converted MK2 to 7.62mm caliber: used by navy and RAF. The L4A4 (1960) is similar to the L4A2 except for a chrome lined barrel. The L4A6 is a converted L4A1 with chrome lined barrel.

In 1941 the MK2 was produced in Canada for the Chinese Nationalist army in 7.92x57mm caliber. A .30-06 version was made in Taiwan.

Be aware that there are a number of different mounts for the Bren gun besides the traditional bipod. There is a tripod mount as well as an antiaircraft mount.

NOTE: The Vickers-Berthier gun is similar in external design, caliber, and appearance as the Bren except it has a different operating mechanism and other minor differences. This gun is made in India and that country used the gun in World War II. It is still in use in that country. This gun is extremely rare as only a few known transferable examples exist. For pre-1968 Vickers-Berthier guns a price of $25,000 in excellent condition would be a good starting place for value.

Bren MK I, Photo Courtesy Private NFA Collection

Pre-1968 (Very Rare)

Exc.	V.G.	Fair
19000	15000	13000

Pre-1986 conversions

Exc.	V.G.	Fair
N/A	N/A	N/A

Pre-1986 dealer samples

Exc.	V.G.	Fair
14000	10000	6000

Lewis 0.303in, Mark 1

This gas operated machine gun is chambered for the .303 British cartridge. Though perfected by an American army officer, Colonel Isaac Lewis (1858-1931), it was first produced in Belgium in 1912 where it was used extensively by British forces during WWI. In fact it was the principal British light machine gun used in WWI. It has a 26" barrel and a rate of fire of about 550 rounds per minute. Called by the Germans the "Belgian Rattlesnake." Magazine capacity is 47- or 97-round drum. Its weight is approximately 26 lbs. Marked

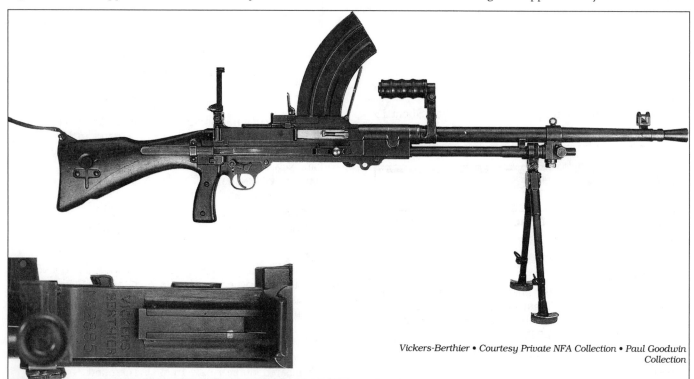

Vickers-Berthier • Courtesy Private NFA Collection • Paul Goodwin Collection

"LEWIS AUTOMATIC MACHINE GUN/MODEL 1914 PATENTED" behind the magazine drum. The gun was produced by BSA and Savage Arms of the U.S. Production stopped in 1925. A number of other countries used the gun as well, such as France, Norway, Japan, Belgium, Honduras, and Nicaragua.

The Lewis MK2 was introduced in 1915 which was a MK1 without the radiator and barrel jacket. The buttstock was removed and spade grips attached for aircraft use. The Lewis MK2* modified the gun to increase the rate of fire to about 800 rounds per minute. See also *United States, Machine Guns, Savage-Lewis M1917.*

Private NFA Collection • Photo by Gary Gelson

Pre-1968

Exc.	V.G.	Fair
15000	14000	12000

Pre-1986 conversions

Exc.	V.G.	Fair
N/A	N/A	N/A

Pre-1986 dealer samples

Exc.	V.G.	Fair
N/A	N/A	N/A

Vickers Mark 1

This British water-cooled machine gun was first produced in 1912 and chambered for the .303 British cartridge. In essence an improved Maxim with the action inverted. It has a 28" barrel with corrugated water jacket and is fed by a 250 cloth belt. Its rate of fire is 450 rounds per minute. Its weight is approximately 40 lbs. It was also used in aircraft and stayed in service in various countries until the 1970s. Besides use in British forces, the gun was sold to South American countries between the two World Wars. Serial number is marked on top rear of water jacket.

Variations of the Vickers Mark 1 are: the Mark 1*, which is an aircraft gun with pierced and louvered barrel jacket for air-cooling. Some of these guns had a rate of fire of about 850 rounds per minute and marked "SU" for "speeded up." There were several other Vickers aircraft variations which incorporated minor modifications. The Vickers was also used on tanks. These variation were designated the Mark 4A, Mark 4B, Mark 6, Mark 6*, Mark 7. A .50 caliber Vickers was also produced for tank and naval use. These gun are designated the .5 inch, Mark 3, and .5 inch Mark 4. These guns had a rate of fire of about 675 rounds per minute and weighed approximately 60 lbs.

NOTE: For the Colt produced version in .30-06 caliber see *United States, Machine Guns.*

Pre-1968

Exc.	V.G.	Fair
20000	18000	17000

Pre-1986 conversions (Non-Martial current U.S. manufacture)

Exc.	V.G.	Fair
10000	8000	7000

Pre-1986 dealer samples

Exc.	V.G.	Fair
N/A	N/A	N/A

British Vickers Mark IV
Courtesy Blake Stevens, The Grand Old Lady of No Man's Land

Hotchkiss Mark I

Although a French design the British army purchased the rights to manufacture the Hotchkiss during World War I. These British guns were known as the Mark 1 and Mark 1* and were built in the Royal Small Arms factory in England. The British Hotchkiss was chambered for the .303 British cartridge. This version was fed by a 30-round metallic strip and had a rate of fire of about 500 rounds per minute. The gun weighed about 27 lbs. Barrel length was 23.5". The British Hotchkiss stayed in service in the British army until 1946. A belt-fed version (Mark I*) for use on tanks used a 250-round belt.

Lewis Mark 2 Aircraft Gun • Paul Goodwin Photo

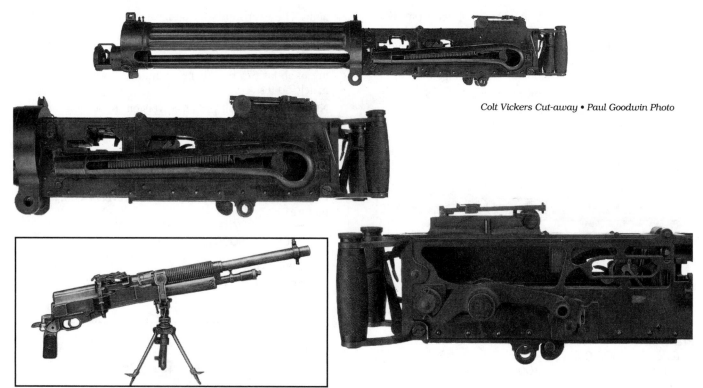

Colt Vickers Cut-away • Paul Goodwin Photo

Courtesy Butterfield & Butterfield

Pre-1968

Exc.	V.G.	Fair
4500	4000	3500

Pre-1986 conversions

Exc.	V.G.	Fair
3000	2500	2000

Pre-1986 dealer samples

Exc.	V.G.	Fair
N/A	N/A	N/A

Besa

Introduced in 1939 this gun was a design bought from the Czech's ZB vz53 and produced in Britain by BSA in a slightly modified form. It was used primarily on tanks. It was an air-cooled gun chambered for the 7.92x57mm cartridge. It was gas operated but with a recoiling barrel. It has a rate of fire of approximately 500 or 800 rounds per minute using a selector switch for high or low rate. Weight of the gun is about 48 lbs. Feeds from a 250-round belt.

There are a number of variations of the initial model. The Mark 2 has some minor modifications. The Mark 3 has a single rate of fire of 800 rounds per minute. The Mark 3* has a single rate of fire of 500 rounds per minute.

Pre-1968

Exc.	V.G.	Fair
7000	6500	6000

Pre-1986 conversions

Exc.	V.G.	Fair
N/A	N/A	N/A

Pre-1986 dealer samples

Exc.	V.G.	Fair
N/A	N/A	N/A

ISRAEL

Israeli Military conflicts, 1870-Present

In the late 19th century Zionist movement called for a Jewish homeland in Palestine. In World War I Britain captured the area and appeared to support this purpose. In 1922 the League of Nations approved the British mandate of Palestine with the result of a large Jewish immigration into the area. This influx was opposed by the Arabs and with the end of World War II the U.N. divided Palestine into Jewish and Arab states. In 1948 the state of Israel was proclaimed. The Arabs rejected this proclamation and the result was the 1948-1949 war between Israel and Lebanon, Syria, Jordan, Egypt, and Iraq. Israel won the war and increased its territory by 50%. Arab opposition continued with subsequent conflicts: the Sinai campaign of 1956, the Six-Day War of 1967, and the Yom Kippur War of 1973. Israel won all of these conflicts. Israel and Egypt signed a peace treaty in 1979 with Israel withdrawing from the Sinai. The balance of the 1980s and 1990s is marked by fierce fighting in Lebanon and with the PLO. In 1993 Israel signed an accord with the PLO for self rule in Gaza and the West Bank. A peace treaty was signed with Jordan in 1994. The area remains highly volatile.

HANDGUNS

NOTE: Israel has used a number of different handguns during its early fight for independence and in the turbulent years after. These handguns included Enfield and Webley revolvers as well as Browning Hi-power, Lugers and P-38 pistols. They also built a modified copy of the Smith & Wesson Military & Police model chambered for the 9x19 cartridge required the use of two three-round half moon clips.

Beretta M1951

This 9mm semiautomatic pistol is the standard Israeli military sidearm. *See Italy, Handguns, Beretta.*

Jericho

A 9mm or .41 Action Express double action semiautomatic pistol with a 4.72" barrel, polygonal rifling, ambidextrous safety and fixed sights. Blued with plastic grips. Weight is approximately 36 oz. Magazine capacity is 16 rounds in 9mm. This pistol is primarily used by the Israeli police and other government agencies generally in 9mm.

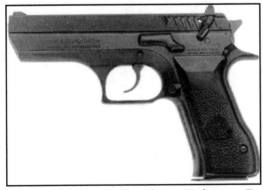

Exc.	V.G.	Good	Fair	Poor
475	400	350	300	200

SUBMACHINE GUNS

NOTE: Prior to the development of the UZI the Israeli used British Sten guns and other World War II submachine guns that were available for purchase on the arms market.

UZI

First produced in Israel in 1953 this submachine gun is chambered for the 9mm cartridge. It is fitted with a 10.14"

barrel and metal folding stock. It has a magazine capacity of 25, 32, or 40 rounds. Empty weight is about 7.7 lbs. Rate of fire is 600 rounds per minute. This gun enjoys widespread use and is found in military and police units all over the world. Marked "UZI SMG 9MM" on left side of receiver.

Pre-1968 (Very Rare)

Exc.	V.G.	Fair
10000	9000	8000

Pre-1986 conversions

Exc.	V.G.	Fair
3000	2500	2300

Vector Uzi pre-1986 conversion

The receiver was produced, marked, and registered by Group Industries, Louisville, KY prior to May 1986. Receiver fixed parts manufacturing and receiver assembly is done by Vector Arms, Inc. of North Salt Lake, UT. A total of 3,300 receivers built. All parts (South African) interchangeable with original IMI guns. Receiver parkerized. All other specifications same as original Uzi.

Pre-1986 conversions

NIB/Exc.	V.G.	Fair
3000	2500	2300

Mini-UZI

First produced in 1987 this is a smaller version of the original UZI. It functions the same as its larger counter part. Accepts

20-, 25-, and 32-round magazines. Rate of fire is about 900 to 1,100 rounds per minute. Weight is about 6 lbs. Overall length is about 14" with butt retracted and 23" with butt extended. Still in production in Israel, some South American countries, and U.S. Special Forces.

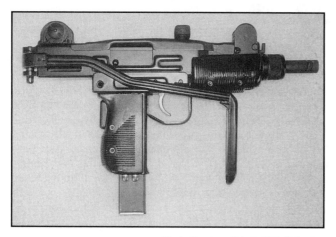

Photo Courtesy Private NFA Collection

Pre-1968

Exc.	V.G.	Fair
N/A	N/A	N/A

Pre-1986 conversions

Exc.	V.G.	Fair
5000	4500	4000

Pre-1986 dealer samples

Exc.	V.G.	Fair
3500	2750	2500

RIFLES

NOTE: During the 1950s Israel converted Mauser 98 rifles to 7.62mm caliber. Some of these were sold as surplus. The Israeli military employed a large number, about 150,000, of Colt-built M16A1 rifles and M16A1 carbines during the 1970s. This weapon is still popular with the IDF today. They also have used FN-built and IMI-assembled FN-FAL rifles. Israeli military forces were even issued AKM rifles. In 1975 the U.S. government sold about 22,000 M14 rifles to the Israeli military.

Galil ARM-Select Fire Assault Rifle

This automatic rifle is produced in Israel and is chambered for the 5.56x45mm cartridge. Similar in appearance to the AK-47 this rifle is fitted with an 18" barrel and folding stock. Magazine capacity is 35 or 50 rounds. Rate of fire is 550 rounds per minute. Model markings on the left side of the receiver are in Hebrew. Weight is approximately 8.7 lbs. First produced in 1971. Still in production.

Photo Courtesy Private NFA Collection

Model ARM Assault Rifle • Courtesy West Point Museum • Paul Goodwin Photo

Pre-1968

Exc.	V.G.	Fair
N/A	N/A	N/A

Pre-1986 conversions

Exc.	V.G.	Fair
10000	7500	7000

Pre-1986 dealer samples (Rare)

Exc.	V.G.	Fair
9000	9000	8500

Galil SAR-Select Fire Assault Rifle

Similar to the SRM but with a folding metal stock and a barrel length of 13". Weight of SAR is about 8.25 lbs.

Photo Courtesy Private NFA Collection

Pre-1968

Exc.	V.G.	Fair
N/A	N/A	N/A

Pre-1986 conversions

Exc.	V.G.	Fair
10000	9000	8500

Pre-1986 dealer samples

Exc.	V.G.	Fair
9000	9000	8500

Model AR

This rifle is an Israeli variant of the AK-47 based on the Valmet. It is also used by the South African military where it is called the R-4 rifle. It is a .223 or .308 caliber semiautomatic rifle with 16" or 19" barrels. Parkerized with the flip "Tritium" night sights and folding stock. The .308 version would bring about a 10% premium.

NIB	Exc.	V.G.	Good	Fair	Poor
2800	2400	2000	1500	900	700

Model ARM

As above, with a ventilated wood handguard and a folding bipod and carrying handle. The .308 will bring about a 10% premium.

NIB	Exc.	V.G.	Good	Fair	Poor
3000	2700	2000	1500	900	700

Galil Sniper Rifle

Introduced in 1983 and similar to the above rifle chambered for the 7.62x51 NATO caliber, with a 20" heavy barrel, adjustable wooden stock, and a 6X40 scope is furnished in addition to the Tritium night sights. Supplied to military in semiautomatic version only. Weight is about 14 lbs. Supplied with two 25-shot magazines and a fitted case.

NIB	Exc.	V.G.	Good	Fair	Poor
8500	7500	6000	4000	3000	2000

IDF Mauser Rifle Model 66SP

This is a bolt action rifle chambered for the .308 Win. cartridge. Adjustable trigger for pull and travel. Barrel length is 27". Specially designed stock has broad forend and a thumb hole pistol grip. Cheekpiece is adjustable as is the recoil pad. The rifle is fitted with an original Swarovsky 6x24 BDC Mil-Spec scope. Supplied with case. This rifle is military issue built by Mauser for the Israel Defense Force in the early 1980s. Less than 100 imported into the U.S by Springfield Armory.

Exc.	V.G.	Good	Fair	Poor
2200	1750	—	—	—

MACHINE GUNS

Israel uses a variety of foreign-built machine guns from the FN MAG, Browning 1919 and Browning .50 caliber heavy machine gun. There are no known transferable Israel machine guns in the U.S.

ITALY

Italian Military Conflicts, 1870-Present

The period of the last quarter of the 19th century was one of the final nationalistic efforts at unification of the Italian states. By the end of the century this effort was achieved. In 1915 Italy entered World War I on the allied side and by the end of the war in 1918 Italy was awarded additional territories, but social unrest and economic discord brought about the rise of fascism, and in 1922 Mussolini seized power. He created a totalitarian state and expand Italian influence through armed aggression into Ethiopia in 1936, Albania in 1939 and entered World War II on the side of the Germans. In 1943 Italy surrendered to the Allies. In 1946, Italy became a republic. By 1947 Italy shed its colonies. The last 50 years has seen a rapid succession of governments tring to govern the country without much success.

HANDGUNS

Modello 1872

This was the first handgun adopted by the Kingdom of Italy's military forces. It was very similar to the French Model 1874 and is chambered for the 10.35mm cartridge. It is fitted with a 6.3" octagon barrel. Cylinder is fluted and grips are checkered wood with lanyard loop. Built by Siderugica Glisenti and others. Weight is about 40 oz. In use by the Italian military from 1872 to 1943.

Exc.	V.G.	Good	Fair	Poor
600	400	300	200	125

System Bodeo Modello 1889 (Enlisted Model)

A 10.4mm caliber revolver with a 4.5" octagonal barrel, and 6-shot cylinder. Built on a Chamelot-Delvigne frame with loading gate on the right side. This revolver was adopted as the Italian service revolver in 1889 and was replaced by the Glisenti in 1910. Manufactured by various Italian arms companies. This revolver, in different configurations, remained in service until 1945.

Courtesy Richard M. Kumor, Sr.

Exc.	V.G.	Good	Fair	Poor
300	200	150	100	75

Modello 1889 (Officers Model)

Essentially the same as the enlisted man's model with a round barrel, non-folding trigger, and conventional triggerguard.

Exc.	V.G.	Good	Fair	Poor
300	200	150	100	75

Glisenti Model 1910

A 9mm Glisenti caliber semiautomatic pistol with a 3.9" barrel, fixed sights, and 7-shot magazine. Weight is about 30 oz. Manufactured from 1910 to 1934. As many as 100,000 of these pistols were produced and used during World War II.

WARNING: *Standard 9x19 ammo must not be shot in this gun.*

Courtesy Faintich Auction Service • Photo Paul Goodwin

Model 1910 with black plastic grips with crown
Courtesy Richard M. Kumor, Sr.

Exc.	V.G.	Good	Fair	Poor
750	500	375	250	150

BERETTA, PIETRO

Model 1915

A 7.65mm caliber semiautomatic pistol with 3.5" barrel, fixed sights and 7-shot magazine. Blued with walnut grips. Weight is about 20 oz. The slide is marked "PIETRO BERETTA BRESCIA CASA FONDATA NEL 1680 CAL. 7.65MM BREVETTO 1915." Manufactured between 1915 and 1922. Used by the Italian military during World War I and World War II. About 65,000 were produced, most of which were not martially marked.

Courtesy Orvel Reichert

Exc.	V.G.	Good	Fair	Poor
350	300	225	150	100

Exc.	V.G.	Good	Fair	Poor
350	300	225	150	100

Model 1919

Similar to Model 1915, in 6.35mm caliber. Manufactured between 1920 and 1939.

Exc.	V.G.	Good	Fair	Poor
350	300	225	150	100

Model 1915 2nd Variation

As above, in 9mm Glisenti caliber with 3.75" barrel. Checkered wood grips. Weight is about 32 oz.

Exc.	V.G.	Good	Fair	Poor
425	350	275	200	125

Model 1923

A 9mm caliber semiautomatic pistol with 4" barrel and 8-shot magazine. Blued with steel grips. The slide is marked, "Brev 1915-1919 Mlo 1923." Exposed hammer. Italian army markings on left grip tang. Some pistols are cut for a shoulder stock. Manufactured from 1923 to 1935. Approximately 10,000 manufactured.

Model 1915/1919

This model is an improved version of the above pistol but chambered for the 7.65mm cartridge. It also incorporates a new barrel-mounting method and a longer cutout in the top of the slide. Produced from 1922 to 1931 for the Italian military with about 50,000 manufactured, most without military markings.

Exc.	V.G.	Good	Fair	Poor
525	425	350	225	150

Model 1931

A 7.65mm caliber semiautomatic pistol with 3.5" barrel and open-top slide. Blued with walnut grips and marked, "RM" separated by an anchor. Issue limited to the Italian navy. Produced from 1931 to 1934 for the Italian navy. Approximately 8,000 manufactured.

Courtesy Orvel Reichert

Exc.	V.G.	Good	Fair	Poor
450	375	275	200	150

Model 1934

As above, with 9mm Corto (Kurz) caliber. The slide is marked, "P. Beretta Cal. 9 Corto-Mo 1934 Brevet Gardone VT." This inscription is followed by the date of manufacture that was given numerically, followed by a Roman numeral that denoted the year of manufacture on the Fascist calendar, which began in 1922. Examples are marked, "RM" (navy), "RE" (army), "RA" (air force), and "PS" (police). Manufactured between 1934 and 1959.

Courtesy Orvel Reichert

Exc.	V.G.	Good	Fair	Poor
375	325	225	150	100

Air Force "RA" marked

Exc.	V.G.	Good	Fair	Poor
550	475	325	225	150

Navy "RM" marked

Exc.	V.G.	Good	Fair	Poor
625	550	375	250	175

Model 1934 Rumanian Contract

See *Romania, Handguns.*

Model 1935

As above, in 7.65mm caliber. A number of these pistols were built and used by the German army during the occupation of Italy in World War II. Some of these pistols are marked with the German army acceptance stamp. Pistols produced in 1944 and 1945 were likely used by the German army without markings. Some of these wartime pistols are marked with Italian navy or air force markings. Production between 1934 and 1943 was about 90,000 pistols. Postwar versions are known. Manufactured from 1935 to 1959.

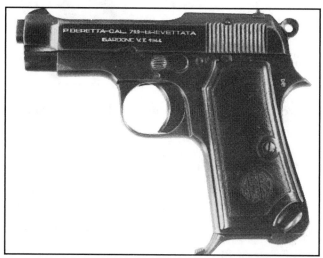

Courtesy Orvel Reichert

Exc.	V.G.	Good	Fair	Poor
375	325	225	150	100

Model 1951

Chambered for the 7.65 or 9mm cartridges, this model was fitted with a 4.5" barrel and had an 8-round magazine. Fixed sights. Weight was about 31 oz. This pistol was used by the Italian military as well as Egypt (Helwan) and Israel. Sold commercially under the name "Brigadier."

Exc.	V.G.	Good	Fair	Poor
300	250	200	100	75

NOTE: For Egyptian copies deduct 50%.

Model 92

A 9mm caliber double action, semiautomatic pistol with a 5" barrel, fixed sights and a 16-round, double-stack magazine. Blued with plastic grips. Introduced in 1976 and is now discontinued. This model was used by the Italian State Police forces. The U.S. military version, the M9, is based on this series.

NOTE: There are a number of different version of this pistol. The main differences lie in the safety type and magazine release, barrel length, and magazine capacity.

NIB	Exc.	V.G.	Good	Fair	Poor
450	400	375	300	250	200

BERNARDELLI, VINCENZO

Model PO 18

A 7.65mm or 9mm Parabellum caliber, double action, semi-automatic pistol with a 4.75" barrel and a 16-shot, double stack, detachable magazine. All-steel construction. Blued with plastic grips. Walnut grips are available for an additional $40. Introduced in 1985. The 7.65mm was designed for commercial sales while the 9mm was for military sales and should be so marked.

NIB	Exc.	V.G.	Good	Fair	Poor
650	550	400	275	200	100

Model PO 18 Compact

As above, with a 4" barrel and a shorter grip frame with a 14-shot, double column magazine. Introduced in 1989.

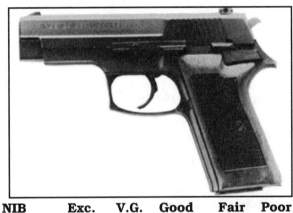

NIB	Exc.	V.G.	Good	Fair	Poor
650	550	400	275	200	100

Twin Villar Perosa guns in simulated aircraft mount • Courtesy Private NFA Collection • Paul Goodwin Photo

SUBMACHINE GUNS

Italy also uses the HK MP5A3 and MP5SD in its police and antiterrorist units.

Villar Perosa Model 1915

This was the first submachine gun adopted by any military force. Chambered for the 9x19mm Glisenti cartridge. Barrel length is 12.5". Its rate of fire was about 1200 rounds per minute. Fed by a 25-round box top mounted magazine. This gun was designed to be mounted in pairs on aircraft, various of type vehicles, and from fixed mounts with its spade grip. Weight of pair is about 14 lbs.

Pre-1968 (Very Rare)

Exc.	V.G.	Fair
25000	22500	20000

Pre-1986 conversions

Exc.	V.G.	Fair
N/A	N/A	N/A

Pre-1986 dealer samples

Exc.	V.G.	Fair
N/A	N/A	N/A

Villar Perosa Model 1918 (Beretta)

This gun is an adapted Villar Perosa into a wooden stock with new trigger mechanism. Most of the original M1915 Villar Perosa's were converted to the Model 1918. Barrel length is 12.5". Magazine capacity is 25 rounds. Rate of fire is about 900 rounds per minute. Select fire. Weight is about 8 lbs. This gun was used by the Italian army from the end of World War I to World War II.

Pre-1968 (Extremely Rare)

Exc.	V.G.	Fair
7500	5000	3000

Pre-1986 conversions

Exc.	V.G.	Fair
N/A	N/A	N/A

Pre-1986 dealer samples

Exc.	V.G.	Fair
N/A	N/A	N/A

Beretta Model 1938A

This Italian-made submachine gun is chambered for the 9mm Parabellum cartridge and was produced from 1938 to about 1950. It was in use by German, Italian, and Romanian armies in different eras. Argentina also purchased a number of Model 38As directly from Beretta. It is fitted with a 12.25" barrel, full rifle-style stock and has a magazine capacity of 10, 20, 30, or 40 rounds. Its rate of fire is 600 rounds per minute. Markings on top of receiver are "MOSCHETTI AUT-BERETTA MOD 1938A BEREVETTO NO 828 428 GARDONE V.T. ITALIA" This weapon was fitted with two triggers: the front trigger fires in the semi-automatic mode, and the rear trigger fires in the automatic mode. A few early models were fitted with a bayonet lug. Weight is about 9.25 lbs.

Private NFA Collection • Photo by Gary Gelson

Pre-1968

Exc.	V.G.	Fair
3750	3300	3000

Pre-1986 conversions

Exc.	V.G.	Fair
2500	2300	2000

Pre-1986 dealer samples

Exc.	V.G.	Fair
2000	1500	1200

Beretta Model 38/42

This is an improved wartime version of the Model 1938 without the barrel shroud. This was a less well finished model than the Model 1938A. Barrel length is a little over 8". Rate of fire is about 550 rounds per minute. Magazine capacity is 20 or 40 rounds. Produced from 1943 to about 1975. Weight is approximately 7 lbs. Marked "M.P. BERETTA MOD 38/42 CAL 9" on the top of receiver. This model was used by Italian and German troops in Italy in the latter stages of World War II. Some of these guns were sold to Romania in 1944.

NOTE: A simplified version of the Model 38/42 is designated the Model 38/44 and features a lighter and more simple bolt design and main operating spring. This main spring is very similar to the one used in the British Sten gun. The Model 38/44 was sold to Syria, Pakistan, Iraq, and Costa Rica, among others following World War II.

Courtesy Richard M. Kumor, Sr.

Pre-1968

Exc.	V.G.	Fair
3500	3000	2500

Pre-1986 conversions

Exc.	V.G.	Fair
N/A	N/A	N/A

Pre-1986 dealer samples

Exc.	V.G.	Fair
1750	1500	1000

Beretta Model 12

Chambered for the 9mm Parabellum cartridge, this sub gun was produced from 1959 to about 1978. It is manufactured basically from steel stampings. Fitted with a bolt that wraps around the barrel. Also fitted with a front vertical hand grip and either a folding metal stock or detachable wood stock. First used by Italian military in 1961. Also used in South America and Africa. Barrel is 7.75" long with a magazine capacity of 20, 30, or 40 rounds. Rate of fire is 500 rounds per minute. Marked "MOD12-CAL9/M PARABELLUM" on the top of the receiver. Weight is about 6.5 lbs.

Pre-1968 (Rare)

Exc.	V.G.	Fair
8000	7000	6500

Pre-1986 conversions

Exc.	V.G.	Fair
N/A	N/A	N/A

Pre-1986 dealer samples

Exc.	V.G.	Fair
4000	3500	3000

Beretta Model 12S

Similar to the Model 12 but with an improved safety system, sights, and folding stock fixture. Production began in 1978 when it replaced the Model 12.

Photo Courtesy Private NFA Collection

Pre-1968

Exc.	V.G.	Fair
N/A	N/A	N/A

Pre-1986 conversions

Exc.	V.G.	Fair
N/A	N/A	N/A

Pre-1986 dealer samples

Exc.	V.G.	Fair
5000	4500	4000

Franchi LF-57

First produced in Italy in 1960, this submachine gun is chambered for the 9mm cartridge. It was placed in service with the Italian navy. Produced until 1980. It is fitted with an 8" barrel and has a magazine capacity of 20 or 40 rounds. Equipped with a folding stock. Rate of fire is about 500 rounds per minute. Marked "S P A LUIGI FRANCHI-BRESCIA-CAL9P" Weight is 7 lbs.

Pre-1968

Exc.	V.G.	Fair
3500	3000	2500

Pre-1986 conversions

Exc.	V.G.	Fair
N/A	N/A	N/A

Pre-1986 dealer samples

Exc.	V.G.	Fair
1500	1300	1000

Beretta Model 93R

Built of the Beretta Model 92 frame and slide, this machine pistol is chambered for the 9mm Parabellum cartridge. It is fitted with a 6.1" barrel with muzzle brake and uses a 15- or 20-round magazine. Can be fitted with a shoulder stock. Rate of fire is about 1,100 rounds per minute. Has a 3-round burst mode, and a small swing-down metal foregrip mounted on the front of the triggerguard. Weight is about 2.5 lbs. Used by the Italian antiterrorist units.

Pre-1968

Exc.	V.G.	Fair
7500	7000	6000

Pre-1986 conversions

Exc.	V.G.	Fair
N/A	N/A	N/A

Pre-1986 dealer samples

Exc.	V.G.	Fair
3500	3000	2500

RIFLES

Prior to 1965 Italy used the U.S. M1 carbine as well as the M1 Garand. Beretta manufactured as large number of these rifles and many are still in use by some military units. Also used by counter-terrorist units is the HK G3 SG1 sniper rifle and the Mauser Model 66 sniper rifle.

VETTERLI

NOTE: See also *Switzerland, Rifles, Vetterli.*

Model 1870 Rifle

This rifle was produced at Brescia and Torino arsenals under license from the Swiss firm Vetterli. It was chambered for the 10.35x47Rmm centerfire cartridge. Single shot and full stock. This rifle was fitted with a sheet steel bolt opening cover which rotates left to right to close over the receiver opening. The barrel was 34" in length with the rear portion hexagonal. Marked on the upper left barrel flat with the maker's name and on the left barrel flat, the date. There is also a short barrel (24") version of this rifle.

Exc.	V.G.	Good	Fair	Poor
400	300	200	100	50

Model 1870 Carbine

Same as above but fitted with a 17.5" barrel. The stock was half stocked with brass or steel forearm bands. The bayonet folded under the barrel with the blade tip inserted into the forearm.

Exc.	V.G.	Good	Fair	Poor
700	600	500	250	100

Model 1870/87 Rifle/Carbine

This rifle was the same as the Model 1870 with the important exception of having been converted to magazine feed. The 4-round magazine was developed by Guiseppe Vitali. The magazine is unusual because the charger had to be fully inserted

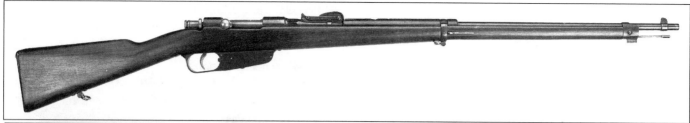

Model 1891 Rifle • Courtesy West Point Museum • Paul Goodwin Photo

and then withdrawn with a string as the cartridge stripped away. Over 1,000,000 of these rifles were issued. A large number of these converted rifles and carbines were sold to Russia. Some of these rifles were converted to 6.5mm caliber and designated the Model 1870/87/15.

Exc.	V.G.	Good	Fair	Poor
700	600	500	250	100

CARCANO

Designed by Salvator Carcano, the Model 1891 was adopted as Italy's standard service rifle in 1892.

Fucile Modello 1891 Rifle

A 6.5x52mm caliber bolt action rifle with a 31" barrel, 6-shot Mannlicher clip loading magazine, full-length stock, split bridge receiver, and a tangent rear sight with a wooden hand-guard and barrel bands retaining the stock. Fitted for a knife-type bayonet. On early versions the barrel behind the rear sights is octagonal. Weight is about 8.5 lbs. Produced at the Brescia and Terni arsenals. On post-1922 examples Roman numerals appear on the upper right barrel flat, denoting the year of the Mussolini rule. Many millions of this rifle were produced through World War II.

Exc.	V.G.	Good	Fair	Poor
225	175	125	75	40

Model 1891 Carbine

Same as above but half stocked with an 18" barrel with folding bayonet attached to the muzzle. Weight is about 6.5 lbs.

Exc.	V.G.	Good	Fair	Poor
165	140	100	50	20

Model 1891 TS (Truppe Speciali)

Similar to the Carbine above but without permanently attached bayonet.

Exc.	V.G.	Good	Fair	Poor
135	110	75	40	20

Model 1891/24 TS Carbine

Similar to the Model 1891 TS but with different rear sights.

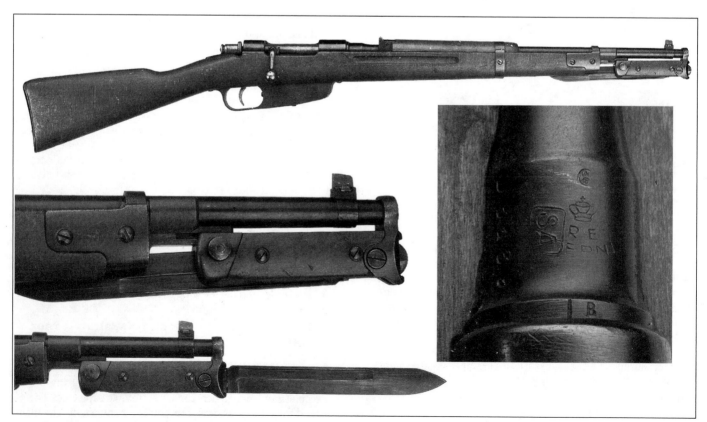

Model 1938 Rifle-Courtesy West Point Museum-Paul Goodwin Photo

Courtesy Richard M. Kumor Sr.

Exc.	V.G.	Good	Fair	Poor
150	125	75	40	20

Model 1891/28 Carbine

M91/28 Carbine with Grenade Launcher.

Courtesy Richard M. Kumor, Sr.

NOTE: Model 91/28 Carbine is rare and will command a substantial premium. Models in excellent condition can sell as high as $5,000. This model is encountered so seldom that prices are not given. Consult an expert prior to a sale.

Model 1938 Rifle (Prototype)

This model is chambered for the 7.35x51mm cartridge and fitted with a 22" barrel. It has a 6-round detachable box magazine. Bent bolt handle. It is full stocked with exposed barrel and bayonet lug. Simple fixed rear sight. Weight is about 7.5 lbs. Produced at the Terni arsenal. Very rare.

Exc.	V.G.	Good	Fair	Poor
N/A	—	—	—	—

Model 1938 Short Rifle

This is the carbine version of the Model 1938 rifle. Barrel length is 22" but fitted with shorter handguard. Weight about 6.5 lbs.

Model 1938 Carbine • Courtesy West Point Museum • Paul Goodwin Photo

Exc.	V.G.	Good	Fair	Poor
175	140	100	60	25

Model 1938 T.S. Carbine

Same as above but with bayonet not permanently attached.

Courtesy Richard M. Kumor, Sr.

Exc.	V.G.	Good	Fair	Poor
150	100	75	40	20

Model 1938 Cavalry Carbine

This model has a 17.75" barrel. It is fitted with a round-up bayonet that fits under the barrel when not deployed. Chambered for the 7.35x53mm cartridge, this carbine was issued to Italian paratroopers in the 1930s. Built by FNA in Brescia and other Italian firms. The rear sight is a fixed 200 meter sight. About 100,000 were produced but it is not often seen in North America. Weight is about 6.5 lbs. Carbines built in Gardone were equipped with grenade launchers.

NOTE: A very scarce carbine. No pricing information available

Exc.	V.G.	Good	Fair	Poor
N/A	—	—	—	—

Model 1941 Rifle

This is a 6.5mm rifle fitted with a 27" barrel and 6-round detachable box magazine. Very similar to the Model 1891 but for length and rear sight. Weight about 8.2 lbs.

Courtesy Richard M. Kumor, Sr.

Exc.	V.G.	Good	Fair	Poor
195	150	120	75	50

Italian Youth Rifle

Smaller version of full size military and chambered for 6.5mm cartridge. Barrel length is 14.4".

NOTE: Add $75 for dedication plaque.

Courtesy Richard M. Kumor, Sr.

Exc.	V.G.	Good	Fair	Poor
450	375	250	150	75

Breda Model PG

Chambered for the 7x57mm rimless cartridge, this is a gas operated self-loading rifle with an 18" barrel and 20-round detachable box magazine. The particular rifle was made by Beretta for Costa Rica and is so marked" GOBIERNO DE COSTA RICA," with the date 1935 and Roman numerals XIII. Weight was about 11.5 lbs. Fitted for a Costa Rican Mauser bayonet.

Paul Goodwin Photo

Exc.	V.G.	Good	Fair	Poor
450	375	250	150	75

Beretta Model BM59-Select Fire Assault Rifle

This select fire rifle closely resembles the U.S. M1 Garand rifle. Chambered for the 7.62x51mm cartridge, it is fitted with a 19" barrel and 20-round magazine. It has a rate of fire of 750 rounds per minute. Weight is about 10 lbs. Marked "P BERETTA BM59" on the top rear of the receiver. Produced from 1961 to 1966. This rifle did see service in the Italian army. There are number of variations to this rifle. They are the BM59 Alpini with folding stock short forearm and bipod for use by Alpine troops. The BM59 Parachutist Rifle with 18" barrel, folding stock and detachable flash hider.

Pre-1968

Exc.	V.G.	Fair
4500	4000	3800

Pre-1986 conversions

Exc.	V.G.	Fair
3500	3250	3000

Pre-1986 dealer samples

Exc.	V.G.	Fair
3000	2750	2500

Beretta AR70/.223-Select Fire Assault Rifle

Chambered for the 5.56x45mm cartridge, this select fire rifle was fitted with a 17.5" barrel and a 30-round magazine. Most were fitted with a solid buttstock while others were fitted with a folding stock. Weight was about 8.3 lbs. Marked "P BERETTA AR 70/223 MADE IN ITALY" on the left side of the receiver. This rifle was not widely adopted. Produced from 1972 to 1980.

Pre-1968 (Rare)

Exc.	V.G.	Fair
12000	8000	8000

Pre-1986 conversions

Exc.	V.G.	Fair
10000	7500	5000

Pre-1986 dealer samples

Exc.	V.G.	Fair
6500	5000	5000

Beretta SC 70-Select Fire Assault Rifle

Similar to the AR 70 and chambered for the 5.56x45mm cartridge. It feeds from a 30-round magazine. The SC 70 has a folding stock and is fitted with a 17.5" barrel. Weight is about 8.8 lbs. The SC 70 short carbine also has a folding stock and is fitted with a 13.7" barrel. Weight is about 8.3 lbs. Both of these rifles are still in production and used by the Italian army since approved for service in 1990.

Model BM59 • Courtesy West Point Museum • Paul Goodwin Photo

Photo Courtesy Private NFA Collection

SC 70 Carbine • Photo Courtesy Private NFA Collection

SC 70 Short Carbine • Photo Courtesy Private NFA Collection

Pre-1968

Exc.	V.G.	Fair
12000	9500	8500

Pre-1986 conversions

Exc.	V.G.	Fair
10000	8000	6500

Pre-1986 dealer samples

Exc.	V.G.	Fair
8000	6500	5500

AR-70

A .223 caliber, semiautomatic rifle with a 17.7" barrel, adjustable diopter sights, and an 8- or 30-shot magazine. Black epoxy finish with a synthetic stock. Weight is approximately 8.3 lbs.

NIB	Exc.	V.G.	Good	Fair	Poor
2500	2200	1900	1500	1000	—

BM-59 Standard Grade

A gas operated semiautomatic rifle with detachable box magazine. Chambered for .308 cartridge. Walnut stock. Barrel length is 19.3" with muzzle brake. Magazine capacity is 5,10, or 20 rounds. Weight is about 9.5 lbs.

NIB	Exc.	V.G.	Good	Fair	Poor
2200	1700	1200	700	400	—

SHOTGUNS

Franchi SPAS12

A 12 gauge slide action or semiautomatic shotgun with a 21.5" barrel and 9-shot magazine. Anodized black finish with a composition folding or fixed stock. Weight is about 9.25 lbs.

NIB	Exc.	V.G.	Good	Fair	Poor
950	800	600	500	400	300

Franchi SPAS 15

Similar to the SPAS 12 but with a detachable 6-round box magazine. Tubular steel folding stock and 18" barrel or fixed stock with 21" barrel. Weight is about 8.5 lbs. Very few imported into the U.S.

NIB	Exc.	V.G.	Good	Fair	Poor
4500	4000	3500	2500	—	—

NOTE: For guns with folding stock and 18" barrel add $1,000.

MACHINE GUNS

Italy used the Maxim Model 1906 and Model 1911. Both of these models were chambered for the 6.5mm cartridge. During World War I Italy purchased a number of Colt Model 1914 guns (Potato Diggers) chambered for the 6.5mm cartridge. When the war ended Italy received a large number of Austrian Schwarzlose Model 1907/12 as war reparations. The first Italian light machine gun was the Breda Model 1924, the forerunner of the Breda Model 30.

After World War II Italy has adopted the U.S. Model 1919A4 and .50 NM2 HB guns, as well as the MG42/59, for which several Italian firms make the components under license.

Beretta M70/78

Similar to the Model 70/223 but fitted with a heavy 17.5" barrel. Magazine capacity is 30 or 40 rounds. Rate of fire is 700 rounds per minute. Marked "P BERETTA FM 70/78 MADE IN ITALY" on left side of the receiver. First produced in 1978 with production ending in 1983.

Pre-1968

Exc.	V.G.	Fair
N/A	N/A	N/A

Pre-1986 conversions

Exc.	V.G.	Fair
N/A	N/A	N/A

Pre-1986 dealer samples (Rare)

Exc.	V.G.	Fair
9000	9000	8500

Revelli Model 1914

This was the first Italian designed machine gun to be made in quantity. It was chambered for the 6.5mm cartridge and fitted with a 26" barrel. It was fed by a unique 50-round magazine with 10 compartments holding 5 rounds each. Rate of fire was about 500 rounds per minute. Weight was 38 lbs. without tripod, 50 lbs. with tripod. The gun was manufactured by Fiat.

Revelli Model 1914 • Courtesy Private NFA Collection • Paul Goodwin Photo

Pre-1968

Exc.	V.G.	Fair
5000	4000	3500

Pre-1986 conversions

Exc.	V.G.	Fair
N/A	N/A	N/A

Pre-1986 dealer samples (Rare)

Exc.	V.G.	Fair
N/A	N/A	N/A

Fiat Model 1928 (SAFAT)

This is a light version of the Revelli Model 1914. Chambered for the 6.5 Carcano cartridge. Magazine is a 20-round magazine. Rate of fire is about 500 rounds per minute. Weight is

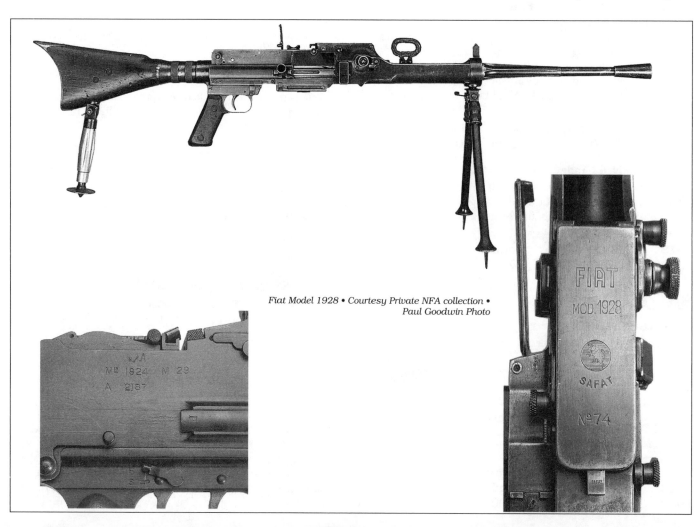

Fiat Model 1928 • Courtesy Private NFA collection •
Paul Goodwin Photo

Fiat Model 35, Courtesy Private NFA Collection • Paul Goodwin Photo

approximately 21 lbs. Only a few thousand were manufactured during its limited production. Very Rare.

Pre-1968

Exc.	V.G.	Fair
N/A	N/A	N/A

Pre-1986 conversions

Exc.	V.G.	Fair
N/A	N/A	N/A

Pre-1986 dealer samples (Rare)

Exc.	V.G.	Fair
N/A	N/A	N/A

Revelli/Fiat Model 35

This is a converted Revelli Model 1914 to 8mm. It is an air-cooled gun. It is fed by a 300-round belt. It's fired from a closed bolt. It was not a successful gun. Weight without tripod was 40 lbs.

Breda Model 30

First produced in Italy in 1930 this machine gun was chambered for the 6.5x52mm cartridge. It is fitted with a 20.3" barrel. Magazine capacity is 20 rounds. Rate of fire is 475 rounds per minute. Marked "MTR LEGG MOD 30....BREDA ROMA" on top of receiver. Weight is about 22 lbs. Production on this model ceased in 1937. This was the primary Italian machine gun of World War II.

Pre-1968

Exc.	V.G.	Fair
10000	9500	9000

Pre-1986 conversions

Exc.	V.G.	Fair
N/A	N/A	N/A

Pre-1986 dealer samples (Rare)

Exc.	V.G.	Fair
5500	5000	4000

Pre-1968

Exc.	V.G.	Fair
5000	4000	3500

Pre-1986 conversions

Exc.	V.G.	Fair
N/A	N/A	N/A

Pre-1986 dealer samples

Exc.	V.G.	Fair
N/A	N/A	N/A

Breda Model 30 with receiver markings • Paul Goodwin Photo

Breda Model 37

Chambered for the 8x59 Breda cartridge this gas operated machine gun had a rate of fire of 450 rounds per minute. It was fitted with a 26.5" barrel and weighs approximately 43 lbs. It was fed with a 20-round strip. Marked "MITRAGLIATRICE BREDA MOD 37" on the left side of the receiver. Produced from 1936 to 1943, this was the standard heavy machine gun of the Italian army during World War II. The Model 37 was considered to be one of the best Italian machine guns used in World War II, mainly because of its reliability and accuracy.

Pre-1968

Exc.	V.G.	Fair
9500	8500	8000

Pre-1986 conversions

Exc.	V.G.	Fair
N/A	N/A	N/A

Pre-1986 dealer samples

Exc.	V.G.	Fair
N/A	N/A	N/A

Breda Model 37 with receiver markings • Paul Goodwin Photo

JAPAN

JAPANESE MILITARY CONFLICTS: 1870-1945

The year 1868 marks the beginning of Japanese adoption of Western civilization and rapid modernization into an industrial and military power. The Japanese military was successful in the First Sino-Japanese War (1894-1895), as well as the Russo-Japanese War (1904-1905). In 1910 Japan annexed Korea and established a puppet-state in Manchuria in 1932. In 1937 the Japanese invaded northern China to begin the Sino-Japanese War (1937-1945). On December 7, 1941 the Japanese bombed Pearl Harbor, thus entering World War II. The war ended in August, 1945. Since the end of World War II the Japanese military has operated on a very small scale.

Bibliographical Note: Little has been written about Japanese military weapons. For a good overview see A.J. Barker, *Japanese Army Handbook*, 1939-1945, 1979.

HANDGUNS

Bibliographical Note: For technical data, history, and photos see Fred Honneycutt, Jr., *Military Pistols of Japan*, 3rd ed., Julian Books, 1994.

Type 26 Revolver

A 9mm caliber double action hinged barrel revolver with a 6-shot cylinder. As this pistol does not have a hammer spur, it only functions in double action. Fitted with a 4.7" barrel. Weight is about 31 oz. Manufactured from 1893 to 1924 in various government arsenals. This revolver was used by NCOs during WWII.

Courtesy Amoskeag Auction Co., Inc.

Exc.	V.G.	Good	Fair	Poor
400	300	200	150	100

4th Year Type Nambu Pistol

This is a quality built semiautomatic pistol chambered for the 8mm cartridge. It is fitted with a 4.7" barrel and has a magazine capacity of 8 rounds. It can be identified by the grip safety located on the front strap and tangent sights. The early models, known as "Grandpa" to collectors, can be identified by a wooden bottom magazine and stock slot. Later pistols, known as "Papa" Nambu, have aluminum bottom magazines and only a very few "Papas" were slotted for stocks. The values shown here are only approximate. Different variations may bring different prices and an appraisal is recommended. Pistols with original wooden stocks are worth considerably more.

Grandpa

Grandpa - Courtesy of James Rankin

Exc.	V.G.	Good	Fair	Poor
5000	3500	2000	1500	800

NOTE: Add $1,500 for original matching shoulder stock-holster.

Papa

Papa - Courtesy of James Rankin

Exc.	V.G.	Good	Fair	Poor
1500	900	650	450	300

Baby Nambu

As above, with a 3.5" barrel. 7mm cartridge is unique to the gun. A much smaller version of the Papa 8mm pistol. It is a well-made piece.

Courtesy Buffalo Bill Historical Center, Cody, Wyoming

Exc.	V.G.	Good	Fair	Poor
2250	2000	1500	1000	750

14th Year Type Nambu Pistol/T-14

Similar to the 4th Year Type but without a grip safety and with grooved grips and a larger triggerguard. Manufactured until 1945. Early guns have a small triggerguard. Later models have a much larger triggerguard. Early guns will bring a premium of 20%. The month and year of production are indicated on the right side of the receiver, just below the serial numbers on both the Type 14 and Type 94 pistols. The guns are dated from the beginning of the reign of Hirohito (Sho-wa period) which stared in 1925. Thus 3.12 means 1928-Dec. and 19.5 means 1944-May.

Courtesy Orvel Reichert

Courtesy Orvel Reichert

Later pistol with large triggerguard • Courtesy Orvel Reichert

Exc.	V.G.	Good	Fair	Poor
350	250	200	150	100

Type 94 Pistol/T-94

An 8mm caliber semiautomatic pistol with a 3.8" barrel and 6-shot magazine. Weight is about 27 oz. This was a service pistol issued in WWII. Most examples are poorly constructed and finished. Manufactured from 1937 to 1945.

Courtesy Orvel Reichert

Courtesy Orvel Reichert

Exc.	V.G.	Good	Fair	Poor
350	300	250	175	125

Hamada Skiki Type 2

Designed in 1942. There were several variations of this pistol chambered for both 7.65mm and 8mm Nambu. Production started in 1944 and continued through the end of the war in 1945.

Courtesy James Rankin

Exc.	V.G.	Good	Fair	Poor
4500	3500	2500	2000	1000

SUBMACHINE GUNS

The Japanese military used Bergmann submachine guns built by SIG. These guns were similar to the MP 18 but chambered for the 7.63 Mauser cartridge and used a box magazine. These gun were fitted for a bayonet. It was not until the late 1930s that the Japanese began a development program to produce their own submachine gun; the first one was the Type 100/40.

Type 100/40

Adopted for use in 1940 this submachine gun is chambered for the 8x21mm Nambu cartridge and fitted with a 9" barrel with perforated jacket, fitted with a bayonet bar. It is mounted on a wooden half stock with tubular receiver made at the Kokura arsenal. These guns will also be seen with a folding stock made at the Nagoya arsenal. It is estimated that some 10,000 guns were built with fixed stocks and about 6,000 were built with folding stocks. Both types had 30-round box magazines. Rate of fire is approximately 450 rounds per minute. Weight was about 7.5 lbs. This model was issued primary to paratroopers.

Pre-1968
Exc.	V.G.	Fair
3500	3000	2500

Pre-1986 conversions
Exc.	V.G.	Fair
N/A	N/A	N/A

Pre-1986 dealer samples
Exc.	V.G.	Fair
N/A	N/A	N/A

Type 100/44

This model was first produced in Japan in 1944. It is chambered for the 8mm Nambu cartridge. The barrel is 9.2" long with a honeycombed barrel jacket without bayonet bar. The side mounted magazine capacity is 30 rounds. Markings are in Japanese on the rear of the receiver. Produced until the end of the war. Weight is about 8.5 lbs. Rate of fire is 800 rounds per minute. Approximately 8,000 were produced at the Nagoya arsenal. This improved version was issued to the infantry.

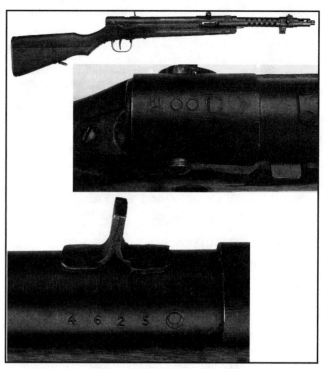

Type 100/44 • Courtesy West Point Museum • Paul Goodwin Photo

Pre-1968
Exc.	V.G.	Fair
3500	3000	2500

Pre-1986 conversions
Exc.	V.G.	Fair
N/A	N/A	N/A

Pre-1986 dealer samples
Exc.	V.G.	Fair
N/A	N/A	N/A

RIFLES

Bibliographical Note: For historical information, technical data and photos see *Military Rifles of Japan*, 4th edition. Fred Honeycutt, Jr., 1993.

Murata Type 13 (M.1880)

This was the first Japanese designed bolt action rifle. This was a single shot rifle with no extractor or safety. Chambered for the 11x60Rmm cartridge with a barrel length of 31.25". One piece full-length stock with two barrel bands. The machinery to build this rifle was purchased from Winchester. The rear barrel flat is stamped with the Imperial chrysanthemum. The left side of the receiver is stamped with Japanese characters.

Exc.	V.G.	Good	Fair	Poor
2000	1500	1000	600	400

Murata Type 16

Same as above but fitted with a 25" barrel for cavalry use.

Exc.	V.G.	Good	Fair	Poor
2200	1650	1200	700	500

Murata Type 18 (M.1885)

An 11mm caliber bolt-action rifle with a 31.25" barrel, and full-length stock secured by two barrel bands. This was an improved version of the Type 13, which added a receiver gas escape ports, a flat-top receiver ring, and a safety. These rifles was used in the Sino-Japanese War of 1894 and the Russo-Japanese War as well.

Courtesy Buffalo Bill Historical Center, Cody, Wyoming

Exc.	V.G.	Good	Fair	Poor
1650	1200	800	200	100

Murata Type 22 (M.1889)

Produced circa 1889 to about 1899 in caliber 8x53Rmm. Fitted with a 29.50" barrel with 8-round tubular magazine located in the forearm. This model was full stocked to the muzzle with straight grip. There were 2 variations of this rifle. The early version had a barrel band forward of the forend band. In the later version this extra band was eliminated. This was Japan's first smokeless powder military rifle and was the standard rifle issued to Japanese forces in the Sino-Japanese War of 1894. It remained in service until the Russo-Japanese War of 1904.

Rifle

Exc.	V.G.	Good	Fair	Poor
1600	1400	1000	300	200

Murata Type 22 Carbine

Introduced in 1894 and fitted with a 19.5" barrel and 5-round magazine. No bayonet fitting. A rare carbine.

Courtesy Richard M. Kumor, Sr.

Exc.	V.G.	Good	Fair	Poor
2200	1900	1400	350	200

Arisaka Type 30 Rifle (aka Hook Safety) (M.1897)

A 6.5x51SRmm Arisaka caliber bolt action rifle with a 31.5" barrel, 5-shot magazine and full-length stock secured by two barrel bands and a wooden upper handguard. This was the first box magazine Mauser-Mannlicher design used by the Japanese military. Straight handle bolt. This was the primary shoulder arm of Japanese troops during the Russo-Japanese War of 1904. Some of these rifles remained in service until WWII. A number of these rifles were sold to Great Britain and Russia during World War I. The Type 30 was also built for Siam (Thailand) and marked by that county's crest on the receiver bridge. It was designed by Nariaki Arisaka. Manufactured from 1897 to 1905. The rifle gets its nickname, "hook-safety", from the prominent hook projecting from the left side of the rear of the bolt.

Exc.	V.G.	Good	Fair	Poor
575	500	375	125	75

Arisaka Type 30 Carbine (aka Hook Safety Carbine)

As above, with a 20" barrel and no upper handguard.

Courtesy Richard M. Kumor, Sr.

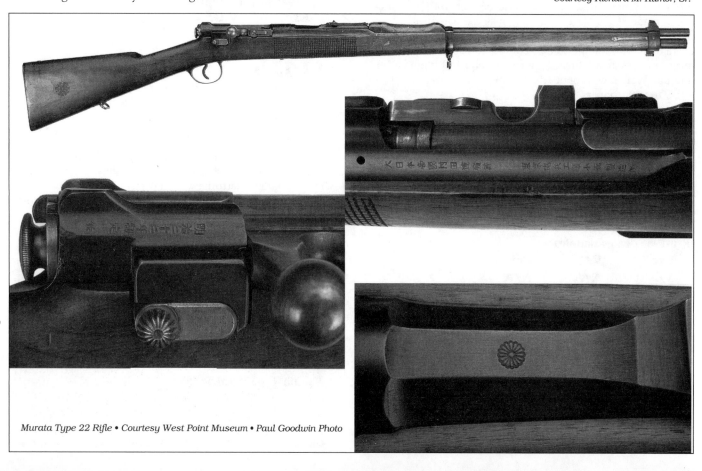

Murata Type 22 Rifle • Courtesy West Point Museum • Paul Goodwin Photo

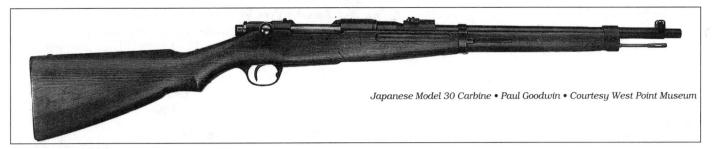

Japanese Model 30 Carbine • Paul Goodwin • Courtesy West Point Museum

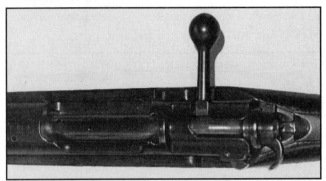

Courtesy Richard M. Kumor, Sr.

Exc.	V.G.	Good	Fair	Poor
600	550	400	150	100

NOTE: Deduct 30% if mum stamping is ground off.

Arisaka Type 35 Navy (M.1902)
Adopted by the Japanese navy in 1902, this was an improved version of the Type 30 rifle. Some main differences are that the hook safety was reduced in length and checkered. The re-

Exc.	V.G.	Good	Fair	Poor
175	150	125	90	65

Arisaka Type 38 Carbine
As above, with a 19" barrel and upper handguard. Equipped for a bayonet. Weight is about 7.25 lbs.

Courtesy Richard M. Kumor Sr.

ceiver included a spring latched bolt cover. Used during the Russia-Japanese of 1904. About 40,000 were built. Many of these were sold to Great Britain and Russian during World War I. All dimensions are the same as the Type 30 rifle.

Exc.	V.G.	Good	Fair	Poor
450	350	250	150	100

Arisaka Type 38 Rifle (M.1905)
A 6.5mm Arisaka caliber bolt action rifle with a 31.5" barrel, 5-shot magazine and large bolt handle. Full-length stock secured by two barrel bands with finger grooves. It was based on the Model 1893 Spanish Mauser. This model was built with a separate sheet steel action cover sliding with the bolt action. This rifle saw extensive use as late as World War II. Some of these rifles were sold to England in 1914 and 1915 and about 600,000 were sold to Russia in 1915 and 1916 in 7mm Mauser caliber. These rifles were originally intended for Mexico and have the Mexican crest of the receiver. These Russian-purchased rifles ended up in Germany in 1917 and were used in the Russian Civil War of 1917. Manufactured from 1905 to 1945. Most production switched to the Type 99 in 7.7mm beginning in 1939.

Exc.	V.G.	Good	Fair	Poor
300	250	175	125	85

NOTE: Deduct 30% if mum stamping is ground off.

Thai Type 38 Conversions
Short Rifle-.30-06

Exc.	V.G.	Good	Fair	Poor
600	475	350	250	150

Half-Stock Carbine-6.5mm

Exc.	V.G.	Good	Fair	Poor
550	425	300	200	100

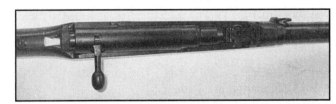

Courtesy Richard M. Kumor Sr.

Arisaka Type 38 Rifle • Courtesy West Point Museum • Paul Goodwin Photo

Arisaka Type 44 Carbine

Similar to the Type 38 carbine but with an 18.5" barrel and folding bayonet that hinged into the forearm. Weight was about 9 lbs.

Courtesy Buffalo Bill Historical Center, Cody, Wyoming

Exc.	V.G.	Good	Fair	Poor
450	350	225	150	100

Arisaka Type 97 "Sniper's Rifle"

The Type 38 with a side-mounted 2.5-power telescope and a bipod. Introduced in 1937. The telescope mounted on each rifle was factory fitted and stamped with the serial number of the rifle. The rear sight was a peep with folding from 400 to 2200 meters. Weight is approximately 11 lbs. with scope.

Courtesy Richard M. Kumor, Sr.

Courtesy Richard M. Kumor, Sr.

Exc.	V.G.	Good	Fair	Poor
2000	1700	1200	600	300

Arisaka Type 99 Short Rifle

A 7.7mm caliber bolt action rifle with a 26" barrel and full-length stock secured by two barrel bands. Non-detachable magazine capacity is 5 rounds. Fitted with a folding wire monopod. Weight is about 8.5 lbs. Adopted for military use in 1939. The rear sight on this rifle was a graduated leaf-type with folding arms to help aiming at aircraft. The monopod and anti-craft sight were phased out as the war progressed.

NOTE: Add 15% for monopod.

Exc.	V.G.	Good	Fair	Poor
175	140	100	80	60

Arisaka Type 99 "Last Ditch" Rifle

This is a Type 99 simplified for easier production. Typical features include a cylindrical bolt knob, a fixed peep sight, no front sight guards and a wooden buttplate. Not all rifles have each of these features.

Exc.	V.G.	Good	Fair	Poor
250	200	150	125	100

Arisaka Type 99 Long Rifle

This variation is the same as the above model but fitted with a 31.4" barrel. Weight is about 9 lbs. This is a scarce variation.

NOTE: Add 30% for monopod and dust cover.

Courtesy Richard M. Kumor, Sr.

Exc.	V.G.	Good	Fair	Poor
500	400	300	100	50

NOTE: Deduct 30% if mum stamping is ground off.

Test Type 1 Paratroop Rifle

Bolt action rifle chambered for 6.5mm Japanese. Barrel length is 19". Cleaning rod is 17-3/16" long. The stock is a two-piece buttstock with full-length handguard and a hinge attached at the wrist. Metal finish is blued. Total number produce is approximately 200-300 rifles.

Exc.	V.G.	Good	Fair	Poor
1800	1500	1000	500	125

Type 100 Paratroop Rifle

Chambered for 7.7mm Japanese cartridge. Barrel length is 25-1/4" long. Blued cleaning rod 21-5/16" long. Rear sight is adjustable from 300m to 1500m. Two-piece buttstock with full handguard can be disassembled with an interrupted-thread connector. Bolt handle is detachable. Metal finish is blued. Total number produced is estimated at 500 rifles.

Exc.	V.G.	Good	Fair	Poor
4500	4000	3000	—	—

Type 2 Paratroop Rifle

Similar to the model above but with a different style of takedown. This model uses a wedge and bail wire connector. This rifle production began in late 1943.

Courtesy Richard M. Kumor, Sr.

Exc.	V.G.	Good	Fair	Poor
1200	1000	700	300	100

Type 99 "Snipers Rifle"

The standard Type 99 with a 25.5" barrel and 4-power telescope.

Exc.	V.G.	Good	Fair	Poor
2000	1700	1200	500	200

Type 5 Semiautomatic Rifle

A 7.7mm semiautomatic rifle with 10-round box magazine patterned after the U.S. M1. Made at the Kure naval arsenal in

1945. It is believed that approximately 20 were made. Prospective purchasers should secure a qualified appraisal prior to acquisition.

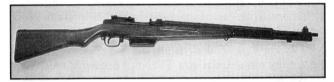

Courtesy Richard M. Kumor, Sr.

Exc.	V.G.	Good	Fair	Poor
22000	19000	14000	—	—

MACHINE GUNS

The Japanese used the Hotchkiss gun during the Russo-Japanese War and later adopted the Model 1914 Hotchkiss. Both of these guns were chambered for the 6.5mm cartridge.

Japanese Type 1

Introduced in 1941 as an improvement over the Type 92. Barrel length is 23" with cooling fins the same diameter through its length. The muzzle is fitted with a flash hider. Fed by a 30-round metal strip and chambered fro the 7.7mm cartridge. Rate of fire is approximately 550 rounds per minute. Weight is about 77 lbs. with tripod.

Pre-1968

Exc.	V.G.	Fair
8500	7500	7000

Pre-1986 conversions

Exc.	V.G.	Fair
N/A	N/A	N/A

Pre-1986 dealer samples

Exc.	V.G.	Fair
N/A	N/A	N/A

Japanese Type 3

Medium air-cooled gun chambered for 6.5x51SR Arisaka cartridge and introduced in 1914. A copy of the Hotchkiss Model 1897. Cooling fins on the barrel. Spade grips and tripod mount with sockets for carrying poles. Weight was about 63 lbs. Barrel length was 29.5". Fed from a metal 30-round strip.

Rate of fire was about 400 rounds per minute. Introduced in 1914.

Pre-1968

Exc.	V.G.	Fair
8000	7000	6500

Pre-1986 conversions

Exc.	V.G.	Fair
N/A	N/A	N/A

Pre-1986 dealer samples

Exc.	V.G.	Fair
N/A	N/A	N/A

Japanese Type 11

First produced in 1922 this is a light air-cooled machine gun chambered for the 6.5x51SR Arisaka cartridge. The gun utilizes a 30-round hopper feed system. The 19" barrel is finned. Weight is about 22.5 lbs. Rate of fire is 500 rounds per minute. Fitted with a bipod.

Pre-1968

Exc.	V.G.	Fair
6000	5000	4500

Pre-1986 conversions

Exc.	V.G.	Fair
N/A	N/A	N/A

Pre-1986 dealer samples

Exc.	V.G.	Fair
N/A	N/A	N/A

Japanese Type 89

This gun was produced in 1929 and is a copy of the British Vickers aircraft gun but chambered for the 7.7x56R (.303 British) cartridge. Weight is about 27 lbs.

Japanese Type 89 Vickers Aircraft • Courtesy Blake Stevens

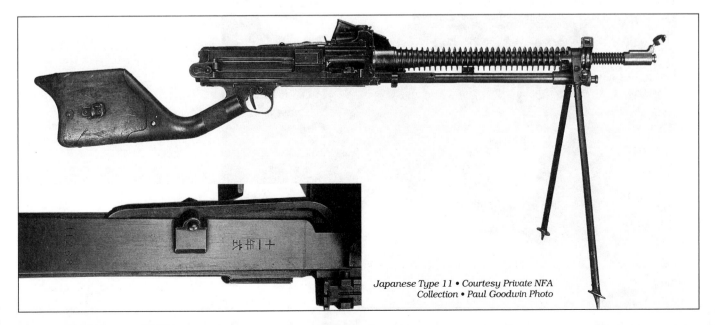

Japanese Type 11 • Courtesy Private NFA Collection • Paul Goodwin Photo

Pre-1968

Exc.	V.G.	Fair
11000	10000	9500

Pre-1986 conversions

Exc.	V.G.	Fair
N/A	N/A	N/A

Pre-1986 dealer samples

Exc.	V.G.	Fair
N/A	N/A	N/A

Japanese Type 92

This is an improved version of the Type 3 gun introduced in 1932. Chambered for the 7.7x58SR (.303 British) cartridge. It was fitted with dropped grips behind and below the receiver instead of spade grips. Barrel length is 28". Fed by a metal 30-round strip. Rate of fire was about 450 rounds per minute. Weight is about 100 lbs. with tripod. Gun alone weighs approximately 60 lbs. The mount was designed so that two men could carry it by means of poles or pipes fitted into the legs of the mount. This was the most widely used Japanese machine gun of World War II.

NOTE: The Type 92 designation was also applied to the Japanese copy of the Lewis gun. See *Great Britain, Machine Gun, Lewis 0.303in, Mark 1.*

Pre-1968

Exc.	V.G.	Fair
9000	8000	7500

Pre-1986 conversions

Exc.	V.G.	Fair
N/A	N/A	N/A

Type 92 • Private NFA Collection • Photo by Gary Gelson

Japanese Model 96 with plaque that reads,"Presented to U.S.M.A. by two former superintendents Gereral Douglas MacArthuer and Lt. Gen. Robert L. Eichelberger captured at Buna, New Guinea, Dec. 27, 1942 • Paul Goodwin Photo • Courtesy West Point Museum

Pre-1986 dealer samples

Exc.	V.G.	Fair
N/A	N/A	N/A

Japanese Type 96

Introduced in 1936 this light air-cooled machine gun is chambered for the 6.5mm cartridge. It was considered an improvement over the Model 11. This model is top mounted box magazine with a 30-round capacity. The cartridges are oiled when loaded into the magazine by an oiler built into the magazine loader. Barrel length is a finned 22" quick change affair with carrying handle. The wood buttstock has a pistol grip. Rate of fire is about 550 rounds per minute. Weight is approximately 20 lbs. These guns are sometimes seen with a 2.5 power scope fitted on the receiver.

Pre-1968

Exc.	V.G.	Fair
6000	5000	4500

Pre-1986 conversions

Exc.	V.G.	Fair
N/A	N/A	N/A

Pre-1986 dealer samples

Exc.	V.G.	Fair
N/A	N/A	N/A

Japanese Type 97

This model was designed in 1937 to fired from a tank or aircraft. It was to replace the Type 92 gun and is chambered for the 7.7mm cartridge. Its barrel length is 28" and the barrel is finned for cooling. Design is similar to the Czech vz 26. This was the first Japanese machine that did not require oiled ammunition. Weight is about 24 lbs. Rate of fire is approximately 500 rounds per minute. Fed by a 30-round box magazine.

Pre-1968

Exc.	V.G.	Fair
7000	6000	5500

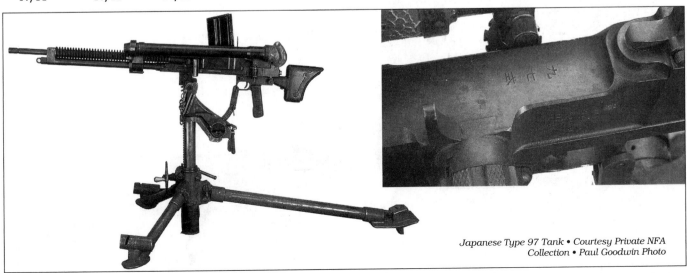

Japanese Type 97 Tank • Courtesy Private NFA Collection • Paul Goodwin Photo

Type 99 BRNO • Courtesy Private NFA Collection • Paul Goodwin Photo

Pre-1986 conversions

Exc.	V.G.	Fair
N/A	N/A	N/A

Pre-1986 dealer samples

Exc.	V.G.	Fair
N/A	N/A	N/A

Japanese Type 98

This is a copy of the German MG 15 ground gun. First used in 1938. Fed by a 75-round saddle drum with a rate of fire of 900 rounds per minute.

Pre-1968

Exc.	V.G.	Fair
8500	7500	7000

Pre-1986 conversions

Exc.	V.G.	Fair
N/A	N/A	N/A

Pre-1986 dealer samples

Exc.	V.G.	Fair
N/A	N/A	N/A

Japanese Type 99

Chambered for the 7.7x58mm Arisaka cartridge, this machine was first produced for the Japanese army in 1939, and is an improved version of the Type 96. It is fitted with a 21.3" quick change barrel and a 30-round top feed magazine. Its rate of fire is 850 rounds per minute. It weighs about 23 lbs. The gun is marked with model and serial number on top of the receiver. The gun has a bipod under the barrel and a monopod under the toe of the buttstock. Production ceased with the end of WWII.

Pre-1968

Exc.	V.G.	Fair
8000	7000	6500

Pre-1986 conversions

Exc.	V.G.	Fair
N/A	N/A	N/A

Pre-1986 dealer samples

Exc.	V.G.	Fair
N/A	N/A	N/A

Japanese Machine Gun Trainer

These guns were built in small machine shops all over Japan in the 1930s and 1940s so that young school-age males could be taught the basic techniques and operations of machine guns. Blowback operation. This gun does in fact fire a reduced load of either 6.5mm or 7.7mm cartridges, as well as blanks and is registered as a machine gun under the NFA. These guns, as a group, are different enough so that no two will be exactly the same. **CAUTION: DO NOT FIRE THIS GUN, IT IS UNSAFE.**

Pre-1968

Exc.	V.G.	Fair
2000	1500	1000

Pre-1986 conversions

Exc.	V.G.	Fair
N/A	N/A	N/A

Pre-1986 dealer samples

Exc.	V.G.	Fair
N/A	N/A	N/A

Japanese Machine Gun Trainer • Paul Goodwin Photo

MEXICO

MEXICAN MILITARY CONFLICTS, 1870 to 1945

The first three quarters of the 19th century were periods of almost constant strife and civil war for Mexico. Beginning in 1876 Mexico was ruled by Porfirio Diaz. The country was relatively stable and at peace for the 35 years of his rule. Beginning in the early 20th century a new generation of revolutionaries demanded power for the people. Such men as Emilliano Zapate and Panco Villa threatened the stability of the government. It was Francisco Madero who overthrew Diaz in 1911. A succession of reformist governments followed with the eventual formation of the PRI party in 1929 and a stable political climate through the Second World War and beyond.

HANDGUNS

NOTE: Other than the Obregon the Mexican military has relied on foreign purchases of its military handguns. The principal sidearm is the Colt Model 1911 in .45 ACP, purchased from the U.S. government. Mexico has also purchased pistols from Heckler & Koch, the P7M13, and numerous Smith & Wesson revolvers and pistols for its police forces.

OBREGON

Pistola Automatica Sistema Obregon

This is a .45 caliber semiautomatic pistol with a 5" barrel. Similar to the Colt M1911A1 but with a combination side and safety latch on the left side of the frame. The breech is locked by rotating the barrel, instead of the Browning swinging link. This unusual locking system results in a tubular front end appearance to the pistol. Originally designed for the Mexican military, it was not adopted as such and only about 1,000 pistols were produced and sold commercially, mostly to Mexican military officers. The pistol is 8.5" overall and weighs about 40 ozs. The magazine holds seven cartridges. This is a rare pistol, therefore an independent appraisal is suggested prior to sale.

Exc.	V.G.	Good	Fair	Poor
4500	2500	1250	750	400

A Mexican Obregon was sold at auction for $4,400. Condition good.
Faintich Auction Service, April 1999

Colt Model 1911A1

This is the standard service pistol of the Mexican military in .45 ACP.

SUBMACHINE GUNS

NOTE: The Mexican military availed itself of the Thompson submachine gun in various models, from the Model 1921 to the Model M1A1. The Mexican government has also purchased directly from the U.S. government a number of M3A1 .45 ACP submachine guns. From Germany the Mexican government purchased the HK MP5 and the HK 53. The MP5 is currently made in Mexico under license from HK.

Mendoza (HM-3)

Developed by Rafael Mendoza in the 1950s this submachine gun is produced by Productos Mendoza S.A. in Mexico City. This is a relatively small select fire gun chambered for the .45 ACP, .38 Super, or 9mm cartridges. Barrel length is 10", although some examples are found with 16" barrels in full automatic fire only. The box magazine capacity is 20 rounds. Rate of fire is about 550 rounds per minute. Weight is about 5 lbs. Stock is tubular steel. An unknown number of these guns are used by the Mexican army.

RIFLES

NOTE: Mexico used a number of different models of the Mauser bolt action rifle. Since the end of World War II, the Mexican military has purchased a number of foreign rifles for military use. These consist of U.S. M1 and M2 carbines, Colt M16A1 rifles in the 1970s, FN-FAL rifles, some of which were assembled in Mexico beginning in 1968 with FN supplied parts. In 1979 Mexico began to produce, under license from HK, the G3 rifle (G3A3 and G3A4).

MAUSER

M1895 Rifle

This was the standard rifle for the Mexican army under the Diaz regime. It is similar to the Spanish Model 1893. Fitted with an almost full stock with straight grip with no finger grooves. Barrel length is 29" and chambered for the 7x57mm cartridge. Rear leaf sight graduated to 2000 meters. Bayonet lug. Magazine capacity is 5 rounds. Weight is about 8.5 lbs. Produced by both DWM and the Spanish firm Oviedo.

Exc.	V.G.	Good	Fair	Poor
150	110	90	60	25

M1895 Carbine

Similar to the Model 1895 rifle except with 17.25" barrel, bent bolt handle and side-mounted sling. No bayonet fittings. Weight is about 7.5 lbs. Some but not all are marked with Mexican crest on receiver ring.

Exc.	V.G.	Good	Fair	Poor
150	100	80	50	25

M1902 Rifle

This model has an improved Model 98 action. Nearly full-length stock with half-length upper handguard. This model was built by DWM and Steyr. Barrel length is 29". Caliber is 7x57mm. Straight bolt handle. Rear sight graduated to 2000 meters. Mexican crest on receiver ring. Weight is about 8.75 lbs.

Exc.	V.G.	Good	Fair	Poor
300	225	170	100	60

M1907 Steyr Rifle

This rifle was fitted with an almost full-length stock with pistol grip. Upper barrel band has a stacking hook. Bayonet lug accepts Model 98 bayonet. Barrel length is 29". Caliber is 7x57mm. Straight bolt. Weight is about 8.75 lbs. Marked, "STEYR.MODEL 1907/DATE" on receiver ring.

Exc.	V.G.	Good	Fair	Poor
300	225	190	140	90

M1910 Rifle

This was the first Mauser produced by Mexico at the *Fabrica Nacional de Cartuchos* and the *Fabrica Nacional de Armas* in Mexico City. Similar to the Model 1902 rifle. Straight grip stock. Bayonet stud for Model 1895 bayonet. Barrel length is 29" and caliber is 7x57mm. Marked on top of receiver ring.

Exc.	V.G.	Good	Fair	Poor
125	100	80	60	20

M1910 Carbine

Very similar to the Model 1895 carbine with the addition of the Model 98 action and barley corn front sights. Mexican crest on receiver ring. Weight is about 8 lbs. Barrel length is 17.5" and caliber is 7x57mm.

Exc.	V.G.	Good	Fair	Poor
125	100	80	70	25

M1912 Steyr Rifle

Mexico bought these rifle directly from Steyr. This model is fitted with a 29" barrel and large receiver ring with straight bolt. Nearly full-length stock with pistol grip. Chambered for the 7x57mm cartridge. Receiver ring marked, "MODEL 1912" over "STEYR" over the date. Weight is about 8.75 lbs.

Exc.	V.G.	Good	Fair	Poor
300	230	175	100	75

M1912 Steyr Short Rifle

This short rifle is the same as the Model 1912 rifle except for turned down bolt handle and barrel length.

Exc.	V.G.	Good	Fair	Poor
300	230	175	100	75

FN M24 Short Rifle

Approximately 25,000 of these rifles were bought from FN by Mexico in 1926 and 1927. This then is the standard FN Model 1924 version with pistol grip stock without finger grooves. Barrel length is 23.5" and caliber is 7x57mm. Weight is about 8.5 lbs.

Exc.	V.G.	Good	Fair	Poor
150	120	90	70	40

FN M24 Carbine

Same as above but with 15.25" barrel and no bayonet fittings. Weight is about 7.5 lbs.

Exc.	V.G.	Good	Fair	Poor
150	130	100	80	50

VZ 12/33 Carbine

This is the Czech export Model 12/33 carbine. Pistol grip stock. Barrel length is 22" and caliber is 7x57mm. Weight is about 8.5 lbs. Marked with Mexican crest on receiver ring.

Exc.	V.G.	Good	Fair	Poor
225	195	170	125	90

MONDRAGON

Model 1908 & Model 1915

Firearms designed by Manuel Mondragon were produced on an experimental basis first at St. Chamond Arsenal in France and later at SIG in Neuhausen, Switzerland. The latter company was responsible for the manufacture of the two known production models: the Model 1908 and 1915.

The Model 1908 Mondragon semiautomatic rifle holds the distinction of being the first self-loading rifle to be issued to any armed forces. Only about 400 of these rifles were delivered to the Mexican army in 1911 when revolution broke out. The rifle was chambered for the 7x57mm Mauser cartridge and featured a 24.5" barrel. It has an 8-round box magazine. Weight is about 9.5 lbs. SIG had several thousand of these rifles left after the Mexicans were unable to take delivery. When WWI got under way the Swiss firm sold the remaining stocks to Germany. These rifle were called the Model 1915 and were identical to the Model 1908 except for the addition of a 30-round drum magazine.

Courtesy Rock Island Auction Company

Exc.	V.G.	Good	Fair	Poor
6000	4000	2000	1000	750

FABRICA NACIONAL DE ARMAS
Mexico, City

Model 1936

This bolt action rifle was chambered for the 7mm cartridge and uses a short-type Mauser action. The rifle is of Mexican design and resembles the Springfield Model 1930A1 in appearance. Barrel length is 19.25" with a 5-round non-detachable magazine. Tangent rear sight with "V" notch. Weight is about 8.25 lbs.

Exc.	V.G.	Good	Fair	Poor
300	270	250	160	110

Model 1954

This Mexican produced and designed rifle also uses a Mauser action but resembles a Springfield Model 1903A3 in appearance. The stock is laminated plywood. Barrel length is 24" and chambered for the 30-06 cartridge. Weight is approximately 9 lbs. Some of these rifles may still be in service.

Exc.	V.G.	Good	Fair	Poor
350	300	250	175	110

MACHINE GUNS

NOTE: The Mexican military has used a variety of foreign-built machine guns. The Madsen Model 1934, the Model 1896 Hotchkiss 7mm machine gun, and the Browning Model 1919.

NORWAY

Norwegian Military conflicts, 1870-Present

In 1870 Norway was ruled by Sweden. An upsurge in Norwegian nationalism forced Sweden to dissolve its ties and grant independence as a constitutional monarchy to Norway in 1905. Norway remained neutral during World War I. However, the country was occupied by Germany from 1940 to 1945 during World War II. Since the end of the war Norway as remained independent economically and socially from the rest of Europe, having rejected membership in the European Union on two occasions.

HANDGUNS

NAGANT

Model 1883 Revolver

Adopted in 1883 this Nagant 6-round revolver has a solid frame with loading gate and mechanical rod ejection. Double action. Chambered for the 9x23R Belgian Nagant cartridge. Barrel is part round and part hexagon and is 5.5" long. Fluted cylinder and checkered wood grips with lanyard loop. Weight is about 32 oz. This model stayed in service until 1940. It was issued to both officers and NCOs.

Exc.	V.G.	Good	Fair	Poor
1250	750	400	275	150

Model 1887/93 Revolver

Similar in appearance to the Model 1883 but chambered for the 7.5x22R Norwegian Nagant cartridge. Barrel length is 4.5". Weight is about 28 oz. In service until 1940.

Exc.	V.G.	Good	Fair	Poor
1250	750	400	275	150

Model 1912/14

All of the Model 1912/14 pistols were produced at the Norwegian arsenal at Konsberg Vapenfabrikk. The official designation of the Norwegian Colt pistol was "COLT AUTOMATISK PISTOL, MODEL 1912, CAL. 11.43 M/M." In 1917 the designation changed to "11.25 M/M AUTOMATISK PISTOL MODEL 1914." The new marking began with serial number 96. For a more detailed explanation of the differences in the Norwegian pistols see Clawson's, *Colt .45 Government Models, 1912 through 1970*.

Table 1:

DATE	Serial Range
1917	1-95
1918	96-600
1919	601-1150
1920	1151-1650
1921	1651-2200
1922	2201-2950

Table 1:

1923	2951-4610
1924	4611-6700
1925	6701-8940
1926	8941-11820
1927	11821-15900
1928	15901-20100
1929	20101-21400
1932	21441-21940
1933	21941-22040
1934	22041-22141
1936	22142-22211
1939	22212-22311
1940	22312-22361
1941	22362-26460
1942	26461-29614
1945	29615-30535
1947	32336-32854

Kongsberg Vapenfabrikk Model M/1912 (Norwegian) copy SN 1-96

(Rarely seen) (99%-100% add 20-30%)

Exc.	V.G.	Good	Fair	Poor
3500	2200	1150	850	600

Kongsberg Vapenfabrikk Model M/1914 (Norwegian) copy SN 97-29614 and 30536-32854

(Numbers must match)

Notice the extended slide stop on the left side • Courtesy Karl Karash

Exc.	V.G.	Good	Fair	Poor
1400	900	750	600	400

Kongsberg Vapenfabrikk Model M/1914 (Norwegian) copy SN 29615 to 30535

(Waffenamt marked on slide and barrel. (Numbers must match.) Waffenamt marked M/1914s outside this range are probably FAKES. (99%-100% add 20-30%.) A little over 900 were produced.

Exc.	V.G.	Good	Fair	Poor
3000	1900	1150	850	600

SUBMACHINE GUNS

Norway uses a copy of the German MP40 designated the M40 chambered for the 9x19mm Parabellum cartridge. The Norwegian military also issued the British Sten gun, as well as the HK MP5A2 and MP5A3. The Norwegian Marines use the Suomi 37/39 submachine gun.

RIFLES

The Norwegian military also uses the HK G3 rifle, the Mauser 98K converted to 7.62x51mm, as well as now obsolete U.S. M1 Garands and U.S. M1 and M2 carbines.

KRAG JORGENSEN
See also *U.S., Rifles, Krag*

NOTE: The Norwegian Krag rifles differ from the U.S. Krags primary in that it does not have a cartridge cutoff. The Norwegian Krags were used by the Norwegian army as its principal long arm until the Germans occupied Norway in 1940. The majority of these rifles were built at Konsberg although some were produced at Steyr and FN Herstal. Norwegian Krags were chambered for the 6.5x55mm Swedish Mauser cartridge.

Model 1894 Rifle

This rifle is full stocked with pistol grip and full-length handguard. Barrel length is 30". Box magazine is located in horizontal position and has a capacity of 5 rounds. Tangent rear sight. Weight is approximately 9 lbs.

Exc.	V.G.	Good	Fair	Poor
1000	750	600	400	150

Model 1923 Sniper

This model is fitted with a full stock and checkered pistol grip. Full-length handguard. Heavy barrel length is 24". Bayonet fittings on nose cap. Micrometer rear sight with aperture. Marked "M.1894" on receiver. Magazine capacity is 5 rounds. Weight is about 9 lbs. Scarce.

Exc.	V.G.	Good	Fair	Poor
3500	2250	1250	650	300

Model 1925 Sniper

Fitted with a 30" heavy barrel similar to the Model 1894 rifle but with checkered pistol grip and micrometer rear peep sight. Weight is approximately 10 lbs. Scarce.

Exc.	V.G.	Good	Fair	Poor
3500	2250	1250	650	300

Model 1930 Sniper

This model has a sporter-style half stock with checkered full pistol grip. Heavy 30" barrel. No bayonet fittings. Micrometer rear sight. Marked "M/1894/30." Weight is approximately 11.5 lbs. Scarce.

Exc.	V.G.	Good	Fair	Poor
3500	2250	1250	650	400

Model 1895 Carbine

This model is half stocked with short handguard and fitted with a 20.5" barrel. Magazine capacity is 5 rounds. Weight is about 7.5 lbs. Very similar in appearance to the U.S. Krag carbine.

Exc.	V.G.	Good	Fair	Poor
1500	850	650	400	200

Model 1897 Carbine

Similar to the Model 1895 carbine except the rear sling swivel is located near toe of buttstock.

Exc.	V.G.	Good	Fair	Poor
1500	850	650	400	200

Model 1904 Carbine

This model has a 20.5" barrel with full stock and upper handguard but no bayonet lug. Weight is about 8.5 lbs.

Exc.	V.G.	Good	Fair	Poor
1500	850	650	400	200

Model 1907 Carbine

Similar to the Model 1907 but with sling swivels located on rear barrel band and buttstock.

Exc.	V.G.	Good	Fair	Poor
1500	850	650	400	200

Model 1912 Carbine

Full stocked with 24" barrel and 5-round magazine. Fitted with a bayonet lug on nose cap. Weight is about 8.5 lbs.

Exc.	V.G.	Good	Fair	Poor
1200	650	450	300	150

MACHINE GUNS

Norway used the Hotchkiss machine gun, chambered for the 6.5mm cartridge, beginning in 1911, as well as the Model 1914 and Model 1918 Madsen guns. The Browning Model 1917 water-cooled gun was used by the Norwegians and designated the Model 29. After World War II the Norwegian military used the Browning Model 1919A4, as well as the MG 34 and MG 42. Currently Norway has adopted the MG 42/59 as its standard machine gun, designated it the LMG 3.

POLAND

POLISH MILITARY CONFLICTS, 1870 TO THE POST-WAR PERIOD

From 1772 to 1918 Poland was part of Prussia, Austria and Russia, and as such it did not exist as an independent state. Following World War I Poland received its independence. In 1920-21 a border dispute led to war with Russia. Poland won some of its claims in the Treaty of Riga. In 1926 Joseph Pillsudski, Chief of State since 1918, assumed dictatorial power. After his death in 1935 a military junta assumed power. In 1939 Nazi Germany invaded Poland, precipitating World War II. After the war a government was established under Soviet auspices. In 1947 government control gave the Communists full control of the country. In 1990 the first free elections were held in Poland with the election of Lech Walesa.

HANDGUNS

RADOM

Fabryka Broniw Radomu

This company was established after World War I and produced military arms for Poland. During WWII the Radom factory was operated by the Nazis. Production was not recommenced after the war.

Ng 30

A copy of the Russian Nagant revolver chambered for the 7.62mm Russian cartridge. Approximately 20,000 were manufactured during 1930 and 1936.

Courtesy Richard M. Kumor, Sr.

Exc.	V.G.	Good	Fair	Poor
2000	1500	800	200	10

VIS-35

A 9mm semiautomatic pistol with a 4.5" barrel, fixed sights and an 8-shot magazine. On this model there is no manual safety; however, a decocking lever is installed that allows the hammer to be safely lowered on a loaded chamber. Versions made prior to WWII are engraved with a Polish eagle on the slide and "FB" and "VIS" are molded into the grips. These prewar pistols are slotted for a holster stock. German production pistols were made without the decocking lever and subsequently without the stripping catch. They also eliminated the stock slot. These pistols were stamped "P35p" and bear the Waffenamt inspector's mark "WaA77." Near the end of the war the take-down was eliminated and the grips were replaced with crude wooden grips. The slide, barrel, and frame are all numbered to each other.

NOTE: Prices quoted are for 1939 dated guns. Earlier years bring a significant premium.

Polish Eagle Model-1936 through 1939

Courtesy Richard M. Kumor, Sr.

Exc.	V.G.	Good	Fair	Poor
1700	1400	900	350	200

Nazi Captured Polish Eagle-Waffenamt Marked

Exc.	V.G.	Good	Fair	Poor
3500	2200	1500	450	300

Nazi Polish Eagle (Navy marked)

Courtesy Richard M. Kumor, Sr.

Will command a premium price

Nazi Production Model

Exc.	V.G.	Good	Fair	Poor
500	400	250	200	175

Nazi Production Model-"bnz" code

This is a late Nazi production with no other slide markings other than "bnz." A rare variation.

Courtesy Richard M. Kumor, Sr.

Exc.	V.G.	Good	Fair	Poor
1600	1400	900	650	500

VIS-35 Reissue

This is an exact copy of the original VIS-35 pistol. Limited to 100 pistols with less than that number imported into the U.S. The importer "Dalvar of USA" is stamped on the barrel.

NIB	Exc.	V.G.	Good	Fair	Poor
2300	—	—	—	—	—

Model 64

A PPK size pistol chambered for the 9mm Makarov cartridge. Rare.

NIB	Exc.	V.G.	Good	Fair	Poor
900	750	600	400	300	—

P-83

This pistol is chambered for the 9x18 (Makrov) cartridge. It is fitted with a 3.5" barrel and has a double action trigger with decocker. Magazine capacity is 8 rounds. Weight is about 25 oz. Black oxide finish. Developed in early 1970s, it is similar to a Marakov pistol except it is built from stampings. Used by Polish army and security forces.

NOTE: A commercial version is chambered for the 9x17 Short (.380) cartridge.

NIB	Exc.	V.G.	Good	Fair	Poor
250	200	—	—	—	—

P-93

Similar to the P-83 differing only in cosmetics but chambered for 9mm Makrov only. The decocking lever is on the frame instead of the slide. Barrel length is 3.9". Black oxide finish.

NIB	Exc.	V.G.	Good	Fair	Poor
350	275	200	150	—	—

MAG-95

This pistol is chambered for the 9mm Para cartridge and fitted with a 4.5" barrel. Magazine capacity is 15 rounds. Trigger is double action with external hammer. Weight is about 38 oz. Black oxide finish. Optional 20-round magazine. In use by Polish forces on NATO duty.

NIB	Exc.	V.G.	Good	Fair	Poor
525	425	—	—	—	—

SUBMACHINE GUNS

NOTE: Poland was supplied with Soviet made PPSh M1941 and PPS M1943 submachine guns.

M1943/52

This gun is a Polish-built modification of the Soviet PPS M1943 submachine gun in 7.63mm caliber. It is select fire and is fitted with a 9.5" barrel. Magazine capacity is a 35-round box. Rate of fire is about 600 rounds per minute. Weight is approximately 8 lbs. Wooden buttstock.

Pre-1968

Exc.	V.G.	Fair
7500	6500	6000

Pre-1986 conversions

Exc.	V.G.	Fair
N/A	N/A	N/A

Pre-1986 dealer samples

Exc.	V.G.	Fair
N/A	N/A	N/A

WZ-63

Introduced in 1964 this submachine gun is a small, almost pistol-size weapon chambered for the 9x18mm Makarov cartridge. It is fitted with a 6" barrel with folding metal butt. The

Polish Wz 29 • Courtesy Richard M. Kumor, Sr.

folding is designed to be used as a front vertical grip, if desired. A noticeable spoon-shaped muzzle compensator is used. Magazine is a box type with 15- or 25-round capacity. Rate of fire is about 600 rounds per minute. Weight is approximately 4 lbs.

Pre-1968

Exc.	V.G.	Fair
10000	9000	8500

Pre-1986 conversions

Exc.	V.G.	Fair
N/A	N/A	N/A

Pre-1986 dealer samples

Exc.	V.G.	Fair
N/A	N/A	N/A

RIFLES

MAUSER

NOTE: Poland began producing Mauser rifles and carbines in the early 1902 at the Warsaw arsenal.

M98 Rifle

This rifle is similar to the German Gew 98 with a tangent rear sight instead of the German style. Nearly full stock with pistol grip and finger grooves on the forend.

Exc.	V.G.	Good	Fair	Poor
300	200	120	90	60

M98AZ Rifle

This rifle is the same as the German Model 98AZ. Polish wood is used on the stock in place of walnut.

Polish M98AZ • Courtesy Richard M. Kumor, Sr.

Exc.	V.G.	Good	Fair	Poor
395	320	250	175	100

Wz 29 Short Rifle

This rifle was built at the Radom factory. Barrel length is 23.6" and caliber is 7.92x57mm. Straight bolt handle. Almost full stock with pistol grip. Tangent leaf rear sight graduated to 2000 meters. Weight is about 9 lbs.

Exc.	V.G.	Good	Fair	Poor
275	190	140	100	60

Wz 98a Rifle

Exc.	V.G.	Good	Fair	Poor
375	300	225	150	90

Wz 29 .22 Caliber Training Rifle

Exc.	V.G.	Good	Fair	Poor
225	180	140	100	80

Kbk 8 Wz 31 .22 Caliber Training Rifle

Exc.	V.G.	Good	Fair	Poor
225	180	140	100	80

Model 1891 Polish Nagant

A 7.62mm caliber bolt action rifle with a 28.75" barrel, 5-shot integral magazine, ladder rear sight and a full-length stock secured by two barrel bands. Blued with a walnut stock.

Polish Model 1891 • Courtesy Richard M. Kumor, Sr.

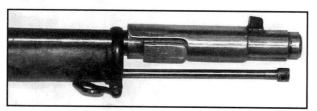

Polish Model 1891 close-up of bayonet and fittings
Courtesy Richard M. Kumor, Sr.

Exc.	V.G.	Good	Fair	Poor
225	175	125	100	75

NOTE: Add $150 to $250 for correct bayonet.

Model 1891/98/25 Polish Nagant

The production of these rifles started in the early 1920s at the Warsaw arsenal. Chambered for the 7.92mm cartridge but fitted with a bayonet lug and stamped with a small crowned Polish Eagle on receiver and bolt. It has a 23.5" barrel with 5-round non-detachable box magazine. Leaf rear sight. Weight is approximately 8 lbs. A very rare variation. Original, unaltered examples will command a premium price.

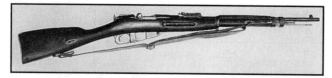

Courtesy Richard M. Kumor, Sr.

Pre-1968

Exc.	V.G.	Fair
30000	27500	25000

Pre-1986 conversions

Exc.	V.G.	Fair
N/A	N/A	N/A

Pre-1986 dealer samples

Exc.	V.G.	Fair
N/A	N/A	N/A

MACHINE GUNS

NOTE: Poland used a variety of foreign-built machine guns prior to World War II. Some of these were the Browning Model 1917s and the BAR. Both of these guns were chambered for the 7.92mm cartridge. After the war Poland used Soviet issued weapons.

Polish BAR (wz 28)

This Polish BAR was chambered for the 7.92x57mm cartridge with skids on its bipod instead of spikes and a bipod attached to the ga regulator instead of muzzle. Barrel length is 24" with AA ring sight base. Approximately 12,000 Polish-built BARs were produced between 1930 and 1939. These guns are marked "R.K.M. BROWNING WZ. 28 P.W.U.F.K. (DATE) (SERIAL NUMBER) located on receiver. A number of these guns (est. 500) saw service in the Spanish Civil War and by German military forces.

Pre-1968

Exc.	V.G.	Fair
15000	13000	11000

Pre-1986 conversions

Exc.	V.G.	Fair
N/A	N/A	N/A

Pre-1986 dealer samples

Exc.	V.G.	Fair
4000	3500	3000

Exc.	V.G.	Good	Fair	Poor
500	450	400	—	—

KbKg Model 1960 or PMK-DGN and PMKM

All of these rifles are copies of AK-47 variations. Both the PMK and PMKM are sometimes fitted with grenade launchers fitted to the muzzle.

PMK-DGM • Courtesy West Point Museum • Paul Goodwin Photo

ROMANIA

Romanian Military Conflicts, 1870-Present

In 1861 the principalities of Moldavia and Walachia (formerly under Russian control) were united to form Romania, which became independent in 1878. In 1881 Romania became the Kingdom of Romania. Romania was involved in the Second Balkan War in 1913 with Serbia, Greece, and Turkey against Bulgaria for a larger share of Macedonia. Romania and its allies defeated Bulgaria. This Balkan conflict helped to hasten the Balkan nationalism that precipitated World War I. In 1916 Romania joined forces with the Allies against Austria-Hungary and Germany. At the conclusion of World War I Romania was ceded additional land, but its history was marked by increased domestic turmoil and violence. In the 1930s the rise of the Iron Guard, a fascist organization, overthrew the Romanian king and established a dictatorship. Romania joined Germany against Russia in 1941. Soviet troops entered Romania in 1944 and shortly after the end of World War II a Communist government took power. While Romania was part of the Soviet empire it maintained a certain independence, especially in its foreign policy. In 1990 an election was held that ousted most of the communists from the government but failed to find solutions to domestic turmoil and strife.

HANDGUNS

Steyr Hahn Model 1911

Chambered for the 9mm Steyr cartridge, this pistol was made by Steyr for the Romanian military in 1913 and 1914, as well as other military forces. This particular model is marked with Romanian crest over 1912 on left of slide. Some of these pistols were used by Romanian military during World War II.

Exc.	V.G.	Good	Fair	Poor
450	375	300	250	150

Beretta Model 1934 Romanian Contract

This model is identical to the Beretta Model 1934 except the slide is marked "9mm Scurt" instead of 9mm Corto. Built for the Romanian military in 1941 with about 36,000 manufactured in Italy.

Exc.	V.G.	Good	Fair	Poor
475	425	325	225	125

Model 74

A Romanian copy of the Walther PP chambered for the 7.65mm (.32 ACP) cartridge. This pistol has an aluminum frame and is similar to the FEG Hungarian R 61 with the exception of a heel-type magazine release.

Exc.	V.G.	Good	Fair	Poor
160	140	125	100	80

Soviet TT33 (Copy)

This model is not fitted with a safety and has no import stamp. It is original military issue.

Exc.	V.G.	Good	Fair	Poor
800	700	600	500	300

NOTE: For pistols with safety and import stamp deduct 75%.

Soviet PM (Copy of Makarov)

Fitted with a safety but with no import stamp.

Exc.	V.G.	Good	Fair	Poor
400	350	300	200	100

SUBMACHINE GUNS

Before 1939 Romania acquired Beretta 9mm Model 1938A submachine guns. After 1939 the Romanian armed forces used the Beretta 38/42 in 9mm Parabellum. Then after the war Romania adopted the Czech vz 24 and vz 26 guns.

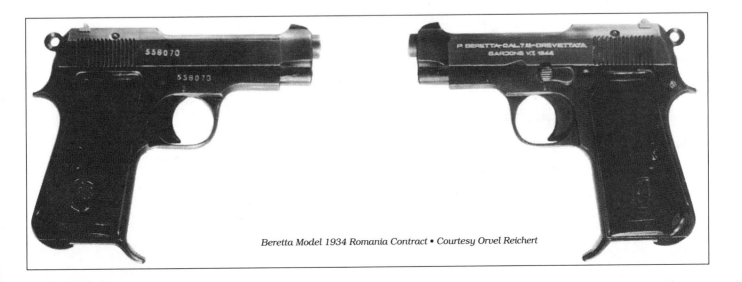

Beretta Model 1934 Romania Contract • Courtesy Orvel Reichert

RIFLES

MANNLICHER

Model 1892

Introduced in 1892 and built by Steyr, this turn bolt rifle is chambered for the 6.5x53Rmm cartridge. This model is full stocked with straight grip and half-length handguard. Fitted with a cleaning rod and bayonet fittings. Barrel length is 28.5". Leaf rear sight. Clip loaded magazine has a 5-round capacity. Weight is about 9 lbs. Marked "OE" over "W.G." on receiver ring and "MD. 1892" on left side of receiver.

Exc.	V.G.	Good	Fair	Poor
200	150	100	75	50

Model 1893

This is an improved version of the Model 1892 with stacking hook added and bolt modifications to prevent faulty assembly. Other specifications are the same as the Model 1892.

Exc.	V.G.	Good	Fair	Poor
175	125	90	75	50

Model 1893 Carbine

This is a short version of the Model 1893 rifle with 17.7" barrel. No handguard and no bayonet fittings. Weight is approximately 7.25 lbs.

Exc.	V.G.	Good	Fair	Poor
300	200	150	100	75

MAUSER

VZ 24 Short Rifle

This model is a copy of the Czech vz 24 Short rifle. The only difference is the Romanian crest on the receiver ring.

Exc.	V.G.	Good	Fair	Poor
325	280	200	140	80

STATE FACTORIES

FPK Sniper Rifle

This model is chambered for the 7.62x54Rmm cartridge and fitted with a modified AKM-type receiver. Magazine capacity is 10 rounds. Buttstock is similar to the Soviet SVD but with a molded cheekpiece. The muzzle brake is of Romanian design. Equipped with a telescope sight. Weight is about 10.5 lbs.

Exc.	V.G.	Good	Fair	Poor
800	700	550	400	200

AKM

Copy of the Soviet AKM except for a noticeable curved front vertical fore grip formed as part of the forend.

Courtesy West Point Museum • Paul Goodwin Photo

Pre-1968

Exc.	V.G.	Fair
8500	8000	7500

Pre-1986 conversions

Exc.	V.G.	Fair
N/A	N/A	N/A

Pre-1986 dealer samples

Exc.	V.G.	Fair
N/A	N/A	N/A

AKM-R

This a compact version of the Soviet AKM with an 8" barrel and side-folding metal butt. Magazine capacity is 20 rounds. Chambered for the 7.62x39mm cartridge. Rate of fire is about 600 rounds per minute. Weight is approximately 7 lbs.

Pre-1968

Exc.	V.G.	Fair
9000	8500	8000

Pre-1986 conversions

Exc.	V.G.	Fair
N/A	N/A	N/A

Pre-1986 dealer samples

Exc.	V.G.	Fair
N/A	N/A	N/A

AK-74

Similar to the Soviet 5.45x39mm version of this model but with a full-length handguard. Forend is fitted with vertical foregrip. Produced with metal or wooden buttstock. Semiautomatic version only.

Exc.	V.G.	Good	Fair	Poor
300	250	200	150	100

MACHINE GUNS

The Romanians used Soviet-built RPDs, SGMs, PK, PKB, PKS, PHTs and the Soviet-made DShK 38/46.

RPK (Romanian Manufacture)

Copy of Soviet RPK

Pre-1968

Exc.	V.G.	Fair
17000	15000	12000

Pre-1986 conversions

Exc.	V.G.	Fair
6500	6000	5500

Pre-1986 dealer samples

Exc.	V.G.	Fair
4500	4000	3500

RUSSIA
Former USSR/Warsaw Pact

RUSSIAN/SOVIET MILITARY CONFLICTS, 1870 to 2000

After the Crimean War, 1854-1856, Russian expansion continued into Caucasus, Turkestan, and eastern Asia. Alexander II was assassinated in 1881. Oppressive imperial rule followed under Alexander III and Nicholas II. The Russo-Japanese War of 1905 led to the Revolution of 1905, the results of which forced Nicholas to grant a Parliament and constitution. World War I led to the collapse of imperial rule and the country was thrown into revolution in 1917. Lenin took control but civil war lasted until 1920 when the Soviet regime emerged victorious. In 1922 Russia became part of the USSR. Despite a non-aggression treaty with Hitler Russia was invaded by Nazi Germany in 1941. Russian military forces fought several famous battles against the Germans throughout the war. In 1945 Russian forces entered Berlin and forced the Allies to partition Berlin and later Germany. From the end of World War II military forces of the USSR and Warsaw Pact nations were engaged in numerous military adventures. Perhaps the best known was the ten year struggle in Afghanistan. In 1991 the USSR collapsed and Russia resumed her autonomy. Since that time Russia has engaged in trying to control rebellious ethnic areas of the country from gaining autonomy, namely Chechnya and Tatarstan.

HANDGUNS

NOTE: Russia contracted for a number of Smith & Wesson revolvers over a period of years. The number of these revolvers purchaed by Russia was about 350,000. These revolvers were made for the Russian military and are covered under *U.S., Handguns, Smith & Wesson*.

NAGANT

Model 1895 "Gas Seal" Revolver

A 7.62mm caliber single or double action revolver with a 4.35" barrel and 7-shot cylinder. As the hammer is cocked, the cylinder is moved forward to engage the barrel breech.

Blued with either walnut or plastic grips. Weight was approximately 28 oz. In service from 1895 to approximately 1947.

This model is called the "Gas Seal" because the gap between the front of the cylinder and the rear of the barrel was closed. The cartridge case was used to close this gap. Built by Nagant Brothers in Liege, Belgium. The Russians also built the gun under license at their arsenal in Tula.

Exc.	V.G.	Good	Fair	Poor
200	150	100	75	50

NOTE: Single action only versions are much less encountered and will command a 50% premium. Prices reflect revolvers that have original finish, and are not arsenal refinished.

Mosin Nagant Model 1895 • Paul Goodwin Photo

Model 1895 Nagant .22 Caliber

As above but chambered for .22 caliber cartridges. Converted at the Tula arsenal from surplus 7.62mm revolvers. Used as a training revolver from 1925 to 1947.

Exc.	V.G.	Good	Fair	Poor
350	300	250	200	100

Model 1895 Nagant (KGB)

This is a standard Nagant with the important exception of a 3.5" barrel and shorter grip frame. Used by the Russian secret police during the Stalin years. Extremely rare. Proceed with caution.

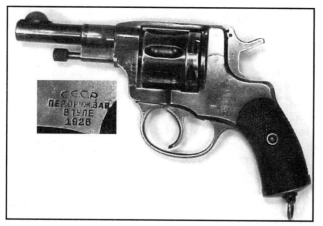

Nagant KGB Model • Courtesy Richard M. Kumor Sr.

Exc.	V.G.	Good	Fair	Poor
2000	1500	1000	—	—

FN 1900 Russian Contract

An unknown number of these FN pistols were purchased by the Russian government. Little information is known. Proceed with caution.

FN Model 1900 Russian Contract Pistol • Courtesy Richard M. Kumor Sr.

Exc.	V.G.	Good	Fair	Poor
1000	700	500	300	200

SOVIET STATE FACTORIES

Tokarev TT30 & TT33

Fyedor Tokarev was a Russian weapons designer who began his career at the Sestroretsk rifle factory in 1907. He was responsible for the development of machine guns, pistols, and automatic rifles. The TT series of pistols were just some of his designs.

In 1930 the TT30 was adopted and in 1933 a slightly modified version, the TT33 was introduced. A 7.62mm semiautomatic pistol with a 4.5" barrel and 8-shot magazine. This model was produced in a number of communist countries. Each country had its own model designation for the pistol; in Poland and Yugoslavia it is called the M57; in Hungary it was known as the M48; in China the M51 and M54; and in North Korea the M68. The North Korean M68 differs from the other Tokarevs in the location of the magazine release and the elimination of the barrel locking link.

NOTE: Add 50% for TT30, for cut-aways add 200%.

TT33

Courtesy Richard M. Kumor Sr.

Exc.	V.G.	Good	Fair	Poor
350	300	250	125	100

Tokarev Model R-3

A training version of the TT Tokarev pistols chambered for the .22 caliber cartridge.

Exc.	V.G.	Good	Fair	Poor
650	550	400	300	150

Tokarev Model R-4

A long barrel target version of the TT Tokarev pistol chambered for the .22 caliber cartridge.

Exc.	V.G.	Good	Fair	Poor
650	550	400	300	150

TK TOZ (Tula Korovin)

A .25 caliber pocket pistol produced by the Soviet arsenal at Tula. Used by military officers and police units.

Exc.	V.G.	Good	Fair	Poor
450	375	300	200	100

Makarov

This semiautomatic pistol is similar in appearance to the Walther PP pistol and is chambered for the 9mm Makarov (9x18mm) cartridge. It has a double action trigger and is fitted with fixed sights. Barrel length is 3.6" and overall length is 6.4". Weight is approximately 25 oz. Magazine capacity is 8 rounds.

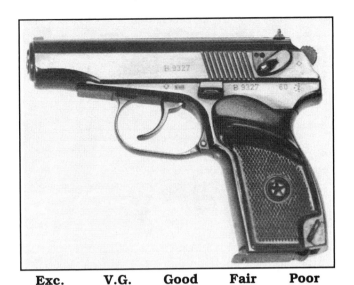

Exc.	V.G.	Good	Fair	Poor
150	100	80	60	50

Stechkin

A select fire pistol chambered for the 9x18 Makarov cartridge. Fitted with a 5.5" barrel and a 20-round magazine. Rate of fire is about 750 rounds per minute. Weight is approximately 36 oz. This was the standard service pistol of the Soviet army between 1955 and 1975. A wooden stock/holster is supplied with the pistol.

NOTE: It is not known how many, if any, of these machine pistols are in the U.S. and are transferable. Prices listed below are estimates only.

Pre-1968 (Extremely Rare)

Exc.	V.G.	Fair
30000	—	—

SUBMACHINE GUNS

PPD-1934/38 (Pistol Pulyemet Degtyarev)

Introduced in 1938 and based on the Bergman MP28 submachine gun. Select fire. The buttstock is wooden. Barrel is 10.5" with perforated barrel jacket and tangent sight. Chambered for the 7.62 Soviet pistol cartridge. Magazine capacity is 25-round box or 71-round drum. Rate of fire is approximately 800 rounds per minute. Weight is about 8.5 lbs.

Pre-1968

Exc.	V.G.	Fair
7500	7000	6000

Pre-1986 conversions

Exc.	V.G.	Fair
N/A	N/A	N/A

Pre-1986 dealer samples

Exc.	V.G.	Fair
N/A	N/A	N/A

PPD-1940

First produced in 1940 this Russian-built submachine gun is chambered for the 7.62 Soviet pistol cartridge. The gun was fitted with a 71-round drum magazine and 10" barrel. The rate of fire was 800 rounds per minute. The serial number and factory code is located on top of the receiver. Weight is about 8 lbs. Production ceased in 1941.

Pre-1968

Exc.	V.G.	Fair
6500	6000	5500

Pre-1986 conversions

Exc.	V.G.	Fair
N/A	N/A	N/A

Pre-1986 conversions

Exc.	V.G.	Fair
N/A	N/A	N/A

Pre-1986 dealer samples

Exc.	V.G.	Fair
N/A	N/A	N/A

PPD-1940 • Courtesy West Point Museum • Paul Goodwin Photo

Pre-1986 dealer samples

Exc.	V.G.	Fair
N/A	N/A	N/A

PPsh-41 (Pistol Pulyemet Shpagin)

This Russian select fire submachine was produced from 1941 until 1947. About five million were built and many were sold throughout the world. Some were converted from the 7.62 pistol cartridge to the 9mm cartridge by Germany. The gun could use a 71-round drum magazine or a 35-round box magazine. Rate of fire was 900 rounds per minute. The barrel was 10.3" long with slotted barrel jacket and weighed almost 8 lbs. Early models had a tangent back sight while most were fitted with a two position flip up rear sight. Markings are located on the receiver.

Courtesy Richard M. Kumor, Sr.

Pre-1968

Exc.	V.G.	Fair
7000	6000	5000

Pre-1986 conversions

Exc.	V.G.	Fair
N/A	N/A	N/A

Pre-1986 dealer samples

Exc.	V.G.	Fair
N/A	N/A	N/A

PPS 1943, Courtesy Steve Hill, Spotted Dog Firearms

PPS 1943, Paul Goodwin Photo

Pre-1968

Exc.	V.G.	Fair
7500	7000	6500

Pre-1986 conversions

Exc.	V.G.	Fair
N/A	N/A	N/A

Pre-1986 dealer samples

Exc.	V.G.	Fair
N/A	N/A	N/A

RIFLES

BERDAN

Berdan Model 1870 (Berdan II)

After Colt had built and supplied the Russians with the first Berdan rifles, BSA of Birmingham, England produced another 30,000. BSA, in 1871 and 1872, also provided the tooling and

PPsh41/Viet Cong • Paul Goodwin Photo

PPS 1943 (Pistol Pulyemet Sudaev)

Chambered for the 7.62 pistol cartridge this full automatic only submachine gun is fitted with a 10" barrel with slotted barrel jacket and 35-round box magazine. The receiver and jacket is stamped out of one piece of sheet steel. The metal butt folds behind the ejection port. Rate of fire is about 700 rounds per minute. Weight is approximately 7.5 lbs. Introduced in 1943 as an improvement over the PPsh-41.

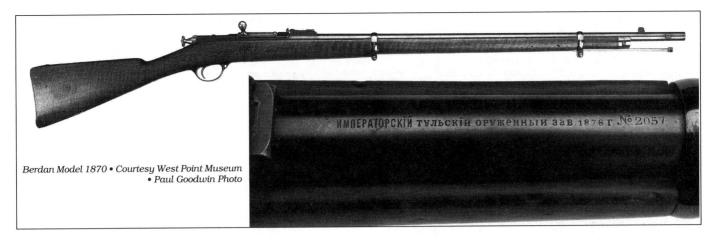

Berdan Model 1870 • Courtesy West Point Museum
• Paul Goodwin Photo

machinery so that the Russians could build their own version of the Berdan. A total of 3,500,000 Russian Berdans were built at their Russian arsenals of Ishevsk, Sestroryetsk, and Tula. This single shot model had a octagon receiver with short bolt handle. Caliber was 10.66x57Rmm with a barrel length of 32.5". Marked with the Russian arsenal on top of the receiver ring flat. These rifles saw service as late as World War I. Some captured Russian rifles were issued to German units during WWI.

Exc.	V.G.	Good	Fair	Poor
750	600	400	300	100

MOSIN-NAGANT

The first Mosin-Nagant rifles were developed at Tula by Sergi Mosin. The feed system was developed by Belgian designer Leon Nagant. The Russians had inadequate production facilities to build these rifles so many of them were produced by Chatelleraut, Remington, and Westinghouse. SIG made barrels for the rifles and Valmet, Tikkakoske rebuilt and modified Russians rifles. The Mosin Nagant was also produced in Poland, Hungary, Romania, and China. For history and technical details see Terence W. Lapin's, *The Mosin-Nagant Rifle*, North Cape Publications, 1998.

Model 1891

A 7.62x54Rmm caliber bolt action rifle with a 31.5" barrel, 5-shot integral magazine, ladder rear sight and a full-length stock secured by two barrel bands. Blued with a walnut stock. The Model 1891, before 1918, was fitted with an octagonal receiver ring with a heavy weight rear barrel section behind the rear sight. Pre-1908 version did not have upper handguards. Post-1908 rifles had sling swivels mounted through slots in the butt and forearm. Weight of these rifles was about 10 lbs. Used extensively in the Russo-Japanese War of 1904-1905. A total of over 9,000,000 of these rifles were built between 1892 and 1922.

Exc.	V.G.	Good	Fair	Poor
150	125	100	75	60

NOTE: Some Model 1891 rifles captured by Austria were converted to take the 8x50R Austrian cartridge. These examples are extremely rare and command a $300 premium.

Model 1891 Dragoon Rifle

Same as above but for a 28.75" barrel. Fitted with a short handguard with sling slots in buttstock and forend. Weight was reduced to about 8.5 lbs. Replaced the Model 1891 rifle as standard issue after 1920.

Exc.	V.G.	Good	Fair	Poor
175	150	125	75	60

Model 1891/30 Rifle

This is an improved version of the Model 1891 Dragoon rifle. The older hexagon receiver is replaced with a cylindrical one. It has a 28.7" barrel with metric rear tangent sights. Front sight is hooded. The bayonet ring was changed to a spring loaded catch type. Five-round magazine. Weight is about 9.7 lbs. Introduced in 1930. Over 17,000,000 of these rifles were produced between 1930 and 1944.

Exc.	V.G.	Good	Fair	Poor
150	125	100	75	60

Model 1891/30 sniper rifle w/3.5 power P.U. scope

This is a Model 1891/30 with a scope attached, and a longer turned down bolt handle.

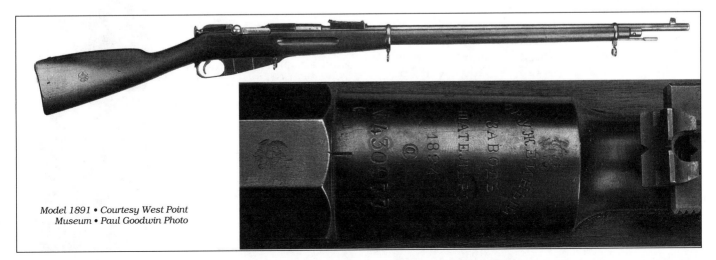

Model 1891 • Courtesy West Point
Museum • Paul Goodwin Photo

NOTE: There are a number of Czech CZ 54 and CZ 57 sniper rifles based on the Mosin, as well as Finnish sniper rifles based on the Mosin. All examples are worth a minimum of 100% premium over the Russian Model 1891/30 PU. Deduct 50% for imported rifles.

Courtesy Richard M. Kumor, Sr.

Exc.	V.G.	Good	Fair	Poor
1200	1000	800	N/A	N/A

Model 1891/30 sniper rifle w/4 power P.E. scope (Rare)

This is a Model 1891/30 with a scope attached.

Close-up of P.E. scope • Courtesy Richard M. Kumor, Sr.

NOTE: Deduct 50% for imported rifles.

Exc.	V.G.	Good	Fair	Poor
2000	1700	1100	N/A	N/A

Model 1907/1910 Carbine

As above, with a 20" barrel and modified sights. No bayonet fittings. Leaf sight is graduated in Russian arshins form of measurement. Weight is a 7.5 lbs.

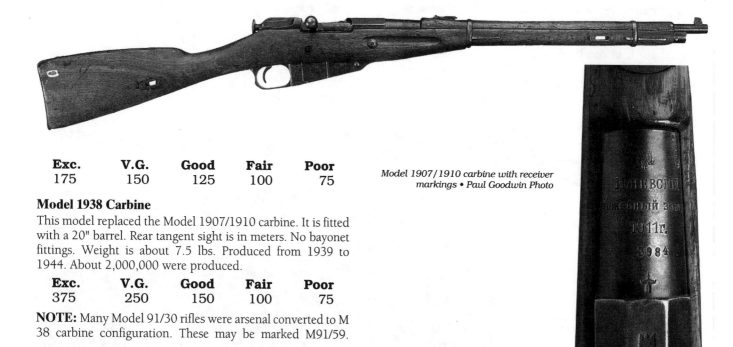

Exc.	V.G.	Good	Fair	Poor
175	150	125	100	75

Model 1938 Carbine

This model replaced the Model 1907/1910 carbine. It is fitted with a 20" barrel. Rear tangent sight is in meters. No bayonet fittings. Weight is about 7.5 lbs. Produced from 1939 to 1944. About 2,000,000 were produced.

Exc.	V.G.	Good	Fair	Poor
375	250	150	100	75

NOTE: Many Model 91/30 rifles were arsenal converted to M 38 carbine configuration. These may be marked M91/59.

Model 1907/1910 carbine with receiver markings • Paul Goodwin Photo

Conversions done in Bulgaria, Czech, and possibly the Soviet Union.

Model 1944 Carbine

This was the last Mosin-Nagant. It was fitted with a folding bayonet hinged at the barrel muzzle. The barrel was about a 1/2" longer than the Model 1938 carbine. With the bayonet this carbine weighed about 9 lbs. This model was copied by the Chinese and designated the Type 53. This model was also made in Poland and Romania.

NOTE: Add 15% for no import markings.

Exc.	V.G.	Good	Fair	Poor
200	150	125	75	50

TOKAREV

M1938 Rifle (SVT)

A 7.62x54Rmm caliber gas-operated semiautomatic or select fire rifle with a 24" barrel with muzzle break and 10-shot magazine (15 rounds in select fire). Cleaning rod in stock. Blued with a two-piece hardwood stock extending the full-length of the rifle. Upper handguard is 3/4 length of barrel. Weight is about 8.5 lbs. Manufactured from 1938 to 1940.

NOTE: Add 300% for Sniper variation.

Courtesy Richard M. Kumor Sr.

Model 1944 carbine with receiver markings • Paul Goodwin Photo

M38 Sniper • Courtesy Richard M. Kumor Sr.

Exc.	V.G.	Good	Fair	Poor
1000	800	600	200	100

M1940 Rifle (SVT)

An improved semiautomatic version of the M1938 with half stock and half-length slotted handguard with a sheet metal handguard and muzzle brake. Ten-round magazine. Weight is about 8.5 lbs.

NOTE: Add 50% for no importer marking. Add 300% for Sniper variation.

CAUTION: All Tokarev SVT carbines encountered with "SA" (Finnish) markings were altered to carbine configuration by their importer and have little collector value. It is believed that few SVT 40 carbines were ever made by the USSR.

Courtesy Richard M. Kumor Sr.

Exc.	V.G.	Good	Fair	Poor
400	350	300	200	150

DRAGUNOV

SVD Sniper Rifle

This model was developed as a replacement for the Mosin-Nagant Model 1891/30 Sniper rifle and introduced in 1963. It is chambered for the 7.62x53R cartridge. It is fitted with a 24.5" barrel with prong-style flash hider and has a skeleton stock with cheek rest and slotted forearm. Semiautomatic with an action closely resembling the AK series of rifles. A PSO-1 telescope sight with illuminated reticle is supplied with the rifle from the factory. This sight is fitted to each specific rifle. Magazine capacity is 10 rounds. Weight is about 9.5 lbs. This rifle is made under license in China, Iran, and Romania.

Exc.	V.G.	Good	Fair	Poor
4000	3500	3000	—	—

SIMONOV

Simonov AVS-36

First built in Russia in 1936 this rifle is chambered for the 7.62x54R Soviet cartridge. Fitted with a 24.3" barrel with muzzle break and a 20-round magazine. This automatic rifle has a rate of fire of 600 rounds per minute. It weighs is 9.7 lbs. Production ceased in 1938.

M1940 Rifle, Courtesy Rock Island Auction Company

Soviet SVD Sniper • Courtesy
West Point Museum • Paul
Goodwin Photo

AVS-36 • Courtesy Steve Hill, Spotted Dog Firearms

Pre-1968

Exc.	V.G.	Fair
10000	9500	9000

Pre-1986 conversions

Exc.	V.G.	Fair
N/A	N/A	N/A

Pre-1986 dealer samples

Exc.	V.G.	Fair
N/A	N/A	N/A

SKS

Introduced in 1946 this 7.62x39mm semiautomatic rifle is fitted with a 20.5" barrel and 10-shot fixed magazine. Blued with oil finished stock and half-length upper handguard. It has a folding blade-type bayonet that folds under the barrel and forearm. Weight is about 8.5 lbs. This rifle was the standard service arm for most Eastern Bloc countries prior to the adoption of the AK47. This rifles was also made in Romania, East Germany, Yugoslavia, and China.

NOTE: The importation of Chinese SKS rifles in very large quanities has resulted in an oversupply of these rifles with the result that prices are less than $150 for guns in excellent condition. However, this situation may change and if that occurs the price will adjust accordingly. Study local conditions before purchase or sale of this firearm.

KALASHNIKOV

Avtomat Kalashnikov AK-47

Designed by Nikhail Kalashnikov and first produced in 1947, the Russian AK-47 is chambered for the 7.62x39mm cartridge and operates on a closed bolt principal. Select fire. The standard model is fitted with a 16" barrel and a fixed beech or birch stock. Early rifles have no bayonet fittings. Magazine capacity is 30 rounds. Rate of fire is 700 rounds per minute. Rear sight is graduated to 800 meters. The bolt and carrier are bright steel. Weight is 9.5 lbs. Markings are located on top rear of receiver. This model was the first line rifle for Warsaw Pact. The most widely used assault rifle in the world and still in extensive use throughout the world.

North Korean AK-47 • Photo Courtesy Private NFA Collection

Pre-1968

Exc.	V.G.	Fair
21000	12000	9500

Pre-1986 conversions

Exc.	V.G.	Fair
6500	6000	5750

Pre-1986 dealer samples

Exc.	V.G.	Fair
5000	4000	3750

AK-S

A variation of the AK rifle is the AK-S. Introduced in 1950 this rifle features a folding steel buttstock which lies under the receiver.

AK-S • Courtesy West Point Museum • Paul Goodwin Photo

Pre-1968

Exc.	V.G.	Fair
21000	12500	9500

Pre-1986 conversions

Exc.	V.G.	Fair
6500	6000	5500

Pre-1986 dealer samples

Exc.	V.G.	Fair
5000	4000	3750

AKM

This variation of the AK-47, introduced in 1959, can be characterized by a small indentation on the receiver above the magazine. Pressed steel receiver with a parkerized bolt and carrier. Laminated wood furniture and plastic grips. The forend on the AKM is a beavertail-style. The rear sight is graduated to 1000 meters. Barrel length and rate of fire was the same as the AK-47 rifle. Several other internal production changes were made as well. Model number is located on the top rear of the receiver. Weight is approximately 8.5 lbs.

Photo Courtesy Private NFA Collection

Pre-1968

Exc.	V.G.	Fair
15000	11500	11000

Pre-1986 conversions

Exc.	V.G.	Fair
6500	6000	5750

Pre-1986 dealer samples

Exc.	V.G.	Fair
8000	8000	7500

AKM-S

In 1960 the AKM-S was introduced which featured a steel folding buttstock as seen on the AK-S. Weight is approximately 8 lbs.

AKM-S • Courtesy West Point Museum • Paul Goodwin Photo

Pre-1968

Exc.	V.G.	Fair
17000	12500	11500

Pre-1986 conversions

Exc.	V.G.	Fair
7500	7000	6500

Pre-1986 dealer samples (Rare)

Exc.	V.G.	Fair
8000	8000	7500

AK-74 Assault Rifle

Similar to the AK-47 but chambered for the 5.45x39mm cartridge. Magazine capacity is 30 rounds. Barrel length is 16.35". Select fire with semiauto, full auto, and 3-shot burst. Weight is about 8.9 lbs. Rate of fire is approximately 650 to 700 rounds per minute.

NOTE: There are no known original Soviet transferable examples in the U.S. Prices below are for pre-86 conversions only using AKM receiver and original parts.

Courtesy Steve Hill and Doug McBeth, A.S.D. Firearms

Pre-1968

Exc.	V.G.	Fair
N/A	N/A	N/A

Pre-1986 conversions

Exc.	V.G.	Fair
9000	8500	8000

Pre-1986 dealer samples

Exc.	V.G.	Fair
N/A	N/A	N/A

AK-74 (Semiautomatic only)

Introduced in 1974 this rifle is chambered for a smaller caliber, the 5.45x39.5mm, than the original AK-47 series. It is fitted with a 16" barrel with muzzle brake and has a 30-round plastic magazine. The buttstock is wooden. Weight is approximately 8.5 lbs.

In 1974 a folding stock version was called the AKS-74, and in 1980 a reduced caliber version of the AKM-SU called the AK-74-SU was introduced. No original military AK-74 are known to exist in this country.

Exc.	V.G.	Good	Fair	Poor
N/A	—	—	—	—

AK-47 COPIES

NOTE: These are copies of the Kalashnikov designs with only minor alterations. Because original military select fire AK assault rifles are so rare this list includes *semiautomatic rifles only* unless otherwise noted. These rifles listed below are built in their country of origin and contain no U.S.-made parts, i.e. receivers, etc. Some of these rifles may not be available to the collector and are listed for reference purposes only.

BULGARIA

AK-47

This is an exact copy of the Russian AK-47.

Exc.	V.G.	Good	Fair	Poor
650	600	500	400	300

AKN-47

This is an exact copy of the Russian AKS.

AKN-47 • Courtesy West Point Museum • Paul Goodwin Photo

Exc.	V.G.	Good	Fair	Poor
800	700	600	500	400

AK-47-MI

This is a copy of an AK-47 fitted with a 40mm grenade launcher.

AK-47-MI • Courtesy West Point Museum • Paul Goodwin Photo

Exc.	V.G.	Good	Fair	Poor
N/A	N/A	N/A	N/A	N/A

AK-74/AKS-74

These are copies of the Russian models. They were also exported in 5.56x45mm caliber.

Exc.	V.G.	Good	Fair	Poor
N/A	N/A	N/A	N/A	N/A

CHINA

See *China, Rifles*

EGYPT

MISR (Maadi)

A copy of the AKM with insignificant dimensional differences. Sometimes seen with single brace folding metal buttstock.

Pre-Ban

Exc.	V.G.	Good	Fair	Poor
1500	1200	950	750	500

ARM

This model is a Misr modified to semiautomatic only. It is fitted with a thumbhole stock. It is usually seen with a 10-round magazine.

Exc.	V.G.	Good	Fair	Poor
300	250	200	150	100

EAST GERMANY

MPiK

A copy of the AK-47 without a cleaning rod.

Exc.	V.G.	Good	Fair	Poor
N/A	N/A	N/A	N/A	N/A

MpiKS

A copy of the AKS without cleaning rod.

Exc.	V.G.	Good	Fair	Poor
N/A	N/A	N/A	N/A	N/A

MPiKM

A copy of the AKM with a cleaning rod. Early models used wooden stocks while later ones used plastic. Not fitted with a muzzle compensator.

Exc.	V.G.	Good	Fair	Poor
N/A	N/A	N/A	N/A	N/A

MPiKMS

Copy of a AKMS without shaped muzzle.

Exc.	V.G.	Good	Fair	Poor
N/A	N/A	N/A	N/A	N/A

KKMPi69

A version of the MPiKM without the gas cylinder. Chambered for the .22 caliber Long Rifle cartridge and used as a training rifle.

Exc.	V.G.	Good	Fair	Poor
N/A	N/A	N/A	N/A	N/A

HUNGARY

See *Hungary, Rifles*

IRAQ

Tabuk

This model is a copy of the Soviet AKM. An export version was built in 5.56mm.

Exc.	V.G.	Good	Fair	Poor
N/A	N/A	N/A	N/A	N/A

NORTH KOREA

Type 58

This model is a copy of the Soviet AK-47 solid receiver without the finger grooves on the forearm.

Type 58 • Courtesy West Point Museum • Paul Goodwin Photo

Pre-1968

Exc.	V.G.	Fair
20000	11000	8500

Pre-1986 conversions

Exc.	V.G.	Fair
5500	5000	4500

Pre-1986 dealer samples

Exc.	V.G.	Fair
5000	4000	3750

Type 68

This is a copy of the Soviet AKM-S with lightening holes drilled into the folding butt.

Exc.	V.G.	Good	Fair	Poor
N/A	N/A	N/A	N/A	N/A

POLAND

See *Poland, Rifles*

ROMANIA

See *Romania, Rifles*

YUGOSLAVIA

See *Yugoslavia, Rifles*

MACHINE GUNS

NOTE: Russia used early Maxim guns against the Japanese during the Russo-Japanese War of 1904-1905. The Russian military also used the Madsen Model 1902 and the Colt Model 1914 during World War I, as well as the Lewis gun.

Model 1905 Maxim

The first machine gun built in Russia at the Tula arsenal. Based on the Belgian Model 1900 Maxim with 28" barrel with smooth bronze water jacket. Fed by a 250-round belt with a 450 rounds per minute rate of fire. Gun weighs about 40 lbs.

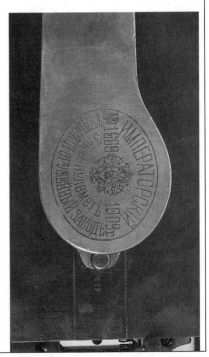

Russian Model 1905 in caliber 7.62mm produced at Tula Arsenal • Courtesy Private NFA Collection • Paul Goodwin Photo

Maxim M1910 • Courtesy Private NFA Collection • Paul Goodwin Photo

Pre-1968

Exc.	V.G.	Fair
15000	12000	10000

Pre-1986 conversions

Exc.	V.G.	Fair
10000	9000	8000

Pre-1986 dealer samples (Rare)

Exc.	V.G.	Fair
N/A	N/A	N/A

NOTE: For matching numbers add a 10% premium.

Model 1910 Maxim (SPM)

This is a Russian-built water-cooled machine gun chambered for the 7.62x54R cartridge. Early guns use a smooth water jacket while later ones used corrugated type. In 1941 these guns were given a large water-filling cap so that ice and snow could be used in extreme conditions. Barrel length is 28". Fed by a 250-round cloth belt. Rate of fire is approximately 550 rounds per minute. Guns weighs about 52 lbs. and the tripod weighs about 70 lbs.

Pre-1968

Exc.	V.G.	Fair
15000	12000	10000

Pre-1986 conversions

Exc.	V.G.	Fair
10000	9000	8000

Pre-1986 dealer samples

Exc.	V.G.	Fair
N/A	N/A	N/A

NOTE: For matching numbers add a 10% premium.

Model DP 28 (Degtyarrev Pulyemet)

This was the first original Russian-designed light machine gun. Developed in 1926 by Vasily Degtyarev at the Tula Arms Factory this gun was chambered for the 7.62x54R Russian cartridge. It was an air-cooled gun with 24" finned barrel. It was fitted with a rifle-style stock and bipod. It was fed with a 47-round flat drum. Rate of fire is approximately 550 rounds per minute. Weight is about 20 lbs. Designed as a light infantry machine gun. Used by all Warsaw Pact countries.

This was the first in a series of DP variants. The DA is an aircraft mounted machine gun. The DT is a tank mounted weapon with a 60-round drum. Others are the DPM, the DTM, and the RP46.

Private NFA Collection • Photo by Gary Gelson

Pre-1968

Exc.	V.G.	Fair
12000	10000	9000

Pre-1986 conversions (or remanufactured guns)

Exc.	V.G.	Fair
8000	7000	6500

Pre-1986 dealer samples (Rare)

Exc.	V.G.	Fair
N/A	N/A	N/A

Model 1939 DS

A heavy machine version of the DP. Limited production.

Model DPM

Introduced in 1944, this is a modification of the DP machine gun by placing the return spring in a tube at the rear of the receiver, sticking out over the butt. A pistol grip was added to facilitate firing. The bipod was attached to the barrel casing. No grip safety but a safety lever in its place. Barrel length is 24" and the drum capacity is 47 rounds. Rate of fire is 550 rounds per minute. Weight is approximately 27 lbs.

DP • Paul Goodwin Photo

Pre-1968

Exc.	V.G.	Fair
13000	11000	10000

Pre-1986 conversions

Exc.	V.G.	Fair
8000	7000	6000

Pre-1986 dealer samples

Exc.	V.G.	Fair
6500	6000	5000

Model RP-46

This gun is a version of the DP series of machine guns and is a metallic belt or magazine fed 7.62mm caliber. It was designed to be used as a company-size machine gun and is fitted with a 24" quick change heavy barrel. Introduced in 1946. Weight is about 29 lbs. Rate of fire is approximately 650 rounds per minute. The North Koreans use this same gun designated the Type 64.

NOTE: Many RP-46s were fitted with DP or DPM components by the Soviets. These components are dated prior to 1946. The prices listed below are for RP-46 guns with RP-46 (1946) components.

Courtesy Steve Hill, Spotted Dog Firearms

Pre-1968

Exc.	V.G.	Fair
17000	16000	15000

Pre-1986 conversions (or remanufactured guns)

Exc.	V.G.	Fair
10000	9000	8000

Pre-1986 dealer samples (Rare)

Exc.	V.G.	Fair
N/A	N/A	N/A

Model RPK

Introduced around 1960 this model is the light machine gun equivalent to the AKM assault rifle. It is fitted with a 23" non-quick change barrel. It uses either a 75-round drum magazine or a 40-round box magazine. It is also capable of using the 30-round magazine of the AK and AKM rifles. This model replaced the RPD as the squad automatic weapon (SAW) of the Soviet army.

Model RPK • Courtesy West Point Museum • Paul Goodwin Photo

Pre-1968 (very rare)

Exc.	V.G.	Fair
17000	15000	12000

Pre-1986 conversions

Exc.	V.G.	Fair
6500	5500	5000

Pre-1986 dealer samples (Rare)

Exc.	V.G.	Fair
4500	4000	3500

Model RPKS

This is the Model RPK with a side folding stock. All other dimensions and specifications are the same.

Pre-1968

Exc.	V.G.	Fair
N/A	N/A	N/A

Pre-1986 conversions

Exc.	V.G.	Fair
6500	5500	5000

Pre-1986 dealer samples (Rare)

Exc.	V.G.	Fair
4500	4000	3500

Model RPK-74

Similar to the RPK but chambered for the 5.45x39mm cartridge. Select fire with 4 positions: safe, semi-auto, full auto, and 3-shot burst. Barrel length is 23.6". Magazine capacity is 45-round box magazine. Also uses a 30-round magazine. Weight is about 12 lbs. and rate of fire is approximately 650 to 700 rounds per minute.

NOTE: There are no known original Soviet transferable examples in this country. Prices below are for conversion using Russian AKM receiver and Russian parts.

Courtesy Steve Hill and Doug McBeth, A.S.D. Firearms

Pre-1968

Exc.	V.G.	Fair
N/A	N/A	N/A

Pre-1986 conversions (A.S.D. Firearms)

Exc.	V.G.	Fair
10500	10000	9500

Pre-1986 dealer samples (Rare)

Exc.	V.G.	Fair
N/A	N/A	N/A

Model PK/PKS (Pulemet Kalashnikova/Stankovy)

This is general purpose air-cooled machine gun that is chambered for the 7.62mm Soviet cartridge. When this gun is mounted on a bipod it is designated the Model PK; when mounted on a tripod it is called a Model PKS. The operating system of this gun is the same as the AK series except turned upside down. It is fitted with a 26" quick change barrel and can be fed by a 100, 200, or 250 metal belt. The rate is fire is about 700 rounds per minute. Weight is approximately 20 lbs. Introduced in 1963.

The PK, when mounted on tanks, is designated the PKT. The PKM is an improved version of the PK with lighter components. The PKMS is a PKM mounted on a tripod. The PKB is a PKM without butt, bipod, pistol grip, or trigger. Instead, a spade grip with trigger is fitted to the receiver.

Pre-1968

Exc.	V.G.	Fair
N/A	N/A	N/A

Pre-1986 conversions (only 1 known)

Exc.	V.G.	Fair
—	43000	—

Pre-1986 dealer samples (Rare)

Exc.	V.G.	Fair
N/A	N/A	N/A

Model DShK M38-M1938/46

Introduced in 1938 this is a heavy air-cooled gas operated machine gun chambered for the 12.7x108mm cartridge. The feed system on the early guns (M1938) uses a rotary mechanism while the later versions (M1939/46) use a conventual lever system. The barrel is 42" and finned with muzzle brake. Fed by a 50-round metal belt. The rate of fire is about 550 rounds per minute. Weight of the gun is approximately 75 lbs. The mount can weigh 250 lbs. This was the primary heavy machine gun in Korea in 1950-1953, and it was used both as a ground gun and an anti-aircraft gun. The gun is mounted on a wheeled carriage or a heavy tripod.

Courtesy Steve Hill, Spotted Dog Firearms

Pre-1968 (very rare)

Exc.	V.G.	Fair
—	35000	30000

Pre-1986 conversions

Exc.	V.G.	Fair
—	27000	—

Pre-1986 dealer samples (Rare)

Exc.	V.G.	Fair
—	20000	20000

Russian RPD • Courtesy Private NFA Collection • Paul Goodwin Photo

NOTE: Many M1938/46 guns were converted from M1938 models. It is extremely difficult to determine when the conversion was done and by whom. Proceed with caution.

Degtyarev RPD

This is a belt machine gun chambered for the 7.62x39mm cartridge. It has a rate of fire of 700 rounds per minute and is fitted with a 100-round disintegrating belt carried in a drum. It has a 20.5" barrel and weighs about 15.6 lbs. This weapon was at one time the standard squad automatic weapon in the Soviet bloc. It was produced in large numbers and is still in use today in southeast Asia and Africa.

Pre-1968 (Very Rare)

Exc.	V.G.	Fair
38000	35000	35000

Pre-1986 conversions

Exc.	V.G.	Fair
20000	18000	16000

Pre-1986 dealer samples

Exc.	V.G.	Fair
20000	20000	20000

Goryunov SG43

This model was the standard Soviet machine gun during WWII. Chambered for the 7.62x54R Soviet cartridge, it is fitted with a 28" smooth barrel and is fed with a 250-round metal link belt. Rate of fire is 650 rounds per minute. Its weight is about 30 lbs. Marked on the top of the receiver. In production from 1943 to 1955.

Pre-1968

Exc.	V.G.	Fair
16000	13000	12000

Pre-1986 conversions

Exc.	V.G.	Fair
14000	13000	12000

Pre-1986 dealer samples

Exc.	V.G.	Fair
N/A	N/A	N/A

Model SGM

A modified version of the SG43 with fluted barrel and cocking handle on right side of receiver. Dust covers on both feed and ejection ports. Barrel length is 28". Weight is approximately 30 lbs. Fed by 250-round metal link belt.

There are variants of the SG43 which are the SGMT, a tank mounted version with electric solenoid. The SGMB is similar to the SGM but with dust covers over feed and ejection ports.

Pre-1968 (Very Rare)

Exc.	V.G.	Fair
16000	15000	14000

Pre-1986 conversions

Exc.	V.G.	Fair
14000	13000	12000

Pre-1986 dealer samples

Exc.	V.G.	Fair
N/A	N/A	N/A

SG 43 • Courtesy Private NFA Collection • Paul Goodwin Photo

SPAIN

Spanish Military Conflicts, 1870-Present

During the middle of the 19th century Spain was occupied with domestic power struggles. In 1868 a constitutional monarchy was established, followed by a republic from 1873 to 1874. Spain lost its last colony, Cuba, with its defeat by the United States in the Spanish-American War of 1898. In 1928 a military dictatorship was established and a second republic was created. Spanish separatists weakened the republic with the result that a Communists government came to power. This helped to create an internal struggle that led to the Spanish Civil War, 1936 to 1939. During this conflict the Germans supported Franco with men and weapons. During World War II Spain sided with the Axis powers but did not enter the war. Franco died in 1975. Spain joined the European Union in 1986. Spain is also a member of NATO.

HANDGUNS

NOTE: Officers in the Spanish military provided their own sidearms during the later half of the 19th century and into the early 20th century. The Spanish government provided guidelines for purchase and many Spanish officers purchased Smith & Wesson and Merwin & Hulbert revolvers. In 1884 the Spanish government directed its military officers corps to purchase the Smith & Wesson .44 Double Action Top Break built by Orbea y Compania of Eibar, Spain. It was designated the Model 1884. There were a number of Spanish gun makers building revolvers during the late 19th century, and many of these handguns were used by the Spanish military but were not marked as such. During WWI Spain provided a number of handguns to Britian, France, and other countries due to the shortage of military side arms in those countries. We only touch on the more significant models.

It is also important to note the various Spanish manufactures sold almost one million copies of the FN/Browning Model 1903 to the French during World War I.

Bibliographical Note: For additional historical information, technical data, and photos see Leonardo Antaris, *Astra Automatic Pistols*, Colorado, 1998.

CAMPO GIRO

Model 1910

Similar to the above, in 9mm Largo. Tested, but not adopted, by the Spanish army.

Exc.	V.G.	Good	Fair	Poor
1200	800	650	500	450

Model 1913

An improved version of the above.

Exc.	V.G.	Good	Fair	Poor
950	750	650	500	450

Model 1913/16

An improved version of the above.

Courtesy James Rankin

Courtesy James Rankin

Model 1913, Courtesy James Rankin

Exc.	V.G.	Good	Fair	Poor
550	450	375	300	200

ASTRA-UNCETA SA

Astra 400 or Model 1921

A 9x23 Bergman caliber semiautomatic pistol with a 6" barrel. Blued with black plastic grips. This model was adopted for use by the Spanish army. Approximately 106,000 were made prior to 1946. Recent importation has depressed the price of these guns.

NOTE: Any with Nazi proofs marks are worth a 100% premium, but caution is advised because there are no known examples, even though about 6,000 pistols were delivered to the German army in 1941.

Courtesy Orvel Reichert

Exc.	V.G.	Good	Fair	Poor
325	275	150	75	40

Astra 300

As above, in 7.65mm or 9mm short. Those used during World War II by German forces bear Waffenamt marks. Between 1941 and 1944 some 63,000 were produced in 9mm Kurz, and about 22,000 were produced in 7.65mm. Approximately 171,000 were manufactured prior to 1947.

Nazi-Proofed-Add 25%.

Exc.	V.G.	Good	Fair	Poor
350	300	200	150	100

Astra 600

Similar to the Model 400, but in 9mm Parabellum. In 1943 and 1944 approximately 10,500 were manufactured. Some of these World War II guns will have Nazi proof stamp and bring a premium. A further 49,000 were made in 1946 and commercially sold.

Exc.	V.G.	Good	Fair	Poor
350	250	200	150	100

ASTRA 900 SERIES

NOTE: The prices listed below include original Astra matching wooden stock/holster numbered to the pistol. For pistols with detachable magazines numbered to the gun add a small premium. For non-matching stock/holster deduct $300 to $500. For Chinese stock/holsters deduct $500. Original Astra stocks are difficult to locate.

Astra Model 900

Introduced in 1928 this is similar in appearance to the Mauser C96 pistol. Fitted with a 5.5" barrel chambered for the 7.63mm cartridge and fitted with a ring hammer. Ten-round box magazine with charger loading. Weight is about 40 oz. Production discontinued in 1955. Between 1928 and 1944 almost 21,000 were manufactured. Some of these pistols (about 1,000) were purchased by German military in France in 1943. No military acceptance marks but can be identified by serial number (see Still, *Axis Pistols*).

NOTE: A large number of Astras exported to China are frequently found in fair to poor condition. Some of these are marked with Chinese characters. During the late 1950s a number of Chinese Astras were brought into the U.S. These pistols appear to be in much better condition.

Exc.	V.G.	Good	Fair	Poor
3000	2750	2500	2000	1000

Astra Model 901

Introduced in 1928 this is similar to the Model 900 (5.5" barrel) but with select fire capability. Fixed 10-round magazine. Many of these pistols were sold to China in the 1930s. Rate of fire is about 900 rounds per minute. Weight is about 44 oz. Only about 1,600 of these pistols were produced. Exceedingly rare. Only a tiny number of these pistols are transferable, perhaps less than 5.

Pre-1968

Exc.	V.G.	Fair
6500	6000	5500

Pre-1986 conversions

Exc.	V.G.	Fair
N/A	N/A	N/A

Pre-1986 dealer samples

Exc.	V.G.	Fair
N/A	N/A	N/A

Astra Model 902

Same as above but with 7" barrel. Some went to China with various military units in the 1930s but most remained in Spain. Weight is approximately 53 oz. About 7,000 of these pistols were built. Very rare in this country for transferable examples. Perhaps less than 10 known.

Pre-1968

Exc.	V.G.	Fair
6500	6000	5500

Pre-1986 conversions

Exc.	V.G.	Fair
N/A	N/A	N/A

Pre-1986 dealer samples

Exc.	V.G.	Fair
N/A	N/A	N/A

Astra 903/903E

This is detachable 10- or 20-round magazine pistol developed in 1932. Fitted with a 6.25" barrel. Select fire. Some of these pistol were sold to China and others went to the German army in France in 1941 and 1942. No German acceptance proofs but can be identified by serial number (see Still). Some 3,000 of this model were produced. It is estimated that less than 15 of these pistols are transferable in the U.S.

Pre-1968

Exc.	V.G.	Fair
7000	6500	6000

Pre-1986 conversions

Exc.	V.G.	Fair
N/A	N/A	N/A

Pre-1986 dealer samples

Exc.	V.G.	Fair
3500	3000	2500

Astra Model 904 (Model F)

Similar to the other 900 series machine pistols but chambered for the 9mm Largo cartridge and fitted with a rate reducer that reduces the rate of fire from 900 rounds per minute to approximately 350 rounds per minute. The Model 904 was first produced in 1933 and was the prototype of the Model F. Only 9 Model 904s were built. About 1,100 Model F pistols were issued, most of which went to the Spanish Guardia Civil. Perhaps less than 10 of these pistols are known to exist on a transferable basis in the U.S.

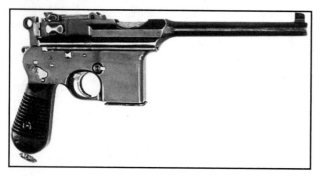

Astra Model F • Courtesy Chuck Karwan

Pre-1968

Exc.	V.G.	Fair
7500	7000	6500

Pre-1986 conversions

Exc.	V.G.	Fair
N/A	N/A	N/A

Pre-1986 dealer samples

Exc.	V.G.	Fair
4000	3500	3000

Astra A-80

A .38 Super, 9mm or .45 caliber double action semiautomatic pistol with a 3.75" barrel and either a 9- or 15-shot magazine depending upon the caliber. Blued or chrome-plated with plastic grips. Introduced in 1982.

NIB	Exc.	V.G.	Good	Fair	Poor
450	350	300	250	200	100

Astra A-90

As above, in 9mm or .45 caliber only. Introduced in 1986.

NIB	Exc.	V.G.	Good	Fair	Poor
400	350	300	250	200	100

LLAMA

Model IX

Chambered for the 7.65mm Para, 9mm Largo, or .45 ACP, this model has a locked breech with no grip safety. Built from 1936 to 1954.

Exc.	V.G.	Good	Fair	Poor
325	275	200	150	100

Model IX-A

This version of the Model IX is fitted with a grip safety. Current production models are chambered for the .45 ACP only. Weighs about 30 oz. with 5" barrel.

Exc.	V.G.	Good	Fair	Poor
275	225	150	125	100

ECHEVERRIA, STAR-BONIFACIO SA

NOTE: These pistols are stamped with a letter code to denote year built. For 1938 the letter "N" up to 1945 the letter "P."

Modelo Militar

Represents the first pistol Star produced that was not a Mannlicher-design copy. This model was copied from the

Colt 1911. It was chambered initially for the 9mm Largo in hopes of securing a military contract. When this contract was awarded to Astra, Star chambered the Model 1919 for the .38 Super and the .45 ACP, and put it on the commercial market. This model is like the Colt 1911—it has a Browning-type swinging link and the same type of lock up. However there is no grip safety, and the thumb safety functions differently. This model was produced until 1924.

Exc.	V.G.	Good	Fair	Poor
300	250	200	175	125

Star Model A

A modification of the Model 1919, chambered for the 7.63 Mauser, 9mm Largo, and the .45 ACP cartridge. The slide is similar in appearance to the 1911 Colt, and the spur hammer has a small hole in it. Early models had no grip safety, but later production added this feature. Some models are slotted for addition of a shoulder stock.

Exc.	V.G.	Good	Fair	Poor
375	275	175	150	100

Star Model M

A select fire version of the Model A. Chambered for .45 ACP cartridge this pistol was built during the 1930s. Some examples were sold to Nicaragua and Argentina. Rate of fire is about 800 rounds per minute. The selector switch is located on the right side of the slide.

Star Model M • Courtesy Chuck Karwan

Pre-1968

Exc.	V.G.	Fair
6000	5500	5000

Pre-1986 conversions

Exc.	V.G.	Fair
N/A	N/A	N/A

Pre-1986 dealer samples

Exc.	V.G.	Fair
3000	2500	2000

Star Model B

Similar to the Model A except that it is almost an exact copy of the Colt 1911. It is chambered for 9mm Parabellum and has a spur hammer with no hole. This model was introduced in 1928. Approximately 20,000 pistols were sold to the German army and about 6,000 to the German navy. These are stamped with acceptance stamps.

Courtesy Orvel Reichert

Exc.	V.G.	Good	Fair	Poor
350	250	200	175	125

Star Model 1941 S

Add 100% to prices listed below for pistols issued to the Spanish air force with box, cleaning rod, instruction sheet, and 2 numbered magazines.

Courtesy Richard M. Kumor Sr.

Exc.	V.G.	Good	Fair	Poor
200	175	150	100	75

Star Model BM

A steel-framed 9mm that is styled after the Colt 1911. It has an 8-shot magazine and a 4" barrel. It is available either blued or chrome-plated.

NIB	Exc.	V.G.	Good	Fair	Poor
350	300	250	200	150	125

Star Model 28

The first of Star's Super 9s. It is a double action semiautomatic chambered for the 9mm Parabellum cartridge. It has a 4.25" barrel and a steel frame. The magazine holds 15 shots. The construction of this pistol was totally modular, and it has no screws at all in its design. It is blued with checkered synthetic grips and was manufactured in 1983 and 1984.

NIB	Exc.	V.G.	Good	Fair	Poor
400	300	250	200	150	100

Star Model 30M

An improved version of the Model 28 that is quite similar in appearance. It was introduced in 1985.

NIB	Exc.	V.G.	Good	Fair	Poor
450	350	300	250	200	125

Star Model 30/PK

Similar to the Models 28 and 30M, with a lightweight alloy frame.

NIB	Exc.	V.G.	Good	Fair	Poor
450	350	300	250	200	125

SUBMACHINE GUNS

The Spanish made a number of submachine guns, both of domestic and copies of foreign guns. The Spanish MP28 II was a copy of the Bergmann MP28 II in 9mm Bergmann caliber. The Model 1941/44 was a copy of the German Erma. Star made a number of submachine in the 1930s which were used on a limited basis in the Spanish Civil War. These were the S135, the RU35 and the TN35, all chambered for the 9x23 Largo cartridge. The first of two of these models had adjustable rates of fire and the last, the TN35, had a rate of fire of about 700 rounds per minute. However, these guns were never standard issue in the Spanish army.

Star Z-45

This design is based on the German MP40 but with the cocking handle on the left side. It was fitted with an 8" barrel that was easily removable and covered by a perforated barrel jacket. The gun has a two stage trigger: pull slightly for single shots and pull more for full automatic fire. Magazine is a 30-round box type. Gun has a rate of fire of about 450 rounds per minute. Weight is approximately 8.5 lbs. Introduced into service in 1944. This weapon is supplied with either a fixed wood stock or folding metal one. The Z-45 was the standard submachine of the Spanish army and was sold to Chile, Cuba, Portugal, and Saudi Arabia.

Pre-1968

Exc.	V.G.	Fair
9500	8500	8000

Pre-1986 conversions

Exc.	V.G.	Fair
N/A	N/A	N/A

Pre-1986 dealer samples

Exc.	V.G.	Fair
N/A	N/A	N/A

Star Z-62

This select fire submachine gun was introduced in 1960 and is chambered for the 9mm Largo or 9mm Parabellum cartridge. It has an 8" barrel with perforated barrel jacket. Folding metal buttstock. The box magazine has a 20-, 30-, or 40-round capacity. Rate of fire is about 550 rounds per minute. Weight is approximately 6.5 lbs. This gun was issued both to the Spanish army and the *Guardia Civil*. Marked "STAR EIBAR ESPANA MODEL Z-62" with the serial number on the left side of the magazine housing. Produced until about 1970.

Pre-1968

Exc.	V.G.	Fair
8500	7500	7000

Pre-1986 conversions

Exc.	V.G.	Fair
N/A	N/A	N/A

Pre-1986 dealer samples

Exc.	V.G.	Fair
3500	3000	2500

Star Z-70

Introduced into the Spanish army in 1971 this select fire sub-machine gun is chambered for the 9x19mm cartridge, and is considered an improved version of the Z-62 with new trigger mechanism. It is fitted with an 8" barrel and has a rate of fire of 550 rounds per minute. Choice of 20-, 30-, or 40-round magazines. Folding metal stock. Weight is about 6.3 lbs. Built by Star Banifacio Echeverria in Eibar, Spain. No longer in production. Used mainly by the Spanish armed forces.

Photo Courtesy Private NFA Collection

Pre-1968

Exc.	V.G.	Fair
N/A	N/A	N/A

Pre-1986 conversions

Exc.	V.G.	Fair
N/A	N/A	N/A

Pre-1986 dealer samples

Exc.	V.G.	Fair
3500	2500	2000

RIFLES

MAUSER

M1891 Rifle

Based on the Turkish Model 1890 rifle with full stock and no handguard. Chambered for 7.65x53mm cartridge with barrel length of 29". Exposed 5-round box magazine. Weight is about 9 lbs.

Exc.	V.G.	Good	Fair	Poor
300	225	180	130	90

M1892 Rifle

Similar to the Model 1891 but with internal charger loaded magazine, improved extractor, and removable magazine floor plate. Chambered for 7x57mm cartridge. Half-length handguard. Barrel length is 29". Weight is about 9 lbs.

Exc.	V.G.	Good	Fair	Poor
350	260	190	130	90

M1892 Carbine

Same action as the Model 1891 rifle but full stock with nose cap, bent bolt handle, sling bar, and saddle ring. Chambered for 5x57mm cartridge. Barrel length is 17.5". Weight is about 7.5 lbs. Built by Loewe.

Exc.	V.G.	Good	Fair	Poor
300	225	180	120	80

M1893 Rifle

Built by Loewe and Oviedo this model is considered to be the "Spanish Mauser." Chambered for the 7.57mm cartridge and fitted with a 29" barrel. Buttstock has straight grip. A charger loading magazine is concealed in the buttstock. The receiver has a charger loading guide in the receiver bridge. Weight is about 8.5 lbs.

Exc.	V.G.	Good	Fair	Poor
175	140	100	80	40

M1893 True Carbine

This is a short version of the Model 1893 rifle with a 21.5" barrel. Fitted with bent bolt and half-length handguard. Weight is about 8 lbs.

Exc.	V.G.	Good	Fair	Poor
275	210	180	110	50

M1895 Carbine

As above but with 17.5" barrel. Weight is about 7 lbs.

Exc.	V.G.	Good	Fair	Poor
300	250	185	110	80

M/G 98 Modified Rifle

Identical to the German G 98 but chambered for the 7x57mm cartridge and fitted with a tangent rear sight. Spanish markings on receiver ring.

Exc.	V.G.	Good	Fair	Poor
275	225	175	120	90

M1916 Short Rifle

This model was built by Fabrica de Armas in Oviedo, Spain from 1916 to 1951. A shortened version of the Model 1893 rifle with 21.75" barrel and chambered for the 7x57mm cartridge. Rear sight graduated to 2000 meters. Almost full stock with upper handguard. Sight protectors on front sight. Spanish crest on receiver ring. Weight is about 8 lbs.

Exc.	V.G.	Good	Fair	Poor
200	150	100	75	40

M1916 True Carbine

Produced at the Oviedo arsenal. Fitted with a 17" barrel chambered for the 7x57mm cartridge. Straight grip stock

Spanish Mauser Model 1893 • Paul Goodwin Photo

with 3/4-length stock and upper handguard. No bayonet fittings. Bent bolt handle. Weight is about 6.75 lbs.

Exc.	V.G.	Good	Fair	Poor
225	160	110	85	50

M1933 Standard Model Short Rifle

This rifle is chambered for the 7x57mm cartridge and fitted with a 22" barrel. Straight grip stock with upper handguard. Tangent leaf rear sight graduated to 2000 meters. Marked with Mauser banner over the date of manufacture on receiver. Weight is about 8.2 lbs.

Exc.	V.G.	Good	Fair	Poor
325	280	220	180	110

M1943 Short Rifle

This model replaced the Model 1916 short rifle. Chambered for the 7.92x57mm cartridge and fitted with a 23.6" barrel. Stock is 3/4-length with pistol grip. Straight bolt handle. Tangent leaf rear sight graduated to 2000 meters. Weight is about 8.5 lbs. Marked with Spanish crest on receiver ring.

Exc.	V.G.	Good	Fair	Poor
250	190	140	90	40

FR 7 Special Purpose Rifle

A arsenal converted (1950s) Model 1916 and Model 43 short rifle with 18.5" barrel. Upper wooden handguard. Chambered for the .308 Winchester cartridge. Weight is about 7.5 lbs. Used by Spanish special forces.

Exc.	V.G.	Good	Fair	Poor
180	140	100	70	50

FR 8 Special Purpose Rifle

Same as above.

Exc.	V.G.	Good	Fair	Poor
180	140	100	70	50

CETME

Cetme Autoloading Rifle (Sport)

A .308 caliber semiautomatic rifle with a fluted chamber, a 17.74" barrel, an aperture rear sight and a 20-round detachable magazine. Black with a military-style wood stock. It is identical in appearance to the H&K 91 assault rifle.

NIB	Exc.	V.G.	Good	Fair	Poor
2500	2000	1500	900	—	—

Model 58

Introduced in 1958 and manufactured by Centro de Estudios de Materials Especiales (CETME) this Spanish-made rifle is similar to the HK G3 rifle and is chambered for the 7.62x51mm cartridge. This is a select fire weapon with a rate of fire of about 600 rounds per minute. The bipod, when retracted, acts as a metal forend. Barrel length is 17". Tangent rear sight. Weight is approximately 11 lbs.

Pre-1968

Exc.	V.G.	Fair
6000	5000	4500

Pre-1986 conversions

Exc.	V.G.	Fair
N/A	N/A	N/A

Pre-1986 dealer samples

Exc.	V.G.	Fair
3000	2500	2000

Santa Barbara CETME Model L

First produced in 1984 this 5.56x45mm select fire rifle was adopted by the Spanish army. It is fitted with a 15.6" barrel and 30-round magazine. It also has a fixed stock. Rate of fire is 650 rounds per minute. Weight is about 7.5 lbs. A short barrel (12.5") carbine version is known as the Model LC. Still in service.

Pre-1968

Exc.	V.G.	Fair
N/A	N/A	N/A

Pre-1986 conversions

Exc.	V.G.	Fair
N/A	N/A	N/A

Pre-1986 dealer samples

Exc.	V.G.	Fair
5000	5000	5000

MACHINE GUNS

In 1907 the Spanish used the 7mm Hotchkiss machine and later the Model 1914, also in 7mm. The Spanish armed forces also adopted the Madsen Model 1902 and Model 1922 guns. During the Spanish Civil War large numbers of foreign machines guns were sent to Spain, including the Soviet Maxim Tokarev, Soviet DP guns, Czech vz26, vz30, and ZB53 as well as other German and Italian machine guns. At the present time the Spanish army uses the MG 42/59 machine gun.

FAO Model 59

This is a Spanish-built gun designed on the Czech ZB26. It is chambered for the 7.62mm cartridge and is belt-fed with 50-round metallic links in a drum. Full automatic fire only. Barrel length is 22" with attached bipod. Gun weighs about 20 lbs. Rate of fire is approximately 650 rounds per minute.

Pre-1968

Exc.	V.G.	Fair
16500	15500	15000

Pre-1986 conversions

Exc.	V.G.	Fair
14000	13000	11000

Pre-1986 dealer samples

Exc.	V.G.	Fair
N/A	N/a	N/A

ALFA Model 1944

This gun was designed for use as a heavy machine gun. Chambered for the 7.92x57 Mauser cartridge and fitted with a 29.5" barrel. Select fire. Fed by a 100-round metallic link belt loaded in a drum. Rate of fire is about 800 rounds per minute. Weight is approximately 28 lbs.

NOTE: The Model 44 was also supplied to Egypt with aluminum cooling fins extending the length of the barrel and large slots in the gas cylinder.

Pre-1968

Exc.	V.G.	Fair
12000	10000	9000

Pre-1986 conversions

Exc.	V.G.	Fair
7500	6500	5500

Pre-1986 dealer samples

Exc.	V.G.	Fair
N/A	N/A	N/A

ALFA Model 55

Introduced in 1955 this is an updated version of the Model 44 chambered for the 7.62mm cartridge and fitted with a shorter 24" ribbed barrel with a lighter tripod. Rate of fire is about 800 rounds per minute. Weight is approximately 28 lbs.

Pre-1968

Exc.	V.G.	Fair
12500	11000	9500

Pre-1986 conversions

Exc.	V.G.	Fair
8000	7000	6000

Pre-1986 dealer samples

Exc.	V.G.	Fair
N/A	N/A	N/A

Ameli

Introduced in 1980 this is a light air-cooled machine gun chambered for the 5.56x45mm cartridge. It is fitted with a 15.75" barrel with slotted jacket, carry handle, and bipod. Barrel is quick change with flash hider. Belt-fed with 100- or 200-round belts. Plastic stock with pistol grip. Rate of fire is about 900 rounds per minute. Weight is approximately 11.5 lbs. Similar in appearance to the MG42 but smaller in size.

Pre-1968

Exc.	V.G.	Fair
N/A	N/A	N/A

Pre-1986 conversions

Exc.	V.G.	Fair
N/A	N/A	N/A

Pre-1986 dealer samples

Exc.	V.G.	Fair
10500	10000	9500

CETME Ameli • Courtesy Chuck Karwan

SWEDEN

Swedish Military conflicts, 1870-Present

As an outcome of the Swedish defeat against France in 1808 Sweden lost Finland to Russia but gained Norway. This union with Norway remained until 1905 when Norway was granted its independence. During the 20th century Sweden avoided involvement in both World Wars and maintained its neutrality during the Cold War. Sweden joined the European Union in 1995.

HANDGUNS

Sweden purchased a small number, about 10,000, of Walther P-38 pistols in 1939, designated the Model 39. Also a limited number of Walther PP pistols were used by the army as well.

Model 1871

The Swedish military issued the Lefaucheux-Francotte 6-shot revolver built by Auguste Francotte in Liege, Belgium and also by Husqvarna. The frame was solid with fixed cylinder and no mechanical ejection. Chambered for the 11mm cartridge and fitted with a 5.9" round barrel. Checkered wooden grips with lanyard loop. Six-round cylinder is non-fluted. Weight is about 41 oz. First adopted by the cavalry and then included other units as well. In use between 1871 and 1890.

Exc.	V.G.	Good	Fair	Poor
1250	750	500	350	200

Model 1863/79

This revolver is a converted pin fire to 11mm centerfire. Octagon barrel is 6.2". Smooth wooden grips with lanyard loop. Built by Lefaucheux in Paris. In use between 1879 and 1890.

Exc.	V.G.	Good	Fair	Poor
700	450	300	175	100

Model 1884

In 1884 the Swedish navy chose the French Model 1873 revolver as its issue sidearm. It was designated the Model 1884. It was chambered for the 11mm cartridge and fitted with a 4.4" half-round half-octagon barrel. Checkered wood grips with lanyard loop. It was built in St. Etienne. Used by the navy from 1884 to 1887.

Exc.	V.G.	Good	Fair	Poor
500	350	250	175	125

HUSQVARNA

Model 1887 Officer's Model

This double action revolver was chosen by the Swedish army as its official sidearm. It was a 6-shot double action Nagant design chambered for the 7.5mm cartridge with fluted cylinder. It was fitted with a 4.5" half-round half-octagon barrel. Checkered wood grips with lanyard loop. Weight is about 24 oz. The first of these revolvers were built by the Nagant brothers in Liege beginning in 1887, and in 1897 these guns were built at Husqvarna as well. Issued until 1947.

NOTE: Between 1897 and 1905 Husqvarna produced about 13,000 of these revolvers. They were delived with a holster, spare cylinder, cleaning rod, and screwdriver. Many of these revolvers were also sold on the commercial market as well.

Exc.	V.G.	Good	Fair	Poor
350	200	150	100	75

Model 1907 (Browning Model 1903)

This pistol is a copy of the FN Browning Model 1903 made for the Swedish army. It is identical in every way to the FN model. This pistol remained in service until 1940. Many were converted to the .380 caliber and imported into the U.S. If converted to .380 caliber reduce values by 50%.

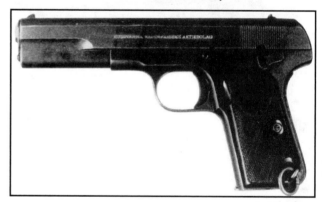

Courtesy Orvel Reichert

Exc.	V.G.	Good	Fair	Poor
350	250	200	150	100

Lahti Model 40

A 9mm caliber semiautomatic pistol with a 5.5" barrel and 8-shot magazine. The grip is cut for a shoulder stock. Designed by Aino Lahti, built by Husqvarna and adopted as the standard Swedish sidearm in 1940.

Exc.	V.G.	Good	Fair	Poor
425	350	275	225	150

SUBMACHINE GUNS

The Swedes used the Thompson submachine gun designated the 11mm Model 40 in limited numbers. They also used the Finnish Suomi (Model 37-39) and the Bergmann Model 34, designated the Swedish Model 39.

Carl Gustav 45

This 9mm weapon was first produced in 1945 in Sweden. This submachine gun is still in use. Models built after 1948 have a 36-round magazine. It is used by the Swedish and Indonesian armies. Some integral silencer version were used by Special Forces in Vietnam. Barrel is 8.25" in length. Fitted with retractable stock. Rate of fire is about 600 rounds per minute. Weight is about 8.5 lbs. This is the principal submachine gun is use by the Swedish army today.

Courtesy Richard M. Kumor, Sr

Carl Gustav M45/B • Photo Courtesy Private NFA Collection

Pre-1968

Exc.	V.G.	Fair
8500	7000	6500

Pre-1986 conversions

Exc.	V.G.	Fair
4750	4250	3750

Pre-1986 dealer samples

Exc.	V.G.	Fair
3500	3000	2500

NOTE: Add 33% for M45/B model which features a different non-removable magazine well, green finish, and improved bolt retention.

RIFLES

MAUSER

NOTE: These Mauser rifles were built either by Mauser, Carl Gustav, or Husqvarna.

M1894 Carbine

Chambered for the 6.5x55mm cartridge and fitted with a 17.5" barrel. Full stocked in European carbine-style with half-length handguard with finger grooves. Turned down bolt. Magazine capacity is 5 rounds. Leaf rear sight. Weight is about 7.5 lbs.

Exc.	V.G.	Good	Fair	Poor
400	350	300	250	200

M1896 Rifle

Action similar to the Model 1894 but with a 29" barrel, full-length stock, half-length upper handguard, and bayonet lug. Magazine capacity is 5 rounds. Weight is about 9 lbs.

Courtesy Rock Island Auction Company

Exc.	V.G.	Good	Fair	Poor
200	150	100	80	60

M1896 Sniper Rifle/M41 AGA scope

This is a Model 1896 rifle with Model 41 AGA scope mounted.

Exc.	V.G.	Good	Fair	Poor
950	800	700	650	500

M1896 Sniper Rifle/M42 AGA scope

This is a Model 1896 rifle with Model 42 AGA scope mounted.

Exc.	V.G.	Good	Fair	Poor
950	800	700	650	500

M1938/40 Short Rifle

This model is a Swedish modified German Kar. 98k converted to 8x63mm machine gun cartridge. The rifle was fitted with a muzzle brake to soften recoil but the cartridge was too powerful for the gun. Four-round magazine. Weight is about 9.5 lbs.

Exc.	V.G.	Good	Fair	Poor
200	150	100	80	50

Swedish "K" with intergral suppressor • Paul Goodwin Photo • Courtesy West Point Museum

M1896 Sniper Rifle/M44 AGA scope

A Model 1896 rifle fitted with a Model 44 AGA scope.

Exc.	V.G.	Good	Fair	Poor
950	850	750	650	500

M1896 Military Target Rifles

A Model 1896 rifle with special micrometer target sights.

Exc.	V.G.	Good	Fair	Poor
295	250	200	150	110

Ljungman AG-42B

Designed by Eril Eklund and placed in service with the Swedish military in 1942—less than one year after it was designed. The rifle is a direct gas-operated design with no piston or rod. It is chambered for the 6.5mm cartridge and has a 24.5" barrel with a 10-round detachable magazine. This rifle has military-type sights and a full-length stock and handguard held on by barrel bands. There are provisions for a bayonet. There is also an Egyptian version of this rifle known as the "Hakim" and a Danish version that was manufactured by Madsen. Our AR-15 rifles use the same type of gas system.

AG-42B action • Courtesy Chuck Karwan

Exc.	V.G.	Good	Fair	Poor
400	325	250	150	100

MACHINE GUNS

The Swedish armed forces have utilized a wide variety of machine guns from several countries. Sweden adopted the Schwarzlose Model 14 in 6.5mm caliber, the Browning Model 1917A1 water-cooled gun (Model 36), the Browning Model 1919A6 (Model 42), the Czech vz26 in 6.5mm caliber (Model 39), and more currently the FN MAG in 7.62mm (Model 58). These early FN MAG guns were chambered for the 6.5x55mm Mauser cartridge.

Swedish Model 36

This is the Swedish version of the Browning Model 1917 water-cooled gun. The gun shown is in a twin anti-aircraft configuration, and is too rare to price.

Pre-1968

Exc.	V.G.	Fair
15,000	12,500	11,000

Pre-1986 conversions

Exc.	V.G.	Fair
N/A	N/A	N/A

Pre-1986 dealer samples

Exc.	V.G.	Fair
4000	3500	3000

Swedish BAR Model 21

Designated the Swedish Kg. (*Kulsprutegevar*, light machine gun) these guns were built in Sweden under license from Colt between 1923 and 1935. Chambered for the Swedish 6.5x55mm cartridge. This model does not have a quick change barrel as originally built. A little over 8,000 of these BARs were built in Sweden during its production life.

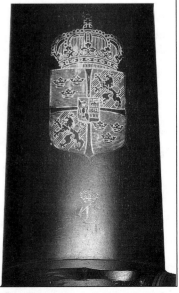

Swedish Model 1936 Twin • Courtesy Private NFA Collection • Paul Goodwin Photo

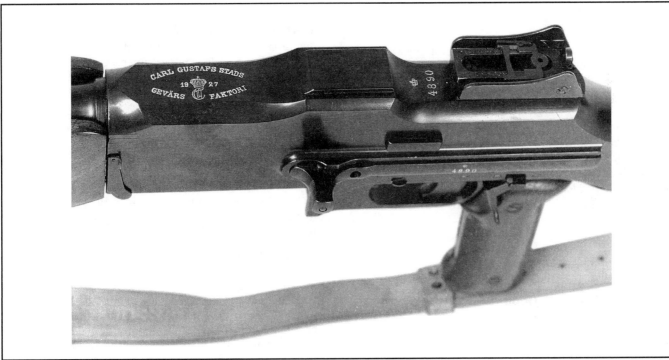

Model 21 Swedish BAR • Private NFA Collection • Photo by Gary Gelson

Pre-1968

Exc.	V.G.	Fair
10000	9500	9000

Pre-1986 conversions

Exc.	V.G.	Fair
N/A	N/A	N/A

Pre-1986 dealer samples

Exc.	V.G.	Fair
4000	3500	3000

Swedish BAR Model 37

The Model 37 Swedish BAR is an improved version of the Model 21 with a screw-on receiver extension that prevented the adoption of a quick change barrel. A total of about 15,000 Model 37s were produced between 1937 and 1944.

NOTE: A number of Model 21s were refitted with quick change barrels and designated the Model 21/37.

Pre-1968 (Very Rare)

Exc.	V.G.	Fair
12000	10000	9000

Pre-1986 conversions

Exc.	V.G.	Fair
N/A	N/A	N/A

Pre-1986 dealer samples

Exc.	V.G.	Fair
3500	3250	3000

SWITZERLAND

Swiss Military Conflicts, 1870 -Present

In 1815 Switzerland was guaranteed perpetual neutrality by the Treaty of Vienna. The Swiss remained neutral in both World Wars. Switzerland is not a member of the UN or the European Economic Area.

National defense is based on a system of universal conscription by which every Swiss male is liable for military duty between the ages of 20 and 50. The Swiss is the only soldier in the world who keeps his equipment, including arms and ammunition, at home, and who performs his obligatory duty each year in civilian clothes. Once his military rifle is issued the Swiss soldier keeps it at home for life.

HANDGUNS

Model 1872

This Swiss Model 1872 is a 10.4mm rimfire revolver with a 6-shot fluted cylinder. It is fitted with a 5.9" octagon barrel. The frame is solid with fixed fluted cylinder and mechanical rod ejection. Checkered wood grips with lanyard loop. The revolver was built by the Belgian firm of Pirlot Freres in Liege. It was issued from 1872 until 1878. Weight is 37 oz. This was the last foreign built handgun to be issued to the Swiss military.

NOTE: This is a very rare revolver as most were converted to centerfire with the Model 1872/78 in 1878.

Exc.	V.G.	Good	Fair	Poor
N/A	—	—	—	—

Model 1872/78

This is a centerfire converted Model 1872 in 10.4mm. This revolver was rarely used by the Swiss military.

Exc.	V.G.	Good	Fair	Poor
N/A	—	—	—	—

Model 1878

This was the first Swiss-made revolver used by the Swiss military. Made in Bern this Schmidt-Galand-type revolver was chambered for the 10.4mm cartridge. The frame was solid with fixed cylinder and mechanical rod ejection. 4.5" octagon barrel. Checkered grips with the Swiss cross on the left side. Weight was about 35 oz. This revolver was issued to cavalry units with about 6,000 in service.

Exc.	V.G.	Good	Fair	Poor
1750	1000	600	350	250

Model 1882

This revolver was similar in appearance to the Model 1878 but was chambered for the smaller 7.5mm cartridge. It was fitted with a 4.5" octagon barrel. Early Model 1882 revolvers were fitted with hard rubber checkered grips while later guns will be seen with grooved wooden grips. This revolver was built in Switzerland at Bern or SIG. Weight is about 27 oz. This model stayed in use in the Swiss military from 1882 to as late as 1950.

Exc.	V.G.	Good	Fair	Poor
750	400	350	175	100

LUGER

WAFFENFABRIK BERN

Switzerland was the first country to adopt the Luger as a military sidearm with its contract purchase of the Model 1900 from DWM. Another contract for the Model 1906 soon followed. Because DWM could no longer supply Switzerland with Lugers during World War I the Swiss firm of Waffenfabrik Bern (W+F Bern) produced its own version based on the Model 1906.

Bibliographical Note: For additional historical information, technical data and photos see Vittorio Bobba, *Parabellum; A Technical History of Swiss Lugers*, Italy, 1996.

NOTE: There are a number of sub-variations of Swiss Lugers that may affect value. It is strongly suggested that thorough research of this model be undertaken prior to a sale.

Model 1906 Bern (Model 1924)

A Swiss-made copy of the German Model 1906 Luger. Made in caliber 7.65mm, fitted with a 4.75" barrel, and marked "WAFFENFABRIK BERN" under the Geneva cross on top of the toggle. The grips on this pistol are unique in that most are checkered walnut with a plain border on the front and rear edges. About 17,000 of these pistols were manufactured. This model was most likely produced between 1918 and 1922, and was built for the Swiss military.

Courtesy James Rankin

Exc.	V.G.	Good	Fair	Poor
3200	2500	2000	1400	1000

Model 1929

Similar to the above, with the exception that the toggle finger pieces are smooth, the grip frame is uncurved, safety lever is a flat configuration and the grip safety is of inordinate size. Fitted with plastic grips. Chambered for caliber 7.65mm. About 30,000 of these pistols were produced. Sold both for military and commercial use.

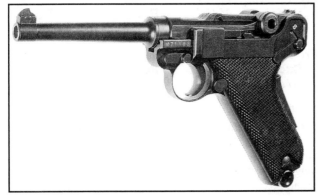

Courtesy James Rankin

Exc.	V.G.	Good	Fair	Poor
2500	2000	1500	1200	900

SIG
Schweizerische Industrie Gesellschaft,
Neuhausen am Rheinfalls, Switzerland

Biographical **Note:** For historical background, technical data, and photos see Lorenz Vetter, *Das grosse Buch der SIG-Pistolen*, Verlag Stocker-Schmid AG, 1995.

NOTE: The P210 pistol was designated the SP47/8 prior to 1957 when it was renamed the P210. There are a number of production changes on this pistol that follow a chronological order.

P210

A 7.65mm or 9mm semiautomatic pistol with a 4.75" barrel and 8-shot magazine. Fixed rear sight. Blued with plastic grips. In 1996 the 9mm version was the only one imported. Weight is about 32 oz. This model was also used by the Danish army (Model 49).

NIB	Exc.	V.G.	Good	Fair	Poor
2300	1500	1300	1100	800	500

NOTE: For 1996 a .22 caliber conversion unit serialized to the gun was available. Add $600 for this option.

P 210-1

As above, with an adjustable rear sight, polished finish and walnut grips. Imported prior to 1987. Weight is about 31 oz.

NIB	Exc.	V.G.	Good	Fair	Poor
2750	2250	1500	1150	800	—

P 210-2 (Swiss Army Model 49-SP47/8)

This model is similar to the P210-1 with the exception that it has a sandblasted matte finish and black plastic grips with fixed sights. Adopted by the Swiss army in 1947 and still in service.

NIB	Exc.	V.G.	Good	Fair	Poor
2000	1750	1350	1000	750	300

P210-3

Introduced in 1950 this model was issued to the Swiss police in Lausanne and Basel. Early examples are polished blue and later examples are sandblasted matte blue. Fixed sights. Production ceased in 1983. Very few of these pistols was sold on a commercial basis. Very scarce.

NIB	Exc.	V.G.	Good	Fair	Poor
N/A	—	—	—	—	—

P210-4

Special model produced for the West German Border Police. Fixed rear sight. Walnut grips on early models and black plastic grips on later models. Early models have blued finish while later models have sandblasted matte finish.

NIB	Exc.	V.G.	Good	Fair	Poor
2000	1750	1350	1000	750	300

P 210-5

A commercial version as above, with an extended length barrel of 5.9" (150mm) or 7.1" (180mm), adjustable rear sight, target trigger, and walnut grips. Front sight is fitted to front of extended barrel, not the slide. Offered in a standard and heavy frame weight. Polished blue finish. Weight is about 35 oz. for standard weight frame.

NIB	Exc.	V.G.	Good	Fair	Poor
3500	2750	1750	1200	800	400

P 210-6

A commercial version as above, with a 4.75" barrel. Front sight is fitted to slide. Adjustable rear sight on some of these variations fixed sight on others. Polished blue finish.

SIG P 210-6 Commercial version • Courtesy SIG Arms

NIB	Exc.	V.G.	Good	Fair	Poor
2750	2250	1500	1250	800	400

P210-7

This model is chambered for the .22 rimfire cartridge and fitted with a 4.75" barrel. Most of the variations of this model are built for commercial and export sales except one variation, built for the West German Border Guards as a practice pistol. Fixed sights. Checkered plastic grips.

NIB	Exc.	V.G.	Good	Fair	Poor
N/A	—	—	—	—	—

P220 (Swiss Army Model P-75)

Swiss army military sidearm. This is a high-quality, double action semiautomatic pistol chambered for .38 Super, .45 ACP , and 9mm Parabellum. It has a 4.41" barrel and fixed sights and features the decocking lever that was originally on the Sauer Model 38H. There are two versions of this pistol: one with a bottom magazine release (commonly referred to as the European model) and the other with the release on the side (commonly referred to as the American model), as on the Model 1911 Colt. The frame is a lightweight alloy that is matte finished and is available in either blue, nickel, or K-Kote finish with black plastic grips. The .45 ACP magazine capacity is 7 rounds and the pistol weighs 25.7 oz.; the .38 Super magazine capacity is 9 rounds and the pistol weighs 26.5 oz.; the 9mm magazine holds 9 rounds and the overall weight is 26.5 oz. This model was manufactured from 1976 and is still in production. The 9mm version in this model is no longer in production. The prices listed below are for guns with a standard blue finish.

NOTE: For the K-Kote finish add $40, for nickel slide add $40.

NIB	Exc.	V.G.	Good	Fair	Poor
750	550	400	300	200	150

SUBMACHINE GUNS

Steyr-Solothurn (Solothurn SI-100 or MP34(o))

See Austria, Submachine Guns, Steyr.

MP41/44

This model was developed by Furrer and built by W+F Bern arsenal between 1936 and 1942. Chambered for the 9mm Luger cartridge. Recoil operated with a toggle system similar to the Luger pistol but turned on its side. Slotted barrel jacket with 10" barrel with forward vertical handgrip and pistol grip wooden stock. Rate of fire is about 900 rounds per minute. Magazine capacity is 40 rounds. Very expensive to produce with the result that less than 5000 guns were manufactured. Weight is about 11.5 lbs.

Pre-1968 (Rare)

Exc.	V.G.	Fair
9000	8000	7000

Pre-1986 conversions

Exc.	V.G.	Fair
N/A	N/A	N/A

Pre-1986 dealer samples

Exc.	V.G.	Fair
N/A	N/A	N/A

MP43/44

The Swiss version of the Suomi with a bayonet lug and flip over rear sight. Built by Hispano Suiza under licence from Finland. Rate of fire is about 800 rounds per minute and weight is approximately 10.5 lbs. Magazine capacity is 50-round box type.

Swiss M43/44 • Courtesy Private NFA Collection • Paul Goodwin Photo

Pre-1968 (Rare)

Exc.	V.G.	Fair
9000	8000	7000

Pre-1986 conversions

Exc.	V.G.	Fair
N/A	N/A	N/A

Swiss MP41 • Courtesy Private NFA Collection • Paul Goodwin Photo

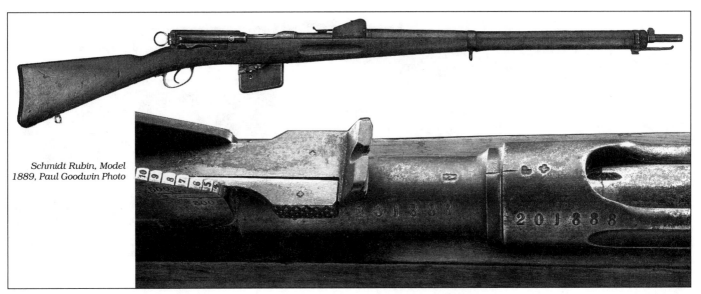

Schmidt Rubin, Model 1889, Paul Goodwin Photo

Pre-1986 dealer samples

Exc.	V.G.	Fair
N/A	N/A	N/A

RIFLES

SCHMIDT RUBIN
Eidgenossische Waffenfabrik Bern
Bern, Switzerland (1875-1993)

Model 1889

A 7.5mm straight pull bolt action rifle with a 30.75" barrel and 12-shot magazine. Blued with a full-length walnut stock secured by two barrel bands. Approximately 212,000 were manufactured.

Exc.	V.G.	Good	Fair	Poor
300	200	175	125	90

Model 1896

As above, with a shortened action. There were approximately 137,000 made.

Exc.	V.G.	Good	Fair	Poor
300	225	200	150	125

Exc.	V.G.	Good	Fair	Poor
250	150	100	80	60

Model 1911 Carbine

As above, with a 23.30" barrel. Approximately 185,000 were manufactured.

Model 1897 Cadet Rifle

Similar to the above, with a shortened stock and reduced weight. Approximately 7,000 were manufactured.

Exc.	V.G.	Good	Fair	Poor
350	250	200	150	100

Model 1900

A shortened version of the Model 1896, with a 6-shot magazine. Approximately 18,750 were manufactured between 1900 and 1904.

Exc.	V.G	Good	Fair	Poor
450	350	300	200	150

Model 1905 Carbine

Similar to the above, without a bayonet. Approximately 7,900 were manufactured.

Exc.	V.G.	Good	Fair	Poor
400	300	250	200	150

Model 1911

A redesigned Model 1896 with a 6-shot magazine and pistol grip stock. Approximately 133,000 were manufactured.

Exc.	V.G.	Good	Fair	Poor
250	150	100	80	60

Model 1931

Similar to the above, with a redesigned block work, 25.7" barrel and 6-shot magazine. Approximately 528,180 were manufactured.

Model 1911 • Courtesy West Point Museum • Paul Goodwin Photo

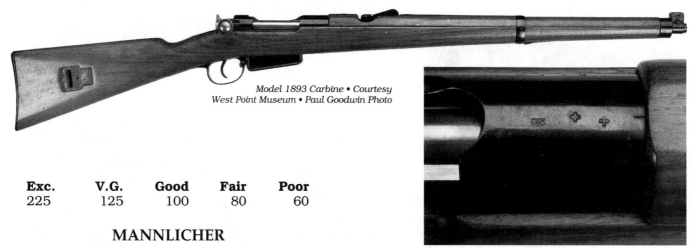

Model 1893 Carbine • Courtesy
West Point Museum • Paul Goodwin Photo

Exc.	V.G.	Good	Fair	Poor
225	125	100	80	60

MANNLICHER

Model 1893 Carbine

This is a Mannlicher straight pull design carbine with a 21.5" barrel chambered for the 7.5x53.5mm cartridge. It was the only Mannlicher adopted by Switzerland. It was fitted with a full-length stock and upper handguard. No bayonet fittings.

Exc.	V.G.	Good	Fair	Poor
400	325	250	200	100

VETTERLI
Bern, SIG, Pfenninger

This rifle was invented by Friderich Vetterli at Neuhausen, Switzerland, in 1867. This was the first bolt action rifle to be used as a military service weapon. It was adopted on January 8, 1869, and predated the Fruwirth by three years. It is chambered for the 10.2 copper based Vetterli rimfire cartridge, the .41 Swiss, or the 10.4x38mm cartridges. It has a 12-round tubular magazine that is loaded through a side gate similar to a Winchester lever action. There is a swinging cover on the loading gate. The finish is blue, with a full-length walnut stock secured by one barrel band and an endcap. There is a full-length cleaning rod located under the barrel. The receiver has a round configuration and the triggerguard has a rear spur. The rifle and its variations were built between 1869 and 1881.

Model 1871 Rifle

Exc.	V.G.	Good	Fair	Poor
—	750	400	200	100

Model 1871 Stuzer (Short Rifle)

This short rifle was fitted with two barrel bands on its 30" barrel. Double set triggers with 9-round magazine. Fitted with a curved buttplate. Weight is about 10 lbs.

Exc.	V.G.	Good	Fair	Poor
850	700	550	400	150

Magazine capacity was 6 rounds and it was charger loaded. The receiver ring is marked with a small Swiss cross.

Model 1871 Carbine

The carbine has an 18.5" barrel with no bayonet fittings. Full stock with 6-round tube magazine. Rear sling swivel behind triggerguard. Weight is about 7 lbs.

Exc.	V.G.	Good	Fair	Poor
—	1500	800	400	200

Model 1878 Rifle

This model was a modified version of the Model 1878. Fitted with a full-length stock with curved buttplate and chambered for the 10.4x42R rimfire cartridge. The rear sight is graduated to 1200 meters. Barrel length is 33" with an 11-round tube magazine in the forend. Built at SIG, Neuhausen, and Bern. Weight is about 10 lbs.

Exc.	V.G.	Good	Fair	Poor
350	300	250	200	100

Model 1881 Rifle

This model is the same as the Model 1878 above with the exception of a 1600 meter graduated rear sight. Weight is about 10 lbs.

Exc.	V.G.	Good	Fair	Poor
350	300	250	200	100

SIG
Schweizerische Industrie Gesellschaft, Neuhausen am Rheinfalls, Switzerland

SSG 2000

This is a high-grade, bolt action, sniping-type rifle chambered for .223, 7.5mm Swiss, .300 Weatherby Magnum, and .308 Winchester. It has a 24" barrel and was furnished without

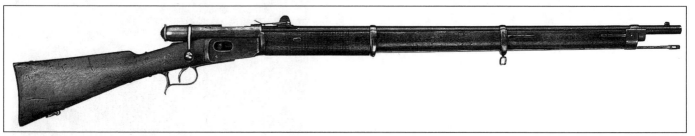

Model 1871 Rifle, Paul Goodwin Photo

sights. It has a 4-round box magazine. The finish is matte blued with a thumbhole-style stippled walnut stock with an adjustable cheekpiece. This model was discontinued in 1986.

NIB	Exc.	V.G.	Good	Fair	Poor
8000	6000	3500	1500	—	—

SSG 3000

Chambered for the .308 Win. cartridge, this model is fitted with a 23.4" barrel and ambidextrous McMillian Tactical stock. Magazine capacity is 5 rounds. Overall length is 46.5", and approximate weight is 12 lbs. This model comes in three different packages. They are listed below.

Level I

Base model with no bipod or scope, but with carrying case.

NIB	Exc.	V.G.	Good	Fair	Poor
2550	2000	—	—	—	—

Level II

At this level a Leupold Vari-X III 3.5-10x40mm Duplex scope and Harris bipod with carrying case.

NIB	Exc.	V.G.	Good	Fair	Poor
3500	2750	—	—	—	—

Level III

Rifle is supplied with a Leupold Mark 4 M1-10x40mm Mil-Dot Scope with Harris bipod and carrying case.

NIB	Exc.	V.G.	Good	Fair	Poor
4500	3500	—	—	—	—

SIG AMT

This is a semiautomatic rifle chambered for .308 cartridge. Fitted with a 19" barrel and wooden buttstock and forearm. Folding bipod standard. Box magazine capacity is 5, 10, or 20 rounds. Weight is about 10 lbs. Built from 1960 to 1974.

Bern Stg 51 Assault Rifle

Developed after the end of World War II the Swiss wanted their own version of a true assault rifle. Waffenfabrik Bern was one of the companies involved in this project. The result was the Stg 51 first built in 1951. This rifle was chambered for the 7.5mm short cartridge, a special cartridge made specifically for this rifle and no longer produced. The rifle is select fire and does so in both models in closed bolt position. A 30-round box magazine supplies the gun that has a rate of fire of about 800 rounds per minute. The barrel is 22.5" in length and is fitted with a muzzle brake/flash suppressor. A mid-barrel bipod is fitted just ahead of the forend. Weight is approximately 10.5 lbs.

A second model of this rifle was also produced with internal modifications and some small external differences. Both models were issued to the Swiss army most likely on a trials basis. Extremely rare.

NOTE: The first model of this rifle will interchange some parts with the German FG 42. The second model will interchange all of its parts with the German FG 42.

Bern Stg 51 (First Model)
Pre-1968

Exc.	V.G.	Fair
25000+	—	—

Pre-1986 conversions

Exc.	V.G.	Fair
N/A	N/A	N/A

Pre-1986 dealer samples

Exc.	V.G.	Fair
N/A	N/A	N/A

Bern Stg 51 (Second Model)
Pre-1968

Exc.	V.G.	Fair
35000+	—	—

Pre-1986 conversions

Exc.	V.G.	Fair
N/A	N/A	N/A

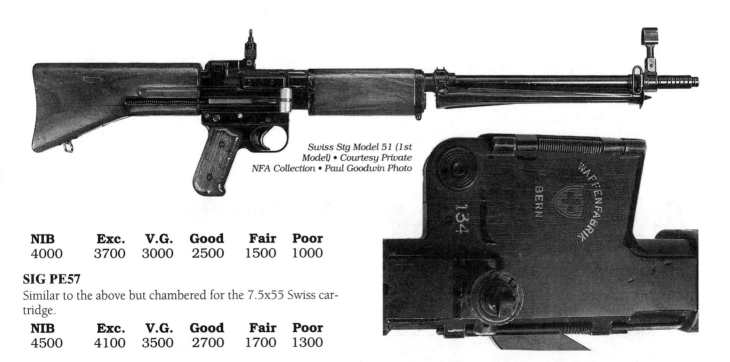

Swiss Stg Model 51 (1st Model) • Courtesy Private NFA Collection • Paul Goodwin Photo

NIB	Exc.	V.G.	Good	Fair	Poor
4000	3700	3000	2500	1500	1000

SIG PE57

Similar to the above but chambered for the 7.5x55 Swiss cartridge.

NIB	Exc.	V.G.	Good	Fair	Poor
4500	4100	3500	2700	1700	1300

Swiss Stg Model 51 (2nd Model) • Courtesy Private NFA Collection • Paul Goodwin Photo

Pre-1986 dealer samples

Exc.	V.G.	Fair
N/A	N/A	N/A

SIG Stgw 57 Assault Rifle

This rifle is a select fire chambered for the 7.5x55mm Swiss cartridge. Barrel length is 23". Box magazine capacity is 24 rounds. Weight is about 12.25 lbs. Adopted by the Swiss army with about 600,000 of these rifles produced between 1957 and 1983. It is based on the German StG 45. The rifle has a pressed steel receiver, folding bipod wood butt, barrel jacket, and carry handle. The muzzle is designed to act as a grenade launcher and compensator. As with all standard issue Swiss military rifles, this rifle will remain in service for the lifetime of the soldier.

Pre-1968

Exc.	V.G.	Fair
9000	8500	8000

Pre-1986 conversions

Exc.	V.G.	Fair
6000	5500	5000

Pre-1986 dealer samples

Exc.	V.G.	Fair
5000	4500	4000

SIG 550

This semiautomatic rifle is chambered for .223 cartridge and fitted with an 18" barrel.

Courtesy Rock Island Auction Company

NIB	Exc.	V.G.	Good	Fair	Poor
9000	7000	5500	3000	—	—

SIG 551

Same as above but fitted with a 16" barrel.

NIB	Exc.	V.G.	Good	Fair	Poor
9500	7500	6500	4000	—	—

SIG SG510-4

There are actually four different version of this rifle. This version fires the 7.62x51mm cartridge and is fitted with a 19.7" barrel. A military version, adopted by the Swiss army, is called the Stgw 57(510-1). Magazine capacity is 20 rounds. Weight is 9.3 lbs. Rate of fire is 600 rounds per minute. Produced from 1957 to 1983. Markings are on left rear of receiver.

PE-57 Assault Rifle • Courtesy Chuck Karwan

Pre-1968 (Rare)

Exc.	V.G.	Fair
9000	8500	8000

Pre-1986 conversions

Exc.	V.G.	Fair
6000	5500	5000

Pre-1986 dealer samples

Exc.	V.G.	Fair
5000	4500	4000

SIG 530-1

This rifle is a scaled down version of the Stgw 57 assault rifle chambered for the 5.56x45mm cartridge. Operated by a gas pistol system instead of a delayed blowback operation. Receiver is pressed steel with synthetic butt and forend. Barrel is 18" in length with compensator and grenade launcher rings. Magazine capacity is 30 rounds. Weight is about 7.5 lbs. Rate of fire is 600 rounds per minute. There is also a folding stock version of this rifle.

Pre-1968

Exc.	V.G.	Fair
N/A	N/A	N/A

Pre-1986 conversions

Exc.	V.G.	Fair
N/A	N/A	N/A

Pre-1986 dealer samples

Exc.	V.G.	Fair
N/A	N/A	N/A

Swiss Model 1911 Maxim • Courtesy Private NFA Collection • Paul Goodwin Photo

SIG SG540

Designed by the Swiss (SIG) and built in Switzerland, and also built in France by Manurhin beginning in 1977. This 5.56x45mm rifle is in service by a number of African and South American countries. It is fitted with an 18" barrel, 20- or 30-round magazine and has a rate of fire of 800 rounds per minute. It is fitted with a fixed stock. Its weight is 7.8 lbs. Marked "MANURHIN FRANCE SG54X" on right side of receiver. This rifle is still in production. There are also two other variants called the SG542 and SG543.

Pre-1968

Exc.	V.G.	Fair
N/A	N/A	N/A

Pre-1986 conversions

Exc.	V.G.	Fair
N/A	N/A	N/A

Pre-1986 dealer samples (Rare)

Exc.	V.G.	Fair
7500	7500	7000

MACHINE GUNS

The Swiss adopted the Maxim machine gun in 1894. The Swiss military also used the Maxim Model 1900. More recently the Swiss have used the FN MAG in addition to its own Swiss-built guns.

Model 1911 Maxim

Built by W+F Bern and chambered for the 7.5x55mm Swiss cartridge. Fitted with a plain steel water jacket, otherwise identical to the German MG 08. This was the standard Swiss heavy machine gun and remained in service until 1951.

Pre-1968

Exc.	V.G.	Fair
10000	9000	8000

Pre-1986 conversions

Exc.	V.G.	Fair
N/A	N/A	N/A

Pre-1986 dealer samples (Rare)

Exc.	V.G.	Fair
N/A	N/A	N/A

Model 11 Heavy

Chambered for the 7.5mm cartridge and fitted with a 28" barrel, this gun has a rate of fire of about 500 rounds per minute. The gun is fed by a 250-round cloth belt. Weight of the gun is approximately 40 lbs. Remained in service until the early 1950s.

Swiss Flab MG29 • Courtesy Private NFA Collection • Paul Goodwin Photo

Pre-1968 (Very Rare)

Exc.	V.G.	Fair
30000	25000	20000

Pre-1986 conversions

Exc.	V.G.	Fair
20000	18000	15000

Pre-1986 dealer samples (Rare)

Exc.	V.G.	Fair
15000	12500	10000

Pre-1968

Exc.	V.G.	Fair
35000	32500	—

Pre-1986 conversions

Exc.	V.G.	Fair
N/A	N/A	N/A

Pre-1986 dealer samples

Exc.	V.G.	Fair
N/A	N/A	N/A

Model Flab MG29

Developed by Adloph Furrer and built in 1929 by W+F Bern, this machine gun was chambered for the 7.5mm Swiss cartridge. Fed by metal belts. It was designed for use on armoured vehicles and for anti-aircraft applications. The gun has a high rate of fire of about 1,100 rounds per minute. Weight is about 20 lbs. Rare.

Model 25 Light

Introduced in 1926 this gun was designed as a light air-cooled gun chambered for the 7.5x55mm Swiss cartridge. The gun uses a toggle action that opens sideways. It is fitted with a 23" barrel with slotted barrel jacket, flash hider, and bipod. The buttstock is wooden. The magazine is mounted on the right side of the gun and has a capacity of 30 rounds. Rate of fire is about 450 rounds per minute. Weight is approximately 24 lbs.

Furrer M25 Light • Courtesy Private NFA Collection • Paul Goodwin Photo

Pre-1968

Exc.	V.G.	Fair
18000	15000	15000

Pre-1986 conversions

Exc.	V.G.	Fair
N/A	N/A	N/A

Pre-1986 dealer samples (Rare)

Exc.	V.G.	Fair
12500	11000	10000

UNITED STATES

U.S. Military Conflicts, 1870-Present

After the end of the American Civil War in 1865 america turned its attention back to westward expansion. The period from 1870 to 1890 were marked by a series of Indian wars that finally ended, for the most part in 1890. the country turned its attention overseas with the annexation of Hawaii in 1898 and Puerto Rico, Guam, and the Philippines in the Spanish-American War of 1898. A brief excursion into Mexico in 1915-1916 combated the Mexican forces of Pancho Villa. In 1917 the U.S. entered World War I on the side of the Allies and withdrew from european involvement at the wars end in November, 1918. with the Japanese attack on Pearl Harbor December 7, 1941 America one again fought against foreign aggression in the Pacific and Europe. As a world power at the end of the war in August, 1945 the U.S. found itself taking a leading role in combating the Communist invasion of Korea in 1950. A cease fire was signed July 27, 1953. After the French defeat in the Indochina war (1946-1954) the U.S. began to increase its presence in South Vietnam and with the Tonkin Gulf Resolution of 1964 the war rapidly escalated. A cease fire in 1973 ended U.S. involvement in Vietnam with the loss of over 55,000 troops. A number of military actions took place such places as Panama (1989) and in 1991 with the Persian Gulf War, Somalia and the Balkans.

Bibliographical Note: There a number of excellent books on general U.S. military firearms. Some of them are Bruce Canfield's, *U.S. Infantry Weapons of World War I*, Mowbry, 2000 and *U.S. Infantry Weapons of World War II*, Mowbry, 1992. Norm Flayderman's, *Flayderman's Guide to Antique American Firearms and Their Values*, 7th edition, Krause Publications, 1998. Thomas Batha, *U.S. Martial .22RF Rifles*, Excalibur Publications, 2000.

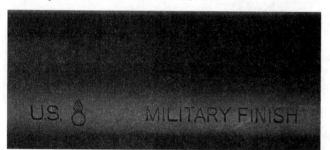

The famous flaming bomb ordance mark with "U.S." stamp.

HANDGUNS

Bibliographical Note: There a number of comprehensive publications on U.S. military handguns some of which are: *U.S. Handguns of World War II, The Secondary Pistols and Revolvers*, Charles W. Pate, Mowbray, 1999. *U.S. Military Automatic Pistols, 1894-1920*, Scott Meadows, Ellis Publications,1993.

COLT

Bibliographical Note: There are a number of excellent books on Colt firearms, many of which cover Colt's military models. A few of these books are: John W. Brunner, *The Colt Pocket Hammerless Automatic Pistols*, Phillips Publications, 1996. Keith Cochrane, *Colt Cavalry, Artillery and Militia Revolvers*, South Dakota, 1987. Kopec, Graham and Moore, *A Study of the Colt Single Action Army Revolver*, California, 1976. For the Colt Model 1911 references see *Colt Model 1911 section*.

NOTE: It should be pointed out that the U.S. military purchased and used a number of different Colt pistols and revolvers over the years. In some cases these handguns will be marked with military acceptance stamps or inspectors stamps. In other cases that may be no markings. The following models are some of the most often encountered military marked Colt handguns.

Early Military Model 1873-1877

The serial number range on this first run of military contract revolvers extends to #24000. The barrel address is in the early script style with the # symbol preceding and following. The frame bears the martial marking "US," and the walnut grips

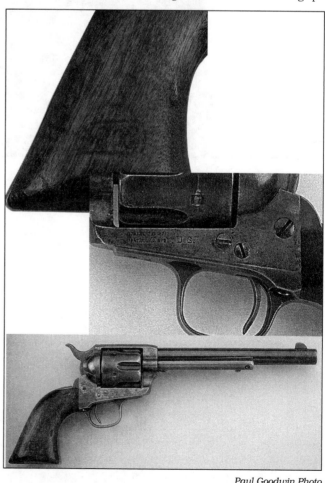

Paul Goodwin Photo

have the inspector's cartouche stamped on them. The front sight is steel as on all military models; the barrel length, 7.5". The caliber is .45 Colt, and the ejector rod head is the bull's-eye or donut style with a hole in the center of it. The finish features the military polish and case colored frame, with the remainder blued. Authenticate any potential purchase; many spurious examples have been noted.

Exc.	V.G.	Good	Fair	Poor
N/A	35000	18000	12000	6000

NOTE: Certain 3-digit and 4-digit serial numbers will command a substantial premium. Seek an expert appraisal prior to sale.

> An Answorth inspected Colt Model 1873 sold at auction for $25,875. Fitted with 7.5" barrel and re-marked "U.S." markings. Possible connection to Battle of the Little Bighorn. Condition was good. Rock Island Auction company, December, 1999

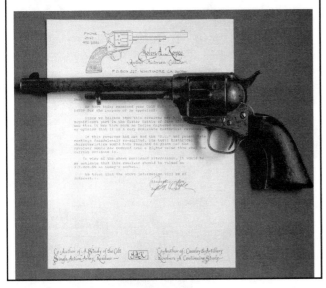

Late Military Model 1878-1891

The later Military Models are serial numbered to approximately #136000. They bear the block-style barrel address without the # prefix and suffix. The frames are marked "US," and the grips have the inspector's cartouche. The finish is the military-style polish, case colored frame; and the remainder, blued. Grips are oil-stained walnut. On the military marked Colts, it is imperative that potential purchases be authenticated as many fakes have been noted.

Exc.	V.G.	Good	Fair	Poor
30000	20000	10000	6000	2500

NOTE: Revolvers produced from 1878 to 1885 will command a premium. Seek an expert appraisal prior to sale.

Artillery Model 1895-1903

A number of "US" marked SAAs were returned either to the Colt factory or to the Springfield Armory, where they were altered and refinished. These revolvers have 5.5" barrels and any combination of mixed serial numbers. They were re-marked by the inspectors of the era and have a case colored frame and a blued cylinder and barrel. Some have been noted all blued within this variation. This model, as with the other military marked Colts, should definitely be authenticated before purchase. Some of these revolvers fall outside the 1898 antique cutoff date that has been established by the govern-

ment and, in our experience, are not quite as desirable to investors. They are generally worth approximately 20 percent less.

Exc.	V.G.	Good	Fair	Poor
7500	5500	3500	2500	1500

Model 1902

This is a U.S. Ordnance contract Model 1878. It has a 6" barrel and is chambered for .45 Colt. The finish is blued, and there is a lanyard swivel on the butt. This model bears the U.S. inspector's marks. It is sometimes referred to as the Philippine or the Alaskan model. The triggerguard is quite a bit larger than standard.

Courtesy Butterfield & Butterfield

Exc.	V.G.	Good	Fair	Poor
5000	4000	2000	1000	600

Model 1889 Navy

The 1889 Navy is an important model from a historical standpoint as it was the first double-action revolver Colt manufactured with a swing-out cylinder. They produced 31,000 of them between 1889 and 1894. The Model 1889 is chambered for the .38 Colt and the .41 Colt cartridges. The cylinder holds 6 shots. It is offered with a 3", 4.5", or 6" barrel; and the finish was either blued or nickel-plated. The grips are checkered hard rubber with the "Rampant Colt" in an oval molded into them. The patent dates 1884 and 1888 appear in the barrel marking, and the serial numbers are stamped on the butt.

NOTE: For 3" Barrel add 20%.

Exc.	V.G.	Good	Fair	Poor
2000	1200	650	450	200

U.S. Navy Model

This variation has a 6" barrel, is chambered for .38 Colt, and is offered in blued finish only. "U.S.N." is stamped on the butt. Most of the Navy models were altered at the Colt factory to add the Model 1895 improvements. An original unaltered specimen would be worth as much as 50 percent premium over the altered values shown.

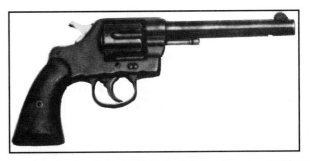

Courtesy Butterfield & Butterfield, San Francisco, California

Exc.	V.G.	Good	Fair	Poor
7500	5000	3000	1000	500

Model 1892 "New Army and Navy"

This model is similar in appearance to the 1889 Navy. The main differences are improvements to the lockwork function. It has double bolt stop notches, a double cylinder locking bolt, and shorter flutes on the cylinder. The .38 Smith & Wesson and the .32-20 were added to the .38 Colt and .41 Colt chamberings. The checkered hard rubber grips are standard, with plain walnut grips found on some contract series guns. Barrel lengths and finishes are the same as described for the Model 1889. The patent dates 1895 and 1901 appear stamped on later models. Colt manufactured 291,000 of these revolvers between 1892 and 1907. Antiques before 1898 are more desirable from an investment standpoint.

NOTE: For 3" Barrel add 20%.

Exc.	V. G.	Good	Fair	Poor
1250	900	500	200	100

U.S. Navy Model

Exc.	V.G.	Good	Fair	Poor
3500	2750	1500	1000	750

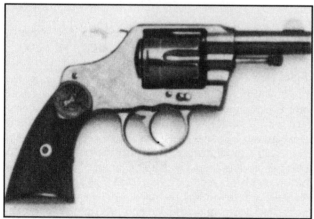

Courtesy Butterfield & Butterfield, San Francisco, California

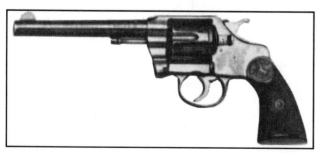

Courtesy Butterfield & Butterfield, San Francisco, California

U.S. Army Model

The initial Army purchase was for 8000 Model 1892 revolvers, almost all of which were altered to add "MODEL 1894" improvements. Unaltered examples will bring a premium.

Exc.	V.G.	Good	Fair	Poor
3000	2200	1250	600	300

Model 1894/96 Army Model

This model is an improved Model 1892 with a better locking mechanism for the cylinder. Many Model 1892 models were

converted in this manner. By the middle of 1897 all U.S. troops were issued the Model 1894 revolver which was the first military handgun to use smokeless powder cartridges. Marked, "U.S ARMY MODEL 1894" on the bottom of the butt. The Model 1896 was identical to the Model 1894. The Model 1901 was the same as the Model 1894 with the addition of a lanyard swivel. The Model 1903 was identical to the Model 1894 with a smaller bore diameter (9.068mm) and a modified grip.

Photo Paul Goodwin

Colt Model 1896 Army with cartouche • Photo Paul Goodwin

Exc.	V.G.	Good	Fair	Poor
2000	1200	500	250	150

Model 1905 Marine Corps

This model is a variation of the Model 1894. It was derived from the late production with its own serial range #10001-10926. With only 926 produced between 1905 and 1909, it is quite rare on today's market and is eagerly sought after by

Colt Double Action collectors. This model is chambered for the .38 Colt and the .38 Smith & Wesson Special cartridges. It holds 6 shots, has a 6" barrel, and is offered in a blued finish only. The grips are checkered walnut and are quite different than those found on previous models. "U.S.M.C." is stamped on the butt; patent dates of 1884, 1888, and 1895 are stamped on the barrel. One hundred-twenty-five of these revolvers were earmarked for civilian sales and do not have the Marine Corps markings; these will generally be found in better condition. Values are similar.

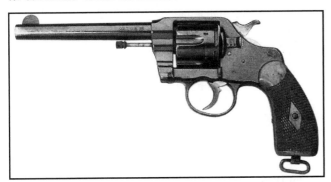

Courtesy Faintich Auction Services, Inc. Photo Paul Goodwin

Exc.	V.G.	Good	Fair	Poor
4500	3500	2000	1500	750

Military Model of 1909 (New Service)

Made both in a commercial and military version this revolver was chambered for the .45 Colt cartridge. fitted with a 5.5" barrel and walnut grips with lanyard swivel. Total military procurement was approximately 20,000 revolvers.

U.S. Army Model 1909, #30000-#50000

Marked "U.S. ARMY MODEL 1909" on butt. A total of about 18,000 were produced for the U.S. Army.

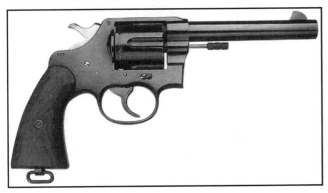

Courtesy Faintich Auction Services, Inc. Photo Paul Goodwin

Exc.	V.G.	Good	Fair	Poor
3000	1500	800	300	200

U.S. Navy Model 1909, #30000-#50000

Same as above with "U.S.N." on butt. About 1,000 were produced for the U.s. Navy.

Exc.	V.G.	Good	Fair	Poor
3500	2000	1000	350	250

U.S. Marine Corps Model 1909, #30000-#50000

Checkered walnut rips,. "U.S.M.C." on butt. About 1,200 were built for the Marine Corps.

Exc.	V.G.	Good	Fair	Poor
4500	2000	1200	650	450

U.S. Army Model 1917, #150000-#301000

Smooth walnut grips, 5.5" barrel, .45 ACP, model designation stamped on butt and barrel. The Model 1917 differed from the Model 1909 in that it had a shorter cylinder for half-moon clips for the .45ACP cartridge, a wider cylinder stop lug on the sideplate, and a tapered barrel instead of a straight barrel. Blued, unpolished finish. Approximately 150,000 were purchased by the U.S. military.

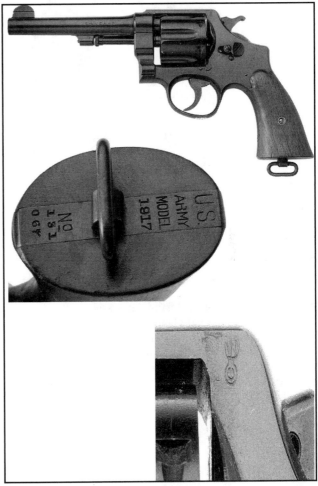

Photo Paul Goodwin

Exc.	V.G.	Good	Fair	Poor
750	600	400	300	225

Official Police (Martially marked)

This model was purchased by the military during World War II in barrel lengths of 4", 5", and 6". It has a polished blue finish. Chambered for the .38 Special cartridge. checkered walnut grips. About 5,000 were purchased by the U.S. Army during WWII The Defense Supply Corporation also purchased about 5,000 revolvers from Colt as well.

Exc.	V.G.	Good	Fair	Poor

Commando Model (Martially marked)

This model, for all intents and purposes, is an Official Police chambered for .38 Special, with a 2" and 4" barrels. This model is has a matted blue finish, no checkering on the cylinder latch or trigger and matt finish on top of frame. checkered plastic grips. Stamped "Colt Commando" on the barrel. There were approximately 50,000 manufactured between 1942-1945 for use in World War II.

NOTE: Add 30% for 2" barrel.

Courtesy Richard M. Kumor, Sr.

Exc.	V.G.	Good	Fair	Poor
550	450	275	150	100

Detective Special (Martially marked)

Chambered for the .38 special cartridge and fitted with a 2" barrel. Blued finish with checkered cylinder latch and trigger. Checkered walnut grips. approximately 5,000 were purchased by armed forces mostly for military intelligence and police units.

Exc.	V.G.	Good	Fair	Poor

Air Crewman Special (Martially marked)

This model was especially fabricated for the Air Force to be carried by their pilots for protection. It is extremely lightweight at 11 oz. The frame and the cylinder are made of aluminum alloy. It has a 2" barrel and is chambered for a distinctive .38 Special cartridge "M41" military cartridge with a chamber pressure of 16,000 pounds per square inch. The finish was blued, with checkered walnut grips. There were approximately 1,200 manufactured in 1951 with special serial numbers A.F. 1 through A.F. 1189.

Exc.	V.G.	Good	Fair	Poor
4500	2500	1500	800	250

COLT SEMIAUTOMATIC PISTOLS

The Colt Firearms Co. was the first of the American gun manufacturers to take the advent of the semiautomatic pistol seriously. This pistol design was becoming popular among European gun makers in the late 1880s and early 1900s. In the United States, however, the revolver was firmly ensconced as the accepted design. Colt realized that if the semiauto could be made to function reliably, it would soon catch on. The powers that be at Colt were able to negotiate with some of the noted inventors of the day, including Browning, and to secure or lease the rights to manufacture their designs. Colt also encouraged the creativity of their employees with bonuses and incentives and, through this innovative thinking, soon became the leader in semiauto pistol sales—a position that they have never really relinquished to any other American gun maker. The Colt semiautomatic pistols represent an interesting field for the collector of Colt handguns. There were many variations with high enough production to make it worthwhile to seek them out.

Model 1900

This was the first of the Colt automatic pistols. It was actually a developmental model with only 3,500 being produced. The Model 1900 was not really a successful design. It was quite clumsy and out of balance in the hand and was not as reliable in function as it should have been. This model is chambered for the .38 Rimless smokeless cartridge. It has a detachable magazine that holds seven cartridges. The barrel is 6" in length. The finish is blued, with a case-colored hammer and safety/sight combination. The grips are either plain walnut, checkered walnut, or hard rubber. This pistol is a Browning design, and the left side of the slide is stamped "Browning's Patent" with the 1897 patent date. Colt sold 250 pistols to the Navy and 300 to the Army for field trials and evaluation. The remaining 3,300 were sold on the civilian market. This model was manufactured from 1900-1903.

NOTE: Civilian Model with Sight/Safety Combination add 40%.

Model 1900 Navy model with sight safety • Paul Goodwin Photo

Standard Civilian Production

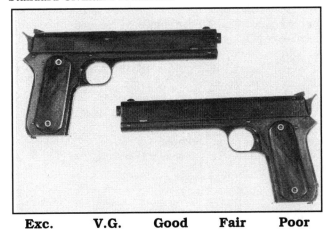

Exc.	V.G.	Good	Fair	Poor
7500	4000	2250	1250	750

U.S. Navy Military Model-250 built

Colt serial numbers 1001 to 1250 with Navy numbers, "U.S.N. 1 TO U.S.N. 250" on the left side of frame.

Exc.	V.G.	Good	Fair	Poor
7500	6000	5000	2500	1000

U.S. Army Military Model-1st contract-100 built

Exc.	V.G.	Good	Fair	Poor
20000	15000	10000	4000	2000

U.S. Army Military Model-2nd contract-200 built

Exc.	V.G.	Good	Fair	Poor
10000	7500	5500	2000	1500

Model 1902 Military Pistol

This model is a somewhat larger, heavier pistol than the 1902 Sporting Pistol. It has the same .38 ACP chambering and 6" barrel, detachable magazine holding 8 rounds. The grip of this model is larger and squared off to accommodate the larger magazine, and it has a lanyard swivel on the butt. There were approximately 18,000 manufactured between 1902 and 1929. The vast majority of these pistols were commercial models.

Early Model with Front of Slide Serrated

Model 1902 U.S. military with early front slide serrations-Paul Goodwin Photo

Exc.	V.G.	Good	Fair	Poor
3500	2000	1250	750	450

Standard Model with Rear of Slide Serrated

Model 1902 military with rear slide serrations • Paul Goodwin Photo

Exc.	V.G.	Good	Fair	Poor
2500	1750	1000	500	400

A Model 1902 Military Standard Model in excellent condition with original box was sold at auction for $3,740. Box was in excellent condition as well. Faintich Auction Services, Inc., September 1998

U.S. Army Marked, #15001-#15200 with Front Serrations-200 built

Exc.	V.G.	Good	Fair	Poor
6000	5000	2500	1250	600

Model 1902 U.S. military with early front slide serrations • Paul Goodwin Photo

Model 1903 Hammerless, .32 Pocket Pistol

Courtesy Orvel Reichert

Model 1903 Hammerless with 4" barrel. • Courtesy Richard M. Kumor, Sr.

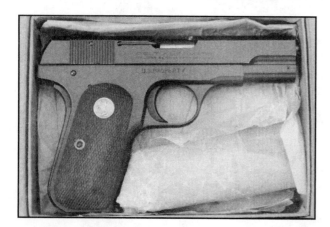

This was the second pocket automatic Colt manufactured. It was another of John Browning's designs, and it developed into one of Colt's most successful pistols. This pistol is cham-

bered for the .32 ACP cartridge. Initially the barrel length was 4"; this was shortened to 3.75". The detachable magazine holds 8 rounds. The standard finish is blue, with quite a few nickel plated. The early model grips are checkered hard rubber with the "Rampant Colt" molded into them. Many of the nickel plated pistols had pearl grips. In 1924 the grips were changed to checkered walnut with the Colt medallions. The name of this model can be misleading as it is not a true hammerless but a concealed hammer design. It features a slide stop and a grip safety. Colt manufactured 572,215 civilian versions of this pistol and approximately 200,000 more for military contracts. This model was manufactured between 1903 and 1945.

NOTE: A number of these pistols were shipped to the Philippine Army as well as other foreign military forces but no clear record of these shipments exist. However, About 24,000 Colt Hammerless pistols were sold to Belgium between 1915 and 1917. Serial numbers for these pistols are available (see Brunner, *The Colt Pocket Hammerless Automatic Pistols*). In addition several thousand Colt .32 pocket pistols as well as Colt .25 and .380 pocket models were shipped to England during World War I. During World War II Colt supplied about 8,000 Colt pocket pistols in various calibers to England in blued and Parkerized finish marked "U.S. PROPERTY". (see Brunner).

NOTE: Early Model 1897 Patent Date add 40%.
Nickel Plated With Pearl Grips add $100.
4" Barrel to #72,000 add 20%.

Civilian Model

Exc.	V.G.	Good	Fair	Poor
550	500	450	300	200

U.S. Military Model

Chambered for .380 caliber only and some of them marked "U.S. Property" on frame, blue or parkerized finish.

NOTE: Pistols issued to General Officers will command a premium. Also blued pistols will command a premium.

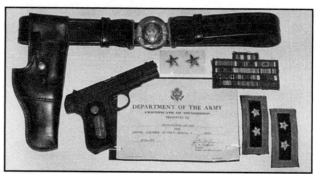

Model 1903 US marked issued to Gen. Ahee. • Courtesy Richard M. Kumor Sr.

Exc.	V.G.	Good	Fair	Poor
1300	950	500	300	250

NOTE: *See also Belgium, Handguns, FN*

Model 1908 Hammerless .380 Pocket Pistol

This model is essentially the same as the .32 Pocket Pistol, chambered for the more potent .380 ACP, also known as the 9mm Browning short. Other specifications are the same. Colt manufactured approximately 138,000 in this caliber for civilian sales. An unknown number were sold to the military.

Standard Civilian Model

Nickel with Pearl Grips add $100.

Exc.	V.G.	Good	Fair	Poor
800	650	475	350	250

Military Model

Some have serial prefix "M", marked "U.S. Property" on frame, blued finish.

NOTE: None of these pistols were originally Parkerized.

Exc.	V.G.	Good	Fair	Poor
1500	1000	750	500	300

Model 1908 Hammerless .25 Pocket Pistol

This was the smallest automatic Colt made. It is chambered for the .25 ACP cartridge, has a 2" barrel, and is 4.5" long overall. It weighs a mere 13 oz. This is a true pocket pistol. The detachable magazine holds 6 shots. This model was offered in blue or nickel-plate, with grips of checkered hard rubber and checkered walnut on later versions. This model has a grip safety, slide lock, and a magazine disconnector safety. This was another Browning design, and Fabrique Nationale manufactured this pistol in Belgium before Colt picked up the rights to make it in the U.S. This was a commercial success by Colt's standards, with approximately 409,000 manufactured between 1908 and 1941.

NOTE: A small number of these pistols were bought by the OSS during World War II from retailers or distributors. These pistol are probably not martially marked. Beware of fakes that are marked by an engraving tool.

Courtesy Orvel Reichert

Civilian Model
Exc.	V.G.	Good	Fair	Poor
500	350	300	200	100

Military Model

"U.S. Property" stamped on right frame. Very rare.

Exc.	V.G.	Good	Fair	Poor
2500	1500	600	450	300

Model 1905 .45 Automatic Pistol

The Spanish American War and the experiences with the Moros in the Philippine campaign taught a lesson about stopping power or the lack of it. The United States Army was convinced that they needed a more powerful handgun cartridge. This led Colt to the development of a .45-caliber cartridge suitable for the semiautomatic pistol. The Model 1905 and the .45 Rimless round were the result. In actuality, this cartridge was not nearly powerful enough to satisfy the need, but it led to the development of the .45 ACP. Colt believed that this pistol/cartridge combination would be a success and was geared up for mass production. The Army actually bought only 200 of them, and the total production was approximately 6,300 from 1905 to 1911. The pistol has a 5" barrel and detachable 7-shot magazine and is blued, with a case-colored hammer. The grips are checkered walnut. The hammer was rounded on the first 3,600 pistols and was changed to a spur hammer on the later models. The right side of the slide is stamped "Automatic Colt/Calibre 45 Rimless Smokeless." This model was not a commercial success for Colt—possibly because it has no safety whatsoever except for the floating inertia firing pin. The 200 military models have grip safeties only. A small number (believed to be less than 500) of these pistols were grooved to accept a shoulder stock. The stocks were made of leather and steel and made to double as a holster. These pistols have been classified "Curios and Relics" under the provisions of the Gun Control Act of 1968.

A Colt Model 1905 with experimental safety was sold at auction for $13,800. British proofs. Possible British Trials pistol. Condition was good.
Rock Island Auction Company, August 1999

Civilian Model

Exc.	V.G.	Good	Fair	Poor
4000	3500	1750	950	400

Military Model, Serial #1-201

Known as the 1907 Contract Pistol, it has a lanyard loop, a loaded chamber indicator, and a grip safety and bears the inspector's initials "K.M."

Exc.	V.G.	Good	Fair	Poor
8500	6500	4500	1500	500

COLT 1911

The Colt Government Model is one of the most recognizable handguns in the world. Its popularity is second only to the Single Action Army among firearm collectors in the world today. It was this pistol that established Colt as the leader among handgun manufacturers. Arguably the advent of this fine pistol was timely from a historic point of view. It appeared in time for the beginning of WWI and was able to prove its worth on the battlefields of Europe and the Pacific in both WWI and WWII. This may have been John Browning's crowning achievement, as this pistol shall always be the most respected of the Colt Auto line. There are over 200 factory variations and the unsurpassed production run from 1911 to the present is still going strong. Total production of Civilian pistols (GOVERNMENT MODELS) was approximately 336,000. The total number of Military pistols from all manufacturers, (including the pistols that Colt made which duplicated the serial numbers assigned to Ithaca, Remington Rand, and Union Switch and Signal) was just under 2.8 Million. The Colt .45 was used in WWI, WWII, the Korean War and Vietnam. However only recently has collector interest become widespread. However along with widespread collector interest has come widespread counterfeiting and fakery. Only by education in depth can the collector "hold his own" with these scoundrels and avoid costly mistakes. There are 4 reference books on the "COLT .45 AUTO PISTOL" so indispensable to collecting .45s that they will be mentioned by name: "Colt .45 Service Pistols, Models of 1911 and 1911A1", "Colt .45 Government Models (Commercial Series)", and "Collectors Guide to Colt .45 Service Pistols, Models of 1911 and 1911A1" all by Charles Clawson. Currently Mr. Clawson's books are all out of print, but hopefully they will be reprinted soon. And "U.S. Military Automatic Pistols 1894-1920" by Edward S. Meadows.

COLT FOREIGN CONTRACT 1911 PISTOLS

NOTE: These foreign contract pistols are included as military pistols despite their commercial serial numbers. The majority of these pistols were used by foreign governments as military, police, or other government agency sidearms.

First Argentine contract C6201-C6400.

Rarely seen better than Good. Many of these pistols have been reblued and parts changed. Reblue = Fair/Poor.

Exc.	V.G.	Good	Fair	Poor
na	1200	700	500	300

Second Argentine contract C20001-C21000.

Most of these pistols have been reblued and had parts changed. Reblue=Fair/Poor.

Exc.	V.G.	Good	Fair	Poor
1800	1200	750	450	250

Subsequent Argentine 1911 contracts after C21000.

Many of these pistols have been reblued and parts changed. Reblue = Fair/Poor.

Exc.	V.G.	Good	Fair	Poor
1800	1200	750	450	250

Canadian Contract (About 5000 pistols from C3000 to C14000)

Many pistols have owners markings applied. (99%-100% add 20-30%)

Exc.	V.G.	Good	Fair	Poor
3000	1800	950	550	300

First and Second British .455 Contract (200 pistols from W19000 to W19200) and 400 from W29001 to W29444.

All "JJ" marked. Many pistols have owners markings applied. (99%-100% add 20-30%)

Exc.	V.G.	Good	Fair	Poor
3500	2100	950	550	300

WWI British Contracts

This series is chambered for the British .455 cartridge and is so marked on the right side of the slide. The British "Broad Arrow" property mark will often be found. These pistols were made in 1915-1918. Some pistols are RAF marked on the left side of the frame.(+30% for RAF.) RAF pistols normally have an endless steel ring through the lanyard loop. Many of these pistols have been reblued (Reblued=Fair/poor) (99%-100% add 20-30%)

Right side of slide stamped"CALIBER .455" / left side of frame stamped "RAF" • Courtesy Karl Karash Collection

Exc.	V.G.	Good	Fair	Poor
2500	1700	750	550	300

French Contract (5000 pistols between C17800 and C28000

Very seldom seen (99%-100% add 20-30%)

Exc.	V.G.	Good	Fair	Poor
4500	2500	1150	750	500

1911 Russian Order

This variation is chambered for .45ACP and has the Russian version of "Anglo Zakazivat" stamped on the frame. There were about 51,100 pistols between serial C21,000 and C89,000 shipped. This variation is occasionally encountered today, And a few have been recently imported from Russia. At least one example is known that bears the Finnish arsenal mark "SA". This pistol may have been captured by the Finns as Russia invaded Finland prior to WWII. There could be thousands of these in warehouses ready to be released on the market. A precipitous drop in value might result. One should be extra cautious if contemplating a purchase, as fakes have been noted. However ORIGINAL pistols in V.G. or better condition are in high demand despite the market uncertainties. (99%-100% add 20-30%)

Exc.	V.G.	Good	Fair	Poor
4000	2600	1750	1100	625

Kongsberg Vapenfabrikk Model M/1914 (Norwegian) copy SN 1-96

(Rarely seen) (99%-100% add 20-30%)

Exc.	V.G.	Good	Fair	Poor
3500	2200	1150	850	600

Kongsberg Vapenfabrikk Model M/1914 (Norwegian) copy SN 97-29,614, and 30,536-32,854

(Numbers must match)

Exc.	V.G.	Good	Fair	Poor
1400	900	750	600	400

Kongsberg Vapenfabrikk Model M/1914 (Norwegian) copy SN 29,615 to 30,535

(Waffenamt marked on slide and barrel. (Numbers must match.) Waffenamt marked M/1914s outside this range are probably FAKES.) (99%-100% add 20-30%)

Exc.	V.G.	Good	Fair	Poor
3000	1900	1150	850	600

MODEL 1911 AUTOMATIC PISTOL, U.S. MILITARY SERIES

Colt Manufacture

Marked "MODEL OF 1911 U.S.ARMY" on right slide, "UNITED STATES PROPERTY" on left front frame until SN 510,000 then above trigger right. Serial number located on right front frame until SN 7,500 Then above trigger right. Pistols have high polish and Fire blue small parts until SN 2400, then finish changed to non-reflective dull blue. Double diamond grips throughout. Lanyard loop magazine (3 types) until about SN 129,000. Thereafter, two-tone magazine.

Model 1911 U.S. Army marked • Paul Goodwin Photo

Below Serial #101 "LARGE" UNITED STATES PROPERTY" and other Unique features.

Unmarked fully blued barrel(99%-100% add 20-30%)

Courtesy Karl Kash Collection

Exc.	V.G.	Good	Fair	Poor
30000	12000	6000	4500	2500

Three Digit "MODEL OF 1911 U.S.ARMY" marked slide. SN 100 Through SN 500.

Unmarked fully blued barrel until SN 400. H (With serifs) marked on rear of barrel hood until SN500. (99%-100% add 20-30%)

Exc.	V.G.	Good	Fair	Poor
12000	6000	4000	2200	1200

Three Digit "MODEL OF 1911 U.S.NAVY" marked slide. SN 501 Through SN 1,000.

H (With serifs) marked on rear of barrel hood (fully blued). Some seemingly original early NAVY pistols have been observed with the later dull finish. These may have been finished, assembled and shipped out of sequence. (Later dull finish in the range where mirror and fire blue is expected, under SN 2400, less 70 (99%-100% add 20-30%)

Exc.	V.G.	Good	Fair	Poor
15000	6000	4000	2200	1200

Model 1911 U.S. Navy marked • Paul Goodwin Photo

Four Digit "MODEL OF 1911 U.S.ARMY" marked slide. With fire Blue parts

SN 1,001 to 1,500, 2,001 to 2,400, After SN 2,400, no fire blue and dull finish. (No fire blue, less 40%) H (With serifs) marked on rear of barrel hood until SN 7,500. Some seemingly original early ARMY pistols have been observed with the later dull finish. These may have been finished, assembled and shipped out of sequence. (Later dull finish in the range where mirror and fire blue is expected, under SN 2400, less 65%) (99%-100% add 20-30%) Exc.V.G.GoodFairPoor 9000 450025001500750 1913 production USMC SN 3501 to 3800 (Rarely seen and often well used) (99%-100% add 20-30%)

Exc.	V.G.	Good	Fair	Poor
7500	3800	2500	1500	950

Four Digit "MODEL OF 1911 U.S.NAVY" marked slide.

SN 1501 to SN 2,000, After SN 2,400, no fire blue and dull finish. H (With serifs until SN 7500, No serifs after SN7500) marked on rear of barrel hood (fully blued). 5 groups: (1,501-2,000, 2,501-3,500, 4,501-5,500, 6,501-7,500, and 8,501-9,500. Some seemingly original early NAVY pistols have been observed with the later dull finish. These may have been finished, assembled and shipped out of sequence. Later dull finish in the range where mirror and fire blue is expected, under SN 2400, less 65%) (Dull finish no fire blue, less 40%, above SN 2400) (99%-100% add 20-30%)

Exc.	V.G.	Good	Fair	Poor
12000	6000	3500	1600	800

Five Digit Colt "MODEL OF 1911 U.S.ARMY" marked slide.

No fire Blue, and dull finish. H (Without serifs) marked on rear of barrel hood until about SN 19500. P (Without serifs) marked on rear of barrel hood, H visible through ejection port from about SN 19500 to SN 24600. H P (Horizontal) visible through eject port from SN 24600 to SN 110,000. H on back of hood +15%. P on back of hood +30%. (99%-100% add 20-30%)

Exc.	V.G.	Good	Fair	Poor
4000	2800	2500	1500	750

1913 production 36401 to 37650 USMC shipment.

Slide marked "MODEL OF 1911 U.S. ARMY" on ALL ORIGINAL USMC shipped pistols. (Any USMC marked 1911 pistol should be considered a FAKE. Same as 5 digit ARMY, but +35% (Rarely seen and Often well used.)

Five Digit "MODEL OF 1911 U.S.NAVY" marked slide.

4 groups: (10,501-11,500, 12,501-13,500, 38,001-44,000, 96,001-97,537) Same as 5 digit ARMY, but +35%

Six Digit "MODEL OF 1911 U.S.NAVY" marked slide.

(109,501-110,000)Similar To 5 digit ARMY, but +25% Springfield Armory "MODEL OF 1911 U.S.ARMY" Dull finish, ALL parts MUST be Springfield made. Made in 4 SN groups: 72571-83855, 102597-107596, 113497-120566. Same as 5 digit ARMY, but +40% (99%-100% add 20-30%) Springfield Armory 72571 to about 75000 with short stubby hammer Same as 5 digit ARMY, but +50% (99%-100% add 20-30%)

Remington UMC "MODEL OF 1911 U.S.ARMY"

Dull finish, ALL parts MUST be Remington made. Similar To 5 digit COLT "ARMY" marked slide, but +35%

1911 Colt "NRA" marked pistol

An unknown number of shipped Colt 1911 pistols were taken from stores and sold to NRA members. These pistols ranged from about SN 70,000 to the high 150,000 range. Pistols were marked N.R.A. under the serial or at the Right front of the frame. The number is unknown, perhaps 300 (99%-100% add 20-30%)

Exc.	V.G.	Good	Fair	Poor
5000	3200	2100	1500	1000

1911 Springfield "NRA" marked pistol

An unknown number of shipped Colt 1911 pistols were taken from stores and sold to NRA members. These pistols ranged from about SN 70,000 to the high 129,000 range. Pistols were marked N.R.A. under the serial or at the Right front of the frame. The number of N.R.A. marked Springfields is unknown, but based on observed pistols it is perhaps 600. (99%-100% add 20-30%)

Exc.	V.G.	Good	Fair	Poor
5000	3200	2100	1500	1000

North American Arms of Montreal QB "1911"

Made for US but none delivered to Army. Less than 100 pistols assembled from parts. Rarely seen. Numbered under left grip and left rear slide. Similar To 5 digit Colt "ARMY" marked slide, but +500% (99%-100% add 20-30%)

Six Digit Colt 1915 - 1919 "MODEL OF 1911 U.S.ARMY" marked slide.

Dull finish. Vertically oriented "P H" or "H P" marked on barrel, visible through eject port from about SN 110,000 to SN 425,000. Interlaced HP (Horizontal orientation) visible through Ejection port from about SN 425,000 to end of 1911 production. Slides marked "MODEL OF 1911 U.S. ARMY" on ALL ORIGINAL USMC shipped pistols. (Any USMC marked

1911 pistol should be considered a FAKE. (99%-100% add 20-30%)

Exc.	V.G.	Good	Fair	Poor
3000	2200	1500	1100	550

SA suspended numbers assigned to Colt, shipped as replacement frames +25%

1916 production with S marked frame, slide, and barrel +60%

1916 production with normally marked frame, slide, and barrel +20%

1917 production 151187 to 151986 USMC shipment +25% (Often well used)

1917 production 185801 to 186200 USMC shipment +25% (Often well used)

1917 production 209587 to 210386 USMC shipment +25% (Often well used)

1917 production 210387 to 215386 Replacement Frames +25% (Rarely Seen)

1917 production 215387 to 216186 USMC shipment +25% (Rarely Seen)

1917 production 216187 to 216586 ARMY transferred from USMC +15% (Rarely Seen)

1917 production 216587 to 217386 USMC shipment +25% (Rarely Seen)

1917 production 223953 to 223990 NAVY (ARMY marked) +15%

1917 production 232001 to 233600 NAVY (ARMY marked) +15%

1918-1919 production with Eagle over number

No inspectors cartouche about 302,000 to end of 1911 production (625,000.) (Black Army, -25% if flaking present, if no flaking present, watch out for reblue.) (99%-100% add 20-30%)

Exc.	V.G.	Good	Fair	Poor
3000	2200	1500	1100	550

4 Digit X Numbered Rework

these pistols were renumbered when their original serial numbers were either defaced, obliterated, or became too light to read during rebuilding or refinishing. the four digit X prefix numbers (X1000 through X4385) were assigned after WWI (1924) and were used by Springfield through 1953. all are considered "Arsenal Refinished""

Exc.	V.G.	Good	Fair	Poor
1000	800	650	475	350

"Military to Commercial Conversions"

Some 1911 military pistols that were brought home by GIs were subsequently returned to the Colt factory by their owners for repair or refinishing. If the repair included a new barrel, the pistol would have been proof fired and a normal verified proof mark affixed to the trigger guard bow in the normal commercial practice. If the pistol was refinished between 1920 and 1942, the slide would probably be numbered to the frame again in the normal commercial practice. these pistols are really a re-manufactured Colt pistol of limited production and should be valued at least that of a contemporary 1911A1 commercial pistol. Very seldom seen. (99%-100% add 30%).

Exc.	V.G.	Good	Fair	Poor
2000	1200	900	500	275

Remington U.S. Model 1911, marked Remington/UMC • Paul Goodwin Photo

SERIAL NUMBERS ASSIGNED TO M1911 AND 1911A1 CONTRACTORS

Year	Serial No.	Manufacturer
1912	1-500	Colt
	501-1000	Colt USN
	1001-1500	Colt
	1501-2000	Colt USN
	2001-2500	Colt
	2501-3500	Colt USN
	3501-3800	Colt USMC
	3801-4500	Colt
	4501-5500	Colt USN
	5501-6500	Colt
	6501-7500	Colt USN
	7501-8500	Colt
	8501-9500	Colt USN
	9501-10500	Colt
	10501-11500	Colt USN
	11501-12500	Colt
	12501-13500	Colt USN
	13501-17250	Colt
1913	17251-36400	Colt
	36401-37650	Colt USMC
	37651-38000	Colt
	38001-44000	Colt USN
	44001-60400	Colt
1914	60401-72570	Colt
	72571-83855	Springfield
	83856-83900	Colt
	83901-84400	Colt USMC
	84401-96000	Colt
	96001-97537	Colt
	97538-102596	Colt
	102597-107596	Springfield
1915	107597-109500	Colt
	109501-110000	Colt USN
	110001-113496	Colt
	113497-120566	Springfield
	120567-125566	Colt
	125567-133186	Springfield
1916	133187-137400	Colt
1917	137401-151186	Colt
	151187-151986	Colt USMC
	151987-185800	Colt
	185801-186200	Colt USMC

Year	Serial No.	Manufacturer
1917	186201-209586	Colt
	209587-210386	Colt USMC
	210387-215386	Colt Frames
	215387-216186	Colt USMC
	216187-216586	Colt
	216587-216986	Colt USMC
1918	216987-217386	Colt USMC
	217387-232000	Colt
	232001-233600	Colt USN
	233601-594000	Colt
1918	1-13152	Rem-UMC
1919	13153-21676	Rem-UMC
	594001-629500	Colt
	629501-700000	Winchester (Assigned)
1924	700001-710000	Colt
1937	710001-712349	Colt
1938	712350-713645	Colt
1939	713646-717281	Colt USN
1940	717282-721977	Colt
1941	721978-756733	Colt
1942	756734-800000	Colt
	S800001-S800500	Singer
	800501-801000	H&R (Assigned)
1943	801001-958100	Colt
	958101-1088725	U.S. S.& S.
	1088726-1208673	Colt
	1208674-1279673	Ithaca
	1279674-1279698	Augusta Arsenal (Renumber)
	1279699-1441430	Remington-Rand
	1441431-1471430	Ithaca
	1471431-1609528	Remington-Rand
1944	1609529-1743846	Colt
	1743847-1890503	Ithaca
	1890504-2075103	Remington-Rand
1945	2075104-2134403	Ithaca
	2134404-2244803	Remington-Rand
	2244804-2380013	Colt
	2380014-2619013	Remington-Rand
	2619014-2693613	Ithaca

MODEL 1911A1 AUTOMATIC PISTOL MILITARY MODEL

COLT MANUFACTURE

Service Model Ace

In 1937 Colt introduced this improved version of the Ace pistol. It utilizes a floating chamber invented by David "Carbine" Williams, the firearm's designer who invented the M1 carbine while serving time in a southern chain gang. this floating chamber gave the Service Model Ace the reliability and feel that the public wanted. the serial number is prefixed by the letters "SM". the external configuration is the same as the Ace, and the slide is marked "COLT SERVICE MODEL ACE .22 LONG RIFLE". Colt sold most to the Army and a few a a commercial basis. There were a total of 13,803 manufactured before production ceased in 1945. (99%-100% finish add 33%).

Parkerized pistols (after about serial # SM3840)

Exc.	V.G.	Good	Fair	Poor
2600	1700	1050	600	450

Blued pistols (before serial # SM3840)

Exc.	V.G.	Good	Fair	Poor
3500	2000	1250	800	600

Transition Model.

SN 700,001 to 710,000. Some pistols below 700,100 rumored to have numbered slides (Not verified.) Made in 1924. Brushed Blue finish, all 1911A1 features (Arched mainspring housing, short checkered trigger, long tang on grip safety, trigger finger cutouts, Full checkered walnut grips, etc.) However they retained the "MODEL OF 1911 U.S. ARMY" slide marking. No verified proof or final inspectors mark on trigger guard bow, interlaced "HP" and "K" marked barrel. (add 30% for 99%-100%)

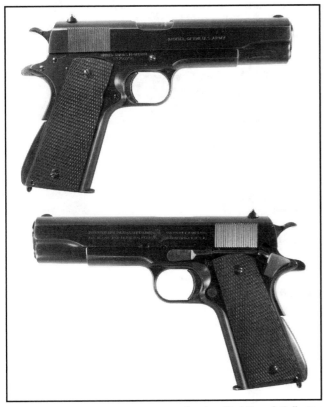

Courtesy Karl Karash Collection

Exc.	V.G.	Good	Fair	Poor
2700	1800	1200	800	550

First Transition Model of 1937.

SN 710,001 to about 711,001. Numbered slide under firing pin stop plate. No "P" marking on frame or slide. Brushed Blue finish, all 1911A1 features (Arched mainspring housing, short checkered trigger, long tang on grip safety, trigger finger cutouts, etc.) However they retained the "MODEL OF 1911 U.S. ARMY" slide marking. Verified proof and final inspectors mark on trigger guard bow. "COLT .45 AUTO" marked magazine floorplate with flattened letters. Extremely rare. (add 40% for 99%-100%)

Exc.	V.G.	Good	Fair	Poor
5000	3900	2700	1800	1250

Second Transition Model of 1937.

About SN 711,001 to 712,349. Numbered slide under firing pin stop plate. "P" marking on frame and top of slide. Brushed Blue finish, all 1911A1 features (Arched mainspring housing, short checkered trigger, long tang on grip safety, trigger finger cutouts, etc.) However they retained the "MODEL OF 1911 U.S. ARMY" slide marking. Verified proof and final inspectors mark on trigger guard bow. "COLT .45 AUTO" marked magazine floorplate with flattened letters. Extremely rare. (add 40% for 99%-100%)

Exc.	V.G.	Good	Fair	Poor
5000	3900	2700	1800	1250

Model of 1911A1, 1938 production.

SN 712,350 to 713,645. Numbered slide under firing pin stop plate. "P" marking on frame and top of slide. No markings on Right side of slide. Brushed Blue finish, all 1911A1 features (Arched mainspring housing, short checkered trigger, long tang on grip safety, trigger finger cutouts, etc.) Right side of frame is marked "M1911A1 U.S. ARMY" forward of the slide stop pin, and "United States Property" behind the slide stop pin. Verified proof and final inspectors mark on trigger guard bow. Most are "H" marked on left side by magazine catch. "COLT .45 AUTO" marked magazine floorplate with flattened letters. Extremely rare. (add 50% to 100% for 99%-100%) So few of these rare pistols have been sold publicly that these prices are intended as a rough guide only.

Exc.	V.G.	Good	Fair	Poor
10000	6500	4000	3000	2000

NOTE: All Military .45 cal. pistols manufactured during and after 1938 are designated and marked "1911A1" and include all the 1911A1 features.

Model of 1911A1, 1939 production. (1939 NAVY)

SN 713,646 to 717,281. Numbered slide under firing pin stop plate. "P" marking on frame and top of slide. No markings on Right side of slide. Brushed Blue finish. Shortened hammer. Right side of frame is marked "M1911A1 U.S. ARMY" forward of the slide stop pin, and "United States Property" behind the slide stop pin. Verified proof and final inspectors mark on trigger guard bow. Most are "H" marked on left side by magazine catch. "COLT .45 AUTO" marked magazine floorplate with flattened letters. Rare. (add 30% for 99%-100%)

Exc.	V.G.	Good	Fair	Poor
3300	2500	1800	900	600

Model of 1911A1, 1940 production. (CSR)

SN 717,282 to 721,977. Numbered slide under firing pin stop plate. "P" marking on frame and top of slide. No markings on Right side of slide. Brushed Blue finish. Shortened hammer. Right side of frame is marked "M1911A1 U.S. ARMY" forward of the slide stop pin, and "United States Property" behind the slide stop pin. Verified proof and final inspectors mark on trigger guard bow. "CSR "(Charles S. Reed) marked on left side below slide stop. "COLT .45 AUTO" marked magazine floorplate with flattened letters. Some pistols may have early brittle plastic grips. Rare. (add 30% for 99%-100%)

Exc.	V.G.	Good	Fair	Poor
3300	2500	1800	900	600

Model of 1911A1, 1941 production. (RS)

SN 721,978 to 756,733. Numbered slide under firing pin stop plate. "P" marking on frame and top of slide. No markings on Right side of slide. Brushed Blue finish through about SN 736,000. Parkerizing was used thereafter until the end of Colt production. Any Colt pistol after about SN 737,000 with a blued finish is likely to be a FAKE. Shortened hammer. Right side of frame is marked "M1911A1 U.S. ARMY" forward of the slide stop pin, and "United States Property" behind the slide stop pin. Verified proof and final inspectors mark on trigger guard bow. "RS "(Robert Sears) marked on left side below slide stop starting at about SN 723,000, ending about 750,500. After 750,500 Pistols were marked WB (Waldemar S. Broberg) "COLT .45 AUTO" marked magazine floorplate with flattened letters. Early pistols may have wood grips, later pistols have hollow back (without ribs) plastic grips. Prices are for Blued finish. (Parkerized finish Less 40%) Rare. (Subtract 5% to 10% for British proofs, most collectors prefer virgin pistols.)(add 30% for 99%-100%)

Exc.	V.G.	Good	Fair	Poor
2700	2200	1500	750	500

Model of 1911A1, 1942 production. (WB)

SN 756,733 to about 856,100. Numbered slide under firing pin stop plate. "P" marking on frame and top of slide. No markings on Right side of slide. Parkerized finish. Shortened hammer. Right side of frame is marked "M1911A1 U.S. ARMY" forward of the slide stop pin, and "United States Property" behind the slide stop pin. Verified proof and final inspectors mark on trigger guard bow. "WB "(Waldemar S. Broberg) marked on left side below slide stop "COLT .45 AUTO" marked magazine floorplate with flattened letters, sand blasted bottom. (Subtract 5% to 10% for British proofs, most collectors prefer virgin pistols.) (add 30% for 99%-100%)

Exc.	V.G.	Good	Fair	Poor
1300	1000	700	600	400

Model of 1911A1, 1942 NAVY.

3982 pistols shipped to Naval supply depots, Oakland CA and Sewalls Point VA. Numbered SN 793658 to SN 797639. Numbered slide under firing pin stop plate. "P" marking on frame and top of slide. No markings on Right side of slide. Parkerized finish. Shortened hammer. Right side of frame is marked "M1911A1 U.S. ARMY" forward of the slide stop pin, and "United States Property" behind the slide stop pin. Verified proof and final inspectors mark on trigger guard bow. "WB "(Waldemar S. Broberg) marked on left side below slide stop "COLT .45 AUTO" marked magazine floorplate with flattened letters, sand blasted bottom. (Subtract 5% to 10% for British proofs, most collectors prefer virgin pistols.) (add 30% for 99%-100%)

Exc.	V.G.	Good	Fair	Poor
2000	1400	950	700	475

Model of 1911A1, Singer Manufacturing Co., Educational Order 1942.

Exactly 500 pistols accepted and shipped. J.K.C. (John K. Clement) marked on left side below slide stop. At least two un-numbered (and not marked United States Property) pistols were made and retained by employees. Slightly dull Blue finish, brown plastic hollow-back grips, un-marked blue magazine, wide spur hammer, checkered slide stop, thumb safety, trigger, and mainspring housing. About one hundred of the original 500 are known. Very Rare and most highly de-

sired. Exercise caution when contemplating a purchase as fakes, improved, and reblued models abound. Be extra cautious with an example that is 98% or better. (add 50% for 99%-100%) (Un-numbered or numbered with out of sequence numbers subtract 50%.) (Subtract 5% to 10% for British proofs, most collectors prefer virgin pistols.) (Reblued, restored subtract 90% to 95%.)

Exc.	V.G.	Good	Fair	Poor
25000	18000	12000	7000	3500

Rock Island Arsenal Replacement numbers.

SN 856,101 to 856,404. Replacement numbers issued to allow a pistol whose number had been defaced or worn away during refinishing to be numbered again. Very rare.

Exc.	V.G.	Good	Fair	Poor
1300	1000	700	600	400

A Colt Model 1911A1 Military cutaway was sold at auction for $1,980. It was marked "RIA." Built in 1943. condition was excellent.
Faintich Auction Service, September, 1998

Model of 1911A1, Military. 1943 production. (GHD marked)

SN 867,00 to about 1,155,000. Colt had their own serial numbers assigned within this range, but in addition, Colt duplicated Ithaca's serial numbers between 865,404 and 916,404 as well as Remington Rand's between 916,405 and 958,100, and US&S's between 1,088,726 and 1,092,896. Numbered slide under firing pin stop plate until about 1,139,000. "P" marking on frame and top of slide. Parkerized. Right side of frame is marked "M1911A1 U.S. ARMY" forward of the slide stop pin, and "United States Property" behind the slide stop pin. Verified proof and final inspectors mark on trigger guard bow. "GHD "(Guy H. Drewry) marked on left side below slide stop. Plain blued or contract magazine. (Subtract 5% to 10% for British proofs, most collectors prefer virgin pistols.) (add 30% for 99%-100%) Colt in Ithaca or Remington Rand range +10%, Colt in U.S.& S range +20%,

Exc.	V.G.	Good	Fair	Poor
1050	850	700	600	400

Model of 1911A1, Commercial to Military Conversions. 1943 production.

(A few WB marked, most GHD marked) SN 860,003 to about 867,000. Numbered slide under firing pin stop plate. "P" marking on frame and top of slide. Commercial markings on Right side of slide. Parkerized finish over previously blued finish. Original Commercial SN peened and restamped with military numbers. Most have the Swartz Grip Safety cutouts in slide and frame but not the Swartz parts. None have the Swartz "Sear Safety". No slides marked "NATIONAL MATCH" have been reported. If any exist, a NM slide pistol would command a premium. Shortened hammer. Right side of frame is marked "M1911A1 U.S. ARMY" forward of the slide stop pin, and "United States Property" behind the slide stop pin. Verified proof and final inspectors mark on trigger guard bow. "GHD "(Guy H. Drewry) marked on left side below slide stop "COLT .45 AUTO" marked magazine floorplate with flattened letters, sand blasted bottom. (Subtract 5% to 10% for British proofs, most collectors prefer virgin pistols.) (add 30% for 99%-100%) (add 10-30% for NM marked slide.

Exc.	V.G.	Good	Fair	Poor
1750	1200	900	700	475

Model of 1911A1, Military with commercial slide. 1943 production. (GHD marked)

SN 867,00 to about 936,000. Numbered slide under firing pin stop plate. "P" marking on frame and top of slide. Commercial markings on Right side of slide. Parkerized finish over previously blued finish (slide only). Most have the Swartz Grip Safety cutouts in slide but not in frame. None have the Swartz parts. Frames are generally new military manufacture Shortened hammer. Right side of frame is marked "M1911A1 U.S. ARMY" forward of the slide stop pin, and "United States Property" behind the slide stop pin. Verified proof and final inspectors mark on trigger guard bow. "GHD "(Guy H. Drewry) marked on left side below slide stop May have "COLT .45 AUTO" marked magazine floorplate with flattened letters with sand blasted bottom or plain blued magazine. Barrels marked "COLT .45 AUTO" (add 30% for 99%-100%) (add 35% Canadian Broad arrow/C)

Exc.	V.G.	Good	Fair	Poor
1250	1000	800	600	400

Model of 1911A1, Canadian Broad Arrow/C marked 1943 production.

1515 pistols (GHD marked) SN 930,000 to about 939,000. Numbered slide under firing pin stop plate. "P" marking on frame and top of slide. Commercial markings on Right side of slide on a few, otherwise blank. Parkerized finish. Right side of frame is marked "M1911A1 U.S. ARMY" forward of the slide stop pin, and "United States Property" behind the slide stop pin. Verified proof and final inspectors mark on trigger guard bow. "GHD "(Guy H. Drewry) marked on left side below slide stop. All appear to have British proofs as well. A few pistols in "Fair" condition have recently been sold without British proofs. These pistols were used in Canadian prisons and recently released. Beware non-British marked pistols in better than "Good" condition as some of these former prison pistols have appeared in "New" condition. Barrels marked "COLT .45 AUTO. Most have plain blued magazine. (add 30% for 99%-100%)

Exc.	V.G.	Good	Fair	Poor
1750	1350	800	600	400

Model of 1911A1, Military. 1944 production. (GHD marked)

SN 1,155,00 to about 1,155,000-1,208,673, and 1,609,529-1,720,000. Un-numbered slide. "P" marking on frame and top of slide. Parkerized. Right side of frame is marked "M1911A1 U.S. ARMY" forward of the slide stop pin, and "United States Property" behind the slide stop pin. Verified proof and final inspectors mark on trigger guard bow. "GHD

"(Guy H. Drewry) marked on left side below slide stop. Barrels marked "COLT .45 AUTO. Plain blued or contract magazine. (Subtract 5% to 10% for British proofs, most collectors prefer virgin pistols.) (add 30% for 99%-100%)

Exc.	V.G.	Good	Fair	Poor
975	825	650	550	350

Model of 1911A1, Military. 1945 production.

(GHD marked but a few were J.S.B. marked and a few were un-inspected.) SN 1,720,000-1,743,846, and 2,244,804-2,368,781. Un-numbered slide. "P" marking on frame and top of slide. Parkerized. Right side of frame is marked "M1911A1 U.S. ARMY" forward of the slide stop pin, and "United States Property" behind the slide stop pin. Verified proof and final inspectors mark on trigger guard bow. "GHD "(Guy H. Drewry) marked on left side below slide stop. Plain blued or contract magazine. Early Barrels marked "COLT .45 AUTO", later examples marked with a "C" in a square. (Subtract 5% to 10% for British proofs, most collectors prefer virgin pistols.) (add 30% for 99%-100%)

Exc.	V.G.	Good	Fair	Poor
1000	850	650	550	350

Model of 1911A1, Military. 1945 production.

(J.S.B.) around SN 2,360,600. Un-numbered slide. "P" marking on frame and top of slide. Parkerized. Right side of frame is marked "M1911A1 U.S. ARMY" forward of the slide stop pin, and "United States Property" behind the slide stop pin. Verified proof and final inspectors mark on trigger guard bow. "JSB" (John S. Begley) marked on left side below slide stop. Plain blued or contract magazine. Barrels marked with a "C" in a square. (Add 100% for J.S.B. marking. (Subtract 5% to 10% for British proofs, most collectors prefer virgin pistols.) (add 30%-50% for 99%-100%)

Exc.	V.G.	Good	Fair	Poor
2000	1500	1100	950	700

Colt, Model Of 1911A1, Military. 1945 Production.

(Un-inspected and usually no ordnance wheel.) around SN 2,360,600. Un-numbered slide. "P" marking on frame and top of slide. Parkerized. Right side of frame is marked "M1911A1 U.S. ARMY" forward of the slide stop pin, and "United States Property" behind the slide stop pin. Verified proof and final inspectors mark on trigger guard bow. Plain blued or contract magazine. Barrels marked with a "C" in a square. (Subtract 5% to 10% for British proofs, most collectors prefer virgin pistols.) (add 30% for 99%-100%)

Exc.	V.G.	Good	Fair	Poor
1600	1200	800	650	400

Ithaca Gun Co. 1943-1945 Production.

FJA inspected, un-numbered slide. Right side of frame is marked "M1911A1 U.S. ARMY" forward of the slide stop pin, and "United States Property" behind the slide stop pin. Plastic Keyes Fibre grips, stamped trigger, flat sided hammer, HS marked barrel, contract magazine. A few early pistols had an I prefix. I few into the 1.28 million range had the "MODEL OF 1911 U.S. Army" on the right side of the slide. (Subtract 5% to 10% for British proofs, most collectors prefer virgin pistols.) (add 30% for 99%-100%) (add 30% for "MODEL OF 1911A1 U.S. ARMY" marked slide.) (add 25% for Dulite finish, below SN 950,000)(add 150% for I prefix)

Exc.	V.G.	Good	Fair	Poor
900	875	750	550	350

Remington Rand Co. 1942-1943 production.

"NEW YORK" (Type I) marked slide. FJA inspected, un-numbered slide. Right side of frame is marked "M1911A1 U.S. ARMY" forward of the slide stop pin, and "United States Property" behind the slide stop pin. DU-LITE (Blued over sand blasting) finish. Plastic Keyes Fibre grips with no rings around screws, Milled trigger, flat sided hammer, "Colt .45 AUTO" marked barrel, contract magazine. Fine checkered mainspring housing. (Subtract 5% to 10% for British proofs, most collectors prefer virgin pistols.) (add 30% for 99%-100%)

Exc.	V.G.	Good	Fair	Poor
1500	1150	900	650	450

Remington Rand Co. 1942-1943 production.

Large "N. Y." (Type II) marked slide. FJA inspected, un-numbered slide. Right side of frame is marked "M1911A1 U.S. ARMY" forward of the slide stop pin, and "United States Property" behind the slide stop pin. DU-LITE (Blued over sand blasting) finish. Plastic Keyes Fibre grips with small rings around screws, Stamped trigger, flat sided hammer, "HS" marked barrel, contract magazine. Fine checkered mainspring housing. (Subtract 5% to 10% for British proofs, most collectors prefer virgin pistols.) (add 30% for 99%-100%)

Exc.	V.G.	Good	Fair	Poor
900	700	600	450	300

A Remington Rand Model 1911A1 pistol was sold at auction for $977.50. Produced in 1943. Condition was excellent with original box. Amoskeag Auction Co., Inc., January, 2000

Remington Rand Co. 1942-1943 Production.

Small "N. Y." (Type III) marked slide. FJA inspected, un-numbered slide. Right side of frame is marked "M1911A1 U.S. ARMY" forward of the slide stop pin, and "United States Property" behind the slide stop pin. Parkerized (Phosphate over sand blasting) finish. Plastic Keyes Fibre grips with small rings around screws, Stamped trigger, flat sided hammer, "HS" marked barrel, contract magazine. Serrated mainspring housing. (Subtract 5% to 10% for British proofs, most collectors prefer virgin pistols.) (add 30% for 99%-100%)

Exc.	V.G.	Good	Fair	Poor
775	675	575	400	275

Remington Rand Co. 1942-1945 Production.

Numbered Presentation pistol (all observed are Type III) marked slide. They were usually disposed of as give-aways to contracting personnel and employees, however several remained in the company safe long after WWII until they were eventually sold. No inspector, un-numbered slide. The only frame marking is a 2 or three digit number above trigger right. Parkerized (Phosphate over sand blasting) finish. Plastic Keyes Fibre grips with small rings around screws, Stamped trigger, flat sided hammer, "HS" marked barrel, contract magazine. Serrated mainspring housing. (add 30% for 99%-100%)

Exc.	V.G.	Good	Fair	Poor
1900	1300	900	700	600

Remington Rand Co. 1942-1945 Production.

ERRS prefix Presentation pistol (all observed are Type III) marked slide. They were usually disposed of as give-aways to contracting personnel and employees, however several remained in the company safe long after WWII until they were eventually sold. No inspector, un-numbered slide. The only frame marking is a 2 or three digit number with the "ERRS" prefix above trigger right. Parkerized (Phosphate over sand blasting) finish. Plastic Keyes Fibre grips with small rings around screws, Stamped trigger, flat sided hammer, "HS" marked barrel, contract magazine. Serrated mainspring housing. Popular wisdom seems to be that "ERRS" meant "Experimental Remington Rand" however there seems to be no evidence to support that notion. The true meaning of ERRS may never be known. (add 30% for 99%-100%)

Exc.	V.G.	Good	Fair	Poor
1900	1300	900	700	600

UNION SWITCH SIGNAL CO.

Swissvale Pennsylvania. 55,000 pistols total delivered in 1943. US&S pistols have become one of the most sought after of all the 1911/1911A1 pistols.

Courtesy Karl Karash Collection

Union Switch Signal Co. 1943 Production. Type I

(No "P" on frame or slide. From SN 1,041,405 to about 1,060,000 with probable overlap. RCD inspected, un-numbered slide. Right side of frame is marked "M1911A1 U.S. AR-

MY" forward of the slide stop pin, and "United States Property" behind the slide stop pin. DU-LITE (Blued over sand blasting) finish. Plastic Keyes Fibre grips with no rings around screws, Stamped, blued trigger, flat sided hammer, "HS" marked barrel, contract magazine. Checkered mainspring housing. (add 30% for 99%-100%)

Exc.	V.G.	Good	Fair	Poor
1700	1300	900	700	500

Union Switch Signal Co. 1943 Production. Type II

("P" on top edge of slide.) From about SN 1,060,000 to about 1,080,000 with probable overlap. RCD inspected, un-numbered slide. Right side of frame is marked "M1911A1 U.S. ARMY" forward of the slide stop pin, and "United States Property" behind the slide stop pin. DU-LITE (Blued over sand blasting) finish. Plastic Keyes Fibre grips with no rings around screws, Stamped, blued trigger, flat sided hammer, "HS" marked barrel, contract magazine. Checkered mainspring housing.(add 30% for 99%-100%)

Exc.	V.G.	Good	Fair	Poor
1700	1300	900	700	500

Union Switch Signal Co. 1943 Production. Type III

("P" on frame and slide in the usual location. From about SN 1,080,000 to 1,096,404 with probable overlap. RCD inspected, un-numbered slide. Right side of frame is marked "M1911A1 U.S. ARMY" forward of the slide stop pin, and "United States Property" behind the slide stop pin. DU-LITE (Blued over sand blasting) finish. Plastic Keyes Fibre grips with no rings around screws, Stamped, blued trigger, flat sided hammer, "HS" marked barrel, contract magazine. Checkered mainspring housing. (add 30% for 99%-100%)

Exc.	V.G.	Good	Fair	Poor
1800	1350	900	700	500

Union Switch Signal Co. 1943 Production. Exp.

About 100 Pistols. ("EXP" on frame partially under right grip. These pistols generally have some defect about them which may have caused them to be rejected and written off. They were generally disposed of as give-aways to contracting personnel and employees. No inspector, un-numbered slide. Some pistols were finished with the DU-LITE process (Blued over sand blasting) that closely resembled the finish of the delivered military pistols. Other EXP marked pistols were blued over such heavy buffing that the pistols have an amateur look about them. This along with the crudeness of the markings might lead one to question the authenticity of the blued EXPs. However most evidence indicates that they are indeed genuine US&S made pistols. Popular wisdom seems to be that "EXP" meant "Experimental" however there seems to be no evidence to support that notion. Plastic Keyes Fibre grips with no rings around screws, Stamped, blued trigger, flat sided hammer, "HS" marked barrel, contract magazine. checkered mainspring housing. (add 30% for 99%-100%) Most have type II slides.

Exc.	V.G.	Good	Fair	Poor
3000	2250	1700	1200	800

7 Digit X Numbered Rework

These pistols were renumbered when their original serial numbers were either defaced, obliterated, or became too light to read during rebuilding or refinishing. the seven digit X prefix numbers (X2693614 through X2695212) were assigned to various arsenals from 1949 to 1957. Some of the reworks are done in small batches and are more distinctive and collectable than the 4 digit X numbers. All are considered "Arsenal Refinished".

Exc.	V.G.	Good	Fair	Poor
1100	850	700	500	350

State of New York Government Model

Serial number 255000-C to about 258000-C with factory roll mark "PROPERTY OF THE STATE OF NEW YORK" with a verified proof and "government model" marking. A few of the parts were leftover military. This is a state militia pistol. (99% to 100% finish add 33%. For the few consecutive pairs know add 15% premium.)

Exc.	V.G.	Good	Fair	Poor
1100	800	600	500	350

Military National Match

these are .45 caliber pistols rebuilt from service pistols at Springfield Armory between 1955 and about 1967. these pistols were built and rebuilt each year with a portion being sold to competitors by the NRA. Each year improvements were added to the rebuild program. Four articles in the "American Rifleman" document these pistols well: August, 1959; April, 1963: June, 1966: and July, 1966. Many parts for these pistols have been available and many "Look Alike" pistols have been built by basement armorers. Pistols generally came with a numbered box or papers. Less box and papers deduct 40%. When well worn these pistols offer little over a standard pistol.

Exc.	V.G.	Good	Fair	Poor
1400	1000	700	550	350

SMITH & WESSON

NOTE: For historical information, photos and technical data see Jim supica and Richard Nahas, *Standard Catalog of Smith & Wesson*, Krause Publications.

.38 Safety Hammerless Army Test Revolver

There were 100 sold to U.S. government in 1890. They have 3rd Model features but are in the 2nd Model serial number range, 41333-41470. Fitted with 6" barrels and marked "US".

CAUTION: Be very wary of fakes. Seek an expert appraisal prior to a sale.

Exc.	V.G.	Good	Fair	Poor
10000	7000	5000	3000	2000

Model 3 American 1st Model

This model represented a number of firsts for the Smith & Wesson Company. It was the first of the top break, automatic ejection revolvers. It was also the first Smith & Wesson in a large caliber (it is chambered for the .44 S&W American cartridge as well as the .44 Henry rimfire on rare occasions). It was also known as the 1st Model American. This large revolver is offered with an 8" round barrel with a raised rib as standard. Barrel lengths of 6" and 7" were also available. It has a 6-shot fluted cylinder and a square butt with walnut grips. It is blued or nickel-plated. It is interesting to note that this model appeared three years before Colt's Single Action Army and perhaps, more than any other model, was associated with the historic American West. There were only 8,000 manufactured between 1870 and 1872.

U.S. Army Order-Serial Number Range 125-2199

One thousand produced with "U.S." stamped on top of barrel; "OWA, on left grip.

Exc.	Fine	V.G	Good	Fair
15000	9000	5500	3250	2500

NOTE: Add 10% premium for original nickel finish.

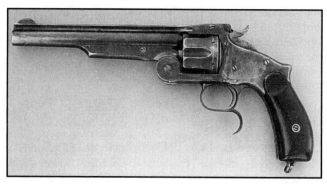
Courtesy Jim Supica, Old Town Station

Model 3 Russian 1st Model-Cyrillic

This model is quite similar in appearance to the American 1st and 2nd Model revolvers. S&W made several internal changes to this model to satisfy the Russian government. The markings on this revolver are distinct; and the caliber for which it is chambered, .44 S&W Russian, is different. There were approximately 20,000 Russian-Contract revolvers. The serial number range is 1-20000. They are marked in Russian Cyrillic letters. The Russian double-headed eagle is stamped on the rear portion of the barrel with inspector's marks underneath it. All of the contract guns have 8" barrels and lanyard swivels on the butt. These are rarely encountered, as most were shipped to Russia. The commercial run of this model numbered approximately 4,655. The barrels are stamped in English and include the words "Russian Model." Some are found with 6" and 7" barrels, as well as the standard 8". There were also 500 revolvers that were rejected from the Russian contract series and sold on the commercial market. Some of these are marked in English; some, Cyrillic. Some have the Cyrillic markings ground off and the English restamped. This model was manufactured from 1871 to 1874.

Russian Contract Model-Cyrillic barrel address

Exc.	V.G.	Good	Fair	Poor
—	7000	3500	2000	—

Model 3 Russian 2nd Model-Foreign contracts

This revolver was known as the "Old Model Russian." This is a complicated model to understand as there are many variations within the model designation. The serial numbering is quite complex as well, and values vary greatly due to relatively minor model differences. Before purchasing this model, it would be advisable to secure competent appraisal as well as to read reference materials solely devoted to this firearm. This model is chambered for the .44 S&W Russian, as well as the .44 rimfire Henry cartridge. It has a 7" barrel and a round butt featuring a projection on the frame that fits into the thumb web. The grips are walnut, and the finish is blue or nickel-plated. The triggerguard has a reverse curved spur on the bottom. There were approximately 85,200 manufactured between 1873 and 1878.

Russian Contract Model

70,000 made; rare, as most were shipped to Russia. Cyrillic markings; lanyard swivel on butt.

Exc.	V.G.	Good	Fair	Poor
—	3500	1750	950	—

1st Model Turkish Contract

.44 rimfire Henry, special rimfire frames, serial-numbered in own serial number range 1-1000.

Exc.	V.G.	Good	Fair	Poor
—	6000	3750	1750	—

2nd Model Turkish Contract

Made from altered centerfire frames from the regular commercial serial number range. 1,000 made. Use caution with this model.

Exc.	V.G.	Good	Fair	Poor
—	4500	2250	1000	—

Japanese Govt. Contract

Five thousand made between the 1-9000 serial number range. The Japanese naval insignia, an anchor over two wavy lines, found on the butt. The barrel is Japanese proofed, and the words "Jan.19, 75 REISSUE July 25, 1871" are stamped on the barrel, as well.

Exc.	V.G.	Good	Fair	Poor
—	3500	1700	950	—

Model 3 Russian 3rd Model -Foreign contracts

This revolver is also known as the "New Model Russian." The factory referred to this model as the Model of 1874 or the Cavalry Model. It is chambered for the .44 S&W Russian and the .44 Henry rimfire cartridge. The barrel is 6.5", and the round butt is the same humped-back affair as the 2nd Model. The grips are walnut; and the finish, blue or nickel-plated. The most notable differences in appearance between this model and the 2nd Model are the shorter extractor housing under the barrel and the integral front sight blade instead of the pinned-on one found on the previous models. This is another model that bears careful research before attempting to evaluate. Minor variances can greatly affect values. Secure detailed reference materials and qualified appraisal. There were approximately 60,638 manufactured between 1874 and 1878.

Turkish Model

Five thousand made of altered centerfire frames, made to fire .44 rimfire Henry. "W" inspector's mark on butt and "CW" cartouche on grip. Fakes have been noted; be aware.

Exc.	V.G	Good	Fair	Poor
—	4500	2700	900	—

Japanese Contract Model

One thousand made; has the Japanese naval insignia, an anchor over two wavy lines, stamped on the bottom of the frame strap.

Exc.	V.G	Good	Fair	Poor
—	3100	1950	850	—

Russian Contract Model

Barrel markings are in Russian Cyrillic. Approximately 41,100 were produced.

Exc.	V.G	Good	Fair	Poor
—	3100	1950	850	—

Model 3 Russian 3rd Model (Loewe & Tula Copies)

The German firm of Ludwig Loewe produced a copy of this model that is nearly identical to the S&W. This German revolver was made under Russian contract, as well as for commercial sales. The contract model has different Cyrillic markings than the S&W and the letters "HK" as inspector's marks. The commercial model has the markings in English. The Russian arsenal at Tula also produced a copy of this revolver with a different Cyrillic dated stamping on the barrel.

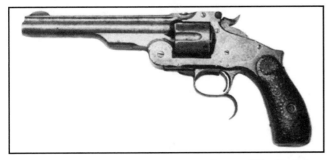

Courtesy Mike Stuckslager

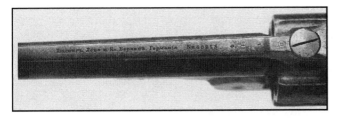

Courtesy Mike Stuckslager

Loewe

Exc.	V.G	Good	Fair	Poor
—	2900	1750	700	—

Tula

Exc.	V.G	Good	Fair	Poor
—	3350	2000	800	—

Model 3 Schofield

In 1870 Major George W. Schofield heard about the new S&W Model 3 revolver and wrote to the company expressing a desire to be an exclusive sales representative for them. At that time S&W was earnestly attempting to interest the government in this revolver and obviously felt that the Major could be of help in this endeavor, perhaps because his brother, General John Schofield, was president of the Small Arms Board. Major Schofield was sent one Model 3 revolver and 500 rounds of ammunition free of charge. After testing the revolver, Schofield felt that it needed a few changes to make it the ideal cavalry sidearm. With the company's approval, Schofield made these changes and secured patents. The company eventually began production of what became known as the Model 3 Schofield 1st Model. The Major was paid a 50 cents royalty per revolver. The eventual production of this model ran to a total of 8,969, with the last one sold in 1878. What was hoped to be the adopted government-issue sidearm never materialized—for a number of reasons. First, the Colt Single Action Army being used by the cavalry had a longer chamber than the S&W and could fire the Schofield ammunition. The Schofield could not fire the longer Colt .45 cartridges. This resulted in disastrous mix-ups on more than one occasion, when Colt ammunition was issued to troops armed with the Schofields. The company was not happy about paying the 50 cents royalty to Major Schofield. Sales of their other models were high; and they simply did not care about this model, so they eventually ceased its production. It was a popular model on the American frontier and is quite historically significant.

Model 3 Schofield 1st Model

The modifications that made this model differ from the other Model 3 revolvers were quite extensive. The Schofield is chambered for the .45 S&W Schofield cartridge. The top break latch was moved from the barrel assembly to the frame. It was modified so that the action could be opened by simply pulling back on the latch with the thumb. This made it much easier to reload on horseback, as the reins would not have to be released. A groove was milled in the top of the raised barrel rib to improve the sighting plain. The extractor was changed to a cam-operated rather than rack-and-gear system. The removal of the cylinder was simplified. There were 3,000 contract Schofields and 35 commercial models. The contract revolvers were delivered to the Springfield Armory in July of 1875. These guns are stamped "US" on the butt and have the initials "L" and "P" marking various other parts. The grips have an inspector's cartouche with the initials "JFEC." There were 35 1st Models made for and sold to the civilian market; these revolvers do not have the "US" markings. The Schofield has a 7" barrel, 6-shot fluted cylinder, and walnut grips. The 1st Model is blued, with a nickel-plated original finish gun being extremely rare.

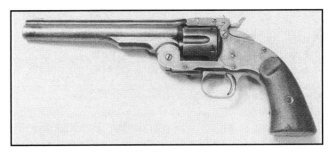

Courtesy Mike Stuckslager

"US" Contract-3,000 Issued

Exc.	V.G.	Good	Fair	Poor
8000	4500	2700	1750	1000

A Smith & Wesson Model 3 Schofield 1st model sold at auction for $54,625. Fitted with a 7" barrel and stamped "S.B.L." cartouche. Condition was excellent. Butterfield & Butterfield, November, 1999

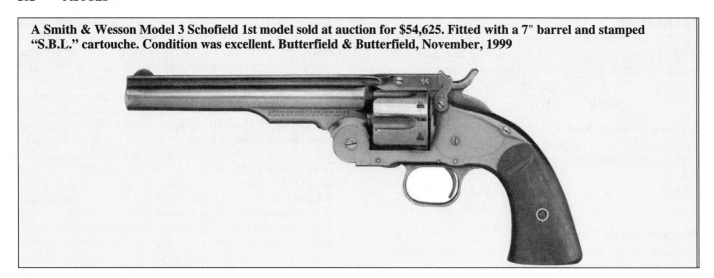

Civilian Model, No "US" markings

35 Made-Very Rare, Use Caution. UNABLE TO PRICE. At least double the military model values. Expert appraisal needed.

Model 3 Schofield 2nd Model

The difference between the 1st and 2nd Model Schofield revolvers is in the barrel latch system. The 2nd Model latch is rounded and knurled to afford an easier and more positive grip when opening the revolver. A group of 3,000 of these revolvers was delivered to the Springfield Armory in October of 1876, and another 2,000 were delivered in 1877. These 2nd Model contract revolvers were all blued. There were an additional 649 civilian guns sold as well. The civilian models were not "US" marked and were offered either blued or nickel-plated. A total of 8,969 Model 3 Schofield 2nd Models were manufactured. The last sale was recorded in 1878.

Courtesy Jim Supica, Old Town Station

"US" Contract-4,000 Issued

Exc.	V.G.	Good	Fair	Poor
7500	4000	2500	1600	950

Civilian Model-646 Made

Exc.	V.G.	Good	Fair	Poor
6250	3600	2150	1400	900

Model 3 Schofield-Surplus Models

Many Schofields were issued to various states under the Militia Act, some of which were used in the spanish American War. After the government dropped the Schofield as an issue cavalry sidearm, the remaining U.S. inventory of these revolvers was sold off as military surplus. Many were sold to dealers such as Bannerman's or Schuyler, Hartley & Graham, two large gun dealers who then resold the guns to supply the growing need for guns on the Western frontier. Schuyler, Hartley & Graham sold a number of guns to the Wells Fargo Express Co. Almost all of these weapons had the barrels shortened to 5", as were many others sold during this period. Some were nickeled plated. Beware of fakes when contemplating purchase of the Wells Fargo revolvers.

Wells Fargo & Co. Model

Exc.	V.G.	Good	Fair	Poor
7000	3750	2500	1500	1000

Surplus Cut Barrel-Not Wells Fargo

Exc.	V.G.	Good	Fair	Poor
3000	1800	1400	1100	800

New Model No. 3 Single Action

Always interested in perfecting the Model 3 revolver D.B. Wesson redesigned and improved the old Model 3 in the hopes of attracting more sales. The Russian contracts were almost filled so the company decided to devote the effort necessary to improve on this design. In 1877 this project was undertaken. The extractor housing was shortened; the cylinder retention system was improved; and the shape of the grip was changed to a more streamlined and attractive configuration. This New Model has a 3.5", 4", 5", 6", 6.5", 7", 7.5", or 8" barrel length with a 6-shot fluted cylinder. The 6.5" barrel and .44 S&W Russian chambering is the most often encountered variation of this model, but the factory considered the 8" barrels as standard and these were kept in stock as well. The New Model No. 3 was also chambered for .32 S&W, .32-44 S&W, .320 S&W Rev. Rifle, .38 S&W, .38- 40,.38-44 S&W, .41 S&W, .44 Henry rimfire, .44 S&W American, .44-40, .45 S&W Schofield, .450 Rev., .45 Webley, .455 MkI and .455 MkII. They are either blued or nickel-plated and have checkered hard rubber grips with the S&W logo molded into them, or walnut grips. There are many sub-variations within this model designation, and the potential collector should secure detailed reference material that deals with this model. There were approximately 35,796 of these revolvers manufactured between 1878 and 1912. Nearly 40 percent were exported to fill contracts with Japan, Australia, Argentina, England, Spain, and Cuba. There were some sent to Asia, as well. The proofmarks of these countries will establish their provenance but will not add appreciably to standard values.

Standard Model-6.5" barrel, .44 S&W Russian

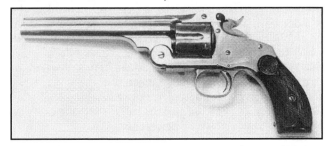

Courtesy Mike Stuckslager

Exc.	V.G.	Good	Fair	Poor
—	3700	2000	1000	—

Japanese Naval Contract

This was the largest foreign purchaser of this model. There were over 1,500 produced with the anchor insignia stamped on the frame.

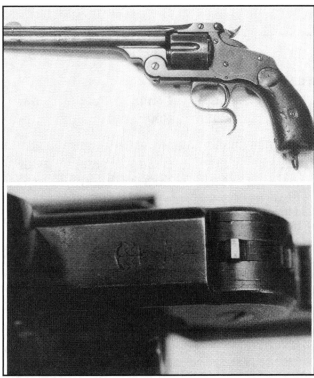

Courtesy Mike Stuckslager

Exc.	V.G.	Good	Fair	Poor
—	3700	2000	1000	—

Japanese Artillery Contract

This variation is numbered in the 25,000 serial range. They are blued, with a 7" barrel and a lanyard swivel on the butt. Japanese characters are stamped on the extractor housing.

Exc.	V.G.	Good	Fair	Poor
—	5000	2500	1250	—

Maryland Militia Model

This variation is nickel-plated, has a 6.5" barrel, and is chambered for the .44 S&W Russian cartridge. The butt is stamped "U.S.," and the inspector's marks "HN" and "DAL" under the date 1878 appear on the revolver. There were 280 manufactured between serial-numbers 7126 and 7405.

Exc.	V.G.	Good	Fair	Poor
—	10000	6000	3000	—

NOTE: Rarity makes valuation speculative.

Australian Contract

This variation is nickel-plated, is chambered for the .44 S&W Russian cartridge, and is marked with the Australian Colonial Police Broad Arrow on the butt. There were 250 manufactured with 7" barrels and detachable shoulder stocks. The stock has the Broad Arrow stamped on the lower tang. There were also 30 manufactured with 6.5" barrels without the stocks. They all are numbered in the 12,000-13,000 serial range.

NOTE: The total number of these revolvers made is greater than the number mentioned but no exact number can be given.

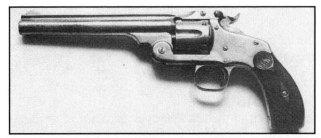

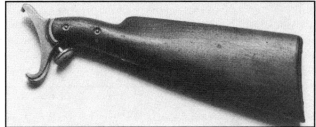

Courtesy Mike Stuckslager

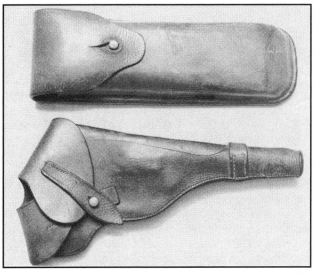

Courtesy Mike Stuckslager

Revolver with stock and holsters

Exc.	V.G.	Good	Fair	Poor
—	8000	4750	2750	—

NOTE: Deduct 40% for no stock.

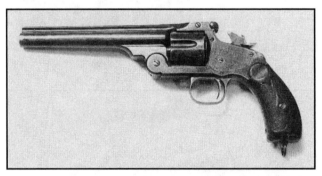

A Smith & Wesson New Model No. 3 Australian with match numbered holster and shoulder stock sold at auction for $12,650. Nickel finish was good. Faintich Auction Service, October 1999

Paul Goodwin Photo

Argentine Model

This was essentially not a factory contract but a sale through Schuyler, Hartley and Graham. They are stamped "Ejercito/Argentino" in front of the triggerguard. The order amounted to some 2,000 revolvers between the serial numbers 50 and 3400.

Exc.	V.G.	Good	Fair	Poor
—	7000	3500	1750	—

Turkish Model

This is essentially the New Model No. 3 chambered for the .44 rimfire Henry cartridge. It is stamped with the letters "P," "U" and "AFC" on various parts of the revolver. The barrels are all 6.5"; the finish, blued with walnut grips. Lanyard swivels are found on the butt. There were 5,461 manufactured and serial numbered in their own range, starting at 1 through 5,461 between 1879 and 1883.

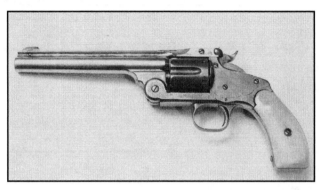

Courtesy Mike Stuckslager

Exc.	V.G.	Good	Fair	Poor
—	7000	3500	1750	—

U.S. Revenue Cutter Service (U.S. Coast Guard)

This model was issued to the U.S. Revenue Cutter Service as a standard issue sidearm. Fitted with 5", 6", or 6.5" barrels. The revolver is not marked but there are known serial numbers that identify this as a military variation. Consult an expert prior to sale, or see *Standard Catalog of Smith & Wesson* page 68 for a list of known serial numbers.

Exc.	V.G.	Good	Fair	Poor
—	12500	5000	2750	—

New Model No. 3 Frontier Single Action

This is another model similar in appearance to the standard New Model No. 3. It has a 4", 5", or 6.5" barrel and is chambered for the .44-40 Winchester Centerfire cartridge. Because

the original New Model No. 3 cylinder was 1-7/16" in length this would not accommodate the longer .44-40 cartridge. The cylinder on the No. 3 Frontier was changed to 1-9/16" in length. Later the company converted 786 revolvers to .44 S&W Russian and sold them to Japan. This model is either blued or nickel-plated and has checkered grips of walnut or hard rubber. They are serial numbered in their own range from 1 through 2072 and were manufactured from 1885 until 1908. This model was designed to compete with the Colt Single Action Army but was not successful.

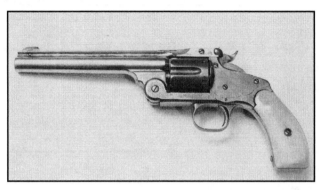

Courtesy Mike Stuckslager

.44-40-Commercial Model

Exc.	V.G.	Good	Fair	Poor
—	5000	2500	1250	—

Japanese Purchase Converted to .44 S&W Russian

Exc.	V.G.	Good	Fair	Poor
—	4000	2000	1000	—

.38 Hand Ejector Military & Police 1st Model or Model of 1899

This was an early swing-out cylinder revolver, and it has no front lockup for the action. The release is on the left side of the frame. This model is chambered for .38 S&W Special cartridge and the .32 Winchester centerfire cartridge (.32-20), has a 6-shot fluted cylinder, and was offered with a 4", 5", 6", 6.5", or 8" barrel in .38 caliber and 4", 5", and 6-1/2" in .32-20 caliber. The finish is blued or nickel-plated; the grips, checkered walnut or hard rubber. There were approximately 20,975 manufactured between 1899 and 1902 in .38 caliber; serial number range 1 to 20,975. In the .32-20 caliber 5,311 were sold between 1899 and 1902; serial number range 1 to 5311.

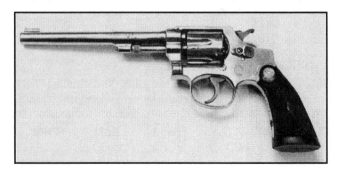

Courtesy Mike Stuckslager

Commercial Model

Exc.	V.G.	Good	Fair	Poor
750	650	600	450	350

U.S. Navy Model

One thousand produced in 1900, .38 S&W, 6" barrel, blued with checkered walnut grips, "U.S.N." stamped on butt, serial number range 5000 to 6000.

Exc.	V.G.	Good	Fair	Poor
1300	1000	700	500	300

U.S. Army Model

One thousand produced in 1901, same as Navy Model except that it is marked "U.S.Army/Model 1899" on butt, "K.S.M." and "J.T.T." on grips, serial number range 13001 to 14000.

Exc.	V.G.	Good	Fair	Poor
1300	1000	700	500	300

.38 Hand Ejector Military & Police 2nd Model or Model of 1902-U.S. Navy Model

Chambered for .38 Long colt cartridge with Navy serial number range 1001 to 2000. Marked "u.s.n." with anchor stamped on butt. Smith & Wesson serial number stamped on front tang in the 25001 to 26000 serial range. Some 1025 revolvers were produced.

Exc.	V.G.	Good	Fair	Poor
1300	1000	700	500	300

.45 Hand Ejector U.S. Service Model of 1917

WWI was on the horizon, and it seemed certain that the United States would become involved. The S&W people began to work with the Springfield Armory to develop a hand-ejector model that would fire the .45-caliber Government cartridge. This was accomplished in 1916 by the use of half-moon clips. The new revolver is quite similar to the .44 Hand Ejector in appearance. It has a 5.5" barrel, blued finish with smooth walnut grips, and a lanyard ring on the butt. The designation "U.S.Army Model 1917" is stamped on the butt. After the war broke out, the government was not satisfied with S&W's production and actually took control of the company for the duration of the war. This was the first time that the company was not controlled by a Wesson. The factory records indicate that there were 163,476 Model 1917s manufactured between 1917 and 1919, the WWI years. After the war, the sale of these revolvers continued on a commercial and contract basis until 1949, when this model was finally dropped from the S&W product line.

Military Model

Exc.	V.G.	Good	Fair	Poor
500	350	300	200	150

Commercial Model

High gloss blue and checkered walnut grips.

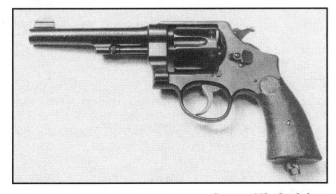

Courtesy Mike Stuckslager

Exc.	V.G.	Good	Fair	Poor
600	450	350	275	200

.455 Mark II Hand Ejector 1st Model

This model was designed the same as the .44 Hand Ejector 1st Model with no caliber stamping on the barrel. It has a barrel length of 6.4". Of the 5,000 revolvers produced and sold only 100 were commercial guns, the rest were military. Produced between 1914 and 1915. The commercial model is worth a premium.

Exc.	V.G.	Good	Fair	Poor
700	575	400	300	200

.455 Mark II Hand Ejector 2nd Model

Similar to the first model without an extractor shroud. Barrel length was also 6.5". Serial number range was 5000 to 74755. Manufactured from 1915 to 1917.

Exc.	V.G.	Good	Fair	Poor
450	300	250	225	175

Model 10 (.38 Military & Police)-Military Marked

This model has been in production in one configuration or another since 1899. It was always the mainstay of the S&W line and was originally known as the .38 Military and Police Model. The Model 10 is built on the K, or medium frame, and was always meant as a duty gun. It was offered with a 2", 3", 4", 5", or 6" barrel. Currently only the 4" and 6" are available. A round or square butt is offered. It is chambered for the .38 Special, 38S&W, and .22 rimfire and is offered in blue or nickel-plate, with checkered walnut grips. The Model designation is stamped on the yoke on all S&W revolvers. This model, with many other modern S&W pistols, underwent several engineering changes. These changes may affect the value of the pistol and an expert should be consulted. The dates of these changes are as follows:

10-None-1957	**10-4-1962**
10-1-1959	**10-5-1962**
10-2-1961	**10-6-1962**
10-3-1961	

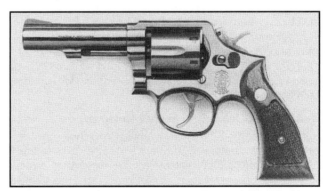

NIB	Exc.	V.G.	Good	Fair	Poor
450	350	250	150	125	90

Victory Model

Manufactured during WWII, this is a Model 10 with a sand-blasted and parkerized finish, a lanyard swivel, and smooth walnut grips. The serial number has a V prefix. This model was available in only 2" and 4" barrel lengths. The Victory Model was discontinued on April 27, 1945, with serial number VS811,119.

Victory Model marked "N.Y.M.I." • Courtesy Richard M. Kumor, Sr.

Exc.	V.G.	Good	Fair	Poor
275	200	150	100	75

Navy marked Smith & Wesson Victory model • Courtesy Amoskeag Auction, Co., Inc.

NOTE: Top strap marked Navy will bring a 75% premium. Navy variation with both top strap and side plate marked will bring a 100% premium. Navy variation marked "N.Y.M.I." will bring a 125% premium. Revolvers marked "U.S.G.C." or "U.S.M.C." will bring a premium of unknown amount. Exercise caution.

Model 11 (.38/200 British Service Revolver)

First produced in 1938 S&W manufactured these revolvers for the British Commonwealth in 4", 5", or 6" barrels. Early models are bright blue later models are parkerized. Square butt with checkered walnut grips. Lend Lease guns marked "UNITED STATES PROPERTY". Production ended in 1945 with 568,204 built. Nicknamed the .38/200 British Service Revolver. Smith & Wesson began producing this model again in 1947 and sold many of these throughout the 1950s and 1960s when production ceased again in 1965. There are several rare variations of this model that will greatly affect its value. Consult an expert if special markings and barrel lengths are encountered.

Exc.	V.G.	Good	Fair	Poor
275	200	150	100	75

USAF M-13 (Aircrewman)

From 1952 to about 1957 the Air Force purchased a large quantity of Model 12s with alloy frames and cylinders. They were intended for use by flight crews as survival weapons in emergencies. This model was not officially designated "13" by S&W, but the Air Force requested these revolvers be stamped "M13" on the top strap. This model was rejected by the Air Force in 1960 because of trouble with the alloy cylinder.

NOTE: Beware of fakes. Seek expert advice before purchase.

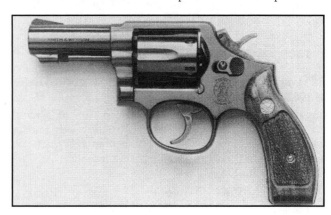

Exc.	V.G.	Good	Fair	Poor
800	750	600	450	250

Model 39 Steel Frame

Semiautomatic pistol chambered for the 9mm cartridge. Fitted with a 4" barrel, walnut stocks, blue finish, and adjustable rear sight. Military version of this pistol has a dull blue finish, no walnut grips, with double action trigger. Manufactured from 1954 to 1966. Some of these military models are found without serial numbers. A special variation was used with a suppressor in Vietnam, and modified with a slide lock for single shot. Named the "Hush Puppy".

NOTE: Pricing does not include the suppressor.

Exc.	V.G.	Good	Fair	Poor
1200	900	700	500	300

Model 56 (KXT-38 USAF)

Introduced in 1962 this is a 2" heavy barrel built on the K-frame. It is chambered for the .38 Special. There were approximately 15,000 of these revolvers built when it was discontinued in 1964. It was marked "US" on the backstrap. A total of 15,205 produced but most destroyed.

NIB	Exc.	V.G.	Good	Fair	Poor
2500	1750	1250	750	500	250

HIGH STANDARD

Model B-US

A version of the Model B with slight modifications to the frame. 14,000 made for the US government 1942-1943. Monogramed hard rubber grips. Blued finish. Black checkered hard rubber grips. Available with a 4.5" round barrel. Type II takedown only.

Exc.	V.G.	Good	Fair	Poor
750	500	275	180	150

Model USA-Model HD

Similar to the Model HD but 4.5" barrel only. Had fixed sights, checkered black hard rubber grips and an external safety. Early models blued; later model parkerized. Introduced 1943; approximately 44,000 produced for the US government.

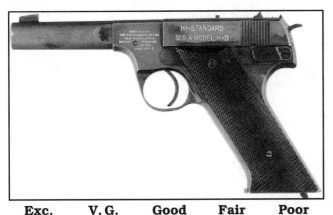

Exc.	V. G.	Good	Fair	Poor
750	550	400	250	175

Model USA-Model HD-MS

A silenced variation of the USA Model HD. Approximately About 2500 produced for the OSS during 1944 and 1945. 6.75" shrouded barrel. Early models blued; later model parkerized. Only a few registered with BATF for civilian ownership. All NFA rules apply.

Model HD-MS • Courtesy Chuck Karwan

Exc.	V. G.	Good	Fair	Poor
6000	5000	—	—	—

HECKLER & KOCH
See also-Germany

H&K Mark 23 model O (SOCOM)

Very similar to the H&K's US government contract pistol developed for US military special operation units. Chambered for the .45 ACP and fitted with a 5.87" barrel, this pistol has a polymer frame with steel slide. Magazine capacity is 10 rounds on civilian models and 12 rounds on military models. Barrel is threaded for noise suppressor. Weight is about 42 oz. Limited availability in fall 1996 to about 2,000 pistols.

NIB	Exc.	V.G.	Good	Fair	Poor
1900	1550	1250	—	—	—

Mk 23 Suppressor

This is the same suppressor as sold to the US military for use on the Mark 23 pistol. This unit can be fitted to the threaded barrel of the MK 23 and be compensated for point of aim. With water the dB sound reduction is 33-35dB. Produced by Knight Armament Corp. of Vero Beach, FL. This suppressor, with a different piston assembly, can be fitted to the USP Tactical.

NIB	Exc.	V.G.	Good	Fair	Poor
1250	—	—	—	—	—

NOTE: Suppressors require a Class III transfer tax. All NFA rules apply to the sale or purchase of these suppressors.

BERETTA
See also-Italy

Model M9 Limited Edition

Introduced in 1995 to commemorate the 10th anniversary of the U.S. military's official sidearm this 9mm pistol is limited to 10,000 units. Special engraving on the slide with special serial numbers. Slide stamped "U.S. 9MM M9-BERETTA U.S.A.-65490".

Standard Model

NIB	Exc.	V.G.	Good	Fair	Poor
750	600	400	300	200	100

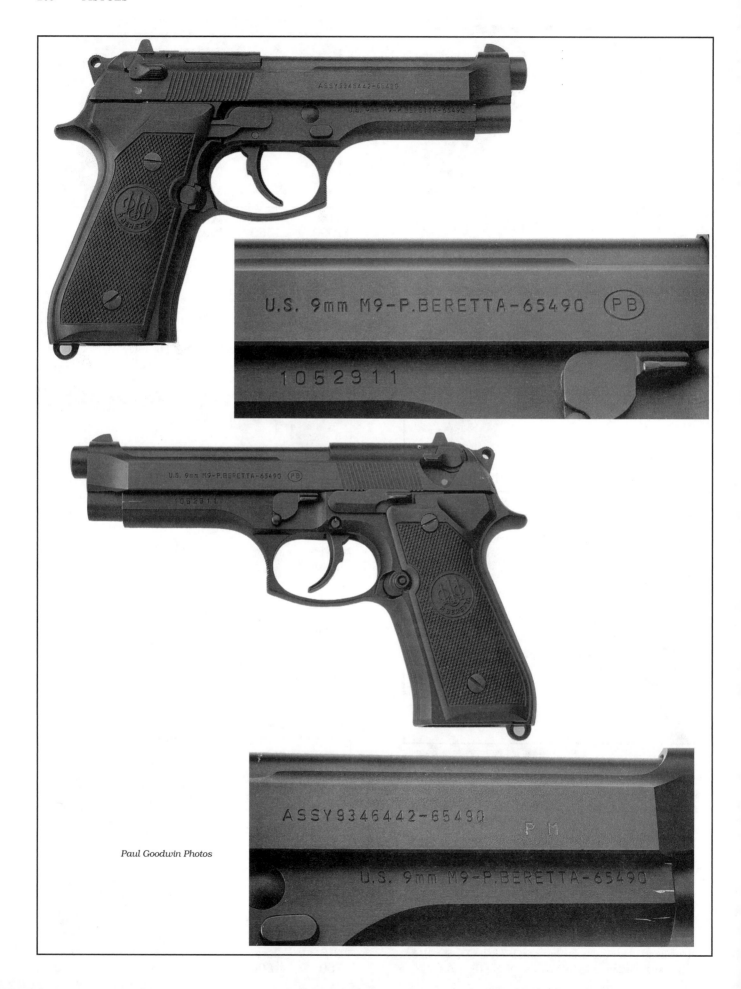

Paul Goodwin Photos

Deluxe Model-Walnut grips with gold plated hammer and grip screws.

NIB	Exc.	V.G.	Good	Fair	Poor
850	700	450	350	200	100

SAVAGE

Model 1907/10/11

Manufactured in 1905 in .45ACP this pistol was tested in the US Army trials. A few were sold commercially. It weighs 32 oz., and has an overall length of 9". Magazine capacity is 8 rounds. Checkered two-piece walnut grips. Blued finish. An improved version was built in 1910 and another version was built in 1911. This last version was a completely re-designed pistol; the Model 1911. Some 288 pistols were built in three different versions. Once the Army Trials were over Savage refinished the pistols with a matte blue finish and sold some of them commercially.

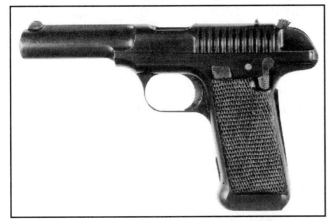

Courtesy James Rankin

Exc.	V.G.	Good	Fair	Poor
5500	4500	3500	2000	1000

Model 1917

This semi automatic pistol is chambered for the 7.65mm cartridge. It is fitted with an external hammer and without the grip safety. The form of the grip frame as been widened. Manufactured between 1917 and 1928. This pistol was sold to the French government during World War I and used by the French military. Approximately 27,000 of these pistols were sold to France. See also *France, Handguns, Savage.*

Exc.	V.G.	Good	Fair	Poor
275	225	175	100	75

STURM, RUGER & CO.

Mark I Target Pistol (US marked)

This is a semi-automatic target pistol with 6.88" barrel and target sights. Stamped "U.S." on top of receiver. First produced in 1956. Blued finish. Rebuilt or refinished pistols may be Parkerized and stamped with arsenal stamp.

Exc.	V.G.	Good	Fair	Poor
800	600	400	250	150

GUIDE LAMP
Division of General Motors

Liberator

A .45 ACP caliber single shot pistol with a 3.5" smooth bore barrel and overall length of 5.5". This pistol is made primarily of stampings and was intended to be air dropped to partisans in Europe during WWII. The hollow grip is designed to hold a packet of four extra cartridges. Originally packaged in unmarked cardboard boxes with an illustrated instruction sheet.

Courtesy Richard M. Kumor, Sr.

NIB	Exc.	V.G.	Good	Fair	Poor
2000	1200	750	400	300	175

SUB-MACHINE GUNS

Bibliographical Note: For historical information, technical data, and photos see Tracie Hill, *Thompson: The American Legend*, Collector Grade Publications, 1996.

Colt 9mm (Model 635)

Based on the M16 this submachine gun is chambered for the 9mm cartridge. It was first produced in 1990. It has the capability of full automatic or 3-round burst. The barrel length is 10.125" with a 20- or 32-round magazine. The gun is fitted with a retractable stock. Weight is about 6.5 lbs. Rate of fire is about 900 rounds per minute. "SMG" and serial number are marked on left side of magazine housing. Used by the U.S. Marine Corp. and other country's military forces

NOTE: See also *U.S., Rifles, M16*

Photo Courtesy Private NFA Collection

Pre-1968

Exc.	V.G.	Fair
N/A	N/A	N/A

Pre-1986 conversions, for OEM add 20%

Exc.	V.G.	Fair
5500	5000	4500

Pre-1986 Dealer samples

Exc.	V.G.	Fair
N/A	N/A	N/A

Ingram Model 10

Chambered for the 9mm or .45ACP cartridge this submachine gun is fitted with a 5.7" barrel and a 30-round magazine. It has a rate of fire of 1,100 rounds per minute. The empty weight is approximately 6.3 lbs. This submachine gun was used by various government agencies in Vietnam. A version chambered for the .380 cartridge is known as the Model 11.

Photo Courtesy Private NFA Collection

Pre-1968

Exc.	V.G.	Fair
1500	1200	1000

Pre-1986 conversions

Exc.	V.G.	Fair
N/A	N/A	N/A

Pre-1986 Dealer samples

Exc.	V.G.	Fair
N/A	N/A	N/A

Reising 50/55

First built in 1941 the gun was chambered for the .45 ACP cartridge. It was first used by Marines in the Pacific but failed to be combat reliable. The Model 50 was fitted with a wooden buttstock and 10.8" barrel. Magazine capacity was 12 or 20 rounds. Rate of fire was 550 rounds per minute. The gun has

a select fire mechanism for single round operation. Marked "HARRINGTON & RICHARDSON WORCESTER MASS USA" on the top of the receiver. Weight was about 6.75 lbs.

The Model 55 is the same mechanism but with a wire folding stock and no muzzle compensator. the weight of the Model 55 was 6.25 lbs. About 100,000 Reising Model 50s and 55s were built between 1941 and 1945 when production ceased.

Courtesy Richard M. Kumor, Sr.

Pre-1968

Exc.	V.G.	Fair
2000	1700	1500

Pre-1986 conversions

Exc.	V.G.	Fair
N/A	N/A	N/A

Pre-1986 Dealer samples

Exc.	V.G.	Fair
1000	750	500

THOMPSON SUBMACHINE GUNS
Text and prices by Nick Tilotta

Thompson Model 1921AC/21A/ 1921/28 Navy

The first Thompson's to come to market were the Model 1921s, manufactured by Colt Patent firearms for Auto Ordnance Corporation in New York, New York. Between March, 1921 and April, 1922 15,000 guns were built. Of those 15,000 manufactured only about 2,400 weapons exist in a transferable state today. Transferable, meaning weapons that can be bought, sold, or traded legally within the U.S. three models of the Model 1921 were produced. The Model 1921A had a fixed front sight and a rate of fire of 800 rounds per minute. The Model 1921AC has a Cutts compensator instead of a fixed front sight and an 800 rounds per minute rate of fire. The Model 1928 Navy was fitted with a Cutts compensator and a heavier actuator that reduced the rate of fire to 600 rounds per minute. All of these Navy models had the number "8" stamped crudely over the number "1" on the left side of the receiver. Of the 15,000 colt Model 1921 produced approximately 25% were Model 1921As, 33% were Model 1921ACs, and 41% were 1928 Navy's. A handful of Model 1927s were manufactured by Colt and left the factory as semi-automatics. However the ATF considers these guns as machine guns and requires that all NFA rules apply. These Model 1927s are quite rare and represent only about 1% of total production. They do not seem to sell for the same dollar figures that the machine guns do.

All Colt manufactured Thompsons were arsenic blued: none were Parkerized. All had walnut stocks, grips, and forearms manufactured by Remington. With the exception of a few prototypes, all Colt Thompsons were chambered for the .45ACP cartridge. All internal parts were nickel plated and all barrels were finned. All weapons had a Lyman rear sight assembly. A removable rear stock was standard. All weapons were marked with a "NEW YORK, USA" address on the right side of the receiver. "COLT PATENT FIREARMS" was marked on the left side of the receiver. these Colt Thompsons would accept a 20 or 30 round box magazine as well as a 50 round "L" drum or 100 round "C" drum. Weight is about 10.75 lbs. Prices below are for original Colt Guns with original parts and finish.

NOTE: Model 1921As, early serial numbers, previous ownership, and documentation can dramatically add to the prices below. In addition, missing components, re-barreled weapons, etc. will see a substantial reduction in price, as these orginal components are almost extinct. Re-finishing or re-bluing will result in a substantial reduction in value by as much as 50%.

Pre-1968

Exc.	V.G.	Fair
25000	17500	12000

Pre-1986 conversions

Exc.	V.G.	Fair
N/A	N/A	N/A

Pre-1986 Dealer samples

Exc.	V.G.	Fair
N/A	N/A	N/A

Thompson Model 1928 Commercial/ 1928A1 Military

The next limited run of Thompson's came just before and right at the beginning of WWII. This version is called the Model 1928AC or commercial model. These weapons were assembled by Savage Arms in Utica, New York, using original Colt internal components. The receivers were still marked with the New York address but void of any "Colt" markings. Most weapons were simply marked, "MODEL 1928". The first of these guns has a blued receivers and blued barrels. The second run had parkerized receivers and blued barrels. These guns are quite rare and command premium prices.

At the outbreak of WWII the demand for the Thompson gun soared. A brake lining facility in Bridgeport, CT was acquired to accommodate the increased demand for production. Three models of Thompsons were born in this WWII era. The first

was the Model 1928A1 Thompson. This version was a copy of the Model 1928 Navy Colt Thompson. Most were parkerized with much less detail paid to fine machining. this gun was assembled in two locations; Utica, NY and Bridgeport, CT. Receivers produced in Utica were marked with an "S" prefix in front of the serial number. Receivers marked with a "AO" prefix were produced in Bridgeport. Receivers were ,marked on the right side, "AUTO ORDNANCE CORPORATION, BRIDGEPORT, CT", no matter where the receiver was manufactured. The Utica, NY plant concentrated its efforts on manufacturing components while the Bridgeport facility concentrated on assemblies. As production increased, the Model 1928A1 lost many of its "unnecessary" components such as the finned barrel, the costly Lyman sight, and finely checkered selector switches. Approximately 562,000 Thompsons were produced in the Model 1928A1 configuration. All of the weapons were Parkerized, and some have finned barrels and some have smooth barrels. Some of these guns were also fitted with Lyman sights, some have a stamped "L" type sight that may or may not have protective ears. As a general rule of thumb most Model 1928 Commercial guns were fitted with a vertical foregrip while most Model 1928A1 guns were fitted with a horizontal forearm, and all had removable butt stocks. Used by Allied forces during WWII. Used both 20 or 30 round box magazines and 50 or 100 round drum magazines.

Thompson Model 1928 Commercial

Pre-1968

Exc.	V.G.	Fair
17500	13500	10000

Thompson Model 1921 with close-up of receiver stamping • Photo Paul Goodwin

Pre-1986 conversions

Exc.	V.G.	Fair
N/A	N/A	N/A

Pre-1986 Dealer samples

Exc.	V.G.	Fair
8000	6000	5000

Thompson Model 1928A1 Military
Pre-1968

Exc.	V.G.	Fair
12000	10000	8500

Pre-1986 conversions

Exc.	V.G.	Fair
N/A	N/A	N/A

Pre-1986 Dealer samples

Exc.	V.G.	Fair
6000	5000	4000

Thompson M1/M1A1

In April, 1942, the M1 Thompson was introduced. It was a simplified version of the Model 1928 with a smooth barrel, stamped rear "L" sight, and a fixed rear stock. the expensive Model 1928 type bolt assembly was modified to simplified machining procedures. the result was a repositioned cocking knob on the right side of the receiver. Some 285,000 M1s were produced before being replaced by an improved version, the "M1A1" in april, 1942. This version of the Thompson has a fixed firing pin machined into the bolt face, and had protective ears added to the rear sight assembly. All M1 Thompsons were fitted with a horizontal forearm and fixed butt stock. Approximately 540,000 M1A1 Thompsons were produced before the end of WWII. All M1 and M1A1 Thompsons used stick or box magazines only.

NOTE: Many of these weapons were reworked by a military arsenal during the war and may have been refinished, however it does not significantly reduce the value of the gun. In addition to the rework many of the serial numbered lower assemblies were not assemblied with the correct serial numbered receiver. Although this may disturb some collectors it should not significanlty devalue the weapon. A very small percentage of these weapons were marked "US PROPERTY" behind the rear sight and this increases the value by as much as $1,000.

Courtesy Richard M. Kumor, Sr.

Pre-1968

Exc.	V.G.	Fair
10500	8500	7000

Pre-1986 conversions

Exc.	V.G.	Fair
N/A	N/A	N/A

Pre-1986 Dealer samples

Exc.	V.G.	Fair
5000	4000	3500

Third Generation Thompson's

In 1975, the Auto Ordnance Corp., West Hurley, New York, began production of the new Model 1928 Thompson. It was an attempt to produce a version of the Thompson for the civilian collector as well as a limited number of law enforcement sales. The early weapons were manufactured from surplus WWII components and were quite acceptable in quality. As time wore on, however, many of the components were of new manufacture and lesser quality. Between 1975 and 1986 approximately 3,200 models of the 1928 were produced. Some of these guns were commemorative models. the weapons had finned barrels, flip-up rear leaf sights, removable stocks, and blued finish. In 1985 and 1986 approximately 600 versions of the M1 Thompson were built. these were actually a version of the M1A1 military Thompson with blued finish. With the exception of a short production run for export in 1992, production of these weapons was banned in May, 1986 by Federal law. All receivers were marked "AUTO-ORDNANCE WEST HURLEY, NEW YORK" on the right side of the receiver and "THOMPSON SUB-MACHINE GUN, CALIBER .45 M1" on the left side. All serial numbers carried the letter "A" suffix. A very limited number of .22 caliber models were produced in the Model 1928 configuration, but had limited success in the market.

Thompson Model 1928-West Hurley
Pre-1968

Exc.	V.G.	Fair
7500	5500	4000

Pre-1986 conversions

Exc.	V.G.	Fair
N/A	N/A	N/A

Pre-1986 Dealer samples

Exc.	V.G.	Fair
3750	2750	2000

Thompson Model M1-West Hurley
Pre-1968

Exc.	V.G.	Fair
6500	4500	3000

Pre-1986 conversions

Exc.	V.G.	Fair
N/A	N/A	N/A

Pre-1986 Dealer samples

Exc.	V.G.	Fair
3250	2500	1500

Thompson Model 1928 .22 caliber-West Hurley
Pre-1968

Exc.	V.G.	Fair
5500	4000	2500

Pre-1986 conversions

Exc.	V.G.	Fair
N/A	N/A	N/A

Pre-1986 Dealer samples

Exc.	V.G.	Fair
3000	2000	1500

UD (United Defense) M42

Built by Marlin for U.S. military forces beginning in 1942 Designed by Carl Swebilius founder of High Standard. Well constructed of excellent materials. Chambered for the 9mm Parabellum cartridge. Select fire with rate of fire was 700 rounds per minute. Barrel length was 10.8". Weight is about 9 lbs. Markings on left side of receiver are;" UNITED DEFENSE SUPPLY CORP/US MODEL 42/MARLIN FA CO NEW HAVEN". Magazine capacity is 20 rounds. Limited quantities produced with an estimate of about 15,000 produced. It seems that the majority built to sold to the Netherlands during WWII with a few shipped to the American OSS for us in Europe and the Far East.

Private NFA collection. • Photo by Gary Gelson

Pre-1968

Exc.	V.G.	Fair
4500	4000	3500

Pre-1986 conversions

Exc.	V.G.	Fair
N/A	N/A	N/A

Pre-1986 Dealer samples

Exc.	V.G.	Fair
N/A	N/A	N/A

US M3

First produced in the U.S. in 1942 this submachine gun was chambered for the .45 ACP or 9mm cartridge (special conversion kit). It is similar in design to the British Sten gun. It was fitted with a 8" barrel and folding metal stock. The box magazine capacity was 30 rounds. The rate of fire was 400 rounds per minute. Weight of the M3 was about 8 lbs. It was produced until 1944. Marked "GUIDE LAMP DIV OF GENERAL MOTORS/US MODEL M3" on top of the receiver. Approximately 600,000 M3s were produced. Built by the Guide Lamp Division of General Motors.

NOTE: A suppressed version of this gun was built for the OSS in World WAr II and used for covert operations in Vietnam as well. Too rare to price.

US M3. • Courtesy Richard M. Kumor, Sr.

Pre-1968

Exc.	V.G.	Fair
6500	6000	5500

Pre-1986 conversions (or current U.S. manufacture)

Exc.	V.G.	Fair
5000	4500	4200

Pre-1986 Dealer samples

Exc.	V.G.	Fair
3500	3000	2000

US M3A1

Similar to the M3 but with significant changes and improvements. This model has a larger ejection port, the retracting handle has been eliminated, a finger hole is used for cocking,

US M3 with silencer • Courtesy Chuck Karwan

disassembly grooves were added, a stronger cover spring was installed, a larger oil can is in the grip, a stock plate and magazine filler were added to the stock, and a guard was added for the magazine catch. First produced in 1944. Approximately 50,000 M3A1s were built. This version was built by Guide Lamp and Ithaca.

US M3A1. • Photo Courtesy Private NFA Collection

Pre-1968

Exc.	V.G.	Fair
9000	8000	7000

Pre-1986 conversions (or current U.S. manufacture)

Exc.	V.G.	Fair
6000	5500	5000

Pre-1986 Dealer samples

Exc.	V.G.	Fair
4000	3500	3000

RIFLES

PEDERSEN, JOHN D.
Denver, CO & Jackson, WY

John D. Pedersen was the inventor and designer of the Pedersen device that consisted of a conversion unit to be installed in a modified Springfield 1903 .30-06 bolt action rifle. This device allowed the rifle to function as a semiautomatic. At the end of World War I the idea was discarded. During the 1920's Pedersen and John Garand began working on a new semiautomatic military rifle for US forces. Pedersen's design was chambered for the .276 caliber and his rifle eventually lost out to Garand's rifle; the M1. The Pedersen rifles and carbines appear to be part of a test group for military trials. Total number built is unknown.NOTE: Thanks to Jim Supica for his research into the Pedersen rifle and carbine which appeared for sale in his Old Town Station Dispatch.

Pedersen Rifle
Chambered for .276 Pedersen cartridge. Marked "PEDERSEN SELF LOADER PA/VICKERS-ARMSTRONG LTD." on the left side of the receiver. In oval over chamber marked "C/2". Rare.

Exc.	V.G.	Good	Fair	Poor
12500	7500	—	—	—

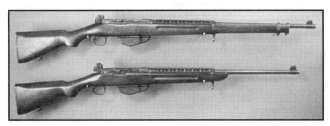

Pedersen rifle at top, carbine at bottom. • Courtesy Jim Supica, Old Town Station

Pedersen Carbine
Same caliber and markings as rifle, but with 23" barrel. Rare.

Exc.	V.G.	Good	Fair	Poor
15000	8500	—	—	—

SPRINGFIELD ARMORY

This was America's first federal armory. It began producing military weapons in 1795 with the Springfield Model 1795 musket. The armory has supplied famous and well known military weapons to the United States military forces throughout its history. The armory was phased out in 1968. The buildings and its collections are now part of the National Park Service.

BIBLIOGRAPHICAL NOTE: For further information, technical, and photos see the following; Robert W.D. Ball, *Springfield Armory Shoulder Weapons, 1795-1968*, Antique Trader Books, 1997. Blake Stevens *U.S Rifle M14 From John Garand to the M21*, Collector Grade Publications. William S. Brophy,

Pedersen Carbine • Courtesy West Point Museum • Paul Goodwin Photo

The Springfield 1903 Rifles, Stackpole Books, 1985. Bruce Canfield, *A Collector's Guide to the '03 Springfield*, Andrew Mowbray Publishers, 1991.

Joslyn Breechloading Rifle • Courtesy West Point Museum • Paul Goodwin Photo

Joslyn Breech-Loading Rifle

Until recently, this rifle was considered a post-Civil War breechloading conversion of a muzzleloading musket, but information developed since the 1970s indicates that this was the first true breechloading cartridge rifle to be made in quantity by a national armory, circa 1864. Actions were supplied to the Springfield Armory by the Joslyn Firearms Co. where they were assembled to newly made rifles designed for the action. In 56-60 caliber, with a 35.5" barrel with three barrel bands, the uniquely shaped lock with eagle ahead of the hammer, U.S./Springfield on the front of the lock, with 1864 at the rear. Walnut stock specially made for the barreled action and lock. Converted to 50-70 centerfire will command approximately $100 more.

Exc.	V.G.	Good	Fair	Poor
2000	1700	1100	700	400

A first Model Allin conversion was sold at auction for $6900. Condition was near excellent with most of the original finish.
Rock Island Auction Company, August 1998

Model 1866 U.S. Breech-Loading Rifle, Allin Conversion, aka Second Model Allin

Produced in 50 caliber centerfire, with a 40" barrel with a 50 caliber liner tube inserted and brazed, walnut stock with three barrel bands with band springs. Differences between the First and Second Model Allin include a lengthened bolt, a firing pin spring, and a stronger internal extraction system. the Breechblock is marked with 1866 over an eagle, while the lock bears standard Springfield markings with either an 1863 or 1864 date. A total of 25,000 Model 1863 percussion muskets were thus altered at the Springfield Armory around 1866.

Exc.	V.G.	Good	Fair	Poor
2000	1500	1200	800	500

Model 1865 U.S. Breech-Loading Rifle, Allin Conversion, aka First Model Allin

Designed in 58 caliber rimfire, with a 40" barrel with three flat barrel bands. the Breechlock is released by a thumb latch on the right side, pivoted upward, with the firing pin contained within the breechblock. 5,000 Model 1861 percussion muskets were altered using this method at the Springfield Armory circa 1865. The breechblock is unmarked, while the lock is marked with the eagle ahead of the hammer, as well as U.S./Springfield, with all specimens dated 1865 at the rear.

Exc.	V.G.	Good	Fair	Poor
4000	3000	2500	1500	1200

Model 1867 U.S. Breech-Loading Cadet Rifle

This model is a .50 caliber centerfire, 33" barrel, two band, scaled down version of the Model 1866 Second Model Allin

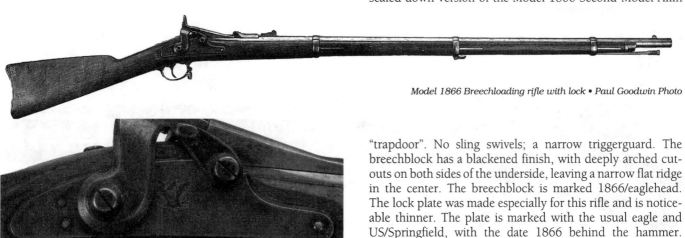

Model 1866 Breechloading rifle with lock • Paul Goodwin Photo

"trapdoor". No sling swivels; a narrow triggerguard. The breechblock has a blackened finish, with deeply arched cutouts on both sides of the underside, leaving a narrow flat ridge in the center. The breechblock is marked 1866/eaglehead. The lock plate was made especially for this rifle and is noticeable thinner. The plate is marked with the usual eagle and US/Springfield, with the date 1866 behind the hammer.

About 424 rifles were produced at the Springfield Armory between 1876 and 1868.

Exc.	V.G.	Good	Fair	Poor
5250	3700	2700	1100	850

Model 1868 Rifle

This is a single shot Trapdoor rifle chambered for the .50 caliber centerfire cartridge. It features a breechblock that pivots forward when a thumblatch at its rear is depressed. It has a 32.5" barrel and a full-length stock held on by two barrel bands. It has iron mountings and a cleaning rod mounted under the barrel. It features an oil-finished walnut stock. The lock is marked "US Springfield". It is dated either 1863 or 1864. The breechblock features either the date 1869 or 1870. There were approximately 51,000 manufactured between 1868 and 1872.

Exc.	V.G.	Good	Fair	Poor
1000	800	650	500	350

Model 1869 Cadet Rifle

This is a single shot Trapdoor rifle chambered for .50 caliber centerfire. It is similar to the Model 1868 with a 29.5" barrel. There were approximately 3,500 manufactured between 1869 and 1876.

Exc.	V.G.	Good	Fair	Poor
1000	850	650	500	450

Model 1870

There are two versions of this Trapdoor breechloader—a rifle with a 32.5" barrel and a carbine that features a 22" barrel and a half-stock held on by one barrel band. They are both chambered for .50 caliber centerfire and feature the standard Springfield lock markings and a breechblock marked "1870" or "Model 1870". There were a total of 11,500 manufactured between 1870 and 1873. Only 340 are carbines; they are extremely rare.

Rifle

Courtesy Milwaukee Public Museum, Milwaukee, Wisconsin

Exc.	V.G.	Good	Fair	Poor
1500	1200	900	700	600

Carbine-Very Rare

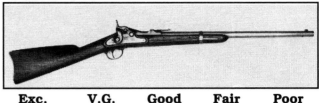

Exc.	V.G.	Good	Fair	Poor
9000	7500	5000	3000	2000

Model 1871 Rolling Block U.S. Army Rifle

This model is a .50 caliber centerfire, 36" barrel, with two barrel bands, rolling block action. Sights, sling-swivels, and most other details as for the Model 1870 Remington U.S. Navy rifle. Case-hardened frame, bright finished iron mountings. Two piece walnut stock. Known as the "locking action" as the hammer went to half cock when the breechblock was closed. No serial numbers. Left side of frame marked "Model 1871". Right side marked with eagle over U.S./Springfield/1872. On the tang, marked "REMINGTON'S PATENT. PAT.MAY 3D, NOV. 15TH, 1864, APRIL 17TH, 1868". About 10,001 rifles were produced between 1871 and 1872 under a royalty agreement with Remington Arms Co.

Exc.	V.G.	Good	Fair	Poor
1600	1300	900	750	500

A Model 1871 rolling block rifle sold at auction for $5175. Condition was near mint for metal and excellent for stock. Rock Island Auction Company, August 1998

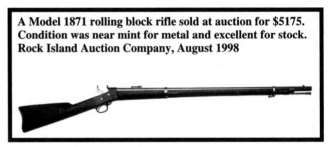

Model 1871 Ward-Burton U.S. Rifle

A .50 caliber centerfire, 32.63" barrel secured by two barrel bands. This is an early bolt action, single shot rifle, with the cartridge loaded directly into the open action, with cocking on the closing of the bolt. Walnut stock, sling swivels on the forward barrel band and the front of the triggerguard. Not serially numbered. The top of the bolt marked, "WARD BURTON PATENT DEC. 20, 1859-FEB. 21, 1871". Left side of the action marked with American eagle motif and "US/SPRINGFIELD" 1,011 rifles and 316 carbines produced at the Springfield Armory basically as a trial weapon.

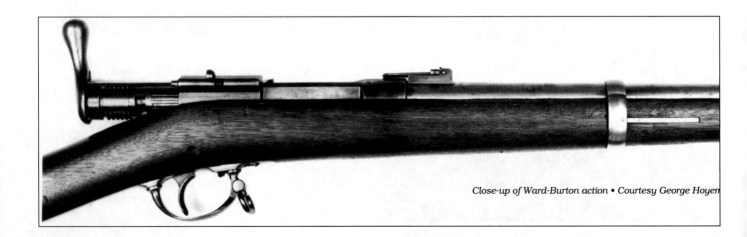

Close-up of Ward-Burton action • Courtesy George Hoyer

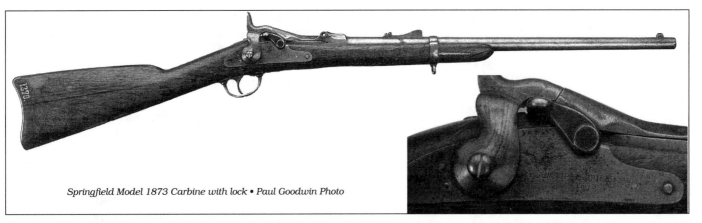

Springfield Model 1873 Carbine with lock • Paul Goodwin Photo

Courtesy Bob Ball

Exc.	V.G.	Good	Fair	Poor
3200	2200	1100	700	500

Model 1873

This is a Trapdoor breechloading rifle chambered for the .45-70 cartridge. The rifle version has a 32.5" barrel with a full-length stock held on by two barrel bands. The carbine features a 22" barrel with a half-stock held on by a single barrel band, and the cadet rifle features a 29.5" barrel with a full length stock and two barrel bands. The finish of all three variations is blued and case-colored, with a walnut stock. The lock is marked "US Springfield 1873". The breechblock is either marked "Model 1873" or "US Model 1873". There were approximately 73,000 total manufactured between 1873 and 1877.

NOTE: Prices listed below are for rifles in original configuration.

Rifle-50,000 Manufactured

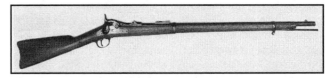

Courtesy Milwaukee Public Museum, Milwaukee, Wisconsin

Exc.	V.G.	Good	Fair	Poor
1250	1000	600	300	200

Carbine-20,000 Manufactured

Exc.	V.G.	Good	Fair	Poor
5000	4000	3000	2000	1000

Cadet Rifle-3,000 Manufactured

Exc.	V.G.	Good	Fair	Poor
1250	1000	750	600	500

Model 1875 Officer's Rifle

This is a high-grade Trapdoor breechloader chambered for the .45-70 cartridge. It has a 26" barrel and a half-stock fas-

Model 1875 Officer's rifle • Courtesy West Point Museum • Paul Goodwin Photo

tened by one barrel band. It is blued and case-colored, with a scroll engraved lock. It has a checkered walnut pistol grip stock with a pewter forend tip. There is a cleaning rod mounted beneath the barrel. This rifle was not issued but was sold to army officers for personal sporting purposes. There were only 477 manufactured between 1875 and 1885.

Exc.	V.G.	Good	Fair	Poor
35000	20000	15000	10000	7500

Model 1875 Lee Vertical Action Rifle

A 45-70 centerfire, 32.63" barrel secured by two barrel bands. Martini-style dropping block action, with a unique, centrally mounted hammer with an exceptionally long spur. In order to open the breech, the hammer must be given a sharp blow with the heal of the hand; the insertion of a cartridge will automatically close the breech, while the hammer is cocked by hand. All blued finish. Stacking and sling swivel on upper band, with sling swivel on triggerguard. Serially numbered 1 through 143 on the internal parts only. Upper tang marked, "U.S. PAT. MAR 16, 1875", no barrel proof marks; inspector's initials "ESA" in an oval on the stock. 143 rifles produced in 1875 at the Springfield Armory basically as a trials weapon.

Exc.	V.G.	Good	Fair	Poor
5500	4000	2500	1500	1000

Model 1877

This is a Trapdoor breechloading rifle chambered for the .45-70 cartridge. It was issued as a rifle with a 32" barrel and a full-length stock held on by two barrel bands, a cadet rifle with a 29.5" barrel, and a carbine with a 22" barrel, half-stock, and single barrel band. This version is similar to the Model 1873. In fact, the breechblock retained the Model 1873 marking. The basic differences are that the stock is thicker at the wrist and the breechblock was thickened and lowered. This is basically a mechanically improved version. There were approximately 12,000 manufactured in 1877 and 1878.

Rifle-3,900 Manufactured

Exc.	V.G.	Good	Fair	Poor
2750	2400	1600	1250	1000

Cadet Rifle-1,000 Manufactured

Exc.	V.G.	Good	Fair	Poor
1500	1300	1000	850	650

Carbine-2,950 Manufactured

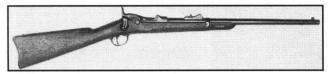

Courtesy Milwaukee Public Museum, Milwaukee, Wisconsin

Exc.	V.G.	Good	Fair	Poor
3000	2500	1800	1250	850

Model 1880

This version features a sliding combination cleaning rod/bayonet that is fitted in the forearm under the barrel. It retained the 1873 breechblock markings. There were approximately 1,000 manufactured for trial purposes in 1880.

Courtesy Milwaukee Public Museum, Milwaukee, Wisconsin

Exc.	V.G.	Good	Fair	Poor
2000	1500	1200	1000	800

> A Model 1880 ramrod bayonet rifle was sold at auction for $6325. Condition was excellent with 98% original blue. Bright case hardening on breechblock.
> Rock Island Auction Company, August 1998

Model 1881 Marksman Rifle

This is an extremely high-grade Trapdoor breechloading rifle chambered for the .45-70 cartridge. It has a 28" round barrel and is similar to the Model 1875 Officer's Rifle in appearance.

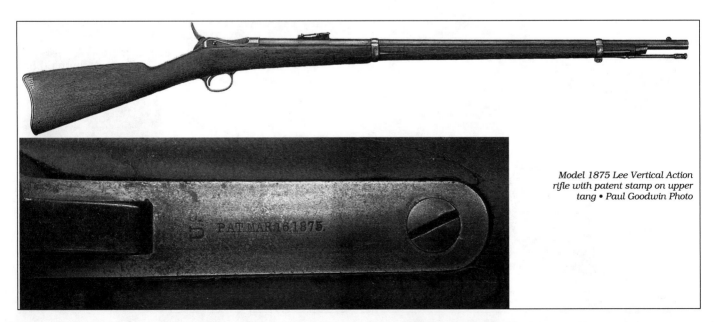

Model 1875 Lee Vertical Action rifle with patent stamp on upper tang • Paul Goodwin Photo

Model 1877 Cadet Rifle • Paul Goodwin Photo

It features a full-length, high grade, checkered walnut stock held on by one barrel band. It has a horn schnabel forend tip. The metal parts are engraved, blued, and case-colored. It has a vernier aperture sight as well as a buckhorn rear sight on the barrel and a globe front sight with a spirit level. There were only 11 manufactured to be awarded as prizes at shooting matches.

CAUTION: This is perhaps the supreme rarity among the Trapdoor Springfields, and one should be extremely cognizant of fakes.

Exc.	V.G.	Good	Fair	Poor
40000	35000	30000	20000	15000

Model 1882 U.S. Magazine Rifle, Chaffee-Reese

A 45-70 caliber centerfire, 27.78" barrel secured by two barrel bands. One of the early bolt action repeaters, with the cartridges carried in a tubular feed in the butt. Iron mountings, with a blued finish, walnut stock, stacking swivel and sling swivel on the upper barrel band, and a sling swivel on the front of the triggerguard. Not serially numbered. Left side of breech marked, "US SPRINGFIELD, 1884", the barrel marked, "V.P." with eagle head proof. Unfortunately, most rifles found are lacking the feed mechanism in the butt, which lowers the value approximately 15%. 753 rifles were produced at the Springfield Armory in 1884.

Exc.	V.G.	Good	Fair	Poor
3000	2500	2000	900	750

Model 1884

This is also a breechloading Trapdoor single shot rifle chambered for the .45-70 cartridge. It was issued as a standard rifle with a 32.75" barrel, a cadet rifle with a 29.5" barrel, and a military carbine with a 22" barrel. The finish is blued and case-colored. This model features the improved Buffington rear sight. It features the socket bayonet and a walnut stock. There were approximately 232,000 manufactured between 1885 and 1890.

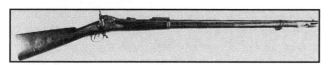

Courtesy Bob Ball

Rifle-200,000

Exc.	V.G.	Good	Fair	Poor
1000	800	600	500	350

A Springfield Model 1884 rifle was sold at auction for $6,037.50. It was the property of Captain Leonard Wood, later General Wood, with a letter dated 1893. Stock cartouche "SWP/1887." Condition was good. Amoskeag Auction Co. Inc., March, 2000

Cadet Rifle-12,000

Exc.	V.G.	Good	Fair	Poor
850	750	600	400	300

Carbine-20,000

Exc.	V.G.	Good	Fair	Poor
1000	850	700	500	400

Model 1886 Experimental "Trapdoor" Carbine, aka Experimental Model 1882 third/fourth type

Apparently both of these designations are misnomers, as the weapon was officially referred to as the "24" Barrel Carbine. Collectors now call it the Model 1886 to conform to the year of manufacture. The most outstanding feature is the almost full length stock with uncapped, tapered forend. The single upper barrel band is fitted with a bent, or wraparound swivel to facilitate insertion in a saddle scabbard. Lower swivel on butt, with a sling ring and bar on the left side. Cleaning rod compartment in the butt. Buffington-type Model 1884 rear sight marked XC on leaf. About 1,000 produced during 1886.

Exc.	V.G.	Good	Fair	Poor
4300	3200	2200	1100	800

Model 1888

This version is similar to its predecessors except that it features a sliding, ramrod-type bayonet that was improved so that it stays securely locked when in its extended position.

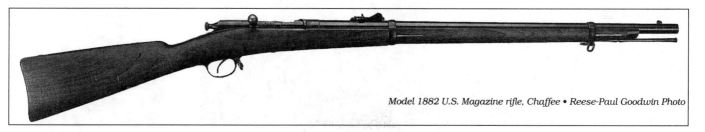

Model 1882 U.S. Magazine rifle, Chaffee • Reese-Paul Goodwin Photo

Springfield Model 1884 • Paul Goodwin Photo

The breechblock was still marked "Model 1884". This was the last Springfield Trapdoor rifle produced. There were approximately 65,000 manufactured between 1889 and 1893.

Courtesy Milwaukee Public Museum, Milwaukee, Wisconsin

Exc.	V.G.	Good	Fair	Poor
750	650	500	350	250

Trapdoor Fencing Musket

This is a non-gun that was used by the Army in teaching bayonet drills. They had no desire to damage serviceable rifles during practice, so they produced this version to fill the bill. There were basically four types produced.

Type I

This version is similar to the Model 1873 rifle without a breech or lock. The finish is rough, and it is unmarked. It was designed to accept a socket bayonet. One should secure a qualified appraisal if a transaction is contemplated. There were 170 manufactured in 1876 and 1877.

Exc.	V.G.	Good	Fair	Poor
800	650	500	400	300

Type II

This version is basically a Model 1884 with the hammer removed and the front sight blade ground off. It accepted a socket bayonet that was covered with leather and had a pad on its point.

Exc.	V.G.	Good	Fair	Poor
500	400	300	250	200

Type III

This version is similar to the Type II except that it is shortened to 43.5" in length. There were approximately 1,500 manufactured between 1905 and 1906.

Exc.	V.G.	Good	Fair	Poor
750	650	450	350	300

Type IV

This version is similar to the Type III except that the barrel was filled with lead. There were approximately 11,000 manufactured between 1907 and 1916.

Exc.	V.G.	Good	Fair	Poor
500	400	300	250	200

Model 1870 Rolling Block

This is a single shot breechloading rifle with a rolling-block action. It is chambered for .50 caliber centerfire and has a 32.75" barrel. It has a full-length forend held on by two barrel bands. The finish is blued and case-colored, with a cleaning rod mounted under the barrel. The stock and forend are walnut. The frame is marked "USN Springfield 1870". There is an anchor motif marked on the top of the barrel. It also features government inspector's marks on the frame. This rifle was manufactured by Springfield Armory under license from Remington Arms Company for the United States Navy. The first 10,000 produced were rejected by our Navy and were sent to France and used in the Franco-Prussian War. For that reason, this variation is quite scarce and would bring a 20% premium. There was also a group of approximately 100 rifles that were converted to the .22 rimfire cartridge and used for target practice aboard ships. This version is extremely rare. There were approximately 22,000 manufactured in 1870 and 1871.

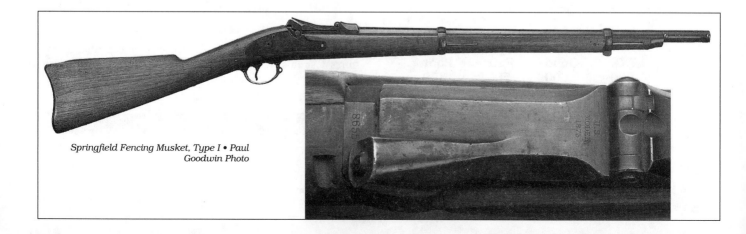

Springfield Fencing Musket, Type I • Paul Goodwin Photo

Courtesy Milwaukee Public Museum, Milwaukee, Wisconsin

Standard Navy Rifle

Exc.	V.G.	Good	Fair	Poor
1000	850	700	500	400

Rejected Navy Rifle

Exc.	V.G.	Good	Fair	Poor
700	600	500	350	250

.22 Caliber

Exc.	V.G.	Good	Fair	Poor
2000	1750	1250	900	750

U.S. Krag Jorgensen Rifle

NOTE: This firearm will be found listed in its own section of this text.

SPRINGFIELD MODEL 1903 & VARIATIONS

These rifles were built by Springfield, Remington, Rock Island Arsenal, and Smith-Carona

Model 1903

This rifle was a successor to the Krag Jorgensen and was also produced by the Rock Island Arsenal. It was initially chambered for the .30-03 cartridge and very shortly changed to the .30-06 cartridge. Its original chambering consisted of a 220-grain, round-nosed bullet. The German army introduced its spitzer bullet so our government quickly followed suit with a 150-grain, pointed bullet designated the .30-06. This model has a 24" barrel and was built on what was basically a modified Mauser action. It features a 5-round integral box magazine. The finish is blued, with a full length, straight-grip walnut stock with full handguards held on by two barrel bands. The initial version was issued with a rod-type bayonet that was quickly discontinued when President Theodore Roosevelt personally disapproved it. There were approximately 74,000 produced with this rod bayonet; and if in an unaltered condition, these would be worth a great deal more than the standard variation. It is important to note that the early models with serial numbers under 800,000 were not heat treated sufficiently to be safe to fire with modern ammunition. There were a great many produced between 1903 and 1930. The values represented reflect original specimens; WWII alterations would be worth approximately 15% less.

Rod Bayonet Version (Original & Unaltered)

Exc.	V.G.	Good	Fair	Poor
25000	20000	15000	12500	10000

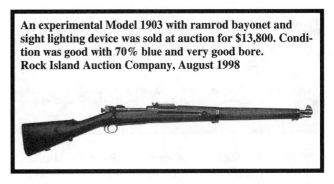

An experimental Model 1903 with ramrod bayonet and sight lighting device was sold at auction for $13,800. Condition was good with 70% blue and very good bore. Rock Island Auction Company, August 1998

Standard Model 1903 (Original & Unaltered)

Exc.	V.G.	Good	Fair	Poor
4800	4000	3000	2000	1000

Model 1903 with Air Service magazine • Courtesy Richard M. Kumor Sr.

NOTE: For standard Model 1903 with Air Service magazine add $350 for magazine to above prices.

Model 1903 Rifle Stripped for Air Service

Special 29" stock, 5.75 upper handguard specially made for this rifle, solid lower barrel band retained by screw underneath, rear sight leaf shortened and altered to open sight with square notch. 25-round extension magazine used. 910 rifles produced during the first half of 1918, with serial numbers ranging between 857000 and 863000; all barrel dated in first half of 1918. A very rare and desirable rifle, with the magazine almost impossible to find. Values shown include magazine.

Exc.	V.G.	Good	Fair	Poor
7500	5000	4000	3000	2000

Model 1903 Mark 1

This version is similar to the original except that it was cut to accept the Pedersen device. This device allows the use of a semiautomatic bolt insert that utilizes pistol cartridges. The rifle has a slot milled into the receiver that acts as an ejection port. The device was not successful and was scrapped. There were approximately 102,000 rifles that were produced with this millcut between 1918 and 1920.

NOTE: The values given are for the rifle alone—not for the device. Rifle must contain all original Mark I parts.

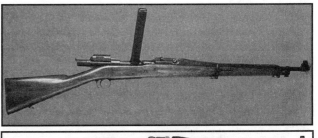

Paul Goodwin Photo

Paul Goodwin Photo

Exc.	V.G.	Good	Fair	Poor
2500	2000	1500	1200	600

Model 1903 Sniper Rifle

Selected Model 1903 rifles were fitted with telescopic sights from 1907 to 1919; apparently 25 rifles so equipped in 1906, but the type of scope has not been definitely identified. If proven original to the period, specimens would be worth more than shown in the values guide. 400 rifles were fitted with the Warner-Swasey Model 1906, 6-power telescope sight in 1911, with the sights marked Model 1908, as well as with the full Warner-Swasey markings. Scope number do not match the rifle numbers. Rifles fitted with this Model 1908 scope will bring approximately 30% more than the values shown. Approximately 5000 rifles were fitted with the Model 1913 Warner-Swasey telescopic sight up to 1919; similar to the Model 1908, they were only 5.2 power. When originally fitted, the scopes were numbered to the rifles'; however, scopes were sold separately from the rifles as surplus and were never numbered. These were later fitted to other weapons and the chance of finding matching numbers greatly decreases. Values shown are for original guns with original, matching telescopes.

Courtesy Bob Ball

Exc.	V.G.	Good	Fair	Poor
6750	5300	4250	2750	1700

Model 1903 A1

This version is a standard Model 1903 rifle that was fitted with a Type C, semi-pistol grip stock. All other specifications were the same.

Exc.	V.G.	Good	Fair	Poor
1000	750	600	500	400

Model 1903 A3

This version was introduced in May of 1942 for use in WWII. It basically consisted of improvements to simplify mass production. It features an aperture sight and various small parts that were fabricated from stampings; this includes the triggerguard, floorplate, and barrel band. The finish is parkerized. This model was manufactured by Remington and Smith Corona.

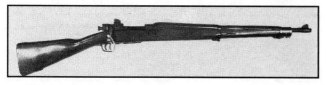

Courtesy Bob Ball

Exc.	V.G.	Good	Fair	Poor
400	350	300	200	100

Model 1903 A4

This is a sniper-rifle version of the Model 1903. It is fitted with permanently mounted scope locks and furnished with a telescopic sight known as the M73B1. This scope was manufactured by Weaver in El Paso, Texas, and was commercially known as the Model 330C. The rifle has no conventional iron sights mounted. this model was built by Remington.

Rifle with WWII M73B1 scope • Courtesy Richard M. Kumor, Sr.

Model 84 scope circa post-Korean War • Courtesy Richard M. Kumor, Sr.

Model 82 scope circa Korea and Vietnam Wars • Courtesy Richard M. Kumor, Sr.

Exc.	V.G.	Good	Fair	Poor
2200	1800	1000	550	350

NOTE: For rifles with M84 scope deduct $250

Model 1903 NRA National Match

This version was based on a standard 1903 service rifle that was selected for having excellent shooting qualities. The parts were then hand-fit, and a special rifled barrel was added that was checked for tolerance with a star gauge. The muzzle of this barrel was marked with a special star with six or eight rays radiating from it. These NRA rifles were drilled and tapped to accept a Lyman No. 48 rear sight. They are marked with the letters "NRA" and have a flaming bomb proofmark on the triggerguard. There were approximately 18,000 manufactured between 1921 and 1928.

NOTE: Prices are for verifiable samples.

Exc.	V.G.	Good	Fair	Poor
3000	2400	2000	1400	800

Model 1903 A1 National Match

Basically the same as the Model 1903 National Match rifle except for the "C" type, or pistol grip stock, without grasping grooves. Bolts and stocks numbered to the receiver. "P" in a circle proof on the underside of the pistol grip, with either a "DAL" in a rectangular cartouche, or S.A./SPG in a square cartouche. Rifles will be found with either a regular or reversed safety. Approximately 11,000 produced with a serial number range from 1285000 to 1532000.

NOTE: Prices are for verifiable samples.

Exc.	V.G.	Good	Fair	Poor
3750	2600	1900	1200	600

Model 1903 Style National Match Special Rifle

This rifle is identical to the National Match, but with a completely different buttstock configuration identical to the Model 1922 NRA. Large shotgun type steel buttplate; full pistol grip. About 150 rifles produced during 1924.

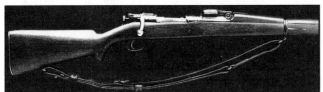

Model 1903 National Match Special Rifle • Courtesy Butterfield & Butterfield

NOTE: Prices are for verifiable samples.

Exc.	V.G.	Good	Fair	Poor
8500	6500	5500	3500	2500

Model 1903 Style "NB" National Match Rifle

This rifle produced with the "B" type stock with more drop than standard, suitable only for off-hand shooting; pistol grip configured with a noticeably squared profile. Deep checkered buttplate. Circle "P" proof in underside of pistol grip. About 195 rifles built between 1925 and 1926.

NOTE: Prices are for verifiable samples.

Exc.	V.G.	Good	Fair	Poor
8500	6500	5500	3500	2500

Model 1903 NRA Sporter

This version is similar to the National Match rifle but features a half-length, Sporter-type stock with one barrel band. It also features the Lyman No. 48 receiver sight. This version was produced for commercial sales. There were approximately 6,500 manufactured between 1924 and 1933.

NOTE: Prices are for verifiable samples.

Exc.	V.G.	Good	Fair	Poor
2600	2200	1800	1400	800

Model 1903 N.B.A. Sporter Rifle

The barrel, action, and sights of this rifle are identical to the Model 1903 NRA sporter rifle above, however it is fitted with a "B" type stock. Grasping grooves and squared pistol grip profile. Circle "P" proof in the underside of the pistol grip. 589 rifles produced at the Springfield Armory during 1925 and 1926.

NOTE: Prices are for verifiable samples.

Exc.	V.G.	Good	Fair	Poor
8500	6500	5500	3500	2500

Model 1903 Heavy Barreled Match Rifles

These rifles were made in a bewildering number of types and variations. Commonly encountered are the style "T" with NRA type stocks. Barrels, which came in three lengths, 26", 28", and 30", measured .860" at the muzzle and 1.250" at the breech, Lyman 48 rear sight; Winchester globe front sight on a modified B.A.R. front band, telescope blocks on the receiver and barrel. Some fitted with adjustable hook type buttplates, set triggers, Garand speed locks, as well as cheekpieces (all commanding premium dollars.) INTERNATIONAL MATCH rifles (worth at least double the values shown) have many

Model 1903 "NB" National Match showing markings • Paul Goodwin Photo

A Rock Island Arsenal Model 1903 sold at auction for $6,875. Condition was excellent plus. Very difficult to find an original unaltered Model 1903 in this condition. Faintich Auction Service, October, 1999

Paul Goodwin Photo

variant features which were changed annually at the request of the individual shooter: these features include palm rests, double set triggers, beaver-tail forends, checkered pistol grips, Swiss style buttplates, etc. Generally the Winchester 5A telescopic sight was used. These rifles are considered rare. Another variation is the 1922 MATCH SPRINGFIELD RIFLE with NRA type stock with grasping grooves, a 24" barrel with service type front sight mount and small base integral with the barrel, as well as telescopic blocks on the barrel. 566 rifles produced at the Springfield Armory between 1922 and 1930.

NOTE: Values shown here are for the standard heavy barrel match rifle without any special features.

Exc.	V.G.	Good	Fair	Poor
7000	5500	4000	2500	1500

Model 1903 Caliber Gallery Practice Rifle "Hoffer-Thompson

This practice rifle differed from the standard issue "03 as follows: the barrel bored and rifled to .22 caliber, the breech chambered for the Hoffer-Thompson cartridge holder, the rear sight graduated to 240 yards, the mainspring shortened, the stocks generally found without cross bolts or the circle "P" on the underside of the pistol grip. Receivers produced after 1901 usually are marked with ".22" on the top of the bridge. About 15,525 rifles were produced at the Springfield Armory between 1907 and 1918.

Exc.	V.G.	Good	Fair	Poor
3250	2200	1400	1000	700

Model 1917

In 1917 when the United States entered WWI, there was a distinct rifle shortage. There were production facilities set up for the British pattern 1914 rifle. This "Enfield" rifle was redesigned to accept the .30-06 cartridge and was pressed into service as the U.S. rifle Model 1917. This rifle appears similar to the British pattern 1914 rifle. In fact, they are so similar that in WWII, when over a million were sold to Britain for use by their Home Guard, it was necessary to paint a 2" stripe around the butt so that the caliber was immediately known. The barrel length is 26", and it has a 5-round integral box magazine. The finish is matte-blue, with a walnut stock. The breech is marked "U.S. Model 1917". This was a robust and heavy-duty rifle, and many are used in the manufacture of large-bore custom rifles to this day. There were approximately 2,200,000 manufactured by Remington and Winchester between 1917 and 1918. The majority were produced at Eddystone, Pennsylvania.

NOTE: Add 30% for Winchester and Remington models.

Exc.	V.G.	Good	Fair	Poor
600	500	350	200	150

Model 1922

This is a bolt-action training rifle chambered for the .22 rimfire cartridge. It appears similar to the Model 1903 but has a 24.5" barrel and a half-length stock without hand guards, held on by a single barrel band. It has a 5-round detachable box magazine. The finish is blued, with a walnut stock. The receiver is marked "U.S. Springfield Armory Model of 1922 Cal. 22". It also has the flaming bomb ordnance mark. There

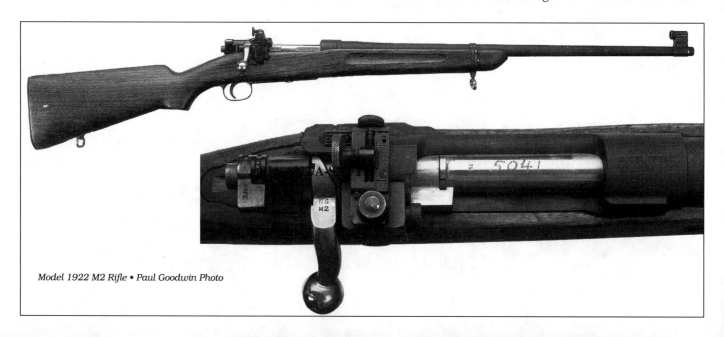

Model 1922 M2 Rifle • Paul Goodwin Photo

were three basic types of the Model 1922: the standard issue type, the NRA commercial type, and the models that were altered to M1 or M2. There were a total of approximately 2,000 manufactured between 1922 and 1924. The survival rate of the original-issue types is not large as most were converted.

Issue Type

Exc.	V.G.	Good	Fair	Poor
800	650	450	250	200

Altered Type

Exc.	V.G.	Good	Fair	Poor
450	350	250	200	150

NRA Type-Drilled and Tapped for Scope

Exc.	V.G.	Good	Fair	Poor
700	550	400	200	150

Model 1922 M1

This version is quite similar to the Model 1922, with a single firing pin that hits the top of the cartridge and a detachable box magazine that does not protrude from the bottom of the stock. The finish is parkerized; and the stock, of walnut. There were approximately 20,000 manufactured between 1924 and 1933.

Unaltered Type

Exc.	V.G.	Good	Fair	Poor
750	650	550	300	200

Altered to M2

Exc.	V.G.	Good	Fair	Poor
450	350	250	200	150

Unaltered NRA Type

Exc.	V.G.	Good	Fair	Poor
650	550	450	300	250

NRA Type Altered to M2

Exc.	V.G.	Good	Fair	Poor
550	500	400	300	250

Model M2

This is an improved version of the Model 1922 M1 that features an altered firing mechanism with a faster lock time. It has a knurled cocking knob added to the bolt and a flush-fitting detachable magazine with improved feeding. There were approximately 12,000 manufactured.

Exc.	V.G.	Good	Fair	Poor
600	500	400	300	200

U.S. Rifle M1 (Garand)

Springfield Armory was one of the manufacturers of this WWII service rifle. It is listed in the Garand section of this text.

Springfield M21 Sniper Rifle

This is the sniper version of the M14 rifle with ART II scope.

M21 with ART II scope and case • Courtesy Richard M. Kumor, Sr.

NOTE: Prices are for verifiable and registered samples.

Exc.	V.G.	Good	Fair	Poor
7000	5500	4000	—	—

KRAG JORGENSEN

The first smallbore, bolt action repeating rifle that used smokeless powder that was adopted by the U.S. government as a service rifle. It was adopted as the Model 1892 and was similar to the rifle being used by Denmark as a service rifle. All of the Krag-Jorgensens were manufactured at the Springfield Armory. There are 11 basic variations of Krag Rifles, and all except one are chambered for the .30-40 Govt. cartridge. They are bolt actions that hold 5 rounds in the unique side-mounted hinged magazine. All of the Krags have walnut stocks and hand guards that are oil-finished. They all have dark gray case hardened receivers and blued barrels. See also *Denmark, Rifles, Krag Jorgensen.*

Bibliographical Note: For historical information, technical data, and photos see Lt. Col. William Brophy's, *The Krag Rifle,* Gun Room Press, 1985.

NOTE: One should be aware that there have been many alterations based on the Krag rifle by many gunsmiths through the years, and the one consistency is that all of these conversions lowered the value of the rifle and rendered it un-collectible. Proceed with caution.

Model 1892

Approximately 24,500 of these rifles produced, dated 1894, 1895, and 1896. They have 30" barrels and are serial numbered from 1-24562. Nearly all were converted to the latter Model 1896, and the original 1st Type is extremely scarce.

1st Type

Serial numbered from 1-1500 and is dated 1894 only. It features a wide upper barrel band and an brass tipped one-piece cleaning rod mounted under the barrel. There is no compartment in the butt, and the muzzle is not crowned and appears flat. The upper hand guard does not extend over the receiver, and the buttplate is flat, without a compartment. One should be wary of fakes and secure expert appraisal if a transaction is contemplated. Unaltered specimens are extremely rare.

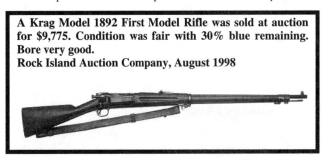

A Krag Model 1892 First Model Rifle was sold at auction for $9,775. Condition was fair with 30% blue remaining. Bore very good.
Rock Island Auction Company, August 1998

Exc.	V.G.	Good	Fair	Poor
18000	15000	12500	6500	3000

2nd Type

Similar to the 1st Type, with a front barrel band that is cut out in the center and does not appear solid. the cleaning rod is a one piece steel type. The serial range is 1500-24562, and the dates 1894 or 1895 are stamped on the receiver and the stock. Again be wary of fakes. This is a rare rifle.

Exc.	V.G.	Good	Fair	Poor
12500	10000	7500	4000	2000

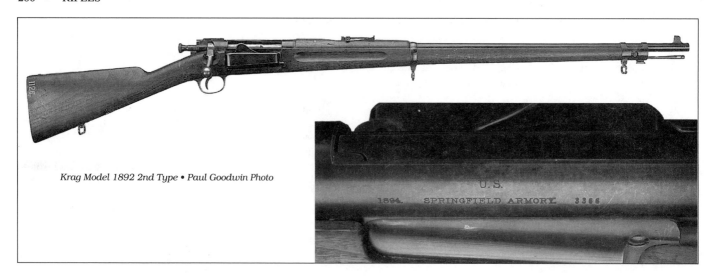

Krag Model 1892 2nd Type • Paul Goodwin Photo

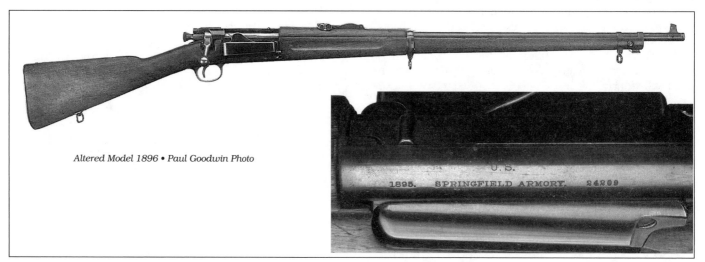

Altered Model 1896 • Paul Goodwin Photo

Model 1892 Altered to 1896 Model

Encompassed nearly the entire production run of the Model 1892 Krag rifle. They still bear the dates 1894, 1895, and 1896 on the receiver; but they do not have a one piece cleaning rod under the barrel but instead a 3 piece type inserted into butt stock, and the hole in the stock has been plugged. The front barrel band was changed. The top hand guard covers the receiver, and the buttplate is curved at the bottom. The muzzle is crowned.

Exc.	V.G.	Good	Fair	Poor
850	550	400	250	150

Model 1895 Carbine (Variation)

Marked "1895" and "1896" on the receiver—without the word Model. They were produced before the Model 1896 was officially adopted, and they are serial numbered from 25000 to 35000. They are similar to the Model 1896 Carbine, with a smaller safety and no oiler bottle in the butt.

Courtesy Richard M. Kumor Sr.

Exc.	V. G.	Good	Fair	Poor
1800	1250	1000	650	400

Model 1896 Rifle

Similar to the altered Model 1892 and has a 30" barrel with the cleaning kit in the butt. The rear sight was improved, and the receiver is marked "U.S. Model 1896" and "Springfield Armory." Lightning cuts were made in the barrel channel to reduce weight. A total of about 62,000 Model 96 rifles were produced in observed same serial number range as the Model 1896 carbine of 37,240 to 108,471. The stock is dated 1896, 1897, and 1898. There were many of these altered to the later stock configurations—in the field or at the Springfield Armory. These changes would lower the value, and one should secure expert appraisal on this model.

Courtesy Richard M. Kumor Sr.

Exc.	V.G.	Good	Fair	Poor
1200	850	500	400	250

Model 1896 Carbine

Similar to the 1896 Rifle, with a 22" barrel and half-length stock held on by one barrel band. There were approximately less than 20,000 manufactured between 1896 and 1898, and the serial number range is 35000-90000. There were many rifles cut to carbine dimensions—be wary of these alterations!

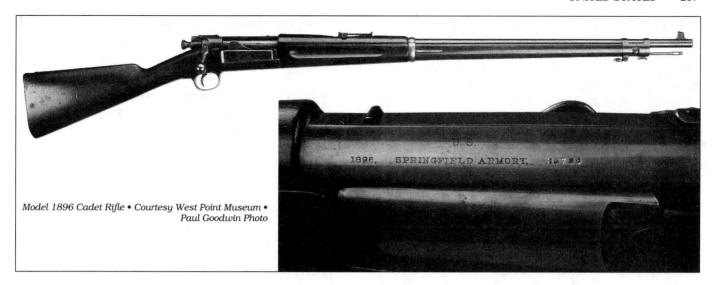

Model 1896 Cadet Rifle • Courtesy West Point Museum •
Paul Goodwin Photo

Courtesy Jim Supica, Old Town Station

Exc.	V.G.	Good	Fair	Poor
1500	950	650	400	200

Model 1896 Cadet Rifle

A rare variation produced for use by the Military Academy at West Point. The dimensions are the same as the 1896 Rifle with a one-piece cleaning rod under the barrel and the 1896-type front band. There were 400 manufactured, and most were altered to standard configuration when they were phased out in 1898. Extremely rare in original and unaltered condition.

Exc.	V.G.	Good	Fair	Poor
—	—	25000	10000	—

Model 1898 Rifle

This model is similar to the Model 1896 in appearance except that the receiver is marked "U.S./Model 1898." The bolt handle was modified, and the sights and hand guards were improved. There were 330,000 manufactured between 1898 and 1903, and the serial number range is 110000-480000.

Courtesy Rock Island Auction Company

Exc.	V.G.	Good	Fair	Poor
1500	1000	500	250	150

Model 1898 Carbine

Similar to the rifle, with a 22" barrel and a bar and ring on the left side of the receiver. There were approximately 5,000 manufactured in 1898 and 1899. The serial range is 118000-134000. Again, be aware that many of the rifles have been converted to carbine dimensions over the years. When in doubt secure an independent appraisal.

Exc.	V.G.	Good	Fair	Poor
3500	2500	2000	950	400

Model 1898 Carbine 26" Barrel

An attempt to satisfy both the infantry and the cavalry. There were 100 manufactured for trial, and the serial range is between 387000-389000. Be wary of fakes.

Exc.	V.G.	Good	Fair	Poor
—	10000	5000	2000	750

Model 1898 Practice Rifle

The only Krag not chambered for the .30-40 cartridge. It is chambered for the .22 rimfire and was designed as a target-practice rifle. It has a 30" barrel and is identical in exterior appearance to the Model 1898 Rifle. The receiver is marked the same as the standard model—with "Cal .22" added. There were approximately 840 manufactured in 1906 and 1907. Serial numbers are above 475,000.

Exc.	V.G.	Good	Fair	Poor
—	3500	1500	700	300

Model 1899 Carbine

The last of the Krags; and it is similar to the 1898, with the "Model 1899" stamped on the receiver and a 2" longer stock. There were approximately 36,000 manufactured between 1900 and 1903. Serial numbers observed are between 222,609 and 362,256. These numbers are part of the Model 1898 rifle series.

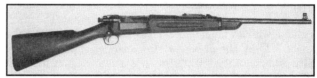

Courtesy Milwaukee Public Museum, Milwaukee, Wisconsin

Exc.	V.G.	Good	Fair	Poor
2000	1500	850	600	350

A Krag Model 1899 Carbine sold at auction for $2,530. Condition was excellent to mint.
Rock Island Auction Company, August 1998

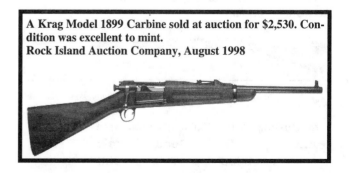

Model 1899 Philippine Constabulary Carbine

Approximately 8,000 modified to accept the knife bayonet at the Springfield Armory and the Rock Island Arsenal. The Springfield pieces are marked "J.F.C." on the stock. This model has a 22" barrel, with the full, but shortened stock of the rifle held on with two barrel bands. One must exercise extreme care as many rifles were altered in a similar manner at later dates.

Courtesy Jim Supica, Old Town Station

NOTE: Prices are for verifiable samples.

Exc.	V. G.	Good	Fair	Poor
—	2500	2000	900	500

Benicia Arsenal Conversion

In the 1920s the Department of Civilian Marksmanship had a number of Krag rifles converted for their use. These are Model 1898 rifles shortened and fitted with Model 1899 Carbine stocks. These conversions are beginning to be regarded as legitimate variations by some collectors of Krag rifles.

Exc.	V.G.	Good	Fair	Poor
—	450	250	175	100

COLT

NOTE: For historical information, technical details, and photos see Blake Stevens' and Edward Ezell's, *The Black Rifle: M16 Retrospective*, Collector Grade Publications, 1994

Berdan Single Shot Rifle (M.1870)

This is a scarce rifle on today's market. There were approximately 30,200 manufactured, but nearly 30,000 of them were sent to Russia. This rifle was produced from 1866-1870. It is a trapdoor-type action chambered for .42 centerfire. The standard model has a 32.5" barrel; the carbine, 18.25". The finish is blued, with a walnut stock. This rifle was designed and the patent held by Hiram Berdan, Commander of the Civil War "Sharpshooters" Regiment. This was actually Colt's first cartridge arm. The 30,000 rifles and 25 half-stocked carbines that were sent to Russia were in Russian Cyrillic letters. The few examples made for American sales have Colt's name and Hartford address on the barrel.

NOTE: For information on Russian built Berdan rifles see *Russia, Rifles, Berdan.*

Courtesy Milwaukee Public Museum, Milwaukee, Wisconsin

Rifle Russian Order, 30,000 Manufactured

Exc.	V.G.	Good	Fair	Poor
—	2000	750	450	—

Carbine Russian Order, 25 Manufactured

Exc.	V.G.	Good	Fair	Poor
—	5500	3000	1250	—

Rifle U.S. Sales, 100 Manufactured

Exc.	V.G.	Good	Fair	Poor
—	5000	2250	1250	—

Carbine U.S. Sales, 25 Manufactured

Exc.	V.G.	Good	Fair	Poor
—	9500	4500	2000	—

Colt-Franklin Military Rifle

This is a rifle that was not a successful venture for Colt. The patents were held by William B. Franklin, a vice-president of the company. This was a bolt-action rifle with a primitive, gravity-fed box magazine. It is chambered for the .45-70 government cartridge, has a 32.5" barrel, and is blued, with a walnut stock. The rifle has the Colt Hartford barrel address and is stamped with an eagle's head and U.S. inspectors marks. There were only 50 of these rifles produced, and it is believed that they were prototypes intended for government sales. This was not to be, and production ceased after approximately 50 were manufactured in 1887 and 1888.

Exc.	V.G.	Good	Fair	Poor
—	8000	4500	2000	—

Lightning Slide Action, Medium Frame

This was the first slide action rifle Colt produced. It is chambered for.32-20,.38-40, and .44-40 and was intended to be a companion piece to the SAAs in the same calibers. The rifle has a 26" barrel with 15-shot tube magazine; the carbine, a 20" barrel with 12-shot magazine. The finish is blued, with case-colored hammer; the walnut stock is oil-finished; and the forend, usually checkered. The Colt name and Hartford address are stamped on the barrel along with the patent dates. There were approximately 89,777 manufactured between 1884 and 1902. The military variant is listed below.

Military Rifle or Carbine

Chambered for .44-40 caliber, fitted with short magazine tube, bayonet lug, and sling swivels. These guns are fitted with various barrel lengths.

Exc.	V.G.	Good	Fair	Poor
—	4500	2000	1000	600

U.S. M14/M14A1

Based on the famous M1 Garand design this select fire rifle is chambered for the 7.62x51mm cartridge. It has a 21.8" barrel and a 20-round magazine. It weighs approximately 11.2 lbs. Rate of fire is about 750 rounds per minute. Marked "US RIFLE 7.62MM M14" on the rear top of the receiver. Production began in 1957 and ceased in 1963. Produced by Harrington & Richardson, Springfield, Winchester, and TRW. The M14A1 version is a light machine gun variant with bipod, folding forward hand grip, and muzzle compensator.

NOTE: A sniper version of this rifle was designated the M21 and fitted with a Leatherwood telescope sight.

Courtesy Richard M. Kumor, Sr.

Pre-1968

Exc.	V.G.	Fair
6500	6300	6000

Pre-1986 conversions (or U.S. manufacture/M1A Springfield Armory)

Exc.	V.G.	Fair
3500	3250	3000

Pre-1986 Dealer samples

Exc.	V.G.	Fair
N/A	N/A	N/A

U.S. M4 Carbine

This is a short barrel version of the M16 with collapsible stock. Chambered for 5.56x45mm cartridge. It is fitted with a 14.3" barrel and has a magazine capacity of 20 or 30 rounds. Its rate of fire is 700 rounds per minute. Weight is about 5.6 lbs. Marked "COLT FIREARMS DIVISION COLT INDUSTRIES HARTFORD CONN USA" on the left side of the receiver with "COLT M4 CAL 5.56MM" on the left side of the magazine housing. In use with American military forces as well as several South American countries.

Photo Courtesy Private NFA Collection

Pre-1968

Exc.	V.G.	Fair
N/A	N/A	N/A

Pre-1986 conversions or OEM/Colt (Rare)

Exc.	V.G.	Fair
9000	7000	6500

Pre-1986 Dealer samples

Exc.	V.G.	Fair
N/A	N/A	N/A

U.S. M16 Standard Rifle

This rifle was first produced in 1964 with many variants following. Chambered for the 5.56x45mm cartridge it has a 20.8" barrel with flash hider. Magazine capacity is 20 or 30 rounds. Weight is 7 lbs. Rate of fire is 800 rounds per minute. Used extensively in Vietnam and now throughout the world. Marked "COLT AR-15 PROPERTY OF US GOVT.M16 CAL 5.56MM" on left side of magazine housing. There is a wide variation in prices and models. Prices listed below are for the standard rifle.

Pre-1968

Exc.	V.G.	Fair
7000	6500	6000

Pre-1986 conversions, for OEM A1 add 40%

Exc.	V.G.	Fair
4500	4300	4000

Pre-1986 Dealer samples

Exc.	V.G.	Fair
2500	2500	2250

U.S. M16 A2

This model is a variation of the M16 Standard rifle with a slower rate of barrel twist and a heavier barrel. A case deflector is mounted on the right side. Sights are an improved version of the standard M16 type. First produced in 1982.

Pre-1968

Exc.	V.G.	Fair
N/A	N/A	N/A

Pre-1986 OEM/Colt

Exc.	V.G.	Fair
9000	8500	8000

Pre-1986 Dealer samples

Exc.	V.G.	Fair
N/A	N/A	N/A

M16 Rimfire Conversion Kits

There are several different conversion kits featuring different designs both adapted by the U.S. military. Both of these kits use a 10 round magazine but are not interchangeable with each other. The first is the Rodman design, known as the Air Force Model, built by OK Industries, New Britain, CT and the second is the M261 built by the Maremont Corp., Saco, ME. TM 9-6920-363-12 issued with the M261 conversion kit. The Atchisson Mark I and Mark II kits and the Atchisson Mark III made by Jonathan Ciener, Inc. are also used by military forces in the U.S. and well as by foreign governments. The Ciener kit was introduced about 1988 and is designed to be used in both the M16 and AR15 rifles, both semi-automatic fire and full auto fire. Rate of fire is between 700 and 800 rounds per minute in the M16.

Ciener Kit Mark III

Exc.	V.G.	Good	Fair	Poor
200	150	—	—	—

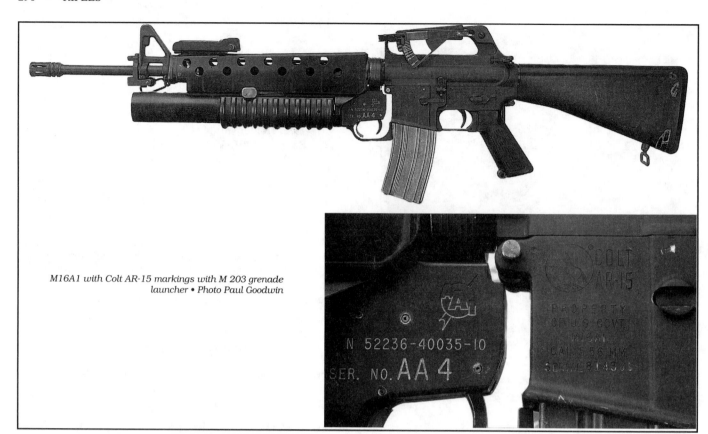

M16A1 with Colt AR-15 markings with M 203 grenade launcher • Photo Paul Goodwin

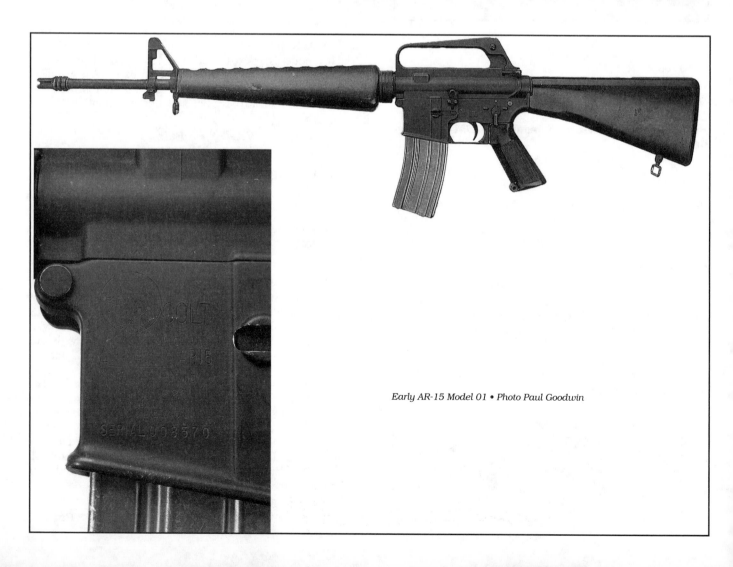

Early AR-15 Model 01 • Photo Paul Goodwin

Colt M16 NOTE: The Colt M16 comes in a variety of configurations (upper receivers) some of which are mentioned here. It is important to note that these configurations are based on the same lower receiver. In the case of civilain ownership the lower receiver is the regestered part of the firearm as far as the BATF is concerned. Therefore, it is possible, with a registered lower receiver, to interchange upper receiver components to a variety of different configurations from 9mm to .223 LMG uppers. Be aware that this interchangeability works best with Colt parts.

AR-15 Sporter (Model #6000)

A semiautomatic rifle firing from a closed bolt was introduced into the Colt product line in 1964. Similar in appearance and function to the military version, the M-16. Chambered for the .223 cartridge. It is fitted with a standard 20" barrel with no forward assist, no case deflector, but with a bayonet lug. Weighs about 7.5 lbs. Dropped from production in 1985.

NIB	Exc.	V.G.	Good	Fair	Poor
1450	1100	850	700	600	400

AR-15 Sporter w/Collapsible Stock (Model #6001)

Same as above but fitted with a 16" barrel and folding stock. Weighs approximately 5.8 lbs. Introduced in 1978 and discontinued in 1985.

NIB	Exc.	V.G.	Good	Fair	Poor
1600	1350	1000	800	600	400

AR-15 Carbine (Model #6420)

Introduced in 1985 this model has a 16" standard weight barrel. All other features are the same as the previous discontinued AR-15 models. This version was dropped from the Colt product line in 1987.

NIB	Exc.	V.G.	Good	Fair	Poor
1600	1350	1000	800	600	400

AR-15 9mm Carbine (Model #6450)

Same as above but chambered for 9mm cartridge. Weighs 6.3 lbs.

NIB	Exc.	V.G.	Good	Fair	Poor
1350	1100	900	750	550	400

Colt AR-15 and Colt Sporter Terminology

There are three different and distinct manufacturing cycles that not only affect the value of these rifles but also the legal consequences of their modifications.

Pre-Ban Colt AR-15 rifles (Pre-1989): Fitted with bayonet lug, flash hider, and stamped AR-15 on lower receiver. Rifles that are NIB have a green label. It is legal to modify this rifle with any AR-15 upper receiver. These are the most desirable models because of their pre-ban features.

Colt Sporters (Post-1989-pre-September, 1994): This transition model has no bayonet lug, but it does have a flash hider. There is no AR-15 designation stamped on the lower receiver. Rifles that are NIB have a blue label. It is legal to modify this rifle with upper receivers made after 1989, i.e. no bayonet lug. These rifles are less desirable than pre-ban AR-15s.

Colt Sporters (Post-September, 1994): This rifle has no bayonet lug, no flash hider, and does not have the AR-15 designation stamped on the lower receiver. Rifles that are NIB have a blue label. It is legal to modify this rifle only with upper receivers manufactured after September, 1994. These rifles are the least desirable of the three manufacturing periods because of their lack of pre-ban military features and current manufacture status.

AR-15A2 (Model #6500)

Introduced in 1984 this was an updated version with a heavier barrel and forward assist. The AR sight was still utilized. Weighs approximately 7.8 lbs.

NIB	Exc.	V.G.	Good	Fair	Poor
1350	1100	900	750	550	400

U.S. Army photo, 101st Airborne, Vietnam, February, 1966

AR-15A2 Govt. Model Carbine (Model #6520)

Added to the Colt line in 1988 this 16" standard barrel carbine featured for the first time a case deflector and the improved A2 rear sight. This model is fitted with a 4-position telescoping buttstock. Weighs about 5.8 lbs.

NIB	Exc.	V.G.	Good	Fair	Poor
1950	1500	1250	950	700	500

AR-15A2 Gov't. Model (Model #6550)

This model was introduced in 1988 is the rifle equivalent to the Carbine. It features a 20" A2 barrel, forward assist, case deflector, but still retains the bayonet lug. Weighs about 7.5 lbs. Discontinued in 1990. USMC model.

NIB	Exc.	V.G.	Good	Fair	Poor
1950	1500	1250	950	700	500

AR-15A2 H-Bar (Model #6600)

Introduced in 1986 this version features a special 20" heavy barrel. All other features are the same as the A2 series of AR15s. Discontinued in 1991. Weighs about 8 lbs.

NIB	Exc.	V.G.	Good	Fair	Poor
1950	1500	1250	950	700	500

AR- 15A2 Delta H-Bar (Model #6600DH)

Same as above but fitted with a 3x9 scope and detachable cheekpiece. Dropped from the Colt line in 1990. Weighs about 10 lbs.

NIB	Exc.	V.G.	Good	Fair	Poor
2250	1900	1500	1200	850	600

Sporter Lightweight Rifle

This lightweight model has a 16" barrel and is finished in a matte black. It is available in either a .223 Rem. caliber (Model #6530) that weighs 6.7 lbs., a (Model #6430) 9mm caliber weighing 7.1 lbs., or a (Model #6830) 7.65x39mm that weighs 7.3 lbs. The .223 is furnished with two five-round box magazines as is the 9mm and 7.65x39mm. A cleaning kit and sling are also supplied with each new rifle. The buttstock and pistol grip are made of durable nylon and the handguard is reinforced fiberglass and aluminum lined. The rear sight is adjustable for windage and elevation. These newer models are referred to simply as Sporters and are _not_ fitted with a bayonet lug and receiver block has different size pins.

NIB	Exc.	V.G.	Good	Fair	Poor
1350	1100	900	650	400	300

NOTE: The Model 6830 will bring about $25 less than the above prices. For post-9/94 guns deduct 30%.

Sporter Target Model Rifle (Model #6551)

This 1991 model is a full size version of the Lightweight Rifle. The Target Rifle weighs 7.5 lbs. and has a 20" barrel. Offered in .223 Rem. caliber only with target sights adjustable to 800 meters. New rifles are furnished with two 5-round box magazines, sling, and cleaning kit.

NIB	Exc.	V.G.	Good	Fair	Poor
1350	1100	900	650	400	300

NOTE: For post-9/94 guns deduct 30%.

Sporter Match H-Bar (Model #6601)

This 1991 variation of the AR-15 is similar to the Target Model but has a 20" heavy barrel chambered for the .223 caliber. This model weighs 8 lbs. and has target type sights adjustable out to 800 meters. Supplied with two 5-round box magazines, sling, and cleaning kit.

NIB	Exc.	V.G.	Good	Fair	Poor
1500	1200	900	650	400	300

NOTE: For post-9/94 guns deduct 35%.

Colt AR-15 (XM16E1)

This rifle was made upon request for foreign contracts. Very rare. Proceed with caution. This variation will command a premium price over the standard AR-15 rifle. Secure an appraisal before a sale.

Courtesy Richard M. Kumor, Sr.

Courtesy Richard M. Kumor, Sr.

Sporter Match Delta H-Bar (Model #6601 DH)

Same as above but supplied with a 3x9 scope. Weighs about 10 lbs. Discontinued in 1992.

NIB	Exc.	V.G.	Good	Fair	Poor
1800	1500	1100	850	600	400

Match Target H-BAR Compensated (Model #6601C)

Same as the regular Sporter H-BAR with the addition of a compensator.

NIB	Exc.	V.G.	Good	Fair	Poor
1250	900	750	—	—	—

Sporter Competition H-Bar (Model #6700)

Introduced in 1992, the Competition H-Bar is available in .223 caliber with a 20" heavy barrel counterbored for accuracy. The carry handle is detachable with target sights. With the carry handle removed the upper receiver is dovetailed and grooved for Weaver-style scope rings. This model weighs approximately 8.5 lbs. New rifles are furnished with two 5-round box magazines, sling, and cleaning kit.

NIB	Exc.	V.G.	Good	Fair	Poor
1500	1300	950	700	500	350

NOTE: For post-9/94 guns deduct 35%.

Sporter Competition H-Bar Select w/scope (Model #6700CH)

This variation, also new for 1992, is identical to the Sporter Competition with the addition of a factory mounted scope. The rifle has also been selected for accuracy and comes complete with a 3-9X rubber armored variable scope, scope mount, carry handle with iron sights, and nylon carrying case.

NIB	Exc.	V.G.	Good	Fair	Poor
1900	1500	1150	850	600	400

Match Target Competition H-BAR Compensated (Model #6700C)

Same as the Match Target with a compensator.

NIB	Exc.	V.G.	Good	Fair	Poor
1250	900	—	—	—	—

AR-15 Carbine Flat-top Heavyweight/Match Target Competition (Model #6731)

This variation in the Sporter series features a heavyweight 16" barrel with flat-top receiver chambered for the .223 cartridge. It is equipped with a fixed buttstock. Weight is about 7.1 lbs.

NIB	Exc.	V.G.	Good	Fair	Poor
1250	1000	800	600	400	300

NOTE: For post-9/94 guns deduct 30%.

AR-15 Tactical Carbine (Model #6721)

This version is similar to the above model with the exception of the buttstock which is telescoping and adjusts to 4 positions. Chambered for the .223 cartridge with a weight of about 7 lbs. A majority of these guns were for law enforcement only.

NIB	Exc.	V.G.	Good	Fair	Poor
1900	1500	1200	—	—	—

Sporter H-Bar Elite/Accurized Rifle (Model #6724)

This variation was introduced in 1996 and features a free floating 24" stainless steel match barrel with an 11 degree target crown and special Teflon coated trigger group. The handguard is all-aluminum with twin swivel studs. Weight is approximately 9.26 lbs.

NIB	Exc.	V.G.	Good	Fair	Poor
1200	1000	800	550	—	—

Armalite AR-18

First introduced in 1966 as a cheaper M16, this select fire rifle was fitted with an 18" barrel and folding metal stock. Magazine capacity was 20, 30, or 40 rounds. Chambered for the 5.56x45mm cartridge this rifle had a rate of fire of 800 rounds per minute. It weight is 7 lbs. Marked "AR 18 ARMALITE" on the pistol grip and "ARMALITE AR-18 PATENTS PENDING" on the left side of the magazine housing. Production ceased in 1979.

Pre-1968

Exc.	V.G.	Fair
4500	4200	4000

Pre-1986 conversions

Exc.	V.G.	Fair
3000	3000	3000

Pre-1986 Dealer samples

Exc.	V.G.	Fair
N/A	N/A	N/A

U.S. CALIBER .30 CARBINE

Bibliographical Note: There are a number of variations, sights, stock configurations, etc. that are too numerous to cover in this publication It is strongly recommended that for additional historical information, technical data, and photos see Larry L. Ruth's, *War Baby!, The U.S. Caliber .30 Carbine*, Collector Grade Publications, 1992.

This carbine was designed by William Roemer, Edwin Pugsley, and others at the Winchester Repeating Arms Company in late 1940 and early 1941. The only feature that can be credited to David Marsh "Carbine" Williams is the short stroke piston design. The U.S. M1 Carbine was produced by a number of manufacturers as listed below. The M1 A1 version was produced by Inland. The selective fire version is known as the Model M2. The exact number of carbines produced is unknown but approximately 6,000,000 carbines were built during World War II.

NOTE: Deduct 50% for imports.

U.S. M3 Carbine

This model is identical to the select fire M2 carbine with the exception of no rear sight and the scope mount to support a variety of scopes for specific uses.

U.S. M3 Carbine • Paul Goodwin Photo

Pre-1986

Exc.	V.G.	Fair
4000	3500	3000

Pre-1986 conversions

Exc.	V.G.	Fair
3000	2750	2500

Pre-1986 Dealer samples

Exc.	V.G.	Fair
2500	2750	2500

M3 Carbine with scope • Courtesy Richard M. Kumor, Sr.

NOTE: For M3 Carbines with infra red scope add $1,000.

U.S. M2 Carbine

First produced in 1942 this select fire rifle is the automatic version of the famous M1 carbine. It has a 17.8" barrel and a 15- or 30-round magazine. It is chambered for the .30 Carbine cartridge (7.62x33mm). Its rate of fire is 750 rounds per minute. Weight is about 5.25 lbs. Marked "U.S.CARBINE CAL .30 M2" on top of chamber. Widely used by American forces during World War II.

Pre-1968

Exc.	V.G.	Fair
4000	3500	3000

Pre-1986 conversions

Exc.	V.G.	Fair
3000	2750	2500

Pre-1986 Dealer samples

Exc.	V.G.	Fair
2500	2750	2500

U.S. M1 Carbine

Introduced in 1941 this is a semiautomatic, gas operated carbine with a 18" barrel and a magazine capacity of 15 or 30 rounds. Half stocked with upper handguard and single barrel band. Bayonet bar located on barrel. Flip up rear sight. Chambered for the .30 U.S. Carbine cartridge. Weight is about 5.25 lbs. Widely used by U.S. military forces during World War II.

NOTE: Prices are for carbines in World War II factory configuration.

Inland

Exc.	V.G.	Good	Fair	Poor
900	700	500	350	250

Underwood

Exc.	V.G.	Good	Fair	Poor
950	750	550	400	275

U.S. M2 Carbine, with selector switch and cartouche • Paul Goodwin Photo

S.G. Saginaw

Exc.	V.G.	Good	Fair	Poor
950	750	550	400	275

IBM

Exc.	V.G.	Good	Fair	Poor
950	750	525	375	250

Quality Hardware

Exc.	V.G.	Good	Fair	Poor
925	725	525	375	250

National Postal Meter

Exc.	V.G.	Good	Fair	Poor
925	725	525	375	250

Standard Products

Exc.	V.G.	Good	Fair	Poor
925	725	525	375	250

Rockola

Exc.	V.G.	Good	Fair	Poor
1000	800	700	425	275

SG Grand Rapids

Exc.	V.G.	Good	Fair	Poor
950	725	550	425	350

Winchester

Exc.	V.G.	Good	Fair	Poor
1250	850	700	500	400

Irwin Pedersen

Exc.	V.G.	Good	Fair	Poor
1500	1000	850	600	500

M1 Carbine Cutaway

Used by factories and military armorer's to facilitate training. Examples with documentation will bring a substainial premium.

M1 Carbinme cutaway • Courtesy Richard M. Kumor, Sr.

Exc.	V.G.	Good	Fair	Poor
1500	1000	850	600	500

M1 Carbine Sniper

This is an M1 carbine with a M84 scope mounted with forward vertical grip. Used in Korea.

Exc.	V.G.	Good	Fair	Poor
1200	950	650	400	300

U.S. M1 A1 Paratrooper Model

The standard U.S. M1 Carbine fitted with a folding stock. Approximately 110,000 were manufactured by Inland between 1942 and 1945. Weight is about 5.8 lbs.

Courtesy Richard M. Kumor, Sr.

Exc.	V.G.	Good	Fair	Poor
1800	1500	1250	1000	650

An M1 Carbine paratrooper model was sold at auction for $1,495. Stamped "INLAND" on barrel. Sling included. Condition was excellent to mint.
Amoskeag Auction Company, August 1999

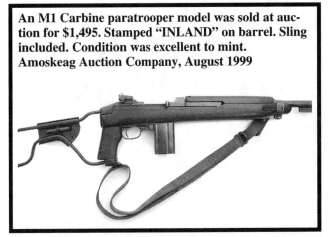

An example of an U.S. M1 Presentation Carbine • Courtesy Richard M. Kumor, Sr.

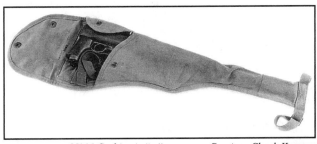

M1A1 Carbine in its jimp case. • Courtesy Chuck Karwan

GARAND
(U.S. M1 Rifle)
U.S. Rifle, CAL. M1 (Garand)

BIBLIOGRAPHICAL NOTE: For further information, technical, and photos see Bruce Canfield, *Complete Guide to the M1 Garand and the M1 Carbine*. Mobray,

An Introduction to U.S. M1 Rifle
By Simeon Stoddard

Adopted in 1936 the M1 remained the standard issue rifle of the United States until it was replaced by the M14 in 1957. It was designed by John C. Garand, who worked for Springfield

Armory from 1919 until his retirement in 1953. During this time Garand concentrated his efforts on the development of a semiautomatic shoulder weapon for general issue to the U.S. armed forces. The M14 rifle, the replacement for the M1, was a compilation of his design work as well.

With the exceptions noted, all values given are for rifles which are in original, as produced condition. Development of the M1 was an ongoing project until it was replaced, as Garand never finished perfecting his basic design. Over 5,400,000 M1 rifles were built, with the majority of them going through a rebuilding process at least once during their service life. During rebuilding, rifles were inspected and unserviceable parts replaced. Parts used for replacement were usually of the latest revision available or what was on hand.

Major assemblies and parts were marked with a government drawing size/part number. This number is often followed with the revision number (see photo above). Barrels were marked, with the exception of early Springfield Armory and all Winchester production, with the month and year of manufacture. It must be remembered that this date only refers to when the barrel was produced, and has nothing to do with when the receiver was produced or the rifle was assembled. This barrel date on "original as produced" rifles should be from 0 to 3 months, before the receiver was produced.

Restored rifles, defined as ones with parts added/replaced to more closely match what they might have been originally, are worth less money than "original as produced" rifles. This difference should be on the order of 30-40% of the values shown, and is due to the low number of rifles of this type. When in doubt, get an appraisal. To tell what parts should be correct, study chapters 5 & 6 of "The M1 Garand: WWII" and chapters 7 & 8 of "The M1 Garand: Post WWII" by Scott A. Duff.

Rebuilt Rifle, any manufacture

Value shown is for rifles with a majority of its parts mixed/replaced. Depending on the type of rebuilding that a rifle went through, rifles could be completely disassembled with no attempt to put parts together for the same rifle. Valued mainly for shooting merits. Bore condition, gaging and overall appearance are important factors.

Exc.	V.G.	Good
650	500	400

DCM Rifles

These rifles should have the correct paperwork and shipping boxes to receive the amounts listed. Prices should be considered to be base price as some DCM M1's fall into the following categories:

Exc.	V.G.	Good
650	550	450

Navy Trophy Rifles

The Navy continued to use the M1 rifle as its main rifle far into the 1960's. They were modified to shoot the 7.62x51 Nato (Winchester) round. This was accomplished at first with a chamber insert, and later with new replacement barrels in the Nato caliber. The Navy modified rifles can be found of any manufacture, and in any serial number range. As a general rule, Navy rifles with new barrels are worth more due to their better shooting capabilities. Paper work and original boxes must accompany these rifles to obtain the values listed.

U.S.N. Crane Depot Rebuild

Exc.	V.G.	Good
1250	1000	900

AMF Rebuild

Exc.	V.G.	Good
1000	900	750

H&R Rebuild

Exc.	V.G.	Good
900	800	700

Springfield Armory Production

Gas trap sn: ca 81-52,000

Values shown for original rifles. Most all were updated to gas port configuration. Look out for reproductions being offered as original rifles! Get a professional appraisal before purchasing.

Exc.	V.G.	Good
40000	35000	25000

M1 Garand Gas Trap close-up • Courtesy Chuck Karwan

Gas tap/modified to gas port

These rifles should have many of their early parts.

Exc.	V.G.	Good
5000	**3500**	**2500**

pre-Dec. 7, 1941 gas port production pn sn: ca 50,000-Apx. 410,000

Exc.	V.G.	Good	Fair	Poor
2000	1500	1000	750	650

WWII Production sn: ca 410,000-3,880,000

Exc.	V.G.	Good	Fair	Poor
1250	1000	900	750	500

POST WWII Production sn: ca 4,200,000-6,099,361

Exc.	V.G.	Good	Fair	Poor
1000	800	650	500	450

Winchester Production

Winchester produced around 513,00 M1 rifles during WWII. Their first contract was an educational order in 1939. This contract for 500 rifles and the gauges and fixtures to produce the rifles. Winchester's second contract was awarded during 1939 for up to 65,000 rifles. Winchester M1's are typified by noticeable machine marks on their parts, and did not have the higher grade finish that is found on Springfield Armory production. Watch for fake barrels, and barrels marked "Winchester" which were produced in the 1960s as replacement barrels.

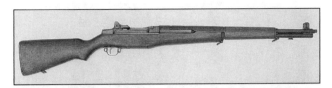

Winchester Educational Contract sn: 100,000-100,500

Exc.	V.G.	Good	Fair	Poor
7500	5500	4500	3500	2500

Winchester sn: 100,501-165,000

Rifles of this serial number range were produced from Jan 1941 until May 1942.

Exc.	V.G.	Good	Fair	Poor
5500	4000	3000	2000	1500

Winchester sn: 1,200,00-1,380,000

Rifles in this serial number range were produced from May 1942 until Aug 1943.

Exc.	V.G.	Good	Fair	Poor
2500	2000	1800	1000	750

Winchester sn: 2,305,850-2,536,493

Rifles in this serial number range were produced from Aug 1943 until Jan 1945.

Exc.	V.G.	Good	Fair	Poor
2250	1850	1250	900	550

Winchester sn: 1,601,150-1,640,000

Rifles in this serial number range were produced from Jan 1945 until June 1945. These are often referred to as Win-13's because of the revision number of the right front receiver leg.

Exc.	V.G.	Good	Fair	Poor
2800	2500	2000	1500	850

Harrington & Richardson Production

Between 1953 and 1956 Harrington & Richardson produced around 428,00 M1 rifles.

Exc.	V.G.	Good	Fair	Poor
1000	750	650	450	350

International Harvester Corp. production

Between 1953 and 1956, International Harvester produced around 337,000 M1 rifles. International at several different times during their production purchased receivers from both Harrington & Richardson and Springfield Armory. Always check for Springfield Armory heat lots on the right front receiver leg.

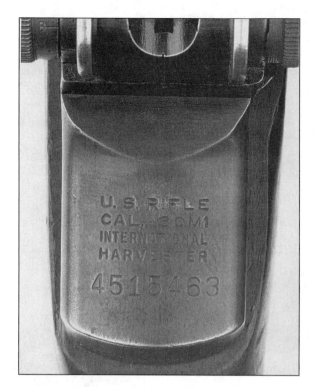

International Harvester Production

Exc.	V.G.	Good	Fair	Poor
1000	750	600	400	350

International Harvester/with Springfield Receiver (postage stamp)

Exc.	V.G.	Good
1800	1250	900

International Harvester/with Springfield Receiver (arrow head)

Exc.	V.G.	Good
1850	1200	1000

International Harvester/with Springfield Receiver (Gap letter)

Exc.	V.G.	Good
1250	1000	900

International Harvester/with Harrington & Richardson Receiver

Exc.	V.G.	Good
1250	1050	850

M1 Experimental w/one piece upper handguard made of fiberglass. •
Courtesy Richard M. Kumor, Sr.

M1 Garand Cutaway

Used by factories and military armorer's to facilitate training.

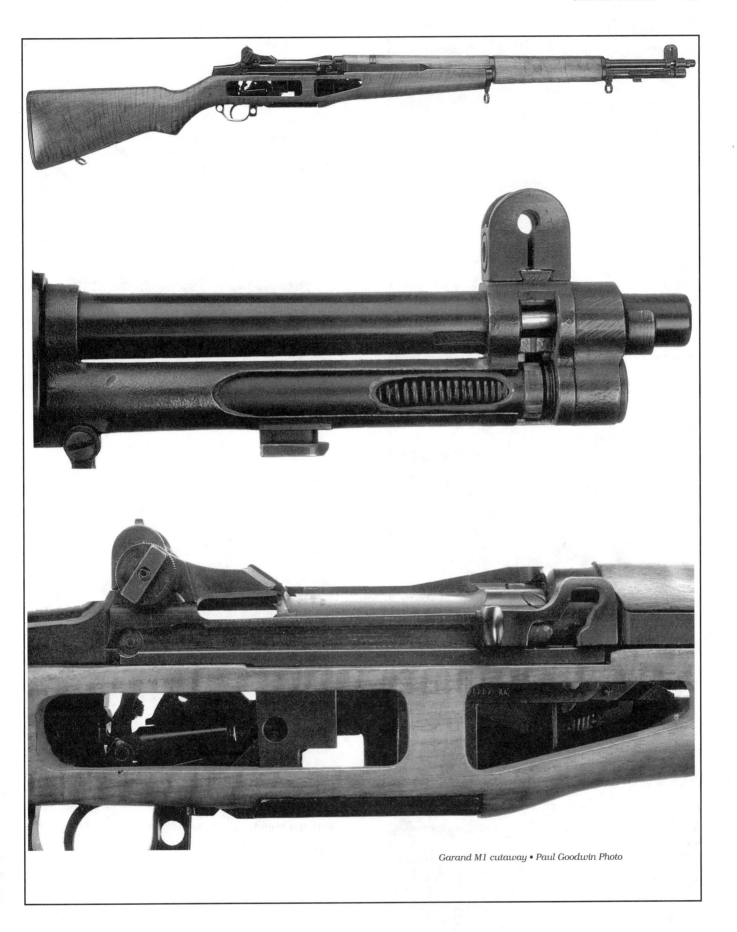

Garand M1 cutaway • Paul Goodwin Photo

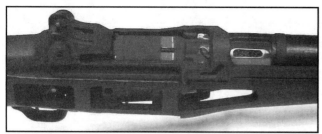

M1 Garand cutaway • Courtesy Richard M. Kumor, Sr.

Exc.	V.G.	Good	Fair	Poor
1500	1000	850	600	500

NOTE: For examples with documentation add 300%.

SCOPE VARIANTS (SNIPER RIFLES)

M1C

Springfield Armory production only. Serial number range is between ca 3,200,000 and 3,800,000. This variant is very rare with only around 7,900 produced. Should be mounted with M81, M82 or M84 scope with 7/8" scope rings. The scopes alone are worth $700 to $800 alone. Ask for government relicense paperwork, and have a serial number check run before purchase is made. If provenance can not be established then rifles are worth the value of their individual parts, under $2000.

M1C serial number markings and cartouche • Paul Goodwin Photo

Exc.	V.G.	Good
10000	8000	5000

MC 1952 (USMC Issue)

Same production range as above. Should be equipped with 1 inch scope mount and Kollmorgen scope. These rifles will command a premium. This is the rarest of the M-1 Snipers.

Courtesy Richard M. Kumor Sr.

Close-up of MC 1952 scope and mount. • Courtesy Richard M. Kumor, Sr.

M1D

This model can be found by any manufacture and in any serial number range. This mounting system was designed by John Garand, and consists of a mounting block on the rear of the barrel. The rear hand guard is shortened and the mount attaches with a large single screw system. The modification could be made on the field repair level. It is not known how many rifles were modified, but it is very likely that they numbered into the tens of thousands. If the rifle does not come with paperwork, it is only worth the value of its parts alone, under $1200. The Model 92 scope is worth between $400 and $500.

Courtesy Richard M. Kumor, Sr.

Exc.	V.G.	Good
2500	2000	1500

National Match

Type I

Produced on Springfield Armory receivers and in serial number ranges from ca 5,800,000 to around 6,090,000. All parts are available to reproduce both types of national match rifles. To obtain values listed these rifles must come with original paperwork.

Exc.	V.G.	Good
3000	2500	1800

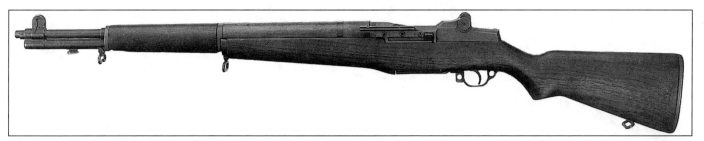

Springfield M1C rifle • Paul Goodwin Photo

Type II

Produced on Springfield Armory receivers, they can be found in any serial number range. These rifles should come with papers to receive values listed.

Exc.	V.G.	Good
8500	6500	5000

KNIGHT'S MANUFACTURING CO.

SR-25 Lightweight Match (U.S. Navy, Mark 11 Model O)

This .308 rifle is fitted with a 20" free floating barrel. No sights. Weight is about 9.5 lbs. Adopted by U.S. Navy. Commercial version is the same except for the markings on the receiver.

NIB	Exc.	V.G.	Good	Fair	Poor
2995	2250	1500	900	—	—

REMINGTON ARMS COMPANY, INC.

U.S. Navy Rolling Block Carbine

A .50-70 caliber single shot rolling block carbine with a 23.25" round barrel. A sling ring is normally fitted to the left side of the frame and sling swivels are mounted on the barrel band and the bottom of the butt. Inspector's markings are to be found on the right side of the frame as well as the stock. Blued, case hardened with a walnut stock. The barrel marked "Remington's Ilion, N.Y. U.S.A." along with the patent dates. Approximately 5,000 were manufactured in 1868 and 1869.

Exc.	V.G.	Good	Fair	Poor
3500	2500	2000	850	350

Model 1867 Navy Cadet Rifle

A .50-45 caliber single shot rolling block rifle with a 32.5" barrel and full length forend secured by two barrel bands. Markings identical to the above with the exception that "U.S." is stamped on the buttplate tang. Blued, case hardened with a walnut stock. Approximately 500 were made in 1868.

Exc.	V.G.	Good	Fair	Poor
—	—	2000	850	350

Rolling Block Military Rifles

Between 1867 and 1902 over 1,000,000 rolling block military rifles and carbines were manufactured by the Remington Company. Offered in a variety of calibers and barrel lengths, the values listed below are for full length rifles. Carbines are worth approximately 40% more.

Courtesy Milwaukee Public Museum, Milwaukee, Wisconsin

Exc.	V.G.	Good	Fair	Poor
—	—	750	400	100

Remington-Keene Magazine Rifle

A bolt-action rifle chambered for the .40, .43, and .45-70 centerfire cartridges with 22", 24.5", 29.25", or 32.5" barrels. It is readily identifiable by the exposed hammer at the end of the bolt. Blued, case hardened hammer and furniture, with a walnut stock. The receiver marked "E. Remington & Sons, Ilion, N.Y." together with the patent dates 1874, 1876, and 1877. The magazine on this rifle was located beneath the barrel and the receiver is fitted with a cut-off so that the rifle could be used as a single shot. Approximately 5,000 rifles were made between 1880 and 1888 in the following variations:

Sporting Rifle-24.5" Barrel

Exc.	V.G.	Good	Fair	Poor
—	1500	750	350	150

Army Rifle

Barrel length 32.5" with a full-length stock secured by two barrel bands. Prices are for martially marked examples.

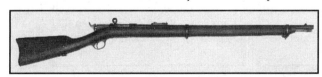

Courtesy Milwaukee Public Museum, Milwaukee, Wisconsin

Exc.	V.G.	Good	Fair	Poor
—	3000	1650	750	300

Navy Rifle

As above, with a 29.25" barrel. Prices are for martially marked examples.

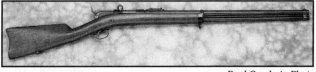

Paul Goodwin Photo

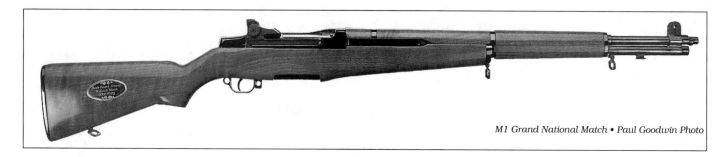

M1 Grand National Match • Paul Goodwin Photo

Exc.	V.G.	Good	Fair	Poor
—	4750	3000	1500	750

Carbine

As above, with a 22" barrel and a half-length forend secured by one barrel band.

Courtesy Milwaukee Public Museum, Milwaukee, Wisconsin

Exc.	V.G.	Good	Fair	Poor
—	3250	1500	750	350

Frontier Model

As above, with a 24" barrel and half-length forend secured by one barrel band. Those purchased by the United States Department of the Interior for arming the Indian Police are marked "U.S.I.D." on the receiver.

Exc.	V.G.	Good	Fair	Poor
—	—	4500	2500	850

Remington-Lee Magazine Rifle

Designed by James Paris Lee, rifles of this type were originally manufactured by the Sharps Rifle Company in 1880. The Remington Company began production of this model in 1881 after the Sharps Company ceased operations. Approximately 100,000 Lee magazine rifles were made between 1880 and 1907. Their variations are as follows:

Model 1879 U.S. Navy Model

Barrel length 28", .45-70 caliber with a full-length stock secured by two barrel bands. The barrel is marked with U.S. Navy Inspector's Marks and an anchor at the breech. The receiver marked "Lee Arms Co. Bridgeport, Conn. U.S.A." and "Patented Nov. 4, 1879." Approximately 1300 were made.

Paul Goodwin Photo

Exc.	V.G.	Good	Fair	Poor
3500	2500	1750	750	250

Model 1882 Army Contract

This model is identifiable by the two grooves pressed into the side of the magazine. The receiver is marked "Lee Arms Co. Bridgeport Conn., U.S.A." and on some examples it is also marked "E. Remington & Sons, Ilion, N.Y. U.S.A. Sole Manufactured & Agents." Barrel length 32", caliber .45-70, full-

length stock secured by two barrel bands. U.S. Inspector's marks are stamped on the barrel breech and the stock. Approximately 750 were made

Paul Goodwin Photo

Exc.	V.G.	Good	Fair	Poor
2500	2000	1750	750	300

Model 1885 Navy Contract

As above, with the inspection markings (including an anchor) on the receiver ring and the left side of the stock. Approximately 1,500 were made.

Exc.	V.G.	Good	Fair	Poor
2500	2000	1750	750	300

Model 1882 & 1885 Military Rifles

Barrel length 32", full-length stock secured by two barrel bands, chambered for .42 Russian, .43 Spanish, .45 Gardner or .45-70 cartridges. The values for those rifles not in .45-70 caliber would be approximately 25% less than those shown below. Approximately 10,000 Model 1882 rifles were made and 60,000 Model 1885 rifles. The two models can be differentiated by the fact that the cocking piece on the bolt of the Model 1885 is larger. The majority of these rifles were made for foreign contracts and commercial sales

Exc.	V.G.	Good	Fair	Poor
—	—	950	400	150

Model 1899

Designed for use with smokeless and rimless cartridges, this model is marked on the receiver "Remington Arms Co. Ilion, N.Y. Patented Aug. 26th 1884 Sept. 9th 1884 March 17th 1885 Jan 18th 1887." Produced from 1889 to 1907 in the following variations:

Military Rifle

Barrel length 29", 6mm USN, .30-40, .303, 7x57mm or 7.65mm caliber with a full-length stock secured by two barrel bands.

Paul Goodwin Photo

Exc.	V.G.	Good	Fair	Poor
—	1000	450	200	100

NOTE: Add $250 if U.S. marked.

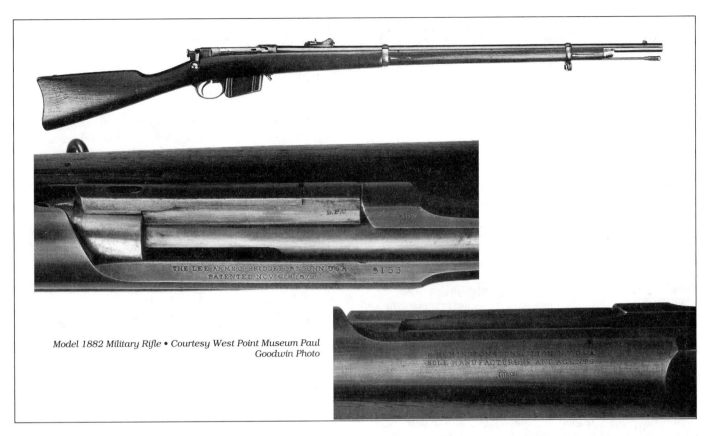

Model 1882 Military Rifle • Courtesy West Point Museum Paul Goodwin Photo

Military Carbine

As above, with a 20" barrel and a 3/4 length carbine stock secured by one barrel band.

Exc.	V.G.	Good	Fair	Poor
—	1500	700	300	100

Remington Lebel Bolt-Action Rifle (Model 1907/1915)

Produced for the French government, this rifle has a 31.5" barrel of 8mm Lebel caliber and a full-length stock secured by two barrel bands. The barrel marked "RAC 1907-15" and the left side of the receiver marked "Remington M'LE 1907-15." Several thousand were manufactured between 1907 and 1915.

Paul Goodwin Photo

Exc.	V.G.	Good	Fair	Poor
—	600	300	150	100

Remington Mosin-Nagant Bolt-Action Rifle

Produced for the Imperial Russian government, this rifle has a 32" barrel of 7.62mm caliber with a full-length stock secured by two barrel bands. The barrel is marked "Remington Armory" with the date of manufacture and the receiver ring is stamped with the Russian coat-of-arms. Approximately 500,000 were made between 1916 and 1918.

Paul Goodwin Photo

Exc.	V.G.	Good	Fair	Poor
—	500	275	100	75

U.S. Model 1917 Magazine Rifle

Produced for the United States government by Eddystone as the principal manufacturer and also by Remington and Winchester. This rifle has a 26" barrel of .30-06 caliber and a full length stock secured by two barrel bands. Those sold to the British government during WWII are often found with a 2" wide red and white painted stripe around their magazine, which was intended to show that they were chambered for the .30-06 cartridge instead of the .303 British cartridge. Total production unknown.

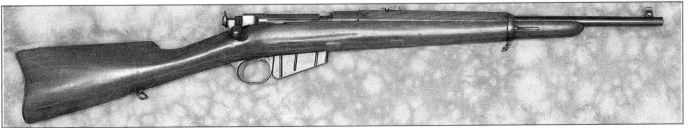

Remington Model 1899 Military Carbine • Paul Goodwin Photo

Paul Goodwin Photo

Exc.	V.G.	Good	Fair	Poor
1200	950	400	150	100

Model 513-T

This is a bolt action .22 caliber training rifle with oil finished walnut stock and checkered steel butt. Barrel length is 26.75" and detachable magazine capacity is 6 rounds. Rear sight is an adjustable Redfield Model 75 RT. Most, but not all, of these rifles are drilled and tapped for telescope mounting blocks. Receiver is stamped "us property". some of these rifles will have the arsenal rebuilder stamped on the barrel. About 70,000 of these rifles were produced under government contract from 1942 to 1944.

Exc.	V.G.	Good	Fair	Poor
750	600	500	300	200

Model 700 (M40)

This is a military version of the commercial Remington bolt action rifle. It was issued without sights and a 10x scope. chambered for the .308 (7.62x51 Nato) cartridge. Barrel length is 24". Magazine capacity is 5 rounds. Walnut stock with oil finish. Scope is a Redfield 3-9X Accu-Range. Buttplate, trigger guard and floorplate are aluminum. Weight is about 14 lbs with scope. Marked, "US RIFLE M40" with the serial number over the chamber. First issued in 1966. Weight is about 9.25 lbs. Primarily used the U.S. Marine Corp.

In 1977 an improved version of this rifle was issued known as the M40A1. Same barrel length and scope butt fitted with a synthetic McMillan camouflage stock, Pachmayr brown recoil pad and steel trigger guard and floorplate. In 1980 the Marine Corp began using Unertl 10X scope with mil-dot reticle with Unertl base and rings.

NOTE: Prices listed below are for verifiable samples.

Exc.	V.G.	Good	Fair	Poor
5000	3500	2500	1500	1000

Remington Model 700P Rifles

Remington's line of law enforcement rifles are also used by a variety of military forces. Rifles purchased under contract will be marked for the country and service of origin. Models purchased by commercial means will not be marked.

Model 700 Police LTR (Lightweight Tactical Rifle)

Fitted with a fluted 20" barrel and chambered for the .308 or .223 cartridge this rifle weighs about 7.5 lbs. Synthetic stock.

NIB	Exc.	V.G.	Good	Fair	Poor
700	550	—	—	—	—

Model 700 Police

This model is fitted with a 26" barrel and chambered for the .308 and .223 cartridges in a short action or 7mm Rem. Mag., .300 Win. Mag., or .300 Rem. Ultra Mag. in a long action. Weight is about 9 lbs. Synthetic stock.

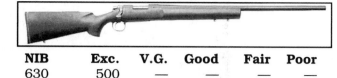

NIB	Exc.	V.G.	Good	Fair	Poor
630	500	—	—	—	—

Model 700 TWS (Tactical Weapons System)

Chambered for the .308 cartridge and fitted with a 26" barrel this model also features a Leupold Vari-X II 3.5x10 scope, a Harris bipod, quick adjustable sling. and a Pelican hard case. Weight of rifle is about 10.5 lbs.

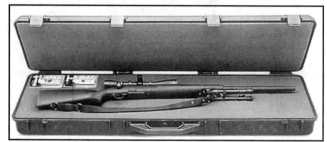

Courtesy Remington Arms

NIB	Exc.	V.G.	Good	Fair	Poor
N/A	—	—	—	—	—

Model 700 VS LH

This model is a left hand version of the Model 700m Police.

NIB	Exc.	V.G.	Good	Fair	Poor
630	500	—	—	—	—

Model 40-XB KS

Two versions of this rifle are offered. In the single shot version it is chambered for the .223, .308, and .300 Win. Mag calibers. In the repeating version it is chambered in the .223 or .308 calibers. All versions are fitted with a 27.25" barrel. Weight is about 10.25 lbs. Martially marked rifles will command a premium over retail prices.

NOTE: Retail prices range from $1,200 to $1,500 depending on configuration and finish.

PARKER HALE

Model 85 Sniper

Built by the Gibbs Rifle Co. in Martinsburg, West Virginia this Parker-Hale designed bolt action rifle is chambered for the .308 cartridge and fitted with a 27.5" barrel with a telescope and bipod. Box magazine capacity is 10 rounds. Weight is about 12.5 lbs. First produced in 1986.

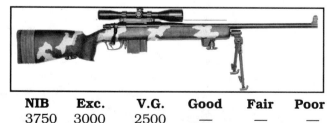

NIB	Exc.	V.G.	Good	Fair	Poor
3750	3000	2500	—	—	—

SAVAGE

Model 1899-D Military Musket

Chambered for .303 Savage only with 28" barrel. Fitted with full military stocks. Produced from 1899 to 1915. Several hundred produced for Canadian Home Guard during WWI. These will have rack numbers on buttplate.

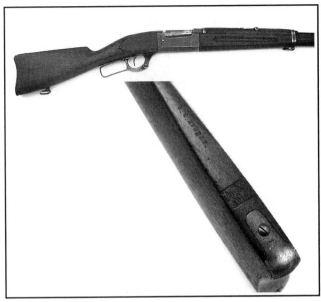

Photo courtesy Amoskeag Auction Company

Exc.	V.G.	Good	Fair	Poor
3000	2000	1500	700	300

WINCHESTER REPEATING ARMS COMPANY

NOTE: The U. S. government purchased many different Winchester rifles over the years for a wide variety of purposes. During World War I the Model 1894 carbine was purchased by the government as well as small numbers of the Model 1907 and the Model 1910 self loading rifles. There is evidence that the U.S. Coast Guard purchased a several thousand of Model 1906 .22 caliber rifles for use during World War I. The Model 52 bolt action rifle was first designed by Winchester in hopes of a government contract as a military training rifle but the end of World War I precluded that goal. During World War II the U.S. government purchased the Winchester Model 74 .22 caliber rifles from 1941 to 1943. It is possible that many Winchester rifles were purchased by the U.S. military for assorted purposes from guard duty to pest control. Many of these rifles will be martially marked and their value increased over the standard civilian rifle.

Bibliographical Note: For more historical information, technical data, and photos see Bruce Canfield's, *A Collector's Guide to Winchester's in the Service.* Also Thomas Henshaw, *The History of Winchester Firearms, 1866-1992,* Winchester Press, 1995. George Madis, *The Winchester Book,* 1985.

Model 1873 Musket

This rifle was fitted with a 30" round barrel and chambered for a variety of calibers at the customers request. Nominal calibers are: .44-40, .38-40, and .32-20. Magazine capacity was 17 rounds. Muskets were fitted with almost full length wooden stocks with cleaning rod. and bayonet fittings. Many of these muskets were sold under contract to foreign governments. Survival rate is very low.

1st Model

Exc.	V.G.	Good	Fair	Poor
N/A	N/A	N/A	N/A	N/A

2nd Model

The dust cover on the Second Model operates on one central guide secured to the receiver with two screws. The checkered oval finger grip is still used, but on later Second Models this is changed to a serrated finger grip on the rear of the dust cover. Second Models are found in the 31000 to 90000 serial number range.

Exc.	V.G.	Good	Fair	Poor
—	—	7500	3500	1250

3rd Model

The central guide rail is still present on the Third Model, but it is now integrally machined as part of the receiver. The serrated rear edges of the dust cover are still present on the Third Model.

Exc.	V.G.	Good	Fair	Poor
—	—	6000	2500	1000

Model 1876

Musket, 32" round barrel with full-length forearm secured by one barrel band and straight grip stock. Stamped on the barrel is the Winchester address with King's patent date. The caliber marking is stamped on the bottom of the receiver near the magazine tube and the breech end of the barrel.

First Model

As with the Model 1873, the primary difference in model types lies in the dust cover. The First Model has no dust cover and is seen between serial number 1 and 3000.

Musket

Exc.	V.G.	Good	Fair	Poor
—	7000	4000	2000	1000

Second Model

The Second Model has a dust cover with guide rail attached to the receiver with two screws. On the early Second Model an oval finger guide is stamped on top of the dust cover while later models have a serrated finger guide along the rear edge of the dust cover. Second Models range from serial numbers 3000 to 30000.

Musket

Exc.	V.G.	Good	Fair	Poor
8000	4000	2000	1000	700

Third Model

The dust cover guide rail on Third Model 76s is integrally machined as part of the receiver with a serrated rear edge on the dust cover. Third Model will be seen from serial numbers 30000 to 64000.

Musket

Exc.	V.G.	Good	Fair	Poor
7500	3500	1750	900	650

Model 1886

Based on a John Browning patent, the Model 1886 was one of the finest and strongest lever actions ever utilized in a Winchester rifle. Winchester introduced the Model 1886 in order to take advantage of the more powerful centerfire cartridges of the time.

Musket, 30" round barrel, musket style forearm with one barrel band. Military style sights. About 350 Model 1886 Muskets were produced. This is the most rare variation of all Winchester lever action rifles.

Musket

Exc.	V.G.	Good	Fair	Poor
—	15000	7500	3000	1500

Model 1895

U.S. Army Musket

U.S. Army Musket, 28" round barrel chambered for the .30-40 Krag. Came equipped with or without knife bayonet. These muskets were furnished to the U.S. Army for use during the Spanish-American War and are "US" marked on the receiver.

Exc.	V.G.	Good	Fair	Poor
—	3000	1500	1000	650

Russian Musket

Russian Musket, similar to standard musket but fitted with clip guides in the top of the receiver and with bayonet. Approximately 294,000 Model 1895 Muskets were sold to the Imperial Russian Government between 1915 and 1916. The first 15,000 Russian Muskets had 8" knife bayonets, and the rest were fitted with 16" bayonets. Some of these rifles went to Spain in its Civil War in 1936-1939.

Exc.	V.G.	Good	Fair	Poor
4000	2500	1000	500	250

Model 1885 (Single Shot)

The High Wall musket most often had a 26" round barrel chambered for the .22 caliber cartridge. Larger calibers were available as were different barrel lengths. The High Wall Musket featured an almost full length forearm fastened to the barrel with a single barrel band and rounded buttplate.

The Low Wall musket is most often referred to as the Winder Musket named after the distinguished marksman, Colonel C.B. Winder. This model features a Lyman receiver sight and was made in .22 caliber.

U.S. and Ordnance markings will appear on rifles purchased by the government.

High Wall Musket

Exc.	V.G.	Good	Fair	Poor
2750	2000	1200	900	700

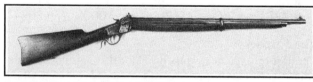

Courtesy Buffalo Bill Historical Center, Cody, Wyoming

Low Wall Musket (WinderMusket)

Exc.	V.G.	Good	Fair	Poor
2250	1500	700	400	250

Winchester Hotchkiss Bolt Action Rifle

This model is also known as the Hotchkiss Magazine Gun or the Model 1883. This rifle was designed by Benjamin Hotchkiss in 1876, and Winchester acquired the manufacturing rights to the rifle in 1877. In 1879 the first guns were deliv-

ered for sale. The Hotchkiss rifle was a bolt-action firearm designed for military and sporting use. It was the first bolt-action rifle made by Winchester. The rifle was furnished in .45-70 Government, and although the 1884 Winchester catalog lists a .40-65 Hotchkiss as being available, no evidence exists that such a chamber was ever actually furnished. Two different types of military configurations will be seen:

1. Carbine, 24" round or 22-1/2" round barrel with military style straight grip stock. Chambered for the 45-55 cartridge.

2. Musket, 32" or 28" round barrel with almost full length military-style straight grip stock. Winchester produced the Model 1883 until 1899, having built about 85,000 guns. Chambered for the 45-70 cartridge.

First Model

This model has the safety and a turn button magazine cut-off located above the triggerguard on the right side. The carbine has a 24" round barrel with a saddle ring on the left side of the stock. The musket has a 32" round barrel with two barrel bands, a steel forearm tip, and bayonet attachment under the barrel. The serial number range for the First Model is between 1 and about 6419.

Army Rifle

These Army models are marked with the inspector stamping of "ESA/1878" on the left side of the stock.

Courtesy Butterfield & Butterfield, San Francisco, California

Exc.	V.G.	Good	Fair	Poor
5500	2500	1500	900	500

Carbine

Exc.	V.G.	Good	Fair	Poor
5500	2500	1500	900	500

Musket

Exc.	V.G.	Good	Fair	Poor
5500	2500	1500	900	500

Second Model

On this model the safety is located on the top left side of the receiver, and the magazine cutoff is located on the top right side of the receiver to the rear of the bolt handle. The carbine has a 22-1/2" round barrel with a nickeled forearm cap. The musket now has a 28" barrel. Serial number range for the Second Model runs from 6420 to 22521.

Carbine

Exc.	V.G.	Good	Fair	Poor
4500	2250	1000	750	500

Musket

Exc.	V.G.	Good	Fair	Poor
4500	2250	1000	750	500

Third Model

The Third Model is easily identified by the two-piece stock separated by the receiver. The carbine is now fitted with a 20" barrel with saddle ring and bar on the left side of the frame.

Close-up of Hotchkiss 1st Model • Courtesy George Hoyem

Close-up of Hotchkiss 2nd Model • Courtesy George Hoyem

Close-up of Hotchkiss 3rd Model action • Courtesy George Hoyem

The musket remains unchanged from the Second Model with the exception of the two-piece stock. Serial numbers of the Third Model range from 22552 to 84555.

Carbine

Exc.	V.G.	Good	Fair	Poor
4250	2500	1000	700	400

Courtesy Butterfield & Butterfield, San Francisco, California

Musket

Exc.	V.G.	Good	Fair	Poor
4250	2500	750	500	300

Winchester-Lee Straight Pull Rifle

This rifle was a military firearm that Winchester built for the U.S. Navy in 1895. The Navy version was a musket type with 28" round barrel and musket style forearm and plain walnut pistol grip stock. In 1897 Winchester offered a commercial musket version for public sale as well as a Sporting Rifle. All of these guns were chambered for the 6mm Lee (.236 Caliber) cartridge. The Sporting Rifle featured a 24" round barrel with plain walnut pistol grip stock and finger grooves in the forearm. Built from 1895 to 1905, Winchester sold about 20,000 Lee rifles; 15,000 were sold to the U.S. Navy, 3,000 were sold in the commercial version, and 1,700 were Sporting Rifles.

NOTE: Commercial and Sporting rifles will not have martial markings, inspector markings, or bayonet fittings.

U.S. Navy Musket

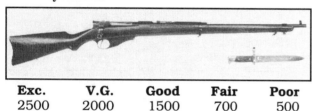

Exc.	V.G.	Good	Fair	Poor
2500	2000	1500	700	500

HARRINGTON & RICHARDSON, INC.

Reising Model 60

A .45 ACP caliber semiautomatic rifle with an 18.25" barrel and a 12- or 20-round detachable magazine. Blued, with a walnut stock. It operates on a retarded blowback system and was developed to be used as a police weapon. Manufactured between 1944 and 1946.

Courtesy Richard M. Kumor, Sr.

Exc.	V.G.	Good	Fair	Poor
1400	1200	500	250	100

Model 65 Military

A .22 l.r. caliber semiautomatic rifle with a 23" barrel and Redfield peep sights. Blued, with a walnut stock. Manufactured between 1944 and 1956.

NOTE: Add 100% if USMC marked.

Courtesy Richard M. Kumor, Sr.

Exc.	V.G.	Good	Fair	Poor
350	300	200	125	90

BARRETT F.A. MFG. CO.

Model 95 (M 107 Sniper Weapon System)

Introduced in 1995 this .50 caliber BMG bolt action model features a 29" barrel and 5 round magazine. Scope optional. Weight is 22 lbs. Adopted by the US Army in 2000 as an anti-material weapon out to 1,500 plus meters. This model differs from the commercial version in that it breaks down into two smaller sections, it is fitted with an 11.5" optical rail, it has one takedown pin, it has a detachable bipod with spiked feet, it is fitted with front and rear iron sights, it has adjustable scope rings.

NIB	Exc.	V.G.	Good	Fair	Poor
4500	4000	3000	2000	—	—

SHOTGUNS

For a more detailed historical and technical account of US military shotguns see Bruce Canfield's, *A Collectors Guide to United States Combat Shotguns*, Andrew Mobray, 1999. Also Thomas F. Swearengen, *The World's Fighting Shotguns*, Vol IV, Ironside International Publishers, 1978.

WINCHESTER

Model 1897 Trench Gun (Model 1917)

Slide action hammer gun 12 gauge, 20" barrel bored to shoot buckshot, plain walnut modified pistol grip stock with grooved slide handle. Solid frame (WWI) or takedown (WWII). Fitted with barrel hand guard and bayonet. This model was furnished to the U.S. Army for trench work in

Winchester Model 1897 Trench Gun • Courtesy Rock Island Auction Company

World War I. It was not listed in Winchester catalogs until 1920. This model was also used in large numbers in WWII, Korea, and Vietnam. Prices below are for US marked guns.

Model 97 Solid Frame-World War I

Exc.	V.G.	Good	Fair	Poor
5000	3500	2000	1000	700

Model 97 Take Down-World War II

Exc.	V.G.	Good	Fair	Poor
4500	3000	1800	800	650

NOTE: Add about $200 for Winchester marked bayonet.

Model 12 Trench Gun

Slide action hammerless gun 12 gauge, 20" barrel bored to shoot buckshot, plain walnut modified pistol grip stock with grooved slide handle. Solid frame or takedown. Fitted with barrel hand guard and bayonet. Finish is blued. This model was furnished to the U.S. Army for trench work in World War I and World War II. Prices below are for US marked guns.

Exc.	V.G.	Good	Fair	Poor
4500	3000	1800	800	650

NOTE: Add about $200 for Winchester marked bayonet.

REMINGTON

Model 10 Trench Gun

Slide action 12 gauge shotgun with 23" round barrel. No checkering on butt stock. Wooden handguard and bayonet lug. Prices below for shotgun only with military markings.

Exc.	V.G.	Good	Fair	Poor
15000	12500	10000	7500	5000

Model 11 Military Riot Gun

This is a 12 gauge 20" barrel shotgun used during WWI. Most were blued some were Parkerized when rebuilt. Military markings with stock cartouche. Many thousands were sold to the military and are often encountered.

Exc.	V.G.	Good	Fair	Poor
1000	800	600	400	200

Model 31 Military Riot Gun

This model was to replace the Model 10. Built in a short barrel (20") riot configuration there were about 15,000 of these shotgun bought by the military but most were in the longer barrel lengths used for training. Stocks were not checkered. Martially marked.

Exc.	V.G.	Good	Fair	Poor
1500	1000	750	500	350

Model 870 Mark I

This is a slide action 12 gauge shotgun with Parkerized finish. Fitted with an 18" round barrel. Prices are for military marked guns.

Exc.	V.G.	Good	Fair	Poor
5000	3500	2000	1250	850

NOTE: The Model 870 is still purchased by the U.S. military in a number of different configurations. The key to the correct designation of these more current shotguns lies with the military markings.

Model 11-87P

This is a semi-automatic 12 gauge shotgun with an 18" barrel and 7 round magazine extension. Fitted with synthetic stock. Purchased by various branches of the U.S. military this shotgun may be found in a number of different configurations. All will be military marked.

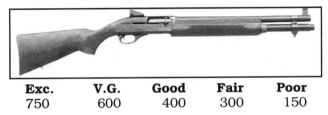

Exc.	V.G.	Good	Fair	Poor
750	600	400	300	150

SAVAGE

Model 720 Military Riot Gun

A semiautomatic 12 gauge shotgun similar in design to the Remington 11 and the Browning A-5. Some 15,000 of these shotgun were sold to the military during WWII. Martially marked. One of the more rare WWII shotguns.

Exc.	V.G.	Good	Fair	Poor
2500	1850	1500	850	500

STEVENS

Model 520 U.S. Marked Trench Gun

A slide action shotgun manufactured from 1930 to 1949. Used extensively in WWII. About 35,000 of these guns were purchased by the government during the war. Blued finish. Trench guns were fitted with metal handguards and bayonet adopters. there is also a military version without handguard called a riot gun. These model will also have military markings. Riot guns will bring less than Trench Guns.

Exc.	V.G.	Good	Fair	Poor
1750	1350	850	500	350

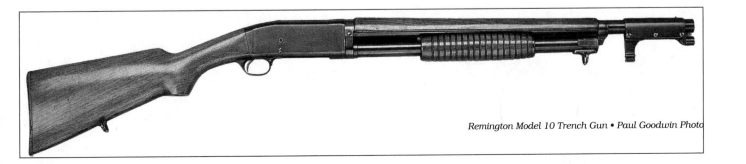

Remington Model 10 Trench Gun • Paul Goodwin Photo

Model 11 Military Riot Gun • Courtesy West Point Museum • Paul Goodwin Photo

Model 520 Trench Gun • Courtesy West Point Museum • Paul Goodwin Photoo

Model 620 U.S. Marked Trench Gun

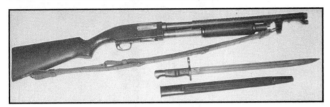

Courtesy Richard M. Kumor Sr.

Exc.	V.G.	Good	Fair	Poor
2000	1600	1100	600	300

NOTE: Add $150 for bayonet.

Stevens .22/.410 Shotgun-Rifle combination

This was the precursor to the Model 24. First made in 1940 with a Tenite stock this combination gun was used by some bomber crews during WWII. According to SAvage records the US government purchased about 10,000 of these guns during the war as well as some years after as some of these guns were marked "USAF".

Exc.	V.G.	Good	Fair	Poor
N/A	—	—	—	—

MOSSBERG

Model 590 Special Purpose (ATP8)

Fitted with a 20" shrouded barrel, bayonet lug, parkerized or blued finish. Speed feed stock and ghost ring sights. Introduced in 1987. Weight is about 7.25 lbs. Military marked. This gun is also offered in a commercial version.

NIB	Exc.	V.G.	Good	Fair	Poor
350	275	200	175	125	100

Model 590A1

A 12 gauge slide action shotgun fitted with an 18" barrel. This model differs from the commercial one by having an aluminum trigger housing instead of plastic, an aluminum safety instead of plastic, and a heavy walled barrel. The finish is Parkerized and military marked.

Exc.	V.G.	Good	Fair	Poor
350	300	250	200	100

ITHACA

For a more detailed description of Ithaca military shotguns see Walter Snyder's book, *Ithaca Featherlight Repeaters...the Best Gun Going: A Complete History of the Ithaca Model 37 and the Model 87*, Cook and Uline Publishing, 1998.

Model 37 Military Marked Trench Gun (WWII)

This is one of the scarcest military shotguns. It was built in three different configurations; 30" barrel, 20" barrel, and 20" barrel with handguard and bayonet lug (Trench Gun). A scarce shotgun, proceed with caution.

Model 37 with 20" barrel and release papers. • Courtesy Richard M. Kumor, Sr.

Exc.	V.G.	Good	Fair	Poor
10000	7500	5000	2500	1500

NOTE: Add $200 for government release papers and 150% for Trench Gun configuration.

Model 37 Military Marked Trench Gun (Vietnam)

Same as above but built from 1962 to 1963. Fitted with 20" barrel. Stock was not checkered and had oil finish. Receiver had "US" stamped. Highest serial number reported is S23710.

Exc.	V.G.	Good	Fair	Poor
3500	2500	1800	900	750

Model 37 Military Marked Trench Gun (Navy Contract)

Similar to the Model 37 Trench gun but built in 1966-1967 for US Navy Ammunition Depot. About 3,000 were built. Based on the Model 37 M&P model.

Exc.	V.G.	Good	Fair	Poor
5000	3500	2500	1250	900

BENELLI

M4 Super 90 (M1014)

Adopted by the U.S. Marine Corps this 12 gauge shotgun features a choice of three modular buttstock and two barrel configurations. Action is semi-auto or slide action. Top mounted Picatinny rail. Barrel length is 18.5". Magazine capacity is 6 rounds. Ghost-ring sights. Black MILSPEC finish. Weight is about 8.4 lbs. Matte black finish. Deliveries in 2000. This model will be available in a modified form for commercial sale after military and law enforcement contracts are filled.

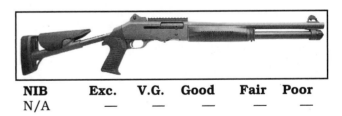

NIB	Exc.	V.G.	Good	Fair	Poor
N/A	—	—	—	—	—

<u>MACHINE GUNS</u>

Bibliographical Note: For historical information, technical data, and photos see James Ballou, *Rock in a Hard Place; The Browning Automatic Rifle*, Collector Grade Publications, 2000. Wahl and Toppel, *The Gatling Gun*, New York, 1965.

Colt Gatling Gun

First invented by American Dr. Richard J. Gatling in 1861 this is a multi-barrel (6 to 10 barrels) hand cranked machine gun. Several different models were developed and built in the 1860s with some used in the American Civil War. Some of these early guns were chambered for the .58 caliber while a few others were chambered for the 1" shell. the classic Gatling gun is the Model 1874 chambered for the .45-70 cartridge. There are several other models such as the Model 1879, Model 1881, the Model 1892, Model 1895, and the Model 1903.

Some of these guns were tripod mounted while others were mounted on gun carriages, and still others were deck mounted for ship-board use. Some of the Gatling guns have exposed barrels while others are enclosed in a brass jacket. The Model 1877 bulldog is fitted with five 18" barrels enclosed in a brass jacket. the Model 1893 Police has six 12" barrels in .45-70 and weighs about 75 lbs. These guns are marked with a brass plate on top of the receiver, "GATLING'S/BATTERY/GUN 9 (PATENT DATES) MADE BY COLT'S/ PT. FIRE ARMS MFG. CO./HARTFORD, CONN.U.S.A.".

NOTE: As an interesting aside Gating guns are still in use by military forces but are now electrically powered (GEC M134/GAU-2B Minigun) and capable of a rate of fire of 6,000 rounds per minute using the 7.62x51 cartridge.

Values for these guns are difficult to establish. Gatling guns in excellent condition in .45-70 caliber can bring between $75,000 to $200,000 and even more.

Colt Model 1895 • Courtesy Butterfield & Butterfield

Colt Gatling Model 1883 • Photo courtesy Butterfield & Butterfield

Colt Model 1895

Designed by John Browning and built by Colt this is a gas operated air-cooled belt fed gun chambered for the .30-03, 6mm USN, and .30-40 cartridges as well as the .30-06 (called the Model 1906 cartridge) in later applications. Rate of fire is about 450 rounds per minute. Called the "potato digger" because of its back and forth motion and proximity to the ground. This was the first non-mechanical firing machine issued to the U.S. military. It saw limited use during the Spanish-American War, the Boxer Rebellion, and as a training gun during World War I.

NOTE: See also *Colt/Marlin Model 1914/1915*

Pre-1968 (Rare)

Exc.	V.G.	Fair
15000	13000	12000

Pre-1986 conversions

Exc.	V.G.	Fair
N/A	N/A	N/A

Pre-1986 Dealer samples

Exc.	V.G.	Fair
N/A	N/A	N/A

NOTE: The .30-03 cartridge was the original and earlier version of the .30-06 cartridge. Guns chambered for the older .30-03 cartridge will function and fire the .30-06 cartridge (accuracy suffers) *but the reverse is not true.* Sometimes the .30-03 cartridge is referred to as the .30-45. Both of these cartridges replaced the older .30-40 Krag as the official military round.

Colt Maxim 1904

This belt fed machine gun was originally chambered for the .30-03 cartridge and then altered to the .30-06. Built on the standard Maxim M1900 pattern. Barrel length is 28.5". Rate of fire is about 500 rounds per minute. Fed by a 250 round cloth belt. Primarily used as a training gun during World War I. A total of 287 of these guns were produced. Weight is approximately 75 lbs

Maxim Model 1904 • Robert G. Segel Collection

Pre-1968 (Very Rare)

Exc.	V.G.	Fair
40000	35000	30000

Pre-1986 conversions

Exc.	V.G.	Fair
N/A	N/A	N/A

Pre-1986 Dealer samples

Exc.	V.G.	Fair
N/A	N/A	N/A

Model 1909 Benet-Mercie Machine Rifle

Developed by the French firm Hotckiss and built in the U.S. by Colt's and Springfield Armory this air cooled gas operated automatic rifle is fed by a 30 round metal strip. Chambered for the .30-06 cartridge. Rate of fire was about 400 rounds per minute. Weight of gun was approximately 27 lbs. This gun was equipped with a Model 1908 Warner & Swasey telescope. This model was used against Mexican bandits in 1915 and 1916 by the U.S. Army and in France during the early stages of World War I. However, it did not prove to be reliable and was soon replaced by the Hotchkiss and Vickers guns. About 670 were produced by both Colt and Springfield.

Model 1909 Benet-Mercie • Robert G. Segel Collection

Pre-1968 (Rare)

Model 1909 Benet • Mercie Warner & Swasey telescope sight • Robert G. Segel Collection

Exc.	V.G.	Fair
6000	5000	4000

Pre-1986 conversions

Exc.	V.G.	Fair
N/A	N/A	N/A

Pre-1986 Dealer samples

Exc.	V.G.	Fair
N/A	N/A	N/A

Browning M1917 & M1917A1

Based on John M. Browning original automatic weapon design it was chambered for the .30-06 cartridge. This water-cooled gun is fitted with a 23.8" barrel and has a rate of fire of 500 rounds per minute using a cloth belt. Its empty weight for the gun only is 33 lbs. The M1917A1 tripod weighs about 53 lbs. Marked "US INSP BROWNING MACHINE GUN US CAL 30 MODEL OF 1917" This gun was produced by various manufacturers from 1917 to 1945.

About 56,000 were built prior to the end of WWI although few saw actual combat service. In the mid 1930s a few minor modifications were made to the gun and it became known as the Model 1917A1. These modifications are as following:

The most important legacy of the Model 1917 Browning is that it led to the use of this gun as the air-cooled Model 1919. During its production life the gun was built by Colt, Remington, and Winchester.

Browning Model 1917 (Westinghouse) • Courtesy Private NFA Collection • Paul Goodwin Photo

Browning Model 1917A1 • Robert G. Segel
Collection

Pre-1968

Exc.	V.G.	Fair
17500	16000	15000

Pre-1986 conversions (Non-Martial current U.S. manu-facture)

Exc.	V.G.	Fair
14000	11000	9500

Pre-1986 Dealer samples

Exc.	V.G.	Fair
N/A	N/A	N/A

Browning M1919 A4

This air cooled gun is chambered for the .30-06 cartridge and fitted with a 23.8" barrel. It has a rate of fire of 500 rounds per minute and is fed with a cloth belt. Weight is about 31 lbs. Marked "BROWNING M1919A4 US CAL .30" on the left side of the receiver. First produced in 1934 it is still in use today. There were a number of earlier variations of this model beginning with the M1919 aircraft gun and several improvements leading to the A4 version.

The Model 1919 was used in WWII as an infantry weapon, tank gun, and even in aircraft (M2). It has seen service all over the world in untold conflicts. Many arms experts think of the A4 version as the definitive .30 caliber machine gun.

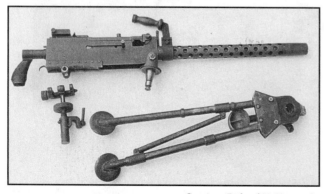

Courtesy Richard M. Kumor, Sr.

Pre-1968

Exc.	V.G.	Fair
10000	9000	9000

Pre-1986 conversions (Non-Martial current U.S. manu-facture)

Exc.	V.G.	Fair
7000	6800	6500

Pre-1986 Dealer samples

Exc.	V.G.	Fair
3500	3500	3000

Browning M1919 A6

This model is a M1919 A4 fitted with a shoulder stock, flash hider, and bipod. Its weight is 32 lbs. Produced from 1943 to 1954. Marked "US INSP BROWNING MACHINE GUN US CAL 30" on the left side of the receiver.

Browning Model 1919A6 • Robert G. Segel Collection

Pre-1968

Exc.	V.G.	Fair
10000	9000	9000

Pre-1986 conversions (Non-Martial current U.S. manu-facture)

Exc.	V.G.	Fair
7000	6800	6500

Pre-1986 Dealer samples

Exc.	V.G.	Fair
3500	3500	3000

Browning M2/M2HB .50

This is an air-cooled .50 caliber machine first produced in 1933. It has a 44.5" barrel and weigh about 84 lbs. Its rate of fire is 500 rounds per minute. It is belt fed. Marked "BROWN-ING MACHINE GUN CAL 50 M2 "on the left side of the receiver. Approximately three million were produced. The gun was produced by Colt, FN, Ramo, Saco, and Winchester.

It is one of the most widely used and successful heavy machines were produced. Besides being utllized as a aircraft, ground and vehicle weapon the M2 is also used as an antiaircraft gun in single, twin, and four barrel configurations. The M2 was additionally configured as a water cooled gun for sustained fire. The commercial designation for this model was the MG 52A. Widely used throughout the world and is still in use today and still in production in the UK, USA, and Belgium.

U.S. Army photograph. Browning BAR in action, January 30, 1951, Korean front

Pre-1968

Exc.	V.G.	Fair
15000	14000	13000

Pre-1986 conversions (Non-Martial current U.S. manufacture)

Exc.	V.G.	Fair
11000	10000	9000

Pre-1986 Dealer samples

Exc.	V.G.	Fair
N/A	N/A	N/A

NOTE: For original M2 water-cooled guns add $10,000 to pre-1968 prices.

Browning Automatic Rifle (BAR)

This is gas operated machine gun chambered for the .30-06 cartridge. Fitted with a 23.8" barrel and a 20-round magazine, it weighs about 16 lbs. Its rate of fire is 500 rounds per minute. Marked "BROWNING BAR M1918 CAL 30" on receiver it was produced from 1917 until 1945 but saw service in the Korean war.

This Browning designed rifle was built by Colt, Marlin, and Winchester. It has several variations from the original M1918 design. About 50,000 Model 1918 BARs saw service in Europe during World War I. The M1918A1 was first built in 1927 and has the butt plate hinged shoulder support. The bipod has spiked feet and is attached to the gas cylinder. It too is select fire. Weight for the M1918A1 is 18.5 lbs. The M1918 A2 was first built in 1932 and is fitted with a bipod with skid feet attached to the flash hider. There is a monopod beneath the butt stock. The rear sight is from a Browning M1919A4 machine gun and is adjustable for windage. This version has a rate of fire regulator that sets the rate between 450 and 650 rounds per minute. Weight for this variation is 19.5 lbs. During World War II approximately 188,000 Model 1918A2 BARs were produced. The last version is called the M1922 and was built in limited numbers. It is similar to the M1918 but with a heavy finned barrel. the bipod is attached to the barrel. Barrel length is 18" with rate of fire of 550 rounds per minute. During its production life the rifle was built by Colt, Marlin, and Winchester.

Photo courtesy Jim Thompson

Pre-1968

Exc.	V.G.	Fair
17500	15000	14000

Pre-1986 conversions

Exc.	V.G.	Fair
10000	9000	8000

Pre-1986 Dealer samples

Exc.	V.G.	Fair
8500	8000	7500

Browning M2 water-cooled anti-aircraft gun • Robert G. Segel Collection

U.S. Army photograph • Browning BAR in action, January 30, 1951, Korean front

Johnson M1941 & 1944

Chambered for the .30-06 cartridge the Model 1941 was fitted with a wooden buttstock while the Model 1944 had a metal stock. Barrel length was 21.8". The M1941 had a rate of fire of 600 rounds while the M1944an adjustable rate of fire between 200 and 900 rounds per minute. Fed by a side mounted 20 box magazine. Weight is about 14 lbs. Produced for the Marine Corps until 1945. Marked "LIGHT MACHINE GUN JOHNSON AUTOMATICS MODEL OF 1941" above the magazine housing. About 10,000 Model 1941 guns were built.

This is an interesting model because it fired from an open bolt for full auto fire and a closed bolt for single shots. The M1941 was built by Cranston & Johnson and the M1944 was built by Johnson.

Johnson Model 1941

Pre-1968

Exc.	V.G.	Fair
10000	9000	9000

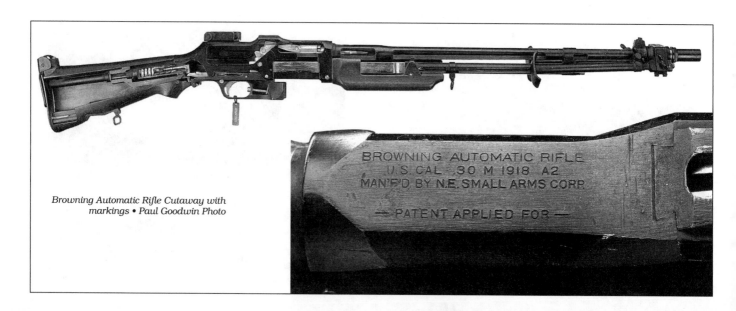

Browning Automatic Rifle Cutaway with markings • Paul Goodwin Photo

BROWNING AUTOMATIC RIFLE
U.S CAL .30 M 1918 A2
MAN'F'D BY N.E. SMALL ARMS CORP.

— PATENT APPLIED FOR —

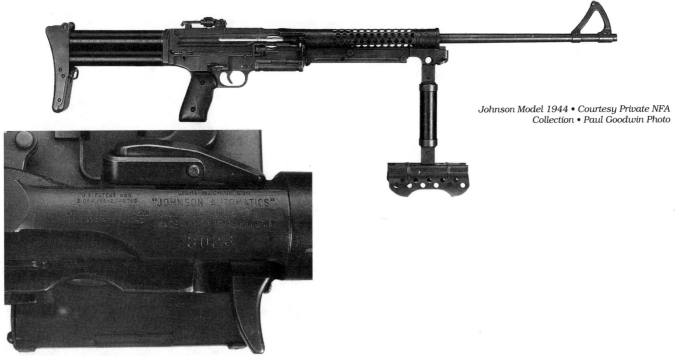

Johnson Model 1944 • Courtesy Private NFA Collection • Paul Goodwin Photo

Pre-1986 conversions

Exc.	V.G.	Fair
N/A	N/A	N/A

Pre-1986 Dealer samples

Exc.	V.G.	Fair
N/A	N/A	N/A

Stoner Model 63/63A

Developed in 1963 as a further evolution to the Model 63 with an improved stainless steel gas system and different style safety per U.S. Marine Corp specifications. This machine gun is chambered for the 5.56x45mm cartridge. It has an overall length of 40.24", a barrel length of 21", and a weight of approximately 11 lbs. Its rate of fire is 700 rounds per minute. It can function as a belt feed gun or can be feed by a top mounted magazine. It was used by both the U.S. Navy and Marine Corps during the Vietnam conflict. Production stopped in the early 1970s. The gun was produced by Cadillac Gage Co.

NOTE: This model is really a weapons system that is capable of a number of different configurations from carbine to machine gun. Also note that Model 63 components will not always interchange with Model 63A guns.

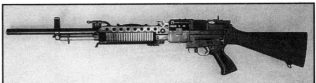

Stoner Model 63A • Photo Courtesy Private NFA Collection

Pre-1968 (Very Rare, less than 6 known)

Exc.	V.G.	Fair
40000	35000	30000

Pre-1986 conversions (Non-martial current U.S. manufacture)

Exc.	V.G.	Fair
35000	30000	25000

Pre-1986 Dealer samples

Exc.	V.G.	Fair
20000	19000	18000

NOTE: Deduct 33% for Stoner Model 63. There are more Model 63s availabe (transferable) than Model 63As.

U.S. M60

Chambered for the 7.62x51mm cartridge this machine gun entered U.S. service in the late 1950s. It was fitted with a 22" barrel and a rate of fire of 550 rounds per minute using a disintegrating link belt system. The weight of the gun is 24.4 lbs.

Stoner Model 63 Carbine • Paul Goodwin Photo • Courtesy West Point Museum

Armalite AR-10 • Courtesy West Point Museum • Paul Goodwin Photo

Used extensively by US forces in Vietnam. Still in production and still in service with U.S. forces (Marine Corp) and many others around the world. the early M60 guns were built by Bridge & Inland.

Pre-1986 OEM/Maremont manufacture

Exc.	V.G.	Fair
20000	17500	15000

Pre-1986 conversions

Exc.	V.G.	Fair
15000	13000	12000

Pre-1986 Dealer samples

Exc.	V.G.	Fair
N/A	N/A	N/A

U.S. M60E3

This is an improved version of the M60 with a lightweight shorter 17" barrel. The forearm is replaced with a forward pistol grip with heat shield. The feed system has been modified to allow the cover to be closed when the bolt is forward. The gas system has been modified as well. Weight has been reduced to about 18 lbs. This model was in service with the U.S. Marine Corp, Navy, and Air Force. Built by both Maremont and Saco.

M60-E3 • Photo Courtesy Private NFA Collection

Pre-1986 OEM/Maremont manufacture

Exc.	V.G.	Fair
25000	24000	23000

Armalite AR-10

Chambered for the 7.62x51mm cartridge, this select fire machine gun was fitted with a 19.8" barrel and had a 20-round magazine. Rate of fire is 700 rounds per minute. Weight is 9 lbs. Marked "ARMALITE AR10 MANUFACTURED BY AL NEDERLAND" on left side of magazine housing. Produced from 1958 to 1961. This gun was adopted by Burma, Portugal, Nicaragua, and Sudan. It was produced in limited numbers.

Pre-1968 (Very Rare)

Exc.	V.G.	Fair
15000	15000	14000

Pre-1986 conversions

Exc.	V.G.	Fair
7500	6500	5000

Pre-1986 Dealer samples

Exc.	V.G.	Fair
2500	2500	2000

Colt/Marlin Model 1914/1915

This was a Browning design that was first produced in 1895. Nicknamed the "Potato Digger" because of its swinging arm bolt driver. It was air cooled and fired a variety of calibers both for the military and commercial sales. The Model 1914 was converted to fire the .30-06 cartridge. Rate of fire was about 450 rounds per minute. Barrel length was 28". Belt feed by 250 round cloth belt. The Model 1915 had cooling fins added to the barrel. The gun was built from 1916 to 1919.

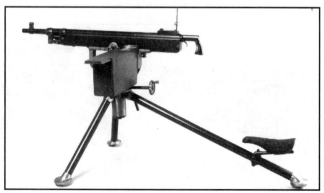

Robert G. Segel Collection

Pre-1968

Exc.	V.G.	Fair
10000	9000	8000

Pre-1986 conversions

Exc.	V.G.	Fair
N/A	N/A	N/A

Pre-1986 Dealer samples

Exc.	V.G.	Fair
N/A	N/A	N/A

Marlin Model 1917

This model is an improved Potato Digger with a gas pistol and cylinder fitted underneath the barrel. Chambered for the .30-06 cartridge. Designed for use in aircraft with long finned aluminum radiator around the barrel, and in tanks with a heavy armored barrel jacket. Barrel length is 28". Fed by a 250 round cloth belt with a rate of fire of approximately 600 rounds per minute. Weight is about 22 lbs.

Pre-1968

Exc.	V.G.	Fair
9000	8000	7000

Pre-1986 conversions

Exc.	V.G.	Fair
N/A	N/A	N/A

Pre-1986 Dealer samples

Exc.	V.G.	Fair
N/A	N/A	N/A

Savage-Lewis Model 1917

This a .30-06 caliber Lewis gun made by Savage during World War I. About 6,000 of these guns were chambered for the .30-06 caliber cartridge and used by the U.S. Marines and Navy until World War I. The U.S. Army purchased 2,500 of the guns but most of these Army guns were used for training purposes. See *Great Britain, Machine Guns, Lewis 0.303in., Mark I.*

Pre-1968

Exc.	V.G.	Fair
15000	14000	12000

Pre-1986 conversions

Exc.	V.G.	Fair
12000	11000	10000

Pre-1986 Dealer samples

Exc.	V.G.	Fair
N/A	N/A	N/A

Colt-Vickers Model 1915

This gun is similar to the British Vickers but built byin Hartford, CT. Many of these Colt Model 1915 guns were rebuilt aircraft guns. About 12,000 were produced by Colt during the period 1915 to 1918 but few of these were original Colt-built ground guns and many of those were destroyed after the war. Therefore, original Colt-Vickers ground guns are very rare and quite desirable. See also Great Britain, Machine Guns, Vickers.

Colt Vickers Model 1915 • Robert G. Segel Collection

Pre-1968 (original Colt ground gun)

Exc.	V.G.	Fair
20000	18000	17000

Pre-1968(Colt rebuilt aircraft gun)

Exc.	V.G.	Fair
14000	12000	10000

Pre-1986 conversions

Exc.	V.G.	Fair
9500	8500	7500

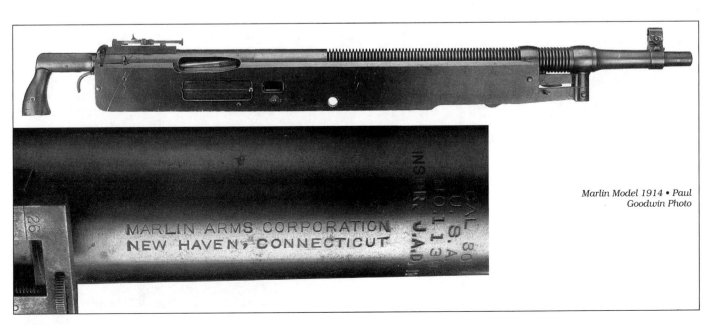

Marlin Model 1914 • Paul Goodwin Photo

Savage-Lewis Gun • Robert G. Segel Collection

Marlin Model 1917 Tank Gun • Courtesy Private NFA Collection
• Paul Goodwin Photo

Colt Vickers Model 1915 with markings • Paul Goodwin Photo

Pre-1986 Dealer samples

Exc.	V.G.	Fair
N/A	N/A	N/A

Colt LMG (RO-750)

First introduced in early 1986 this M16A2 light machine gun was designed as a squad automatic weapon (SAW). SAWs are designed to provide a more sustained fire capability than the standard M16 rifle. Similar in appearance to the M16A2 rifle this model features a 20" heavy barrel upper with square handguard and vertical handgrip. The lower receiver fires from an open bolt full auto only and is marked, "SAFE AND FIRE". The fixed stock houses a hydraulic buffer and special spring to reduce the rate of fire to about 650 rounds per minute. Weight is 12.75 lbs. Fed by standard 30 round M16 magazine or other high capacity devices such as the 100 round Beta C magazine. In use by the U.S. Marine Corp. and other military forces around the world. Still in production. It is estimated by knowledgeable sources that there are less than 20 transferable examples in this country.

Pre-1968

Exc.	V.G.	Fair
N/A	N/A	N/A

Pre-1986 OEM (Rare)

NIB	Exc.	V.G./Fair
15000	12500	N/A

Pre-1986 Dealer samples

Exc.	V.G.	Fair
N/A	N/A	N/A

WHAT'S IT LIKE: THE COLT LMG

With a rate of fire of about 650 rounds per minute, a weight of 13 lbs, and a very large barrel diameter this machine gun this extremely accurate out to 400 yards and beyond. Equipped with a mini A.C.O.G. scope in 3 power by Trijicon this gun was able to consistently score hits with 10 and 15 rounds burst on target from 400 yards with ease. This gun needs a quality scope like the Trijicon to bring out its full capabilities. This kind of accuracy with a light machine gun is nothing short of amazing. Recoil is very light with the result that aim is not disturbed during fire. All of this in full automatic fire. Even with sustained burst from a 100 round Beta C magazine heat dissipation was excellent as was accuracy. The open bolt system and the heavy 20" barrel makes this gun a very effective SAW. Many who have fired both the FN Minimi and the FN Mag prefer the Colt LMG for its accuracy and ease of operation. Only a handful of transferable examples exist in this country due to the small window between introduction of this gun in very early 1986 and the May, 1986 ban on additional transferable machine guns to the civilian market.

YUGOSLAVIA-SERBIA

Yugoslavian-Serbian Military Conflicts, 1870-Present

Once part of Turkey, then an autonomous state, Serbia became a kingdom in 1882. After the Balkan Wars of 1912 and 1913 Serbia emerged as a Balkan power. The Assassination of Austrian Archduke Francis Ferdinand by a Serbian nationalist precipitated World War I when Austria declared war on Serbia. After the war, Serbia became part of what is now Yugoslavia. During World War II Serbia allied itself with the Germans. After the war Serbia became a republic of Yugoslavia in 1946. In the early 1990s Serbia wanted greater independence from Yugoslavia with the result of war in that region between Bosnia, Croatia, and Yugoslavia. The area is still unsettled.

Yugoslavia's existence began after World War I when it officially became identified as Yugoslavia in 1929. This period was marked by regional tensions and border disputes. In 1939 Yugoslavia aligned itself with the axis powers. The country was invaded by Germany in 1941 and partisan forces led by Marshal Tito battled the Germans and then each other in civil war to determine control of the country after the Germans were driven out in 1944. In 1945 Tito came to power and ruled until his death in 1980. In 1990 the communist party ceded control with Serbian president Milosevic eventually coming to power. In 1995 Serbia, Croatia, and Bosnia signed a treaty ending its conflict.

NOTE: In the 1870s military arms were produced at Kragushevat, the national arsenal in Serbia. In the 1920s it was often referred to as Voini Techiki Zavod. This factory was destroyed during World War II. Production of weapons since World War II is at the state arms factory of Zavodi Crena Zastava, Kragujevac, often shortened to "ZCZ." After 1990 the name was changed to Zastava Arms

HANDGUNS

At the end of World War I Yugoslavia acquired a large number of Austrian Model 12 Steyr pistols in 9mm. The Yugoslavians have also used the FN-built M1935 pistol in 9x19 caliber.

Model 1875

This is a double action solid frame with fixed cylinder and mechanical rod ejection. Cylinder holds 6 rounds and is chambered for the 11mm cartridge. Checkered wood grips with lanyard loop. Octagon barrel is 6.2" long. Built by Auguste Francotte in Liege, Belgium. In use from 1875 to 1919.

Exc.	V.G.	Good	Fair	Poor
800	500	350	200	125

Model 1876

This model is built on a modified Lefaucheux-Chaineux solid frame with swing out cylinder. The non-fluted cylinder is chambered for the 11mm cartridge. The half-round half-octagon barrel is 4.4". Checkered wood grips with lanyard loop. Built by Manufacture d'Ares, St. Etienne, France. In service with the Serbian army from 1876 to 1919.

Exc.	V.G.	Good	Fair	Poor
750	500	350	200	125

Model 1891

Built on the Nagant Model 1887 frame, this double action model is chambered for the 7.5mm cartridge. Fluted cylinder. The 4.5" barrel is 3/4 octagon and 1/4 round. Checkered grips with lanyard loop. Built by the Nagant brothers in Liege, Belgium. The Serbian army used this revolver from 1891 to 1945. Revolver has cyrillic markings on the frame.

Exc.	V.G.	Good	Fair	Poor
2000	1000	500	350	225

Model 1898

This revolver is the same as the Austrian Model 1898, built by Rast & Gasser in Wien (Vienna), Austria. This model was built on the Schmidt-Galand double action solid frame with swing-out 8-round cylinder with multiple ejection. Chambered for the 8mm cartridge and fitted with a 4.5" round barrel. Checkered wooden grips with lanyard loop. Weight is about 33 oz.

Exc.	V.G.	Good	Fair	Poor
400	200	150	120	90

Model 1910 FN Browning

Adopted by Serbia and used in World War I. Chambered for 7.65mm cartridge and fitted with a 3.5" barrel. Magazine capacity is 7 rounds. Weight about 21 oz. The principal difference between this model and its predecessors is that the recoil spring on the Model 1910 is wrapped around the barrel. This gives the slide a more graceful tubular appearance instead of the old slab-sided look. This model has the triple safety features of the 1906 Model 2nd variation and is blued with molded plastic grips. The pistol has the Yugoslavian crest on the slide and cyrillic lettering on slide. This model was adopted by police forces and some military units around the world. It was manufactured between 1912 and 1954.

Courtesy Orvel Reichert

Exc.	V.G.	Good	Fair	Poor
400	250	200	150	125

Model 1922 FN Browning

Adopted by Yugoslavia in the 1930s in 9mm short (.380). Fitted with a 4.5" barrel and a magazine capacity of 9 rounds. Fitted with a grip safety. Yugoslavian crest on top of slide. Weight is about 25 oz. Approximately 60,000 of these pistols were produced for the Yugoslavian military between 1922 and 1925. These pistols were also used by the German occupation forces but are not marked with German acceptance or proof stamps.

Exc.	V.G.	Good	Fair	Poor
650	500	400	300	150

Tokarev copy (Model 70)

This is a Yugoslavian copy of the Soviet TT33 in 9x19mm.

Exc.	V.G.	Good	Fair	Poor
500	400	300	200	100

Tokarev copy (Model 57)

This is a Yugoslavian copy of the Soviet Tokarev but with a 9-round magazine in 7.62x25mm.

Exc.	V.G.	Good	Fair	Poor
1200	850	700	500	200

Tokarev copy (Model 65 for export)

This is a copy of the Tokarev in 9mm Parabellum.

Exc.	V.G.	Good	Fair	Poor
500	400	300	200	100

SUBMACHINE GUNS

Prior to World War II Yugoslavia adopted the Erma submachine gun. After the war Yugoslavia used the German Mp38 and Mp40. The Yugoslavian army also used British Sten guns and Beretta submachine guns as well. As a communist state the Yugoslavians were supplied with Soviet PPDs and PPSh41 guns.

Yugoslav Model 49

Similar in appearance to the Soviet PPsh-41 this gun is chambered for the 7.62 Soviet cartridge. Barrel is 10.5" and the rate of fire is 700 rounds per minute. It is fitted with a wooden stock. Weight is approximately 9.4 lbs.

Photo Courtesy Private NFA Collection

Pre-1968

Exc.	V.G.	Fair
7500	7000	6500

Pre-1986 conversions

Exc.	V.G.	Fair
5500	4500	4000

Pre-1986 dealer samples

Exc.	V.G.	Fair
5500	4500	4000

Yugoslav Model 56

The Model 56 is chambered for the 7.62 cartridge, and is fitted with a metal folding stock and 9.8" barrel. Magazine capacity is 35 rounds. Weight is about 6.6 lbs. Rate of fire is 600 rounds per minute.

Photo Courtesy Private NFA Collection

Pre-1968

Exc.	V.G.	Fair
8500	7500	6000

Pre-1986 conversions

Exc.	V.G.	Fair
6500	5500	5000

Pre-1986 dealer samples

Exc.	V.G.	Fair
3500	3200	3000

RIFLES

MAUSER

NOTE: Most of these early Mauser rifles were used by the Serbian armed forces through World War I. The Model 24 was adopted by Yugoslavia.

M78/80 Rifle

A modified G 71 rifle with 30.7" barrel with two barrel bands. Turn bolt action. Single shot in 10.15x62.8mm caliber. Weight is about 10 lbs. Fitted with a long receiver tang to support rearward bolt travel. Marked in cyrillic or German on left side rail.

Exc.	V.G.	Good	Fair	Poor
395	325	280	200	—

M1884 Koka Carbine

Chambered for 10.15mm black powder cartridge and fitted with an 18.375" barrel with turn bolt action. Tubular magazine holds 5 rounds. Full-length stock with front sling swivel on left side of barrel band and real swivel on bottom on buttstock near wrist. Weight is about 8 lbs. Marked "MODEL 1884" on right side of butt. About 4,000 were built by Mauser at its Oberndorf factory.

Exc.	V.G.	Good	Fair	Poor
395	340	300	250	200

M1899 Rifle

Produced by DWM with full-length stock with straight grip. Barrel length is 19". Chambered for 7x57mm cartridge. Adjustable rear sight graduated to 2000 meters. Serbian crest marked on receiver ring. Magazine capacity is 5 rounds. Weight is about 9 lbs.

Exc.	V.G.	Good	Fair	Poor
325	285	240	190	100

M1889c Rifle

Chambered for either the 7.92x57mm cartridge or the 7x57mm cartridge and fitted with a 23.25" barrel with full-length stock with pistol grip with finger grooves. Magazine capacity is 5 rounds. Weight is about 8.5 lbs. Straight bolt handle. Marked with Serbian crest on receiver ring.

Exc.	V.G.	Good	Fair	Poor
300	260	210	150	90

M1908 Carbine

This 7x57mm caliber model is fitted with a full-length pistol grip with finger grooves. Barrel length is 17". Upper handguard extends to the lower barrel band. Bolt handle is bent. No bayonet fittings. Weight is about 6.8 lbs.

Exc.	V.G.	Good	Fair	Poor
385	320	280	210	90

M1910 Rifle

This is the standard export German Model 1910 rifle. Fitted with a 29.13" barrel and full-length stock with pistol grip. The nose cap has a bayonet lug on its bottom. Chambered for the 7x57mm cartridge. Weight is about 9 lbs. Marked with Serbian crest on receiver ring.

Exc.	V.G.	Good	Fair	Poor
325	280	200	130	80

M90 (t) Short Rifle

A Yugoslavian model that was received from the Turks following WWI. Rebarreled for 7.92x57mm and cut to 23.25". Magazine capacity is 5 rounds. Tangent rear sight graduated to 2000 meters. Weight is about 8.5 lbs.

Exc.	V.G.	Good	Fair	Poor
300	250	200	130	80

M03 (t) Short Rifle

Same as above but with 23" barrel.

Exc.	V.G.	Good	Fair	Poor
300	230	190	110	70

M24 Short Rifle

This model has a full-length stock with pistol grip. Upper handguard goes from the receiver to upper barrel band. Fitted with 23.25" barrel and chambered for the 7.92x57mm cartridge. Tangent rear sight graduated to 2,000 meters. Weight is about 8.5 lbs. Yugoslavian crest over model designation on left side of receiver.

Exc.	V.G.	Good	Fair	Poor
300	220	180	90	40

M24 Carbine

Similar to the above model but with 16.75" barrel. Bayonet fittings are on nose cap. Weight is about 7.25 lbs.

Exc.	V.G.	Good	Fair	Poor
350	290	230	150	80

FN M30 Short Rifle

This model has a full-length stock with pistol grip. Straight bolt handle. This model is the standard FN Model 1930 configuration.

Exc.	V.G.	Good	Fair	Poor
250	180	110	70	40

FN M24 Carbine

Full stock with pistol grip and 17.5" barrel. Caliber is 7.5x57mm. Turn bolt action. Tangent leaf sight graduated to 1,400 meters. Yugoslavian crest of top of receiver ring. Weight is about 8 lbs.

Exc.	V.G.	Good	Fair	Poor
250	180	110	70	40

M1948 98k Short Rifle

This model is similar to the German 98k carbine. Almost full-length stock with pistol grip and short upper handguard. Hooded front sight with tangent leaf sight to 2000 meters. Chambered for 7.92x57mm with 5-round magazine. Weight is about 10 lbs. Communist Yugoslavian crest on receiver ring.

Exc.	V.G.	Good	Fair	Poor
200	150	100	80	50

M24/52C Short Rifle

The is an arsenal reconditioned Model 24 short rifle with communist Yugoslavian crest on receiver ring.

Exc.	V.G.	Good	Fair	Poor
190	140	95	70	40

Model 59/66

This is a Yugoslavian copy of the Soviet SKS rifle. The major difference between the two is a gas shut-off valve on the gas cylinder and an integral grenade launcher fitted to the barrel.

Exc.	V.G.	Good	Fair	Poor
1500	1200	850	500	250

Model 64

This is a Yugoslavian copy of the Soviet AK-47 but with a 19.7" barrel with built-in grenade launcher sights that pivots on the barrel.

Pre-1968

Exc.	V.G.	Fair
16000	14000	12000

Pre-1986 conversions

Exc.	V.G.	Fair
N/A	N/A	N/A

Pre-1986 dealer samples

Exc.	V.G.	Fair
N/A	N/A	N/A

NOTE: Add 20% for folding stock.

Zastava M70B1

This Yugoslavian copy of the AK-47 rifle was first produced in 1974. It is chambered for the 7.62x39mm cartridge and is fitted with a 16.2" barrel. It rate of fire is 650 rounds per minute. Weight is about 8 lbs. This model features a folding grenade sight behind the front sight. When raised it cuts off the gas supply to the cylinder redirecting it to the launcher. This is the standard Yugoslav service rifle. Still in production.

Pre-1968

Exc.	V.G.	Fair
N/A	N/A	N/A

Pre-1986 conversions

Exc.	V.G.	Fair
N/A	N/A	N/A

Pre-1986 dealer samples

Exc.	V.G.	Fair
7500	6500	5500

M70B1 (Semiautomatic version)

Exc.	V.G.	Good	Fair	Poor
2000	1500	900	600	300

M70AB2

Copy of the Soviet AKM-S. See *Russia, Rifles.*

M76 Sniping Rifle

This is an copy of a Soviet AKM with a 21.5" barrel and wooden butt. The rifle is fitted with iron sights and a telescope mount. Semiautomatic operation. Chambered for the 8x57mm cartridge. Weight is about 9.5 lbs. Prices listed below are for rifles with correct matching military scope.

M76 with correct military scope • Courtesy Steve Hill

Exc.	V.G.	Good	Fair	Poor
5000	4500	3500	—	—

NOTE: For rifles without scope deduct $1,500. For rifles with commercial scopes but marked M76B deduct $1,000. For rifles in .308 caliber without scope deduct 70%.

M77B1 (Semiautomatic)

Copy of the Soviet AKM with a fixed wooden butt; straight 20-round magazine, and 16.4" barrel. Weight is about 8.5 lbs. Prices listed are for semiautomatic version.

Exc.	V.G.	Good	Fair	Poor
2250	1650	1100	800	300

M77 B1 Assault Rifle

Copy of the Soviet AKM with a fixed wooden butt, straight 20-round magazine, and 16.4" barrel. Rate of fire is about 700 rounds per minute. There are examples in this country chambered for .308 and .223. Weight is about 8.5 lbs.

NOTE: For rifles chambered for .223 add 75% premium.

Pre-1968

Exc.	V.G.	Fair
N/A	N/A	N/A

Pre-1986 conversions

Exc.	V.G.	Fair
N/A	N/A	N/A

Pre-1986 dealer samples

Exc.	V.G.	Fair
4500	4000	3500

MACHINE GUNS

Between the two World Wars Yugoslavia used the Schwarzlose M07/12, the Maxim 08, and the Madsen. After World War II Yugoslavia used the MG34 and MG 42 as well as some Soviet machine guns. The principal Yugoslavian machine is its own produced MG 42 designated the Model 53.

Yugoslavia also acquired several thousand U.S.-made Browning Model 1919 machine guns prior to 1964 as well as the .50 M2 HB Browning heavy machine gun.

ZB30J

This was the primary light machine gun used by Yugoslavian forces prior to World War II. It is a modified copy of the Czech ZB30 gun chambered for the 7.92mm cartridge. The primary difference between the ZB30 and ZB30J is the knurled barrel ring in front of the receiver on the ZB30J.

Pre-1968

Exc.	V.G.	Fair
20000	18500	17000

Pre-1986 conversions

Exc.	V.G.	Fair
16500	15500	14000

Pre-1986 dealer samples

Exc.	V.G.	Fair
N/A	N/A	N/A

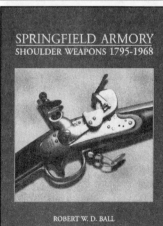
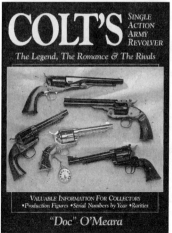

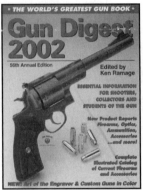

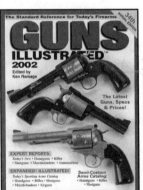

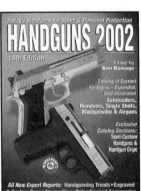